This book is dedicated to Mary, Queen of Apostles, an ancient title for the Mother of God and the particular Marian devotion of the Daughters of St. Paul. Mary is the Queen of Apostles because she was the first apostle, the first to give Jesus to the world. From heaven, Mary continues to invite us to become more like her Son and to receive Christ fully in our minds, wills, and hearts.

May Mary, Queen of Apostles, protect, guide, and bless all who read this book. Through her intercession, may we all receive the strength, love, joy, and peace that comes through Christ so that we may one day join all the saints in heaven.

Thank you

⚜

In Memory of Fr. James T. Edwards

Dr. Lambros and Mrs. Chilimigras

Anthony and Catherine Lussier

The Hunt Family

Joseph Toan and Mary Frances Bùi

In Memory of Helen M. Ravarino

Mike and Tanya Stinson

María Céspedes

John Robert Mathews

Mark Floersch

With profound gratitude to all those whose generosity and
support have made this book possible.
—Daughters of St. Paul

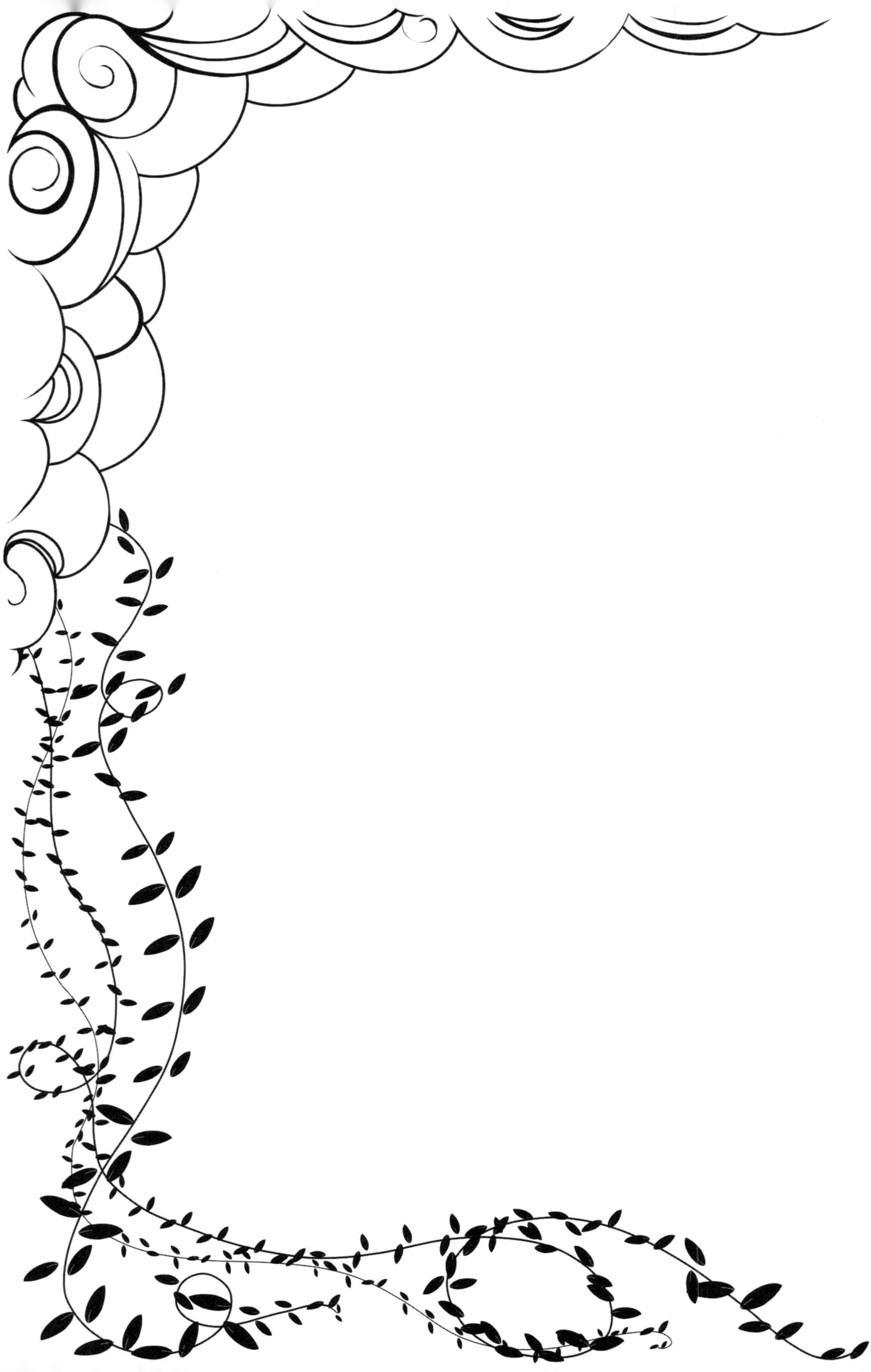

in Caelo et in Terra

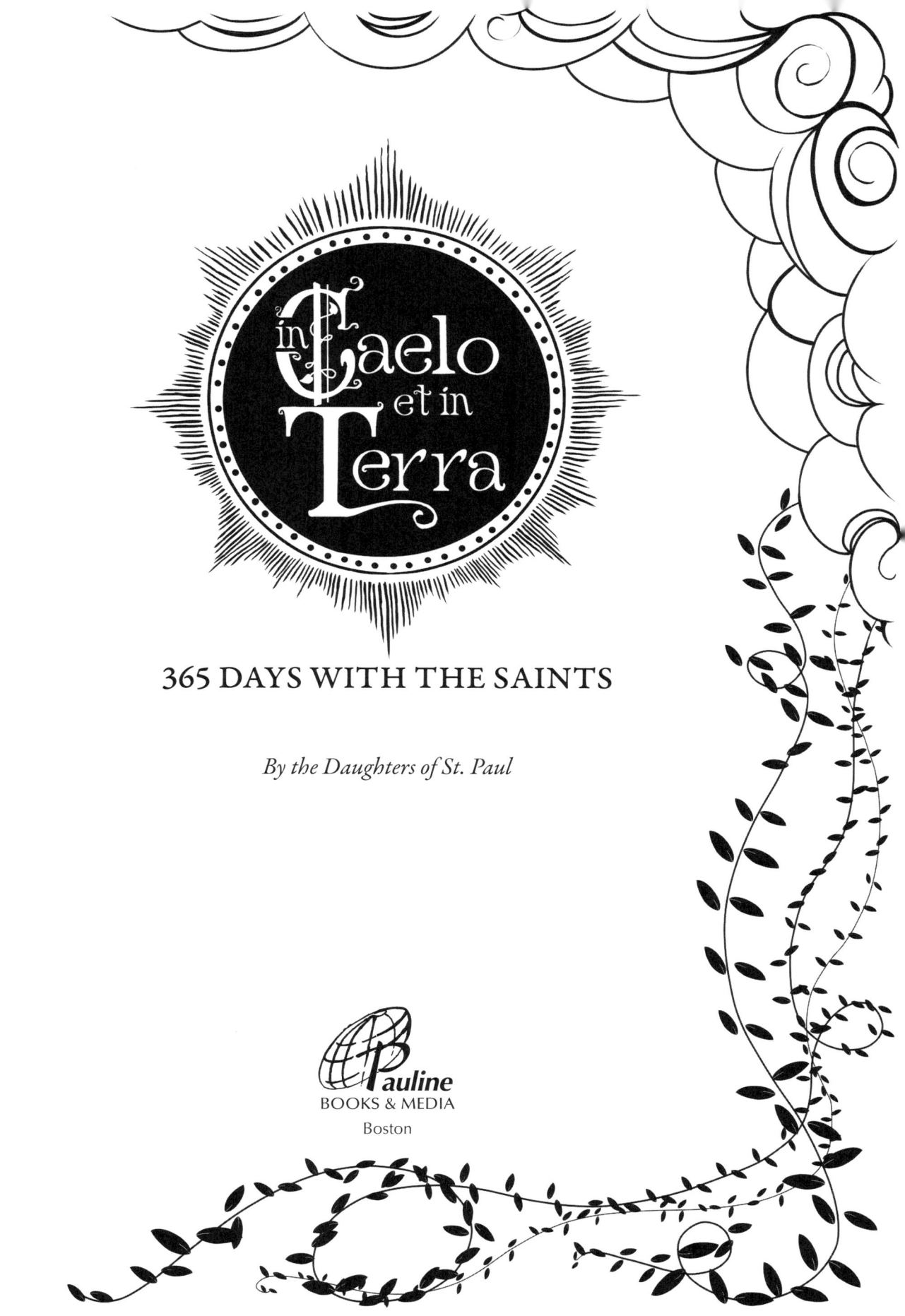

365 DAYS WITH THE SAINTS

By the Daughters of St. Paul

Pauline
BOOKS & MEDIA
Boston

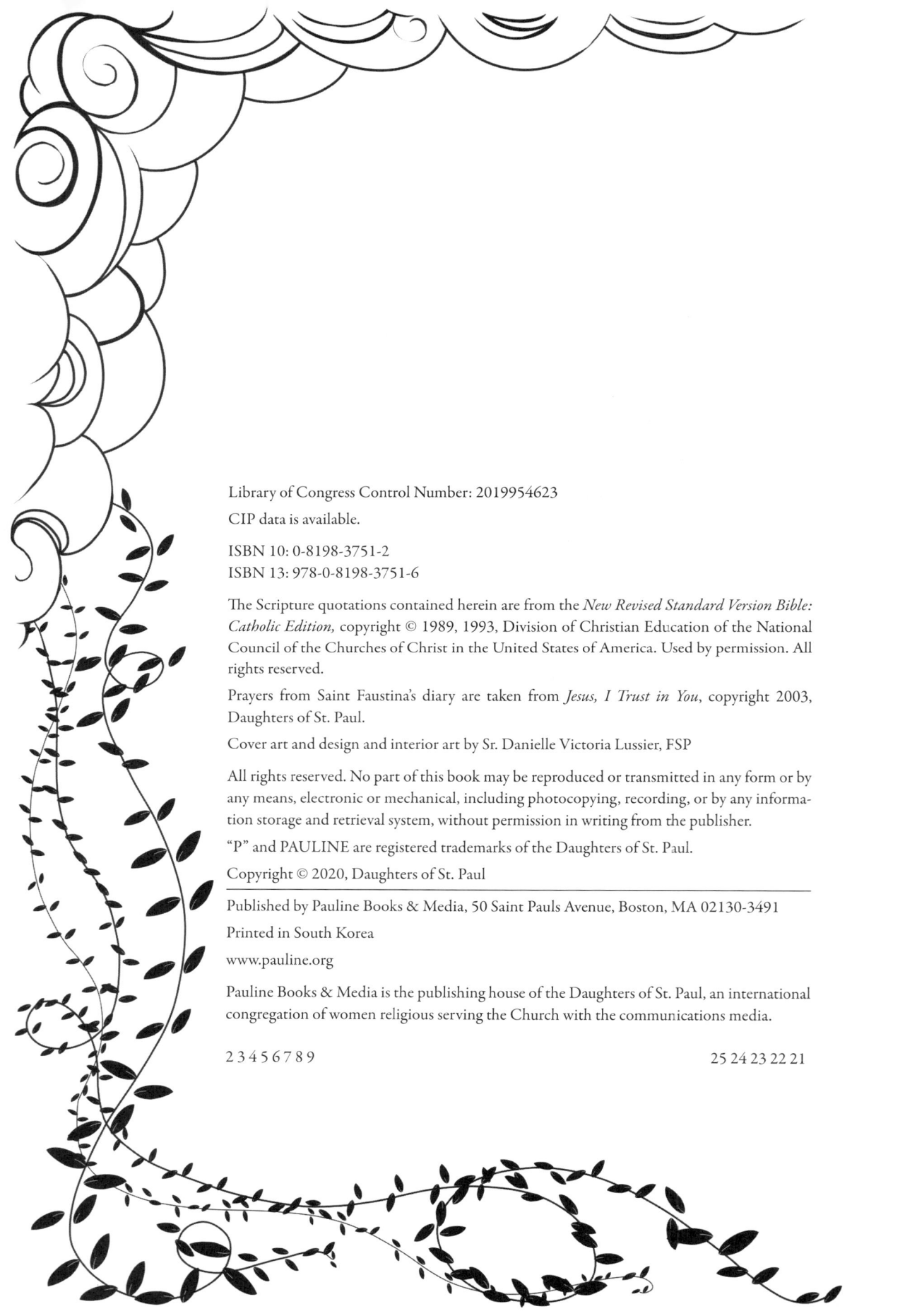

Library of Congress Control Number: 2019954623

CIP data is available.

ISBN 10: 0-8198-3751-2
ISBN 13: 978-0-8198-3751-6

The Scripture quotations contained herein are from the *New Revised Standard Version Bible: Catholic Edition,* copyright © 1989, 1993, Division of Christian Education of the National Council of the Churches of Christ in the United States of America. Used by permission. All rights reserved.

Prayers from Saint Faustina's diary are taken from *Jesus, I Trust in You*, copyright 2003, Daughters of St. Paul.

Cover art and design and interior art by Sr. Danielle Victoria Lussier, FSP

All rights reserved. No part of this book may be reproduced or transmitted in any form or by any means, electronic or mechanical, including photocopying, recording, or by any information storage and retrieval system, without permission in writing from the publisher.

"P" and PAULINE are registered trademarks of the Daughters of St. Paul.

Copyright © 2020, Daughters of St. Paul

Published by Pauline Books & Media, 50 Saint Pauls Avenue, Boston, MA 02130-3491

Printed in South Korea

www.pauline.org

Pauline Books & Media is the publishing house of the Daughters of St. Paul, an international congregation of women religious serving the Church with the communications media.

2 3 4 5 6 7 8 9   25 24 23 22 21

CONTENTS

Preface xi

January 2

February 33

March 62

April 93

May 123

June 154

July 184

August 215

September 246

October 276

November 307

December 337

Appendix of Prayers 369

List of Contributors 381

Index of Names 385

Index of Feast Days 391

Index of Patron Saints 403

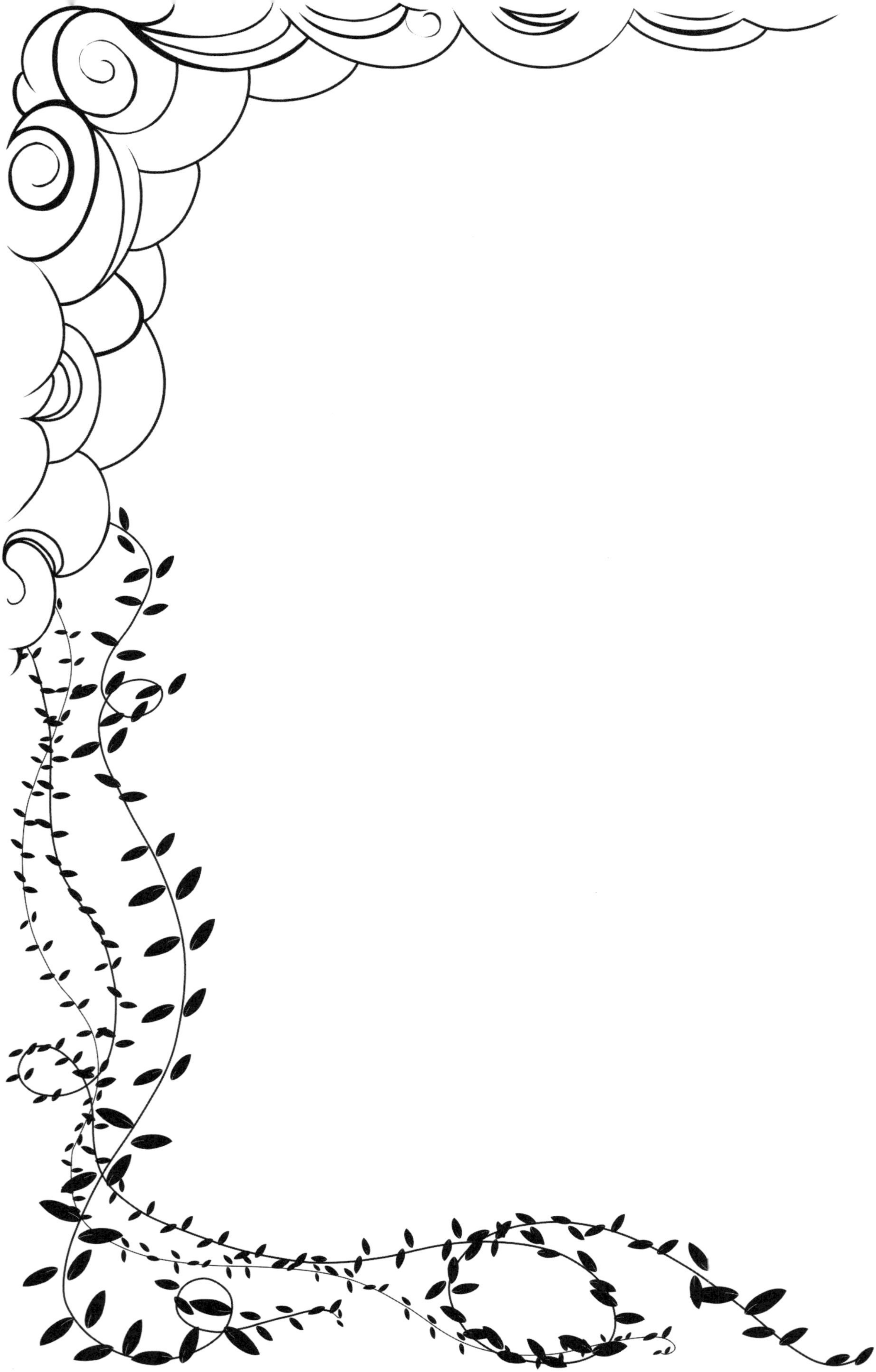

PREFACE

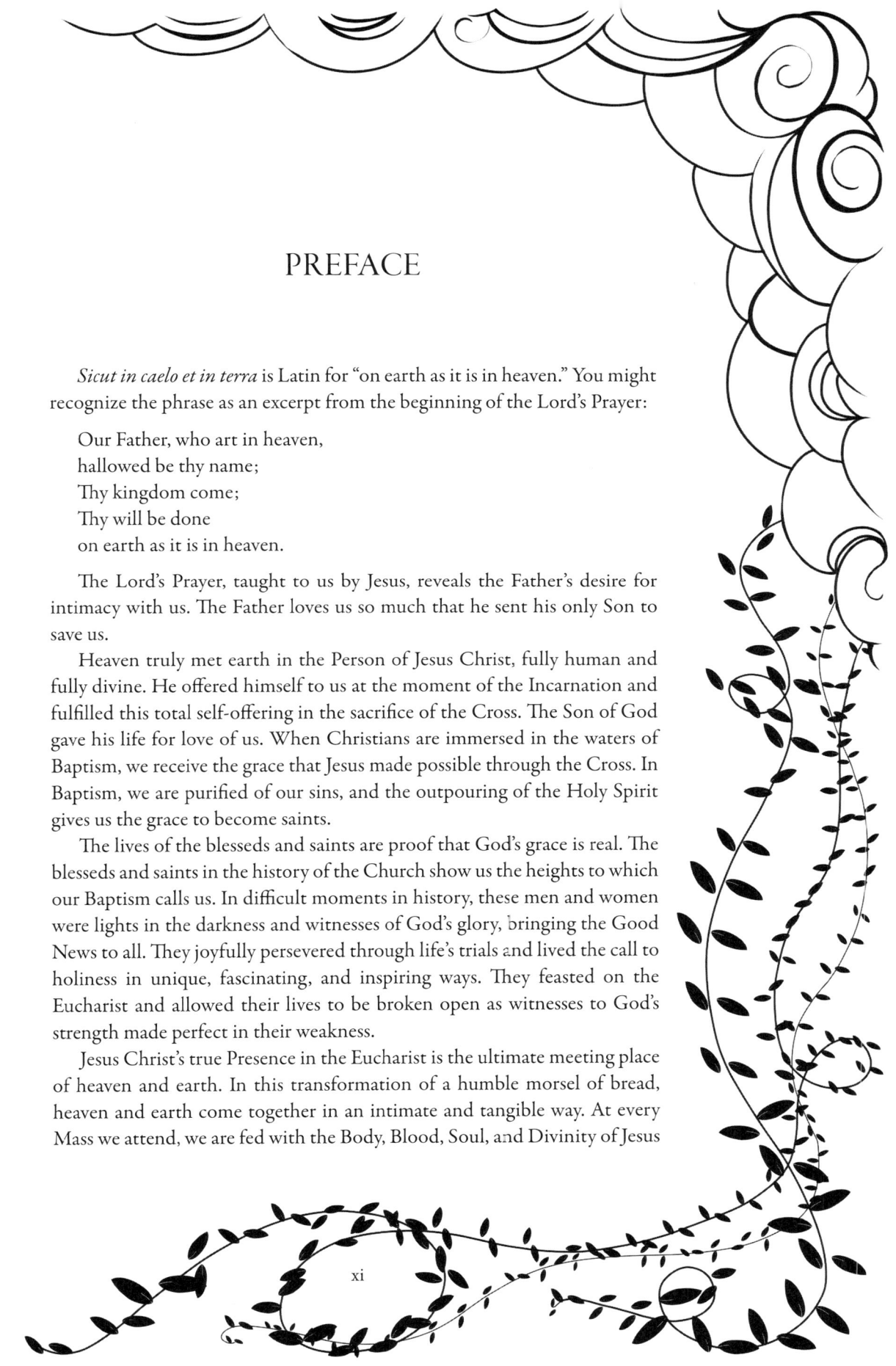

Sicut in caelo et in terra is Latin for "on earth as it is in heaven." You might recognize the phrase as an excerpt from the beginning of the Lord's Prayer:

Our Father, who art in heaven,
hallowed be thy name;
Thy kingdom come;
Thy will be done
on earth as it is in heaven.

The Lord's Prayer, taught to us by Jesus, reveals the Father's desire for intimacy with us. The Father loves us so much that he sent his only Son to save us.

Heaven truly met earth in the Person of Jesus Christ, fully human and fully divine. He offered himself to us at the moment of the Incarnation and fulfilled this total self-offering in the sacrifice of the Cross. The Son of God gave his life for love of us. When Christians are immersed in the waters of Baptism, we receive the grace that Jesus made possible through the Cross. In Baptism, we are purified of our sins, and the outpouring of the Holy Spirit gives us the grace to become saints.

The lives of the blesseds and saints are proof that God's grace is real. The blesseds and saints in the history of the Church show us the heights to which our Baptism calls us. In difficult moments in history, these men and women were lights in the darkness and witnesses of God's glory, bringing the Good News to all. They joyfully persevered through life's trials and lived the call to holiness in unique, fascinating, and inspiring ways. They feasted on the Eucharist and allowed their lives to be broken open as witnesses to God's strength made perfect in their weakness.

Jesus Christ's true Presence in the Eucharist is the ultimate meeting place of heaven and earth. In this transformation of a humble morsel of bread, heaven and earth come together in an intimate and tangible way. At every Mass we attend, we are fed with the Body, Blood, Soul, and Divinity of Jesus

Christ—the life with the power to transform us. Like the saints, we too are invited to embrace the spiritual transformation to which God calls us. We are invited to become food for others and to claim our unique place within the Body of Christ in order to make manifest God's kingdom of heaven on earth.

Transformation in Christ through the Eucharist is central to our life as religious sisters with the Daughters of St. Paul. We produced this book to help readers to foster deeper bonds with the holy men and women in heaven who show us how to live in Christ here on earth. Our hope is that the saints' lives will help you to discover your own story in Christ, develop new friendships, and feel encouraged to call on the saints' intercession. About thirty of our sisters prayed for you as they wrote, edited, designed, and illustrated this book. And all of our sisters in all of our convents and Pauline Books & Media bookstores around the world are praying for you.

As you pray through this book, we pray that it will build you up in faith and inspire hope in your life. We pray that it challenges you to live more deeply the call to holiness in God's good plan for your life. May we all be evermore united in Jesus Christ, Way for our will, Truth for our mind, and Life for our hearts—and may God's will be done on earth as it is in heaven.

Your sisters in Christ,
Daughters of St. Paul

"For everyone, each day is a chain of little things, a succession of minutes, continuous occasions of trials, difficulties, and precious little moments. One who knows how to sanctify everything weaves his life with golden thread."

— Blessed James Alberione

JANUARY 1

Saint Basil the Great

c. 330–January 1, 379
Feast: January 2 (with Saint Gregory Nazianzen)
Patron: Russia, monks, tailors

Basil came from a family of saints. His parents are Saint Basil the Elder and Saint Emmelia of Caesarea. Four of their ten children also became saints: Basil, Macrina, Gregory of Nyssa, and Peter. Basil studied in Athens, where he became close friends with Saint Gregory Nazianzen. After this, Basil had a spiritual awakening that led him to focus on his interior life. He visited various monasteries and later established his own. He wrote a Rule for monks that became the foundation of monastic life in the East. His Rule influenced Saint Benedict who wrote the Rule that would influence the West.

Basil eventually left the monastery to become a hermit. However, Archbishop Eusebius of Caesarea soon summoned him to refute Arius' teachings that Christ was not divine. Basil had much success in refuting Arianism and in 370 became a bishop himself. Basil also wrote important works that helped the Church articulate the dogma of the Trinity. As bishop, Basil was known for his tireless work for the sick and the poor, for whom he built many soup kitchens and a huge hospital. He was so beloved by Christians and non-Christians alike that upon his death, the entire city mourned.

Reflection

Basil's life shows us the importance of the Christian family. He was raised in an atmosphere of holiness by devout parents. Faith flourishes in direct proportion to the flourishing of Christian families. How can I support family life in society today?

Prayer

Saint Basil the Great, pray that as Catholics we might hold fast to the faith and witness it to others, especially through holiness in our families. Amen.

JANUARY 2

Saint Gregory Nazianzen

c. 325–c. 390
Feast: January 2 (with Saint Basil the Great)
Patron: Rhetoricians, philosophers

Gregory was born to pious parents, Saint Gregory the Elder and Saint Nonna. In fact, everyone in Gregory's immediate family is a canonized saint. Gregory is known for his close friendship with Saint Basil, whom he met in rhetorical school. It's no wonder then that young Gregory grew to be a very holy man, surrounded as he was by models of sanctity.

Gregory was shy, and most likely would have shunned public life and embraced life as a hermit given the choice. However, at the behest of his father, Gregory was ordained a priest and later became a bishop. Though shy, he had a gift for apologetics and speaking and was particularly known for his sermons on the Trinity. Called the "Theologian," Gregory was an outspoken critic of Arianism and was later named a Doctor of the Church. But Gregory's intellectual prowess was not the focus of his energies. For him, following God's will was most important. In the last years of his life, this focus led Gregory to submit his resignation as bishop and retire to a life of solitude. Today, his remains are buried in Saint Peter's in Rome.

Reflection

Gregory was a man of great integrity who, through much personal sacrifice, dedicated his life to the Church and to the truth. Setting aside personal preferences, Gregory worked untiringly for the people of God. Like holy and hardworking Gregory, how can I grow closer to Christ and become more Christ-like?

Prayer

Saint Gregory Nazianzen, you put God before all else and tirelessly lived your life in service to the truth. Help me to look beyond my own interests to help bring others to you. Amen.

JANUARY 3

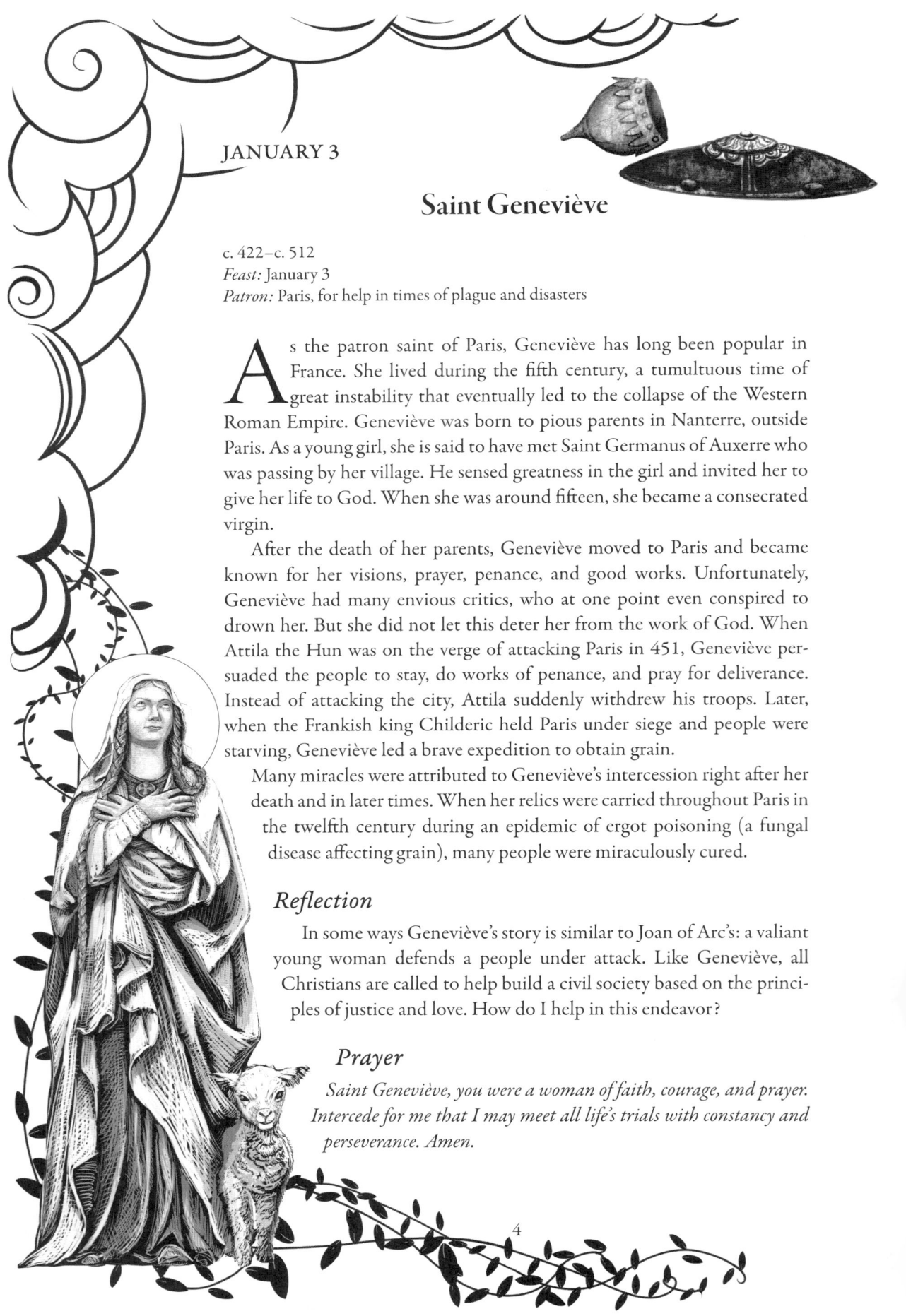

Saint Geneviève

c. 422–c. 512
Feast: January 3
Patron: Paris, for help in times of plague and disasters

As the patron saint of Paris, Geneviève has long been popular in France. She lived during the fifth century, a tumultuous time of great instability that eventually led to the collapse of the Western Roman Empire. Geneviève was born to pious parents in Nanterre, outside Paris. As a young girl, she is said to have met Saint Germanus of Auxerre who was passing by her village. He sensed greatness in the girl and invited her to give her life to God. When she was around fifteen, she became a consecrated virgin.

After the death of her parents, Geneviève moved to Paris and became known for her visions, prayer, penance, and good works. Unfortunately, Geneviève had many envious critics, who at one point even conspired to drown her. But she did not let this deter her from the work of God. When Attila the Hun was on the verge of attacking Paris in 451, Geneviève persuaded the people to stay, do works of penance, and pray for deliverance. Instead of attacking the city, Attila suddenly withdrew his troops. Later, when the Frankish king Childeric held Paris under siege and people were starving, Geneviève led a brave expedition to obtain grain.

Many miracles were attributed to Geneviève's intercession right after her death and in later times. When her relics were carried throughout Paris in the twelfth century during an epidemic of ergot poisoning (a fungal disease affecting grain), many people were miraculously cured.

Reflection

In some ways Geneviève's story is similar to Joan of Arc's: a valiant young woman defends a people under attack. Like Geneviève, all Christians are called to help build a civil society based on the principles of justice and love. How do I help in this endeavor?

Prayer

Saint Geneviève, you were a woman of faith, courage, and prayer. Intercede for me that I may meet all life's trials with constancy and perseverance. Amen.

JANUARY 4

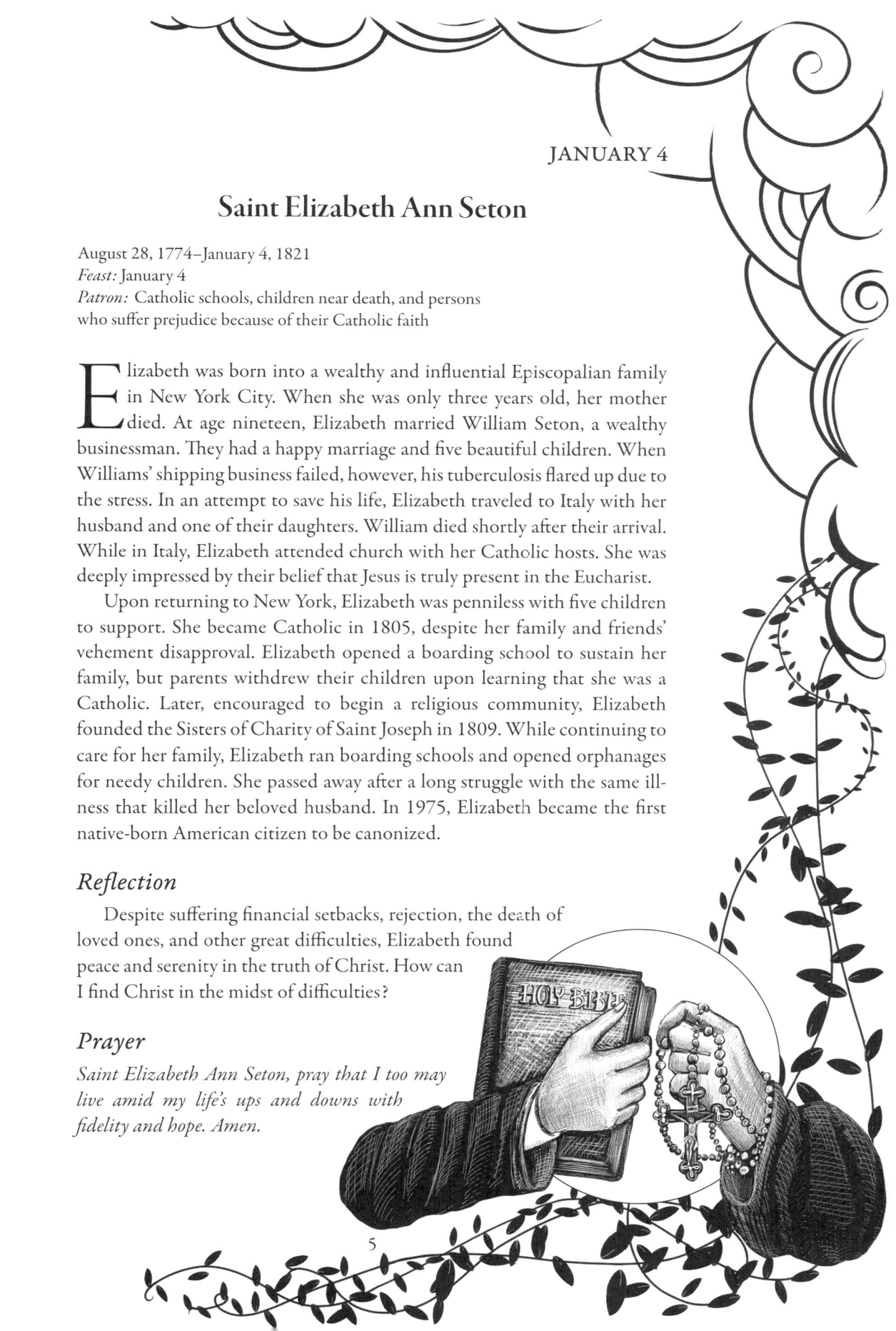

Saint Elizabeth Ann Seton

August 28, 1774–January 4, 1821
Feast: January 4
Patron: Catholic schools, children near death, and persons who suffer prejudice because of their Catholic faith

Elizabeth was born into a wealthy and influential Episcopalian family in New York City. When she was only three years old, her mother died. At age nineteen, Elizabeth married William Seton, a wealthy businessman. They had a happy marriage and five beautiful children. When Williams' shipping business failed, however, his tuberculosis flared up due to the stress. In an attempt to save his life, Elizabeth traveled to Italy with her husband and one of their daughters. William died shortly after their arrival. While in Italy, Elizabeth attended church with her Catholic hosts. She was deeply impressed by their belief that Jesus is truly present in the Eucharist.

Upon returning to New York, Elizabeth was penniless with five children to support. She became Catholic in 1805, despite her family and friends' vehement disapproval. Elizabeth opened a boarding school to sustain her family, but parents withdrew their children upon learning that she was a Catholic. Later, encouraged to begin a religious community, Elizabeth founded the Sisters of Charity of Saint Joseph in 1809. While continuing to care for her family, Elizabeth ran boarding schools and opened orphanages for needy children. She passed away after a long struggle with the same illness that killed her beloved husband. In 1975, Elizabeth became the first native-born American citizen to be canonized.

Reflection

Despite suffering financial setbacks, rejection, the death of loved ones, and other great difficulties, Elizabeth found peace and serenity in the truth of Christ. How can I find Christ in the midst of difficulties?

Prayer

Saint Elizabeth Ann Seton, pray that I too may live amid my life's ups and downs with fidelity and hope. Amen.

JANUARY 5

Saint John Neumann

March 28, 1811–January 5, 1860
Feast: January 5
Patron: Sick children, immigrants, Catholic schools

Born in Bohemia, young John Neumann was eager to become a missionary to immigrants in North America. After completing his seminary studies, he overcame a number of obstacles to arrive in New York in 1836. Bishop Jean Dubois welcomed him, ordained him, and immediately sent him to minister in the Buffalo area. Sometimes caring for several parishes at a time, John traveled on horseback both near and far to visit people in need. John loved being a diocesan priest, but soon he felt called to make religious vows as a Redemptorist priest. He made his religious profession in Baltimore in 1842.

Ten years later, having served in various positions—including temporary leadership of the United States province—a reluctant John was named bishop of Philadelphia. It was an enormous diocese. Characteristically fired with determination, John set to work. As bishop, he made it a point to focus on the people and their needs—delegating administration to others whenever he could. John learned several languages well enough to give spiritual help to various immigrant groups. Under his leadership, the Philadelphia parochial school system was established. He also wrote a catechism, fostered Eucharistic devotion, and his three-to-four-day parish visits were true spiritual renewals. John worked hard but never complained, for he loved serving the people. On a winter afternoon in 1860, John collapsed in the street and expired. Grief-stricken Philadelphians knew they had lost a saint.

Reflection

John Neumann's brief life pulsed with passion for the spiritual well-being of God's people. He tirelessly dedicated every moment of his life to serving God and his people. Do I live in a way that is passionately dedicated to God's will for me?

Prayer

Saint John Neumann, your deep awareness that Jesus was the center and hope of your life urged you on. Help me to center my life around Jesus. Amen.

JANUARY 6

Saint André Bessette

August 9, 1845–January 6, 1937
Feast: January 6 (U. S.), January 7 (Canada)
Patron: Sick, devotion to Saint Joseph

To the world, Alfred Bessette was a failure. Born into a poor Canadian family and orphaned by the time he was twelve, he was plagued by sickness from birth. To make matters worse, the illiterate young man found it difficult to keep a job. Farmhand, cobbler, blacksmith, baker, factory worker; he tried them all without success. But Alfred had two secret strengths: his profound faith and his deep devotion to Saint Joseph. At the age of twenty-five, through the help of an encouraging priest, he finally found his vocation as a Brother of Holy Cross, taking the name Brother André.

For the next forty years, the humble and uneducated Brother André served as doorkeeper of Notre-Dame College in Montreal. Word spread of the prayerful doorkeeper's deep holiness as physical and spiritual healings began to take place in answer to his prayers. Crowds flocked to see André and miracles multiplied. As many as 435 cures were documented in just one year. Brother André always gave the credit to Saint Joseph, encouraging his visitors to seek the saint's intercession with God. André convinced his superiors to build a tiny chapel in honor of Saint Joseph. Over time, it was enlarged and improved, finally becoming today's Oratory of Saint Joseph, the largest shrine dedicated to the saint in the world. Brother André Bessette died at age ninety-one. No less than one million people attended the funeral of this quiet man who walked a simple path to God.

Reflection

Brother André's life is proof that holiness doesn't require special talents or great learning. He knew that God simply desires a loving and trusting heart. Do I believe that great things can happen when I trust in God?

Prayer

Saint André Bessette, pray that the Lord will give me faith and love as strong as yours. Amen.

JANUARY 7

Saint Raymond of Peñafort

1175–January 6, 1275
Feast: January 7 (U. S.), January 8 (Canada)
Patron: Lawyers, especially canon lawyers

Born to a noble family in Spain near Barcelona, Raymond felt called to become a diocesan priest. He studied both civil and canon law, and then taught for fifteen years in Bologna. While in Italy, Raymond was inspired by the preaching of Blessed Reginald of Orleans, a member of the Dominicans, a new religious order. Raymond eventually received the Dominican habit in 1222. At the request of Pope Gregory IX, Raymond produced a collection of Church laws that became the standard until 1917. He also helped Saint Peter Nolasco establish the Mercedarians, a religious order of men with the mission of freeing Christians captured by Muslims.

Raymond was also a renowned preacher who attracted many vocations to the Dominicans and converted many others. Evangelization was an important goal for him so he established schools of Arabic language so Dominicans would be able to preach to the people of Spain and Northern Africa in their native tongues. In 1238 Raymond was elected the third Master General of the Dominicans. He gave of himself totally by visiting all the houses of the order, traveling on foot. After a life spent in total dedication to God, he died peacefully in Barcelona.

Reflection

Raymond's work in codifying her laws was a great contribution to the Church. Canon law is meant to assure that the Church's life is lived in an ordered way for the greatest good of all the members, especially the poor. It involves rights as well as responsibilities. Canon law is not an end in itself but can help us to be better disciples.

Prayer

Saint Raymond of Peñafort, pray for us that we will know how to blend justice with mercy, and love with truth. Through your prayers, may we come to know Jesus Christ more deeply and follow him with greater fidelity. Amen.

JANUARY 8

Blessed Eurosia Fabris Barban

September 27, 1866–January 8, 1932
Feast: January 8
Patron: Large families, vocational discernment

Called Rosina by her family, Eurosia Fabris grew up near Vicenza, Italy. After only two years of primary education, she left school to help her parents on their farm and at home. Nevertheless, she learned to read and write. A religious girl, she studied the catechism and read her Bible and works by the saints. Believing she was not called to marriage, Rosina turned down several marriage proposals. However, she reconsidered her vocation when a neighbor died in 1885 and Rosina stepped in to care for the deceased woman's two small children. After prayer and discernment, she decided to marry the children's father, Carlo Barban.

Rosina and Carlo had nine more children together. The Barbans were not wealthy, but they created a warm and welcoming Christian home. Rosina, now called "Mamma Rosa," lived simply, developed a deep prayer life, and cared for the poor, sick, and orphaned, as well as her own family. Mamma Rosa became a Third Order Franciscan. She took great joy in seeing three of her sons enter the priesthood. Widowed in 1930, Mamma Rosa died of natural causes just two years later. Many of her family members attended her beatification in 2005.

Reflection

Eurosia showed great openness to vocation: first to her own, and later to that of her children. Eurosia is a good example to all Christian parents of someone who lived her vocation well and encouraged her children to do the same. How can I support vocations in my family, parish, and diocese?

Prayer

Blessed Eurosia Fabris, pray that I remain open to God's call for me and for my loved ones. God's plans may not match my own, but God always wills the best for everyone. Amen.

JANUARY 9

Blessed Alix LeClerc

February 2, 1576–January 9, 1622
Feast: October 22
Patron: Education of young women

Alix was born to a wealthy family in the Lorraine region of what is now France. She lived a carefree life indulging in parties and entertainment and had little interest in her faith until she reached her late teens. However, during a serious illness, Alix read about the faith and began to contemplate the futility of this lifestyle. She slowly began to focus her attention completely on God. One day, Alix had a vision of the Blessed Mother holding a child. Mary said to Alix, "Take this child and make him grow." Alix's vision was a sign of her vocation to educate children.

On Christmas night in 1597, with the support of her spiritual director, Saint Peter Fourier, Alix founded the Congregation of Notre Dame: Canonesses of Saint Augustine. The next year, she opened the first of what would be many schools dedicated to the free education of girls. For so long, Alix had dreamed of educating young girls, and her schools attracted many students. However, the new congregation also met great opposition because at that time it was unusual for women religious to be outside of a cloistered convent. But Alix put her trust firmly in the Lord and endured misunderstanding and persecution with patience, knowing that her work was in the hands of God.

Reflection

Alix lived a life wholly dedicated to the work the Lord entrusted to her through the words of the Blessed Mother. She trusted in God's plan even when she was met with opposition. Do I trust that God is with me even in times of hardship?

Prayer

Blessed Alix LeClerc, please help me to grow in patience and serenity in the face of misunderstanding and difficulty. Please ask God to give me the grace to be more focused on others rather than on myself. Amen.

JANUARY 10

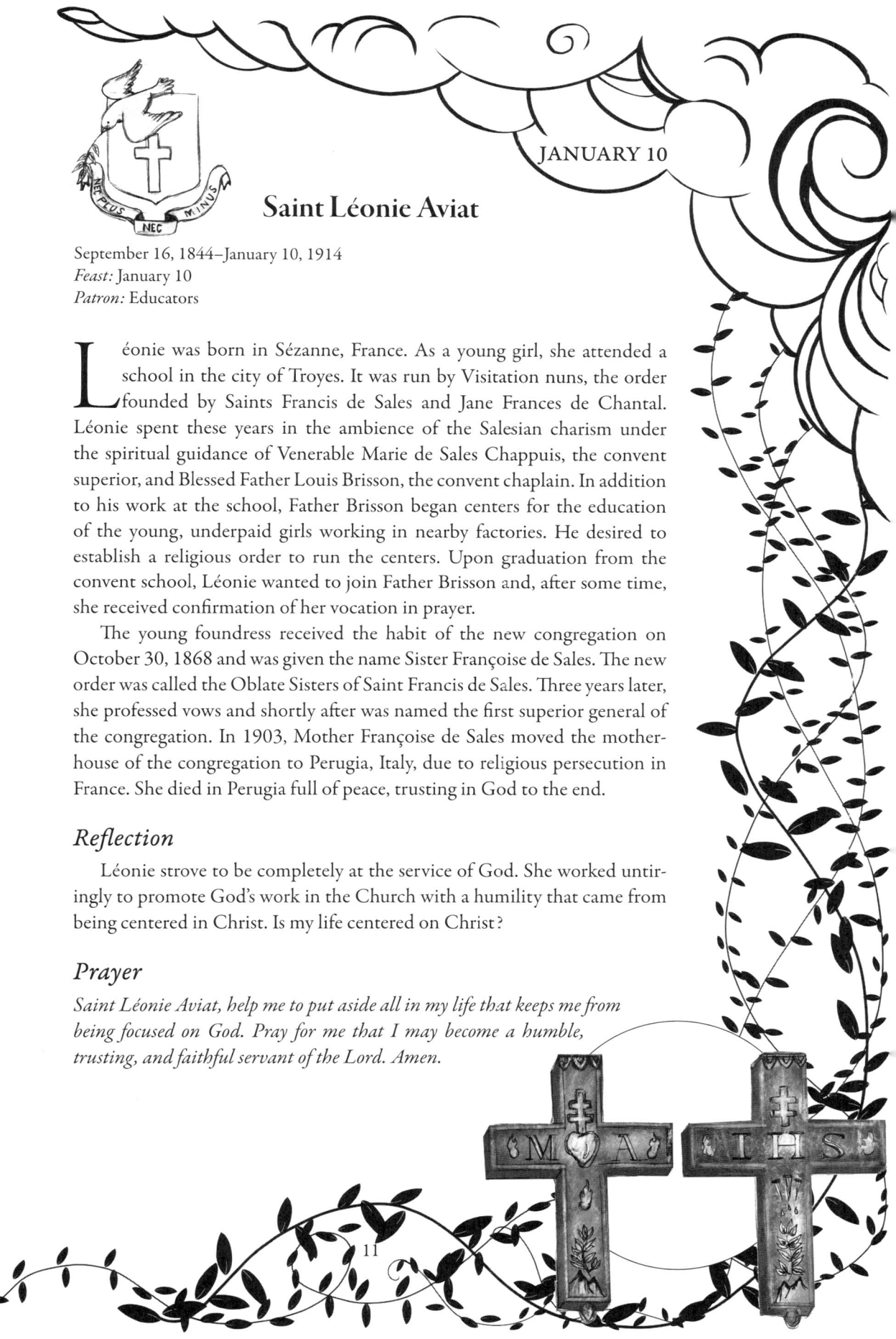

Saint Léonie Aviat

September 16, 1844–January 10, 1914
Feast: January 10
Patron: Educators

Léonie was born in Sézanne, France. As a young girl, she attended a school in the city of Troyes. It was run by Visitation nuns, the order founded by Saints Francis de Sales and Jane Frances de Chantal. Léonie spent these years in the ambience of the Salesian charism under the spiritual guidance of Venerable Marie de Sales Chappuis, the convent superior, and Blessed Father Louis Brisson, the convent chaplain. In addition to his work at the school, Father Brisson began centers for the education of the young, underpaid girls working in nearby factories. He desired to establish a religious order to run the centers. Upon graduation from the convent school, Léonie wanted to join Father Brisson and, after some time, she received confirmation of her vocation in prayer.

The young foundress received the habit of the new congregation on October 30, 1868 and was given the name Sister Françoise de Sales. The new order was called the Oblate Sisters of Saint Francis de Sales. Three years later, she professed vows and shortly after was named the first superior general of the congregation. In 1903, Mother Françoise de Sales moved the motherhouse of the congregation to Perugia, Italy, due to religious persecution in France. She died in Perugia full of peace, trusting in God to the end.

Reflection

Léonie strove to be completely at the service of God. She worked untiringly to promote God's work in the Church with a humility that came from being centered in Christ. Is my life centered on Christ?

Prayer

Saint Léonie Aviat, help me to put aside all in my life that keeps me from being focused on God. Pray for me that I may become a humble, trusting, and faithful servant of the Lord. Amen.

JANUARY 11

Saint Aelred of Rievaulx

c. 1110–January 12, 1167
Feast: January 12
Patron: Friendship

Aelred was born in Hexham, England. As a young adult, he was a member of the royal household of King David of Scotland. He earned not only the respect but also the friendship of the king, who promoted him to royal steward and wanted him to become a bishop. Aelred valued David's friendship and trust, but he also treasured the call from God that he was discerning in his life, and it was not to be a bishop.

Around 1134, Aelred entered the Cistercian monastery at Rievaulx. He was much beloved by the monks and soon served as director of novices as well as abbot of the new monastery at Ravesby in Lincolnshire. Then he was elected abbot of Rievaulx, a position that gave him responsibility for hundreds of monks and for the abbots of all the Cistercian monasteries in England. Aelred fulfilled this responsibility admirably, traveling extensively to visit the monasteries. During his travels, Aelred saw his friend King David one last time before the king died.

Aelred was an excellent preacher and a prolific writer. His writings include both historical and spiritual works, one of the most famous being *Spiritual Friendship*. Aelred patiently suffered various illnesses toward the end of his life, a testament to the gentle and humble way he lived.

Reflection

Aelred was a humble and open person, who used his position of responsibility not to gain power but to relate to people. He valued human friendship but placed the greatest value on his relationship with God. How do I make my relationship with God a priority in my life?

Prayer

Saint Aelred of Rievaulx, through your intercession, may my friends and I grow closer to Christ through a holy friendship. Amen.

JANUARY 12

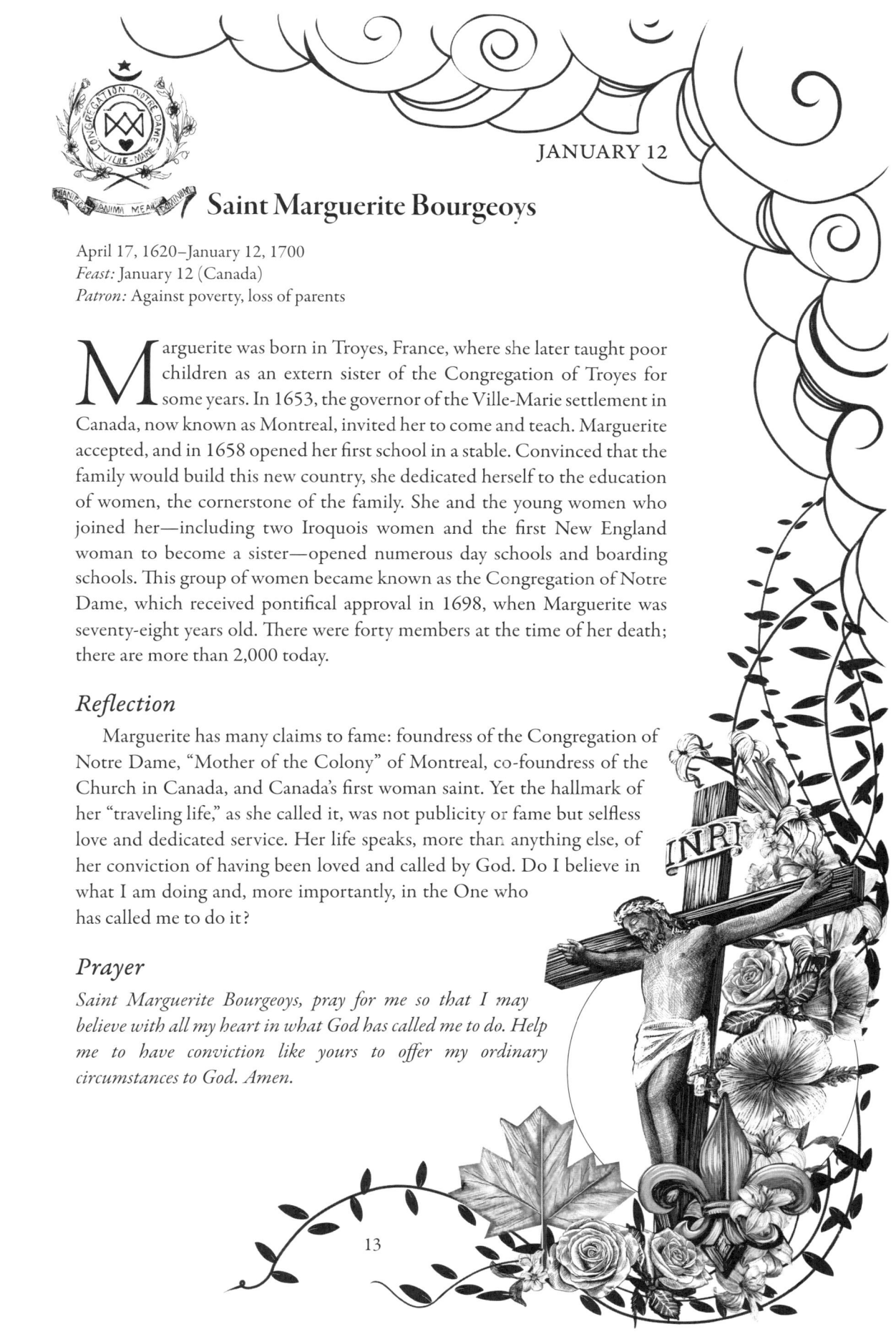

Saint Marguerite Bourgeoys

April 17, 1620–January 12, 1700
Feast: January 12 (Canada)
Patron: Against poverty, loss of parents

Marguerite was born in Troyes, France, where she later taught poor children as an extern sister of the Congregation of Troyes for some years. In 1653, the governor of the Ville-Marie settlement in Canada, now known as Montreal, invited her to come and teach. Marguerite accepted, and in 1658 opened her first school in a stable. Convinced that the family would build this new country, she dedicated herself to the education of women, the cornerstone of the family. She and the young women who joined her—including two Iroquois women and the first New England woman to become a sister—opened numerous day schools and boarding schools. This group of women became known as the Congregation of Notre Dame, which received pontifical approval in 1698, when Marguerite was seventy-eight years old. There were forty members at the time of her death; there are more than 2,000 today.

Reflection

Marguerite has many claims to fame: foundress of the Congregation of Notre Dame, "Mother of the Colony" of Montreal, co-foundress of the Church in Canada, and Canada's first woman saint. Yet the hallmark of her "traveling life," as she called it, was not publicity or fame but selfless love and dedicated service. Her life speaks, more than anything else, of her conviction of having been loved and called by God. Do I believe in what I am doing and, more importantly, in the One who has called me to do it?

Prayer

Saint Marguerite Bourgeoys, pray for me so that I may believe with all my heart in what God has called me to do. Help me to have conviction like yours to offer my ordinary circumstances to God. Amen.

JANUARY 13

Saint Hilary of Poitiers

c. 310–c. 368
Feast: January 13
Patron: Children with disabilities, lawyers, and the sick

Hilary was born to a wealthy family in Poitiers, Gaul. He was married and had a daughter, Abra, when he converted from paganism to Christianity after reading the Scriptures. Around 345, he was baptized with his wife and daughter at the Easter Vigil. Hilary was so highly respected by the people that he was asked only a few years later to become bishop of Poitiers. He was ordained and immediately became involved in the heated Arian controversy, which denied that Jesus was both human and divine.

Unfortunately, while Hilary was bishop, Emperor Constantius, the son of Constantine, continually meddled in the Church's affairs and promoted Arianism. Despite the likely consequences, Hilary refused to align with the Arian bishops. Unsurprisingly, he was exiled to Phrygia in 356. While in exile, he took advantage of his extra time to write twelve books entitled *On the Trinity, Against the Arians*. Hilary returned to Gaul in 360 or 361 and continued to preach against Arian views, helping many to understand the error of Arianism. Sulpicius Severus, a writer of sacred history, remarked of Hilary that the entire French nation had been delivered from heresy through his intervention. Pope Pius IX formally recognized him as a Doctor of the Church in 1851.

Reflection

Hilary showed prudence and moderation in his efforts to overcome the Arian heresy. Instead of complaining, Hilary accepted his exile and made the best of it. And while knowing the dangers, he continued to defend the truth and accept the consequences with patience. Do I defend the truth of the Gospel with both tenacity and prudence?

Prayer

Saint Hilary of Poitiers, help me to be wise in my defense of the faith, charitable to those who disagree with me, and merciful with all. Amen.

JANUARY 14

Blessed Peter Donders

October 27, 1809–January 14, 1887
Feast: January 14
Patron: Those rejected by religious orders, factory workers

Peter Donders was born in Tillburg, Holland. Because of his family's poverty, he received little schooling. From a young age, Peter had to do farm work and work in a factory to help support his family. Peter wanted to become a priest and, finally, with the support of some local priests, he entered the diocesan seminary at the age of twenty-two. On June 5, 1841 he was ordained a priest. Soon after his ordination, he traveled to the Dutch mission in Suriname, South America, arriving in Paramaribo. He ministered to the poor and plantation slaves. He worked to improve their appalling conditions and baptized over 1,200 people before volunteering to serve the leper colony at Batavia. There, he personally nursed the lepers and worked with the civil government to better the conditions of the leper colony.

In 1866, the Redemptorists arrived to take over the mission in Suriname. Peter had always wanted to become a religious priest, but he had been refused admission to the Redemptorists as a young man. God's providence provided another chance. He asked to be admitted to the congregation and took vows just one year later. He then spent several years ministering to the Indian people of Suriname, learning the native language and catechizing them. When his health failed, he was eventually transferred back to the leper colony where he spent the rest of his life nursing the sick.

Reflection

Peter risked his life for his faith, serving lepers and making long, dangerous missionary journeys. Peter's life demonstrates a zeal and selfless dedication to proclaiming Jesus Christ despite challenges. What am I willing to risk to witness to the Gospel?

Prayer

Blessed Peter Donders, help me to keep my eyes on the Lord despite setbacks and challenges. May my life always proclaim the Gospel of Jesus Christ to those I encounter. Amen.

JANUARY 15

Saint Arnold Janssen

November 5, 1837–January 15, 1909
Feast: January 15
Patron: Society of the Divine Word, missionaries

Arnold Janssen was born in Goch, Germany, the second of ten children. He entered the seminary and studied science and mathematics. He was ordained in 1861 and then was a teacher for twelve years. While teaching, Arnold became more aware of the universal mission of the Church and the needs of the faithful around the word. He felt called by God to do something new.

In the 1870s, legislation was passed that severely restricted the Church in Germany. In the midst of a chaotic and difficult time for the Church, Arnold saw possibility. He proposed beginning a seminary to prepare priests for the missions. Many thought Arnold was imprudent, but he said in response, "The Lord challenges our faith to do something new, precisely when so many things are collapsing in the Church."

Trusting in the providence of God and with the support of several bishops, Arnold moved across the border to Steyl, Holland. In 1875, he founded the Divine Word Missionaries in an old, rundown inn. Four years later, the first two missionary priests left for China. Arnold added religious brothers to his society and co-founded two orders of religious women, the Missionary Sisters Servants of the Holy Spirit and the cloistered Missionary Sisters Servants of the Holy Spirit of Perpetual Adoration. Today, thousands of men and women in these societies continue the work Arnold began.

Reflection

God opened Arnold's heart to the spiritual needs of the world, preparing him for a mission that would bring light in the midst of a dark period in the Church. Do I have the courage to hope in something new when everyone else only sees problems?

Prayer

Saint Arnold Janssen, you are a reminder that God is always at work in the Church and in the world. Help me to have faith in this reality, especially in difficulties. Amen.

JANUARY 16

Saint Joseph Vaz

April 21, 1651–January 16, 1711
Feast: January 16
Patron: Sri Lanka

Joseph Vaz was born in Benaulim, Goa, on the southwestern coast of India. His parents were Catholic converts who belonged to the Brahmin caste. Joseph was a bright student who learned both Portuguese and Latin and studied rhetoric, philosophy, and theology. From a young age, he was known for his devotion and would spend many hours before Jesus in the tabernacle. Joseph was ordained a priest in 1676. With a group of clergy, Joseph started a religious order patterned on the Oratory of Saint Philip Neri. He was well respected and soon became the superior of the order.

Although he loved his priestly work, Joseph had a heart for the missions. He longed to help Catholics on the island of Ceylon, now Sri Lanka. The Dutch controlled the area and refused to allow priests to minister to the people. Nevertheless, Joseph obtained permission to go to Ceylon and left in disguise with a former family servant. He barely survived the dangerous trip, but as soon as he recovered, he began to help the people, supporting himself by begging. Dutch persecutions soon forced Joseph to move to the Kandy region, an area still controlled by Buddhists. There, the Buddhist king jailed him, but after gaining his respect, Joseph was released and continued to minister to the people. Joseph died in Kandy among the people he had served with great love.

Reflection

Joseph lived a simple, poor life in imitation of Jesus with little thought for his own comfort or safety. How can I strive to dedicate all my energies to doing God's will in my life?

Prayer

Blessed Joseph Vaz, help me to live a simple life close to the poor and downtrodden. Like you, may I seek to live a holy life that gives glory to God. Amen.

JANUARY 17

Saint Anthony of Egypt

c. 251–c. 356
Feast: January 17
Patron: Butchers, gravediggers, skin diseases

The founder of Christian monasticism, Anthony dedicated all of his adult life to solitude and prayer. We know details of his life from a biography written by his friend Saint Athanasius, who spent some time in his monastic community.

Anthony was born into a wealthy Egyptian family. He had not yet turned twenty years old when his parents died, leaving him to take care of his younger sister. One day, when Anthony went to church, he heard from Matthew's Gospel, "If you wish to be perfect, go, sell your possessions, and give the money to the poor . . . then come, follow me" (Mt 19:21). Anthony felt that God was addressing these words directly to him.

Immediately, Anthony gave away the wealth he had inherited from his parents. He entrusted his sister to the care of a local convent. Then, from the age of twenty-one, Anthony lived as a hermit for many years. He interrupted his solitude only to teach the Christians who followed him into the desert. Many people attributed healings to Anthony's prayers. Eventually, Anthony founded a monastic community and would visit the monks and give them encouraging exhortations. For all his life, Anthony endured numerous temptations. However, despite these temptations, he persevered in following Christ until he breathed his last.

Reflection

Anthony devoted his life to prayer and fasting as a hermit. When he experienced strong temptations and struggles, he intensified his prayer and commitment to God. How can I be steadfast in my prayer even when it's difficult?

Prayer

Saint Anthony of Egypt, you always kept the attention of your heart fixed on Christ. Help me to focus more completely on God. Amen.

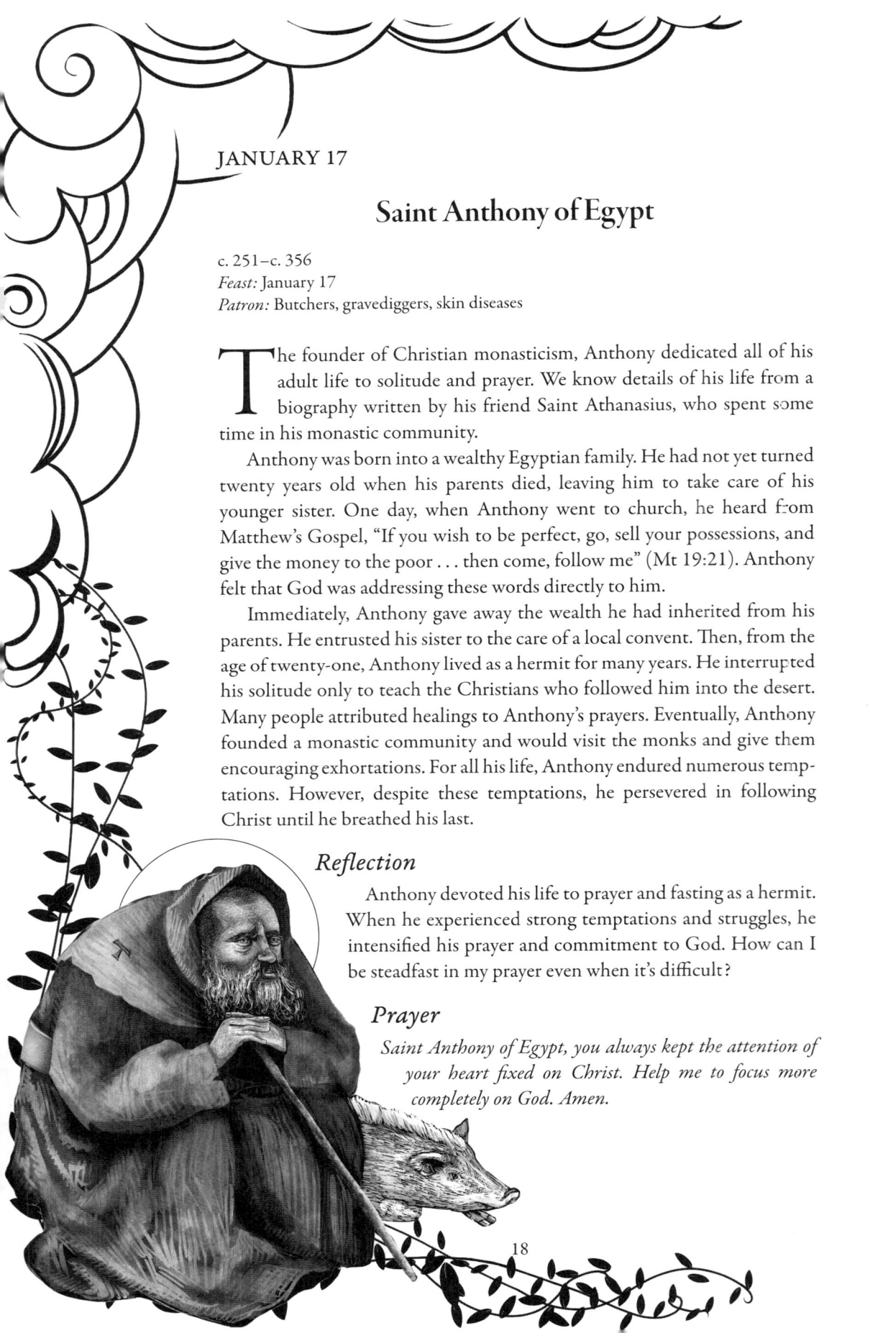

JANUARY 18

Blessed Regina Protmann

1552–January 18, 1613
Feast: January 18
Patron: Congregation of Saint Catherine of Alexandria, works of charity

Regina Protmann was born to a wealthy family at the time of the Reformation in the city of Braunsberg, in what is now northern Poland. At age nineteen, a time when most young woman would have been thinking about marriage, Regina was moved to dedicate her life to God and serve the sick and poor.

In 1571, Regina began working with other women inspired by her vision and together they formed an innovative new order, the Congregation of Saint Catherine of Alexandria. Her vision of a perpetually vowed religious community in direct engagement with the world was unusual for the time. Most women religious observed a strict enclosure. However, inspired by the Holy Spirit, Regina set out to found a community in which an active life was blended with a life of prayer and contemplation.

In 1583, with the support of the local Jesuits and her bishop, Regina wrote a Rule for her new congregation. More young women were inspired to join the new order and to give their lives to prayer, service to the sick, and the education of the young. To this day women of this order are dedicated to serving the people of God.

Reflection

Regina had a new vision for religious life that united contemplation with action. Although her inspiration from the Holy Spirit took some time to be understood, she remained patient and humble. Am I patient when I am misunderstood?

Prayer

Blessed Regina Protmann, pray that I may grow in the virtue of patience and trust in the Lord in all circumstances. Like you, may I balance my busy life with prayer and service. Amen.

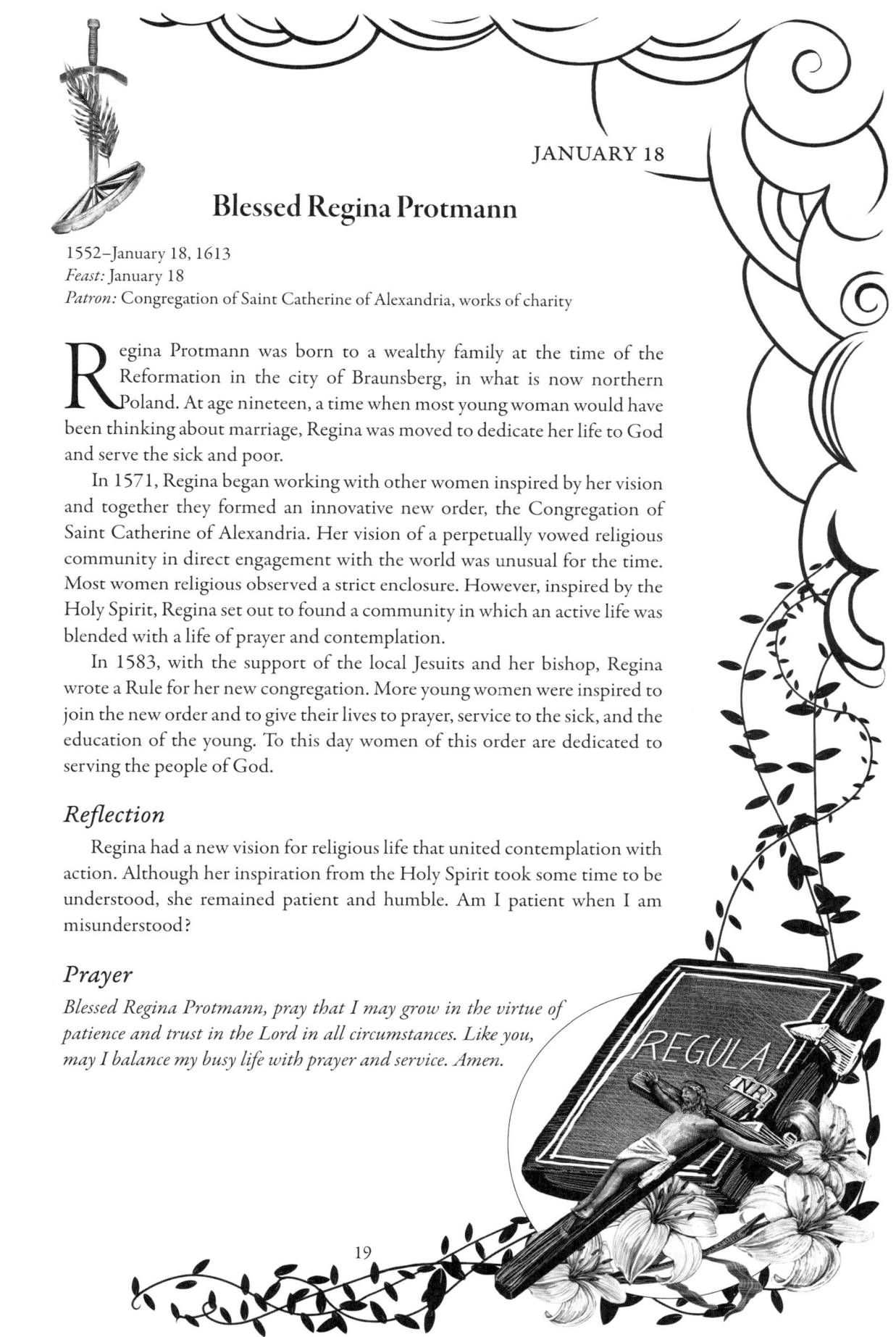

JANUARY 19

Saint Fabian

c. 200–January 20, 250
Feast: January 20
Patron: Potters

Fabian was a farmer who happened to visit Rome at the time of a papal election in 236. While he was observing the proceedings, legend has it that a dove descended on his head. People took this as a sign of God's favor, so Fabian, a layman and a farmer, was elected pope.

After being ordained a priest and bishop, Fabian served as pope for fourteen years during a mostly peaceful time. He is said to have divided Rome into seven sections and assigned a deacon to each section so the people could be better served. Fabian also had a great regard for the bodies of the martyrs. He brought the bodies of Saints Pontian and Hippolytus from Sardinia to Rome and had work done on the catacombs so that the martyrs could be appropriately honored. He also sent seven bishops as missionaries to evangelize the people of Gaul. Shortly after Decius became the Roman emperor in 249, he began to persecute the Church. Fabian died heroically as a martyr during that time.

Reflection

Fabian carefully preserved the martyrs' bodies to honor them and to help the Church remember them. With an eye for the future growth of the Church, he also sent out missionaries. With these actions, Fabian demonstrated the importance of balancing a respect for the past with an eye always to the future. Fabian shows how the Church is always called to be on the move—evangelizing and spreading the kingdom of God—but also that new growth is always rooted in tradition.

Prayer

Saint Fabian, you courageously gave your life to witness to Jesus and his Gospel. Pray for us that the Church today might go forward with courage while holding on to its precious heritage. Amen.

JANUARY 20

Saint Sebastian

c. 263–c. 288
Feast: January 20
Patron: Archers, athletes, soldiers

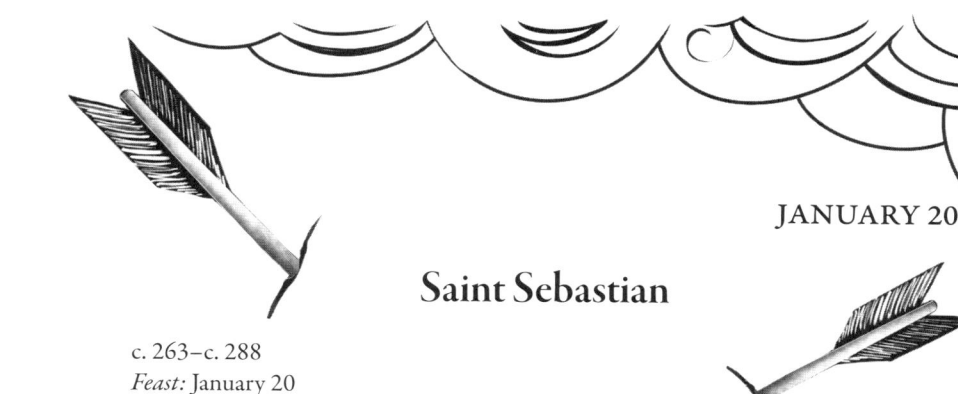

Legend has it that Sebastian grew up in Milan. He entered the army in Rome and eventually became an officer in the imperial army. A man filled with faith, Sebastian knew that being a Christian was dangerous. But he nevertheless regularly tried to share the faith without fear and won many converts. When it was discovered that Sebastian was a Christian, he appeared before the emperor Diocletian. Sentenced to death by arrows, he miraculously survived with the help of Saint Irene, who nursed him back to health.

Rather than going into hiding after his recovery, however, it is said that Sebastian instead sought out the emperor and chastised him for persecuting the Christians. The emperor, after getting over his shock at seeing the healthy man before him, sentenced Sebastian to be clubbed to death. For this reason, Sebastian is sometimes referred to as "the saint who was martyred twice." He was buried in a cemetery on the Appian Way, close to where a basilica, *San Sebastiano Fuori le Mura*, was later built in his name. For centuries after Sebastian's death, many who sought his intercession against the plague were healed.

Reflection

Sebastian's martyrdom has captured the imagination of many artists who memorialized the legend of his death as a young man pierced for his faith with a barrage of arrows. His courage and tenacity in the face of persecution, depicted in these beautiful works of art, can be a source of inspiration for all Christians who suffer for what they believe.

Prayer

Saint Sebastian, may my faith become so strong that I am willing and able to endure any hardship that comes my way. Please pray for all Christians who endure violence, martyrdom, and persecution for believing in Jesus. Amen.

JANUARY 21

Saint Agnes

c. 291–c. 304
Feast: January 21
Patron: Chastity, virgins, rape victims, gardeners

Tradition relates that Agnes was only twelve or thirteen at the time of her martyrdom. Already at this young age, her love for Jesus Christ guided her life. When persecution of the Christians broke out in Rome (it is uncertain which persecution), Agnes was sentenced to death.

Legend has it that the judge sent Agnes to a house of prostitution, but her hair grew long enough to cover her naked body. It is said that a man who tried to look at her was struck blind. Her persecutors then tried to burn her at the stake; when that failed, they beheaded her. Because her name is similar to the Latin *agnus* (lamb), she is often represented with a lamb, as a symbol of her purity of heart. A centuries-old tradition on her feast day involves the blessing of two lambs whose wool is then used to make palliums. Palliums are bands of cloth worn by the pope and archbishops over the neck, shoulders, and chest. They symbolize the pastoral office of the Church, and the Good Shepherd for whom Agnes gave her life.

Reflection

We know very little about Agnes' life and death. But from what we do know emerges the "one thing necessary": single-hearted passion for God and undivided resolve in following him. This led her not only to physical martyrdom, but also to the daily martyrdom of surrendering herself to God and choosing his love in every moment. Agnes shows that loving single-heartedly is not a one-time choice: it means to choose to love again and again.

Prayer

Saint Agnes, you loved Jesus the Good Shepherd in life and in death. Help me to choose his love every day. Amen.

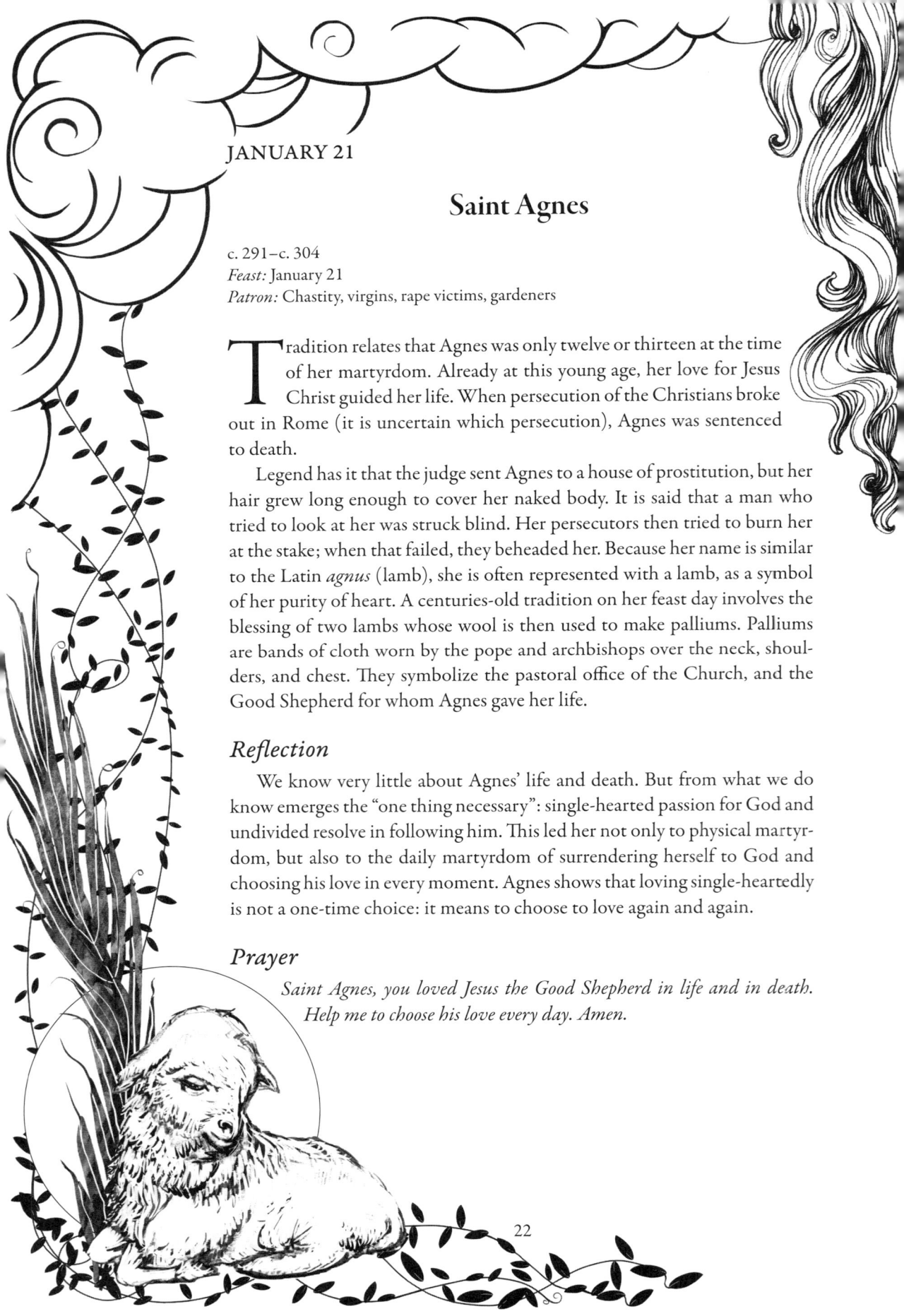

JANUARY 22

Saint Vincent of Saragossa

Died c. 304
Feast: January 22
Patron: Vinedressers, vinegar makers, winemakers

Much of what is known about Vincent's life comes from a poem written about a hundred years after his death by a man named Prudentius. Vincent was a holy and dedicated deacon from northeastern Spain. He was instructed in the faith by the bishop Valerius, who entrusted the young deacon with many responsibilities.

During the persecutions of the Roman Emperor Diocletian, Vincent and Bishop Valerius were brought before Dacian, the governor of Spain. Because Valerius had a speech impediment, Vincent spoke eloquently in his place in defense of the faith. Perhaps due to his powerful speech, Vincent was sentenced to death whereas Valerius was merely exiled. Vincent was forced to endure brutal torture, including being roasted on a gridiron, torn with iron hooks, and, finally, thrown into a dungeon. Inspired by his courage, pious Christians visited Vincent in jail and attended to his wounds. With bold love for the faith, Vincent converted his jailer, but, soon after, he succumbed to his terrible injuries. His body and even the instruments of his torture were preserved and venerated after Vincent's courageous martyrdom.

Reflection

A young man strong in faith and courage, Vincent faced his martyrdom knowing that life in Christ is more powerful than death. His death was an inspiration to his fellow Christians and continues to inspire us to this day. How can I make better use of my time as a preparation for eternity?

Prayer

Saint Vincent of Saragossa, help me to courageously face all life's challenges with the tenacity and conviction with which you faced death. Pray for me, that I may boldly walk along the path of life and prepare for my eventual death. Amen.

JANUARY 23

Saint Marianne Cope

January 23, 1838–August 9, 1918
Feast: January 23
Patron: Hansen's disease, outcasts, those with HIV/AIDS, Hawaii

Barbara Koob was born to a poor farming family in Germany. One year later, the family immigrated to Utica, New York, where her father changed their surname to Cope. When her father could no longer work due to illness, Barbara got a factory job to help support the family. In her heart, however, she nourished a strong desire to serve God as a religious sister.

In 1862, Barbara finally was able to enter the Sisters of Saint Francis in Syracuse, New York. She received the habit and was called Sister Marianne. She began teaching and soon became principal of several elementary schools in New York. Sister Marianne also helped to establish two of the first hospitals in central New York where she lovingly cared for the patients.

After Sister Marianne had been elected the provincial of her community, a priest wrote to her in 1883 on behalf of Hawaii's king and queen. He had asked various religious congregations for help to care for people with leprosy (now called Hansen's disease). Mother Marianne accepted the invitation and went to Hawaii with six other sisters. Soon after her arrival, she was asked to manage Malulani Hospital in Maui. In November 1888, Mother Marianne went to Kalaupapa on the island of Molokai to care for women and girls who had leprosy. She knew that she would most likely never return. There, she met Saint Damien, who had spent his life caring for the lepers. The priest was very ill and died a few months later. For the next thirty years, Mother Marianne totally dedicated herself to caring for the people on Molokai.

Reflection

Mother Marianne always saw Jesus in everyone she met. She once said, "I do not think of reward; I am working for God, and do so cheerfully." Am I willing to help others and to generously serve those in need?

Prayer

Saint Marianne Cope, pray that I might see the face of Christ in everyone I meet, and treat all with love. Amen.

JANUARY 24

Saint Francis de Sales

August 21, 1567–December 28, 1622
Feast: January 24
Patron: Writers, confessors, the deaf, journalists, the press, teachers

Francis was born the eldest in a wealthy noble family in the Savoy region of France. His father was a severe man who hoped Francis would pursue a career in public service. Francis greatly desired to be a priest but, knowing his father's desires, he patiently waited to reveal his vocation to his family. Soon after acquiring his doctorate at the prestigious University of Padua, a relieved Francis was able to obtain permission from his father to become a priest.

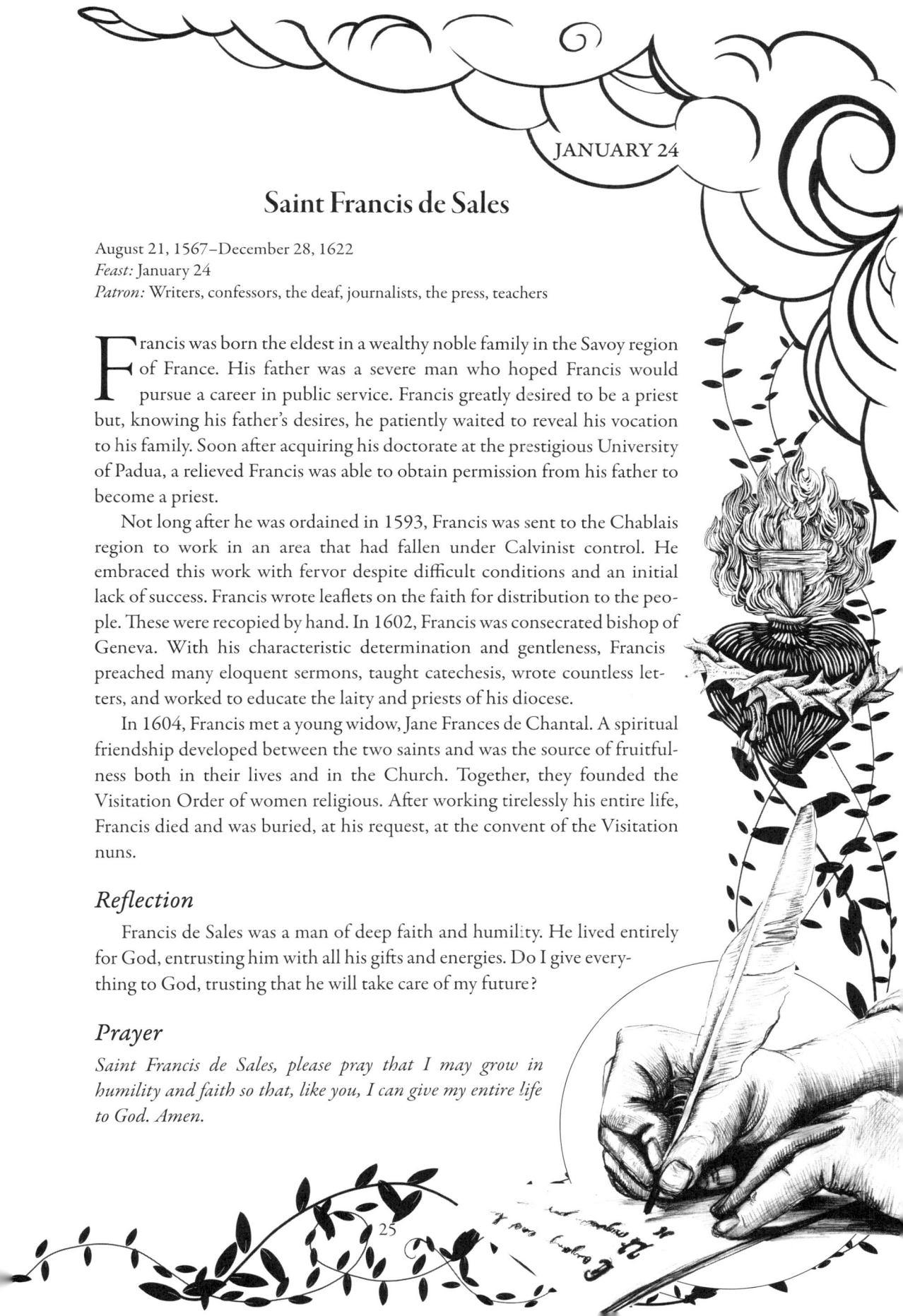

Not long after he was ordained in 1593, Francis was sent to the Chablais region to work in an area that had fallen under Calvinist control. He embraced this work with fervor despite difficult conditions and an initial lack of success. Francis wrote leaflets on the faith for distribution to the people. These were recopied by hand. In 1602, Francis was consecrated bishop of Geneva. With his characteristic determination and gentleness, Francis preached many eloquent sermons, taught catechesis, wrote countless letters, and worked to educate the laity and priests of his diocese.

In 1604, Francis met a young widow, Jane Frances de Chantal. A spiritual friendship developed between the two saints and was the source of fruitfulness both in their lives and in the Church. Together, they founded the Visitation Order of women religious. After working tirelessly his entire life, Francis died and was buried, at his request, at the convent of the Visitation nuns.

Reflection

Francis de Sales was a man of deep faith and humility. He lived entirely for God, entrusting him with all his gifts and energies. Do I give everything to God, trusting that he will take care of my future?

Prayer

Saint Francis de Sales, please pray that I may grow in humility and faith so that, like you, I can give my entire life to God. Amen.

JANUARY 25

Saint Paul, the Apostle

c. 6–c. 67
Feasts: January 25 (Conversion), June 29 (Saints Peter and Paul)
Patron: Authors, journalists, the press, publishers, missionaries, public relations, travel

Paul was a deeply religious Jew—a Pharisee persecuting the early Christians out of misguided devotion—when he encountered the risen Christ on the road to Damascus. In that powerful moment, Christ revealed himself to Paul and turned his life upside down. Paul was captured by Christ's love and transformed into his apostle. He devoted the rest of his life to the mission of proclaiming Christ to the world.

To preach the Gospel, Paul traveled tens of thousands of miles on foot and by sea. He was imprisoned, stoned, and beaten for the sake of the Gospel. Yet for Paul, his greatest suffering was his concern for the early Christian communities that were struggling. He was a passionate man with whom it wasn't always easy to work. Paul sometimes provoked controversy and rejection. Despite the many hardships he faced, Paul never lost his passion to preach the Gospel. Paul gave us the earliest books of the New Testament—his letters to the various Christian communities he founded. In them, Paul personally and creatively reveals his warm pastoral heart, his practical theology, and his Christ-centered spirituality. Paul's desire to complete the gift of his life to Christ was fulfilled when he was martyred in Rome.

Reflection

The key to understanding Paul is his relationship with Christ. Captivated by Christ on the road to Damascus, Paul's life goal was to allow himself to be transformed into Christ, so that Christ could fully live, act, speak, and love through him. What is my life's goal? Is it Christ-centered?

Prayer

Saint Paul, your heart overflowed with the love of the Lord Jesus Christ. Show me how to let Christ's love grow in me so that I, too, may witness to Christ's unfathomable love. Amen.

JANUARY 26

Saints Timothy and Titus

First Century
Feast: January 26
Patron: Timothy: Stomach, intestinal disorders; Titus: United States Army Chaplain Corps

Both of today's saints were associates of Saint Paul. The Acts of the Apostles first mentions Timothy during Paul's second missionary journey. Timothy "was well spoken of by the believers in Lystra and Iconium. Paul wanted Timothy to accompany him" (Acts 16:2–3). Timothy joined Paul, and the young man became a missionary and one of the pillars of the early Church. Paul names Timothy as a co-sender of six of his letters and highly praises him: "I have no one like him" (Phil 2:20). In the year 64, Paul commissioned Timothy to govern the Church in Ephesus.

Titus was another important companion and co-worker of Paul. Titus accompanied him to the Council of Jerusalem, which decided that Gentile Christians did not have to follow all Jewish practices. At one point Paul sent Titus to the Corinthians to help calm the waters after some controversy. Tradition holds that Paul made Titus a bishop to govern the Church on the island of Crete. Though attributed to Paul, the pastoral letters to Timothy and Titus in the New Testament were probably written by an anonymous author later in the first century. They contain valuable guidance for the Church's pastors.

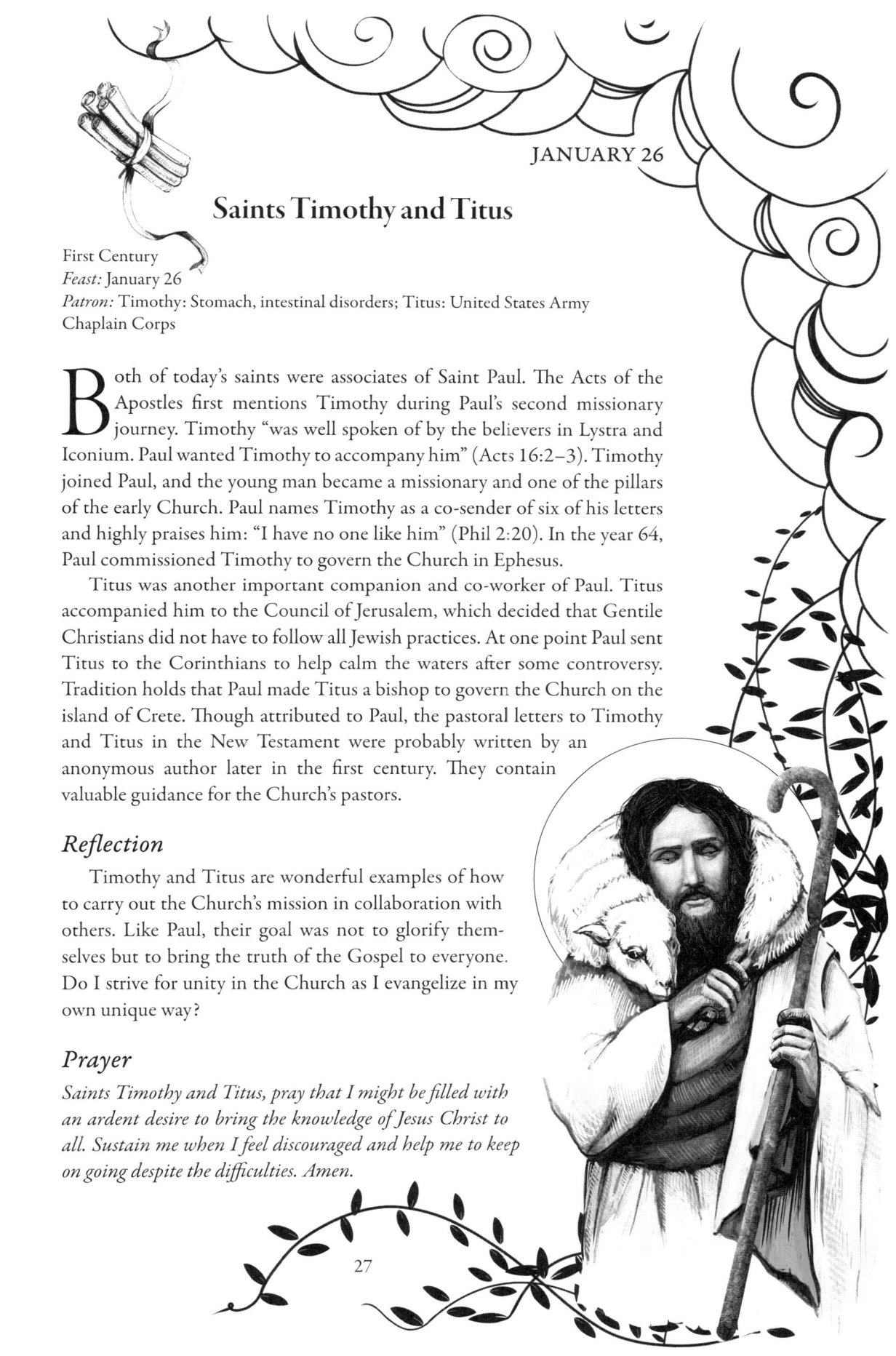

Reflection

Timothy and Titus are wonderful examples of how to carry out the Church's mission in collaboration with others. Like Paul, their goal was not to glorify themselves but to bring the truth of the Gospel to everyone. Do I strive for unity in the Church as I evangelize in my own unique way?

Prayer

Saints Timothy and Titus, pray that I might be filled with an ardent desire to bring the knowledge of Jesus Christ to all. Sustain me when I feel discouraged and help me to keep on going despite the difficulties. Amen.

JANUARY 27

Saint Angela Merici

c. 1474–January 27, 1540
Feast: January 27
Patron: Sick and people with disabilities

Angela was the fifth of six children in a middle-class farming family in northern Italy. When she was young, Angela learned about the saints from her father who would read aloud their stories. She had a special devotion to Saint Ursula, who, according to legend, was a young virgin and princess who died a martyr. Unfortunately, Angela knew sorrow at an early age. Three brothers, one sister, and both her parents died when Angela was a young girl. Angela and her remaining sister went to live with an uncle.

After her uncle died, Angela became a lay Franciscan, returning to her hometown of Desenzano. Angela observed a great need for the education and care of poor young women. In her time, women who did not marry or enter religious life often ended up on the streets as prostitutes or beggars. Together with some other women, Angela began to care for and educate women in need. In 1535, when Angela was in her sixties, her "Company of Saint Ursula" was officially established in Brescia. Angela wanted her companions to live, work, and pray among the people they served. Four years after her death, the Company became a religious congregation, the first women's teaching order in the Church.

Reflection

Angela was a determined woman who clearly perceived the needs of others and allowed those needs to move her. No doubt she was so sensitive to others' needs because she had experienced the gentleness, love, and sensitivity of God toward her. Her life demonstrates the charity that flows from knowing and loving a God who is attentive to each person's needs.

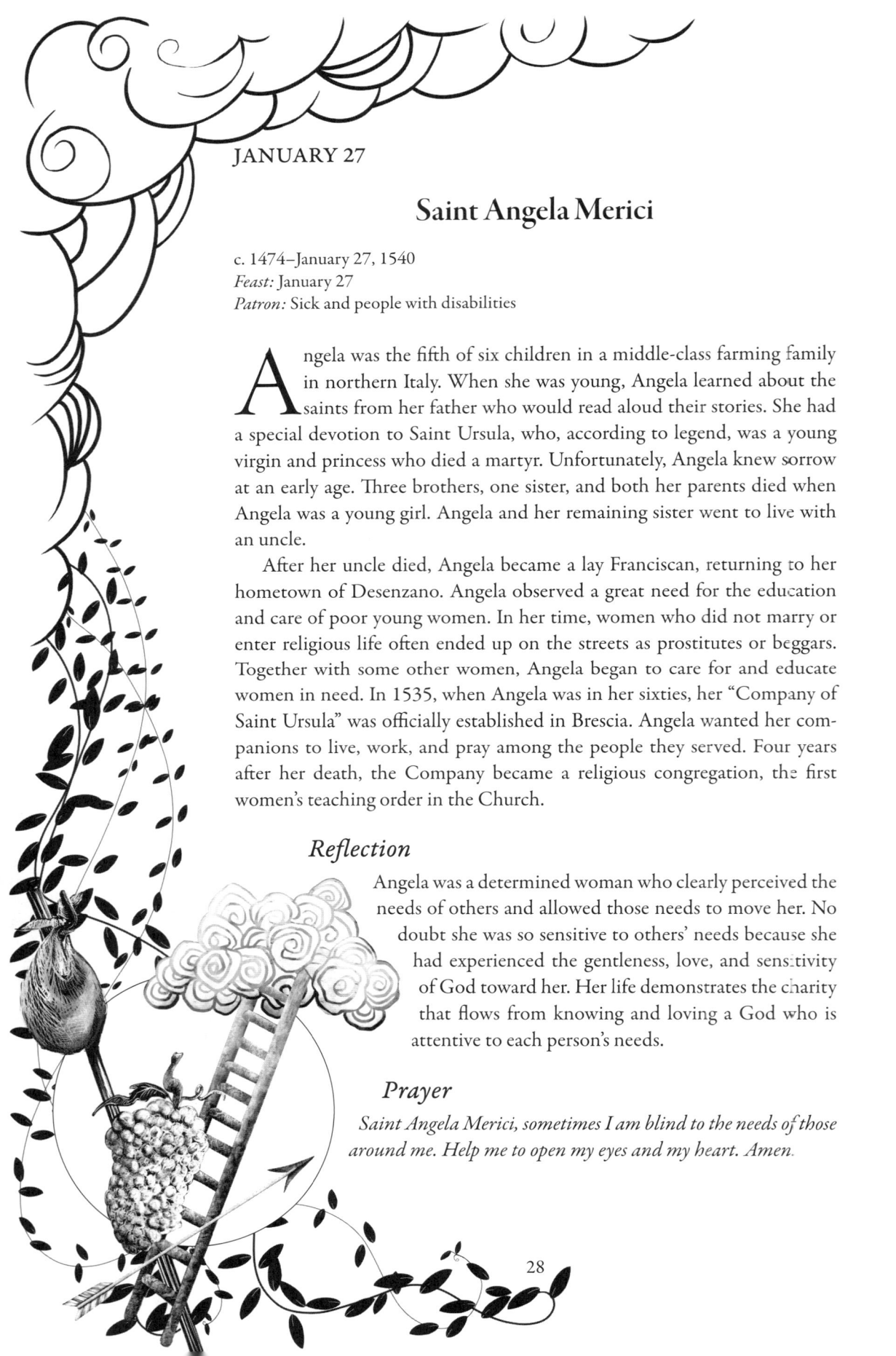

Prayer

Saint Angela Merici, sometimes I am blind to the needs of those around me. Help me to open my eyes and my heart. Amen.

JANUARY 28

Saint Thomas Aquinas

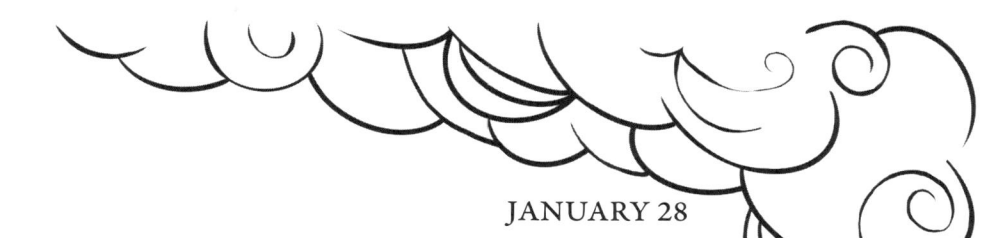

c. 1225–March 7, 1274
Feast: January 28
Patron: Catholic universities, scholars, schools, students, theologians

Very rarely does a figure appear on the stage of history whose life will influence many ages to come. Thomas Aquinas was such a person. As a brilliant young man from a noble Italian family, Thomas had many options before him. But he was attracted to the fledgling Dominicans whose mission was to preach and teach the Gospel. Against the wishes of his family, Thomas insisted on joining the controversial new religious order.

Thomas was so quiet that his classmates dubbed him "the dumb ox." But Saint Albert the Great noticed the silent student's intelligence. And when Thomas finally began to teach and preach, the students and faculty at the University of Paris took notice. Using the writings of Aristotle to throw light on Christian teachings, Thomas forged a new way in philosophy and theology. Thomas' work became a guiding star in theology. He was also deeply contemplative and composed beautiful Eucharistic hymns that are still sung today. Three months before his death, Thomas had a mystical experience at Mass, after which he stopped writing. Thomas said that in comparison with what he had seen, all his work now seemed to him like straw.

Reflection

Thomas is not a saint because of his academic career but because of his virtue. Though his dazzling intellect could have opened many other doors, Thomas chose to live a humble life dedicated to God. He walked great distances across Europe when he traveled, ate simply, and faithfully lived his religious vows. Prayer was the center not only of his studies but also of his entire life. What can I do to make prayer more central in my own life?

Prayer

Saint Thomas Aquinas, you sought divine wisdom in order to teach truth to others. Help me to grow in wisdom and love. Amen.

JANUARY 29

Blessed Timothy Giaccardo

June 13, 1896–January 24, 1948
Feast: October 19
Patron: Evangelization with modern media

From the age of seven, Joseph Giaccardo felt a strong desire to become a priest. While Joseph was studying in the seminary, Blessed James Alberione (see November 26) was his spiritual director. Joseph was fascinated by Alberione and his desire to start a men's religious order, the Society of Saint Paul, dedicated to spreading the Gospel with the most modern forms of media available. But since the Society was not yet an officially recognized religious congregation, Joseph was advised to either join the seminary and certainly become a priest or face an uncertain future with Father Alberione. After much prayer, Joseph entrusted his priestly vocation to God and joined the small but growing group. In 1919, he was indeed ordained to the priesthood. The next year, he pronounced his vows with the Society of Saint Paul and took the name Timothy.

Timothy quickly became Father Alberione's right-hand man. His strong devotion to the Eucharist and to Mary made him a good spiritual father to the young men and women joining Father Alberione. What would be called "the Pauline Family" eventually included five religious congregations, one lay association, and four secular institutes. Timothy was instrumental in helping to found the third religious congregation, the Pious Disciples of the Divine Master. Timothy died of leukemia at the age of fifty-one, offering his life for the sisters of that congregation.

Reflection

Timothy Giaccardo believed very strongly in the importance of using modern media to spread the Gospel. He was even willing to risk his lifelong desire to become a priest in order to participate in this mission. God calls all Christians to use media for good and to spread the Good News to the entire world. Do I use media for good purposes?

Prayer

Blessed Timothy Giaccardo, pray that I may use social media and technology only in ways that bring myself and others closer to God. Amen.

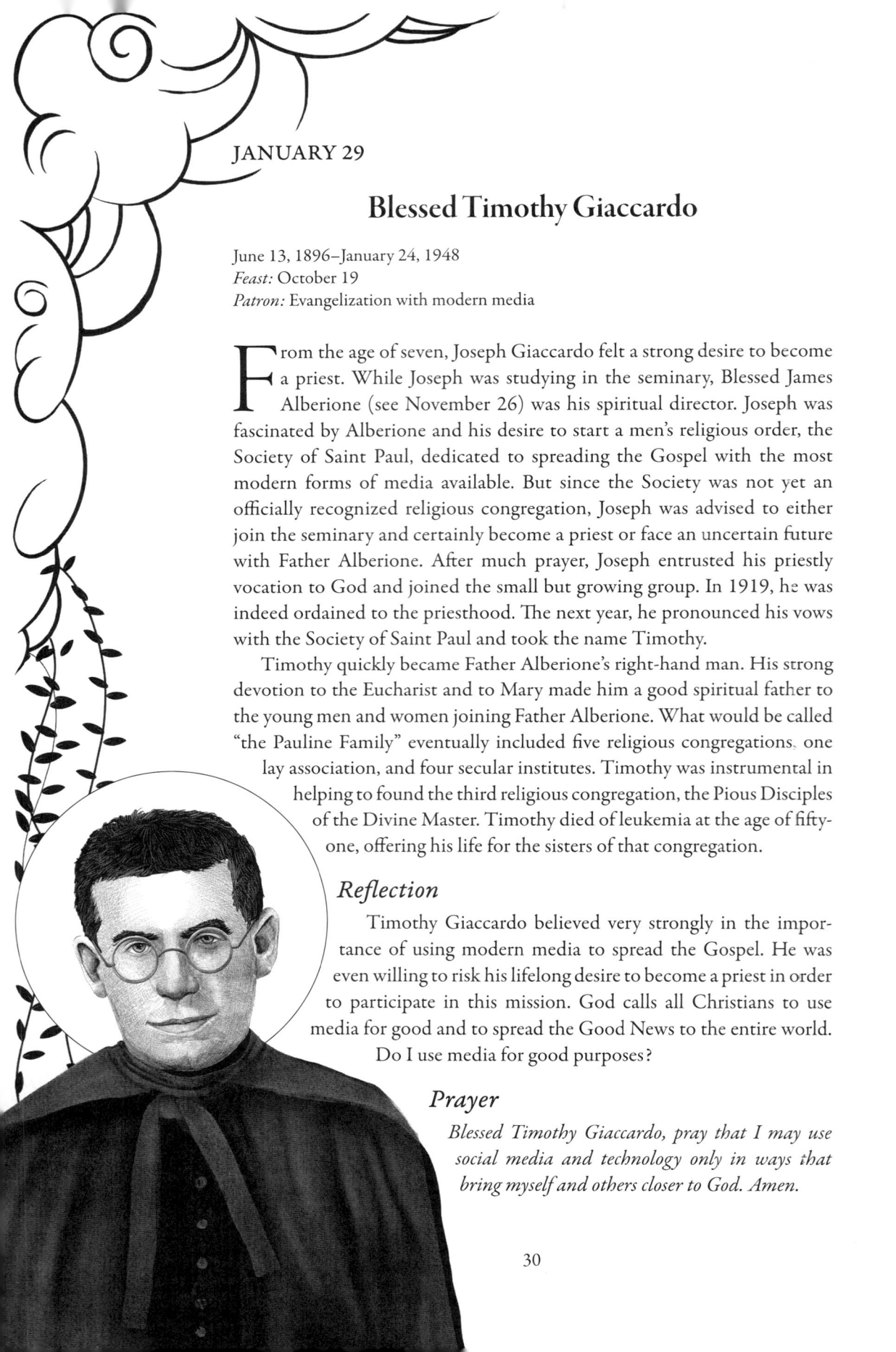

JANUARY 30

Blessed Laura Vicuña

April 5, 1891–January 22, 1904
Feast: January 22
Patron: Abuse victims

Laura was born to an aristocratic family in Santiago, Chile. The Chilean Civil War in 1891 forced her family to flee soon after Laura's birth. They took refuge in the south of the country until Laura's father died suddenly, leaving his wife, Mercedes, and his two young daughters behind. Mercedes took her daughters to Argentina to look for work. She found employment with a violent rancher named Manuel Mora. Mercedes, looking for security for her children, became his mistress.

With Manuel's financial help, Laura was able to attend a school run by the Salesian Sisters. She demonstrated an exceptional love for God and received her first Communion with fervor. Laura began to understand the immoral situation her mother was living in, so she prayed fervently and even offered her life to Jesus, praying that her mother would stop living with Manuel. When Laura returned home during school vacations, Manuel would make sexual advances toward her. Laura resisted his abuse, but then Manuel would beat her savagely. One day, Manuel's mistreatment of Laura, already weak in health, turned lethal. On her deathbed, Laura revealed to her mother that she had offered her life with the intention that she leave Manuel. Moved by her daughter's profound love for her, Mercedes tearfully agreed to leave him. And she kept her promise.

Reflection

Laura lived a life of complete devotion to her family and to God. At a very young age, she understood the importance of giving all for God. Laura demonstrated a Christ-like love for her mother, seeking her moral good. How do I seek the good of family members who may have strayed from the faith?

Prayer

Blessed Laura Vicuña, may I have a heart full of love like yours! Please pray for the daily conversion of my heart as well as for my loved ones. Amen.

JANUARY 31

Saint John Bosco

August 16, 1815–January 31, 1888
Feast: January 31
Patron: Apprentices, laborers, schoolchildren, and editors

John Bosco was born in Piedmont, Italy, to a poor farming family. As a boy he would attract crowds of people by performing magic tricks and acrobatics. Then he would teach them the catechism. After he was ordained a priest, he opened "oratories"—places of prayer, study, and apprenticeship—to keep boys out of prison and off the streets. Fondly called "Don Bosco," John founded the Salesians of Don Bosco, the Salesian Sisters, and the Association of Salesian Cooperators to continue this work of caring for the youth.

John's life and work were characterized by ingenuity, a fun-loving spirit, and a deep tenderhearted love for others. He used to go around Turin looking for boys who needed help. One day he came upon a group of boys gambling in the street. He asked if he could play with them. Soon he had won all their money! He told them that if they promised to come to the Oratory for Mass that coming Sunday, he would give them back their money. The boys promised, John returned the money, and the next Sunday several of them appeared at the Oratory. By the time of John's death, 250 Salesian houses had been established, serving 130,000 children. Today, all over the world, thousands of Salesians continue the work Don Bosco began.

Reflection

John Bosco wanted above all to bring people to Christ. To do this, he used the gifts God had given him: creativity, humor, and a love for the young. He was not afraid to start small, nor was he afraid to let God do big things. What gifts has God given me? How is he calling me to use them?

Prayer

Saint John Bosco, help me to surrender my gifts back to God so that he may shine through me. Amen.

FEBRUARY 1

Saint Brigid of Ireland

c. 451–c. 525
Feast: February 1
Patron: Ireland, nuns, dairy workers, infants

Brigid, whose name takes many forms, is Ireland's most famous female saint. She was born in southeast Ireland, the daughter of a pagan chieftain named Dubthach (an old form of Duffy) and Brocessa, a Christian slave who was said to have been baptized by Saint Patrick.

According to legend, Brigid was an industrious but problematic young slave, since she freely bestowed household goods on itinerant beggars. It is said that her father, Dubthach, once took her to the king's compound, planning to sell her. He briefly left Brigid alone in his chariot but when he returned, his jeweled sword was gone—given to a passing beggar. Dubthach marched Brigid inside and denounced her to the king. But seeing Brigid's holiness, the king convinced Dubthach to give his daughter her freedom.

When she reached adulthood, Brigid gave her life to God, but not by living unmarried at home as others did. She gathered seven like-minded friends and recruited a priest to instruct them in the religious life. Then, with the bishop's approval, the group professed vows and started a community. Later, Brigid traveled throughout Ireland, founding other communities. One of these, Kildare, became a famous center of learning and craftsmanship. Brigid lived most of her life at Kildare, and from there she passed into eternity.

Reflection

Brigid was a woman of strong personality and warm hospitality, who never lost the common touch. Although she promoted studies and the arts, she was usually found tending the flocks, working in the dairy, or cooking a meal. This may be why she was likened to the Blessed Mother and called "Mary of the Gael." Am I faithful in the ordinary things of life?

Prayer

Saint Brigid of Ireland, when I feel distaste for mundane tasks, help me do them gladly, for the love of God. Amen.

FEBRUARY 2

Saint Ansgar

c. 801–865
Feast: February 3
Patron: Scandinavia

Ansgar was born in northern France around the year 801. As a child he was educated at a Benedictine monastery and later chose to become a monk. He soon became known for his fervent and effective preaching. His superiors recognized in Ansgar the passion and charisma of a natural evangelizer. As a young man in his twenties, Ansgar was sent with just one other brother as a missionary to Denmark. Shortly after, Ansgar was also welcomed by King Björn to be a missionary in Sweden and is credited with building the first church there.

Ansgar was then called back and made bishop of Hamburg in Germany. Pope Gregory IV soon made him an archbishop and appointed him the papal legate to the Scandinavian countries, which is why Ansgar is sometimes called the "Apostle to the North." As bishop, Ansgar organized missions to the Scandinavian countries that he also often attended himself. But as much as Ansgar desired to see Christianity spread in the north, he would not witness it in his lifetime. As the Frankish empire declined, missions to Scandinavia ended and many of the people returned to paganism. But Ansgar did not let disappointment overshadow his other endeavors. He oversaw the building of churches, founded a monastery, and built a library. He was truly loved by the people for his deep charity and kindness that were rooted in the security of knowing and believing in God's love.

Reflection

Ansgar devoted his entire life to spreading the Gospel. His heart was on fire with the love of Jesus and he fervently desired that others would come to know God. Is my heart on fire with love for God? What can I do to grow in love for God?

Prayer

Saint Ansgar, pray for the revitalization of the faith in Scandinavia, the people so close to your heart. Please help me to love the Gospel and desire to share it with others as you did. Amen.

FEBRUARY 3

Saint Blaise

Died c. 316
Feast: February 3
Patron: Illnesses of the throat, wild animals, wool combers

Over the centuries, many legends have arisen around the circumstances of Blaise's life and death. He was most likely a native of Sebastea, Armenia, and the son of rich and noble parents. A physician and philosopher, Blaise was respected for his charity and attentive care of the sick of the city. Known for his gentleness and while still a young man, Blaise was made the bishop of Sebastea.

According to legend, Blaise had to flee to a nearby cave and live as a hermit during a time of persecution. He lived peacefully with the wild animals and cured their ailments. One day, hunters captured Blaise. As he was being led to prison, a mother whose child was choking on a fish bone implored his help. She set her son before Blaise and the boy was immediately healed. Continuing on the way to prison, Blaise then met a woman whose pig was captured by a wolf. Blaise commanded the wolf to let go of the pig, and the wolf obeyed. The woman gratefully visited Blaise in prison, bringing him food and candles. Both these stories likely contributed to the tradition of the blessings of throats with candles on the feast of Saint Blaise. Before he died a martyr's death, Blaise bravely faced beatings and his flesh was torn with metal combs. Finally, he was beheaded.

Reflection

Blaise brought healing and peace to others through his strong relationship with the Lord. An ardent follower of Jesus, Blaise truly became like Christ. Even as he was led to a grisly death, he focused on the needs of those around him. Am I attentive to the needs of those around me?

Prayer

Saint Blaise, help me become more like Jesus. Pray that I may leave behind my own needs and wants and focus on those around me. Like you, may I be a healing presence to all those I meet. Amen.

FEBRUARY 4

Saint John de Britto

March 1, 1647–February 4, 1693
Feast: February 4
Patron: Vegetarians, missionaries

Many people have heard of Saint Francis Xavier, the famed Jesuit missionary to India and China. Nearly one hundred years after Francis Xavier's missions, the lesser known but equally zealous John de Britto followed his missionary path to India. John grew up in Lisbon amid the Portuguese aristocracy. At the age of fifteen, John entered the Jesuits. Throughout his time of study and formation, his desire to be a missionary grew and deepened. John was ordained in 1673, and less than two months later was sent to Goa, a Portuguese colony in western India.

The Indian social system divided people into castes, with Christians often being members of the lowest caste. So, John adopted the lifestyle of an Indian ascetic, dressing in yellow and eating vegetarian meals, which enabled him to associate with members of all castes. He also learned the local languages and immersed himself in the culture so that he could preach the Gospel in terms the people would understand.

Gradually, the people accepted John and his teachings. Members of all castes, a prince included, began converting to Christianity. But John also faced many difficulties—among them an arrest, a threat to his life, time in prison, and a brief return to Portugal where his superiors tried to convince him not to go back to India. John insisted upon returning to the people he loved, however, and was eventually beheaded in the province of Oriyur.

Reflection

John had an experience of God that he wanted to share with the people of his day. But he knew he had to approach them in a way they would understand. He became one of them, to tell them about the God who became one of us. How is God inviting me to enter someone else's world today?

Prayer

Saint John de Britto, pray for all missionaries. Help me to realize my call to be a missionary of God's love to the people in my life today. Amen.

FEBRUARY 5

Saint Agatha

c. 235–c. 251
Feast: February 5
Patron: Breast cancer patients, fire victims

Born to a wealthy Christian family, Agatha committed herself to living as a virgin dedicated to Christ from a young age. Ancient legends tell us both of her family's great generosity to the poor of their village and of Agatha's great physical beauty. When a pagan official came to know of her, he proposed marriage. Since she was not interested in either renouncing her faith (a necessary condition of the marriage), or in dispensing with her promise of virginity to the Lord, she rejected his proposal. In an attempt to change her mind, the man had her locked in a local brothel. The brothel's mistress, however, wouldn't allow Agatha to stay for very long because her presence, loud prayers, and insistence on purity were bad for business. Still unwilling to submit to the official's proposal, Agatha was then imprisoned and subjected to many tortures, including having her breasts cut off. Throughout all she suffered, Agnes continued to pray aloud to Jesus, eventually commending her spirit to him in her final moment of death.

Reflection

Agatha was resolved to live according to the values she held most dear. Nothing was able to convince her to act contrary to what she understood to be God's will for her. I know that my own resolve to remain united to God is often weak. What societal pressures do I give in to?

Prayer

Jesus, you inspired Saint Agatha with such a profound love for you that nothing could keep her heart from you. Increase in me the gifts of faith, hope, and love for you, so that I might remember always to turn to you in my most difficult moments. Amen.

FEBRUARY 6

Saint Paul Miki

c. 1564–February 5, 1597
Feast: February 6
Patron: Japan

Paul was born near Osaka, Japan into a noble family. His parents converted to Christianity when he was only about five years old. He received his early education from the Jesuits and entered their seminary at twenty years of age. He was an effective preacher who proclaimed that following Jesus was the way for all people to find happiness and salvation.

Paul had nearly completed his preparation for ordination when authorities arrested him along with twenty-four other Christians. They were all sentenced to death by crucifixion. In Nagasaki, as the group was led to their death, two other Christians who had tried to comfort them were added to the group. From the cross, Paul gave his final homily in which he comforted his companions, renewed his total fidelity to Christ, and professed his forgiveness of his persecutors. He also prayed that his death would strengthen the faith of those who lived on after him. His example in his life, suffering, and death inspired many others to follow Christ, even to the point of death.

Reflection

Paul Miki's martyrdom and the over three thousand Christians who have died for their faith throughout Japan's history bore abundant fruit for the Church in Japan. For nearly three hundred years, during which Christians in Japan were forbidden to practice their faith, thousands of Japanese Christians preserved and passed on their faith in Jesus at great risk to themselves. How strong is my faith?

Prayer

Saint Paul Miki, you gave your life for the Gospel that you proclaimed. By the help of your prayers, may we recognize that our deepest happiness comes from following Jesus and growing in his love. Amen.

FEBRUARY 7

Saint Jerome Emiliani

1481–February 8, 1537
Feast: February 8
Patron: Orphans, abandoned children

Jerome was born in Venice to aristocratic parents, Angelo Emiliani and Eleanor Mauroceni. As a young soldier in the Venetian army he did not pay much attention to living his faith and led a sinful life. One day, however, Jerome was captured in battle and thrown into a dungeon. He turned to God in his time of need and made a vow to the Blessed Mother that if he survived, he would lead a better life. Jerome made a miraculous escape from prison with the help of Our Lady and from then on dedicated his life to the service of God.

After returning home, Jerome was ordained a priest in 1518. In a time of serious famine and plague, he immediately set to work helping those in need. Jerome rented a house and began taking in homeless children. He spent the rest of his life founding orphanages and homes for needy children, the sick, and the unfortunate. Men soon joined him in his charitable work, and the group was known as the Company of the Servants of the Poor. In 1537, Jerome died while helping the sick during an epidemic in the city of Somasca. His community almost disbanded after his death, but it remained together and later would be recognized by the Church as the Order of the Clerics Regular of Somasca, or the Somascan Fathers.

Reflection

Once Jerome returned to the practice of the faith, he never looked back. All of his energies, gifts, and skills were fully devoted to living out his love for Christ in service to the sick and poor. How do I respond to the needs of the poor in my everyday life?

Prayer

Saint Jerome, pray that I may seize opportunities to go out of myself so that my life might become one of service and love. Amen.

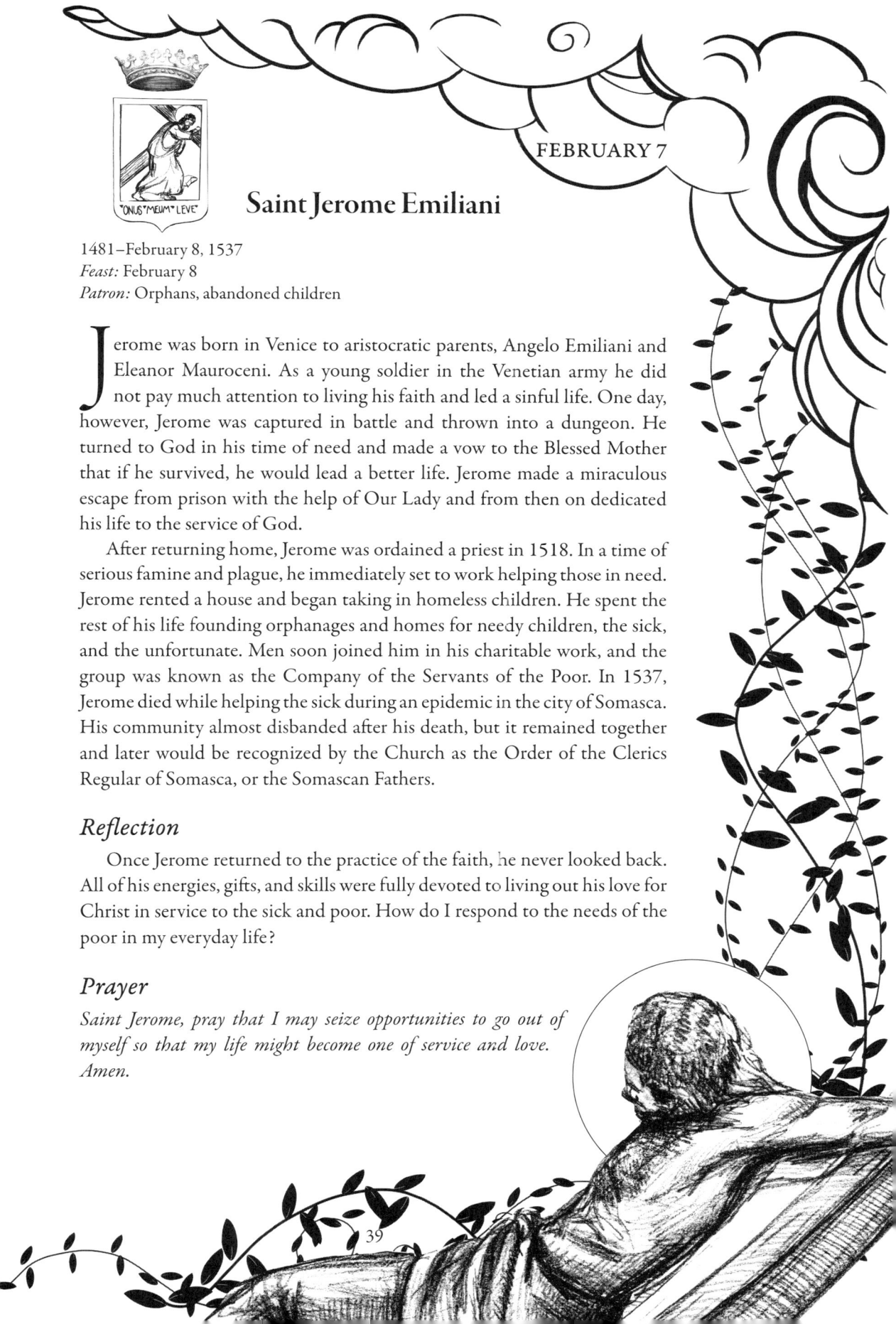

FEBRUARY 8

Saint Josephine Bakhita

c. 1869–February 8, 1947
Feast: February 8
Patron: Sudan, South Sudan, human trafficking survivors, those who suffer racial discrimination

As a young child, Bakhita was kidnapped from her village in Sudan and sold into slavery. The trauma of the experience wiped out all memory of her family name and she became known by her kidnappers' nickname for her: *Bakhita*, "the fortunate one." After suffering inhuman treatment at the hands of several captors, Bakhita was sold to the Italian consul and eventually moved to Italy with his family. There, she became the governess for the Michieli family. Although still a slave, the Michieli family treated her with greater respect, educated her, and introduced her to the Catholic faith, which resonated deeply in her heart.

Despite her great suffering, Bakhita always had a deep sense of awe at the majesty of creation—a wonder that ultimately led her to embrace faith in God and Christian discipleship. At the age of twenty-one, Bakhita was baptized and took the name Josephine. Soon after, despite the protestations of the Michieli family, Bakhita was granted her freedom under Italian law and discerned a call to become a consecrated religious with the Canossian Sisters. Just six years after her baptism she professed her vows. Mother Josephine, as she was called, bore witness to the healing love of God for the next fifty years, serving others with simplicity and compassion.

Reflection

Josephine Bakhita endured unbelievable suffering while remaining hopeful. She is a model of feminine strength, courage, forgiveness, and compassionate service. How does her life's example inspire me?

Prayer

Saint Josephine Bakhita, pray that I might discover God's presence amidst even the most difficult experiences. I entrust to your prayers all those who suffer at the hands of others. May I always respect the dignity of every person as a child of God. Amen.

FEBRUARY 9

Saint Apollonia

Died c. 249
Feast: February 9
Patron: Dentists, toothaches

According to an account Saint Dionysius of Alexandria wrote of her death, Apollonia was an elderly, respected deaconess in Alexandria, Egypt. She was seized, along with several others, during a terrible riot that led to a persecution of the Christians of the city. Apollonia was beaten very badly, causing the loss of most of her teeth. Some accounts describe her persecutors pulling all her teeth out with pincers. (For this reason, Apollonia is often depicted in art holding a tooth in a pair of pincers or wearing a tooth on a necklace.)

The people then built a pyre of fire and threatened the dignified, aged woman with death if she did not worship pagan gods. Apollonia asked for a moment to consider but then immediately threw herself into the fire. Saint Augustine explained the difficulty of Apollonia causing her own death by maintaining that the Holy Spirit must have given her special direction to do so, as under most circumstances it is not right to hasten one's own death. Apollonia's bravery was recognized and became revered at once. Through the centuries, a multitude of churches have claimed to hold relics of her teeth. She has been called upon for help with all dental problems.

Reflection

Apollonia willingly accepted martyrdom rather than betray the God she worshiped and loved. She shows us the wisdom and courage that can come with age. How often do I reflect on the gifts of the Holy Spirit, particularly the gift of fortitude?

Prayer

Saint Apollonia, pray that I may grow in the virtue of fortitude. May I be as courageous as you were in following Christ, particularly when I face sacrifice, discomfort, and the dying to self that prepares me for my death and eternal life. Amen.

FEBRUARY 10

Saint Scholastica

c. 480–c. 547
Feast: February 10
Patron: Nuns, childhood seizures, good sibling relationships; her name is also invoked against storms and rain

Scholastica was the twin sister of Saint Benedict and the foundress of the feminine branch of the Benedictines. According to tradition, Scholastica established and supervised a monastery of nuns five miles away from Monte Cassino, the monastery of her brother, Benedict. Scholastica only visited Benedict once a year. They met outside of his monastery because women were not allowed to enter Monte Cassino. However, though they saw each other rarely, the sibling saints lived their religious life with fervor and encouraged one another in holiness.

In the book *Dialogues*, Saint Gregory the Great recounts the last meeting between the two saints. Scholastica had a feeling that her death was near, so she asked her brother to stay the night rather than return to the monastery. Benedict refused because it was against the monastery's Rule. Scholastica proceeded to pray quietly and almost immediately, a fierce storm broke out. Benedict chastised his sister for trying to get him to stay, but she calmly replied that God had granted her what her brother had refused. Benedict relented, and the two siblings spent the rest of the night speaking of spiritual things. In the morning, Scholastica returned to her monastery.

She died three days later. After her death it is said that her brother saw her soul rising to heaven as a dove. Benedict buried his beloved sister in a tomb that had been prepared for him.

Reflection

Scholastica was a woman in love with the Lord. Love for God led both her and her brother, Benedict, to a life of contemplation and prayer, and together they allowed God to transform them into saints. What people in my life encourage me to holiness?

Prayer

Saint Scholastica, help me to love God so much that my love extends to all people in my life. And may all of my relationships encourage holiness. Amen.

FEBRUARY 11

Saint Bernadette Soubirous

January 7, 1844–April 16, 1879
Feast: April 16
Patron: Shepherds, the sick, the town of Lourdes, devotion to Our Lady

High in the Pyrenees on February 11, 1858, fourteen-year-old Bernadette Soubirous was collecting wood near the River Gave. Suddenly, she heard a strong wind and saw a beautiful young woman wearing a long white veil and a white robe with a blue sash. Astounded, Bernadette pulled out her rosary and began to pray.

Over the next few weeks Bernadette returned to the grotto. Crowds began to flock there too. During Bernadette's vision on February 24, the lady said, "Penance! Penance! Penance! Pray to God for sinners!" The next day the lady told Bernadette, "Go and drink at the spring and wash yourself in it." Although no spring was there, Bernadette began to dig. She found only mud until, finally, water began to trickle out of the ground. Within a day a spring had begun to flow. On March 25, Bernadette asked the lady's name. The lady replied, "I am the Immaculate Conception." The beautiful young woman was Mary, the Mother of God. Eventually a chapel was built on the location of the appearances, as Mary had requested. Miraculous healings and cures began to occur in the spring at Lourdes.

Bernadette later became a Sister of Charity at Nevers, France. In her short life—she died at thirty-five from tuberculosis—she had to endure many trials, just as Mary had told her: "I do not promise to make you happy in this life, but in the next." In 1933, Pope Pius XI canonized Bernadette on December 8, the Feast of the Immaculate Conception.

Reflection

Bernadette did not cling to the extraordinary things she had witnessed. She knew she was only a messenger, an instrument whom God used to bring peace and healing to many people. Do I know how to humbly step back as Bernadette did, and give glory to God?

Prayer

Saint Bernadette Soubirous, pray that I may always give glory to God in all life's circumstances. Amen.

FEBRUARY 12

Blessed Aloysius Stepinac

May 8, 1898–February 10, 1960
Feast: February 10
Patron: Croatia

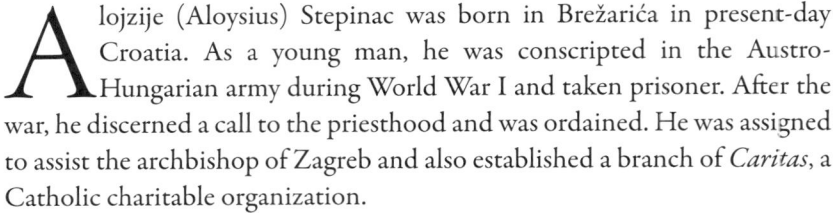

Alojzije (Aloysius) Stepinac was born in Brežarića in present-day Croatia. As a young man, he was conscripted in the Austro-Hungarian army during World War I and taken prisoner. After the war, he discerned a call to the priesthood and was ordained. He was assigned to assist the archbishop of Zagreb and also established a branch of *Caritas*, a Catholic charitable organization.

While still in his thirties, Aloysius was consecrated bishop of Zagreb. A popular and active bishop, Aloysius opened many parishes and led pilgrimages. During World War II, he preached vehemently against the Nazi's racial laws and provided aid and shelter to Jewish citizens and refugees. After the war, the communists began a crackdown on the Church, executing many priests and religious. Along with other Croatian bishops, Aloysius issued a pastoral letter demanding government respect for human rights and the protection of religious liberties.

In 1945, Aloysius survived an assassination attempt. In an effort to be rid of him once and for all, the communists tried Aloysius for "war crimes" and other offenses. He was sentenced to sixteen years of hard labor. Ill and under house arrest from 1951 until his death, he remained steadfast in his defense of the Church and prayed for his persecutors. Pope Pius XII elevated him to cardinal while he was still under house arrest. Aloysius died in 1960 and an examination of his remains suggests he had been poisoned by his captors.

Reflection

Aloysius led the people of Zagreb through perilous political times. A leader under both fascists and communists, he struggled to discern God's call amid great peril. Do I trust in the faithfulness of God even in the midst of danger and difficulty?

Prayer

Blessed Aloysius Stepinac, you gave totally of yourself to defend the faith. Like you, may I respond to God's call in my life with prudence and fortitude. Amen.

FEBRUARY 13

Saint José Sánchez del Río

March 28, 1913–February 10, 1928
Feast: February 10
Patron: Children, adolescents, and persecuted Christians

José Sánchez del Río grew up in Sahuayo, Michoacán, Mexico. José loved his faith and had a special devotion to Our Lady of Guadalupe. While José was still young, the government began persecuting the Church: seizing property, closing schools, and even executing priests. In a popular uprising known as the Cristero War, many Catholics fought to defend their faith.

Strongly devoted to his faith, José longed to join the movement. He was finally allowed to become a flag bearer for the *Cristeros*. Just a few months later, he was captured in battle. José's captors threatened him with death if he did not renounce his faith and the *Cristero* cause. But José remained firm and told his captors that he had been ready to die for his faith from the beginning.

After many failed attempts to intimidate him, José was sentenced to death. Soldiers flayed the soles of his feet and forced him to walk on salt and then through town. Mocking him the whole way, the soldiers made him stand before his own grave and told him he could go free if he denounced Christ. When José refused with the cry, *"Viva Cristo Rey!"* or "Long live Christ the King!" he was summarily executed on the spot.

Reflection

José Sánchez del Río was only fourteen when he was martyred, but he displayed incredible courage. Courage like his is not ordinary but supernatural and can come only from God. How often do I think to ask God for the gift of courage? What in my life would change if I had the courage to live my faith as boldly as José?

Prayer

Christ our King, through the intercession of Saint José Sánchez del Río, grant us the grace to live courageously, remembering that you are always with us. Amen.

FEBRUARY 14

Saints Cyril and Methodius

Cyril: c. 827–February 14, 869
Methodius: c. 815–April 6, 884 or 885
Feast: February 14
Patron: Europe, Slavic peoples, New Evangelization, Ecumenism

Cyril and Methodius were born in Thessalonica, in present-day Greece. Both brothers were very intelligent. Cyril (born Constantine) studied the sciences, and Methodius worked in local government. Both brothers entered the same monastery where they lived for several years, but in 863 they were sent on mission to Moravia to preach the Gospel.

Cyril and Methodius had great success in Moravia. The brothers invented a Slavic alphabet that enabled them to translate the Mass and the Bible into the common language of the people. At that time, the use of the vernacular in liturgy was unusual in the Western Church, so their success was met with disapproval from German bishops in the area. Cyril and Methodius were summoned to Rome. There they were received by Pope Adrian II, who approved the Slavic liturgy and announced that the brothers would be ordained as bishops.

Unfortunately, Cyril was unable to return to Moravia and died in Rome. Methodius returned to Moravia but faced constant opposition. At one point, Pope John VIII reversed earlier papal approval of the Slavonic liturgy. Methodius was again summoned to Rome and convinced the pope to restore the Slavic liturgy. Methodius defended the use of the vernacular in liturgy until the end of his life— even facing jail and brutal treatment. The brothers were venerated for many years in their local regions. In 1880, Pope Leo XIII formally introduced their feast into the Roman calendar.

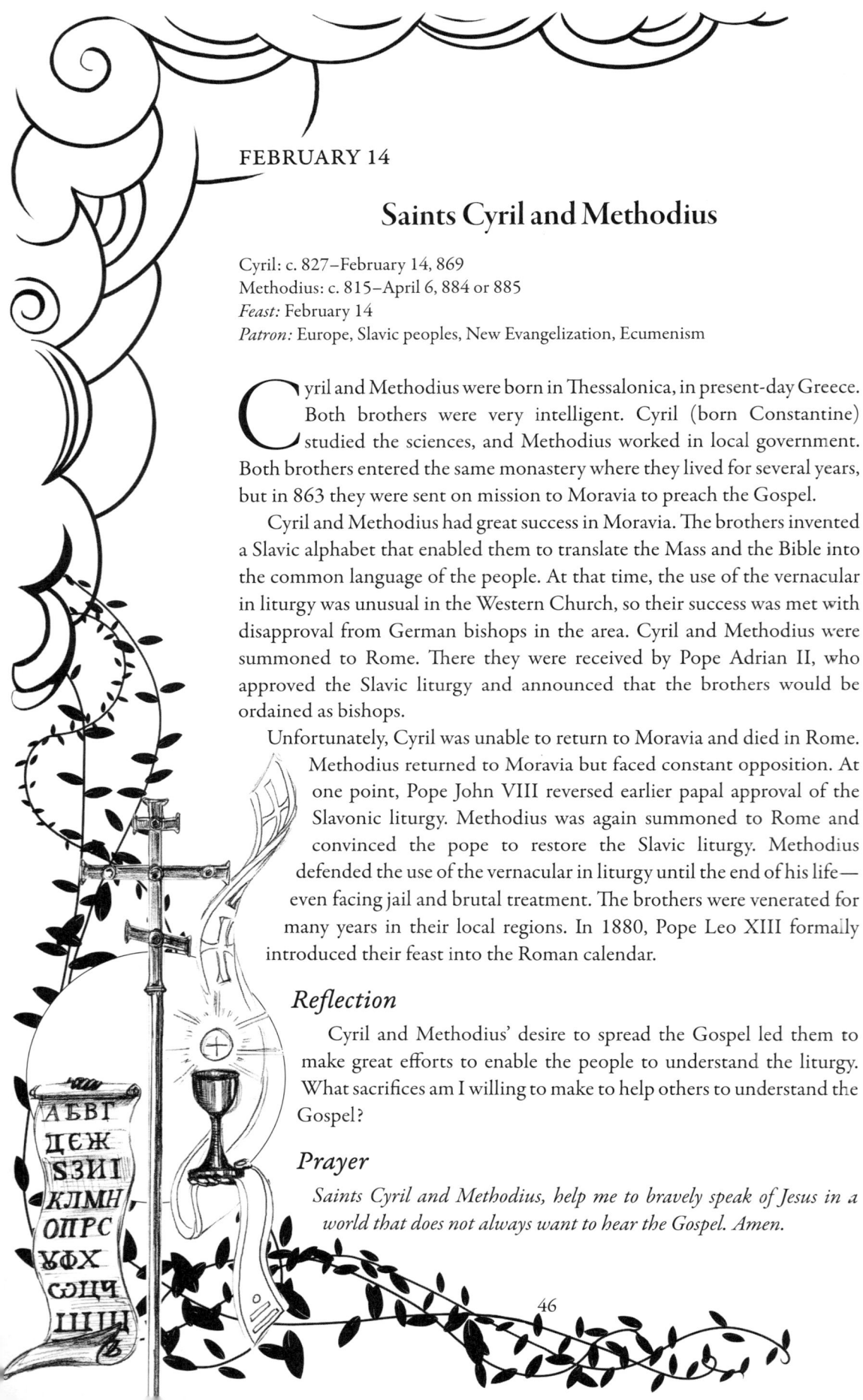

Reflection

Cyril and Methodius' desire to spread the Gospel led them to make great efforts to enable the people to understand the liturgy. What sacrifices am I willing to make to help others to understand the Gospel?

Prayer

Saints Cyril and Methodius, help me to bravely speak of Jesus in a world that does not always want to hear the Gospel. Amen.

FEBRUARY 15

Saint Claude de la Colombière

February 2, 1641–February 15, 1682
Feast: February 15
Patron: Devotion to the Sacred Heart

Claude was born into a noble family in southeastern France. As a teenager, Claude felt a call to the priesthood but was reluctant to follow it. After much prayer, he ultimately determined to follow God's will. Claude entered the Jesuit novitiate in Avignon. He studied philosophy and later became a professor. After Claude was ordained, he was known for his fresh and inspired sermons.

When Claude professed his solemn vows, he was appointed superior of the community at Paray-le-Monial in Burgundy. During his time there, Claude met Saint Margaret Mary Alacoque. He became her confessor and spiritual director, and she confided to him her visions and revelations regarding the Sacred Heart of Jesus. Claude already had a strong personal devotion to the Sacred Heart that helped him to discern that Margaret Mary's visions were from God.

Claude was then sent to London to be the preacher to the Duchess of York. The situation in England was very tense because of mounting anti-Catholic hysteria, but Claude's fervent preaching brought many Protestants back to the Church. In 1678, Claude was accused of being involved in a plot to kill King Charles II and was thrown in jail. Claude was able to return to France in 1681, but his health had seriously deteriorated. Less than a year later, he passed away in Paray-le-Monial. Margaret Mary said she knew when he died that his soul went directly to heaven.

Reflection

Claude, a man in love with the Heart of his Savior, spread devotion to the Sacred Heart of Jesus with enthusiasm. Am I devoted to the Sacred Heart? How do I show my love for the Heart of Jesus?

Prayer

Saint Claude de la Colombière, help me to always love the Heart of Jesus more than anything else in life. Amen.

FEBRUARY 16

Saint Margaret of Cortona

1247–February 22, 1297
Feast: February 22
Patron: Loss of parents, midwives, single mothers, single laywomen

Margaret was born in Laviano, Italy. Her mother died when she was a child, and her father married a woman who was abusive toward Margaret. When she was sixteen, Margaret ran away from home with a nobleman who had promised to marry her. She soon gave birth to a son. She lived with the nobleman for nine years, hoping they would marry. However, their relationship came to a tragic end when he was found dead, most likely murdered.

Margaret tried to return to her father, but he rejected her. Thankfully, Margaret and her son found refuge with two noblewomen associated with a Franciscan community in Cortona. After a few years, Margaret entered the Order of Penitents (later known as the Third Order Franciscans). Her son soon followed suit.

Though initially unwelcome in Cortona, Margaret was eventually recognized by the people for her holiness. She lived a life of penance, received many mystical visions, and preached repentance. Margaret also cared for the sick, opening a hospital staffed by a group of tertiary sisters she gathered around her. They were often referred to as "le poverelle," Italian for "the little poor ones." After her death, Margaret was immediately recognized as a saint but was not canonized until 1728 by Pope Benedict XIII.

Reflection

Margaret faced difficulty in her early life, but God watched over her and guided her with his love. When Margaret began to comprehend her heavenly Father's love, she gave up all else and turned to him with a humble heart. Do I contemplate God's love for me and allow his love to influence my choices?

Prayer

Saint Margaret of Cortona, help me to turn to God's mercy when I fall into sin. Pray that I may live a more penitential life as you did. Amen.

FEBRUARY 17

Seven Holy Founders of the Servite Order

Thirteenth Century
Feast: February 17
Patron: The Servite Order, devotion to Our Lady

In thirteenth century Florence, a group of seven wealthy noblemen banded together to give their lives to the Lord. At first, they joined the Confraternity of the Blessed Virgin Mary. Then, upon Mary's request in a vision, they decided to withdraw from the city and dedicate themselves to a life of prayer and penance.

The men left Florence. Mary then appeared to them a second time and encouraged them to wear a black habit and adopt the Rule of Saint Augustine. From then on, they were called the Servants of Mary. All were ordained to the priesthood except for Alexis Falconieri, who wanted to be a lay brother. The order combined a monastic life with active ministry, praying, caring for the poor, teaching, and preaching. The men also sought to spread devotion to Mary. As the group grew, they started foundations in many countries. Today the Servites are found throughout the world.

Reflection

The Servites developed a spirituality of service with a strong Marian connection. Just as Mary called herself the servant of the Lord, the friars sought to imitate her by living lives of service to the Lord. In doing so, they experienced the paradox in Jesus' words, "whoever wishes to become great among you must be your servant" (Mk 10:43). Prayer, poverty, and penance are joined to this spirit of service. How do I live a spirit of service in union with Mary?

Prayer

Seven Holy Founders, intercede for us. May your example inspire us to readily give of ourselves and in so doing further the spread of the kingdom of God on earth. Amen.

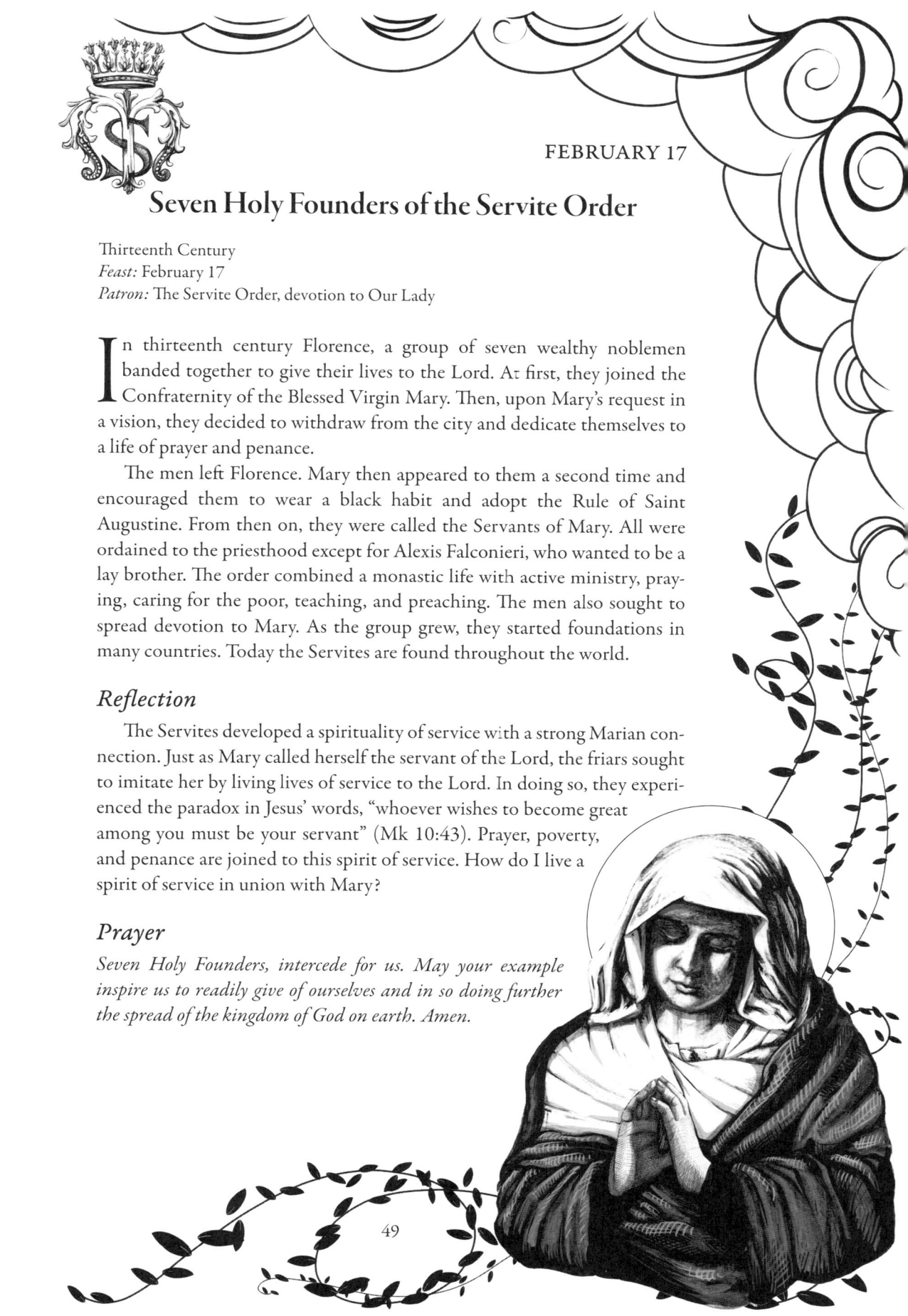

FEBRUARY 18

Blessed John of Fiesole (Fra Angelico)

c. 1400–February 18, 1455
Feast: February 18
Patron: Artists

Popularly known as Fra Angelico, today's saint is recognized throughout the world for his early Renaissance paintings and frescoes. But this rich artistic heritage is only part of his legacy. Born near Florence, Italy, Guido di Pietro always had a gift for painting. Before he joined the Dominicans, he was already recognized for his talent and could have sought fame and fortune. Instead, he and his younger brother both entered the Dominicans at Fiesole around 1420.

Receiving the new name of Fra John of Fiesole, he soon began his life's work preaching the Gospel through art. His illuminated manuscripts and religious paintings became known for a simple, prayerful style. John believed that to portray Christ, one needed to become Christ-like, and so he always preceded his time of painting with a time of prayer. Around 1436, he moved with several other friars to the Convent of San Marco in Florence. Under the patronage of the Medici family, he painted some of his most important works. Later, Pope Eugenius IV invited him to Rome, where he painted frescoes in two of the Vatican chapels. When he died, he was buried in the church of Santa Maria Sopra Minerva in Rome.

Reflection

The world knows Fra Angelico as an early Renaissance painter whose works brought beauty into the lives of many people. During his lifetime, he impressed his contemporaries with his paintings, but even more with his holiness and humility. Today, he is known for the way he gave—and still gives—God to the world. What will be my life's legacy? What do I want it to be?

Prayer

Blessed Fra Angelico, your goal was to be Christ-like in order to depict Christ. Help me to allow the Holy Spirit to "paint" Christ on the canvas of my life. Amen.

FEBRUARY 19

Saint Geltrude Caterina Comensoli

January 18, 1847–February 18, 1903
Feast: February 18
Patron: Youth

Geltrude Comensoli was born in Italy, the fifth of ten children. Her parents brought her to church to be baptized on the day she was born and named her Caterina. From a very young age, Caterina had an intense devotion to the presence of Jesus in the Blessed Sacrament. She was so in love with the Eucharist that one day she slipped out of her house and secretly received her first Communion at the local parish!

When she reached the age of fifteen, Caterina joined the convent of the Sisters of Charity, founded by Saint Bartolomea Capitanio. Much to her disappointment, she fell ill and had to leave the convent. She began to do domestic work but maintained a rigorous life of prayer, penance, and charity. With her confessor's permission, she soon took a vow of chastity on the Feast of Corpus Christi in 1878.

After her parents died, Caterina felt free to follow an inspiration from the Holy Spirit to begin a religious congregation devoted to the Blessed Sacrament. She received permission from her local bishop as well as from Pope Leo XIII. In 1882, the Congregation of the Sacramentine Sisters of Bergamo officially began. She took the religious name of Sister Geltrude of the Blessed Sacrament. A little over ten years later, Geltrude was finally united in heaven with Jesus, whom she had adored for so long in the Blessed Sacrament.

Reflection

Geltrude accepted life's ups and downs, knowing that her Eucharistic Lord was guiding her. Do I trust in the Lord even when it seems like his plans for me are not making sense?

Prayer

Saint Geltrude Comensoli, intercede for me that I may entrust myself to God's plan for my life. Help me to grow in my love for Jesus in the Eucharist. Amen.

FEBRUARY 20

Saint Robert Southwell

1561–February 21, 1595
Feast: February 21
Patron: Persecuted Christians

This gentle priest and poet was born in England during a time of persecution against Catholics. His parents sent him across the Channel to study at Douai and then Paris. Robert wanted to become a Jesuit but was denied at first. Finally, he entered the Jesuit novitiate in Rome. In 1586, two years after ordination, Robert and another Jesuit, Henry Garnet, arrived on a secluded English coast to minister to clandestine Catholics in and around London.

Robert had no illusions about his likely fate. However, he managed to exercise six years of fruitful ministry, overseeing the underground publication of catechisms and devotional books. He spent his daytime hours writing works of doctrine, devotion, and poetry in the home of a nobleman who was imprisoned in the Tower of London. By night, Robert carried out his priestly ministry in and around London. It was only when one of the queen's officials coerced a Catholic into betraying him that Robert was apprehended and imprisoned.

Writing to the Jesuit superior general while en route to England, Robert had stated that while he ardently desired the divine reward, "the flesh indeed is weak . . . it even recoils." Robert endured over ten rounds of torture without revealing the identity of Catholics to whom he had given the Sacraments. He was hanged at Tyburn, after declaring with his Savior: "Into your hands I commend my spirit" (Lk 23:46).

Reflection

Robert Southwell knew his human weakness, but the Lord blessed his desire to remain silent under torture in order to protect those to whom he had ministered. Do I have the courage to live my faith even when it may have negative consequences?

Prayer

Lord Jesus, when I am faced with the prospect of suffering, I ask you to help me endure it for love of you and your people, as Saint Robert Southwell did. Amen.

FEBRUARY 21

Saint Peter Damian

1007–1072
Feast: February 21
Patron: Headache sufferers

Peter was born to a poor noble family in Ravenna, Italy, in 1007. His parents died not long after, and an elder brother took him in, but treated him severely. Another brother, a priest, rescued Peter from this situation and provided for his education. Peter soon had a flourishing academic career. In the midst of his success, Peter heard God calling him to leave the world and enter the monastery.

In 1035, Peter joined the monastery at Fonte Avellana and was recognized for his holiness and intelligence. He was so fervent in his penances, however, that he became ill. After recuperating, Peter was named prior of Fonte Avellana. He was well known for his vehement arguments for reform in the monasteries and in the universal Church. In 1057, Pope Stephen IX made Peter cardinal of Ostia, an office he very reluctantly accepted.

Peter never quite escaped public life again. Pope Alexander II eventually gave him permission to return to Fonte Avellana to live as a simple monk, but Peter was often called upon for diplomatic missions. In between missions, he is said to have spent his time praying, studying, and making wooden spoons. On his way back from one mission, Peter fell sick and died. He was never formally canonized, but, in 1828, Leo XII pronounced him Doctor of the Church and introduced his feast into the Roman calendar.

Reflection

Peter was in love with prayer and contemplation, not so that he could be alone, but so that he could be with God. This close relationship with God led Peter out of the monastery he loved and into public life. Do I allow God to lead me wherever he most needs me?

Prayer

Saint Peter Damian, pray that I might not only accept life's beautiful moments but also embrace every moment as God's loving will. Amen.

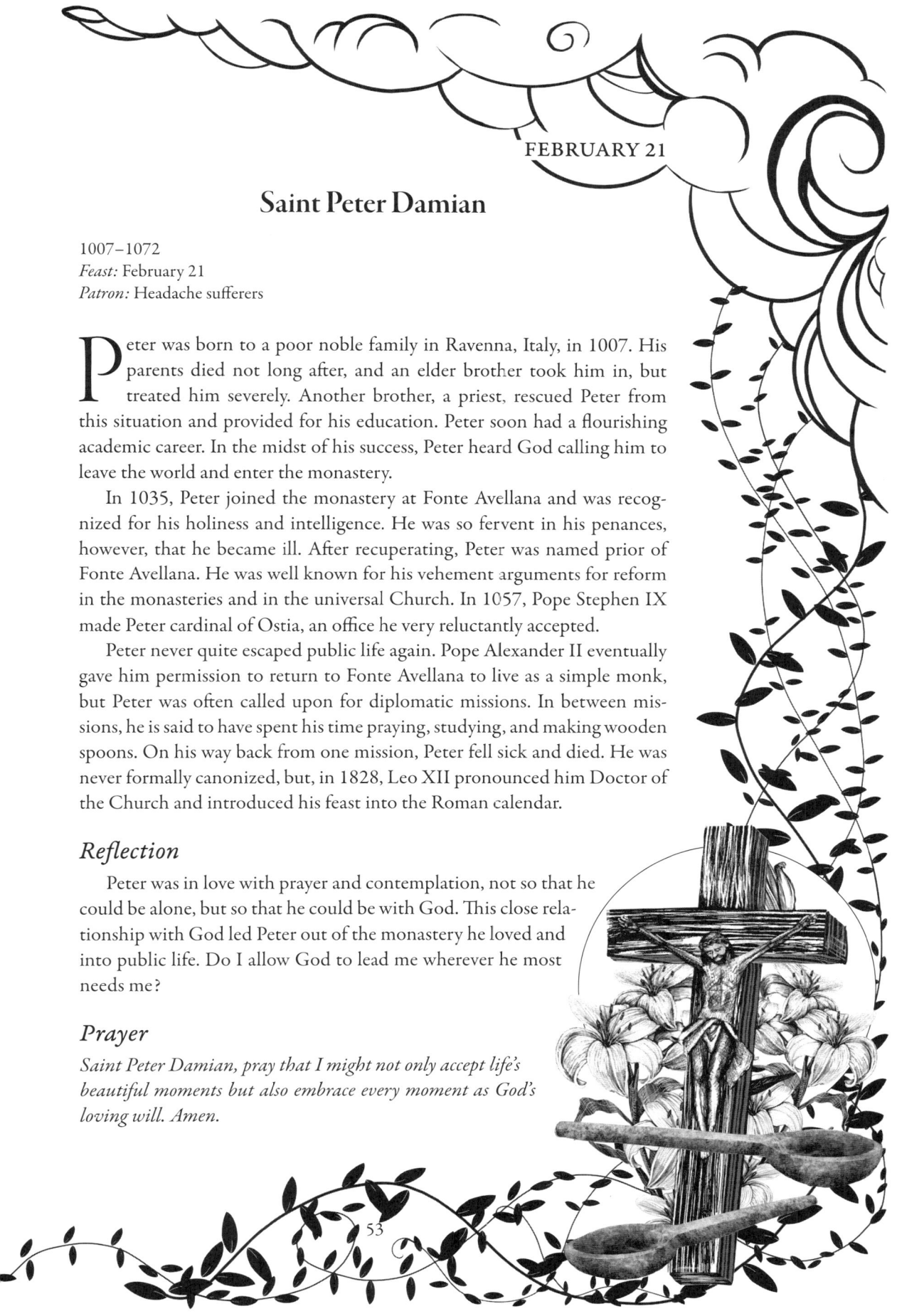

FEBRUARY 22

Saint Maria Faustina Kowalska

August 25, 1905–October 5, 1938
Feast: October 5
Patron: Devotion to Divine Mercy

Helena Kowalska was an unlikely mystic. The third of ten children born into a Polish farming family, she had very little formal education. At age seven, Helena heard God's call to religious life. As she grew older, Helena asked to enter religious life, but her parents did not support her. However, after seeing a vision of Jesus while at a dance with her sister, Helena decided to enter the convent. She was refused several times before being accepted by the Sisters of Our Lady of Mercy in Warsaw. There, she received the name Sister Maria Faustina. Faustina worked hard at domestic duties and prayed intensely. But just as often, she was ill. Some sisters doubted that she was truly sick, and this added to Faustina's sufferings.

On February 22, 1931, Jesus appeared to Faustina and entrusted her with the task of making his Divine Mercy known. He asked that his image be painted, as Faustina had seen him, with one red and one white ray emanating from his chest—symbols of the blood and water that flowed from his pierced heart on Calvary. The words "Jesus, I trust in you" were to be inscribed under the image. Jesus also requested a yearly celebration of Divine Mercy on the first Sunday after Easter. Faustina spent the rest of her short life overcoming many obstacles to carry out Jesus' wishes before she died of tuberculosis at age thirty-three.

Reflection

Sister Faustina was a simple farm girl who often was not taken seriously by her superiors or her sisters in the convent. But she believed in God's power working in her and became a living witness to God's incredible mercy. Do I trust in God's mercy?

Prayer

Saint Maria Faustina Kowalska, help me to offer Jesus' mercy to others so that I may receive it more fully myself. Amen.

FEBRUARY 23

Saint Polycarp

c. 69–c. 155
Feast: February 23
Patron: Earaches

The *Martyrdom of Polycarp* is not only the earliest authentic account of a martyrdom, it is also an engaging story to read. A gentle old man full of faith and fervor, Polycarp had been the bishop of Smyrna for almost fifty years. He was so beloved that even the police sent to arrest him were reluctant to do so. When they came knocking on his door, he greeted them, gave them something to eat, and asked that they allow him some time for prayer. The account tells us that he prayed for two hours, "having made mention of all that had at any time come in contact with him, both small and great, illustrious and obscure, as well as the whole Catholic Church throughout the world."

He was then brought to the arena where the Roman governor urged him to swear the oath to Caesar and say, "Down with the atheists!" (that is, the Christians). Polycarp looked around at the bloodthirsty crowd, and with a sweep of his hand indicating them all, said "Down with the atheists!" The official then urged him to renounce Christ. But Polycarp replied, "Eighty-six years I have served him, and he never did me any injury; how then can I blaspheme my King and my Savior?" With such a spirit, Polycarp's heroic martyrdom greatly inspired the Church of Smyrna and the surrounding area. His life and courageous faith continue to inspire today.

Reflection

Polycarp met death with serenity and grace. He did not cower in fear before his executioners but trusted completely that God would help him bear the trial. When difficulties and trials come into my life, do I entrust myself to God?

Prayer

Saint Polycarp, pray for us that we, too, might have the courage to bear witness to Jesus Christ in our lives today, knowing that our present trials will lead us to eternal glory. Amen.

FEBRUARY 24

Blessed Nikolaus Gross

September 30, 1898–January 23, 1945
Feast: January 15
Patron: Miners, journalists

Nikolaus Gross was born near Essen, Germany. The son of a blacksmith, Nikolaus became a coal miner. He pursued his higher education despite long hours in the mine. He was happily married to Elizabeth Koch, with whom he had seven children. He was a devoted father and raised his children in the Catholic faith.

In 1919 Nikolaus joined Saint Anthony's Miners' Association, the major Catholic union for German miners. He rose through the ranks of the union and was eventually named editor-in-chief of its influential newspaper. Nikolaus boldly wrote that Catholic workers' religious and moral beliefs required them to reject Nazism. The Nazi government banned the paper in 1938. Following the ban, Nikolaus published pamphlets for Catholic workers to encourage them in their faith. By 1940, the Nazis were interrogating Nikolaus and searching his home.

Nikolaus received information about a plot to assassinate Adolf Hitler in July 1944. Though he played no role in the attempt, Nikolaus was arrested on August 12, 1944. His wife noted signs of torture when she visited him in prison. He relied on prayer to strengthen him. Nikolaus was hanged on January 23, 1945 and denied a Christian burial. His body was cremated, and his ashes were thrown over a sewage farm. Nikolaus was beatified by Saint John Paul II on October 7, 2001.

Reflection

Nikolaus was an ordinary family man whose Catholic faith shaped his beliefs regarding the social and political issues of his day. He did not keep his convictions to himself. Rather, his Catholic values transformed his work and family life. How does my Catholic faith infuse my work and family life?

Prayer

Blessed Nikolaus Gross, like you, may I imitate you by allowing my Catholic faith to permeate my family life, my work, and all other aspects of my life. Amen.

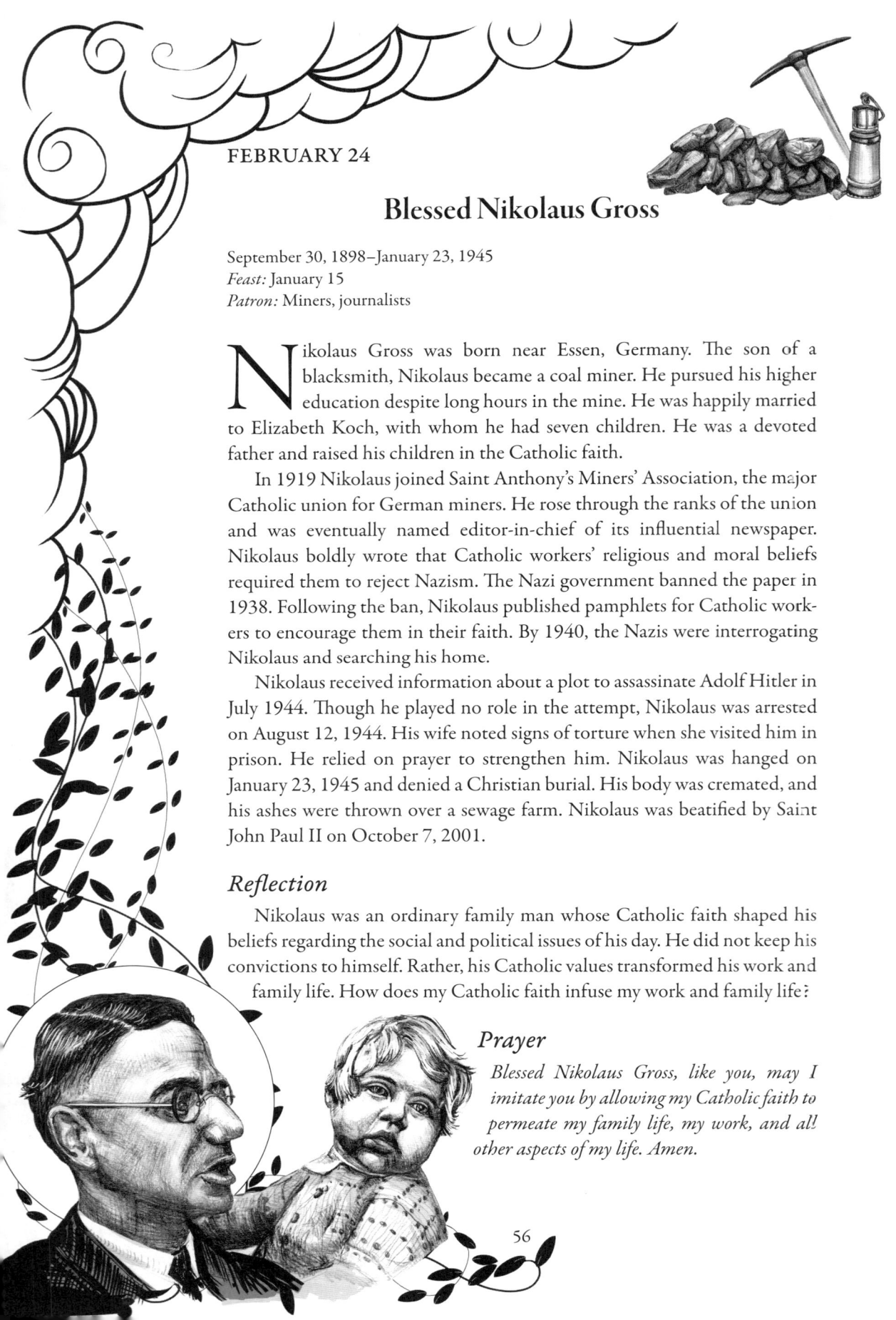

FEBRUARY 25

Blessed Maria Ludovica De Angelis

October 24, 1880–February 25, 1962
Feast: February 25
Patron: Children and adolescents

Antonina De Angelis was born in a small village in Abruzzo, Italy. She was the oldest of eight children. She was a sensitive child who loved nature and people, especially children. Antonina was drawn to a life totally dedicated to God and was deeply inspired by the life of Saint Mary Joseph Rossello, foundress of the Institute of the Daughters of Our Lady of Mercy. She entered this order in 1904 and took the name Sister Maria Ludovica.

Three years later, Sister Ludovica was sent on mission to Buenos Aires, Argentina. She spent fifty-four years at the Children's Hospital spreading the message of God's love to everyone: sick children, hospital staff, and the sisters with whom she lived and worked. Her loving presence created a strong family atmosphere. The phrase she most often repeated was, "Do good to all, no matter who it may be." Her burning love for God and her ardent faith moved her to seek donors who could aid in the expansion of the hospital to include operating rooms, medical equipment, and a home for convalescing children. When Sister Ludovica died, the hospital was renamed after her in gratitude for all she had done.

Reflection

Blessed Maria Ludovica allowed herself to become a true instrument of God's mercy to all, especially the young and the sick. She recognized the incredible gift of God's love for her as well as the fact that so many are hungry for his love! How do I assist people I know who are sick and in special need of God's love?

Prayer

Heavenly Father, help me to be on the lookout for the many signs of your love for me, and to readily share that love in big and small ways with all those I meet. Amen.

FEBRUARY 26

Saint Paula Montal Fornés

October 11, 1799–February 26, 1889
Feast: February 26
Patron: Teachers

Paula grew up in a small town near Barcelona on the coast of Spain. The eldest of five children, she had a great love for the Blessed Mother. When she was only ten, her father passed away. She had to leave school and help her mother provide for the family. Her experience helped her to value education for young girls.

When Paula was thirty, she opened a school for girls in the town of Figueroa near the French border. She believed that when women are not provided an education, it leads to the breakdown of the family. Paula strove to provide a wholesome and comprehensive Christian education for the girls in her school. Gradually, Paula felt called by God to open more schools in Spain, and more women joined her in her mission.

Almost twenty years after she opened her first school, Paula founded a congregation of women religious called The Daughters of Mary, Sisters of the Pious Schools. Paula was inspired by Saint Joseph of Calasanz, the founder of the Piarists, a religious congregation of men dedicated to educating poor children. She based much of her new congregation's life on his teachings and spirituality. At the time of Paula's death there were more than three hundred sisters in the congregation and nineteen schools dedicated to the education of young women.

Reflection

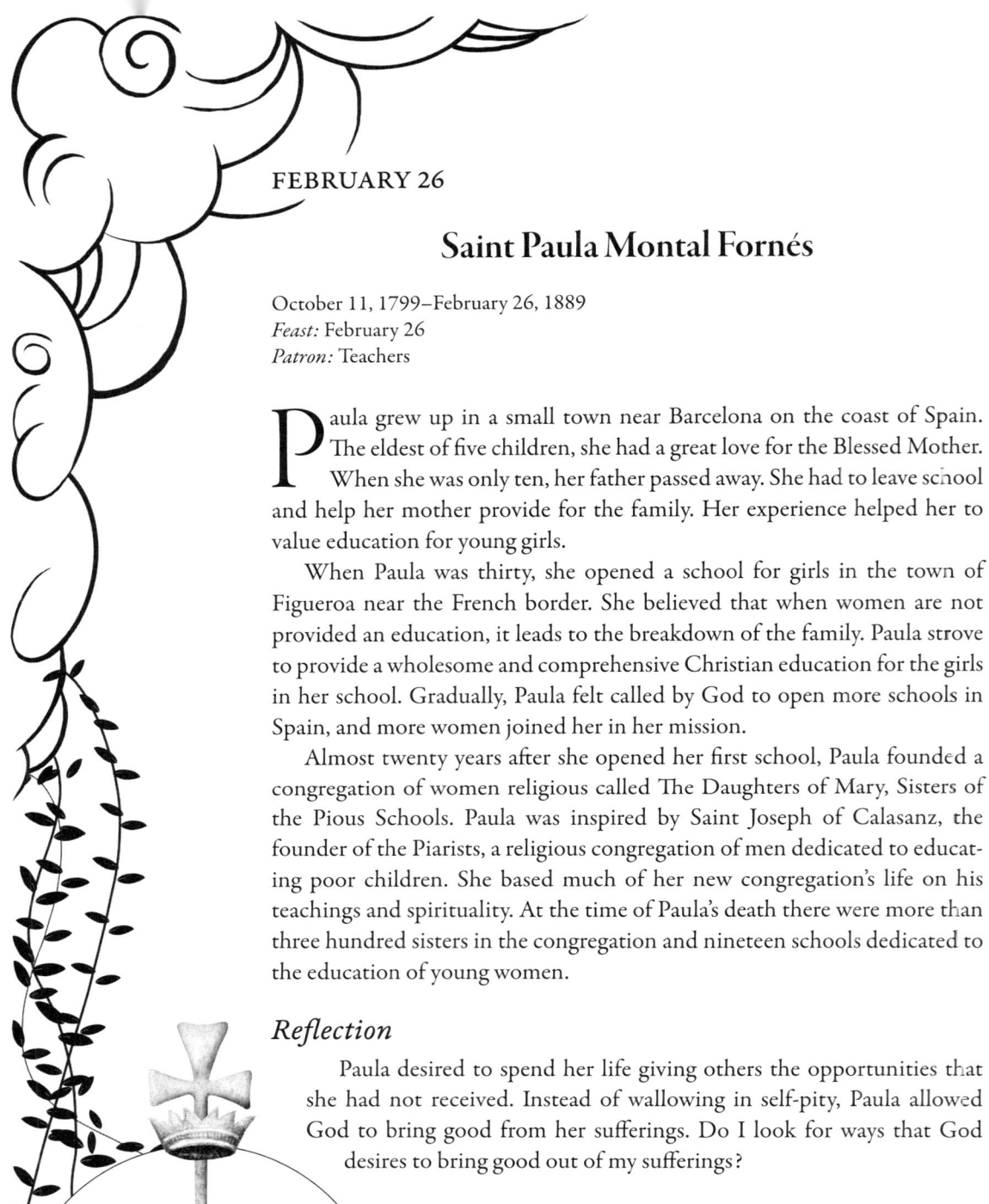

Paula desired to spend her life giving others the opportunities that she had not received. Instead of wallowing in self-pity, Paula allowed God to bring good from her sufferings. Do I look for ways that God desires to bring good out of my sufferings?

Prayer

Saint Paula Montal Fornés, please pray that I may see how difficulties or injustices I may have suffered can be a source of comfort to others who are suffering. Amen.

FEBRUARY 27

Blessed Maria Caridad Brader

August 14, 1860–February 27, 1943
Feast: February 27
Patron: Missionaries, teachers, and catechists

Maria Josefa Carolina Brader, an only child, was born in Switzerland. Devoted to the Blessed Mother, she was highly intelligent. Her widowed mother ensured that she received the best education possible. To her mother's dismay, Maria Josefa entered a cloistered Franciscan convent at age twenty. She took Mary Charity of the Love of the Holy Spirit (or Sister Caridad) as her religious name. Sister Caridad then began teaching at the convent school.

In 1888, Sister Caridad answered a call for missionaries in Ecuador. She served there, and later in Colombia, as a teacher and children's catechist. Despite difficult conditions, she zealously served the poor, the outcast, and those who did not know Christ. Seeing the great need for missionaries in South America, Sister Caridad felt called by God to found the Congregation of the Franciscan Sisters of Mary Immaculate. The congregation attracted many vocations from Switzerland and local communities and soon spread to several other countries.

Mother Caridad, as she was now known, viewed prayer and contemplation as necessary to sustain her and her sisters in their missionary work. She spent a great deal of time in Eucharistic adoration, seeking direction for her congregation's mission. Following her death in Colombia in 1943, her grave became a place for pilgrimage and devotion.

Reflection

Mother Caridad knew she could not carry the Gospel message to the people she loved without first growing close to Jesus in prayer. She nurtured her missionary spirit in Eucharistic adoration. Do I seek direction and solace from Jesus in the Eucharist?

Prayer

Blessed Maria Caridad Brader, like you, may I never let my day's activities and responsibilities, however noble, take second place to my relationship with Christ in prayer. Amen.

FEBRUARY 28

Blessed Carlo Gnocchi

October 25, 1902–February 28, 1956
Feast: October 25
Patron: Orphans, sick children

Carlo was born near Milan, Italy. His father, Enrico Gnocchi, was a marble worker, and his mother, Clementina Pasta, was a seamstress. Carlo was introduced to the mystery of suffering at a young age. When he was five, Carlo's father passed away from lung disease. Within the next ten years, Carlo also lost both of his older brothers, Mario and Andrew. As a teenager, Carlo showed interest in the priesthood, and with a local priest's encouragement, Carlo entered the seminary and was ordained when he was in his early twenties. He began working as a parish priest until he was appointed spiritual director at the Institute Gonzaga.

At the start of World War II, Carlo volunteered to serve as a chaplain. He performed his duties heroically and gathered letters and the belongings of the wounded and dying so he could return them to their families. After the fighting ended, Carlo visited the families of those who had died and returned the mementos. As he witnessed the continued suffering after the war, Carlo decided to do something for the most vulnerable and innocent victims of war: he started the Pro Juventute Foundation, opening centers all over Italy for children with disabilities or who were orphaned or ill. Carlo died at the young age of fifty-three. As he lay dying, Carlo continued to think of others, asking to donate his corneas to two blind children who were guests in one of his houses.

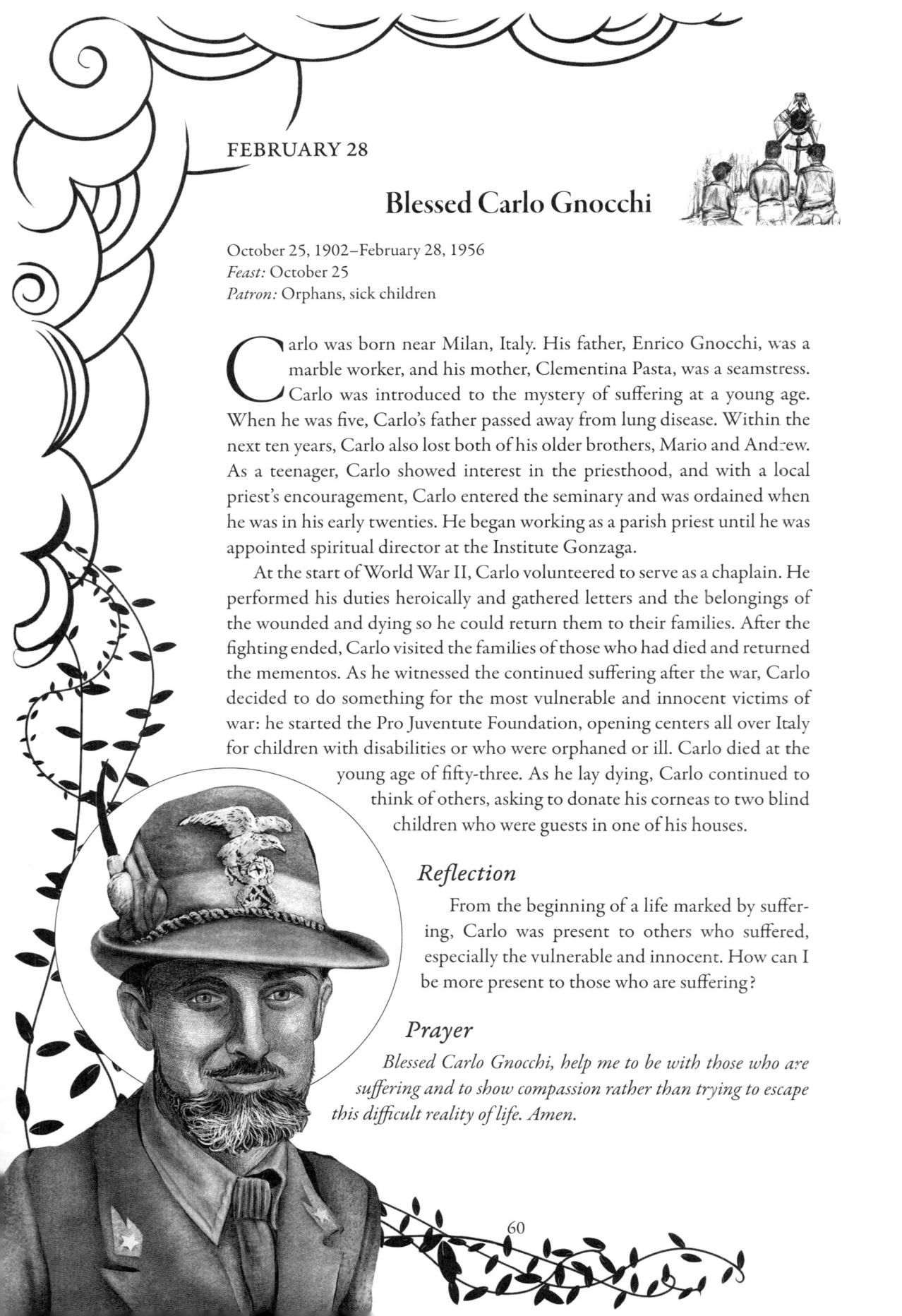

Reflection

From the beginning of a life marked by suffering, Carlo was present to others who suffered, especially the vulnerable and innocent. How can I be more present to those who are suffering?

Prayer

Blessed Carlo Gnocchi, help me to be with those who are suffering and to show compassion rather than trying to escape this difficult reality of life. Amen.

FEBRUARY 29

Blessed Miriam Teresa Demjanovich

March 26, 1901–May 8, 1927
Feast: May 8
Patron: Sisters of Charity of Saint Elizabeth, universal call to holiness

Sister Miriam Teresa is one of the lesser-known of the American "blesseds." Teresa was born and raised in New Jersey, the youngest child of Ruthenian immigrants from what is now Slovakia. She helped take care of her parents, then graduated from college and taught for a year before entering the Sisters of Charity. It seems that her spiritual director was quickly impressed with her holiness. While she was still a novice, he asked her to write conferences for him, anonymously, which he preached to the sisters in formation. Only after her death did he reveal that she was the author of the conferences.

Still a novice, she became very ill and was hospitalized. After having her tonsils removed, she was readmitted to the hospital. Her health worsened, and she was eventually operated on for appendicitis, but died two days later. She had been allowed to make her religious profession *in articulo mortis* (in danger of death) before the surgery. In this way, at only twenty-six years of age, Miriam Teresa died as a professed member of the Sisters of Charity.

Reflection

Sister Miriam Teresa's writings evidence her holiness. One of her key insights would be highlighted at Vatican II, which would be held forty years after her death. Writing about what we now refer to as the universal call to holiness, she insisted that everyone, no matter his or her state in life, is called to close union with God. What can I do to remind myself that I am called to holiness?

Prayer

Blessed Miriam Teresa Demjanovich, you felt called to encourage everyone to strive for union with God. Help me to be attentive to God's invitations for me to draw closer to him. Amen.

MARCH 1

Saint David of Wales

c. 520–c. 589
Feast: March 1
Patron: Wales

David was born in southwest Wales. He is thought to have been the son of Non, a pious young woman, and King Sant of South Wales. He was raised by his mother and eventually became a monk. David was described as tall and strong and must have been a natural leader, for with the help of several companions he founded a number of monasteries in southern Wales. The monks' lifestyle was austere, their sustenance consisting of vegetables and water.

In sixth-century Celtic lands there were almost no urban centers, so monasteries were the chief centers of culture, material aid, and evangelization. The monks' grueling farm labor supported themselves and the local poor, as well as the many travelers who sought hospitality. David and his followers gave spiritual help as well—evangelizing their fellow Celts in Wales, Cornwall, Ireland, and Brittany.

Legends grew up around David. It was said, for example, that once, when he was speaking in public, the ground under his feet swelled into a hill so everyone could see and hear him! He passed away at a monastery he had founded near his birthplace. The date was March 1, which over time became both his feast day and a Welsh national holiday.

Reflection

According to tradition, one of David's last exhortations was: "Be joyful; keep your faith and your creed. Do the little things that you have seen me do." This expression, "Do the little things" calls to mind Jesus' words: "Whoever is faithful in a very little is faithful also in much" (Lk 16:10). Am I faithful in the little things?

Prayer

Saint David of Wales, as I go through my day—whether hectic or tranquil—help me to remember the importance of doing small things well. Amen.

MARCH 2

Saint Agnes of Bohemia

c. 1205–c. 1282
Feast: March 2
Patron: Czech Republic

Agnes was born into a royal family that included two saints: Saint Hedwig of Silesia, her aunt, and Saint Elizabeth of Hungary, her cousin. Agnes' parents, King Ottokar I and Queen Constance of Bohemia, tried to arrange a marriage for her. But Agnes wanted to dedicate herself totally to God. She managed to refuse her suitors, including Emperor Frederick II, by writing to Pope Gregory IX to receive permission to dedicate herself solely to Christ.

Two Franciscan friars who had come to Prague told Agnes about Saint Clare and the Poor Ladies. Their way of life appealed to the young princess who wrote to Clare and invited her to send some nuns. Agnes built a convent and a hospital for them. Then she shocked the high society she lived among when, in 1236, she entered Clare's new order. She fully embraced her new life of extreme poverty and dedication to the poor. Clare wrote to Agnes: "Although you, even more than others, could have enjoyed the splendors, honor, and esteem of the world . . . you despised all these things and with your whole heart and soul aspired to a life of most holy poverty and bodily self-denial, to choose a nobler spouse, our Lord Jesus Christ." Saint John Paul II canonized Agnes in 1989.

Reflection

Agnes had all that the world could offer, but she freely walked away from it for the love of Jesus Christ. We, too, can have access to the greater goods of the Spirit—if we want them. Is there something in my life that blocks me from a closer following of Christ?

Prayer

Saint Agnes of Bohemia, pray for all Christians so that we may set our hearts on the greater gifts, the gifts of the Spirit. Amen.

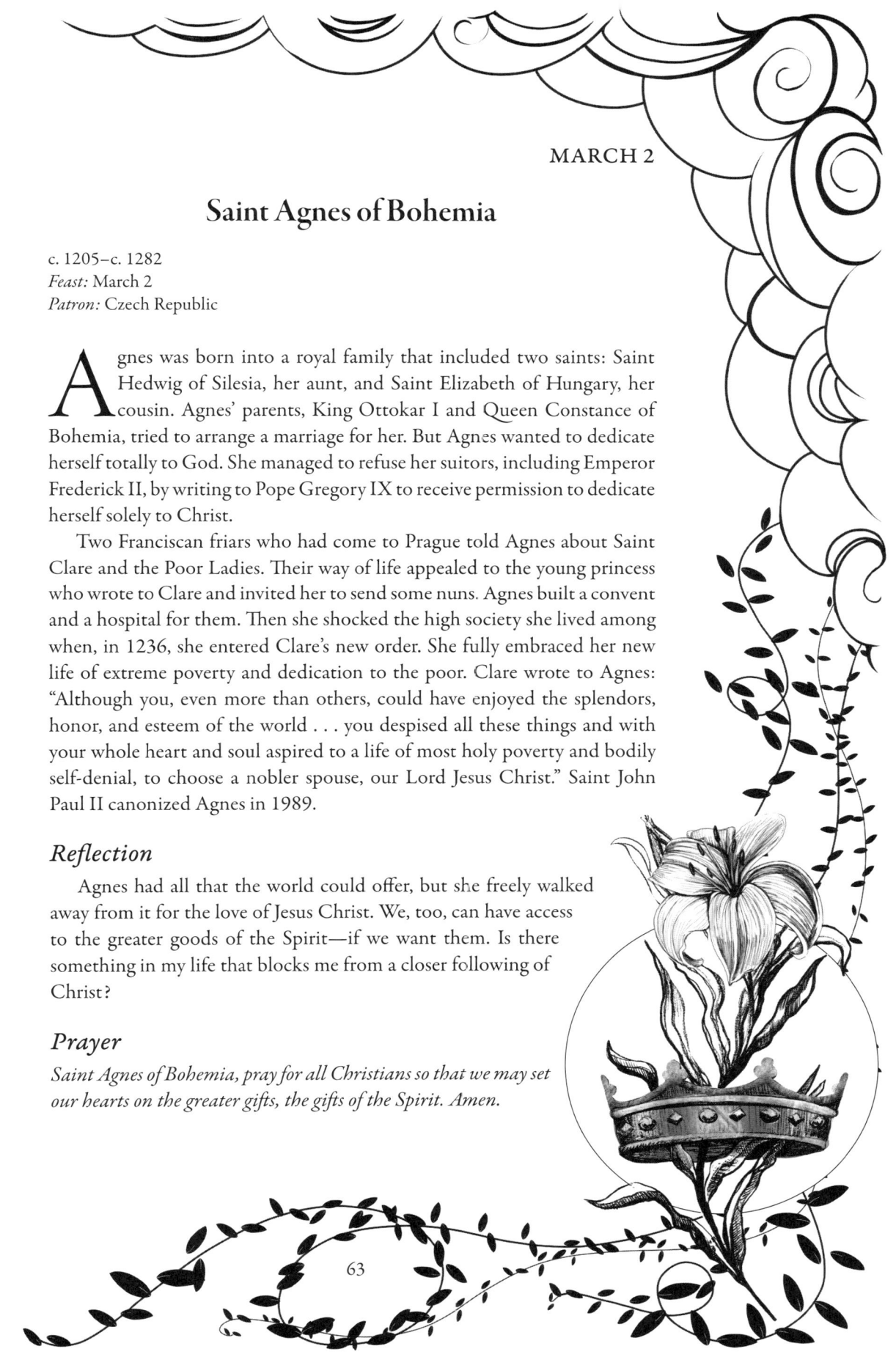

MARCH 3

Saint Katharine Drexel

November 26, 1858–March 3, 1955
Feast: March 3
Patron: Philanthropists, racial justice

Katharine, called "Kate" by her family, was the second daughter of Francis, a wealthy Philadelphia banker, and Hannah Drexel. Kate's mother died shortly after her birth, and she and her sister Elizabeth were raised by their stepmother, Emma Bouvier Drexel. Kate's parents taught their children that the family's vast wealth was a gift to be shared. Once, on a trip with her family out west, Kate was moved by the poverty of many Native Americans who lived on reservations. She also was distressed by the situations many Black Americans suffered due to racial prejudice and injustice. She began to consider what God was asking her to do with her life and with the fortune she would inherit from her parents.

When Katharine's parents died within two years of one another, she and her sisters were left with an enormous trust fund. She traveled to see Pope Leo XIII in the hope that he would provide guidance. While there, Katharine asked the pope to send priests to staff the missions she had begun to support. The pope replied, "Why not become a missionary yourself?"

With her spiritual director's guidance, Katharine decided to begin a new congregation. In 1891, with several young women, Katharine founded the Sisters of the Blessed Sacrament to minister specifically to Native Americans and Black Americans. Katharine never used her family inheritance to support her order but instead financially supported schools, missions, and dioceses around the country. With her sisters, she opened approximately sixty schools, including Xavier University in New Orleans.

Reflection

Katharine Drexel left a rich legacy to the world including love for the Eucharist, quality education for the needy, and total giving of self and resources to serve the victims of social injustice. How can I work for justice and carry out the vital ministry of prayer?

Prayer

Saint Katharine Drexel, through your prayers may society's neediest obtain help to lead dignified and fruitful lives. Amen.

MARCH 4

Saint Casimir

October 3, 1458–March 4, 1484
Feast: March 4
Patron: Poland and Lithuania

Casimir, the third of thirteen children, was the son of King Casimir IV of Poland and Elizabeth of Austria. When Hungarian noblemen petitioned Casimir IV to appoint his son Casimir as their new ruler, the king sent the young teenager into battle to claim the throne. The prince's army was outnumbered from the start. To make matters worse, some of his troops deserted. Young Casimir, who hadn't wanted to fight or be crowned king in the first place, prudently chose instead to order a retreat. His father, shamed and upset by the prince's failure, wouldn't allow him to return to Kraków. Instead, he exiled Casimir to the castle of Dobzki for three months. Never again would Casimir agree to go to war.

Casimir was an unusual prince. He had no desire for wealth, power, or prestige. He defended the needy and the oppressed and found joy in giving away his possessions. He lived simply and spent much of his day in church, assisting at Mass and praying. The prince often secretly returned there at night, kneeling before the locked doors in worship. He was especially known for his devotion to the passion of Jesus and his great love for the Blessed Mother. Although the king tried to get him to marry, he was unsuccessful. Casimir had made a vow of celibacy in order to dedicate himself more fully to God. He died at the age of twenty-six, after having contracted tuberculosis, and miracles were reported at his tomb.

Reflection

More than just a prince, Casimir was a disciple of the Lord Jesus. He never allowed political and cultural pressures to sway him. What pressures do you experience in your faith life?

Prayer

Saint Casimir, help me to live my Catholic faith as you did—especially when I feel pressured in any way to do otherwise. Amen.

MARCH 5

Blessed Aniela Salawa

September 9, 1881–March 12, 1922
Feast: March 12
Patron: Health care workers

Aniela was born into a large, poor family in a village near Kraków, Poland. As a child, she was often sick and unable to help with heavy work, which made her feel inadequate and useless. She moved to Kraków when she was a teenager to begin working as a housemaid. Aniela lived a carefree life and was not interested in her faith until her older sister Theresa died. This event changed Aniela's perspective and from then on she focused on her prayer life. She tried to enter the cloister, but her poor health and lack of a dowry prevented her.

Aniela accepted this as God's will and continued to serve faithfully as a maid. She took a vow of chastity, attended daily Mass, and became a Third Order Franciscan. When World War I began, in addition to her regular work, Aniela served in hospitals tending to wounded soldiers. The appreciative soldiers were so fond of Aniela that they called her the "young, saintly lady." In 1916, Aniela was falsely accused of stealing from her employer. She lost her job and within a short time fell seriously ill. She tried to go to the hospital but was discharged because the symptoms of her illnesses, stomach pains and most likely multiple sclerosis, were not apparent. Abandoned by most friends and family, Aniela spent the last years of her life cared for by the Saint Zita Association.

Reflection

Aniela suffered great misunderstanding and physical pain during her life. But she did not focus on her own suffering. What inspires you to hope in God when you are in pain?

Prayer

Saint Aniela Salawa, please pray that I can accept the little sufferings of my daily life as you did, especially when I feel misunderstood and rejected by others. Amen.

MARCH 6

Saint Colette

January 13, 1381–March 6, 1447
Feast: March 6
Patron: Women seeking to conceive a child, expectant mothers, sick children

Nicolette ("Colette") Boylet was born to devout parents in Corbie, in Burgundy, France. From an early age the girl's spiritual gifts were apparent. She was always drawn to God and wanted to become a religious. She tried to join the Benedictines and the Poor Clares, but when this did not work out, she continued to dedicate herself to prayer as an anchoress. She lived in a small room attached to a church until she began to feel called by God to another mission: to renew the Franciscan Order.

Colette also worked many miracles during her lifetime, especially for the benefit of pregnant women and mothers and their children.

After some fruitless efforts in her hometown, Colette established her first Poor Clare monastery in Besançon. She founded several monasteries in her lifetime and influenced the renewal of many more. As happens with any reform, Colette met with great opposition, but she persevered despite the resistance. The nuns in her monasteries followed a very strict rule of absolute poverty, fasting, penance, and prayer. After her death, the nuns following Colette's primitive observance became known as the Poor Clare Colettines.

Reflection

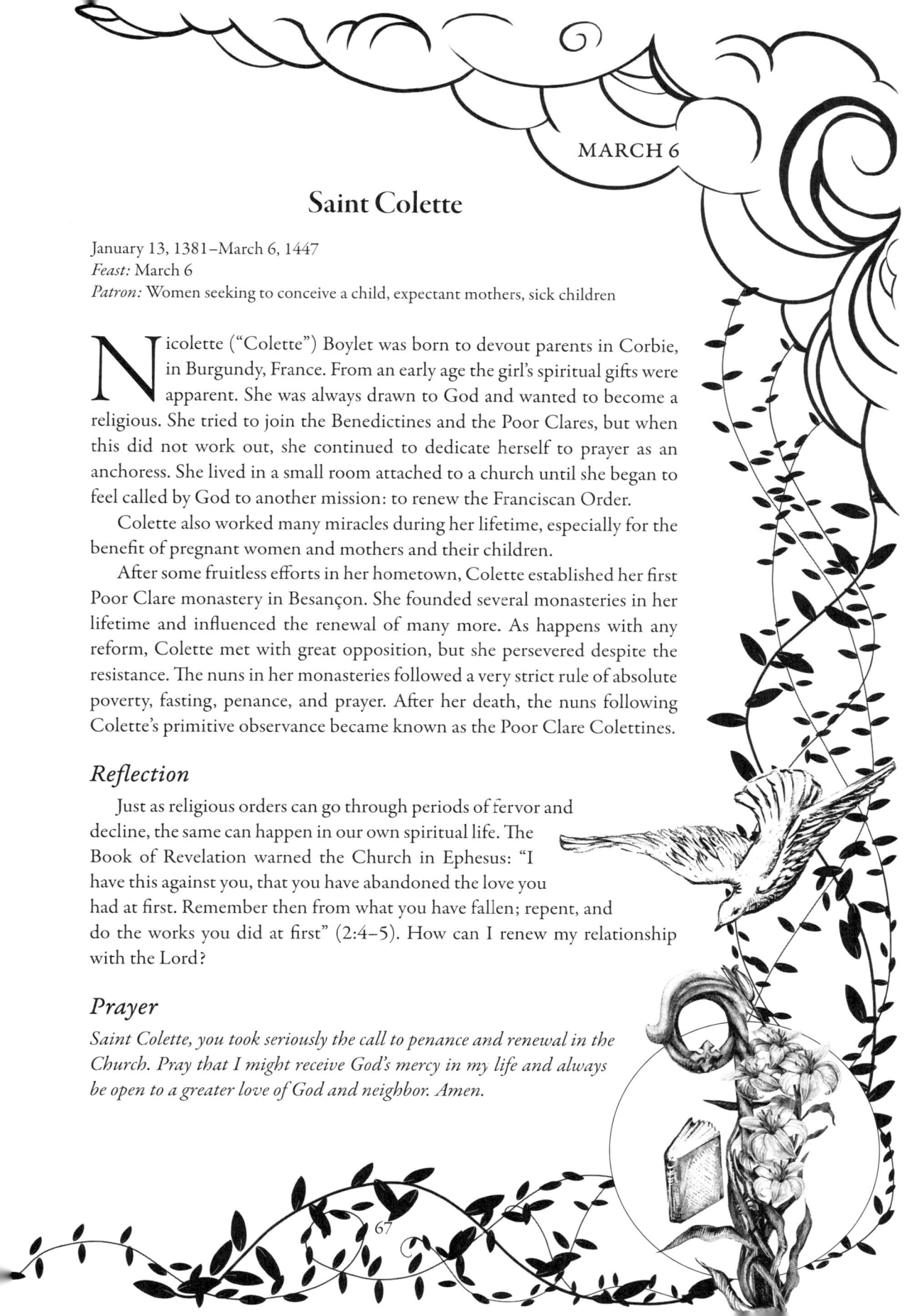

Just as religious orders can go through periods of fervor and decline, the same can happen in our own spiritual life. The Book of Revelation warned the Church in Ephesus: "I have this against you, that you have abandoned the love you had at first. Remember then from what you have fallen; repent, and do the works you did at first" (2:4–5). How can I renew my relationship with the Lord?

Prayer

Saint Colette, you took seriously the call to penance and renewal in the Church. Pray that I might receive God's mercy in my life and always be open to a greater love of God and neighbor. Amen.

MARCH 7

Saints Perpetua and Felicity

Died c. 203
Feast: March 7
Patron: Mothers, expectant mothers, ranchers, and butchers

Perpetua and Felicity were both catechumens from Carthage. They were arrested along with three other Christians and thrown in prison. Perpetua, a twenty-two-year-old Roman noblewoman, was nursing an infant son at the time. Felicity, a slave, was eight months pregnant. We know of these brave women from a narrative account that includes a diary believed to have been written by Perpetua.

After their arrest, Perpetua's father, a pagan, pleaded with his favorite child to renounce Christianity for the sake of her family. Perpetua refused, saying that just as a pot is called a pot, she was a Christian and could not deny that reality. Perpetua's father continued to beg her to offer the required sacrifice to the Roman gods. Although Perpetua was distressed that her father was upset, she refused.

Felicity, meanwhile, prayed night and day to give birth before the catechumens were to be led to their deaths. She preferred to die with her fellow Christians rather than be spared due to her condition. Her prayers were answered, and a sympathetic Christian woman took her new baby girl and cared for her. On the day of their deaths, Perpetua and Felicity were led out into an amphitheater of cheering crowds and thrown about by a wild heifer. Then the two women, along with the other catechumens, were presented to the crowd and their throats were cut.

Reflection

Perpetua and Felicity were young, new mothers, who faced martyrdom with astounding grace and courage. The women loved their children, but they also had great faith and knew that they would be reunited with them in heaven. How do I show my love for the gift of my faith?

Prayer

Saints Perpetua and Felicity, pray that I might always put God first, even before the good things in my life. Amen.

MARCH 8

Saint John of God

March 8, 1495–March 8, 1550
Feast: March 8
Patron: Booksellers, heart ailments, hospitals, sick, nurses

John was born in Montemor-o-Novo, Portugal, to two loving Christian parents who are thought to have been of Jewish ancestry. When he was eight, John disappeared from the family home. What exactly happened is unclear, but John's mother died of grief shortly after and his father joined the Franciscans. Young John was left homeless in Spain until he was taken in by another family. He was given a basic education and began working as a shepherd.

When he was twenty-two years old, John decided to enlist in the army. He fought under Emperor Charles V in various parts of Europe for eighteen years. During this time, the strong faith of his childhood gave way to a life of recklessness. Then the preaching of Saint John of Ávila helped John return to the practice of his faith. Soon after, he decided to spend the rest of his life doing penance.

John lived in poverty for several years before he rented a house in Spain and began to run a shelter and hospital for the poor. Townspeople, impressed by John's sanctity, began to help his efforts materially. The local bishop told him he should be called John of God. John was soon joined by several other men, and the Hospitaller Order of Saint John of God began. On his fifty-fifth birthday, John died as he was praying on his knees before a crucifix in his room.

Reflection

John knew suffering at a young age and struggled with sin for much of his life. But once he was converted, John dedicated his entire life to God. Do I trust that God, in his mercy, can bring good out of my past, even if I have many regrets?

Prayer

Saint John of God, please pray that despite my sinfulness, I may give myself more completely to God so that I may serve him and those in need. Amen.

MARCH 9

Saint Frances of Rome

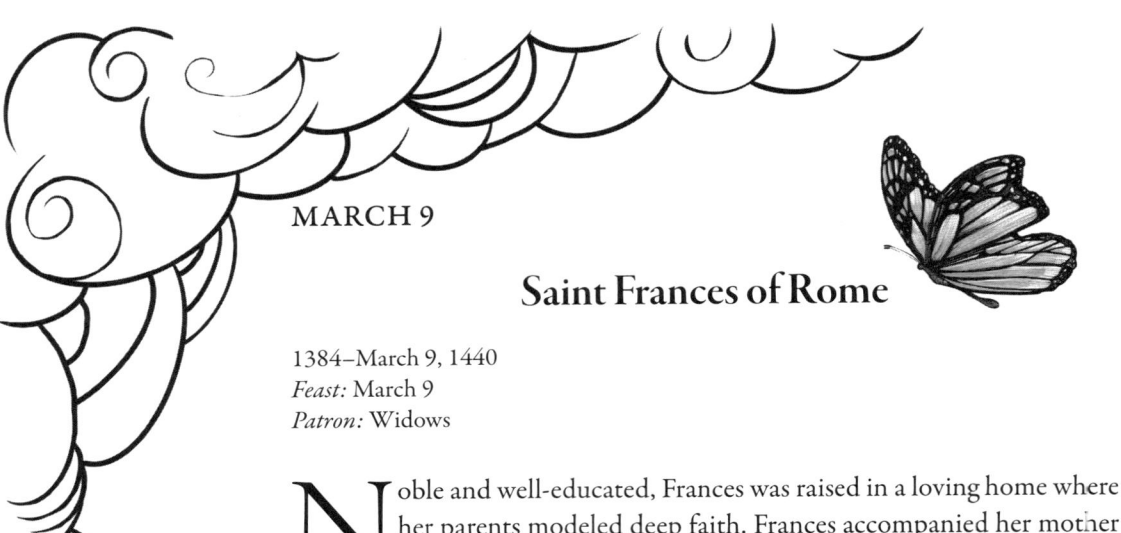

1384–March 9, 1440
Feast: March 9
Patron: Widows

Noble and well-educated, Frances was raised in a loving home where her parents modeled deep faith. Frances accompanied her mother when she visited the poor areas of Rome and learned from her how to manage a household with elegance and common sense. When she was young, Frances expressed to her father her desire to enter religious life, but he told her that he had already arranged for her to marry Lorenzo Ponziani, the commander of the pope's troops in Rome. Frances was devastated, but her spiritual director influenced her to see it as God's will for her to become holy as a wife and mother.

During her forty years of marriage, Frances was greatly devoted to her husband and three children. She dedicated all of her time to her family and to caring for the needy, even opening her palace to the sick and poor in times of war and famine. Other wealthy women began to imitate this holy woman's example, and Frances eventually founded a lay congregation of Benedictine Oblates, now known as the Oblates of Saint Frances of Rome. After her husband's death, Frances joined the community, thus fulfilling her desire to offer her life to God as a religious.

Reflection

Frances' life shows us what it means to be holy and to seek God's loving plan for us. A human, weak and frail like all of us, her life nevertheless shows that obedience to God is better than sacrifice and that God is never outdone in generosity to those who love him. How do I seek to know what God desires of me when it goes against my own immediate desires?

Prayer

Saint Frances of Rome, pray that I might know and accept God's will for me even when I find it difficult. Amen.

MARCH 10

Saint John Ogilvie

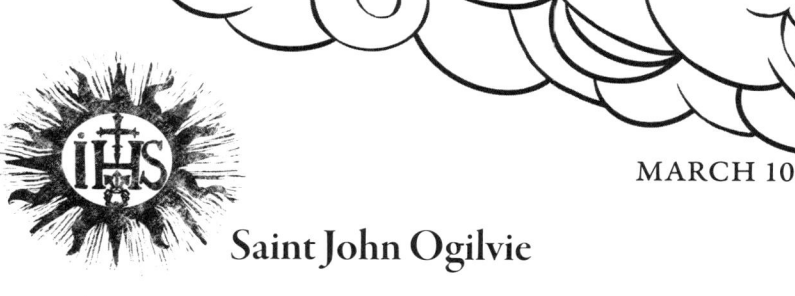

1579–March 10, 1615
Feast: March 10
Patron: Scotland

John Ogilvie was born into a noble family in Banffshire, Scotland, at a time when many people zealously supported the Reformation. John's mother was Catholic, and two of his uncles were Jesuits. But John's mother died when he was young, and he was raised as a Calvinist. When John was a teenager, his father sent him to study in Europe. There, he witnessed public debates between Calvinists and Catholics. John reflected, asked questions, and at seventeen decided to enter the Catholic Church.

John soon answered God's call to become a Jesuit. After his ordination, he prevailed upon his superior general to send him to Scotland despite the intense persecution of Catholics there. Calling himself John Watson, the disguised Ogilvie arrived on an isolated coast and began an undercover ministry that kept him on the move for several months. He even dared to reach out to former Catholics. When capture inevitably came, it was followed by five months of imprisonment, punctuated by periods of torture and three court trials.

John's refusal to identify clandestine Catholics, as well as his clear replies to questioning and his lively wit, impressed the public and even his guards. But this was not enough to spare his life. John was hanged as a traitor for upholding the pope's primacy in spiritual matters.

Reflection

John desired the salvation of all. Two Scripture quotes helped John find his way into the Church: "Come to me, all you . . ." (Mt 11:28), and "God our Savior . . . desires everyone to be saved" (1 Tm 2:3–4). I may not have John Ogilvie's courage and sense of humor, but I can share his desire for the salvation of all.

Prayer

God our Father, through the sacrifice of Jesus, your Son, and the prayers of Saint John Ogilvie, I pray for the salvation of all humankind. Amen.

MARCH 11

Saint Marie-Eugénie de Jésus

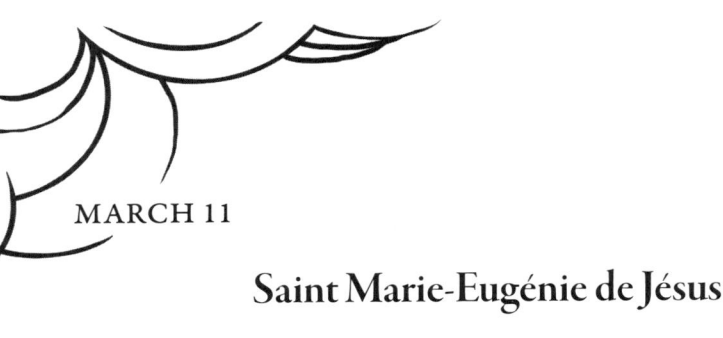

August 25, 1817–March 10, 1898
Feast: March 10
Patron: Educators, students

Anne-Eugénie Milleret de Brou came from a wealthy, nominally Catholic family that did not practice their faith. But when she received her first Communion at age twelve, Anne-Eugénie had a mystical experience of Jesus. It helped sustain her when her father went bankrupt, her parents separated, and her mother died when Anne-Eugénie was only fifteen.

When Anne-Eugénie was nineteen, she attended the Lenten exercises at Notre Dame Cathedral in Paris led by the famous preacher Henri-Dominique Lacordaire, O.P. She understood that God was calling her to give herself completely to him. The next year, with the help of her confessor, Father Combalot, Eugénie discerned she would help him to found a new institute of sisters. In 1839 this dream became a reality with the founding of the Religious of the Assumption. Their mission focused on education, especially of the poor, in order to put Christ at the center of human society. The new congregation grew quickly and flourished, spreading throughout the world. Mother Marie-Eugénie had the gift of two close friendships in this work: Kate O'Neill, who became Sister Therese Emmanuel, and Father Emmanuel d'Alzon, who began the institute for men: the Augustinians of the Assumption.

Reflection

Mother Eugénie's life shows us the beauty of spiritual friendship, which is rooted in love for Jesus, our supreme Friend, who said: "I have called you friends" (Jn 15:15). Eugénie's style of leadership also emphasized collaboration. She inspired others, drawing them into the mission instead of imposing burdens on them. How can her example help me to improve my relationships?

Prayer

Saint Marie-Eugénie, you inspired people by the way you radiated Christ, who was the center of your life. Pray that we, too, might allow the light of Christ to shine through our lives. Amen.

MARCH 12

Saint John Berchmans

March 13, 1599–August 13, 1621
Feast: August 13
Patron: Altar servers, students

With Saints Aloysius Gonzaga and Stanislaus Kostka, John Berchmans is one of a trio of young Jesuit saints who are models for young people. John was born in Diest in Flanders and was raised in a devout Catholic family. As a boy he liked to get up early and serve Mass before going to school. In 1616 he entered the Jesuits and did well in his studies. His main goal was to strive for holiness. He often said, "If I don't become a saint when I am young, I shall never become one." John sought holiness in doing well the ordinary things of life. In particular he valued observing the Jesuit Rule and fidelity in little things.

In the summer of 1621, after finishing philosophy studies in Rome, John caught a virulent form of malaria known as the Roman fever and died at the age of twenty-two. He was canonized in 1888. The required miracle occurred at a convent in Grand Coteau, Louisiana, in which John appeared to a novice of the Order who was deathly sick and told her she would be healed.

Reflection

John's spirituality of seeking holiness in little things was similar to that of Saint Thérèse of Lisieux. Like her, he practiced a way of spiritual simplicity that led him closer to God day by day. All of us are called to be saints, and the way to holiness for most of us is that same little way of fidelity to God in daily life.

Prayer

Saint John Berchmans, you were faithful to Christ's example of humility, purity, and love for the Blessed Virgin Mary. Help us to follow your example in the ordinary events of our lives. Amen.

MARCH 13

Saint Dulce Lopes Pontes

May 26, 1914–March 13, 1992
Feast: August 13
Patron: Brazil, the poor

Maria Rita de Souza Brito Lopes Pontes came from an upper-middle class family in Salvador, Bahia, Brazil. A childhood visit with her aunt to the poorest areas of her city had a profound impact on Maria. As a teenager she invited the poor and sick into her family home and asked neighbors to help her care for them. In 1933 she entered the Missionary Sisters of the Immaculate Conception of the Mother of God. In religious life, Maria took her late mother's name: Dulce.

In 1937 Sister Dulce founded Salvador's first Christian workers' movements: the Saint Francis Labor Union and the Labor Society of Bahia. She also opened a school for working-class children and provided food and medical assistance to the poor, initially sheltering them in abandoned houses. In 1949, with her superior's blessing, she began to care for people in their convent's chicken yard, which Sister Dulce converted into a makeshift hospital. In 1960 that yard became the site of the 150-bed Saint Anthony's Hospital.

In 1959 many of the charitable works that Sister Dulce founded were consolidated into the Charitable Works Foundation of Sister Dulce, a major Brazilian health and social service organization still in operation. Sister Dulce was nominated for the Nobel Peace Prize. Afflicted for years with severe respiratory problems, she died after a long hospitalization and a visit from Saint John Paul II. Sister Dulce, often called an "angel" during her lifetime, was canonized in 2019.

Reflection

Sister Dulce was transformed by the suffering she saw around her. It moved her to give her life in charitable service to her brothers and sisters in need. How do I respond to the suffering of others?

Prayer

Saint Dulce of the Poor, pray that I become more attentive to the needs of the people I encounter. Like you, may I be an "angel" to those in need, even in small ways. Amen.

MARCH 14

Saint Matilda

c. 895–March 14, 968
Feast: March 14
Patron: Parents, large families, misbehaving children

Matilda was born to a noble family in Germany. At the time it was customary for young girls to be educated in convents, so she was sent to the convent of Erfurt where her grandmother was the abbess. The religious atmosphere of her upbringing had an obvious impact on Matilda because she grew to be very devout. When she was a teenager, she was married to Henry, the son of the Duke of Saxony.

Matilda had a good influence on her husband who admired and loved his beautiful, faithful wife. They had five children together: Otto, Henry, Bruno, Gerberga, and Hedwig. Matilda would eventually become queen of Germany when Henry was elevated to the throne, but she did not change her simple lifestyle. Matilda gave away large sums of money to charity, and Henry never questioned her generosity.

When Henry died, Otto became king despite Matilda's desire to see her second son, Henry, on the throne. Matilda later faced persecution from both Otto and Henry because they believed she was wasting the kingdom's riches on the poor. Matilda gave up her inheritance to appease her sons and went to live in the country home of her birth. Matilda eventually was asked to return to the court and forgave her sons for their mistreatment. Toward the end of her life, Matilda spent most of her time in the various monasteries she had helped found with her generous contributions. Becoming seriously ill, Matilda traveled to a convent in Quedlinburg. When she died, she was buried at her husband's side. Immediately after her death, she was honored as a saint by the local people.

Reflection

Matilda lived a life of great privilege, but she used her riches selflessly, generously lavishing her abundance on others in need. When I experience abundance, in talents or material things, how do I share them?

Prayer

Saint Matilda, help me to be generous with what I have. Pray that I may give of myself and my possessions with a generous heart as you did. Amen.

MARCH 15

Saint Clement Mary Hofbauer

December 26, 1751–March 15, 1820
Feast: March 15
Patron: Vienna and Warsaw

Clement Mary Hofbauer was born in Tasswitz, Moravia (now the Czech Republic). He was one of twelve children, and his father died when he was only six years old. Clement wanted to become a priest, but his family couldn't afford the required studies. So Clement worked as a baker's assistant, then as a baker in a monastery, studying Latin in his spare time. For some years he lived as a hermit, then returned to his work as a baker. In 1784 he made a pilgrimage to Rome where he asked to enter the Congregation of the Most Holy Redeemer, or the Redemptorists.

For the next thirty-seven years, Clement devoted himself to the Redemptorist mission of evangelization in Poland and Austria—to such an extent that he is known as the second founder of the Redemptorists and the Apostle to Vienna. In Poland, he and his brother Redemptorists opened a shelter for boys, a school for boys, and a school for girls. They started the "perpetual mission" at their parish, which included daily Masses, sermons, prayer services, and confession. When political turmoil drove them out of Poland in 1808, Clement returned to Austria, where he served as a confessor, preacher, and hospital chaplain. When he died, Pope Pius VII lamented, "Religion in Austria has lost its chief support."

Reflection

Clement is known as the "second founder" of the Redemptorists, even though his foundation in Poland was forced to close and he died before establishing a foundation in Austria. It was not primarily his works that earned him this title, but his love for God that turned into intense enthusiasm for making God known. I may not be the founder or the "second founder" of anything, but this same love can burn in my heart.

Prayer

Saint Clement Mary Hofbauer, no matter what you were doing, your love for God could not be contained. Pray for me, that my love for God may spill over into everything I do. Amen

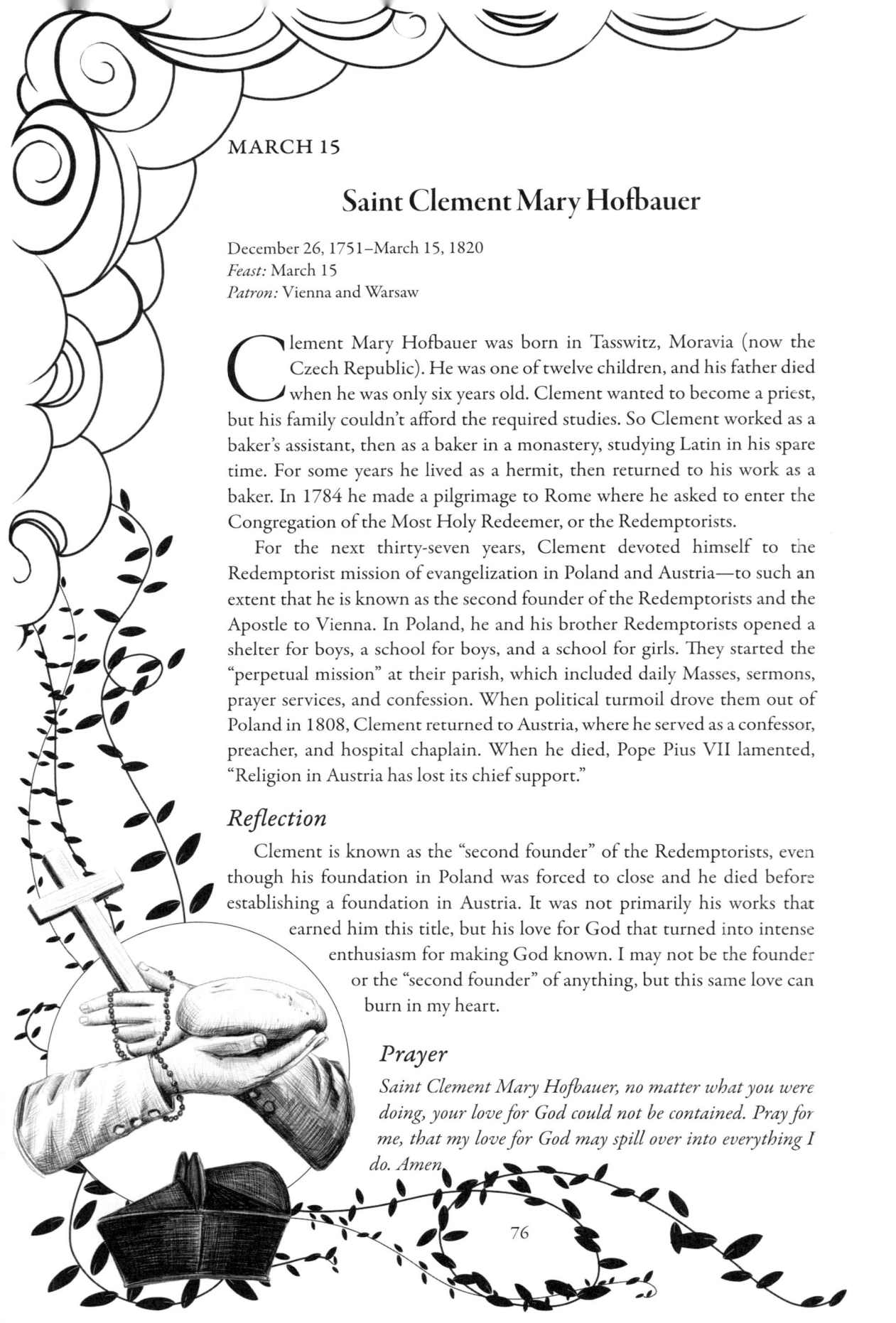

MARCH 16

Saint Louise de Marillac

August 12, 1591–March 15, 1660
Feast: May 9
Patron: Widows, social workers

Raised by her father in an aristocratic French family, Louise never knew her mother because her parents were not married. As a teenager, she was drawn to the spiritual life and tried to enter a convent, but she was not accepted. A few years later she married Antoine le Gras. They had one son, Michel. Louise still longed to be a nun, but on Pentecost 1623, she had a mystical experience in which the Lord told her that in due time she would be able to make vows of chastity, poverty, and obedience. About three years later her husband died.

Louise was fortunate to have Saint Francis de Sales for her spiritual director, and later Saint Vincent de Paul. They guided her in her new vocation. She collaborated with Vincent to become a co-founder of the Daughters of Charity. Working zealously for the poor, the new order quickly spread throughout France and the whole world. She urged the sisters to always have a great heart for the poor and to live together in love and unity. Upon her death, her congregation had forty houses in France.

Reflection

Louise's life shows us how a fervent interior life spills over into works of mission. She had a deeply rooted spirituality based on the French school, popular in the seventeenth century. This approach emphasized union with Christ through living his mysteries. Each person can reflect a particular aspect of Jesus. Louise focused on Jesus' deep love and concern for the poor. Which aspect of Jesus' life most inspires my spiritual life?

Prayer

Saint Louise de Marillac, pray for me that I might reflect Jesus to each person I meet. Help me to discover the particular way that Jesus wants me to follow him, so that I, too, might spend my life loving and serving him in others. Amen.

MARCH 17

Saint Patrick

c. 387–c. 461
Feast: March 17
Patron: Snakebites, engineers, Ireland, Nigeria

Patrick was born into a noble Roman family in Britain. Although his family members were active Christians, he was not interested in religion. When he was sixteen years old, Patrick was kidnapped by Irish raiders and sold as a slave. He later revealed that his deep loneliness and suffering led him to remember the Christian truths he had learned as a child and to turn to God in prayer. After six years, Patrick fled his captors and returned home.

Though he was glad to be home, Patrick felt God calling him to return to Ireland to be a missionary. After his studies, he was ordained a priest. He was consecrated bishop and returned to Ireland around 432. Difficulties and suffering met Patrick in his missionary work, but soon large numbers of the Irish were baptized. Patrick educated and formed them in the spiritual life. He introduced monastic life to the Irish—and they responded with generous fervor. He built churches and monasteries, organized dioceses, and created the infrastructure of the Church in Ireland. Patrick worked there for about thirty years. One hundred years after Patrick's death, the Irish had responded to God so wholeheartedly that Ireland was renowned as the "isle of saints and scholars."

Reflection

Although his ministry consumed much of his attention and energy, Patrick spent long periods of time with God in prayer. Sacred Scripture was an important element of his spiritual life. When he prayed with the Scriptures, he experienced God's revelation and Presence. They nourished him so deeply that his writings were filled with biblical phrases. How does Scripture inspire my prayer life?

Prayer

Please pray for me, Saint Patrick, that I may discover God's life-giving presence in Scripture. Help me to open my mind and heart to be nourished by his word. Amen.

MARCH 18

Saint Cyril of Jerusalem

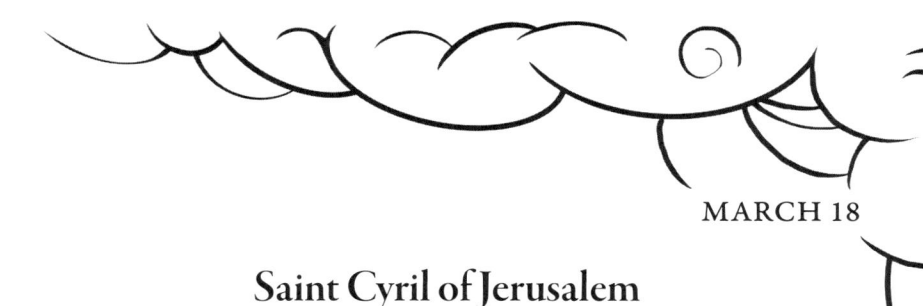

c. 315–c. 386
Feast: March 18
Patron: Catechists

Cyril was born in Jerusalem, probably of Christian parents. Well-educated in his youth, he was ordained a priest by Saint Maximus and, a few years later, succeeded him as the bishop of Jerusalem. Cyril was known for his moderate temperament, but immediately upon becoming bishop he found himself caught up in jurisdiction disputes inherited from his predecessor, as well as with theological controversies with Acacius, the Arian bishop of Caesarea.

In the over thirty years of Cyril's service as bishop of Jerusalem, he was investigated by a local synod, found guilty of selling Church property to give alms to the famine-stricken poor, suspected of doctrinal error, and exiled from his diocese three times. He spent sixteen years in exile. Cyril was named a Doctor of the Church in 1883 by Pope Leo XIII largely for his *Catechetical Lectures* delivered to adult catechumens. It is considered one of the first systematic presentations of Christian theology.

Reflection

The political upheaval and theological struggles that Cyril dealt with were a little different from what we experience today. Conciliatory by nature, Cyril suffered immensely from the factionalism of his day that often ended in bitter recriminations. In disputes he was accused by both parties as being too sympathetic to the other side. And today Cyril is a saint and Doctor of the Church. When arguments about "right" belief lead to factions, labeling, and a culture of communications that doesn't reverence all parties in the discussion, Cyril's example suggests that we take a step back and seek to understand and work together. How do I respond to conflict, especially when it comes to issues of faith?

Prayer

Saint Cyril of Jerusalem, may I serve the Church as you did, in a way that is upright, just, and fair. Amen.

MARCH 19

Saint Joseph

First Century
Feasts: March 19 (Husband of Mary), May 1 (the Worker)
Patron: Fathers, workers, immigrants, unborn children, the dying, virgins, the universal Church, and many countries, including Austria, Belgium, Canada, Croatia, Slovenia, and Peru

Although Saint Joseph is one of the most popular saints in the Church calendar, we know little about his life. But we do know the most important thing, his secret of holiness: Joseph always did what God wanted him to do. "When Joseph awoke from sleep, he did as the angel of the Lord commanded him" (Mt 1:24). Sometimes he had to struggle to discern God's will, but when he received divine guidance, he acted promptly. Joseph's mission was to support Mary and Jesus. As the foster father of Jesus, Joseph brought him up as a devout Jew and taught him the skills of a carpenter and builder.

Joseph loved his family and provided for Jesus and Mary through his hard work. His silence helps us to realize the profound interior life he lived. Tradition tells us that he died in the presence of Jesus and Mary, so he is invoked as the patron of a holy death, one that leads to eternal life. Just as Joseph provided for the Holy Family, he also provides for the extended family that Jesus established: the Church.

Reflection

The Gospels do not record any words of Joseph, but they do record his deeds. In this way, Joseph testifies to what Jesus taught us: "Not everyone who says to me, 'Lord, Lord,' will enter the kingdom of heaven, but only the one who does the will of my Father in heaven" (Mt 7:21). Joseph was not a man who drew attention to himself. Instead, along with Mary, he drew others to Jesus. How can I live in such a way that I draw attention to Jesus?

Prayer

Saint Joseph, patron of the universal Church, pray that all peoples will come to know and believe in Jesus. Amen.

MARCH 20

Saint María Josefa Sancho de Guerra

September 7, 1842–March 20, 1912
Feast: March 20
Patron: Congregation of the Servants of Jesus, sick and homebound

Throughout her childhood, María Josefa had a profound devotion to the Eucharist and the Blessed Mother. When she was eighteen, she decided to join a contemplative community of nuns. Heartbroken when she came down with typhus and could not enter the monastery, she often repeated, "I was born with a religious vocation."

Later, she discerned that the Lord was calling her not to the contemplative life but to an active religious life, and she entered another community of sisters in Madrid. When it came time for her first profession of vows, however, she began to have strong doubts that this was God's will. María Josefa consulted with several spiritual directors, including Saint Anthony Mary Claret, and made a difficult decision.

Now twenty-nine years old, María Josefa and four other women, with their bishop's permission, established a new community called the Congregation of the Servants of Jesus, dedicated to taking care of the sick and homebound. In 1898, María Josefa fell ill. Despite her intense suffering, she continued to direct her nearly one thousand sisters through letters, urging them each to grow in intimacy with Jesus. When she died in 1912, news quickly traveled through the city of Bilbao that a saint had died.

Reflection

María Josefa led a life of intense determination to do whatever God asked of her, no matter how arduous. She was on fire with a special love for the Sacred Heart of Jesus, and he was able to use her to bring his tenderness and care to many lonely and suffering people, even while she was suffering herself. How may God wish me to use my gifts for the sake of others?

Prayer

Saint María Josefa, pray for me that I might always seek the will of God. Help me to become more aware of the needs of others. Amen.

MARCH 21

Saint Óscar Romero

August 15, 1917–March 24, 1980
Feast: March 24
Patron: Christian communicators, persecuted Christians, El Salvador, the Americas

As a boy, Óscar Arnulfo Romero wanted to be a priest. This dream led him first to the local seminary, then to Rome for further studies and ordination in 1942. Returning to his home country of El Salvador, he labored as a parish priest in San Miguel and also worked as the bishop's secretary for over twenty years. In 1970 he became an auxiliary bishop, and in 1974 he took over the diocese of Santiago de María. His pastoral goals were to evangelize the people and also to help the poor. He would drive to the fields in a jeep with loudspeakers and preach to the farm workers.

In 1977 Óscar became the archbishop of San Salvador. Then his good friend, Father Rutilio Grande, S.J., a social activist, was murdered by Salvadoran soldiers. Although Óscar was already advocating for the poor, this event led him to become even more outspoken. He denounced the corrupt government and pressed for social justice. This aroused hostility among many in power. The day after he gave a particularly rousing homily in opposition to government killings, an assassin shot Óscar through the heart as he celebrated Mass in the chapel of Divine Providence Hospital.

Reflection

Óscar never wanted to be a political figure. He was a man of prayer who had deeply developed his interior life based on the spirituality of Opus Dei, as recorded in his diary. As a bishop, he felt a greater responsibility to take action. This was not at odds with his prayer life, but flowed from his commitment to Jesus Christ. How can I strengthen my commitment to Jesus?

Prayer

Saint Óscar Romero, you show us that our commitment to Christ leads us to make a gift of ourselves to those in need. Pray for us that we might generously respond to the needs of the people of our day and lead them to the light of Christ. Amen.

MARCH 22

Saint Rafqa Pietra Choboq Ar-Rayès

June 29, 1832 – March 23, 1914
Feast: March 23
Patron: Against illness, loss of parents

Saint Rafqa (whose name can be translated as "Rebecca") is one of the most beloved saints of the Maronite Rite of the Catholic Church. She was an only child and her parents lovingly taught her the faith. When Rafqa was seven, she suffered greatly when her mother died. A few years later, her father experienced severe financial difficulties and sent her to Damascus to work as a household servant.

When Rafqa returned home, her father had remarried. By this time, she had grown to be a beautiful, humorous, and joyful young woman. Both her new stepmother and an aunt had plans to marry her off, but Rafqa wanted to enter religious life. She finally was able to enter the convent of Our Lady of Deliverance in Bikfaya. After overcoming some crises in her congregation and joining a new monastery, Saint Simon el-Qarn in Aitoshe, she made her final vows in 1872.

In 1885, Rafqa began to pray to share in Jesus' sufferings, and her prayer was granted. She eventually became blind and paralyzed—a reality she endured for years with joy and serenity. Upon her death, an abundance of miracles of healing occurred.

Reflection

Regardless of her life's circumstances, Rafqa found joy in trying to always do God's will. This deep spiritual joy made her a blessing to be around—both for those who knew her during her life, and for those who have received miracles through her intercession since her death. Joy is a fruit of the Holy Spirit and is possible even in times of sorrow. How might I become a more joyful presence in my daily circumstances?

Prayer

Saint Rafqa, please pray for me to be open to the action of the Holy Spirit and receptive to the joy that he desires to give me. Amen.

MARCH 23

Saint Turibius de Mogrovejo

November 16, 1538–March 23, 1606
Feast: March 23
Patron: Peru, Latin American bishops, social justice, and rights of indigenous peoples

Turibius was born in León, Spain, to a wealthy family. After completing his studies, he became a judge who was known for his virtue. The king recognized his piety and asked that Turibius be appointed archbishop of Lima, Peru. Turibius protested that he was only a layman, but the pope gave special permission for him to receive ordination, and he was quickly ordained a priest and then a bishop.

Taking his new office very seriously, Turibius sailed to Peru and discovered that he had much work to do. Many people in his diocese had been baptized but had received no catechesis. He also clashed with local Spanish authorities over the treatment of the indigenous people in his diocese. Undaunted, Turibius journeyed to visit every church in his huge archdiocese several times—his first trip taking seven years due to the wild, mountainous countryside.

Turibius dedicated his time to administering the Sacraments, teaching the indigenous people in their own language, and uniting the ecclesial administration in Peru through regular councils, despite opposition from local Spanish authorities. During one of his many visits to a remote parish in his archdiocese, Turibius fell ill and died.

Reflection

When Turibius was chosen to be the archbishop, he struggled with feelings of unworthiness. He was not even a priest! Why had God chosen him? He eventually realized he would need to rely on the grace of God. How often do I despair because I see only what I can do alone? How would my perspective change if I relied less on myself and more on God's grace?

Prayer

God, let us never be discouraged by our weaknesses, but rather view our unworthiness as opportunities to let you work in and through us. Amen.

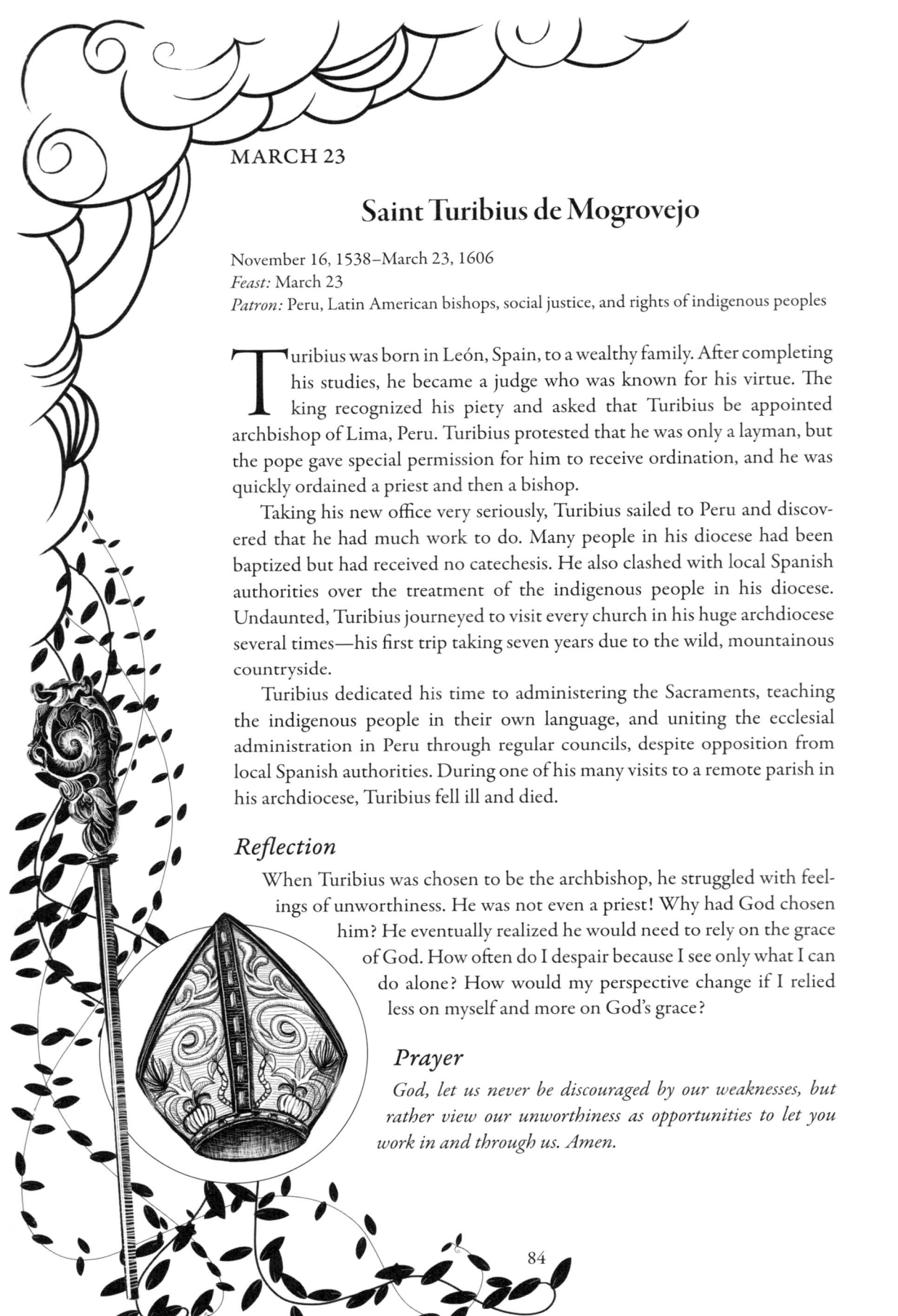

MARCH 24

Saint Catherine of Sweden

c. 1331–March 24, 1381
Feast: March 24
Patron: Unborn children, prevention of miscarriage

Catherine of Sweden was the fourth of eight children of Saint Bridget. When Catherine was about thirteen or fourteen years old, her father arranged for her to be married. Catherine, a very devout young woman, recognized a similar devotion in her husband, and she convinced him that they should live a life of celibacy. Together, they devoted themselves to works of charity and to prayer. Catherine accompanied her mother to Rome and on several other pilgrimages. Undoubtedly, Catherine's spirituality was influenced by her mother's mystical experiences focusing on the passion and death of Christ.

During one of their trips, Catherine received word that her husband had died. Since her father had died several years earlier, Catherine joined her mother in her work of founding the Order of the Most Holy Savior, until Saint Bridget's death in 1373. During a period of painful schism in the Church, Catherine remained faithful to the pope and testified before a judicial commission in support of him. After her mother's death, Catherine worked to get the necessary permissions from the Holy See for her mother's religious congregation, now known as the Brigittines. She then returned to Sweden and became the abbess of Vadzstena.

Reflection

Catherine of Sweden found creative and generous ways of serving God far beyond what was expected of her. Sometimes, it can be easy for us to do the minimum in any situation, whether spiritual, work-related, or in our relationships. What are some concrete ways I can become more generous today?

Prayer

Saint Catherine of Sweden, intercede for us, so that we may come to embrace a greater love for Christ Crucified, and be inspired to a greater generosity. Amen.

MARCH 25

Saint Gabriel the Archangel

Feast: September 29
Patron: Broadcasters, communications media, messengers, postal employees, radio workers, telephone workers

Angels are purely spiritual, immortal creatures that have been present from the beginning of salvation history. Angels are mentioned repeatedly throughout the Old and New Testament. Though they are not human and cannot be officially canonized, the archangels are informally known as "saints" because they are holy and in heaven.

The word "angel" means messenger, and of all the angels in the Bible, Gabriel holds a special place. Gabriel is the angel who brought Mary the good news that God was asking her to become the Mother of God: "Do not be afraid, Mary, for you have found favor with God. And now, you will conceive in your womb and bear a son, and you will name him Jesus" (Lk 1:30–31). Countless paintings and other images of the Annunciation have made Gabriel a popular angel.

Gabriel also announced to Zechariah the birth of John the Baptist. The angel appears in the Old Testament as well, especially in the Book of Daniel. There, he instructs Daniel about how to understand the visions and messages he has received from God. Gabriel has a special role as communicator. He teaches and imparts wisdom and knowledge about the things of God.

Reflection

Mary responded to Gabriel's message from God with complete faith: "Here am I, the servant of the Lord; let it be with me according to your word" (Lk 1:38). Although we might not get extraordinary messages from angels, God communicates with us in various ways, and can give us insight and wisdom through the angels. How can I make more space in my life for prayer so I can pay attention to the urgings of the Holy Spirit?

Prayer

Saint Gabriel, patron of the modern means of communication, ask Jesus, our Divine Master and Shepherd, that the Church may use these powerful means to bring the Gospel to everyone. Amen.

MARCH 26

Saint Marie-Alphonsine Danil Ghattas

October 4, 1843–March 25, 1927
Feast: March 25
Patron: Dominican Sisters of the Most Holy Rosary of Jerusalem, devotion to Mary

Soultaneh Marie, which means "Mary the Queen," was a Palestinian Christian born in Jerusalem. In 1858, she entered the Sisters of Saint Joseph of the Apparition. Two years later, she took her vows and received the name Marie-Alphonsine. After professing her vows, she taught catechism and promoted devotion to the Rosary.

Then, on January 6, 1874, the Feast of the Epiphany, the Blessed Mother appeared to Marie-Alphonsine in a vision. Mary urged Marie-Alphonsine to establish a new religious congregation for Arab girls. Marie-Alphonsine did so but wanted to remain hidden in this work. With the help of her spiritual director, Father Youssef Tannous, the Sisters of the Rosary began with seven young women.

After several years, Marie-Alphonsine received permission to enter the new community. For the rest of her life she dedicated herself to the mission of teaching and pastoral work, especially spreading devotion to Mary and the Rosary. Father Youssef told her to write her memoirs, including Mary's apparitions to her. None of her sisters knew of the visions, however, until Marie-Alphonsine died on the feast of the Annunciation. Pope Francis canonized her in 2015.

Reflection

Today in the Holy Land, the birthplace of Jesus, Christians are sadly a small minority due to persecution, economic hardship, and rising Islamic fundamentalism. Many families who have lived there for generations have had to leave Palestine. Marie-Alphonsine's life testifies to the deep devotion of these Christians. Let us ask her intercession that Christianity might be free to take deeper root in the Holy Land.

Prayer

Saint Marie-Alphonsine Danil Ghattas, intercede for Christians in the Holy Land and for the spread of the Catholic faith. Pray for an end to all hatred and violence, so that all people may live together in holiness and peace. Amen.

MARCH 27

Blessed Alberto Marvelli

March 21, 1918–October 5, 1946
Feast: October 5
Patron: Young people, politicians

Alberto Marvelli grew up in Rimini, Italy, the second of six children. He graduated with an engineering degree in 1941 and started teaching, but soon the tides of war would disrupt life as he knew it. Rimini was devastated by Allied bombing, and Alberto's family fled to a nearby town. After every bombing, Alberto would risk his life to bicycle to Rimini, bringing food and blankets to help those in need and to pray with the wounded and dying. He often returned late at night, without coat or shoes or even his bicycle, all of which he had given away.

Alberto voluntarily joined the Nazi engineering organization that was using forced labor to build fortifications against the Allies. Knowing some German and having an engineering degree, Alberto was able to have some level of authority. He used inside information to warn of raids, and his official stamp to help young men avoid deportation to Germany.

The Germans soon realized what he was doing and arrested him. Alberto, under cover of hugging a friend goodbye, slipped him the official stamp, which the friend used to secure Alberto's release.

After the war, Alberto took the lead in rebuilding Rimini and soon decided to go into politics. One evening, however, as he was bicycling to a meeting regarding the election, he was accidentally hit by a truck and died. He was only twenty-eight years old.

Reflection

Alberto's father died when he was a young teenager, and this experience drew him to the spiritual life. He also read the life of Pier Giorgio Frassati, whom he admired and wanted to imitate. Alberto was convinced that he could become holy in his everyday life. Which saints inspire me to live a holier life?

Prayer

Blessed Alberto, inspire men and women of integrity to get involved in political life so that they can use the values of the Gospel to help shape society. Amen.

MARCH 28

Saint Stephen Harding

c. 1060–March 28, 1134
Feast: April 17
Patron: The Cistercian Order

Born in England, Stephen is honored as one of the founders of the Cistercian Order. As a young boy, he entered the monastery of Sherburn—today Sherborne—where it is likely that he became a monk. For reasons unknown, as a young man he left the monastery and went to Scotland, then to France and Italy. Eventually, he returned to France and became a monk at the Abbey of Molesme.

Later, seeking a more rigorous way of life, Stephen left the Abbey of Molesme with two others, Robert and Alberic. At first, they lived in solitude, but then twenty-one other monks from Molesme joined them, so they moved to Citeaux. The Cistercians were dedicated to a life of prayer, penance, and work. Stephen became the abbot in 1108, but most of the members left because the rigorous life was too difficult for them. It seemed that the new foundation would not survive.

But then, almost miraculously, in 1112 Saint Bernard of Clairvaux joined them with thirty followers. From then on, the Cistercians expanded throughout Europe. Stephen was a major force leading their growth. He was a good organizer and knew how to blend monastic discipline with charity and prudence, as exemplified in the order's constitution, which he wrote, the *Carta caritatis*, or "Charter of Love."

Reflection

Stephen could have easily quit when almost all the monks left the monastery. Did God want him to continue or not? His prayer was answered when Bernard and his men appeared. Stephen pressed on, and the Cistercian Order still flourishes today. When I must make difficult decisions, do I ask God to show me the way?

Prayer

Saint Stephen Harding, pray that I may not give up when things are tough, but that I may turn to God for the grace I need to persevere. Amen.

MARCH 29

Saint Margaret Clitherow

c. 1553–March 25, 1586
Feast: March 26
Patron: Converts, businesswomen

Margaret was born to Protestant parents in York, England. In 1571, she married a wealthy butcher, John Clitherow, who came from a Catholic family but practiced Anglicanism, the state religion. His brother, William, a Catholic priest, perhaps influenced Margaret's conversion to Catholicism a few years later.

John was tolerant of Margaret's religious views and allowed her to raise their children in the faith, use their home to hide Catholic priests, and have Mass celebrated there. At that time, attending Mass was illegal and harboring priests was punishable by death, but Margaret had such a great love for Jesus and the Mass that she was undeterred by the dangers. She was known for her wit and beauty and was so well liked by her neighbors and servants that many knew her secrets and yet refused to betray her.

However, Margaret was finally arrested in 1586. She refused a trial because she wanted to spare her loved ones the pain of testifying against her. She was consequently sentenced to be pressed to death by heavy rocks. As she was led to her execution, she boldly proclaimed that she was dying not for treason but for the love of Jesus.

Reflection

Saint Margaret Clitherow understood the importance of handing on her faith to her children, and her sacrifice was not in vain: inspired by the heroic witness of their mother, two of her sons became priests and her daughter became a nun. How important is the faith in my family life? How do I share it with those I love?

Prayer

Dear Lord, make my family members and me holy. May we always be a living sign of your love in the world. Amen.

MARCH 30

Saint Mary Euphrasia

July 31, 1796–April 29, 1869
Feast: April 24
Patron: Travelers

Rose Virginie Pelletier was born during the French Revolution. In an effort to escape the persecution of Catholics, her parents and siblings lived on an island off the coast of France. Her father baptized Rose, since all the priests in the area had been hunted down and killed. As she grew, she witnessed her father, a doctor, and her mother doing all they could to help the poor. After her father died, the family moved back to the mainland, and Rose was sent to a boarding school. She was devastated when her mother died, and she only learned of it after the funeral.

When she left school, Rose joined the Sisters of Our Lady of Charity. There, she cared for girls and women in difficulty and took the name Sister Mary Euphrasia. Some years later, she became superior of the convent and helped to form a contemplative group of sisters called the Magdalens.

In 1835, Mother Mary Euphrasia received the pope's approval to establish a new congregation, known today as the Sisters of the Good Shepherd. The new congregation had both contemplative and apostolic branches. She served as the general superior of the new congregation for thirty-three years and oversaw its rapid expansion.

Reflection

As with many saints, Mother Mary Euphrasia's childhood experiences had a great effect on her later ministry. Because of her own suffering, grief, and loneliness, she could empathize with others. She often said, "One person is of more value than a world." Mother Mary Euphrasia's compassionate love for others continues to be an inspiration for us all.

Prayer

Mother Mary Euphrasia, obtain for us the grace we need to truly see the value of each person—created by God and loved by the Good Shepherd. Amen.

MARCH 31

Blessed María de San José

April 25, 1875–April 2, 1967
Feast: April 2
Patron: Nurses

When Laura Evangelista Alvarado Cardozo received Jesus in her first Holy Communion at the age of thirteen, she expressed her desire to belong totally to him and made a private vow of chastity. Forever after, she considered herself a bride of Christ and immediately set about doing his work, especially among the poor children of Venezuela. Laura desired to enter a cloistered convent, but most of the religious orders had been suppressed by the government. Instead, with the permission of her confessor, Father Vicente Lopez Aveledo, Laura made a vow of perpetual virginity on December 8, 1892.

When an epidemic broke out, Laura and Father Vicente worked to set up a little hospital. Laura drew in many other young women to volunteer. The group became known as the Samaritans. In the years following, Laura formed this small group into a congregation of sisters, the Augustinian Recollects of the Heart of Jesus, dedicated to the care of the sick, elderly, and orphans. She became known as Mother María de San José. Before her death at the age of ninety-two, she had founded thirty-seven homes for the elderly and orphans. She was the first native of Venezuela to be beatified.

Reflection

When we discover a great restaurant or a new favorite movie, we can't wait to share it with others. Mother María de San José knew something much greater: she knew God's love. This love led her to desire that all outcasts experience God's love as well. Do I allow God to express his love for me to the point that I desire to share it?

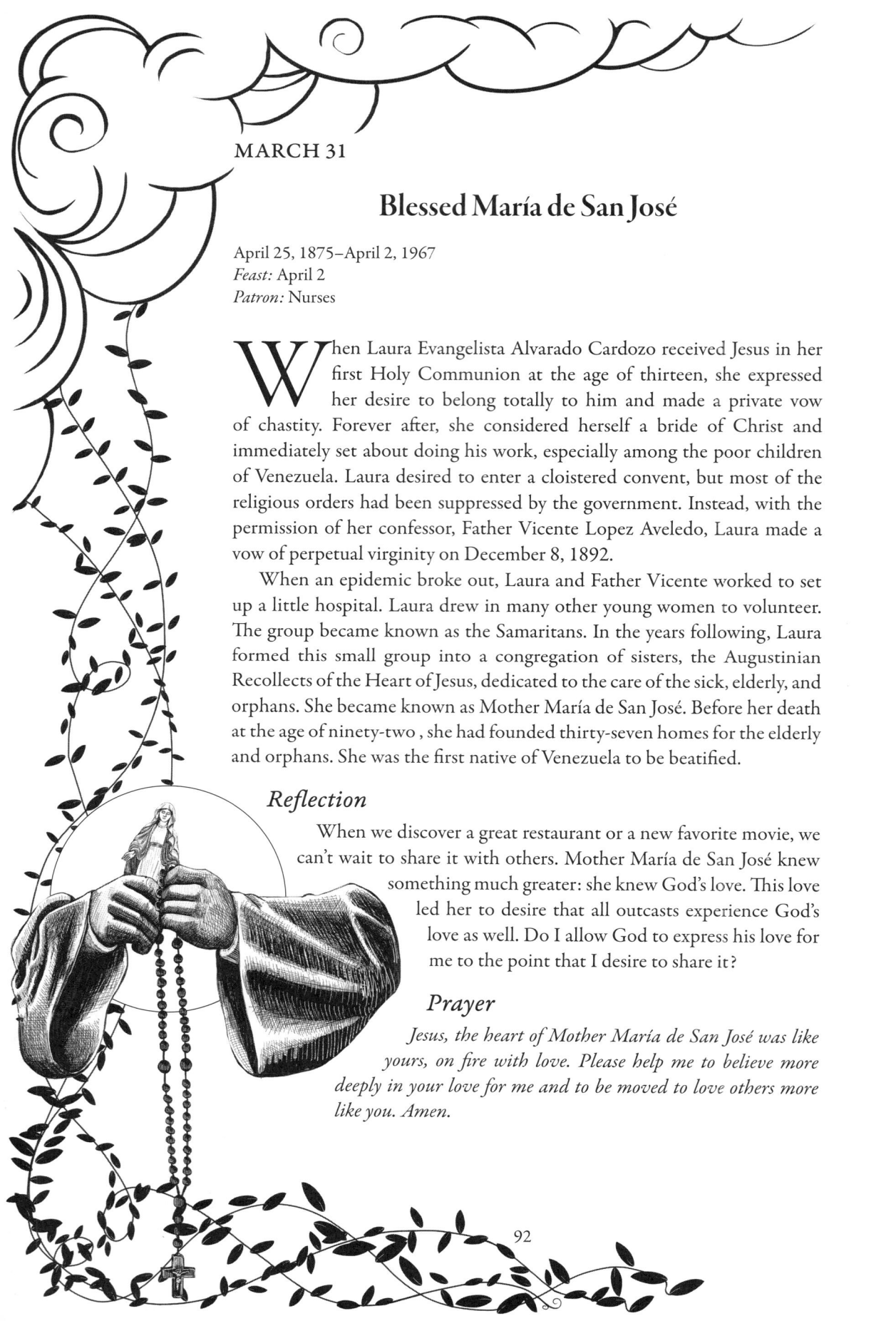

Prayer

Jesus, the heart of Mother María de San José was like yours, on fire with love. Please help me to believe more deeply in your love for me and to be moved to love others more like you. Amen.

APRIL 1

Saint Mary of Egypt

c. 344–c. 421
Feast: April 1
Patron: Penitents, chastity, skin diseases, overcoming addiction

When she was twelve years old, Mary of Egypt ran away from her Christian family to the city of Alexandria. There, she spent the next seventeen years of her life as a prostitute. One day, she saw a large crowd making a pilgrimage to Jerusalem for the feast of the Exaltation of the Cross, and she spontaneously decided to join them. Mary traded sexual favors during the voyage to Jerusalem in exchange for her passage.

Some days after Mary arrived in Jerusalem, the true Cross was to be displayed for public veneration. Mary followed the crowds, intrigued. When she came to the door of the church, an invisible wall prevented her from passing through. After trying several times and witnessing everyone else easily passing through, she realized she was being excluded because of her sinfulness. She was moved to tears with deep contrition for her sins, and looking up, saw an icon of the Blessed Mother. Mary begged the Blessed Mother to help her to reform her life. After receiving the Sacraments, Mary went into the desert and lived as a hermit, fasting and praying for the rest of her life.

Reflection

Mary grew up in a Christian home and her upbringing came back to her at the moment of her conversion. She knew the significance of the Cross because she had been taught it. With God's grace, Mary's life became a beautiful testament to the fact that no one is ever outside the reach of God's love. How firmly do I believe that God is always ready to forgive my sins?

Prayer

Jesus, I thank you that you never give up on us. Help me always to stay close to you. I entrust to you my prayers for my dear ones who have closed themselves off from your love. Amen.

APRIL 2

Saint Francis of Paola

March 27, 1416–April 2, 1507
Feast: April 2
Patron: Naval Officers, against fire, mariners, plague, sailors, sterility, travelers

A childless couple in Paola, Italy, had prayed for a child through the intercession of Saint Francis of Assisi. When God answered their prayers, the couple named their newborn son Francis. When Francis was thirteen, he lived in a nearby Franciscan friary for a year. There he learned to read, write, and how to live the Franciscan lifestyle of poverty and simplicity.

Afterward he led an austere life as a hermit. Eventually joined by others, they called themselves The Poor Hermits of Saint Francis of Assisi. Later, Francis changed their name to the Order of Minims, indicating that he wanted his order to be seen as the least of all. The basic Rule consisted of humility, charity, and penance. Aside from the monastic vows, a fourth was added—a perpetual Lenten fast that excluded meat, dairy, and eggs.

The local people eventually built a church and monastery for Francis' growing community. While it was erected, Francis worked a number of miracles, including the restoration of life for injured construction workers. In 1481, at the request of the dying King Louis XI, Francis traveled barefoot to France. Although the king wanted to be healed, Francis helped him to accept his death in peace. Francis died several decades later on Good Friday.

Reflection

Francis of Paola worked many miracles "in the name of charity." He healed a blind person; restored a child's disfigured, eyeless face; and brought people back to life. He also had the gift of prophecy. These were graces that God does not bestow on many. But God gives abundant graces to some people for the sake of everyone. What gifts has God given me for the sake of others?

Prayer

Saint Francis of Paola, you used the gifts God gave you to help others in the name of charity. Pray that I may always use the gifts God has given me to help others in need. Amen.

APRIL 3

Saint Pedro Calungsod

c. 1654–April 2, 1672
Feast: April 2
Patron: Filipino youth, altar servers, catechists, the Philippines, Guam

Pedro was born in the Visayas region of the Philippines. As a teenager, he attended a boarding school run by the Jesuits. There he learned catechism, how to pray, and other practical skills. An opportunity arose for Pedro to go to Guam as a missionary with one of the Jesuits, Blessed Diego Luis de San Vitores.

In Guam, Pedro and the other catechists worked to evangelize the indigenous Chomorro people. Many people accepted the faith and were baptized. Yet opposition arose when someone started to spread rumors that the baptismal water caused sickness. Since some baptized babies had died, the rumor caught on.

One day, Pedro and Father Diego were visiting a village and baptized a baby with the mother's consent. But the father, who was hostile to Christianity, flew into a rage when he found out. He attacked and killed both men. Pedro could have saved himself by fleeing, but he did not want to leave Father Diego. Pope Benedict XVI canonized Pedro in 2012.

Reflection

Pedro Calungsod was only about seventeen years old when he died. Some people might think that he threw his life away. But in his short life he made a huge impact on the Church. At his beatification, Saint John Paul II quoted the Book of Wisdom: "Being perfected in a short time, they fulfilled long years" (4:13). What matters in the sight of God is not *how long* we live, but *how* we live. Pedro fulfilled the mission given him by God. I don't know how long God wants me to live, but I do know *how* God wants me to live.

Prayer

Saint Pedro Calungsod, you dedicated yourself to the evangelization of the Chomorro people with great love. Pray that the Gospel might continue to spread throughout the whole world. Amen.

APRIL 4

Saint Isidore of Seville

c. 560–April 4, 636
Feast: April 4
Patron: Internet

Isidore was an incredibly learned man, a great scholar. He grew up in a Christian home where he also was steeped in the classical culture of the Roman world. He became a priest and in 599 was named bishop of Seville, succeeding his brother Saint Leander. The social and economic situation was difficult, as the people were struggling to prosper under the rule of the Visigoths after the Roman Empire had collapsed. The Visigoths were Arians, but in 587 their king, Reccared, had become a Catholic. This gave a great impetus to the growth of the Catholic Church in Spain.

Isidore took full advantage of this ripe moment for evangelization. As bishop, he wrote many books, including a massive encyclopedia in which he brought together knowledge from all branches of study. Because of his scholarly efforts, Isidore later was named a Doctor of the Church, the last of the Latin Fathers. But despite his love for study, Isidore always strove to meet the pastoral needs of his people. In blending these two things, Isidore gave a great model for a contemplative life not turned in on itself, but open to the needs of his flock.

Reflection

Isidore had an encyclopedic knowledge of the world that could be compared to today's online search engines. He could have used his intelligence for many things, but Isidore always put his knowledge at the service of God and his people. Isidore's great passion, to use knowledge for God, still inspires us today.

Prayer

Saint Isidore of Seville, pray that we may seek not only a human knowledge limited to this world but also divine wisdom that reveals the ultimate meaning of life. Help us to use technology for the glory of God and the good of the human person. Amen.

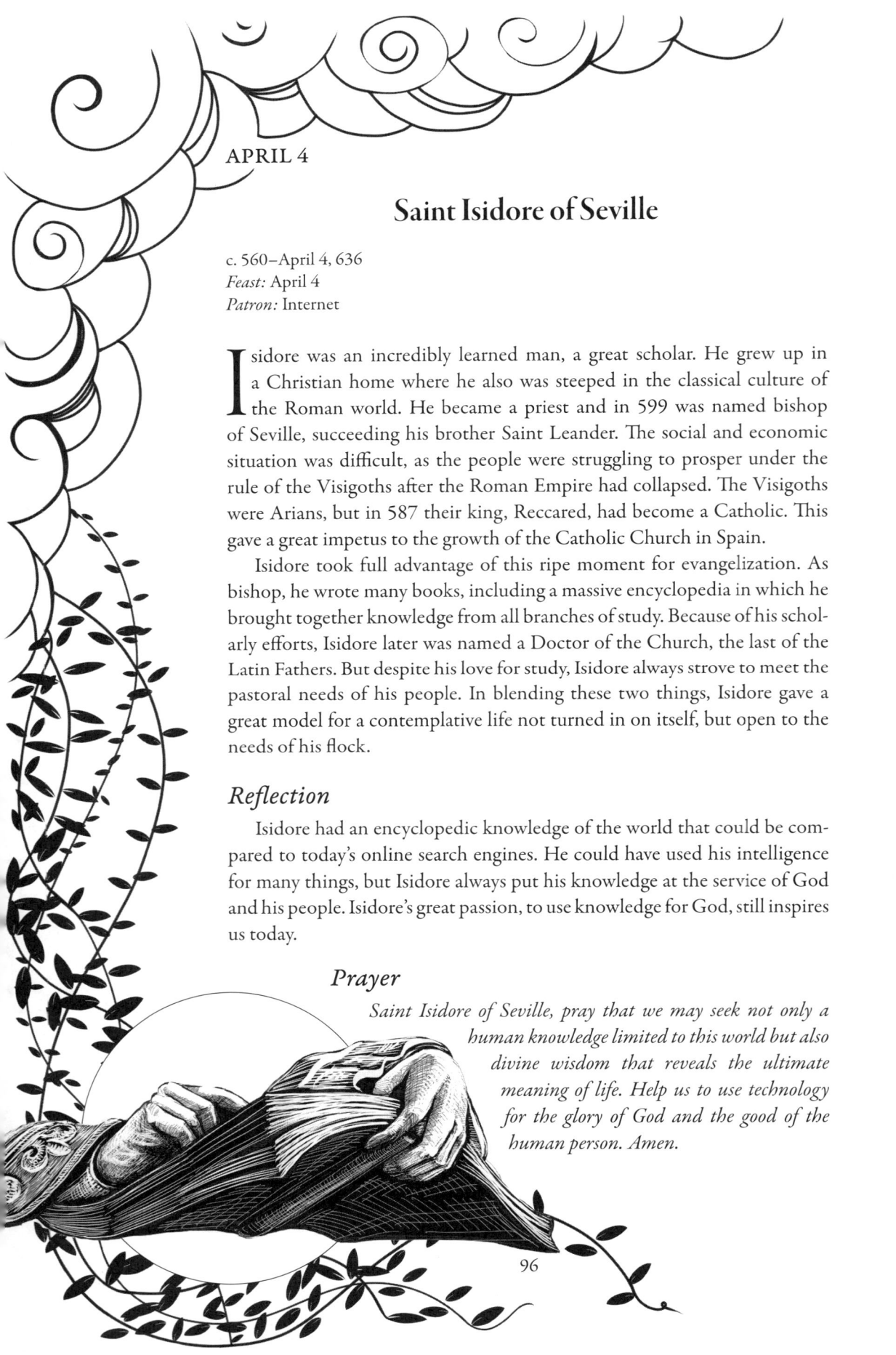

APRIL 5

Saint Vincent Ferrer

January 23, 1350–April 5, 1419
Feast: April 5
Patron: Builders, tilemakers, brickmakers, roofers, reconciliation, protection against epilepsy and headaches

Born in Valencia to a well-to-do family, Vincent received a good education and entered the Dominicans at age seventeen. His early years in the order were spent chiefly studying and teaching. In 1378 the Great Western schism began. The newly elected Urban VI so antagonized the cardinals that they convened to declare his election invalid and choose a new "pope." Their appointee took the name Clement VII and established his court at Avignon. In 1394 Clement's successor, who called himself Benedict XIII, invited Vincent to be his advisor and confessor. Believing Benedict to be the true pope, Vincent accepted the role.

In 1398, Vincent became deathly ill. While he was ill, he had a vision of Christ and Saints Dominic and Francis of Assisi who told him to travel and preach. After recovering, Vincent soon left Avignon and preached for twenty years. Journeying from one region of Western Europe to another, he drew huge crowds, whom he urged to reform their lives. It is said that he prepared for his sermons while kneeling before a crucifix and gazing at Jesus' wounds. Despite his great success, however, he was tormented by a sense of his own unworthiness. Vincent's preaching mission lasted until his death, which took place in Brittany in 1419.

Reflection

Despite Vincent's personal convictions about Benedict XIII's legitimacy as pope, at some point he appealed to him to resign. Benedict refused and was eventually deposed. Sources disagree about Vincent's role in healing the Great Western schism, but this much is certain: Vincent desired unity and reconciliation in the Church.

Prayer

Saint Vincent Ferrer, you accomplished great things despite your sense of unworthiness. Help me to aim to do good—especially as a peacemaker—no matter how inadequate I may feel. Amen.

APRIL 6

Saint Teresa of the Andes

July 13, 1900–April 12, 1920
Feast: April 12
Patron: Young people, the ill

Born into a loving family in Santiago, Chile, Juana Fernández Solar was a lively girl. Her character was marked by a loving spirit as well as a stubborn streak and vanity. In her childhood she read *The Story of a Soul,* the autobiography of Saint Thérèse of Lisieux. This impressed her and planted in her the desire to become a Carmelite nun.

After Juana made her first Communion, she seriously resolved to follow the path of holiness. She did her best to correct her faults and show love to others. In her teenage years, she taught religion and helped the needy in the parish. On May 7, 1919, she entered the Carmel and lived her new life with great intensity and zeal. Now called Teresa of Jesus, she began to write many letters, sharing with friends and family her spiritual insights. But she also knew that she was going to die young. She shared with her confessor that God had told her of her impending death. Soon after, she was struck with a bad case of typhus. Seeing that her condition was fatal, her superiors allowed her to make her profession of vows early, even though she had not completed the novitiate. Devotion to her spread after her death, and she was canonized the first Chilean saint by Saint John Paul II on March 21, 1993.

Reflection

Though she was only nineteen years old when she died, Teresa became a saint because she focused on one goal with laser-like intensity: holiness. We can learn from her the importance of setting our priorities so that God has first place in our lives.

Prayer

Saint Teresa of the Andes, your love for Jesus enabled you to turn away from self-centered desires and give yourself totally to him. Pray that I might also make a sincere gift of myself to God and to others. Amen.

APRIL 7

Saint John Baptist de La Salle

April 30, 1651–April 7, 1719
Feast: April 7
Patron: Teachers

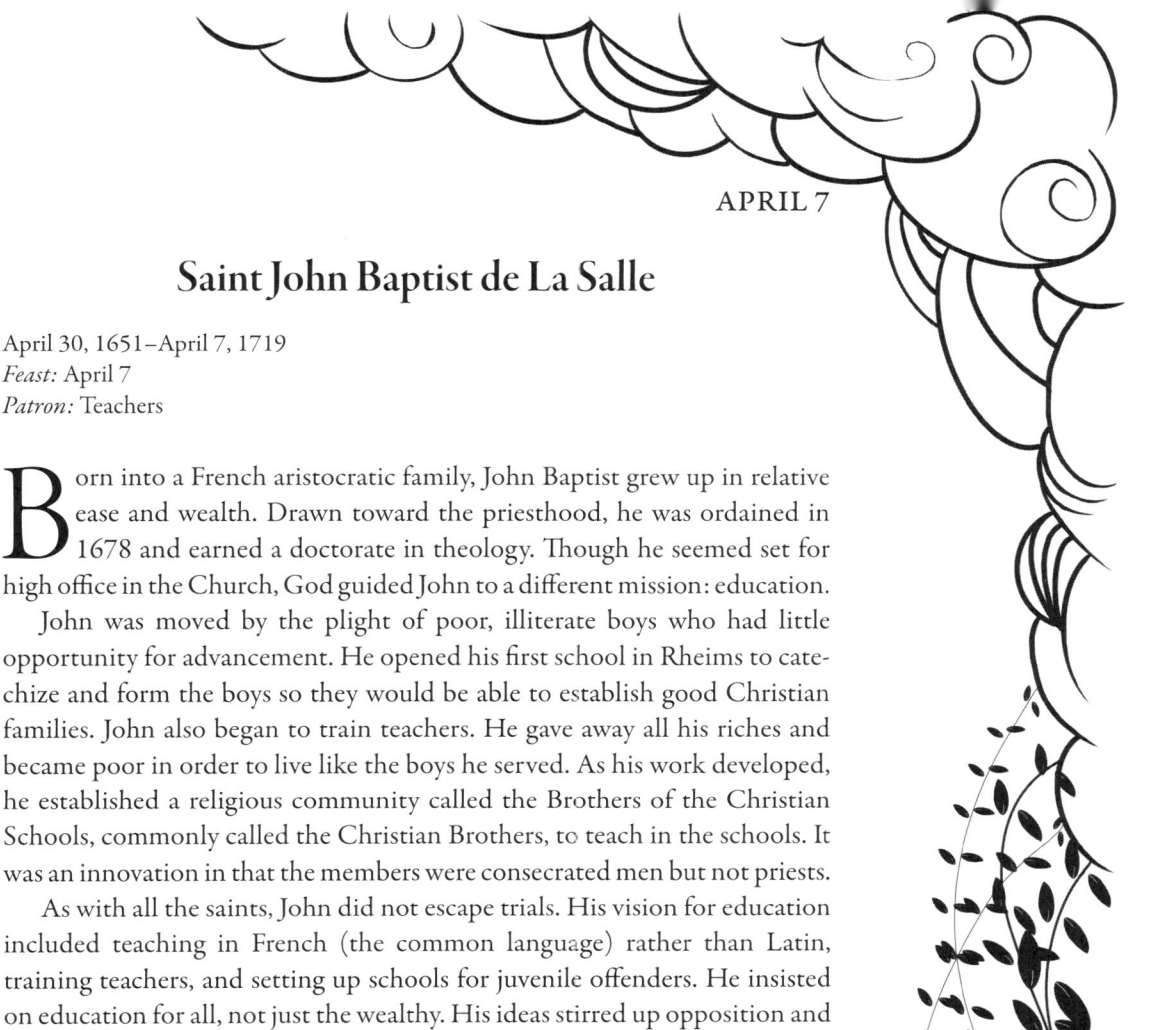

Born into a French aristocratic family, John Baptist grew up in relative ease and wealth. Drawn toward the priesthood, he was ordained in 1678 and earned a doctorate in theology. Though he seemed set for high office in the Church, God guided John to a different mission: education.

John was moved by the plight of poor, illiterate boys who had little opportunity for advancement. He opened his first school in Rheims to catechize and form the boys so they would be able to establish good Christian families. John also began to train teachers. He gave away all his riches and became poor in order to live like the boys he served. As his work developed, he established a religious community called the Brothers of the Christian Schools, commonly called the Christian Brothers, to teach in the schools. It was an innovation in that the members were consecrated men but not priests.

As with all the saints, John did not escape trials. His vision for education included teaching in French (the common language) rather than Latin, training teachers, and setting up schools for juvenile offenders. He insisted on education for all, not just the wealthy. His ideas stirred up opposition and controversy. But John persevered, and his work spread from France to many other countries. Today, thousands of Christian Brothers and their associates continue the educational mission that John began.

Reflection

John understood the great value of education not only for success in this present life but also for our ultimate goal: heaven. He believed that all who follow Christ in simplicity of heart would also help to bring others to eternal life. How do I share the gift of faith with others?

Prayer

Lord, let the light of your truth guide me. Help me so that the faith I profess may grow through the love in my heart. Amen.

APRIL 8

Saint Julie Billiart

July 12, 1751–April 8, 1816
Feast: April 8
Patron: Against poverty, paralysis

Julie was born the sixth of seven children, in Cuvilly, France. Although there were no schools for girls in her village, she quickly learned to read and write. Julie had even memorized the entire catechism by the time she was seven. At the same age, she began teaching other children who were too poor to attend school. At fourteen, she made a private vow of chastity, desiring to live totally for God.

One night in 1774, Julie and her father were sitting at home when suddenly a shot was fired into the house. No one was hurt, but she suffered from shock and her health declined until she was completely paralyzed at the age of thirty. Even so, she continued to teach catechism and to give spiritual direction from her bed. Some years later, she met Françoise Blin de Bourdon, a wealthy French noblewoman. Though Julie was still bedridden, the two women became close friends and together they co-founded the Sisters of Notre Dame de Namur.

One day, a priest who was a friend of the community asked Julie to pray a novena to the Sacred Heart. When the novena ended, he invited Julie to stand up and walk—and she did. Julie immediately began to extend her teaching apostolate and to gather more women around her who were dedicated to the education of children. Her sisters are active all over the world to this day.

Reflection

Julie Billiart was given a special gift for learning and teaching, and she spent her life sharing this gift with others, regardless of the difficulties that came her way. God has entrusted me with special gifts too. What are they? How do I use these treasures entrusted to my care?

Prayer

Heavenly Father, Saint Julie always trusted in your goodness and desired to follow your will. Through her intercession, help us to follow her example. Saint Julie, pray for us. Amen.

APRIL 9

Blessed Marguerite Rutan

April 23, 1736–April 9, 1794
Feast: April 9
Patron: Nurses, persecuted Christians, prisoners

Marguerite Rutan was born in Metz, France. She was the eighth of fifteen children. Her father was a stonecutter and her mother educated the children in the faith. From her childhood years, Marguerite manifested an unusual piety. When she was twenty-one, she decided to enter the Daughters of Charity of Saint Vincent de Paul. Marguerite was overjoyed when two of her sisters also joined the Daughters of Charity but, to her distress, they both died young.

In 1779, Marguerite began working in a hospital in Dax, a city near Saint Vincent de Paul's birthplace. By the time she arrived, she had acquired experience as both a religious and a nurse. With her background and organizational skills, Marguerite was able to help develop the hospital. A new chapel was also constructed. Besides caring for the sick, she reached out to street children and abandoned pregnant women. She also distributed food and alms to families in need.

In 1789, the French Revolution began, and the country was plunged into turmoil. False testimony led to Marguerite's arrest on Christmas Eve in 1793. The following April Marguerite was tried and condemned to death for refusing to renounce her faith. She went to the guillotine with dignity, entrusting her life into the hands of Mary.

Reflection

Marguerite Rutan lived through an unstable and troubling period in France. The French Revolution profoundly changed her home country and personally touched Marguerite, leading to her suffering and martyrdom. In the midst of difficulty, she sought only to follow Christ and to serve her brothers and sisters. How can I continue to show love to others when my life becomes difficult?

Prayer

Saint Marguerite Rutan, pray that I might have the courage to love in all circumstances. Amen.

APRIL 10

Saint Gemma Galgani

March 12, 1878–April 11, 1903
Feast: April 11
Patron: Pharmacists, orphans, those with back and spinal pain, injuries, and illnesses

Gemma Galgani was born in Camigliano, a small town in Tuscany, Italy. The fourth of eight children, she lost both parents before the age of twenty. Left in poverty with her siblings, Gemma was sustained by her strong love of Jesus and vibrant prayer life. Gemma struggled with ill health all her life, but it gradually grew worse. A serious illness in her spine led to hearing loss and paralysis. On the verge of death, she received a miraculous cure and attributed it to the intercession of the young Passionist saint, Gabriel Possenti.

Gemma ardently desired to become a Passionist nun, but even after her cure, her persisting weak health prevented her from entering. Bitterly disappointed, Gemma resolved to live a quiet life of simple humility. She joined the Passionists' third order and devoted herself in a special way to Jesus crucified. Gemma experienced mystical visions and, in 1899, she received the stigmata. A few years later, her spinal disease reoccurred, and she died at the age of twenty-five.

Reflection

Saint Gemma Galgani suffered many disappointments during her life. From the death of close loved ones to terminal illness, she faced obstacles at every turn. She was even denied entrance to the religious order to which she profoundly longed to belong. Yet she died with no regrets, handing her life over to Jesus and giving herself totally over to him. How do I react in the face of disappointment? Am I able to see God's hand in everything and accept all that happens in an attitude of loving joy?

Prayer

Faithful God, make us love you more and more through the disappointments we encounter each day. May every obstacle bring us closer to you. Amen.

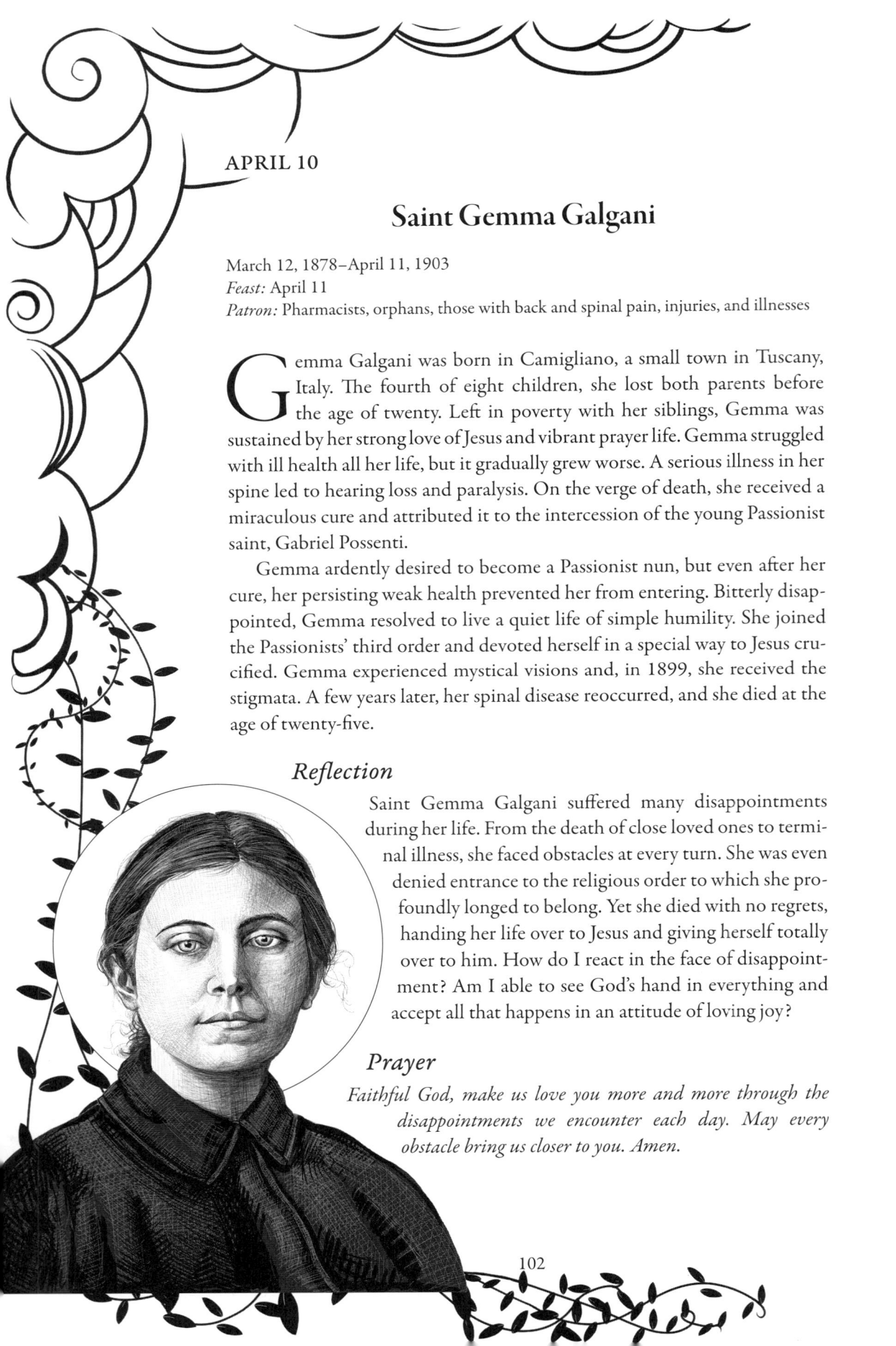

APRIL 11

Saint Stanislaus of Szczepanów

July 26, 1030–April 11, 1079
Feast: April 11
Patron: Poland, the last sacraments

Born in Szczepanów in the diocese of Kraków, Stanislaus received an excellent religious education from his parents. After their death, he took to heart the call of Jesus: he gave away his inheritance and entered the priesthood. He served as a pastor, a preacher at Kraków's cathedral, and both vicar and bishop of the diocese of Kraków.

As bishop, Stanislaus worked energetically to build up his diocese and remove corruption. This led him into conflict with King Bolesław II of Poland over a piece of Church property, as well as over Bolesław's immoral way of life. Anxious for justice to be done, Stanislaus was also concerned for the king's soul. However, his arguments, threats, prayers, and tears were ineffective, and he was eventually forced to excommunicate the king. Bolesław was furious. He followed Stanislaus to the Chapel of Saint Michael in a suburb of Kraków and killed him as he was celebrating Mass. Thus, Stanislaus joined the sacrifice of his life intimately to Christ's sacrifice on the Cross.

Reflection

Stanislaus stands out as one who lived the ever-present tension between Church and state with integrity, working both to reform the Church and to call the state to greater justice and compassion. Stanislaus lived through many difficult and tense situations and conflicts—one that cost him his life. But he never forgot who he was: a son of God called to live in the love of the Father. Stanislaus' radical sense of identity in God can inspire us to live with integrity and call others back to their true identity as children of God.

Prayer

Saint Stanislaus of Szczepanów, pray for me so that in the tensions and conflicts of my life I might see myself and others as children of the Father. Amen.

APRIL 12

Saint Giuseppe Moscati

July 25, 1880–April 12, 1927
Feast: November 16
Patron: Bachelors, physicians

The seventh of Francesco and Rosa Moscati's nine children, Giuseppe grew up near Naples, Italy. He graduated from the University of Naples in 1903 with a degree in medicine and surgery. During his career as a doctor, he served as superintendent of a prominent hospital in Naples, earned a doctorate in and taught physiological chemistry, and engaged in extensive medical research. He could have had a glowing academic career and was offered a tenured professorship, but he turned it down, presumably so he could continue his work at the hospital.

Giuseppe was not concerned with positions or accomplishments. He was concerned about *people*. He had a profound conviction that his role as a physician was not just to heal his patients' bodies, but to lead them to Christ, the Divine Physician, who could heal their souls. His firm but gentle faith led many people back to the Sacraments. He had a heart for the poor, often treating them without charge and paying for their prescriptions. Giuseppe never married. After a life of dedicated service and constant prayer, he died quietly at his office, in between seeing patients.

Reflection

Throughout Giuseppe's seemingly ordinary life runs the thread of an extraordinary union with Christ. This union transformed his life: his workday became a day lived for God, his sick patients became the suffering Christ, and each relationship became an act of love for God. How does Giuseppe's example invite me to open the "ordinariness" of my life to the transforming power of a closer relationship with Christ?

Prayer

Saint Giuseppe Moscati, teach me how to live in Christ so he can live in me! Pray that I might become generous with my time and my heart as you were with yours. Amen.

APRIL 13

Saint Martin I

c. 600–September 16, 655
Feast: April 13
Patron: The poor

Martin became pope in 649, and he was the last of the popes to be venerated as a martyr. In his short pontificate, Martin dealt with the Monothelite heresy, which denied that Jesus Christ had a human will. He called a council in Rome that condemned the error. The Eastern emperor, Constans II, supported the false teaching and had written in support of it. That document was also condemned, but Constans retaliated. He tried to gather support for his ideas from the bishops. When this failed, the emperor sent soldiers to kidnap and imprison the pope. Martin was condemned to death, but the patriarch of Constantinople interceded on his behalf and saved him from execution. Martin endured many sufferings. At one point he was paraded through the streets in chains while crowds of people ridiculed and tormented him. Through it all, he never compromised the truth and steadfastly upheld the Gospel. He died in prison as a result of his mistreatment.

Reflection

In one of Martin's letters that still exist today, he laments that his former friends and family members had forgotten him. His martyrdom did not happen all at once but dragged on through two painful years of suffering. His plaintive remark about being forgotten reminds us that the saints are human too and suffered not only from physical pain but from loneliness and abandonment. Martin's suffering helps us to reflect on the people in our own lives who might be suffering in some way. Is there someone I know who I can reach out to in order to lighten their burden?

Prayer

Saint Martin, you courageously defended the truth of the Catholic faith despite the sufferings you had to endure. Pray for us that we might understand how important truth is, and always cherish our faith even in the face of opposition or ridicule. Amen.

APRIL 14

Blessed Margaret of Castello

1287–April 13, 1320
Feast: April 13
Patron: Pro-life groups, those who are unwanted and abandoned

Margaret of Castello was born to a noble family in Metola, Italy, in the thirteenth century, and she certainly did not have an easy life. She was born blind, hunchbacked, and with dwarfism. Her parents were so ashamed of her severe physical disabilities that they sent her away and put her in a room with no doors after she turned six years old. There were only two windows in the room: one through which she received food and one that opened into the chapel next door. Through the second window, she would listen to the Mass and receive Communion.

When Margaret was about twenty years old, her parents took her to a popular shrine to pray for a cure. When she was not miraculously healed, her parents abandoned her in the street. Despite her great suffering, Margaret resolved to accept whatever God permitted. She learned how to beg from the poor of the city and was taken in by several families who recognized her piety. Eventually, Margaret became a Dominican Tertiary and spent the rest of her life performing works of charity, especially visiting prisoners, helping the sick, and comforting the dying.

Reflection

Today, someone like Margaret might easily become a victim of abortion because of such disabilities. Every human person is made in the image and likeness of a loving God who desires to be in relationship with each one of his children. Building a culture of life begins with recognizing those who are closest to us and seeing their worth, especially those who would be easy to ignore.

Prayer

Blessed Margaret of Castello, you know what it is like to be unwanted. Intercede for me, that I may always remember the infinite love that God has for each of his beloved children. Amen.

APRIL 15

Saint Juliana of Cornillon

c. 1191–April 5, 1258
Feast: April 6
Patron: Devotion to the Eucharist

Juliana was born near Liège, Belgium. She lost her parents at age five and was sent with her sister Agnes to live in the convent of Mont-Cornillon. Juliana was very intelligent, and she learned to read the Church Fathers in Latin. She also developed a deep love for Jesus in the Eucharist and soon asked to enter religious life.

Starting when she was sixteen, Juliana had several mystical experiences during Eucharistic adoration. In her visions she would see an image of the full moon with one dark stripe across it. She realized that the moon represented the liturgy of the Church and the dark part was a lack or absence. God was telling Juliana that a special liturgical celebration of the Eucharist was needed in the Church.

After some time, Juliana spoke about her revelations with trusted friends and a priest who consulted diocesan theologians. Eventually, Bishop Robert Torote decided to initiate the celebration of the feast of Corpus Christi in the diocese of Liège. In the midst of this success, Juliana also experienced opposition from some clergy in her diocese as well as from her superior. She accepted this suffering and remained serene even when she had to leave her convent. Juliana lived the last ten years of her life in various Cistercian monasteries, continuing to spread Eucharistic devotion.

Reflection

One year after Juliana of Cornillon died, Pope Urban IV decreed that the feast of Corpus Christi should be celebrated by the whole Church. She did not live to see the universal Church celebrate the Eucharistic feast, but she undoubtedly rejoiced from heaven. How can I follow Juliana's example of humility and patience when I try to implement my desires for the future?

Prayer

Saint Juliana of Cornillon, pray that I might more deeply appreciate the amazing gift of Jesus' Body and Blood in the Eucharist. Amen.

APRIL 16

Saint Benedict Joseph Labre

March 26, 1748–April 16, 1783
Feast: April 16
Patron: Homeless, mentally ill

Although each saint's life is unique, the life of this saint is quite unusual. Born in northern France and the eldest of fifteen children, Benedict had good educational opportunities. But from a young age he showed himself to be only interested in learning about God; he was unusually attracted to solitude and penance.

When Benedict was sixteen, he began his initial attempts to enter the monastery, although he had to first overcome his parents' opposition. Feeling the desire for a strict monastic life and convinced that he had a vocation, he tried to enter several different Trappist and Carthusian monasteries. However, every time Benedict tried to live the monastic life, his health would break down, possibly from anxiety or scruples.

Eventually, Benedict realized that God was calling him to a different kind of life. So he became a wandering pilgrim. Living poverty and self-denial to an extreme degree, Benedict begged his way from shrine to shrine throughout Europe. Once, he stopped at a farmhouse near Lyons, France, and stayed in the room where Saint John Vianney would be born, only three years after Benedict's death. The last six years of Benedict's life were spent in Rome. He prayed in churches, gave away any money that was given him, and lived on the streets poorly clad and eating very little, until he died.

Reflection

Benedict Joseph Labre is invoked by those suffering from various mental and emotional disturbances. Although he was never diagnosed, Benedict may have suffered from mental illness. However, everything in his life served to bring him closer to God. Do I believe that God can use anything and everything in my life for my ultimate good?

Prayer

Saint Benedict Joseph Labre, pray that I might learn from your single-hearted devotion to God. Amen.

APRIL 17

Saint Kateri Tekakwitha

1656–April 17, 1680
Feast: July 14 (U. S.), April 17 (Canada)
Patron: Ecology, environment, indigenous peoples of the Americas

Kateri was born in upstate New York, the daughter of a Christian Algonquin mother and a Mohawk chief. When she was four, relatives took her in when both she and her parents contracted smallpox. Her parents and little brother died, and Kateri was partially blinded and scarred.

Several years later, Jesuit missionaries came to Kateri's village and she was overjoyed to learn more about the loving God her mother had told her about as a child. Though her relatives did not approve of her new faith, Kateri chose to be baptized in 1676. The villagers began to persecute Kateri ruthlessly. Her relatives were particularly angry that she refused to marry. After some time, Kateri fled to a Christian native village near Montreal where she could practice her faith in peace.

Upon her arrival in Montreal, Kateri met some Ursuline religious sisters and felt called by God to begin her own religious order. Her confessor discouraged her but eventually allowed her to make a vow of virginity. Kateri soon became a spiritual leader in her new village through her simple life, devoted prayer, kindness, and generosity. The intensity of her penances—a common practice among converts—weakened her health. Kateri died at the age of twenty-three or twenty-four. Upon her death, a priest reported that the smallpox scars disappeared from her face and she was radiant.

Reflection

Kateri Tekakwitha, called the "mystic of the wilderness," loved her people and customs. She liked to go off alone in the woods to pray, making a "chapel" by carving a cross in a tree trunk. Kateri's fidelity and courage in integrating her Mohawk lifestyle and Christian faith amazed those who came to know her.

Prayer

Saint Kateri Tekakwitha, teach us how to live a pure and simple life. Amen.

APRIL 18

Blessed Marie-Anne Blondin

April 18, 1809–January 2, 1890
Feast: April 18 (Canada)
Patron: The Sisters of Saint Anne, education of the poor

Esther Blondin was born into a poor farming family in Quebec, Canada. Her parents were deeply faithful and taught her a love for the Eucharist. Like many people in her area, Esther was illiterate. At age twenty-two, Esther worked as a housemaid for the Congregation of Notre Dame. There, she enrolled in the sisters' school and learned to read and write.

Esther felt called by God to religious life and to the work of helping others learn to read. She asked to enter the convent and was accepted, but had to leave due to poor health. Undaunted, Esther became a teacher in a parochial school for girls. Seeing a need, she asked her local bishop's permission to start a congregation dedicated to teaching both boys and girls together, an innovation at the time. The Congregation of the Sisters of Saint Anne was founded in 1850 and Esther took the religious name Mother Marie-Anne.

The bishop soon sent the sisters a chaplain, Father Louis-Adolphe Maréchal, who caused a great deal of trouble for Mother Marie-Anne. He eventually had her removed from all positions of authority and she was relegated to a life of obscurity doing laundry and other domestic tasks. She accepted all this in serenity and peace, writing in her spiritual testament to her sisters, "May the Holy Eucharist and perfect abandonment to God's will be your heaven on earth."

Reflection

Mother Marie-Anne Blondin could have become bitter over the way she was treated, but she saw it as God's Providence for her life. She found meaning in contemplating the Cross of Christ and, in her humility, gave an example of virtue and strength. How do I respond to the trials I encounter in my life?

Prayer

Blessed Marie-Anne Blondin, pray that I might follow your example and find happiness and peace along the sometimes thorny way of life. Amen.

APRIL 19

Saint Adalbert of Prague

c. 956–April 23, 997
Feast: April 23
Patron: Poland, Czech Republic, Hungary

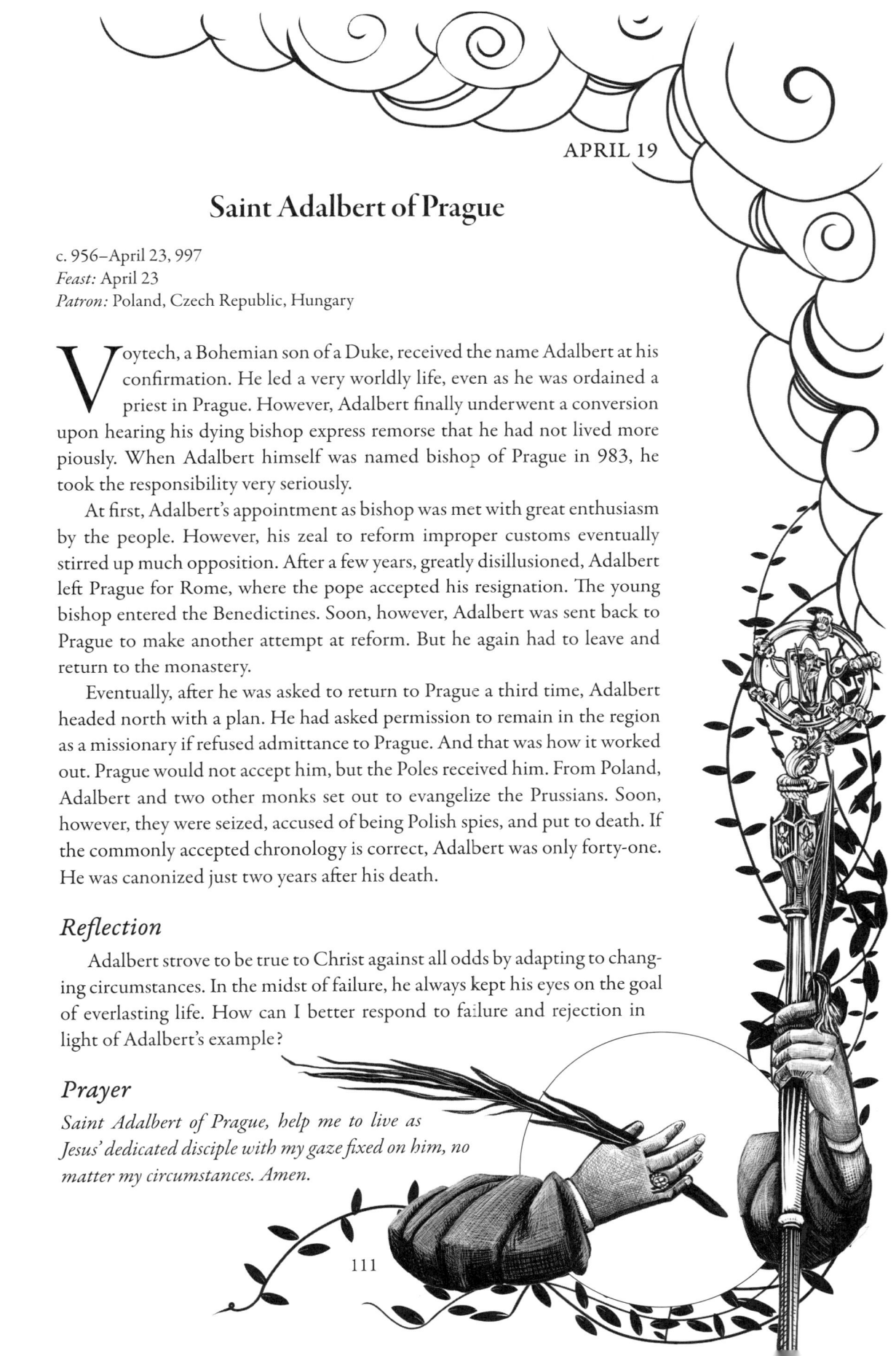

Voytech, a Bohemian son of a Duke, received the name Adalbert at his confirmation. He led a very worldly life, even as he was ordained a priest in Prague. However, Adalbert finally underwent a conversion upon hearing his dying bishop express remorse that he had not lived more piously. When Adalbert himself was named bishop of Prague in 983, he took the responsibility very seriously.

At first, Adalbert's appointment as bishop was met with great enthusiasm by the people. However, his zeal to reform improper customs eventually stirred up much opposition. After a few years, greatly disillusioned, Adalbert left Prague for Rome, where the pope accepted his resignation. The young bishop entered the Benedictines. Soon, however, Adalbert was sent back to Prague to make another attempt at reform. But he again had to leave and return to the monastery.

Eventually, after he was asked to return to Prague a third time, Adalbert headed north with a plan. He had asked permission to remain in the region as a missionary if refused admittance to Prague. And that was how it worked out. Prague would not accept him, but the Poles received him. From Poland, Adalbert and two other monks set out to evangelize the Prussians. Soon, however, they were seized, accused of being Polish spies, and put to death. If the commonly accepted chronology is correct, Adalbert was only forty-one. He was canonized just two years after his death.

Reflection

Adalbert strove to be true to Christ against all odds by adapting to changing circumstances. In the midst of failure, he always kept his eyes on the goal of everlasting life. How can I better respond to failure and rejection in light of Adalbert's example?

Prayer

Saint Adalbert of Prague, help me to live as Jesus' dedicated disciple with my gaze fixed on him, no matter my circumstances. Amen.

APRIL 20

Saint Beuno

Sixth or seventh century
Feast: April 21 (April 20 in Wales)
Patron: Epileptics, sick animals

Little is known about Saint Beuno. Early biographers often confused him with a distant cousin of the same name, who lived two or three generations earlier and was the subject of many legends.

Beuno is believed to have been born around 545 into a royal family in the Welsh kingdom of Powys. He received a good education, became a priest, and for many years traveled about as an itinerant monk and hermit. Around 616 he settled on land given to him in Clynnog, in northwestern Wales, where he built a monastery. Like Saint David, who had labored a little farther south not long before, Beuno and his followers carried out missionary activity in the vicinity of his monastery, as well as in neighboring regions and on nearby islands.

One story about Beuno of Clynnog concerns a young noblewoman who fell in love with a carpenter. Her father gave her to the young man in marriage. But the carpenter abandoned the girl, who was then brought to Beuno. The saint introduced her to the consecrated life, which apparently appealed to her so much that she opted to make that her state even after her wayward husband had been located.

Reflection

When Beuno died at Clynnog, he became famous as an intercessor for the sick, especially epileptics and even sick animals. Pilgrims would sleep on or near the saint's tomb in the hope of a cure, and it was said that many miraculous healings resulted. Even though few facts are known about this saint, we can be inspired by his tender heart and care for others, even from heaven.

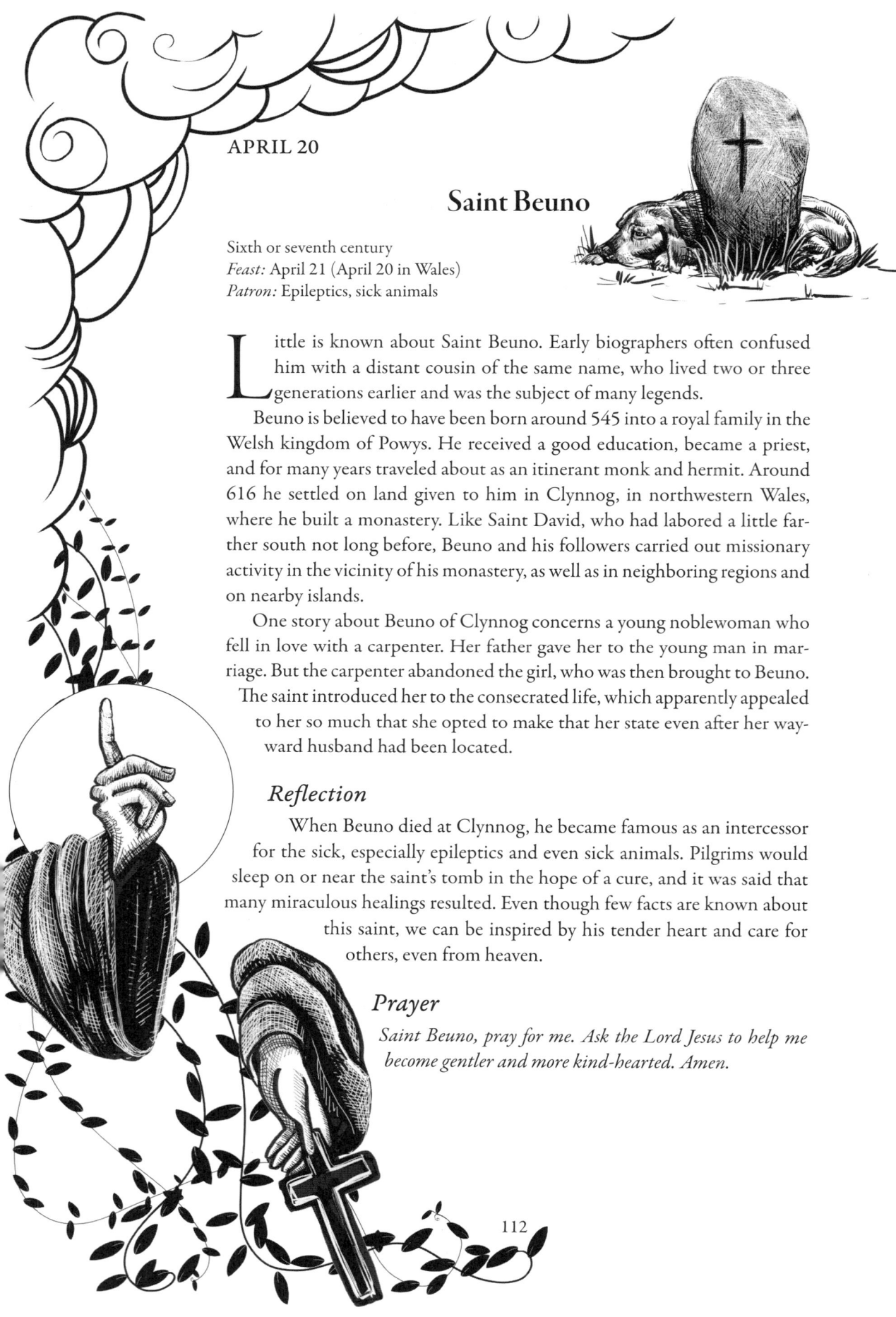

Prayer

Saint Beuno, pray for me. Ask the Lord Jesus to help me become gentler and more kind-hearted. Amen.

APRIL 21

Saint Anselm of Canterbury

c. 1033–April 21, 1109
Feast: April 21
Patron: Theologians, teachers, philosophers

An important thinker and writer, Anselm serves as a bridge from the patristic age to the early Middle Ages. Born into a wealthy family in Aosta, a city in northern Italy, Anselm was a bit aimless as a young man. But at the age of twenty-seven, he entered the monastery of Bec in Normandy. He studied deeply and began to write important theological works in the form of dialogues and meditations. He was elected the abbot; then, in 1093, he was appointed the archbishop of Canterbury. Everything went well until Anselm made clear that he would defend the Church from the political intrusion of King William II and then Henry I. For this, he twice suffered exile from his see.

Anselm's work *Cur Deus Homo* (Why God Became Man) was a groundbreaking theological study of Jesus Christ and his saving death on the Cross. In the *Proslogion,* Anselm made what is known as the ontological argument for God's existence. His argument has been engaged by philosophers for centuries. He was made a Doctor of the Church in 1720 by Pope Clement XI.

Reflection

Anselm penned the famous phrase "faith seeking understanding." By this he meant to encourage believers to always seek a deeper knowledge of God. Anselm knew that he could never fully penetrate the divine mysteries, but he could grow in understanding them. Divine truth can be approached from different angles, which is why there are different schools of theology in the Church. All of this can inspire us to a deeper study of the faith. Reading or rereading the *Catechism of the Catholic Church* would be a good place to start!

Prayer

Saint Anselm, you were both a pastor and a theologian. Pray that I may ponder the mysteries of our faith so as to live them more deeply. Amen.

APRIL 22

Saint Mary Elizabeth Hesselblad

June 4, 1870–April 24, 1957
Feast: June 4
Patron: Seekers of the true faith, ecumenism, nurses, home health care workers

Born into a large Lutheran family in Sweden, even as a child, Mary Elizabeth was troubled at the lack of unity among Christian churches. One day as she walked alone in a quiet forest, she begged the Lord to show her the truth. He would, by a circuitous path. In 1888, at the age of eighteen, she immigrated to New York City to work as a nurse. She cared for many people who were Catholic and became interested in their faith.

On a trip to Brussels in 1900, Mary Elizabeth witnessed a Corpus Christi Eucharistic procession. She did not want to be part of it, but while everyone around her knelt, she heard in her heart, "I am the One whom you seek." Mary Elizabeth responded to the call and within two years she became a Catholic and offered her life to God. In Rome she lived with a Carmelite community in a house where Saint Bridget of Sweden had founded the Brigittines. Mary Elizabeth was inspired to revive that ancient Order. She began a new group of Brigittines that gradually grew and spread around the world. During World War II, Mary Elizabeth sheltered Jewish refugees and saved at least a dozen from death.

Reflection

Mary Elizabeth was an ardent seeker of truth, and this led her to the Catholic faith. Her life shows us that goodness and virtue flow from the truth, and ultimately the Truth is Jesus Christ. Mary Elizabeth, who knew that her beliefs mattered greatly, lived by the light of Scripture: "the righteous live by their faith" (Hab 2:4). Do I believe that faith leads me to the truth and the truth leads to deeper faith?

Prayer

Saint Mary Elizabeth Hesselblad, pray for us that all Christians may believe with one heart and live out that faith in works of loving service. Amen.

APRIL 23

Saint George

Died c. 303
Feast: April 23
Patron: Soldiers, farmers, shepherds, butchers, Boy Scouts, horses, equestrians, saddle makers, the Bulgarian army, European Romani peoples, England, Georgia (the country), Greece, Lithuania, Serbia, Spain, Syria, Montenegro, Portugal, Palestine

Many legends surround the life of Saint George, but very little is known for certain. We do know that he came from Lydda in Palestine, was a Roman soldier, and was martyred in the early fourth century. Because he was a Roman soldier, he could have easily escaped death by simply denying that he was a Christian. But George stood fast in his faith, even in the face of death.

In Western art, George is usually pictured as a medieval knight on horseback, slaying a dragon. He appears in many fictional tales as the hero who saves maidens and towns, kills dragons, and even comes back to life after being killed. In parts of the Middle East, he is venerated by Muslims as well as Christians. He is called, in Greek, a "megalomartyr," meaning "really great martyr." The long list of people who claim him as their patron is evidence that he was and still is a well-loved saint.

Reflection

Devotion to Saint George has been very strong throughout many centuries, which means that his life and death made a deep impression on many people throughout the ages. Though later stories of his life are not always factual, they indicate that George was known for his courage. He showed valor in standing up for the faith, but also in protecting the innocent and defending the weak.

Prayer

Lord, we pray for the grace to follow the example of Saint George, who was courageous in the face of persecution and remained true to you even to death. Help us to resist the temptation to avoid difficulties and instead to hold firm to what we know we are called to do. Amen.

APRIL 24

Saint Fidelis of Sigmaringen

c. 1577–April 24, 1622
Feast: April 24
Patron: Lawyers, those away from the Church

Mark Rey was born in Germany during the difficult time of religious conflict between Catholics and Protestants. Even as a young man he focused on prayer, the practice of virtue, and holiness. He studied philosophy and law at the university of Freiburg and became a lawyer. Known as "the poor man's lawyer" because he took on cases for the needy, he became disillusioned with the injustices of the legal system at the time.

Leaving the law profession, Mark gave his wealth away and decided to become a priest. He was ordained in 1612 and entered the Capuchins shortly after that, taking the name Fidelis. He eventually became the superior of several monasteries and dedicated himself to caring for the poor, the sick, and the downtrodden. He was later sent to Switzerland to preach to those who had fallen away from the Catholic Church, especially followers of Calvin and Zwingli. Martyred by a band of extremists at Seewis, he died praying for them in a spirit of forgiveness. Fidelis was canonized in 1746 by Pope Benedict XIV.

Reflection

The name Fidelis speaks of fidelity, and Fidelis was faithful to God and to his vocation. Despite the strident opposition he often met, he kept on preaching the word of God, in season and out of season. He often would spur himself to greater zeal by recalling the sufferings that Jesus bore for our sake. If at times we start to feel apathetic in our spiritual life, the example of this heroic saint can inspire us to keep on going and to offer everything to Jesus with great love.

Prayer

Saint Fidelis, pray for that we might never grow tired in the service of God, but work with all our might to spread the Gospel to the people of today. Amen.

APRIL 25

Saint Mark, the Apostle

First Century
Feast: April 25
Patron: Venice, Italy, Egypt, Coptic Church, lions, notaries, lawyers, captives, prisoners, glaziers, and stained-glass workers

According to tradition, the Last Supper took place in the evangelist Mark's family home. It is thought that when Judas returned with the soldiers, the young Mark may have run to Gethsemane to warn Jesus. In the Gospel of Mark, a young man runs away naked in the confusion surrounding Jesus' arrest in Gethsemane (see Mk 14:51–52). Many believe he was the evangelist Mark.

Mark is also assumed to be the "John Mark" who appears in the Acts of the Apostles as the cousin of Barnabas. He was invited to accompany Barnabas and Paul on a missionary journey through Asia Minor. Despite his good intentions, Mark was unprepared for the rigorous trip and he returned home. Paul refused to take him along on the next trip, taking Silas instead. Mark did accompany Barnabas to Cyprus and later become a valuable friend to Paul during his years of imprisonment. Mark also became a disciple of Peter whose recollections of Jesus are contained in Mark's Gospel. According to tradition, Mark founded the Church in Alexandria, Egypt, and was martyred around the year 68.

Reflection

Mark's life could represent the life of all believers. Usually family is the first influence on faith, and in youth the attraction of Jesus and his teachings become personal. In our desire to follow Christ, we may want to do great things for him. We are not always successful, but effort and perseverance, faithfulness and grace help us mature into true witnesses. In what way could I witness to the Gospel in my own life?

Prayer

Saint Mark, your Gospel is often represented by the symbol of a lion because it proclaims Jesus who is the great "lion of Judah" (see Rev 5:5). Ask for us the courage to stand by our King. Amen.

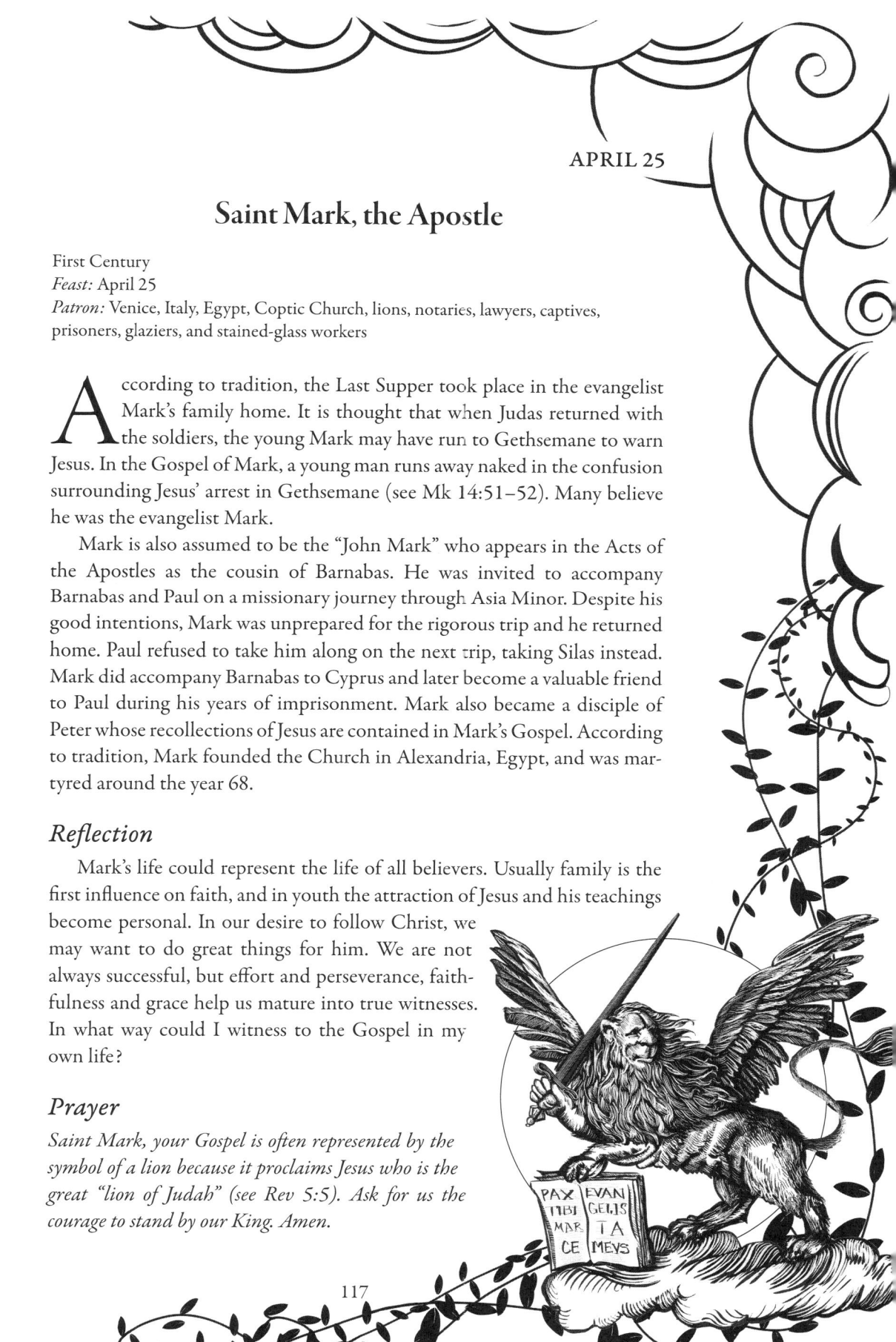

APRIL 26

Saint Louis de Montfort

January 31, 1673–April 28, 1716
Feast: April 28
Patron: Preachers, those devoted to Mary, those who serve the poor

In his short life of forty-three years, Louis de Montfort accomplished great things for God that still inspire us today. Devout from his youth, he became a priest and dedicated himself to working with the poor. Burning with a great desire to bring people the word of God, he became an itinerant preacher in the French countryside. Three congregations claim Louis as their founder: the Company of Mary, Daughters of Wisdom, and Brothers of Saint Gabriel.

His motto, "God alone," inspired Louis to do everything for the glory of God. Louis was influenced by the French school of spirituality with its emphasis on the Incarnation and the Person of Jesus Christ. Louis' great devotion to Mary sprang from his love for Jesus, for he saw Mary as the path to Christ: "To Jesus through Mary." A key feature of his devotion is total consecration to Mary, which accompanies devotion to the holy Rosary. His book *The Secret of the Rosary* and several others remain in print even today.

Reflection

As a young man, Saint John Paul II was greatly influenced by de Montfort's *True Devotion to Mary*. The pope even took his motto, "Totus Tuus" (I am all yours), from that book. Saint Louis de Montfort's love for Mary can also inspire us to reflect on Mary's role in our lives. In what ways can I grow in my devotion to our Blessed Mother?

Prayer

Saint Louis de Montfort, your love for Jesus and Mary led you to become an outstanding preacher of the word of God. Intercede for me that my words and actions may radiate to others the love of Jesus Christ, drawing them to him through Mary. Amen.

APRIL 27

Saint Zita

c. 1218–April 27, 1278
Feast: April 27
Patron: Domestic workers, homemakers, lost keys, people ridiculed for their piety, victims of assault, single laywomen, waiters, waitresses

Zita, born in a village of northern Italy, was raised in the Catholic faith by her pious mother. When she was twelve years old, Zita began working as a servant for the wealthy Fatinelli family. She was convinced that her hard work could help her grow in holiness and that she could do God's will by serving well. She would rise in the early hours to pray and attend Mass.

Surprisingly, Zita's holiness and hard work did not earn her the respect of her fellow servants and employees. They strongly disliked her and assumed she was showing off. But over time everyone realized Zita's devotion was sincere, and they came to love her. Because of her loyalty and hard work, Zita was eventually placed in charge of the household. As head servant, she took her responsibilities very seriously, while also caring for the poor who came to the house for alms. She spent her free time in prayer, having a particularly strong devotion to the Eucharist. Many miracles took place even during her lifetime. Zita prayerfully foresaw her own death, which enabled her to prepare well for it at age sixty.

Reflection

Zita spent her entire life devoted to hard work because she believed that through this, she could serve God. She led a simple life in close communion with God and saw even the most menial household tasks as opportunities to be mindful of God's presence. How often do I tune out during the routine parts of my day, moving through necessary tasks on autopilot? How can I take the time to be intentional about my work, recalling God's presence with me?

Prayer

God, help me to use the tedious, everyday tasks of my life to grow closer to you. Amen.

APRIL 28

Saint Peter Chanel

July 12, 1803–April 28, 1841
Feast: April 28
Patron: Oceania

As a boy, Peter was a shepherd on his family's farm near Belley, France. His religious devotion impressed the parish priest, who helped Peter get a good education. He entered the seminary, was ordained in 1827, and began ministering in a parish. Peter liked to read letters that French missionaries sent home, which stirred his own missionary vocation. He joined the Marists hoping to be sent overseas but was first assigned to teach at the seminary.

After five years his dream came true and he led a band of Marists to Oceania. He started working on the island of Futuna, but with little success. He didn't know the language and had to adapt to an unfamiliar way of life. Yet he persevered. The local chief, strongly opposed to Christianity, became irate when his son asked to be baptized. The chief sent a band of men to kill Peter by clubbing him to death. But within a year or so after his martyrdom, the people accepted the faith and the Church grew greatly.

Reflection

Peter was encouraged by a priest who saw his potential. How many people have gone on to great things in life because someone believed in them! In our daily lives we can easily overlook the good points of others. But if we try to notice their talents and draw them out, we can encourage others to grow.

In what ways can I encourage and support the people I live and work with?

Prayer

Saint Peter Chanel, you didn't give in to discouragement when your missionary efforts seemed to bear no fruit. Pray that I might see the potential in my own and others' lives, so we might all grow to be the saints God calls us to be. Amen.

APRIL 29

Saint Catherine of Siena

March 25, 1347–April 29, 1380
Feast: April 29
Patron: Italy, Europe, nurses and the sick; against fire, sexual temptation, illness, miscarriages

Catherine Benincasa was the second youngest of twenty-five children born to her parents. Only half of her siblings survived childhood, so she was familiar with loss. From a young age, Catherine had mystical visions and felt drawn to give her life to God. But her parents had other plans. When they began to arrange a marriage for her, Catherine resisted and took up extreme ascetical practices to demonstrate her firm resolve. Her parents eventually gave up and Catherine became a Dominican tertiary, living the Dominican spirituality within her family home.

For three years, Catherine lived in silence and solitude in a room in her family home. After a mystical experience of union with Jesus, Catherine felt called to leave solitude and began to help the sick and serve the poor. Gradually, people were attracted by her holiness and many prominent people sought her advice. She dictated at least fifteen letters to Pope Gregory XI, insisting that he move back to Rome from Avignon—and he eventually relented. Around this time, Catherine began work on her *Dialogues*, the book of her meditations and revelations. Catherine died in Rome after a three-month-long illness. She was only thirty-three. She was canonized in 1461 and named a Doctor of the Church in 1970.

Reflection

Catherine was gifted with a desire to be alone with God and a conviction that this was interiorly possible regardless of what was happening exteriorly. Through all the activity in Catherine's life, she managed to remain united to the Lord. She found peace and joy in union with Jesus. How might God be inviting me to a deeper relationship with him?

Prayer

Saint Catherine of Siena, pray that I might be attentive to God's Spirit within me and trust that he knows what will bring me fulfillment, peace, and joy. Amen.

APRIL 30

Saint Pius V

January 17, 1504–May 1, 1572
Feast: April 30
Patron: Church reform, catechists, liturgical formation

Antonio Ghislieri began his life as a shepherd in the fields of northern Italy and ended it as the shepherd of the Universal Church. A Dominican who became pope in 1566. One of the foremost leaders of the Catholic Reformation, Pius implemented the Council of Trent with zeal and helped clarify what it meant to know and follow Christ during confusing times. To reform the liturgy, he had the Roman Breviary revised and published a new Roman Missal for the Latin Rite, which would be the norm until Vatican II. To promote correct doctrine, he issued the *Roman Catechism,* authorized a revision of the Latin Vulgate Bible, and called for a new edition of the *Summa Theologiae* of Saint Thomas Aquinas, whom he made a Doctor of the Church.

Pius lived a holy and austere life, knowing that the Church's problems ultimately sprang from a lack of holiness. However, Pius was not an able politician and his zeal for reform was sometimes excessive, as seen in his harsh treatment of the Jews, and the power given to the Inquisition. He also excommunicated Queen Elizabeth, which only worsened persecution of English Catholics. But when the Ottoman Turks threatened Europe, Pius urged Catholics to pray the Rosary, and he attributed the victory at Lepanto to Mary's intercession.

Reflection

Pius V teaches us that a holy life is the starting point to renew the Church. In that sense, the evangelical Catholicism of today, inspired by Saint John Paul II, is very much in the spirit of Pope Pius V. How can I grow in holiness in order to contribute to the renewal of the Church?

Prayer

Saint Pius V, pray for us that we may always be open to receive and follow the inspirations of the Holy Spirit, who leads us to holiness. Amen.

MAY 1

Saint Peregrine Laziosi

c. 1265–May 1, 1345
Feast: May 4
Patron: People who have cancer, AIDS, or any other serious illness

Peregrine was born in Forli, northern Italy, to a wealthy family. When he was a young man, like many in his hometown, Peregrine belonged to an anti-papal political faction. One day, the head of the Servite Order, Saint Philip Benizi, came to his city on behalf of the pope to seek reconciliation. During an outdoor meeting, the incensed Peregrine verbally abused Philip and struck him across the face. Instead of retaliating, Philip turned so Peregrine could strike the other side of his face.

Peregrine soon repented of his actions and a few years later joined the Servites. It's not clear if he became a priest, but it seems more likely he remained a brother in the Servites. Peregrine eventually returned to his hometown, where he devoted himself to prayer and care for the poor. When in his sixties, Peregrine suffered from cancer of the leg and was told his leg had to be amputated. The night before his surgery, Peregrine spent hours in prayer. He had a vision in which Jesus came down from the Cross and touched the cancerous area. The next day, to the doctors' amazement, his leg was completely healed. After Peregrine's death twenty years later, miraculous healings were attributed to his intercession.

Reflection

Peregrine Laziosi was revered as a living saint when news of his healed leg spread through the city. But he continued living simply and humbly. His attitude reminds us that the proper response to answered prayers is to thank and glorify God. Do I thank God for his gifts to me?

Prayer

Dear Lord, help me to receive the gifts you lovingly bestow on me with humble gratitude. Amen.

MAY 2

Saint Athanasius

c. 296–May 2, 373
Feast: May 2
Patron: Theologians, those who uphold the truth of the Christian faith

As a young man, Athanasius spent some time with Saint Anthony of the Desert to learn the ways of the spiritual life. That formation served him well, for Athanasius became one of the most important defenders of the Christian faith at a time when the early Church was finding a way to teach clearly about who Jesus is. Athanasius accompanied Bishop Alexander of Alexandria to the Council of Nicea in 325. The Council upheld the divinity of Jesus Christ and condemned Arianism, the false teaching that Jesus was not divine. Despite the Council's clear teaching, Arianism spread widely, especially because it was supported by the emperors.

In 328, Athanasius became bishop of Alexandria. He constantly struggled to uphold the true teaching about Jesus Christ. Four emperors exiled Athanasius for a total of seventeen years. Athanasius spent years hiding from his enemies who wanted him dead. Even when it seemed as if Arianism could triumph, Athanasius never gave up. He wrote important theological works, including *De Incarnatione* (On the Incarnation of the Word), and a biography of Saint Anthony, which helped Christian monasticism to grow. In 381, after Athanasius' death, the Council of Constantinople reaffirmed that Jesus is fully human and fully divine.

Reflection

Athanasius could have compromised the truth about Jesus Christ to accommodate the Arians. But he knew that would have destroyed the Christianity, for if Jesus is not fully human and fully divine, he could not have saved us. Athanasius' life reminds us that it is never easy to be Catholic. Like Athanasius, how can I be true to what the Church teaches and still love those who may not understand?

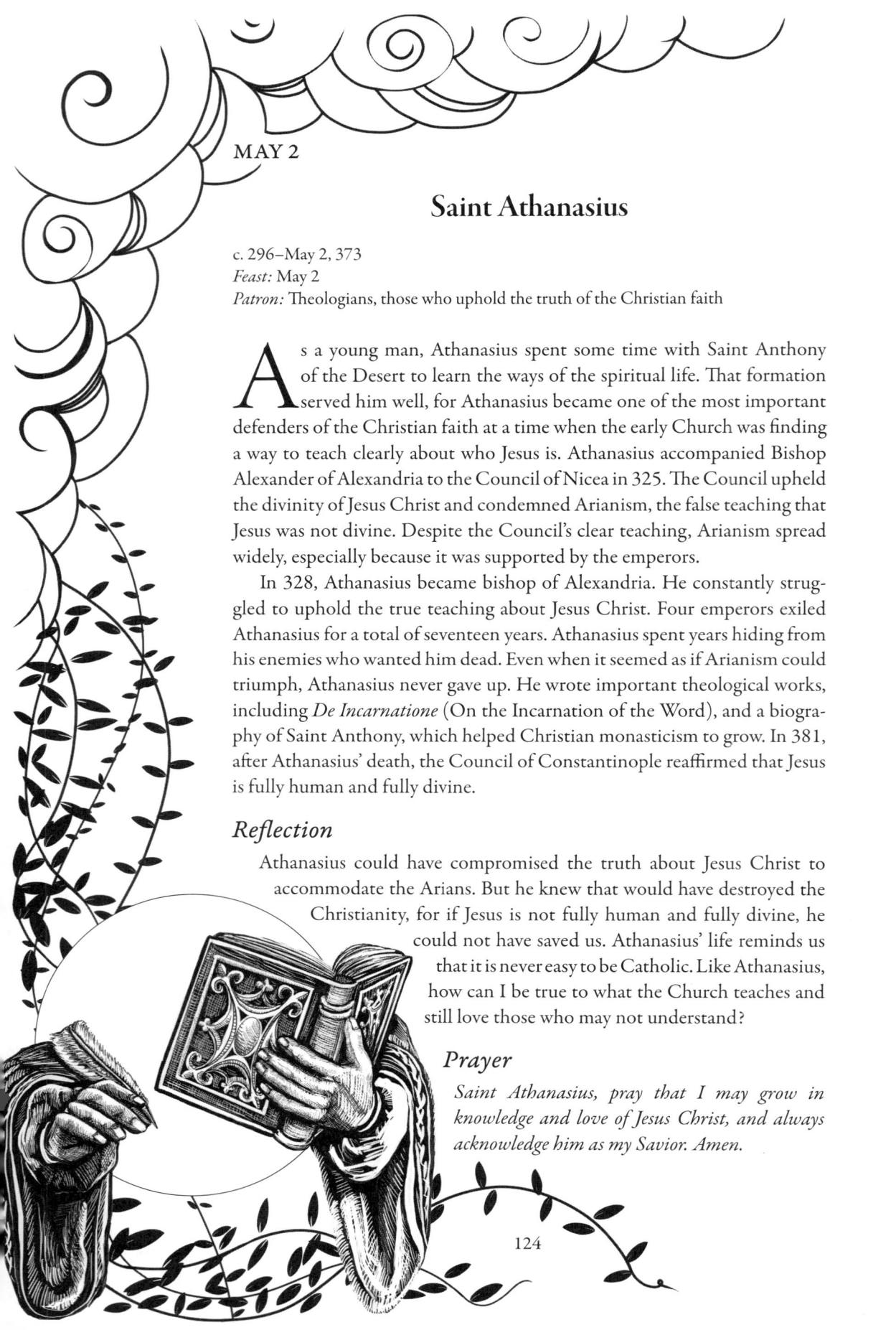

Prayer

Saint Athanasius, pray that I may grow in knowledge and love of Jesus Christ, and always acknowledge him as my Savior. Amen.

MAY 3

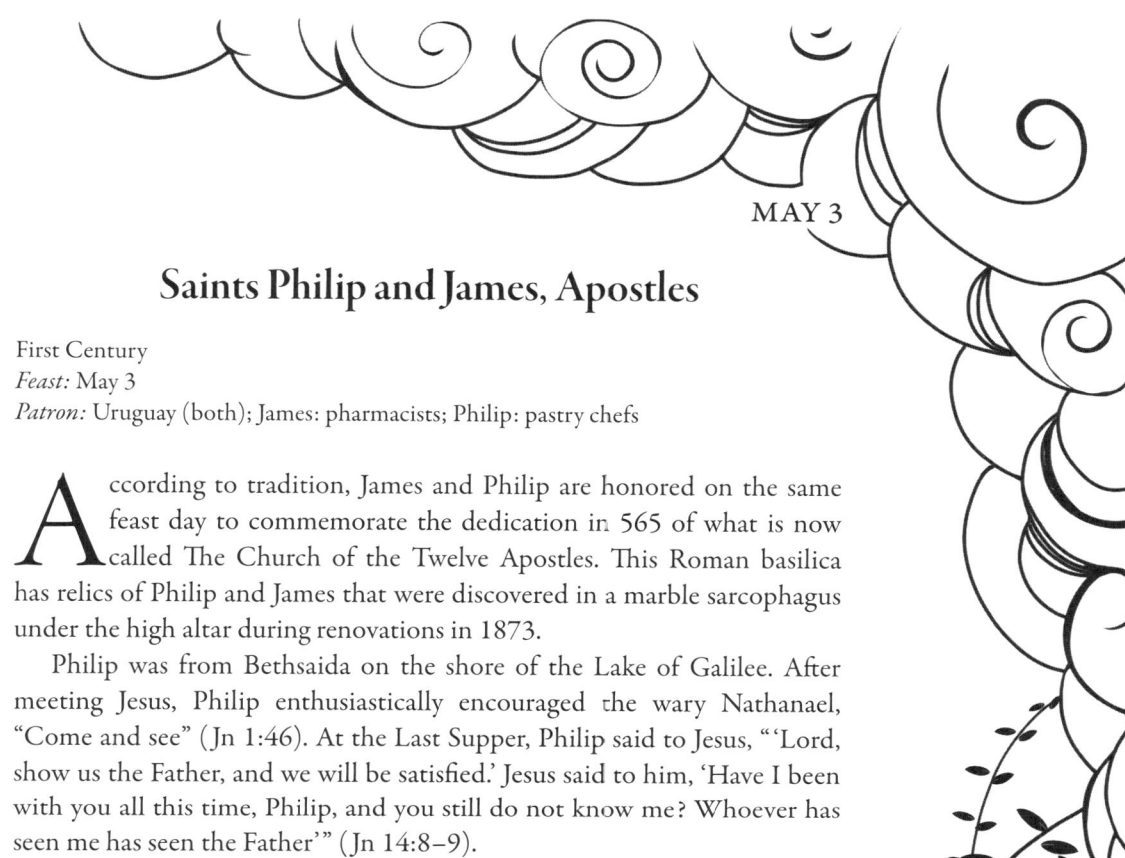

Saints Philip and James, Apostles

First Century
Feast: May 3
Patron: Uruguay (both); James: pharmacists; Philip: pastry chefs

According to tradition, James and Philip are honored on the same feast day to commemorate the dedication in 565 of what is now called The Church of the Twelve Apostles. This Roman basilica has relics of Philip and James that were discovered in a marble sarcophagus under the high altar during renovations in 1873.

Philip was from Bethsaida on the shore of the Lake of Galilee. After meeting Jesus, Philip enthusiastically encouraged the wary Nathanael, "Come and see" (Jn 1:46). At the Last Supper, Philip said to Jesus, "'Lord, show us the Father, and we will be satisfied.' Jesus said to him, 'Have I been with you all this time, Philip, and you still do not know me? Whoever has seen me has seen the Father'" (Jn 14:8–9).

James, the son of Alphaeus, is sometimes called James the Less, to distinguish him from the other Apostle James, the son of Zebedee. Although it's disputed, tradition identifies James the Less as the man who was related to Jesus and became a leader of the Church in Jerusalem. According to the Jewish historian Josephus, James was martyred around the year 62.

Reflection

We don't know that much about Philip or James, but we honor them because the apostles hold a special place in our faith. We are "built upon the foundation of the apostles and prophets, with Christ Jesus himself as the cornerstone" (Eph 2:20). The Church, built on that foundation, offers us stability in every troubled time. Jesus gave us the Church as part of his plan for salvation. As the Church, we are his body now.

Prayer

Saints Philip and James, you willingly gave your lives to testify to Jesus Christ. Pray that we might be apostles in our time who draw others to Jesus. Amen.

MAY 4

Blessed Marie-Léonie Paradis

May 12, 1840–May 3, 1912
Feast: May 4 (Canada)
Patron: Archdiocese of Sherbrooke, Canada; domestic workers

Holiness doesn't mean doing great things but doing ordinary things with great love. Blessed Marie-Léonie Paradis understood that very well. Born May 12, 1840, in L'Acadie, Quebec, Virginie-Alodie was drawn to the religious life. On February 21, 1854, she entered the Marianites of Saint-Laurent, Montreal, a feminine branch of the Holy Cross Congregation. A dedicated teacher, she went to the United States where she worked in New York, Michigan, and Indiana. In the meantime, however, something was tugging at her heart. Slowly, she discovered a desire to serve Jesus Christ in his priests.

In 1874 Marie-Léonie returned to New Brunswick and began domestic service at Saint Joseph's College, in collaboration with Father Camille Lefebvre, C.S.C. Her dedication inspired many young women to join her in this work. In 1880, she began a new congregation, the Institute of the Little Sisters of the Holy Family. Their mission is to serve the Church by assisting priests materially and morally. Marie-Léonie's life was marked by intense dedication to her work, up to the day she died. With their motto, "Piety and dedication," her sisters today continue her witness to the face of the Servant Christ.

Reflection

Marie-Léonie saw no service as too small or unimportant. The domestic tasks she did with such love—whether laundry, cooking, washing dishes, etc.—may have been taken for granted at times, but that didn't bother Marie-Léonie, because it was her way of making a gift of herself. She reminds us that we can become holy no matter what our work is, as long as we do it with love.

Prayer

Blessed Marie-Léonie, pray that I might spend myself gladly for the sake of Jesus Christ, keeping in mind the words of Saint Paul: "The love of Christ urges us on" (2 Cor 5:14). Amen.

MAY 5

Saint Florian

c. 250–c. 304
Feast: May 4
Patron: Firefighters, Austria, Poland, chimney sweeps, brewers, soap boilers; protection from dangers from fire, floods, and drowning.

Florian lived near the town of Enns in what is now Austria. He enlisted in the Roman army and soon became an officer and civil administrator. During the reign of Emperor Diocletian, Florian refused to carry out orders to persecute the Christians. Choosing not to remain silent about his faith, Florian voluntarily presented himself as a Christian to the soldiers of the Roman governor, Aquilinus.

Florian was originally sentenced to death by burning at the stake. Standing on the pyre, it is said that he challenged the Roman soldiers to light the fire, saying, "If you do, I will climb to heaven on the flames." Apprehensive, his persecutors decided to instead scourge and flay Florian, and throw him into the river with a stone around his neck. He is said to have been martyred not far from the spot where the Enns River flows into the Danube. A holy Christian woman recovered his body and buried it. Many miracles, particularly regarding protection from fire, were attributed to Florian's intercession.

Reflection

Florian's life is a reminder that our submission to earthly authority must be tempered and informed by our faith. Service to God took precedence in Florian's life. He realized that he owed his loyalty to God before all else. How do I allow my faith to nurture me in my family life and inform my political opinions? My choices at work? How can I put God before all else in my life?

Prayer

Christ, King of the Universe, inspire me to serve you before all else. Help me to respect lawful authority and give me the gifts of counsel and prudence so that I may know how to best honor them. Amen.

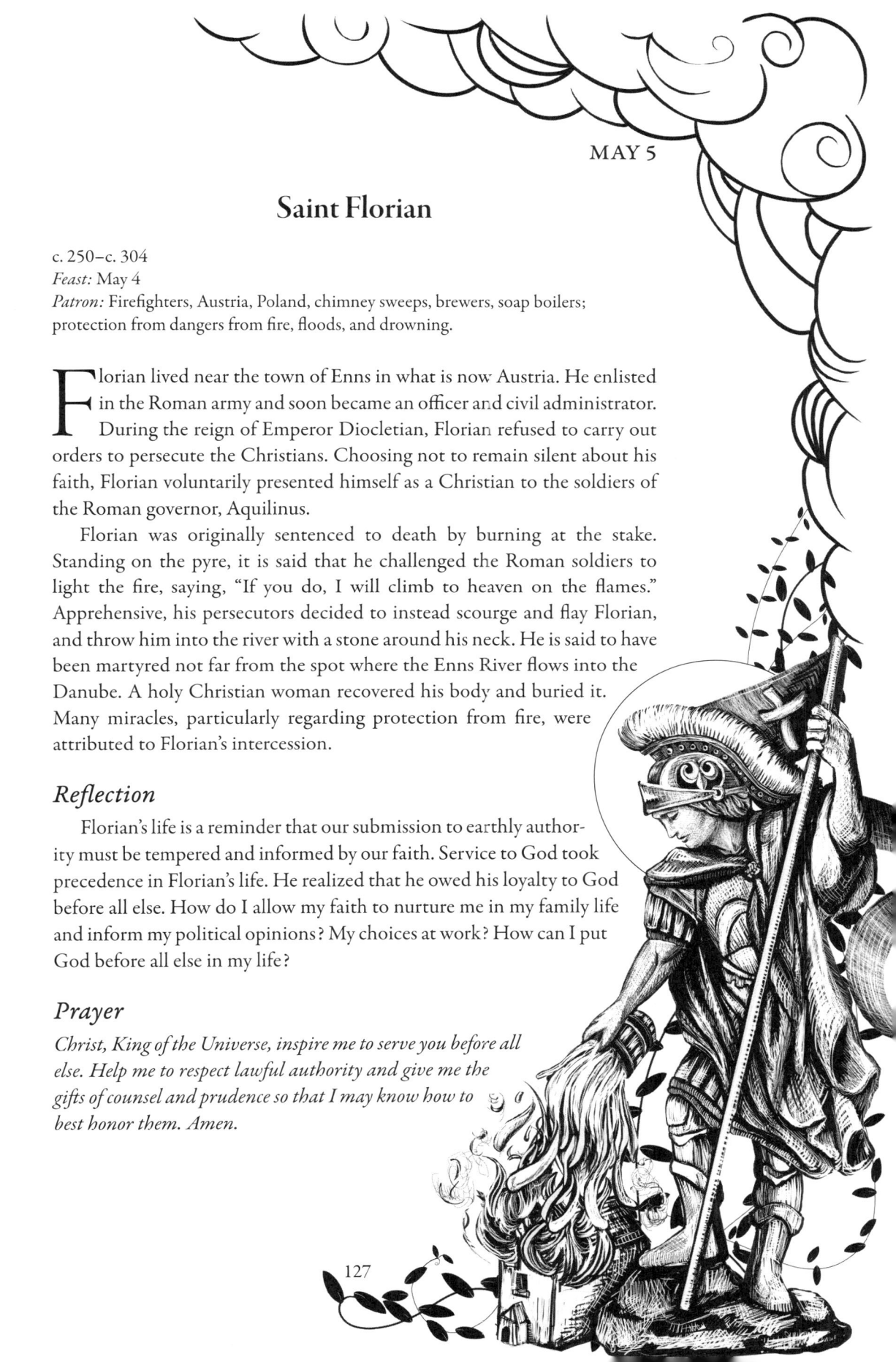

MAY 6

Saint Dominic Savio

April 2, 1842–March 9, 1857
Feast: May 6
Patron: Troubled teens

One of ten children born to a hardworking family in Piedmont, northern Italy, Dominic showed great devotion from an early age. He was allowed to receive his first Communion at age seven, though the usual age was twelve. On that day he made a few resolutions for his life. One became his life's motto: "Death, but not sin!" Despite his youth, that single-hearted desire for holiness guided the rest of his life.

When Dominic was twelve, his parents allowed him to go to the Oratory of Saint Francis de Sales, a school for boys started by Saint John Bosco. Dominic got along well with the other boys and became a good influence on them. Bosco noticed his goodness and guided his spiritual growth. With the help of some friends, Dominic started a sodality in honor of Mary Immaculate. Dominic had poor health, and in early 1857 he became sick with a cough and his condition worsened. His father came to bring him home, where Dominic died peacefully, just short of his fifteenth birthday.

Reflection

After hearing John Bosco preach one day about becoming a saint, Dominic resolved to seek holiness of life even more than before. Bosco advised him to carry out his ordinary duties well. After that, Dominic decided to do little things to honor God's love for him. His spirituality is similar to the Little Way of Saint Thérèse of Lisieux—a path to holiness that all of us can take.

Prayer

Saint Dominic Savio, you showed great love for Jesus and Mary. Pray for us that we too might learn to value the things that really matter, and strive for holiness each day of our lives. Amen.

MAY 7

Saint François de Montmorency Laval

April 30, 1623–May 6, 1708
Feast: May 6 (Canada)
Patron: Bishops of Canada

Saint Marie of the Incarnation said of Bishop Laval, "He is the most austere man of this world, the most detached from worldly possessions. He gives away everything and lives in poverty." François' spirit of poverty was a choice as he was born into the prominent Montmorency family in France. As a boy, he began studies for the priesthood. When his two older brothers died, François inherited the family estate and title. Despite intense pressure from his family, François eventually renounced his patrimony and gave his rights to another brother.

François had always dreamed of becoming a missionary and, after a failed attempt to go to Asia, he was asked to go to Quebec in 1658. He was ordained a bishop and became the vicar apostolic of New France. François threw himself into the arduous work of forming a frontier Church. Braving harsh conditions, he often traveled long distances to assist the people and the priests. He had to confront the civil authorities to insure justice for the indigenous population. He also supported Catholic education and built the large seminary of Quebec. Worn out by his labors, he resigned as bishop in 1688. He continued to be a friend of the poor until his death.

Reflection

François de Montmorency Laval could have chosen to live an easy life in France on his family's estate. Instead, he not only chose the priesthood, but he also willingly traveled to a rugged outpost, enduring many privations. He lived the first beatitude, "Blessed are the poor in spirit, for theirs is the kingdom of heaven" (Mt 5:3). François' example can inspire us to live in a spirit of detachment from our possessions.

Prayer

Saint François de Montmorency Laval, pray for us that we might seek first the kingdom of God, trusting that all other things will be given us besides. Amen.

MAY 8

Blessed Catherine of Saint Augustine

May 3, 1632–May 8, 1668
Feast: May 8 (Canada)
Patron: Canada

Catherine de Longpré was born in Normandy, France. From a young age she had mystical experiences and was intensely attracted to a life of prayer and devotion to God. As a young teenager, she entered the Augustinian Hospitaller Sisters of the Mercy of Jesus. And when she was just sixteen, Catherine volunteered to go to Quebec to help the colonists of New France and the native peoples. Her family opposed the idea, but Catherine was resolute and set sail in 1648. On the ship she contracted the plague and was close to death, but she experienced a miraculous recovery and attributed it to Mary's intercession.

After arriving in Canada, Catherine worked in the Hôtel-Dieu, a hospital established for the people of Quebec. Though Catherine suffered from ill health and great internal turmoil, she lived a life of great virtue and was recognized for her holiness. The spirituality of the recently martyred Jesuit, Father Jean de Brébeuf, appealed to her, and she took him as her model. When she died at the young age of thirty-six, she offered her life for the people of New France. For this reason, Catherine is honored as one of the six founders of the Catholic Church in Canada. Saint John Paul II beatified her on April 23, 1989.

Reflection

Catherine combined a deep life of prayer with service of others. Her contemplative life was not self-focused but spilled over into a life of apostolic service. Her life is an example of someone who gave herself completely to God and to others. How do I let my prayer impact my relationship with others?

Prayer

Blessed Catherine, pray for me that I, too, might grow in both the spirit of prayer and service. Amen.

MAY 9

Saint Mary Domenica Mazzarello

May 9, 1837–May 14, 1881
Feast: May 13
Patron: The sick, educators

During the violent and bloody days of Italy's unification, when anti-clericalism swept through Italy, another drama was played out in the backwaters of Piedmont. A poor young woman dreamed of something far more radical: the ideal of a life totally given over to God, spent in service of the poor. Mary Mazzarello had the virtues and deep faith of the hardworking farmers from whom she came. The pastor of her parish, Father Pestarino, asked her to join a group of girls called the Daughters of Mary Immaculate. Mary led the group in learning how to sew.

One day Mary had a vision of a building with a large courtyard, filled with girls and interiorly heard the words, "These are my children—I entrust them to you." Not long after, she met Saint John Bosco and began to collaborate with him in caring for and educating poor girls. Mary became the foundress and first superior of the feminine branch of the Salesians, the Daughters of Mary, Help of Christians. Under her wise guidance, the group flourished and has since spread worldwide.

Reflection

When Mary Mazzarello was in her small sewing group, she had no inkling that God would inspire her to start a religious order that would one day have thousands of members in almost one hundred countries. That happened by God's power not hers. Do I really believe that God can multiply the fruit of my small efforts to serve his people? How can this encourage me to acts of kindness?

Prayer

Saint Mary Mazzarello, you were filled with a spirit of faith and joy. Pray for me that in the difficulties of life I may more intentionally entrust myself to God. Amen.

MAY 10

Saint Damien of Molokai

January 3, 1840–April 15, 1889
Feast: May 10
Patron: Hawaii, outcasts, and those suffering from Hansen's disease or HIV/AIDS

Joseph de Veuster was born in Belgium to a simple, hardworking farming family. As a young man, Joseph followed his brother into the Congregation of the Sacred Hearts of Jesus and Mary and was given the religious name of Damien. His brother was set to go to Hawaii as a missionary priest, but when he fell ill Damien eagerly volunteered to take his place. For years, Damien worked among the native Hawaiians before volunteering to serve on the quarantined leper colony of Molokai.

Originally, a rotation of missionaries was set to go to the island to prevent the priests from contracting the disease. However, Damien bravely volunteered to go permanently. He wanted to be a priest the people could trust, someone who was not afraid of their illness. For sixteen years, he lived side by side with the people. He wrote passionate letters to authorities asking for material aid for his people. A father to the people he was called to serve, Damien worked tirelessly to support them spiritually and materially. Soon other volunteers, including Mother Marianne Cope, began to arrive to lend aid. Damien contracted leprosy at the age of forty-nine, but he died peacefully, knowing that his work would continue. Damien described himself as the "happiest missionary on earth."

Reflection

Damien of Molokai braved death to serve the people of God. He made no distinction between himself and the poor, ill, and exiled people he happily served. In my family, workplace, and neighborhood, how can I become a more authentic witness of the Gospel?

Prayer

Jesus, like Saint Damien of Molokai, help me to follow your example. Help me to reach out to others and give myself generously to others in need. Amen.

MAY 11

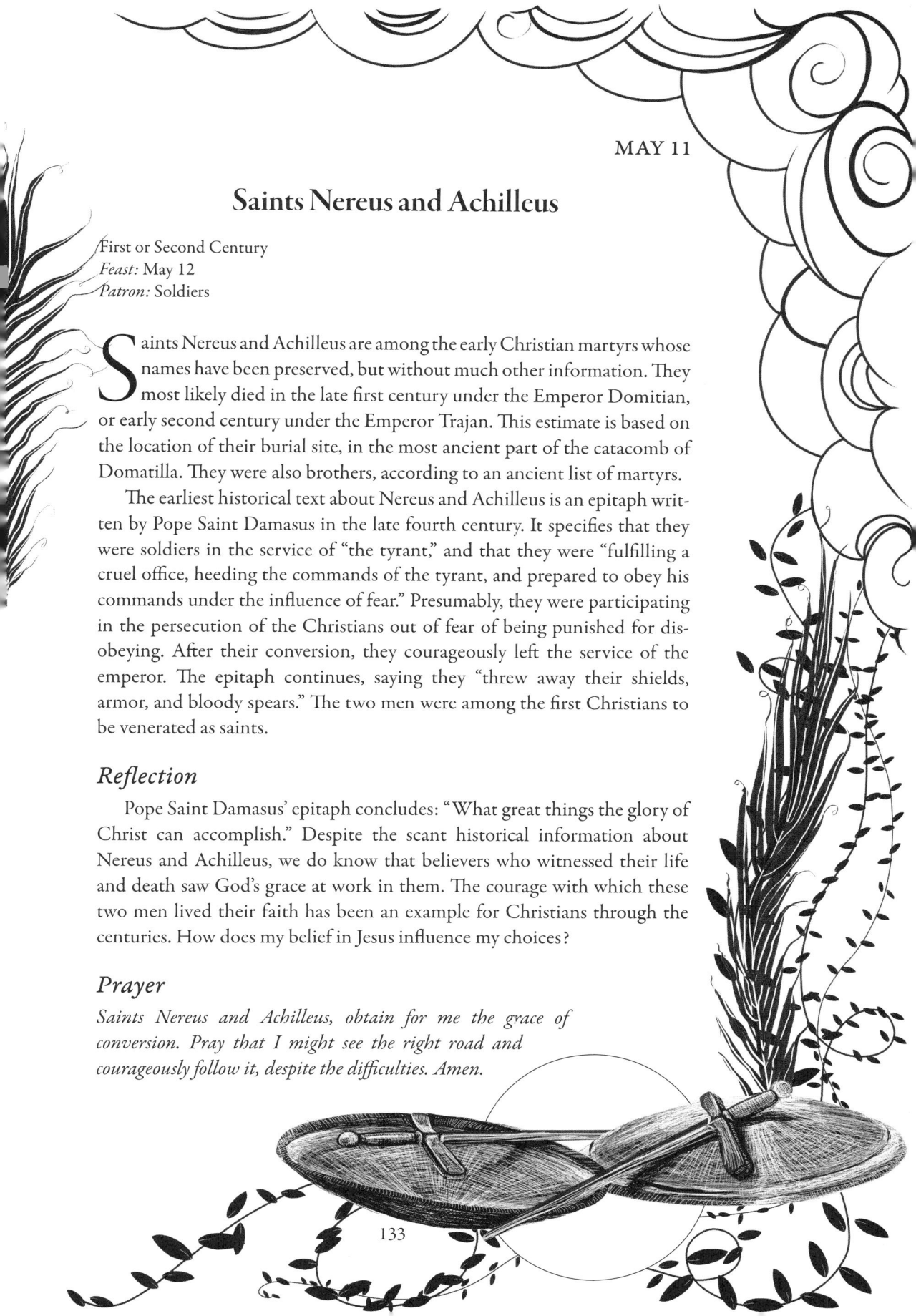

Saints Nereus and Achilleus

First or Second Century
Feast: May 12
Patron: Soldiers

Saints Nereus and Achilleus are among the early Christian martyrs whose names have been preserved, but without much other information. They most likely died in the late first century under the Emperor Domitian, or early second century under the Emperor Trajan. This estimate is based on the location of their burial site, in the most ancient part of the catacomb of Domatilla. They were also brothers, according to an ancient list of martyrs.

The earliest historical text about Nereus and Achilleus is an epitaph written by Pope Saint Damasus in the late fourth century. It specifies that they were soldiers in the service of "the tyrant," and that they were "fulfilling a cruel office, heeding the commands of the tyrant, and prepared to obey his commands under the influence of fear." Presumably, they were participating in the persecution of the Christians out of fear of being punished for disobeying. After their conversion, they courageously left the service of the emperor. The epitaph continues, saying they "threw away their shields, armor, and bloody spears." The two men were among the first Christians to be venerated as saints.

Reflection

Pope Saint Damasus' epitaph concludes: "What great things the glory of Christ can accomplish." Despite the scant historical information about Nereus and Achilleus, we do know that believers who witnessed their life and death saw God's grace at work in them. The courage with which these two men lived their faith has been an example for Christians through the centuries. How does my belief in Jesus influence my choices?

Prayer

Saints Nereus and Achilleus, obtain for me the grace of conversion. Pray that I might see the right road and courageously follow it, despite the difficulties. Amen.

MAY 12

Saint Pancras

c. 289–c. 304
Feast: May 12
Patron: Children, against headaches, false witnesses, and perjury

According to tradition, Pancras was born in Syria and went to Rome with an uncle after his parents died. Pancras and his uncle converted to Christianity in Rome. At the age of fourteen, Pancras was caught up in the vicious persecution launched by the Emperor Diocletian. Pancras was beheaded because he refused to deny Christ.

Pancras became a popular martyr, and devotion to him spread throughout Europe, especially in England. Saint Augustine of Canterbury dedicated the first church he had built in England to Pancras. According to Saint Gregory of Tours' *Glory of the Martyrs*, it was believed that God would punish anyone who swore a false oath on the relics of Saint Pancras. By the thirteenth century, it was a widespread practice to swear oaths in court on Saint Pancras' relics.

Reflection

Through his martyrdom, Pancras testified to his Catholic faith and proved himself a faithful witness to Jesus Christ. The power of his example undoubtedly led many people to testify truthfully in court cases. Thus, because of Pancras justice continued to be served for many centuries after his death. This reminds us that the good we do has a ripple effect that may continue after our death and influence the lives of many other people. Our actions have effects into eternity, with God's grace inspiring people to live holy lives. We don't know how our own actions will affect others, but we do know that if we act in truth and justice, the lives of others can change for the better.

Prayer

Saint Pancras, pray for us that we may always speak the truth with integrity and justice toward others. You courageously professed your faith in Christ; pray that when we have the occasion to witness to Christ, we may not deny him. Amen.

MAY 13

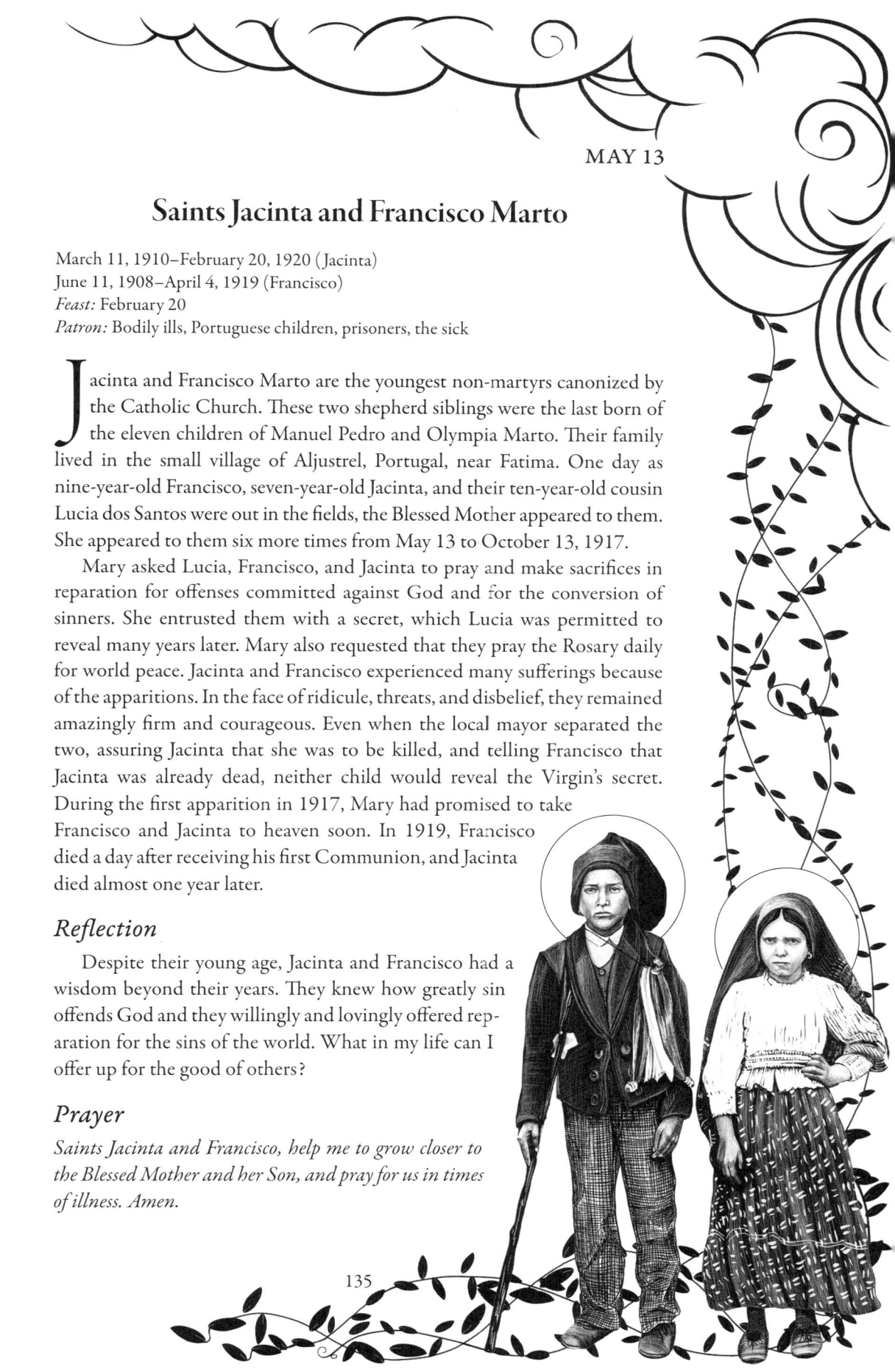

Saints Jacinta and Francisco Marto

March 11, 1910–February 20, 1920 (Jacinta)
June 11, 1908–April 4, 1919 (Francisco)
Feast: February 20
Patron: Bodily ills, Portuguese children, prisoners, the sick

Jacinta and Francisco Marto are the youngest non-martyrs canonized by the Catholic Church. These two shepherd siblings were the last born of the eleven children of Manuel Pedro and Olympia Marto. Their family lived in the small village of Aljustrel, Portugal, near Fatima. One day as nine-year-old Francisco, seven-year-old Jacinta, and their ten-year-old cousin Lucia dos Santos were out in the fields, the Blessed Mother appeared to them. She appeared to them six more times from May 13 to October 13, 1917.

Mary asked Lucia, Francisco, and Jacinta to pray and make sacrifices in reparation for offenses committed against God and for the conversion of sinners. She entrusted them with a secret, which Lucia was permitted to reveal many years later. Mary also requested that they pray the Rosary daily for world peace. Jacinta and Francisco experienced many sufferings because of the apparitions. In the face of ridicule, threats, and disbelief, they remained amazingly firm and courageous. Even when the local mayor separated the two, assuring Jacinta that she was to be killed, and telling Francisco that Jacinta was already dead, neither child would reveal the Virgin's secret. During the first apparition in 1917, Mary had promised to take Francisco and Jacinta to heaven soon. In 1919, Francisco died a day after receiving his first Communion, and Jacinta died almost one year later.

Reflection

Despite their young age, Jacinta and Francisco had a wisdom beyond their years. They knew how greatly sin offends God and they willingly and lovingly offered reparation for the sins of the world. What in my life can I offer up for the good of others?

Prayer

Saints Jacinta and Francisco, help me to grow closer to the Blessed Mother and her Son, and pray for us in times of illness. Amen.

MAY 14

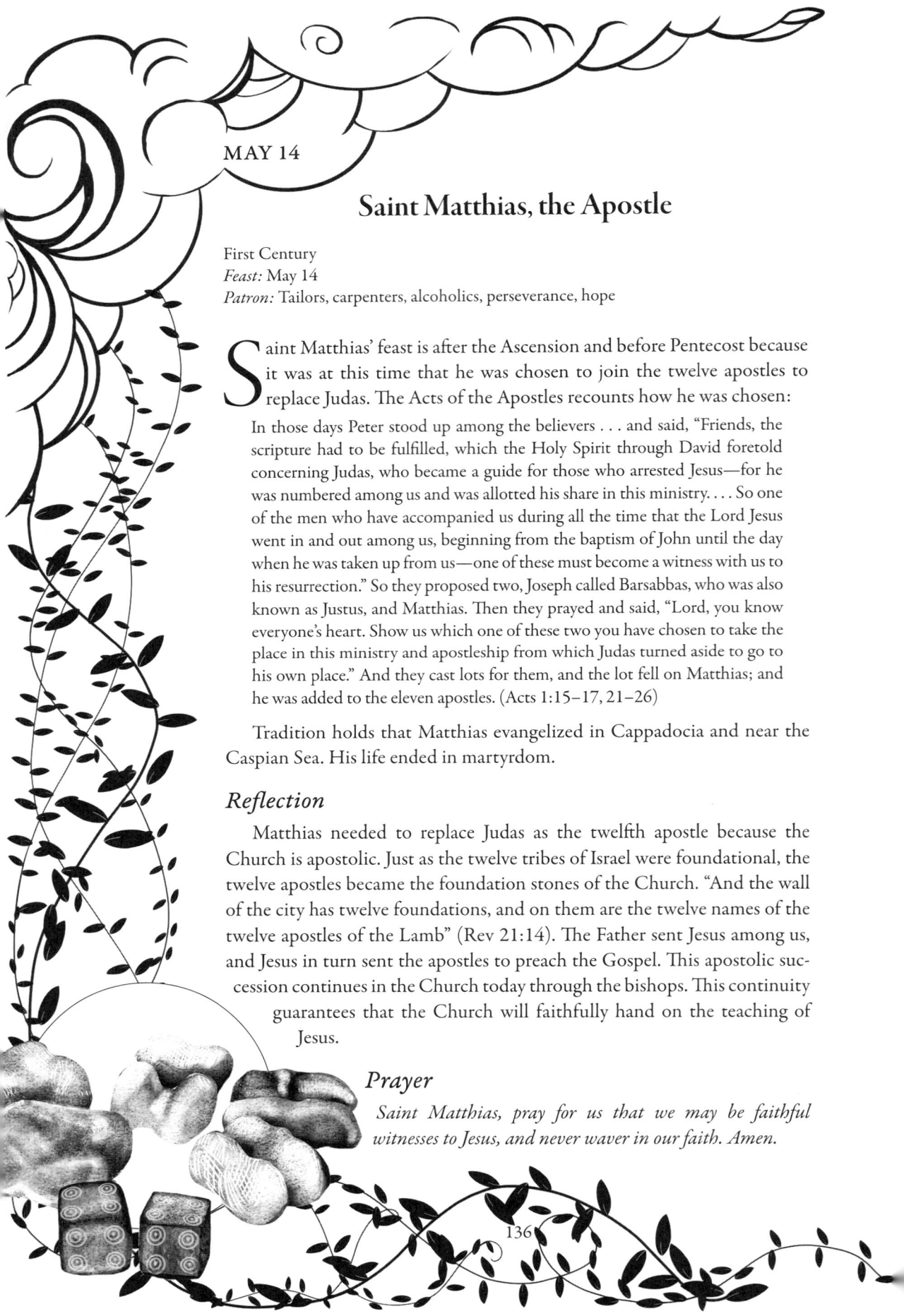

Saint Matthias, the Apostle

First Century
Feast: May 14
Patron: Tailors, carpenters, alcoholics, perseverance, hope

Saint Matthias' feast is after the Ascension and before Pentecost because it was at this time that he was chosen to join the twelve apostles to replace Judas. The Acts of the Apostles recounts how he was chosen:

> In those days Peter stood up among the believers . . . and said, "Friends, the scripture had to be fulfilled, which the Holy Spirit through David foretold concerning Judas, who became a guide for those who arrested Jesus—for he was numbered among us and was allotted his share in this ministry. . . . So one of the men who have accompanied us during all the time that the Lord Jesus went in and out among us, beginning from the baptism of John until the day when he was taken up from us—one of these must become a witness with us to his resurrection." So they proposed two, Joseph called Barsabbas, who was also known as Justus, and Matthias. Then they prayed and said, "Lord, you know everyone's heart. Show us which one of these two you have chosen to take the place in this ministry and apostleship from which Judas turned aside to go to his own place." And they cast lots for them, and the lot fell on Matthias; and he was added to the eleven apostles. (Acts 1:15–17, 21–26)

Tradition holds that Matthias evangelized in Cappadocia and near the Caspian Sea. His life ended in martyrdom.

Reflection

Matthias needed to replace Judas as the twelfth apostle because the Church is apostolic. Just as the twelve tribes of Israel were foundational, the twelve apostles became the foundation stones of the Church. "And the wall of the city has twelve foundations, and on them are the twelve names of the twelve apostles of the Lamb" (Rev 21:14). The Father sent Jesus among us, and Jesus in turn sent the apostles to preach the Gospel. This apostolic succession continues in the Church today through the bishops. This continuity guarantees that the Church will faithfully hand on the teaching of Jesus.

Prayer

Saint Matthias, pray for us that we may be faithful witnesses to Jesus, and never waver in our faith. Amen.

MAY 15

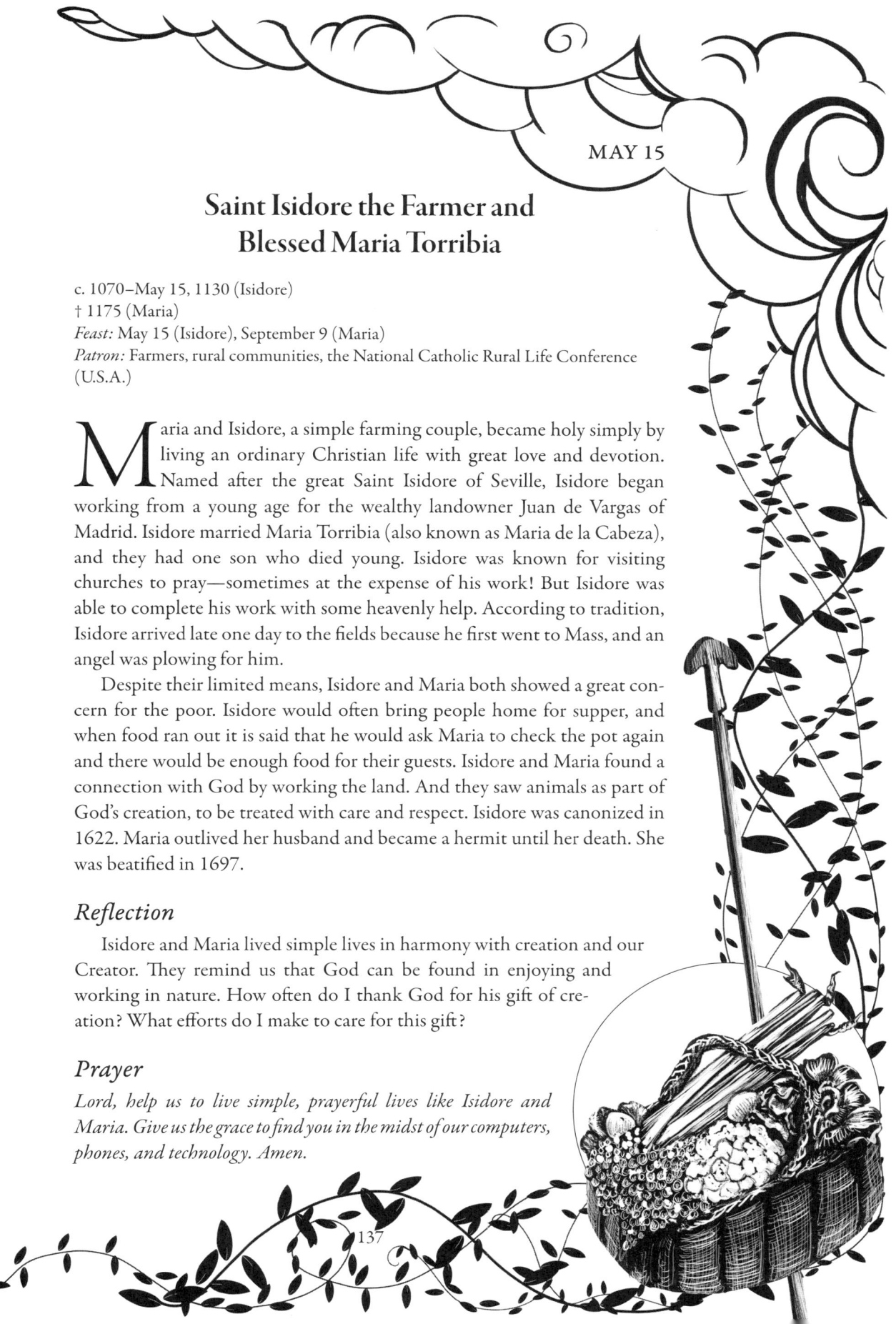

Saint Isidore the Farmer and Blessed Maria Torribia

c. 1070–May 15, 1130 (Isidore)
† 1175 (Maria)
Feast: May 15 (Isidore), September 9 (Maria)
Patron: Farmers, rural communities, the National Catholic Rural Life Conference (U.S.A.)

Maria and Isidore, a simple farming couple, became holy simply by living an ordinary Christian life with great love and devotion. Named after the great Saint Isidore of Seville, Isidore began working from a young age for the wealthy landowner Juan de Vargas of Madrid. Isidore married Maria Torribia (also known as Maria de la Cabeza), and they had one son who died young. Isidore was known for visiting churches to pray—sometimes at the expense of his work! But Isidore was able to complete his work with some heavenly help. According to tradition, Isidore arrived late one day to the fields because he first went to Mass, and an angel was plowing for him.

Despite their limited means, Isidore and Maria both showed a great concern for the poor. Isidore would often bring people home for supper, and when food ran out it is said that he would ask Maria to check the pot again and there would be enough food for their guests. Isidore and Maria found a connection with God by working the land. And they saw animals as part of God's creation, to be treated with care and respect. Isidore was canonized in 1622. Maria outlived her husband and became a hermit until her death. She was beatified in 1697.

Reflection

Isidore and Maria lived simple lives in harmony with creation and our Creator. They remind us that God can be found in enjoying and working in nature. How often do I thank God for his gift of creation? What efforts do I make to care for this gift?

Prayer

Lord, help us to live simple, prayerful lives like Isidore and Maria. Give us the grace to find you in the midst of our computers, phones, and technology. Amen.

MAY 16

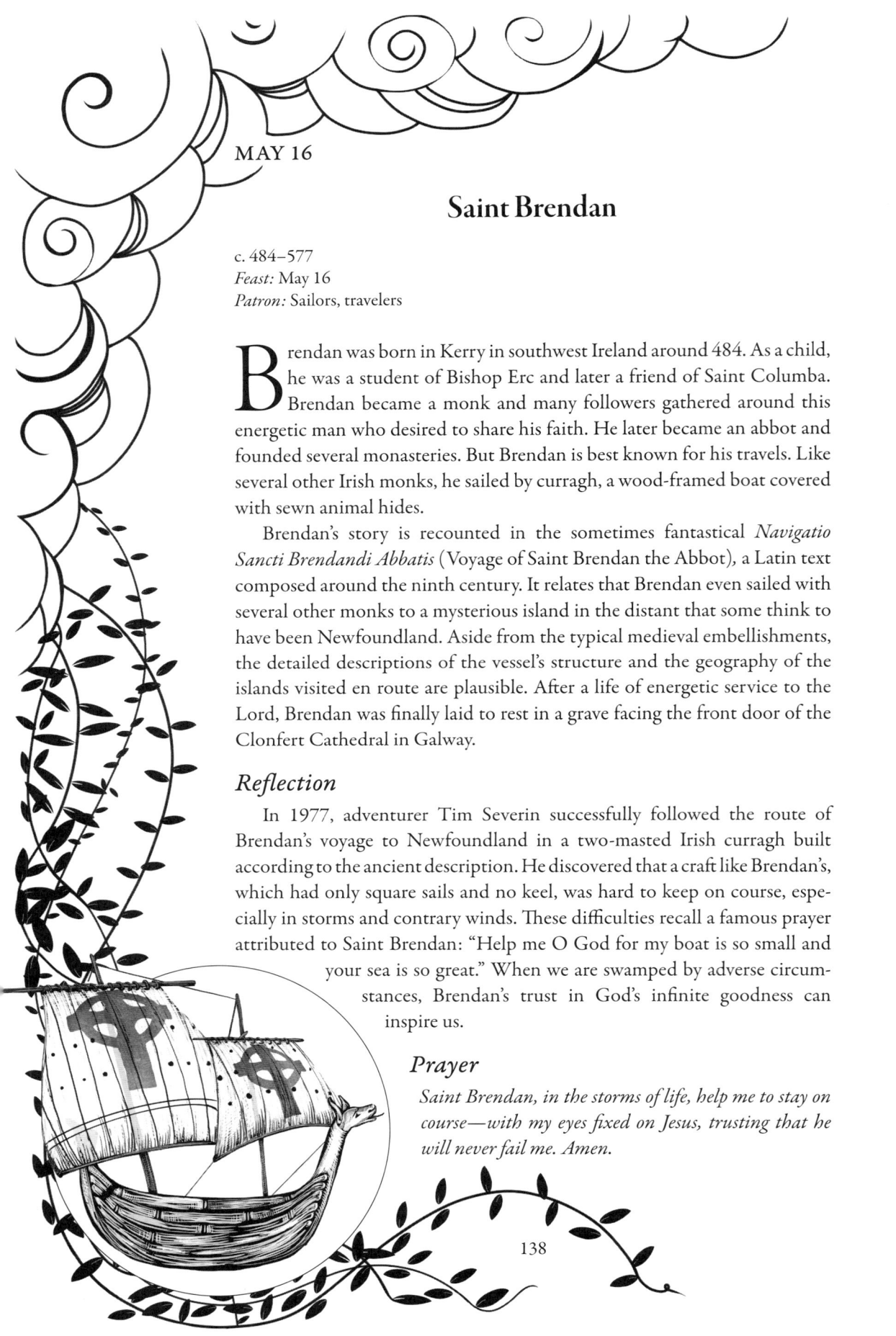

Saint Brendan

c. 484–577
Feast: May 16
Patron: Sailors, travelers

Brendan was born in Kerry in southwest Ireland around 484. As a child, he was a student of Bishop Erc and later a friend of Saint Columba. Brendan became a monk and many followers gathered around this energetic man who desired to share his faith. He later became an abbot and founded several monasteries. But Brendan is best known for his travels. Like several other Irish monks, he sailed by curragh, a wood-framed boat covered with sewn animal hides.

Brendan's story is recounted in the sometimes fantastical *Navigatio Sancti Brendandi Abbatis* (Voyage of Saint Brendan the Abbot), a Latin text composed around the ninth century. It relates that Brendan even sailed with several other monks to a mysterious island in the distant that some think to have been Newfoundland. Aside from the typical medieval embellishments, the detailed descriptions of the vessel's structure and the geography of the islands visited en route are plausible. After a life of energetic service to the Lord, Brendan was finally laid to rest in a grave facing the front door of the Clonfert Cathedral in Galway.

Reflection

In 1977, adventurer Tim Severin successfully followed the route of Brendan's voyage to Newfoundland in a two-masted Irish curragh built according to the ancient description. He discovered that a craft like Brendan's, which had only square sails and no keel, was hard to keep on course, especially in storms and contrary winds. These difficulties recall a famous prayer attributed to Saint Brendan: "Help me O God for my boat is so small and your sea is so great." When we are swamped by adverse circumstances, Brendan's trust in God's infinite goodness can inspire us.

Prayer

Saint Brendan, in the storms of life, help me to stay on course—with my eyes fixed on Jesus, trusting that he will never fail me. Amen.

MAY 17

Saint Dymphna

Seventh Century
Feast: May 15
Patron: Family harmony, the mentally ill, those with epilepsy, those who have suffered nervous breakdowns, and mental health professionals

According to tradition, Dymphna was born in the early seventh century. She was the daughter of a pagan Celtic king and a devout Christian mother. She was baptized by Saint Gerebernus, who later became her confessor. Upon the tragic death of Dymphna's mother, her father was inconsolable. Increasingly unstable, his attention turned toward Dymphna, who bore a striking resemblance to her beautiful mother. Realizing the danger this posed, Gerebernus advised that Dymphna flee. Accompanied by Gerebernus, along with the court jester and his wife, Dymphna traveled to Gheel in northern Belgium. They arrived at Saint Martin's oratory and decided to live there as hermits, in prayer and penance.

Dymphna's father, however, tracked her down and demanded that she return with him. Dymphna refused, and Gerebernus encouraged her to remain resolute. Enraged, the king ordered that both be killed. The king's men killed Gerebernus but could not bring themselves to kill the princess. Deranged, the king beheaded Dymphna himself.

Reflection

For centuries Dymphna has been invoked for those who suffer mental illness. A church was built in the fourteenth century in Gheel to honor the saint and enshrine her relics, and a small infirmary was attached to the church to care for the mentally ill. Through Dymphna's intercession, many healings occurred when people would bring their loved ones to the church. To this day, the people of Gheel have a deep empathy for the mentally ill and maintain a custom of welcoming them into their homes.

Prayer

Jesus, help me to welcome and see each person I meet as my brother or sister. Grant me patience and help me to be gentle and try to understand those who suffer psychologically. Amen.

MAY 18

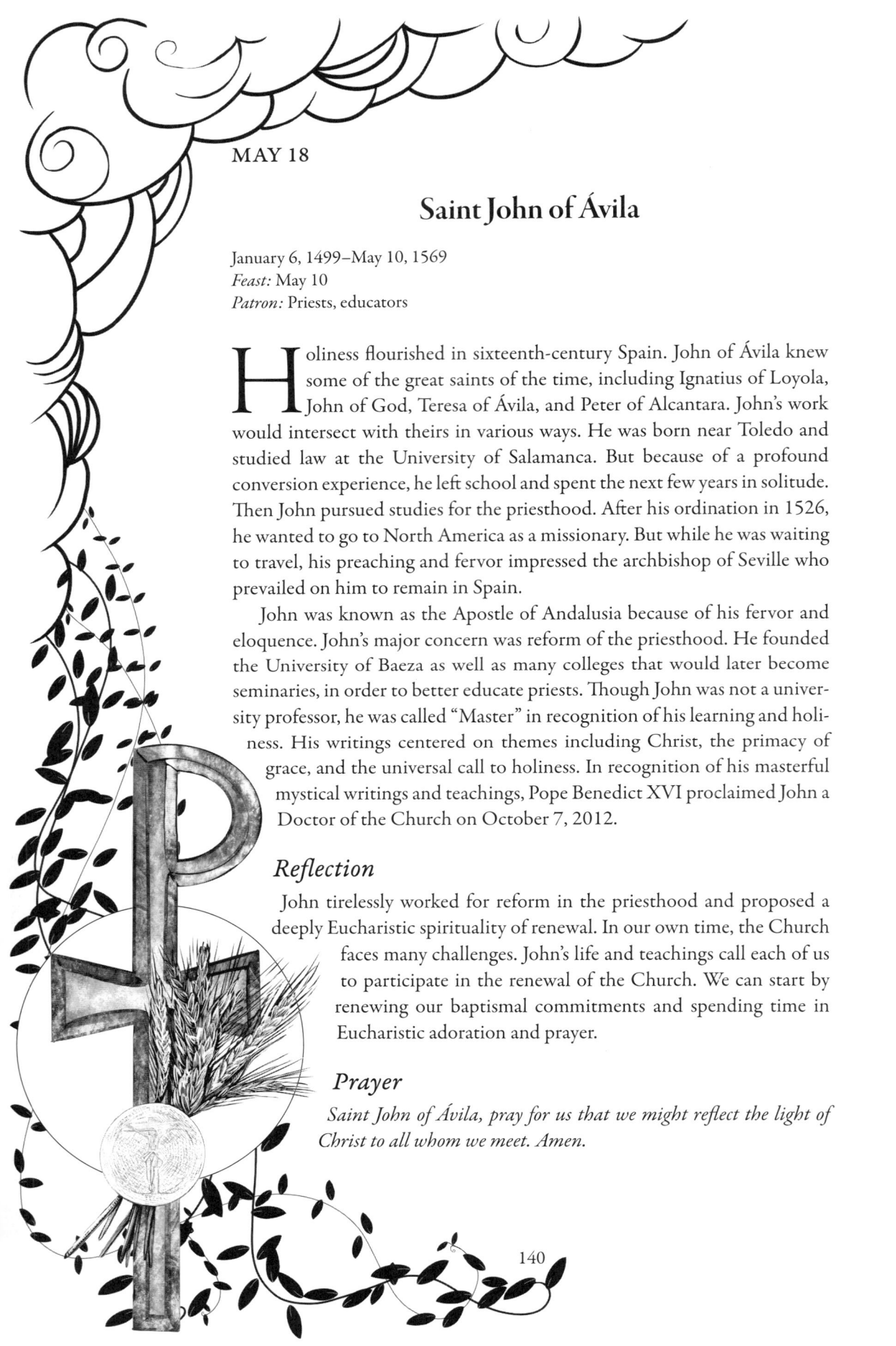

Saint John of Ávila

January 6, 1499–May 10, 1569
Feast: May 10
Patron: Priests, educators

Holiness flourished in sixteenth-century Spain. John of Ávila knew some of the great saints of the time, including Ignatius of Loyola, John of God, Teresa of Ávila, and Peter of Alcantara. John's work would intersect with theirs in various ways. He was born near Toledo and studied law at the University of Salamanca. But because of a profound conversion experience, he left school and spent the next few years in solitude. Then John pursued studies for the priesthood. After his ordination in 1526, he wanted to go to North America as a missionary. But while he was waiting to travel, his preaching and fervor impressed the archbishop of Seville who prevailed on him to remain in Spain.

John was known as the Apostle of Andalusia because of his fervor and eloquence. John's major concern was reform of the priesthood. He founded the University of Baeza as well as many colleges that would later become seminaries, in order to better educate priests. Though John was not a university professor, he was called "Master" in recognition of his learning and holiness. His writings centered on themes including Christ, the primacy of grace, and the universal call to holiness. In recognition of his masterful mystical writings and teachings, Pope Benedict XVI proclaimed John a Doctor of the Church on October 7, 2012.

Reflection

John tirelessly worked for reform in the priesthood and proposed a deeply Eucharistic spirituality of renewal. In our own time, the Church faces many challenges. John's life and teachings call each of us to participate in the renewal of the Church. We can start by renewing our baptismal commitments and spending time in Eucharistic adoration and prayer.

Prayer

Saint John of Ávila, pray for us that we might reflect the light of Christ to all whom we meet. Amen.

MAY 19

Saint Dunstan

c. 910–May 19, 988
Feast: May 19
Patron: Jewelers, goldsmiths, locksmiths

Although Saint Augustine of Canterbury brought Christianity to the Anglo-Saxons, for centuries the most popular Anglo-Saxon saint was Dunstan. Approximately three hundred years after Augustine concluded his labors, Dunstan was born into a noble family in Wessex, the only Saxon kingdom that had survived the Viking invasions. He studied at the monastery of Glastonbury near his birthplace and became a monk and hermit, developing skills as an illuminator of manuscripts, a worker of metals, and a musician.

In 943, King Edmund appointed Dunstan abbot of Glastonbury. The new abbot made Glastonbury a great center of learning and revitalized other monasteries. As members of the royal family followed one another on the throne in sometimes rapid succession, Dunstan tried to advise each of them. Not all of them took this well. King Edwy, whose life was a scandal, actually banished the abbot.

In 960, Edwy's successor, King Edgar, appointed Dunstan archbishop of Canterbury. For two decades, the zealous archbishop carried out many reforms. Then in his final years—still at Canterbury—he devoted himself to prayer, handicrafts, and the instruction of the boys in the cathedral school. In 988, Dunstan had a vision of angels who told him that he would die soon. He passed away shortly after with a prayer of thanksgiving on his lips.

Reflection

Dunstan was at the forefront of reform in both Church and state. But he knew that any reform one initiates must begin with oneself. Dunstan's relationship with God was the source of his ability to bring order and renewal to those around him. How can I grow in my relationship with God and witness to the beauty of following of Christ?

Prayer

Saint Dunstan, pray that I may know where a change in my heart can benefit those around me. Amen.

MAY 20

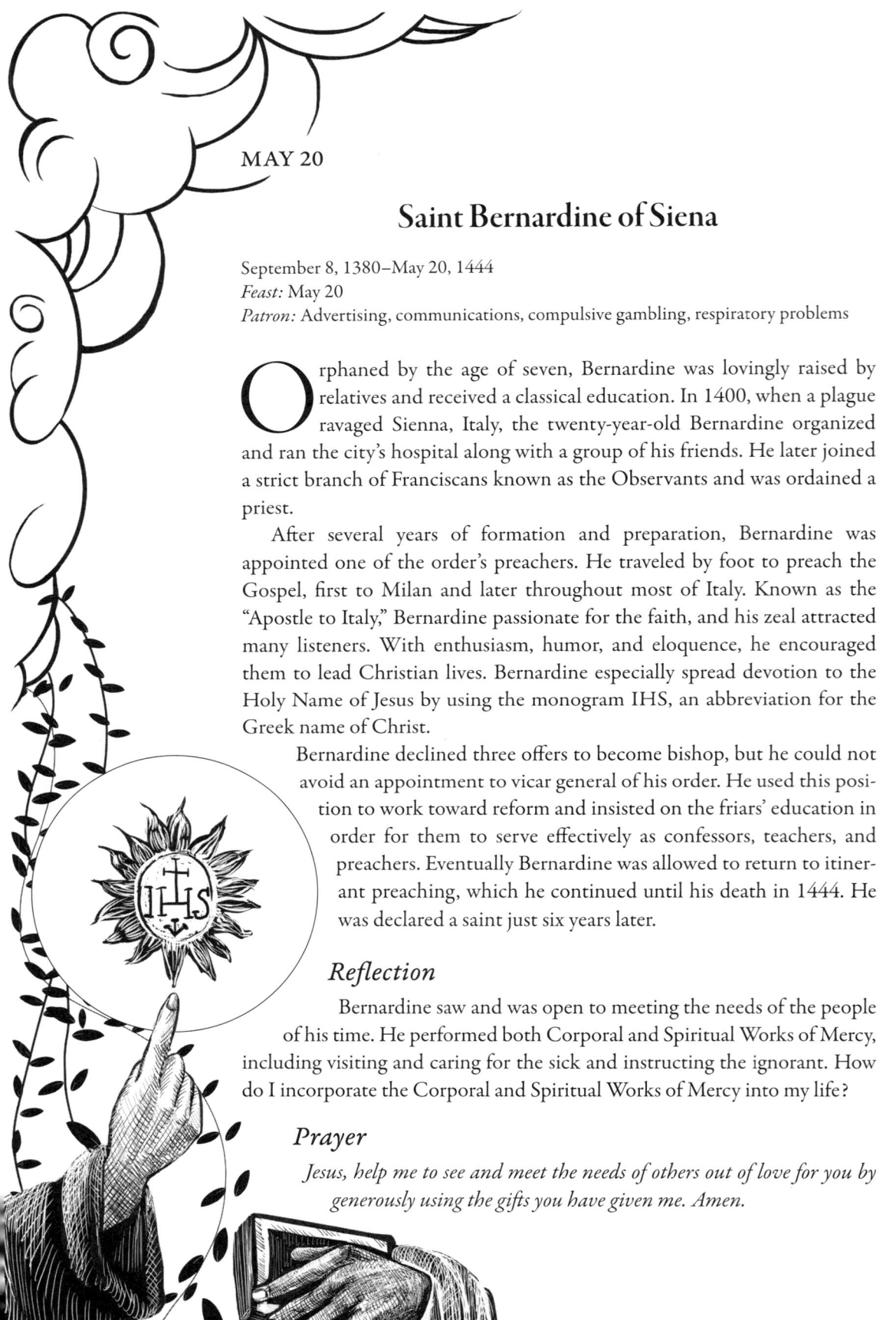

Saint Bernardine of Siena

September 8, 1380–May 20, 1444
Feast: May 20
Patron: Advertising, communications, compulsive gambling, respiratory problems

Orphaned by the age of seven, Bernardine was lovingly raised by relatives and received a classical education. In 1400, when a plague ravaged Sienna, Italy, the twenty-year-old Bernardine organized and ran the city's hospital along with a group of his friends. He later joined a strict branch of Franciscans known as the Observants and was ordained a priest.

After several years of formation and preparation, Bernardine was appointed one of the order's preachers. He traveled by foot to preach the Gospel, first to Milan and later throughout most of Italy. Known as the "Apostle to Italy," Bernardine passionate for the faith, and his zeal attracted many listeners. With enthusiasm, humor, and eloquence, he encouraged them to lead Christian lives. Bernardine especially spread devotion to the Holy Name of Jesus by using the monogram IHS, an abbreviation for the Greek name of Christ.

Bernardine declined three offers to become bishop, but he could not avoid an appointment to vicar general of his order. He used this position to work toward reform and insisted on the friars' education in order for them to serve effectively as confessors, teachers, and preachers. Eventually Bernardine was allowed to return to itinerant preaching, which he continued until his death in 1444. He was declared a saint just six years later.

Reflection

Bernardine saw and was open to meeting the needs of the people of his time. He performed both Corporal and Spiritual Works of Mercy, including visiting and caring for the sick and instructing the ignorant. How do I incorporate the Corporal and Spiritual Works of Mercy into my life?

Prayer

Jesus, help me to see and meet the needs of others out of love for you by generously using the gifts you have given me. Amen.

MAY 21

Saint Cristóbal Magallanes and Companions

July 30, 1869–May 25, 1927
Feast: May 21
Patron: Mexico

Cristóbal (or Christopher) was a parish priest in his home town of Totatiche, Mexico, during the anti-Catholic persecution that occurred in the early twentieth century. With severe laws limiting religious freedom, Plutarco Calles and other government leaders tried to stamp out the Catholic faith and prevent priests from ministering to their flock. Cristóbal nonviolently resisted the government's coercive policies by erecting a seminary in Totatiche and secretly ministering to people.

On May 21, 1927, while on his way to celebrate Mass at a farm, Cristóbal was apprehended. Distributing his possessions to his executors, he expressed forgiveness for his persecutors. He was shot to death four days later without a trial. Right before he died, he said, "I am innocent, and I die innocent. I forgive with all my heart those responsible for my death, and I ask God that the shedding of my blood serve the peace of our divided Mexico." The other martyrs in the group included twenty-one priests and three laymen, killed between 1915 and 1937. Saint John Paul II canonized them during the jubilee year in 2000.

Reflection

Cristóbal and his companions showed total dedication to Christ and the Church. They willingly gave up their lives rather than deny their faith. Their courage can help us give witness to others in the ordinary events of life and to bravely face persecution for our faith. How do I respond to those who do not understand my Catholic faith?

Prayer

Saint Cristóbal Magallanes and companions, pray for us who live in a secular society that often holds values that conflict with the Gospel. Help us to have the courage and conviction to bear witness to Jesus even in difficult situations. Amen.

MAY 22

Saint Rita of Cascia

1381–May 22, 1457
Feast: May 22
Patron: Desperate situations, difficult marriages, healing of wounds, loneliness, parents

Rita was born in an Italian village just outside of Cascia that was wracked by constant feuding. She married Paolo Mancini and the couple had two sons before her husband was violently murdered. Rita forgave his murderers and sought reconciliation. But her teenage sons stubbornly planned their revenge. Rita prayed that God would prevent them from perpetuating the tragic cycle of violence. Both of her sons fell ill, their hearts still full of hate. But before they died, they repented their desire for revenge.

Alone in the world, Rita sought to enter the convent but was adamantly refused. Legends hint of a miracle that changed the sisters' minds: perhaps that Rita was able to reconcile two feuding families, or that three saints miraculously led her past the barred doors of the convent into the chapel, where the surprised sisters found her. Whatever the miracle, the sisters finally allowed Rita to enter. As a religious, Rita's desire to share everything with Jesus deepened. Praying with this desire before the crucifix one Good Friday, Rita felt a thorn from the crucifix's crown of thorns mystically pierce her forehead. The painful wound remained with her for the rest of her life. Rita was canonized on May 24, 1900 by Pope Leo XIII who proclaimed her "The Precious Pearl of Umbria."

Reflection

Rita of Cascia is rightly called "saint of the impossible" because, with God's grace, she didn't just survive several near-impossible situations, but used them as stepping stones to holiness. Immediately after her death, so many miracles were attributed through this humble woman's intercession that she became famous for her heavenly compassion for those who, like her, struggle with unbearable situations.

Prayer

Saint Rita of Cascia, you trusted in God's love for you even in desperate situations. Help us to discover anew God's love for us in our daily life. Amen.

MAY 23

Saint Bede the Venerable

c. 672–May 25, 735
Feast: May 25
Patron: Scholars and historians

Bede was a remarkable Benedictine monk who lived a simple and contemplative life that significantly impacted the culture. He was born in the Ango-Saxon kingdom of Northumbria. At an early age, Bede's parents sent him to the monastery to study. Rarely leaving the monastery confines, Bede spent the rest of his life in the monasteries of Wearmouth and Jarrow, dedicating himself to learning and prayer.

After Bede's ordination to the priesthood at age thirty, he immersed himself in scholarly pursuits. He wrote more than forty books, including sermons, poetry, and biblical commentaries. His most famous work, *Ecclesiastical History of the English People,* earned him the title "Father of English History." Bede was considered the most learned man of his time but was also noted for his humility. Proclaimed a Doctor of the Church in 1899 by Pope Leo XIII, Bede is the only native-born Englishman so honored. His title "Venerable" comes from the inscription on his tomb in Durham Cathedral: "Here are buried the bones of the Venerable Bede."

Reflection

An outstanding scholar of his time, Bede was familiar with the writings of such classical Roman authors as Virgil, Ovid, and Horace. He sought to use what was good and valuable in their works in order to develop a Christian culture that would later flourish in Europe. The study of classical culture can help us to grow in virtue, learn about the ideas of great thinkers, and grow in wisdom. What can I do to grow in my knowledge of the classics?

Prayer

Saint Bede the Venerable, you understood the importance of study and the good use of the mind. Pray for us that our minds might be sanctified in the truth as we grow in both wisdom and love. Help us to creatively lead others to Jesus by knowing how to explain the Gospel. Amen.

MAY 24

Blessed Louis-Zéphirin Moreau

April 1, 1824–May 24, 1901
Feast: May 24 (Canada)
Patron: Diocese of Saint-Hyacinthe, Sisters of Saint Joseph of Saint Hyacinthe, Sisters of Saint Martha, bishops of Canada

Born on a farm in Quebec, Louis was a sickly child prone to illness. His parents sent him to the seminary, but he was forced to drop out because of poor health. His bishop even advised him to give up the idea of the priesthood. But driven by his dream, Louis went to Montreal and was ordained by Bishop Ignace Bourget. Influenced by Bourget's emphasis on prayer, Scripture, and devotion to the Eucharist and to Mary, Louis grew in the spiritual life.

In 1852 Louis was sent to the newly-created diocese of Saint-Hyacinthe to work as secretary for the bishop there. He also started the Union of Saint Joseph, a society to help the needy. After working with several bishops, in 1876 Louis was appointed bishop even though the previous bishop had not recommended Louis. The next twenty-five years proved Louis to be a model bishop. He founded the Sisters of Saint Martha and co-founded the Sisters of Saint Joseph of Saint Hyacinthe. Saint John Paul II beatified him on May 10, 1987.

Reflection

Louis' motto was: "I can do all things in Christ who strengthens me" (see Phil 4:13). At two crucial points in his life—ordination to be a priest and then a bishop—he was discouraged by his own bishops. Yet Louis trusted in Jesus and went ahead, convinced it was God's will. Sometimes others may not believe in us. But God does. And God will give us the grace to do his will despite the obstacles.

Prayer

Blessed Louis, pray that I might look only to God for the strength and courage I need, even if other voices might try to discourage me. Amen.

Saint Gregory VII

c. 1021–May 25, 1085
Feast: May 25
Patron: Church reform

In every age, God raises up men and women to lead the Church through difficult times and to challenge her to holiness. Pope Gregory VII was one such man. Known as Hildebrand before his election to the papacy, Gregory lived in a turbulent time of political and moral corruption. In this climate, he served as a capable and wise administrator and adviser under five popes. His talent did not go unnoticed: during the funeral of Pope Alexander II, the people and clergy began to cry out, "Let Hildebrand be pope!" The college of cardinals formally elected him to the pontificate that same day, April 22, 1073.

Gregory immediately began to address the strained relations with the Eastern Church, the issue of clerical celibacy, and the corruption in the Church's hierarchy. His efforts led to conflict with the Emperor Henry IV. Gregory demanded justice regarding Church property and autonomy in the appointment of bishops. Henry resisted, setting up an antipope, marching on Rome, and forcing Gregory into exile. Despite these personal and political costs, Gregory persevered in the work of reform. This master administrator and diplomat died in Salerno; his last words were, "I have loved justice and hated iniquity; therefore I die in exile."

Reflection

Gregory is not a saint because of his administrative skills or political savvy but because of his love for Jesus Christ. Because he loved, he put himself and all his gifts and energies at the service of the Church, despite her imperfection. Gregory teaches us to see beyond the limitations and the humanity of the Church to the One who is at the heart of the Church, Jesus Christ.

Prayer

Pope Saint Gregory VII, teach me to love Jesus Christ and his Church—his gift to us. Amen.

MAY 26

Saint Philip Neri

July 12, 1515–May 26, 1595
Feast: May 26
Patron: Rome, U.S. Army Special Forces, comedians, joy, humor

Philip was the youngest son of a noble family of Florence. At an early age he was apprenticed to a wealthy uncle, but after a religious conversion in his eighteenth year, he moved to Rome. To support himself, Philip became a tutor, but he also dedicated his time to charitable works among the poor, the sick, and the prostitutes of the city. After finishing the necessary studies, he was ordained a priest in 1551.

With a truly pastoral heart, Philip began his lifelong apostolate. Every day he would walk about the city engaging people in conversation, helping them deepen their commitment as Christians. Many people, especially the young, would join him on little pilgrimages around Rome. These were occasions of much prayer, song, and innocent fun. Out of this work arose the Congregation of the Oratory in 1575. On the feast of Corpus Christi in 1595, after having spent the day hearing confessions, Philip announced to his brother priests, "Last of all we must die." That next morning, with a joy-filled heart, Philip very quietly breathed his last.

Reflection

Philip Neri was often likened to Socrates, the Greek philosopher who traveled around engaging those he met in conversation in order to challenge them to take life seriously, prepare for heaven, and do all with joy. He exhibited the most attractive elements of an evangelizer: creativity of expression, tireless patience, dedication to duty, gracious sensitivity, and joy. Known as the "Apostle of Rome," his life illustrates the need of constant reeducation in the faith.

Prayer

Saint Philip, man of engaging fervor and grace, help us recognize our talents and use them to attract others to a life of faith. Amen.

MAY 27

Saint Augustine of Canterbury

Died c. 604
Feast: May 27
Patron: England

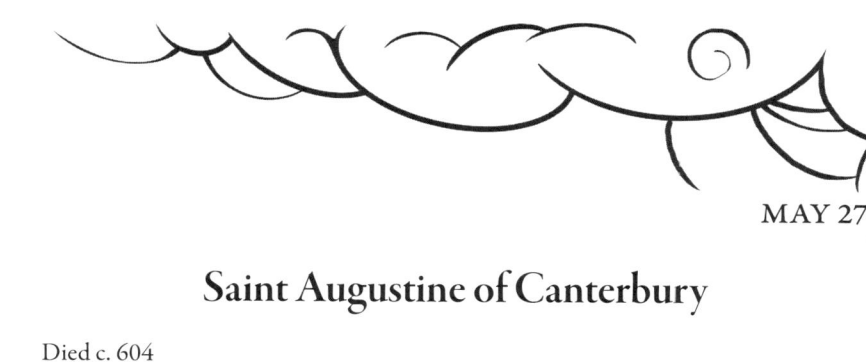

There are times when, by the grace of God, "nobody" unexpectedly becomes "somebody." Augustine, or Austin, of Canterbury is one such example. This soft-spoken monk was serving as prior in a Roman monastery when Pope Gregory the Great asked him to evangelize the Anglo-Saxons. In the spring of 597, accompanied by forty Italian and Frankish clergy—and probably already consecrated a bishop—Augustine arrived on an island off the English coast. Britain had been partially Christianized during the Roman occupation. By Augustine's time, however, the Christians (chiefly Celts) had greatly diminished in number.

Upon his arrival, Augustine met with King Ethelbert, a powerful pagan, and his wife Bertha, a Frankish Christian. The king showed no interest in Christianity. However, he permitted Augustine and his monks to settle in Kent and to preach. After a time, King Ethelbert was inspired by the example of Augustine and the other monks and asked for Baptism. He was followed by thousands of his subjects. Augustine established three dioceses despite opposition from the Welsh bishops, who prevented Augustine from carrying out some of Pope Gregory's plans. Around 604, after a life of arduous work for the Gospel, the Lord called his servant home. Augustine was buried in an abbey he had built, which is now named after this unlikely and inspiring first Archbishop of Canterbury.

Reflection

Augustine had not been eager to leave the monastery and evangelize the English. But he obeyed Pope Gregory and did his best, frequently writing to the pope for advice and adapting to adverse circumstances. How do I respond to any difficulties I experience in my vocation?

Prayer

Saint Augustine of Canterbury, help me to accept generously the tasks I find less appealing. Pray that I don't allow my preferences to impair my response. Amen.

MAY 28

Saint Madeleine Sophie Barat

December 13, 1779–May 25, 1865
Feast: May 25
Patron: Teachers, school girls

From her earliest years, Madeleine Sophie had always wanted to belong to God. The turmoil of the French Revolution prevented her from entering the Carmelites. Meanwhile, her brother Louis, who became a priest, taught her Latin, Greek, theology, and much more. The excellent education Sophie received from her brother enabled her to fulfill her dream of educating children.

In 1800, Sophie felt called by God to found the Society of the Sacred Heart. She established schools, slowly at first, but many more began to eventually spring up. The society expanded throughout Europe and even extended to Africa and North America, when Sophie sent Saint Philippine Duchesne to the United States. Due to her wisdom and good administration, Sophie led the Society for the rest of her life. She knew how to delegate and how to choose and form good collaborators. Her main goal, however, was to form the sisters in a profound spiritual life. As she would often say, "Be humble, be simple, and bring joy to others. When Jesus is the reason for your actions, he will act by his Spirit in you."

Reflection

Because a fire swept through her hometown on the night she was born, friends and family called Sophie "a child of fire." But the fire that burned in her heart was a deep love for Jesus and a desire to offer reparation for sins, especially the sacrileges committed during the French Revolution. Her desire to spread the love of Jesus was her deeper reason for focusing on education. She wanted to form children in the faith first of all and inspire them with love and zeal. How do I share the love of Jesus?

Prayer

Saint Madeleine Sophie Barat, pray for us that we too may have a heart united to Jesus so that others may experience his love. Amen.

MAY 29

Saint Hubert

c. 656–May 30, 727
Feast: November 3
Patron: Hunters, hunting dogs, foresters, mathematicians, opticians, and metalworkers

The eldest son of the Duke of Aquitaine, Hubert enjoyed a carefree life and especially loved to hunt. A legend about him says that one Good Friday, instead of going to church, he went hunting as usual. Pursuing a large white stag, Hubert was amazed when the stag turned to reveal a cross between its antlers. At the same time, he heard a voice beckoning him to convert. Hubert did exactly that and sought out Saint Lambert, bishop of Maastricht, for instruction and guidance.

When Hubert's young wife died in childbirth, he felt God's call to study for the priesthood. After his ordination, Bishop Lambert sent him on a pilgrimage to Rome. While Hubert was away, the bishop was martyred for speaking out against the Frankish prince who was in an adulterous relationship. The pope appointed Hubert as the new bishop. Hubert exercised his pastoral ministry with dedication and love. He evangelized people who had never heard the Gospel, including those living in remote areas of the Ardennes forest. His dedication to the poor, his love of prayer, and his zeal made him a beloved bishop. After Hubert's death, he was one of four saints, known as the Four Holy Marshals, who were appealed to as intercessors in the medieval Rhineland.

Reflection

Just as God had pursued him, Hubert went from hunting game to hunting souls for Christ. His example can inspire us to abandon any obsession with useless pursuits in order to pursue the desires of God's heart. What distractions in my life keep me from focusing on God and eternal life?

Prayer

Saint Hubert, pray for us so that in all of our life's pursuits, we may set our sights on our ultimate goal: heaven. Amen.

MAY 30

Saint Joan of Arc

January 6, 1412–May 30, 1431
Feast: May 30
Patron: France, military members, service women, virgins, prisoners

Joan of Arc was born to tenant farmers in northwestern France during the turbulent Hundred Years' War between England and France. From age twelve, Joan began to receive visions and hear the voices of saints, particularly Saints Michael the Archangel, Margaret of Antioch, and Catherine of Alexandria. Gradually, the voices revealed to Joan her divine mission to lead the armies of France to victory. Illiterate and powerless, Joan nevertheless had faith in the power of God. She resolved to help Charles VII, the contested heir of the French crown, take his throne in spite of English opposition.

Through gifts of prophecy and vision, Joan eventually managed to persuade the desperate Charles VII to accept her help and went on to win a decisive battle at Orléans. The people believed she was sent by God to help them, and French morale increased as her popularity grew. Consequently, Joan was able to lead a successful military campaign and saw Charles VII crowned king of France in 1429. However, a year later she was captured and handed over to the English. Seeking to rid themselves of France's beloved Maid of Orléans, Joan was condemned by pro-English clergy to burn at the stake. As the flames surrounded her, this brave nineteen-year-old girl asked for a crucifix and died with her gaze fixed on it, calling out the name of Jesus.

Reflection

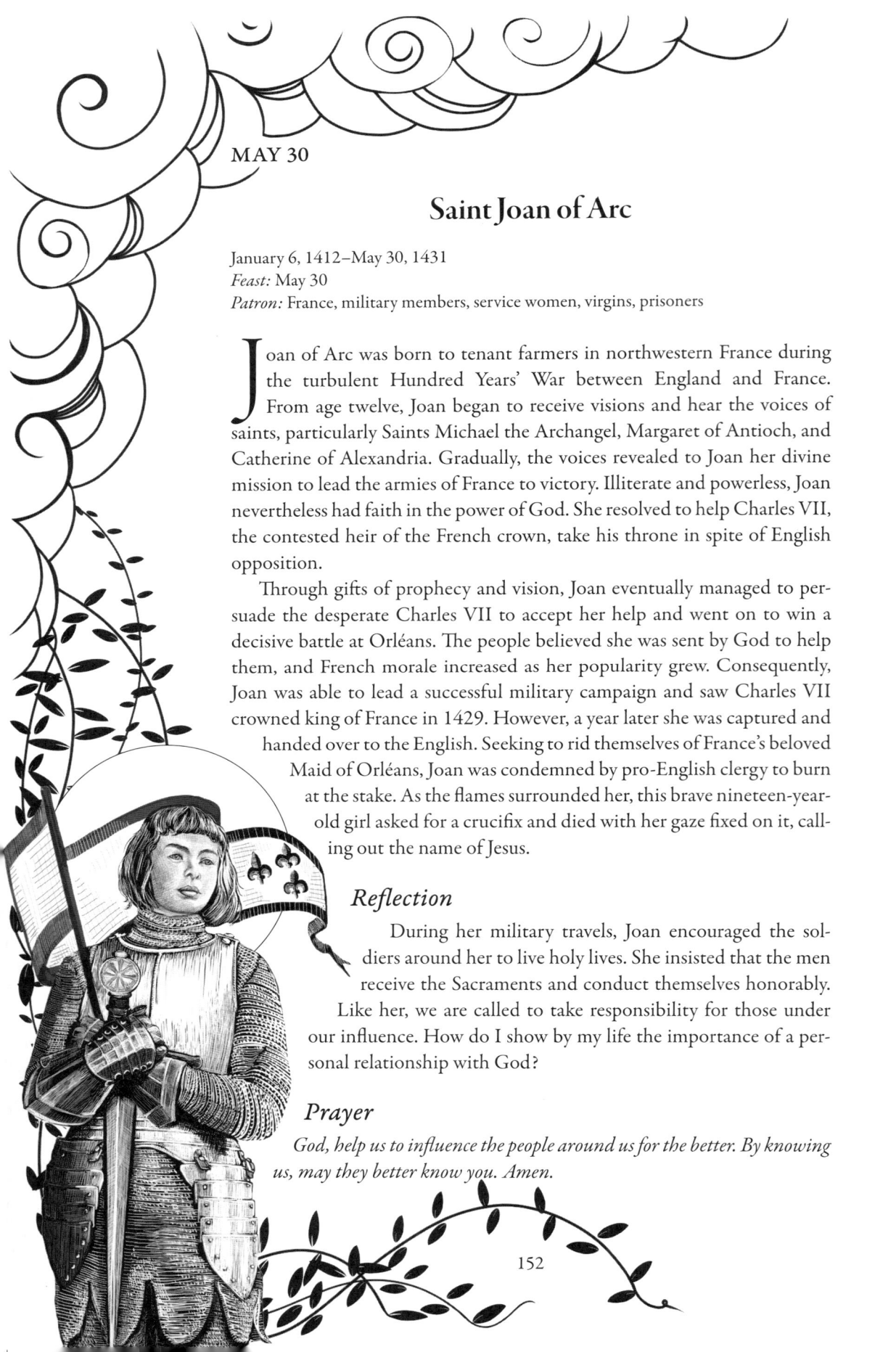

During her military travels, Joan encouraged the soldiers around her to live holy lives. She insisted that the men receive the Sacraments and conduct themselves honorably. Like her, we are called to take responsibility for those under our influence. How do I show by my life the importance of a personal relationship with God?

Prayer

God, help us to influence the people around us for the better. By knowing us, may they better know you. Amen.

MAY 31

Saint Mary Magdalene de' Pazzi

April 2, 1566–May 25, 1607
Feast: May 25
Patron: Against bodily ills and sickness, help in living a chaste life

Mary Magdalene is not well known, but she made a great contribution to the mystical tradition of the Church. She was born in Florence to a prominent family and baptized as Caterina. From a young age she had a deep prayer life. In 1582 she entered the Carmelite convent of Santa Maria degli Angeli in Florence. She chose it because the convent was known for a very rigorous life, and because the nuns were allowed to receive Holy Communion daily, an uncommon practice at that time.

Now called Sister Mary Magdalene, she began to experience intense mystical experiences after having suffered a serious illness. She did not write them down herself, but when she fell into ecstasy she would begin speaking. Her confessor asked that the other nuns transcribe her words. Her words filled five volumes that have a very distinctive oral quality and at times can seem like a drama being acted out. Love for Jesus was at the core of Mary Magdalene's interior life, and she suffered to see how many people were indifferent to his love for them. She died at the age of forty-one and was canonized in 1669.

Reflection

Mary Magdalene would sometimes ring the bells of the convent and cry, "Come and love Love!" Driven by this zeal, she longed for others to love God and encouraged her sisters to love Jesus with all their hearts. Her ardent love for Jesus can help us reflect on our own love for him. How do I respond to Jesus' love for me?

Prayer

Saint Mary Magdalene de' Pazzi, pray for us that our hearts might burn ardently with love for Jesus and the desire to make him known. Do not let us abandon Love. Amen.

JUNE 1

Saint Justin Martyr

c. 100–c. 165
Feast: June 1
Patron: Philosophers, speakers, those who write in defense of the faith (apologists)

A Gentile from Samaria, Justin's passionate search for truth led him to study philosophy. But his efforts left him unsatisfied. He recounted in his writings that one day he met an old man by the seashore. The man talked to Justin about philosophy's limitations in knowing God, the prophets, and Jesus Christ. Justin began to consider Christianity, and he soon converted. He eventually traveled to Rome and instructed many in the faith, continuing to wear the cloak of a philosopher. He wrote several works but only a few survived: *First Apology*, *Second Apology*, and *Dialogue with Trypho*. In his writings Justin described the baptismal rite and the Mass of his day.

Justin's fervent and public affirmation of the Christian faith soon brought him into conflict with the authorities. His trial before the Roman prefect Rusticus is preserved in the *Acts* of his martyrdom. At one point in the *Acts*, Justin affirms his belief in heaven. Rusticus responds, "You imagine then that you shall go to heaven and be rewarded there?" Justin then declares, "I do not suppose it, but I know and am fully persuaded of it."

Reflection

Justin teaches us that the truth matters. He was among the first in a long line of Catholic thinkers who have used philosophy to support the truths of faith. Justin's intellectual endeavors were no mere academic exercise. He gave his life in witness to Jesus Christ rather than deny the truth. What place does the pursuit of truth have in my life?

Prayer

Saint Justin, at your trial you testified to the hope of eternal life. Pray for us that one day we may join you in the blessedness of heaven. Amen.

JUNE 2

Saints Marcellinus and Peter

Died c. 303
Feast: June 2
Patron: Persecuted Christians

These two saints were widely honored in the early Church because of their heroic martyrdom under Diocletian. Marcellinus was a priest and Peter an exorcist. Legend says that Peter had been imprisoned for declaring his faith. While there, he freed the jailer's daughter from an evil spirit. The jailer, his family, and many of the other prisoners converted, and Marcellinus baptized them. This infuriated the Romans who ordered their execution, carried out in the forest so that no one would honor their relics.

However, God had other plans. Two Christian women found the bodies of Macellinus and Peter and buried them after receiving a vision from their relative, the martyr Tiburtius, accompanied by Marcellinus and Peter. The Catacombs of Marcellinus and Peter, located outside Rome, contain a rich collection of early Christian paintings. The fourth-century Pope Damasus wrote an epitaph for their tomb. Constantine built a basilica in their honor, and in 827 Pope Gregory IV transferred their relics to present-day Germany.

Reflection

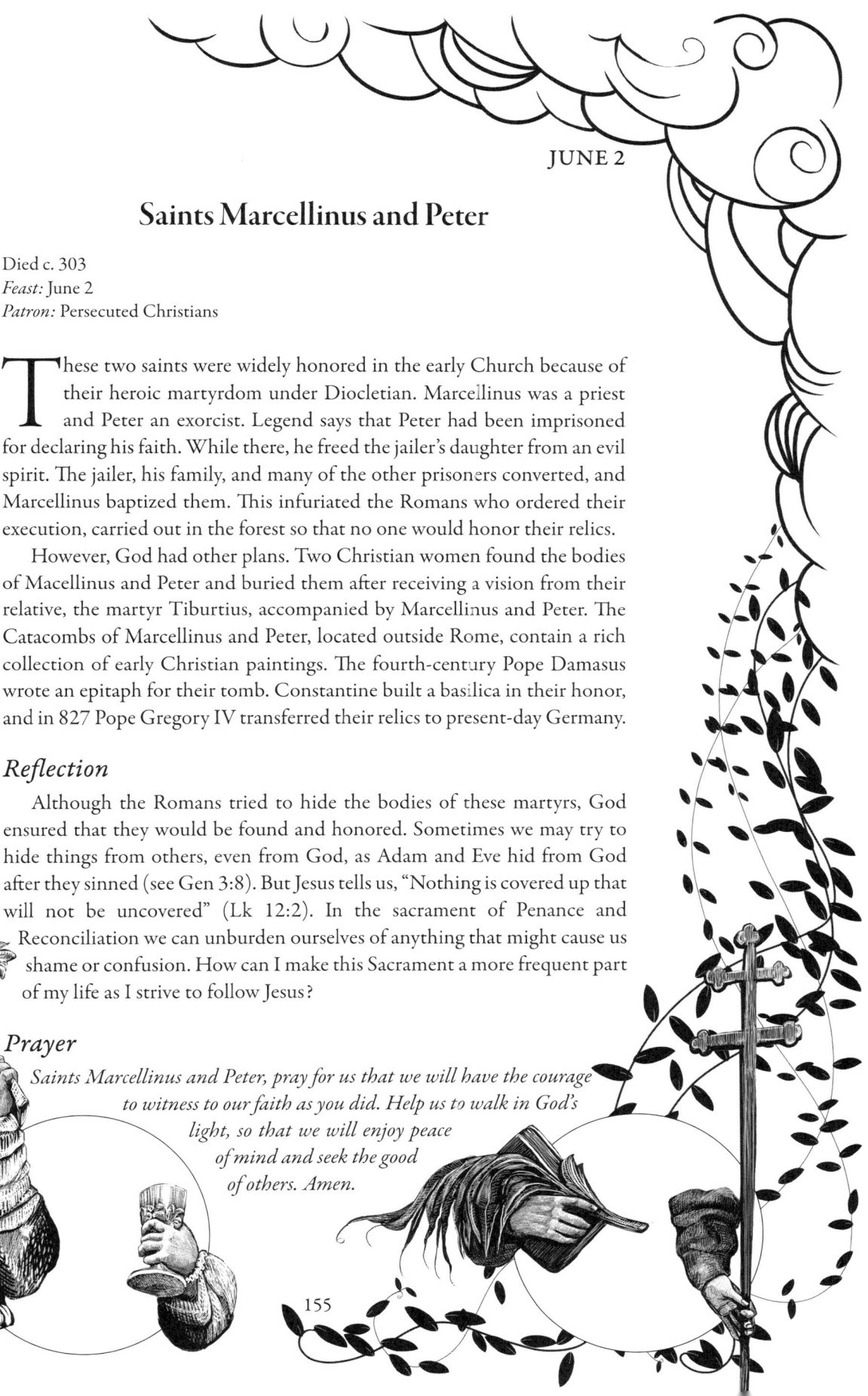

Although the Romans tried to hide the bodies of these martyrs, God ensured that they would be found and honored. Sometimes we may try to hide things from others, even from God, as Adam and Eve hid from God after they sinned (see Gen 3:8). But Jesus tells us, "Nothing is covered up that will not be uncovered" (Lk 12:2). In the sacrament of Penance and Reconciliation we can unburden ourselves of anything that might cause us shame or confusion. How can I make this Sacrament a more frequent part of my life as I strive to follow Jesus?

Prayer

Saints Marcellinus and Peter, pray for us that we will have the courage to witness to our faith as you did. Help us to walk in God's light, so that we will enjoy peace of mind and seek the good of others. Amen.

JUNE 3

Saint Charles Lwanga and Companions

c. 1860–June 3, 1886
Feast: June 3
Patron: Uganda, youth, catechumens

Charles Lwanga had been baptized just over six months when he willingly and courageously accepted martyrdom along with twenty-one other young men. Christian missionaries had recently come to Buganda (now Uganda), a fertile field for the Gospel. King Mutesa welcomed them. But after he died, his son, King Mwanga II, was opposed to the new religion. Many of the pages in the royal court had converted, and this complicated the king's habit of demanding sexual favors. His chief steward, Joseph Mukasa, a Christian, reproached the king for his abuse and for the murder of an Anglican bishop. Mwanga killed Joseph in turn. Charles replaced Joseph in his office. But Charles also opposed the king and protected the young pages from Mwanga's sexual advances.

Mwanga soon decided to round up Charles and his pages. Those who admitted they were Christians were forced to march over thirty miles to a place where they were burned to death. As the leader, Charles was made to die a slow death, but he said, "You are burning me, but it is as if you are pouring water over my body." In 1964 Saint Paul VI canonized this group of twenty-two martyrs who all died between 1885 and 1887. During this time of persecution, both Anglicans and Catholics were killed.

Reflection

A photo of twenty of the young martyrs was taken when they visited a Catholic mission. Their youth is striking. God's grace can transform anyone into heroes and saints. On our own, trusting in ourselves, we can't do it. But the Holy Spirit who works in us can do what we cannot. In what ways can my actions, great and small, be heroic if I trust in God?

Prayer

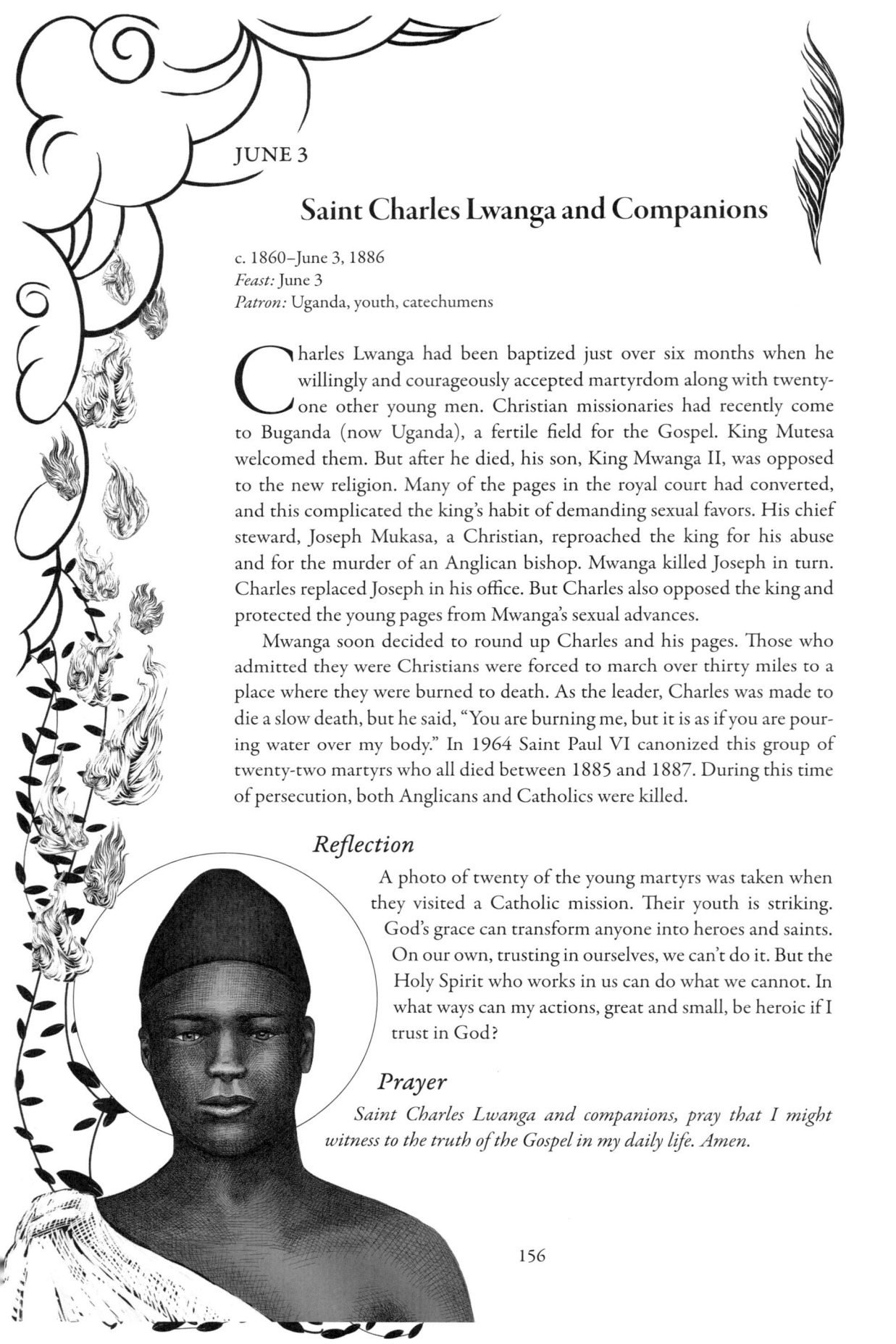

Saint Charles Lwanga and companions, pray that I might witness to the truth of the Gospel in my daily life. Amen.

JUNE 4

Saint Filippo Smaldone

July 27, 1848–June 4, 1923
Feast: June 4
Patron: Deaf people, mute people

The oldest of seven children, Filippo was born in Naples, Italy. While studying for the priesthood, he began to minister to people who were deaf and mute. After Filippo was ordained a priest, he was able to devote himself completely to this ministry. At one point, while he was ministering to the sick, Filippo caught cholera. He was miraculously cured through the intercession of Our Lady of Pompeii.

Filippo's work was not easy, and he eventually became discouraged because of his apparent lack of success. He was tempted to give up and instead go to the foreign missions, but his spiritual director helped him through this crisis. Filippo recognized that God wanted him to stay in Italy and work for the deaf. In 1885, Filippo went to Lecce and founded an institute for the deaf and mute with Father Lorenzo Apicella and a group of sisters. Soon a new congregation developed: the Salesian Sisters of the Sacred Hearts. Despite constant problems and difficulties, the institute gradually expanded. Filippo died knowing that the important work he had begun would be continued.

Reflection

Filippo joined concern for the poor and needy with a profound life of prayer. He had a special devotion to the Eucharist and founded a group dedicated to adoration: the Eucharistic League of Priest Adorers and Women Adorers. Before Jesus in the Eucharist, Filippo received the insight and strength to carry out his work among the deaf, mute, and poor. He believed in Jesus' words: "Those who abide in me and I in them bear much fruit, because apart from me you can do nothing" (Jn 15:5). What gives me the strength to do God's will?

Prayer

Saint Filippo Smaldone, pray for us that we might spend time in prayer with you and trust in the Lord who is the giver of all good gifts. Amen.

JUNE 5

Saint Boniface

c. 674–June 5, 754
Feast: June 5
Patron: Germany, brewers

Named Wynfrith at birth, Boniface was an Englishman who would be forever known as the Apostle of Germany. He became a Benedictine monk and in 716 went from England on his first mission to Frisia. After about a year he returned home due to difficult conditions. But he soon left again, this time for Rome, where he met Pope Gregory II. Recognizing his potential, the pope gave him the name Boniface and sent him to Germania.

Boniface's work largely consisted of a first proclamation of the Gospel to the pagan Germanic tribes. He is famous for felling the Donar Oak, a large tree dedicated to Thor and venerated by the pagan people. When Boniface was not struck by lightning after felling the tree, many were baptized. Upon hearing of his success, Pope Gregory II recalled Boniface and consecrated him bishop. Traveling widely, Boniface established dioceses throughout the region, as well as many monasteries. In his old age, Boniface continued his dangerous work until, along with a group of fifty-two other Christians, he died at the hands of a band of angry looters. Boniface had foreseen and accepted his death and was found next to a slashed copy of Ambrose's *The Advantage of Death*.

Reflection

Boniface helped spread and establish Christianity in Germany. It required hard, dangerous work, but Boniface was willing to give all for the Gospel. Today, it is up to us to continue the work of evangelization, so that the seeds sown long ago will continue to bear fruit. How does what I do speak of Christ to those who may not know him?

Prayer

Saint Boniface, your zeal for the Gospel made you a tireless missionary. Pray for us that we too may feel the urgency to bring the light of Christ to those who do not yet know him. Amen.

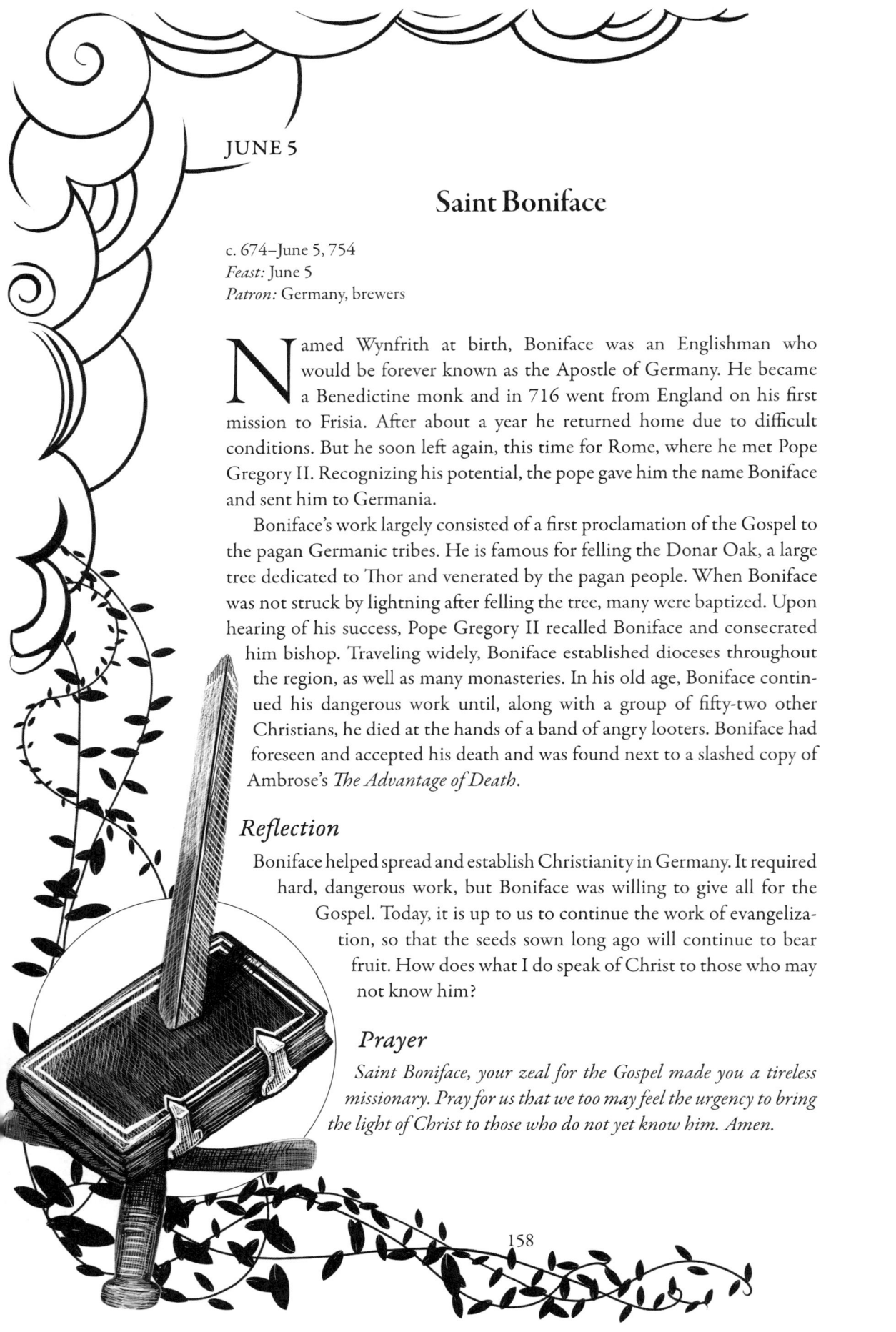

JUNE 6

Saint Norbert

c. 1080–June 6, 1134
Feast: June 6
Patron: Safe delivery of babies, for peace, Bohemia

God doesn't usually strike people with a lightning bolt to get their attention, but it happened to Norbert. Born to a noble family in the German town of Xanten, he led a frivolous life in his youth. He was ordained a subdeacon only as a way to further his earthly fortunes. One day during a storm, lightning struck the horse Norbert was riding and it threw him to the ground, knocking him unconscious. Shaken, he reflected on his worldly life and this led to his complete conversion.

Norbert adopted a strict regimen of prayer and penance, and eventually his holiness of life drew followers. He became a priest and worked as an itinerant preacher. The Church needed reforms among the clergy, and various heretical ideas were spreading. Norbert preached to counteract the false ideas and began a reform movement for the clergy. When he was in France, a bishop allowed him to establish a foundation at Prémontré. On Christmas Day 1121, he and forty companions professed vows. That was the beginning of the Canons Regular of Prémontré, or Norbertines. The order soon spread throughout Europe. In 1126, Norbert became the bishop of Magdeburg in Germany, where he continued to carry out renewal efforts until his death.

Reflection

Jesus said, "The kingdom of heaven is like yeast that a woman took and mixed in with three measures of flour until all of it was leavened" (Mt 13:33). Norbert's work of renewal worked like yeast: it stirred up greater fervor in the Church to build God's kingdom. In our day, too, the Church needs renewal. How might I contribute to that effort by my own daily conversion?

Prayer

Saint Norbert, pray that my efforts to love God and my neighbor might serve to build up the Church in today's world. Amen.

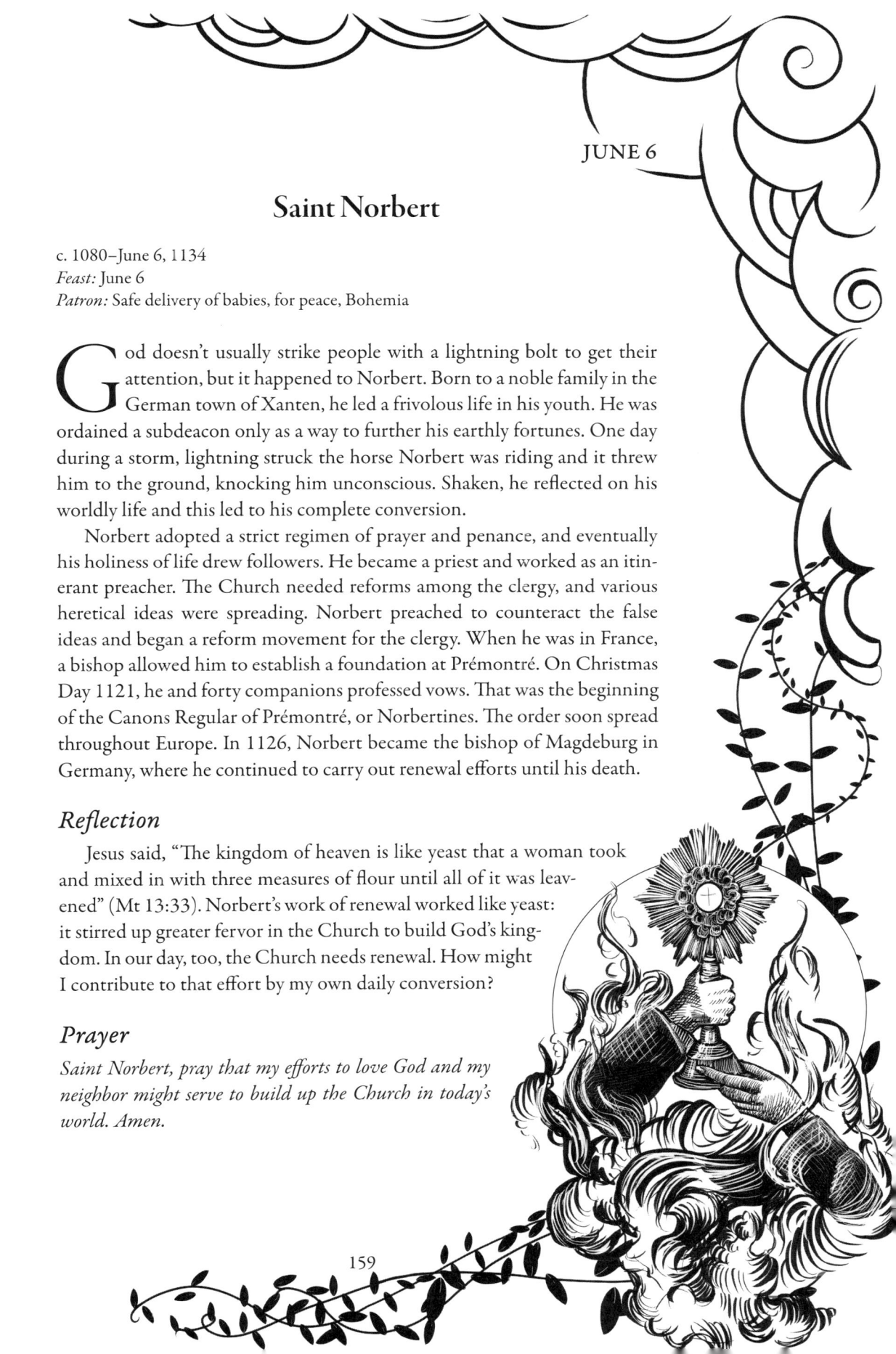

JUNE 7

Saint Clotilda

c. 474–June 3, 545
Feast: June 3
Patron: Brides, adopted children

Saint Clotilda was a princess, the daughter of the king of the Burgundians. She married King Clovis of the Franks. Uncertainty surrounds the details of her life because, from the sixth century onward, many epic narratives were written about the marriage of Clovis and Clotilda, with contradictory information. Her story is intermingled with the history of conflicts of the time, including that between Catholicism and Arian sects.

We do know, however, that Clotilda was Catholic while Clovis was pagan. Before marrying Clovis, a promise was secured that Clotilda could practice her faith. She did so and had her children baptized despite the occasional protests of her husband. Clotilda prayed fervently for her husband's conversion. Finally, at a battle near Cologne, Clovis prayed to "the God of Clotilda" and promised to be baptized if he were victorious—he was. The baptism of Clovis and many of the Franks led to the spread of Christianity in the West.

Reflection

While one would think that the life of royalty would be a pleasant one, Clotilda had much to suffer in her life. After the death of her husband, fighting arose among her sons. Deeply saddened, Clotilda left court to retire to Tours, near the tomb of Saint Martin of Tours. According to legend, one time after praying all night to prevent one of her sons from killing the other, a storm arose that stopped the battle. Clotilda's example of suffering love can inspire us to believe in the power of God to transform the lives of our loved ones, even when things seem hopeless.

Prayer

Saint Clotilda, you persevered in evangelizing your family in the midst of many difficulties. Help us to persist in praying for our families, knowing that God brings change when we least expect it. Amen.

JUNE 8

Saint Columba

c. 521–June 9, 597
Feast: June 9
Patron: Ireland, Scotland, missionaries, bookbinders

Descended from kings through both parents, Columba was born into a powerful clan in Donegal in Northern Ireland, a generation or two after Saint Patrick's time. His name means "dove" in Latin. Actually, it may have been a nickname, for he was a gentle youth who loved to study the Scriptures and write poetry. Columba became a monk and spent about fifteen years as an itinerant preacher. During this time, he also founded the monasteries of Derry, Durrow, and Kells. With the build of a warrior, Columba had strength and endurance that enabled him to live and promote an austere lifestyle.

At forty-two, Columba abruptly left Ireland with twelve companions. According to one account, his kinsmen had avenged an injustice that had angered him, and the monk went into exile to atone for the loss of life. The little group sailed to a Scottish island, where they built a monastery and Columba wrote a monastic rule. From this base, the future Iona, they traveled in small groups to bring the Gospel to the Celts and Picts. Eventually, when Columba's strength began to fail, he returned to Iona to take up scholarly pursuits. In his declining years he remained as gentle and peaceful as he had been in his youth.

Reflection

Whatever the reason for his exile—reparation, flight, or pure missionary zeal—Columba made the best of his changed circumstances and accomplished much good. His biographer drew attention to how well he used his time: not a waking hour passed that Columba was not praying or carrying out some other useful activity. How much time do I dedicate to the Lord?

Prayer

Saint Columba, when my circumstances seem less than ideal, teach me how to rise above the situation and truly make the best of it. Amen.

JUNE 9

Saint Ephrem the Syrian

c. 306–June 9, 373
Feast: June 9
Patron: Spiritual directors, pastors, hymn writers

Ephrem is called "the harp of the Holy Spirit" because of the beauty and depth of his writings. Born into a Christian family in Nisibis, Mesopotamia (in modern Turkey), Ephrem was baptized and later became a deacon. Extremely prolific, his hymns were not only beautiful but also instructed people in the faith. He wrote much on the Virgin Mary, whom he saw as the New Eve and as a figure of the Church. He was one of the first of the early Marian writers to express a deep love and personal devotion to Mary. He speaks of her as "the fruitful vine, by whom we are brought from death to life."

Ephrem moved to Edessa when the Persians invaded his homeland. There he continued to live an ascetical life and use his great talents to teach and catechize, especially through his hymns. Besides his writing and teaching, Ephrem also ministered to the people in Edessa. He died as a result of his work helping victims of the plague that struck the city in 373.

Reflection

At a time when many people were illiterate, Ephrem composed hymns that could be used as catechetical tools. In the fourth century, many errors were being promoted, such as the Arian heresy. Ephrem's hymns dealt with these errors in a way that people could understand. He used the best means of his day to evangelize. In our time we can take Ephrem's example and use our modern means of communication to spread the Gospel.

Prayer

Saint Ephrem, you wrote beautifully about the Virgin Mary. Pray for me that I too may grow in my love and devotion to her, the great Mother of God. Amen.

JUNE 10

Saint Catherine of Bologna

September 8, 1413–March 9, 1463
Feast: March 9
Patron: Artists

Catherine was born into a wealthy family in Bologna. Around the age of ten, she was sent to Ferrara to live at the court of Nicholas III d'Este as a lady-in-waiting to his daughter Margaret. There Catherine received a good education, learning Latin and studying the arts, especially music, poetry, painting, and writing. In the midst of luxury, however, Catherine felt drawn to God. Eventually she left the court to live with a group of devout women. Later, she and some of the women formed a monastic community that followed the Rule of Saint Clare of Assisi. She was then asked to become abbess of the sisters and open a foundation in Bologna, which she obediently did.

In religious life, Catherine experienced great consolations, but also endured dark periods when it seemed as if God had abandoned her. At one point, troubled by her sins, she made a devout confession and afterward had a profound experience of God's divine mercy that affected her deeply. Catherine wrote a treatise called *The Seven Spiritual Weapons*, in which she offered practical advice to her sisters and shared some of what she had learned through her own spiritual struggles. When she was near death, she assured her grieving sisters that she would help them from heaven.

Reflection

Catherine's experience of divine mercy made a profound impression on her and gave direction to the rest of her life. Each of us can experience the same mercy Catherine experienced when we let God into our hearts. No matter what our past has held, when we repent, the greatest sins dissolve before the rays of God's mercy.

Prayer

Saint Catherine of Bologna, pray that, like you, we may receive an abundant outpouring of God's generous mercy and grace. Amen.

JUNE 11

Saint Barnabas, the Apostle

First Century
Feast: June 11
Patron: Cyprus, peacemakers, weavers, against hailstorms

Though Barnabas was not one of the original twelve, he is referred to as an apostle because of the great missionary work he carried out in the early Church. In Scripture, we first meet Barnabas, a Jewish convert living in Jerusalem, when he sells a piece of land and presents the profits to the apostles (see Acts 4:36–37). Born Joseph, the apostles nickname him Barnabas, meaning "son of encouragement," which gives us insight into his personality!

Perhaps due to his gift of encouragement, Barnabas saw the potential in Saint Paul before others did. When Paul arrived in Jerusalem after his conversion and found that the Christian community feared him (see Acts 9:26), Barnabas introduced Paul to the apostles. Later, Barnabas searched out Paul in Tarsus and asked him to accompany him to Antioch to preach the Gospel (see Acts 11:25). Together, the two men traveled to many places, including Cyprus, Syria, and Greece. Bringing the Gospel to many people, they worked miracles and faced challenges. Eventually, the two friends had a disagreement and decided to go their separate ways. Barnabas continued his missionary work with his relative, John Mark, who is traditionally believed to be the author of the Gospel of Mark. According to tradition, Barnabus' life ended when he was stoned to death by his countrymen at Salamis, in Cyprus.

Reflection

Saint Luke describes Barnabas as "a good man, full of the Holy Spirit and of faith" (Acts 11:24). Barnabas' love for God and others made him a fervent preacher of the Gospel. Certainly, his joyful, encouraging disposition also made his preaching more credible. How can I be an encouragement to others?

Prayer

Saint Barnabas the Apostle, pray that I might become more aware of how I'm called to be an encouragement to those around me. Amen.

JUNE 12

Blessed Anna Maria Taigi

May 29, 1769–June 9, 1837
Feast: June 9
Patron: Wives, mothers

Outwardly, Anna Maria Taigi seemed like an ordinary wife and mother. But she lived a very intense prayer life that included extraordinary phenomena. Born in Siena, her family moved to Rome when she was a little girl. She married Dominic Taigi, a good man with a difficult character marked by unpredictable fits of anger. Anna Maria knew how to handle her husband and they had a holy, loving marriage despite their difficulties.

However, Anna Maria did not begin her marriage close to God. At first, she led a vain life until she had a conversion experience and made a good confession. She became a Third Order Trinitarian and found a spiritual director. As her prayer life developed, God gave her many gifts, including mystical visions and the ability to prophesy the future. Hearing of these gifts, many sought her counsel, including the pope. Though she was the target of calumny and jealousy, Anna Maria always remained focused on God's will and the essentials of holiness: prayer, penance, and love of God and neighbor. Pope Benedict XV beatified her in 1920.

Reflection

The mystical phenomena in her life might lead us to dismiss Anna Maria as an odd saint who defies imitation. But her love for difficult people is a lesson we all could learn. To love even those who seem unlovable is the test of a true follower of Jesus, who said, "For if you love those who love you, what reward do you have? Do not even the tax collectors do the same?" (Mt 5:46).

Prayer

Blessed Anna Maria Taigi, pray that we may show God's love to all we meet, even if they seem unlovable to us. Amen.

JUNE 13

Saint Anthony of Padua

c. 1195–June 13, 1231
Feast: June 13
Patron: Amputees, faith in the Blessed Sacrament, infertility, lost articles, preachers

If we think of Saint Anthony only when we lose car keys or wallets, we will miss his true greatness. He was born in Lisbon as Fernando Martins de Bulhões. At age fifteen, he joined the Canons Regular of Saint Augustine and spent several years in study. When he venerated the bodies of the first Franciscan martyrs, he decided to join that new order. Fernando traveled to Italy and became a friar. Known as Anthony, he went to Morocco hoping to become a martyr too, but he got sick and had to return to Italy.

Anthony then attended the General Chapter meetings at Assisi in 1220 and there met Saint Francis. Though very learned, Anthony did not broadcast his abilities and went generally unnoticed by his fellow friars. He was assigned to Monte Paolo, a monastery near Forli, and spent his days in hiddenness. One day, surprisingly, he was prevailed upon to preach at an ordination of both Dominicans and Franciscans. The power and fervor of his words stunned the audience and after that Anthony preached constantly. Steeped in Scripture, his words persuaded people to live a holy life. Pope Pius XII named him a Doctor of the Church in 1946.

Reflection

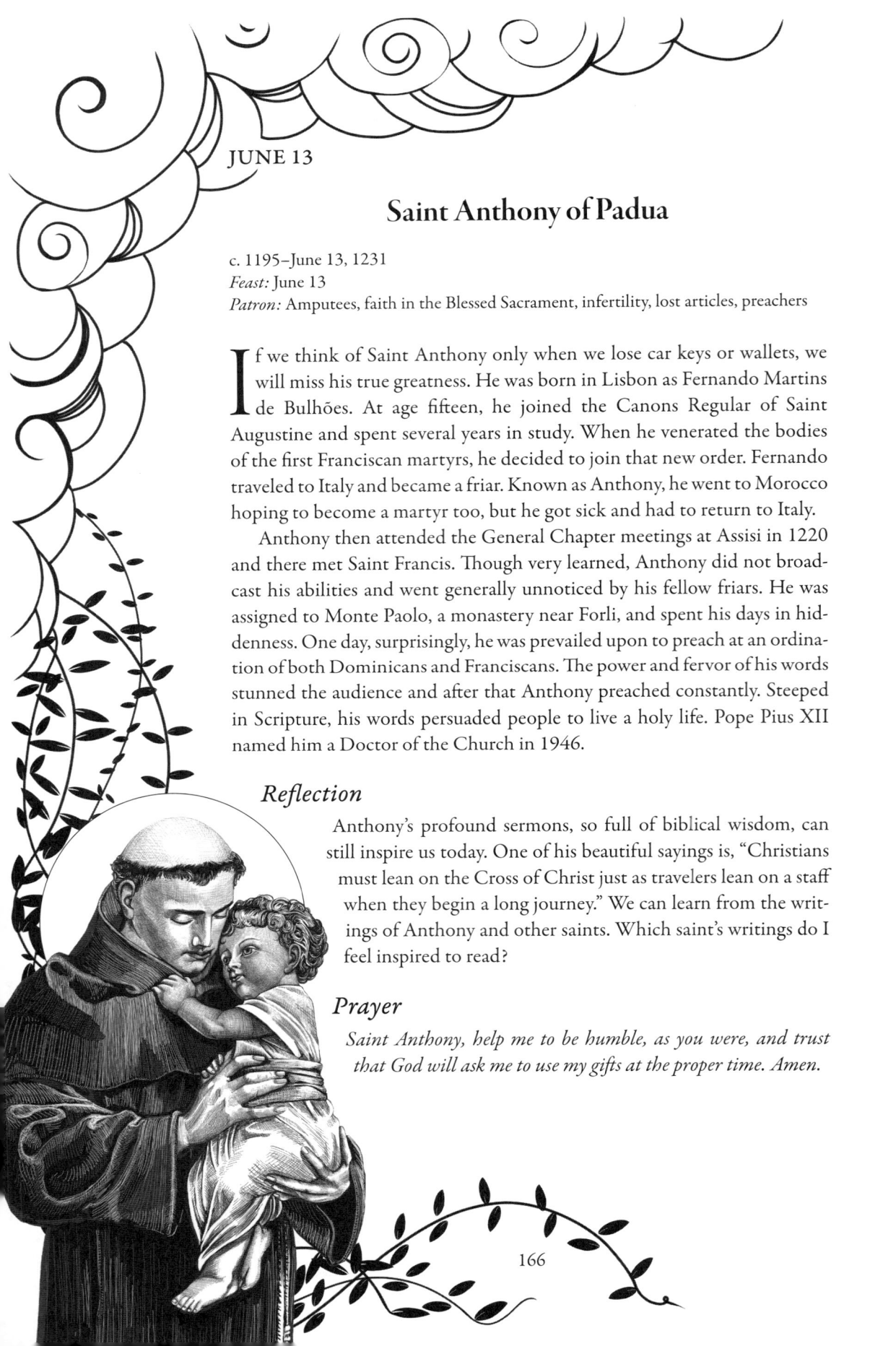

Anthony's profound sermons, so full of biblical wisdom, can still inspire us today. One of his beautiful sayings is, "Christians must lean on the Cross of Christ just as travelers lean on a staff when they begin a long journey." We can learn from the writings of Anthony and other saints. Which saint's writings do I feel inspired to read?

Prayer

Saint Anthony, help me to be humble, as you were, and trust that God will ask me to use my gifts at the proper time. Amen.

JUNE 14

Saint Germaine Cousin

1579–1601
Feast: June 15
Patron: The disabled, the physically unattractive, and victims of abuse

Born in southern France near Toulouse, Germaine suffered from disfigurement and paralysis of her right hand. Her mother died when she was an infant, and her father soon married a woman who hated Germaine and abused her terribly. Her stepmother fed her scraps of food and forced her to sleep under the stairs and in the stable. Each day, Germaine spent long hours caring for the family's sheep. In the fields, Germaine learned to talk to God, spending much of the time in prayer. She attended Mass daily, entrusting her flock to divine providence. And though the area was riddled with wolves, she never lost a single sheep.

At first, Germaine's neighbors thought she was eccentric and mocked her piety. But children liked her, and she delighted in speaking to them about God. The adults eventually became convinced of her holiness and her stepmother even invited her back home to live with the family. Germaine refused, however, content with her simple life of close communion with God. After she died at age twenty-two, the people of her village often prayed to her in time of need and many miracles occurred through her intercession.

Reflection

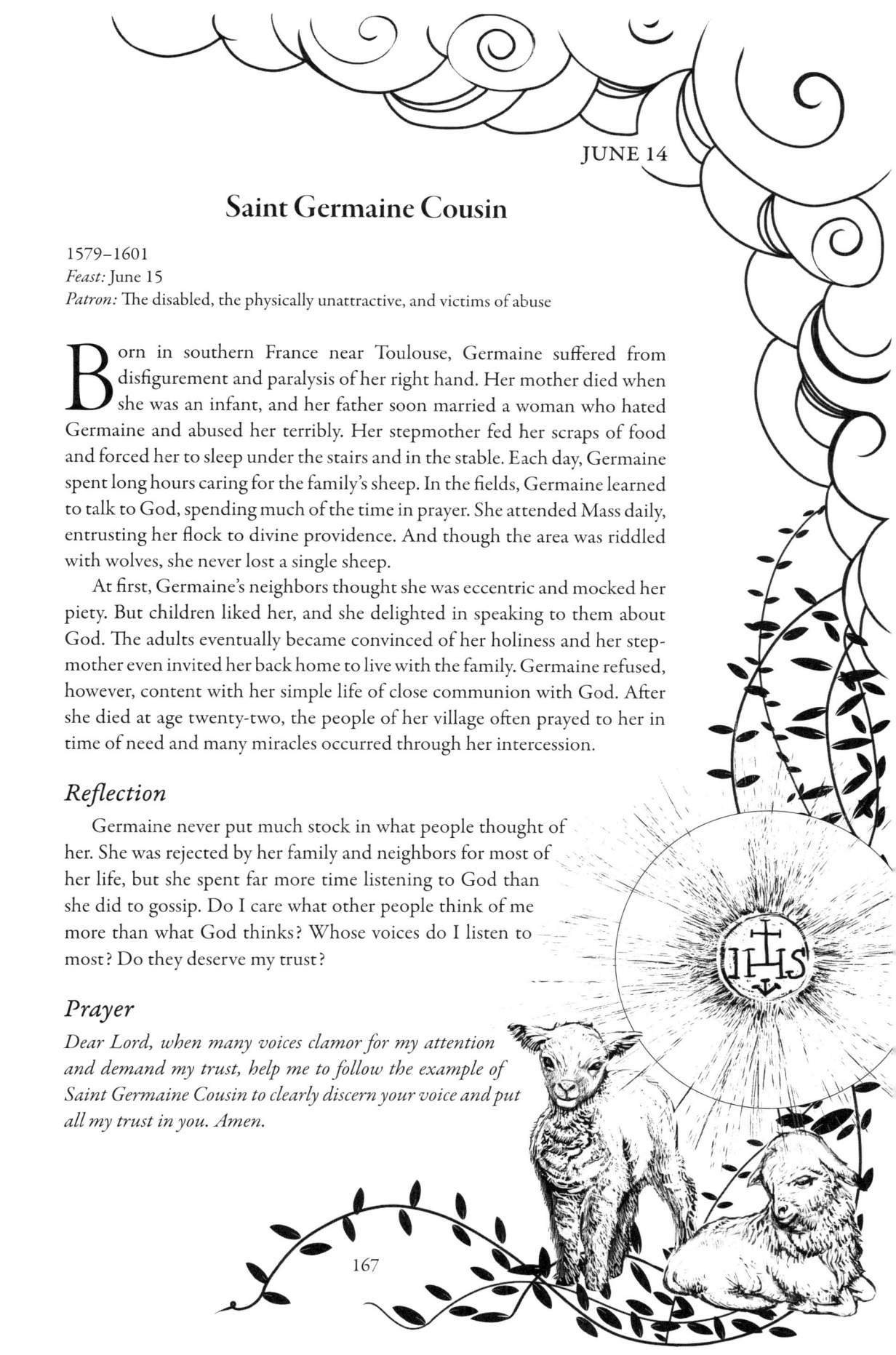

Germaine never put much stock in what people thought of her. She was rejected by her family and neighbors for most of her life, but she spent far more time listening to God than she did to gossip. Do I care what other people think of me more than what God thinks? Whose voices do I listen to most? Do they deserve my trust?

Prayer

Dear Lord, when many voices clamor for my attention and demand my trust, help me to follow the example of Saint Germaine Cousin to clearly discern your voice and put all my trust in you. Amen.

JUNE 15

Blessed Clemente Vismara

September 6, 1897–June 15, 1988
Feast: June 15
Patron: Myanmar, missionaries

Born in the Lombardy region of Italy, Clemente Vismara was orphaned as a small child. During World War I he fought in the Italian army, earning medals for courage. His wartime experiences confirmed his desire to become a missionary priest. He entered the Institute of Foreign Missions of Milan, now known as the Pontifical Institute for Foreign Missions (PIME).

After his ordination in 1923, Clemente left for Burma (now Myanmar). In the remote region where he served, he faced many difficulties: the climate was harsh, opium addiction common, and women and children were treated like property. In the territory assigned to Clemente, Buddhism was the predominant religion, and no one was Catholic. Undeterred, Clemente endeared himself to the people with his good will. He turned away no one who sought his assistance and was especially dedicated to widows and orphans.

During his nearly sixty-five years in Burma, Clemente founded five missionary districts, taught trades, evangelized, introduced agricultural improvements, established factories, and built chapels and schools. He wrote many letters and articles that raised awareness and support for his missions. When the holy man with the striking white beard, often called the "Patriarch of Burma," died at age ninety-one, crowds of people attended his funeral. He was beatified by Pope Benedict XVI in 2011.

Reflection

Clemente was a joyful man who loved his vocation as a missionary priest. Though elderly when he died, Clemente never got old. He remained passionate about his calling until his death, giving his entire life in service to others. How can I give my all in service to God and others whatever my age?

Prayer

Blessed Clemente Vismara, pray that I too might remain young at heart and fulfill my vocation through a life given in joyful service to others. Amen.

JUNE 16

Blessed Francisca de Paula de Jesús

1808–June 14, 1895
Feast: June 14
Patron: The poor, victims of slavery

Known as Nhá Chica, Francisca de Paula de Jesús is a favorite saint of Brazil. Born a poor slave in São João del Rei, Francisca had a difficult start in life materially. But spiritually she was blessed. Her mother had her baptized and instilled a deep faith in her. When Francisca was a young teenager, her family was freed from slavery. However, her mother died shortly after. A strong-willed girl, Francisca not only survived but thrived. Though she had few resources, she refused marriage proposals and decided to live a simple life in a humble two-room house.

Francisca regularly invited the poor to her home and radiated love and warmth to everyone. People began to affectionately call her Nhá Chica, or Aunt Francie. When a brother left her a considerable inheritance, Nhá Chica used the money for her charitable projects. Nhá Chica was deeply devoted to Mary and worked to spread this devotion to others as she helped the poor. She even had a shrine built to the Blessed Mother, known as Our Lady of Conception Sanctuary. Nhá Chica was buried there after her death, and popular devotion to this "Mother of the Poor" grew. Thousands flocked to her beatification in 2013.

Reflection

Nhá Chica's life is a testimony to the power of faith and trust in God. Poor and illiterate, she had nothing when her mother died. Yet, because of her great trust, she had everything. Do I trust that the Lord can work through my gifts and limitations?

Prayer

Saint Francisca de Paula de Jesús, pray for us that we might entrust ourselves wholly to Jesus and spend ourselves in helping the needy in our midst. Amen.

JUNE 17

Blessed Hildegard Burjan

January 30, 1883–June 11, 1933
Feast: June 12
Patron: Politicians, pregnant mothers who are ill

Modern politicians are not often called "saints." But Hildegard Burjan, a laywoman and legislator, defies this generalization. Hildegard came from a middle-class German family of Jewish origin. While studying for her doctorate in philosophy, she met and married Alexander Burjan. As a student, Hildegard had grappled with Christianity. After nearly dying from kidney disease in 1908, Hildegard set aside her doubts and converted to Catholicism. Hildegard and Alexander then moved to Vienna and she became pregnant. Doctors advised the couple to have an abortion due to her health problems. Hildegard refused and continued the difficult pregnancy. She gave birth to a healthy daughter, Lisa.

Influenced by Pope Leo XIII's social encyclical, *Rerum Novarum*, Hildegard began to discern how she could help the poor. She founded associations to help workers and their families. In 1918 she entered politics and, the following year, became one of the first women elected to the Austrian parliament. A gifted politician, Hildegard devoted herself to issues such as welfare, workers' rights, and education initiatives. In 1919 Hildegard founded *Caritas Socialis*, a group of religious sisters who provided social services and spiritual care to the needy. Having accomplished much in her short life, Hildegard died at age fifty and was beatified in 2012.

Reflection

Hildegard's Catholic faith informed her public and private life. Catholic social teaching was the foundation for Hildegard's life, and her inspired work continues today. How do I live my faith both personally and politically?

Prayer

Blessed Hildegard Burjan, your faith shaped your responses to the challenging situations faced by your family, community, and constituents. Pray that I too might look to the Church for guidance when making difficult decisions. Amen.

JUNE 18

Saint María Guadalupe García Zavala

April 27, 1878–June 24, 1963
Feast: June 24
Patron: Nurses

Born in the town of Zapopan in Mexico, María Guadalupe García Zavala never planned to become a religious sister. In fact, at the age of twenty-three she was engaged to be married. But she could not deny the strong pull of the call of God to give herself totally to him as a religious. After praying and consulting with her spiritual director, María discerned that the Lord was inviting her to found a new congregation of religious sisters. The new community, founded in 1901, was named the Handmaids of Saint Margaret Mary and the Poor, in honor of the saint who popularized the devotion to the Sacred Heart of Jesus. The women who joined would be nurses in hospitals and care for the physical and spiritual needs of all people.

Soon after the congregation's founding, however, Mexico began to experience great political turmoil that included the persecution of Catholics. María, affectionately known as Madre Lupita, took risks to protect priests who were in danger. The community helped to hide several priests, including the Archbishop of Guadalajara. Madre Lupita and her sisters served anyone who came to them for help, including anti-Catholics. When the hospital where the sisters worked ran out of supplies, Madre Lupita would go out to beg for donations. After a long illness, she died at age eighty-five, but her earthly work continues through her religious sisters, who now have convents in five countries.

Reflection

Madre Lupita was courageous and bold with the love she showed in her hospitals, caring even for those who were persecuting Catholics. She truly lived Jesus' command to love her enemies (see Lk 6:35). In what ways can I be loving toward those I find difficult and hope for their good?

Prayer

God, help me to be like Saint María Guadalupe, always looking for the good in people so that I may love them as you do. Amen.

JUNE 19

Saint Romuald

c. 950–June 19, 1027
Feast: June 19
Patron: The Camaldolese Order, contemplative life

The son of the Duke of Ravenna, Romuald was a carefree youth without much religious devotion. However, after witnessing his father kill another man in a duel, Romuald entered a nearby monastery to do penance for what his father had done. Soon, however, even the monastic life was not enough and Romuald craved a life of greater solitude and austerity. He began to wander around Italy and live as a hermit near Benedictine monasteries so that he could join the monks in liturgical prayer.

During his travels, Romuald reformed and established many monasteries. In 1012, he received some land that was called the "Camaldoli," in Tuscany. There, Romuald realized his dream of founding an order of hermits who would not live in total isolation but would have some form of community life. The order became known as the Camaldolese. Romuald drew on elements he found in Saint John Cassian and other Fathers of the Desert, whose works were recommended by the Rule of Saint Benedict. Romuald's rule is very brief and distills the essence of the hermit's life: silence, contemplation, and prayer with the word of God, especially the psalms. Romuald lived and died according to one of his favorite sayings from Saint Benedict: "Prefer nothing, absolutely nothing, to the love of Christ."

Reflection

While few are called to the rigors of the Camaldolese life, we are all called to holiness. We can learn from Romuald that no matter the particular work we are entrusted with, we can dedicate ourselves to it radically, with love for God and our neighbor. All Christians can commit to a regular program of prayer and reading God's word in the Scriptures.

Prayer

Saint Romuald, pray for us that as we live our ordinary lives in the world, we may keep our eyes fixed on Jesus and our hope for eternal life. Amen.

JUNE 20

Saint Paulinus of Nola

c. 354–June 22, 431
Feast: June 22
Patron: Politicians

Paulinus was born into a wealthy, politically connected family near Bordeaux, France. Due to his many talents, he rose quickly through the political ranks, becoming the governor of Campania, Italy, when he was only in his twenties. He married Therasia, a Christian, and soon became a Christian too. The couple lived a simple, poor, evangelical life. They had one child, a baby boy, who died a few days after birth. After this, the couple began to sell their property, giving the proceeds to the poor.

Paulinus was ordained a priest, and after his wife died, was elected bishop of Nola in Campania. An outstanding pastor, he dedicated himself especially to caring for the needs of the poor. The people loved him, and he ministered with intense pastoral care for twenty-two years. He led a penitential life and was much devoted to prayer, particularly *lectio divina*. Saint Gregory the Great wrote about Paulinus' example in the *Dialogues*. Paulinus' political experience helped him as he led the Church during the decline of the Roman Empire. He had a vast network of friends, including many famous saints such as Augustine, Ambrose, Martin of Tours, and Jerome. He wrote many letters to them, which are precious for the picture they give us of Christian life in those times.

Reflection

In Paulinus we can see the truth of the adage, "Grace perfects nature." Endowed with many talents, Paulinus used them wholly for God. He didn't leave behind his secular knowledge but instead used it for the good of the Church. How do I use the talents I possess to build up God's kingdom?

Prayer

Saint Paulinus, you were born into fortunate circumstances, but you used your gifts, both material and spiritual, to help the poor. Pray for me that I too may use my talents for God and for the good of others. Amen.

JUNE 21

Saint Aloysius Gonzaga

March 9, 1568–June 21, 1591
Feast: June 21
Patron: Youth, students, Jesuit novices, AIDS patients, AIDS caregivers

Aloysius Gonzaga's powerful Italian family was deeply involved in the world of politics, war, and wealth. He was the eldest son of the Marquis of Castiglione and had to grow up quickly as the family heir. Aloysius began military training at age four and later studied ancient languages and many other subjects. In 1577, Aloysius went to serve in the Medici court. The court's decadence did not impress Aloysius, and he resolved to avoid offending God at all costs. When he returned home, Aloysius received both spiritual guidance and his first Communion from Saint Charles Borromeo, who was visiting his diocese.

After reading about Jesuit missionaries, Aloysius dreamt of joining the Society of Jesus. However, his father adamantly refused. After several years he finally relented, and Aloysius entered the Jesuits in 1585. In formation, Aloysius was helped to find balance in his severe practices of penance, and he grew in the spiritual life. In 1591, a plague broke out in Rome. Aloysius begged his superiors to allow him to care for the victims. He contracted the plague and recovered. That same year, the twenty-three-year-old Aloysius heard in prayer that he would die soon, and he began to prepare. He died as he had predicted, on the octave of Corpus Christi.

Reflection

Aloysius saw beyond the wealth, privilege, and power surrounding him and chose what was truly important. God became the center of his life. He deepened his love for God with prayer, penance, and spiritual reading, and he never looked back. How can I deepen my relationship with God?

Prayer

Saint Aloysius Gonzaga, please obtain for me the grace to be faithful to prayer, penance, and spiritual reading so that I may draw always closer to God. Amen.

JUNE 22

Saint Thomas More

February 7, 1478–July 6, 1535
Feast: June 22
Patron: Attorneys, civil servants, court workers, lawyers, politicians

Born into a wealthy family, Thomas became a lawyer like his father, and he was elected to the British Parliament in 1504. He married Jane Colt and they had four children. When Jane died, Thomas married Alice Middleton, a widow with a daughter. Together they lovingly cared for their blended family.

Known for his sterling character, complete honesty, and dedicated service, Thomas swiftly rose from one office to another and gained the favor of King Henry VIII. Thomas opposed the ideas of Martin Luther and others who were influencing England. Initially the king did too, but then the matter of his divorce and remarriage changed everything. When Henry declared himself head of the Church in England, he demanded that Thomas sign the Oath of Supremacy. Thomas refused. But the king would brook no opposition. After a dishonest trial, Thomas was condemned and sentenced to death. As he climbed the scaffold, he said, "I die the king's good servant, but God's first."

Reflection

The movie *A Man for All Seasons* wonderfully portrays Thomas' struggle to remain true to his conscience. In one scene, he is being led to his cell in the Tower of London while in the background people dance at a party. Thomas resolutely turns away from the revelries. In the eyes of the world, Thomas had everything—wealth, prestige, family. But he knew that God had to come first, even if it cost him his life. What am I willing to let go of for my faith?

Prayer

Saint Thomas More, pray for me that I might always be true to my conscience and that my conscience may be correctly formed according to the teaching of the Catholic faith. Help me to live as a person of integrity. Amen.

JUNE 23

Saint John Fisher

c. 1469–June 22, 1535
Feast: June 22
Patron: Bishops

Born in Yorkshire, John was educated in the finest schools in England. He earned a doctorate in theology at the University of Cambridge and then was ordained a priest. During this time, he is said to have tutored the young Prince Henry, who would later play a decisive role in his life. When John was named bishop of Rochester, he continued to lead an ascetical life and had a special interest in helping the poor.

In 1527, Henry VIII asked a group of bishops for their opinions on the validity of his marriage to Catherine of Aragon. Fisher replied assuring him that the marriage was valid. This was not the response the king wanted. Like Saint Thomas More, John also refused to sign the Oath of Supremacy that made Henry the head of the Church in England. The enraged king consigned John to the Tower of London and denied him the Sacraments, including the right to make his last confession. On the day of his execution, the physically weakened bishop boldly declared to the crowd, "Christian people, I come hither to die for the faith of Christ's holy Catholic Church."

Reflection

John Fisher was the only bishop of England who stood against the king. Abandoned by his fellow Catholics who should have supported him, John wasn't alone because Jesus was with him. His heroic example of courage can inspire us to stand up for the truth, even when others may oppose us. How does the way I live witness to my being a disciple of Jesus?

Prayer

Saint John Fisher, pray for us who live in times when religious freedom and truth are often attacked. Help us to hold fast to the Catholic faith, even if others abandon it, knowing that Jesus, the Way, the Truth, and the Life, will sustain us through it all. Amen.

JUNE 24

Saints Zechariah and Elizabeth

First Century
Feast: September 23 (November 5 on some calendars)
Patron: Infertility

Zechariah and Elizabeth were the parents of Saint John the Baptist. Zechariah was a priest of the order of Abijah, and Elizabeth was a descendant of Aaron (see Lk 1:5). Unable to conceive a child, they continued to pray. One day when Zechariah had entered the Holy of Holies in the Temple to offer the sacrifice, the Angel Gabriel appeared to him. The angel told Zechariah that he and Elizabeth would soon have a son. Zechariah doubted Gabriel's words and was struck dumb. But later the aged Elizabeth did conceive and gave birth to a son, John.

After the Annunciation, Mary hastened to help the older woman. Elizabeth then spoke words that are now part of the prayer, the Hail Mary: "Blessed are you among women, and blessed is the fruit of your womb" (Lk 1:42). When John was born, Zechariah could speak again, and he broke into a hymn of praise known as the Benedictus, which the Church prays every morning in the Liturgy of the Hours. Zechariah and Elizabeth's son, John, grew up to be the forerunner of Jesus, the Messiah.

Reflection

John the Baptist described himself as "the voice of one crying out in the wilderness: 'Prepare the way of the Lord'" (Mt 3:3). Saint Augustine once observed that the voice was John, but the Word was Christ. In this light, Zechariah's silence can be seen not simply as a punishment, but also as a preparation for the coming Word of God. A silent father gave life to a child who would become the voice. Those nine months of silence between Zechariah and Elizabeth bore fruit in two prayers still commonly used today.

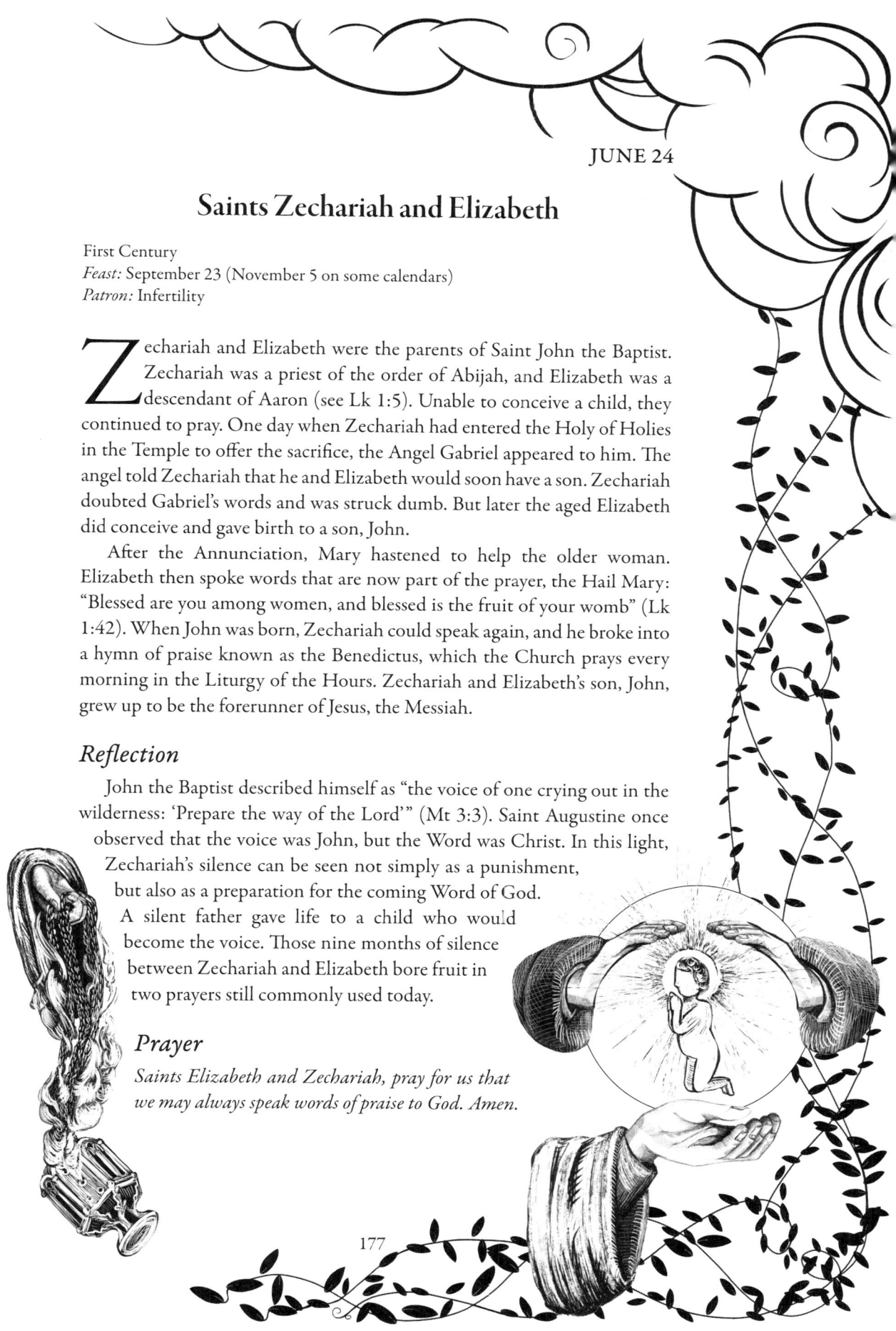

Prayer

Saints Elizabeth and Zechariah, pray for us that we may always speak words of praise to God. Amen.

JUNE 25

Blessed Vasyl Velychkovsky

June 1, 1903–June 30, 1973
Feast: June 27 (Canada)
Patron: Prison ministry, the Ukrainian Catholic Church

Vasyl is one of a group of Ukrainian Catholic martyrs whom Saint John Paul II beatified in 2001. Vasyl entered the Redemptorists and was ordained a priest in 1925. He had a gift for preaching missions, which were very successful and attracted many people. When World War II broke out, Vasyl continued to minister to the people, but life under the Nazi and Soviet occupation was very difficult. In 1940, the Soviets arrested and then later released Vasyl for leading a public procession on the Feast of Our Lady of Perpetual Help.

Finally, in 1945, Vasyl was captured and sentenced to death. But right before the scheduled execution, his sentence was changed to ten years of hard labor in the coal mines. Even there, he managed to conduct a secret ministry among the prisoners. Upon release, he organized the underground Church in Lviv. The pope appointed him a bishop and he was secretly ordained by Metropolitan Josyf Slipyj, who had also been in the gulag. In 1969, Vasyl was arrested again and spent several more years in prison, where he suffered chemical, physical, and mental torture. He was exiled after that and was invited to Winnipeg, Canada, where he died a martyr's death as a result of what he had suffered.

Reflection

The persecution that Vasyl and the other Ukrainian martyrs suffered can spur us to be more grateful for the gift of religious freedom. The martyrs gave their lives for the precious gift of faith. May we never take our own faith for granted but strive to practice it ever more faithfully.

Prayer

Blessed Vasyl, intercede for the persecuted Christians of our day, that they may be strengthened and that their sufferings may bear great fruit for the Gospel. Amen.

JUNE 26

Saint Josemaría Escrivá

January 9, 1902–June 26, 1975
Feast: June 26
Patron: Diabetics, ordinary life

Born in Barbastro, Spain, from a young age Josemaría sensed God was calling him to a special vocation. One day, after seeing a friar's bare footprints left in the snow, he felt that God wanted something from him. He spent years asking God what it was, even after his ordination in 1925. God finally answered the young priest's prayer a few years later during a retreat in Madrid. Josemaría realized God was entrusting him with a new vocational path in the Church, a way for ordinary people to become holy amid everyday life. Josemaría called this path *Opus Dei* or "Work of God." As *Opus Dei* developed, it was opened to men and women, married and single, priests and laity.

Turmoil and civil war in 1930s Spain led to the persecution of Catholics. Members of *Opus Dei* dispersed, and their founder went into hiding. When Josemaría returned to Madrid, he continued his pastoral work and wrote what is now a classic spiritual work, *The Way,* before moving to Rome. Suffering from diabetes, from which he was eventually and inexplicably cured, Josemaría traveled extensively to expand *Opus Dei*. Receiving definitive Vatican approval in 1950, *Opus Dei* had spread all over the world by the time Josemaría died unexpectedly of a heart attack.

Reflection

Josemaría understood that the "Work of God" was indeed God's work, not his own invention. He knew that God calls everyone to his service. During a turbulent time in Spain's history, Josemaría opened to priests and laity alike a new path to holiness. Is there a particular spirituality in the Church that attracts me and helps me to grow closer to God?

Prayer

Saint Josemaría Escrivá, pray I never become discouraged that my life is too "ordinary" for God to work through me. Amen.

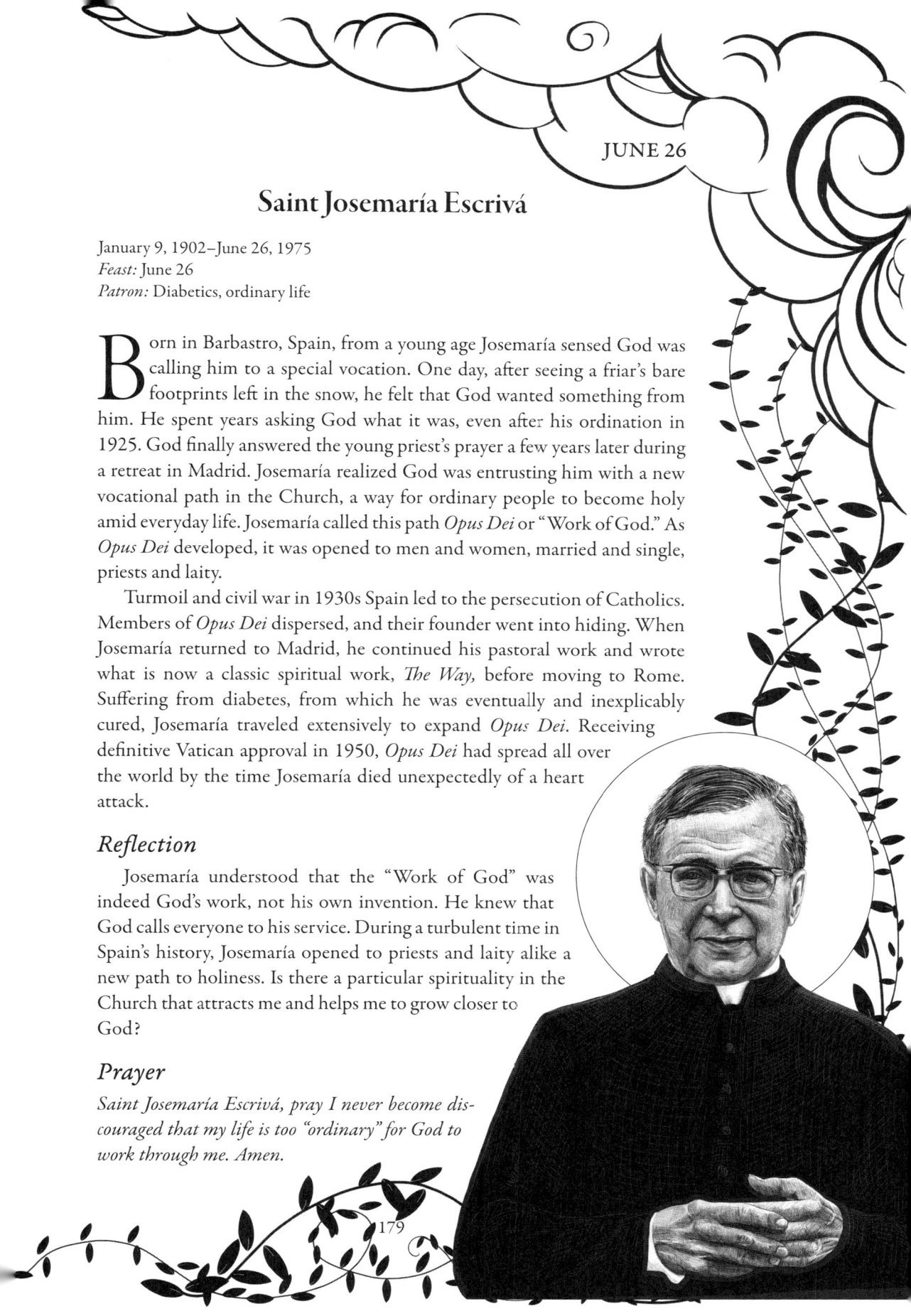

JUNE 27

Saint Cyril of Alexandria

c. 378–June 27, 444
Feast: June 27
Patron: Unity

Cyril didn't want to pick a fight. But as the bishop of Alexandria, Egypt, he was at the center of one of the biggest theological arguments to ever rock the Church. A bishop named Nestorius, the patriarch of Constantinople, started to preach that people should not call Mary the Mother of God, but only the Mother of Christ. Nestorius was trying to preserve the truth that Jesus is both God and man, fully divine and fully human. But Nestorius went too far and in effect split Jesus into two separate persons, one divine and one human.

Cyril vehemently opposed the teaching of Nestorius. If what Jesus did as man was not a divine action, then Jesus' suffering and death did not save us. Cyril explained with great theological depth and clarity that Jesus has two natures, divine and human. And those natures are united in only one Person—the second Person of the Trinity. So, we can indeed call Mary the Mother of God because the Person she gave birth to was the Son of God incarnate. Cyril presided at the Council of Ephesus in 431, which affirmed the truth that Mary is the Mother of God.

Reflection

Cyril gives us hope. He was a profound theologian, strongly passionate for the truth, but he was also impulsive and combative—faults he tried to correct during his life. Nevertheless, he shows us that the Holy Spirit can operate in the Church even in the midst of our human faults and failings. The Church is not a society of the perfect, but the communion of saints, some already in the glory of heaven, and others still struggling on earth.

Prayer

Saint Cyril of Alexandria, pray for us that we will always hold fast to the truth of the Gospel. Amen.

JUNE 28

Saint Irenaeus

c. 134–c. 202
Feast: June 28
Patron: Apologists; theologians; Archdiocese of Mobile, Alabama

Irenaeus was a highly influential writer, bishop, and theologian of the early Church who was born in Asia Minor. He was a student of Saint Polycarp, who had known some of the apostles as Irenaeus would later note in his letters. Irenaeus traveled to Gaul and was ordained a priest in Lyons where he would become bishop around 180.

As bishop, Irenaeus wrote an important work titled *Adversus Haereses* (Against Heresies). The Church in Gaul had been troubled by the false teachings of the Gnostics, who claimed to have a secret knowledge that had to be gained for salvation. In his five-volume book, Irenaeus explained Christian teachings in light of Scripture and the apostolic tradition, underlining that the true teaching was passed on through the bishops in the Church. Irenaeus was also one of the first theologians to develop the parallel between Eve and Mary. He described Mary's role as the New Eve, undoing the damage from original sin and cooperating in the redemptive work of Christ. According to a later but uncertain tradition, Irenaeus died a martyr.

Reflection

The name Irenaeus means "man of peace," and although he was involved in controversies, Irenaeus was a peacemaker. He persuaded Pope Victor I to lift a ban of excommunication that had been imposed on some Eastern Christians who didn't accept the Western date for Easter. Irenaeus' example can inspire us to be peacemakers amidst conflicts that can arise even among members of the faithful.

Prayer

Saint Irenaeus, intercede for us that we too may be peacemakers and seek unity. Pray that those who turn to violence to achieve their goals may be converted to the way of love and follow Jesus who taught us to love one another. Amen.

JUNE 29

Saint Peter, the Apostle

First Century
Feast: June 29 (February 22, Chair of Peter)
Patron: Popes, fishermen, net makers, ship builders, Rome

Simon Peter was not the first person one might expect Jesus to choose as the leader of his Church and the first pope. Born in Bethsaida, Simon managed a fishing business with his brother Andrew, along with James and John, the sons of Zebedee. One day, Andrew introduced him to Jesus, and nothing would ever be the same. Upon meeting Simon, Jesus changed his name to the Aramaic word for "rock" saying, "You are to be called Cephas" (Jn 1:42). Peter, the English translation of Cephas, is derived from *petra,* the Greek word for rock.

Jesus and Peter share a special closeness throughout the Gospels. He is one of the few to see Jesus transfigured on Mount Tabor (see 2 Pet 1:16–18). He is also the first apostle to recognize Jesus as the Messiah, the Son of God (see Mt 16:16). But the Gospel writers also recount several instances when Peter speaks and behaves rashly. Before Jesus' crucifixion, Peter even denies three times that he knows Jesus. After the resurrection, Jesus appears to the disciples and asks Peter three times, "Do you love me?" (see Jn 21:15–19). Jesus' three questions evoke Peter's three denials and reveal God's love and forgiveness. Transformed by the miracle of the resurrection, Peter went on to preach the Gospel until his martyrdom.

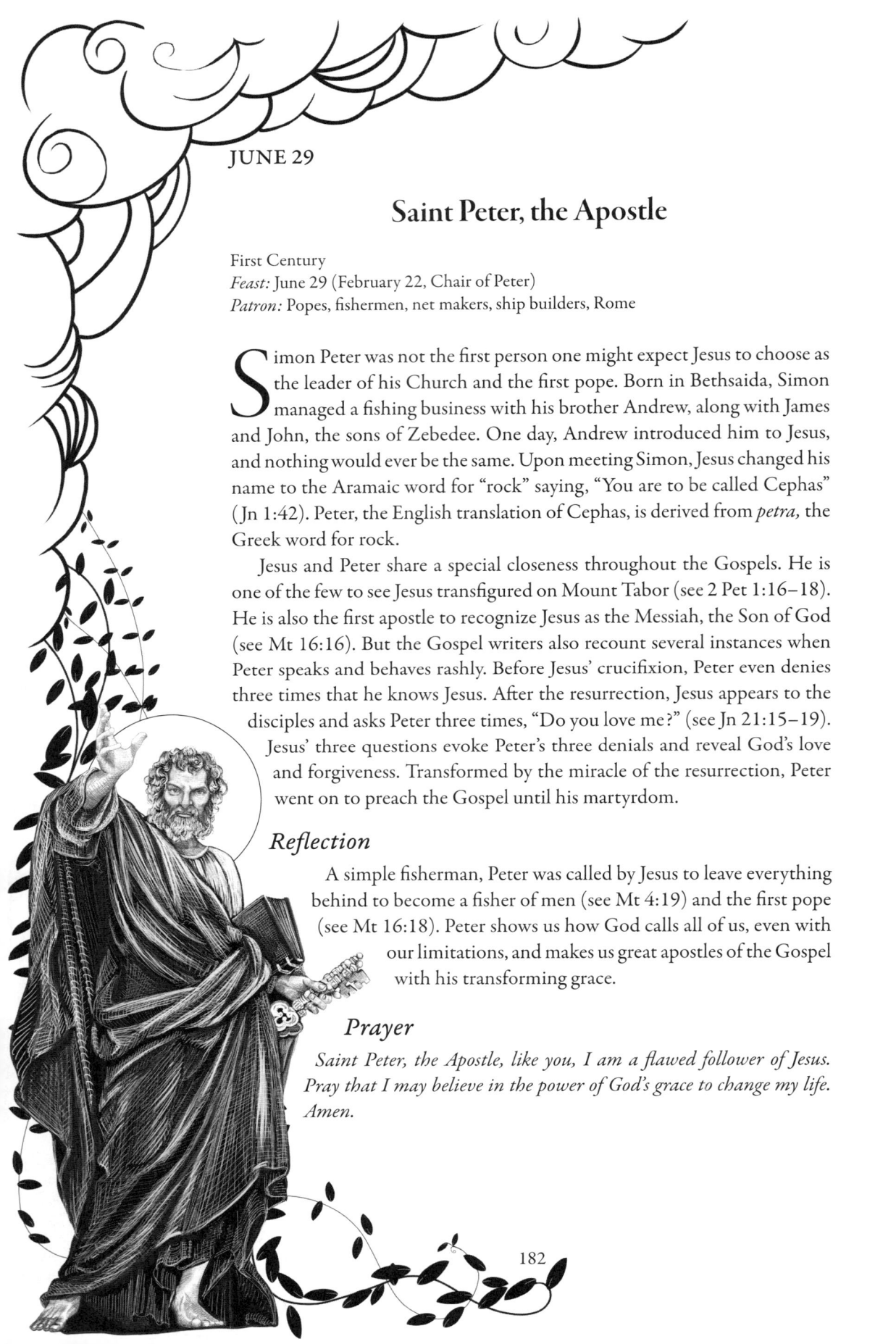

Reflection

A simple fisherman, Peter was called by Jesus to leave everything behind to become a fisher of men (see Mt 4:19) and the first pope (see Mt 16:18). Peter shows us how God calls all of us, even with our limitations, and makes us great apostles of the Gospel with his transforming grace.

Prayer

Saint Peter, the Apostle, like you, I am a flawed follower of Jesus. Pray that I may believe in the power of God's grace to change my life. Amen.

JUNE 30

Saint Tarcisius

Third Century
Feast: August 15
Patron: First Communicants, altar servers

Most of the information we know about this saint comes from the fourth-century inscription Pope Damasus I had carved on Tarcisius' grave in the Catacombs of Saint Callixtus. According to tradition, he was a young acolyte during the persecution of the Emperor Valerian. Though young, he asked to bring the Holy Eucharist to imprisoned Christians awaiting martyrdom. While he was walking along Rome's Appian Way, a crowd of non-believers stopped the young boy. Suspecting Tarcisius was a Christian, the mob demanded to see what he was carrying. Tarcisius, determined to save the Eucharist from sacrilege, courageously refused to surrender his precious parcel. Enraged at his resistance, the men encircled Tarcisius and beat him to death with clubs and stones. The Roman Martyrology records the tradition that every trace of the Blessed Sacrament vanished when Tarcisius' lifeless body was searched. It explains that the consecrated Host became part of Tarcisius' own body as he offered up his life in imitation of Christ.

Reflection

Though the details of his story are uncertain, we know that Tarcisius gave his life as a testimony to his faith in the Real Presence of Jesus in the Holy Eucharist. He was convinced beyond a doubt that the Eucharist is the Body, Blood, Soul, and Divinity of the Lord Jesus. His profound faith reaches across the centuries to inspire and enliven our own belief in the Real Presence. We know how much we need Jesus in our lives. How grateful we can be as Catholics to have such ready access to his special sacramental presence in each of our churches.

Prayer

Saint Tarcisius, help me never to take the gift of the Holy Eucharist for granted. May I receive and adore Jesus with always greater faith and love. Amen.

JULY 1

Saint Junípero Serra

November 24, 1713–August 28, 1784
Feast: July 1
Patron: Latinos in America, missionaries, California, the Serra Club

This Spanish missionary led a varied and exciting life. Born Miguel José, he entered the Franciscan monastery in Palma, Spain, at the age of seventeen. Upon his profession, he took the name Junípero in memory of the brother companion of Saint Francis. After his ordination, he obtained a doctorate in theology and then volunteered to be a missionary to New Spain. Arriving in Vera Cruz in 1749, Junípero and his companions declined horses and walked to Mexico City—a trip of about 250 miles.

Junípero was a determined and fiery missionary who continued to walk—some six thousand miles, despite asthma and an injured foot—to serve the people of God. He learned the languages of the indigenous people and translated catechisms to aid in his work of evangelization. A man of his time, some of his methods are now considered controversial. However, Junípero worked in the best way he knew to protect the rights of the people he served. In what is now Mexico and California, he worked in many missions and founded nine. After a long life of hard work, Junípero died at Mission San Carlos and was buried in the sanctuary of a church he had built.

Reflection

Junípero Serra freely volunteered to take on some very challenging positions, with both physical and intellectual demands. He traveled across the world because of his desire to make Jesus known and loved by all. Junípero wanted to be a good father to those he was called to serve. How might Jesus be calling me out of my comfort zone today?

Prayer

God our Father, you blessed the work of Saint Junípero Serra because it was done out of love for your Son. Help me to do everything with love as my primary motivation. Amen.

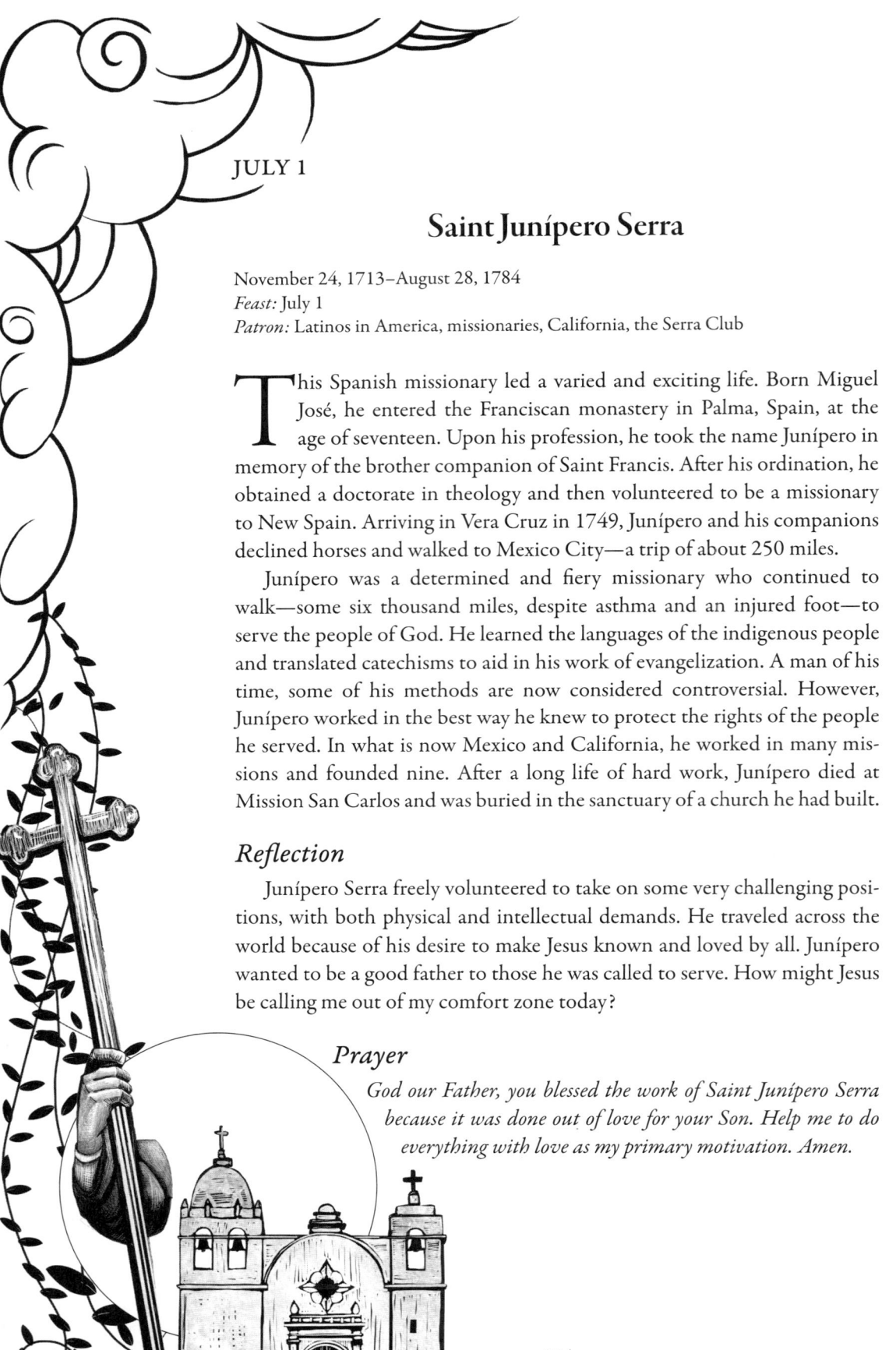

JULY 2

Saint Oliver Plunkett

November 1, 1625–July 1, 1681
Feast: July 1
Patron: Peace and reconciliation

Oliver was born in Loughcrew, Ireland, a little less than a century after Saints Thomas More and John Fisher were martyred under the reign of Henry VIII. Due to the anti-Catholic persecution in Ireland, Oliver studied in Rome and was ordained a priest in 1654. He stayed in Rome, teaching and ministering to the sick. In 1669 he became a bishop and returned to Ireland, traveling incognito.

Oliver attended to his flock for several years, building up the educational infrastructure and confirming tens of thousands of people. His letters from that time reflect his warm personality and pastoral concern. However, in 1673 persecution against Catholics flared once again and Oliver had to go underground. In late 1679, he was jailed on trumped-up charges that he was part of a plot to orchestrate a French invasion of England. Oliver was brought to London to stand trial. He refused to plead guilty and accuse others, though it might have saved his life, saying, "I'd rather die ten thousand deaths than wrongfully to take away one farthing of any man's goods, one day of his liberty, or one minute of his life." He was the last of the Catholic martyrs to die in England.

Reflection

Oliver took full advantage of the short window of time when he could minister relatively freely to his flock. He wrote, "This is the time for doing good." A few years later, Oliver watched as the English drove his priests into hiding and tore down schools built just recently in his diocese. Nevertheless, he entrusted everything to God. Oliver's example can inspire us when we too feel disappointed in life.

Prayer

Saint Oliver Plunkett, pray that we may never lose heart and that we may have the courage to keep on serving God and helping others. Amen.

JULY 3

Saint Thomas, the Apostle

First Century
Feast: July 3
Patron: India, East Indies, architects, construction workers, seekers

Thomas was also called Didymus, which means "twin" in Greek. He was one of the twelve apostles. Thomas was present at many of the important moments of Jesus' life, including the raising of Lazarus from the dead (see Jn 11:6). At the Last Supper, Thomas asked Jesus, "How can we know the way?" and Jesus responded, "I am the way, and the truth, and the life" (Jn 14:5–6).

Thomas is commonly known as "Doubting Thomas" because after the resurrection, Jesus appeared to all the apostles when Thomas was absent. After the apostles reported that they had seen Jesus, Thomas declared that he would not believe it unless he saw it for himself. The risen Lord then appeared to Thomas and invited him to touch his wounds. Stunned, Thomas cried out in faith, "My Lord and my God!" (Jn 20:28).

After Pentecost, Thomas went on apostolic journeys preaching the Gospel. According to tradition, he traveled to Persia and as far south as India, where he was martyred. When Portuguese explorers arrived in southern India in the fifteenth century, they found a Christian community that claimed to have been founded by Saint Thomas.

Reflection

Thomas the Apostle doubted the witness of the other apostles, but when he saw Jesus face to face, he wholeheartedly proclaimed his faith. We may not be able to place our hands into the wounds of Jesus, but the Lord meets us where we are and gives us reason to exclaim, "My Lord and my God!" How often do I stop to give thanks to God throughout the day?

Prayer

Lord, in moments of doubt, help me to recognize your presence. Amen.

JULY 4

Saint Elizabeth of Portugal

1271–July 4, 1336
Feast: July 4 (July 5 in U. S.)
Patron: Brides, victims of adultery and jealousy, those falsely accused, Franciscan tertiaries

Elizabeth (also known as Isabel), was born in Saragossa, Spain. Daughter of King Pedro III of Aragon and Queen Constantia, she was named after her great-aunt, Saint Elizabeth of Hungary. At the age of twelve she married King Dinis of Portugal who had many interests including poetry, agriculture, and, unfortunately, other women. Denis even insisted that Elizabeth raise his children born from other women. Despite her husband's disrespect, Elizabeth chose to trust in God and lovingly cared for all of Denis' children.

Elizabeth was a strong queen who put her faith into action, building convents, hospitals, and shelters. When others would laud her generosity, she would simply reply, "God made me queen so that I may serve others." She was also known as the "Angel of Peace" because she negotiated peace and exercised her influence to settle several disputes. At one point, Elizabeth even rode out onto a battlefield to stop her embittered son Alfonso from marching on Lisbon to dethrone his father who favored one of his other sons. She spent her last days as a Franciscan tertiary living near a Poor Clare convent she had founded at Coimbra. Elizabeth worked for peace until her death.

Reflection

Elizabeth of Portugal busied herself with prayer and good works even as she faced personal sorrows. She once wrote, "On whom but God can I lean?" Elizabeth's life shows us how to rely on the deep anchor of prayer amid life's disappointments. How do I find peace in the painful situations of my life?

Prayer

Saint Elizabeth of Portugal, pray for us that we may turn to God confidently despite all the difficulties that might assail us. Amen.

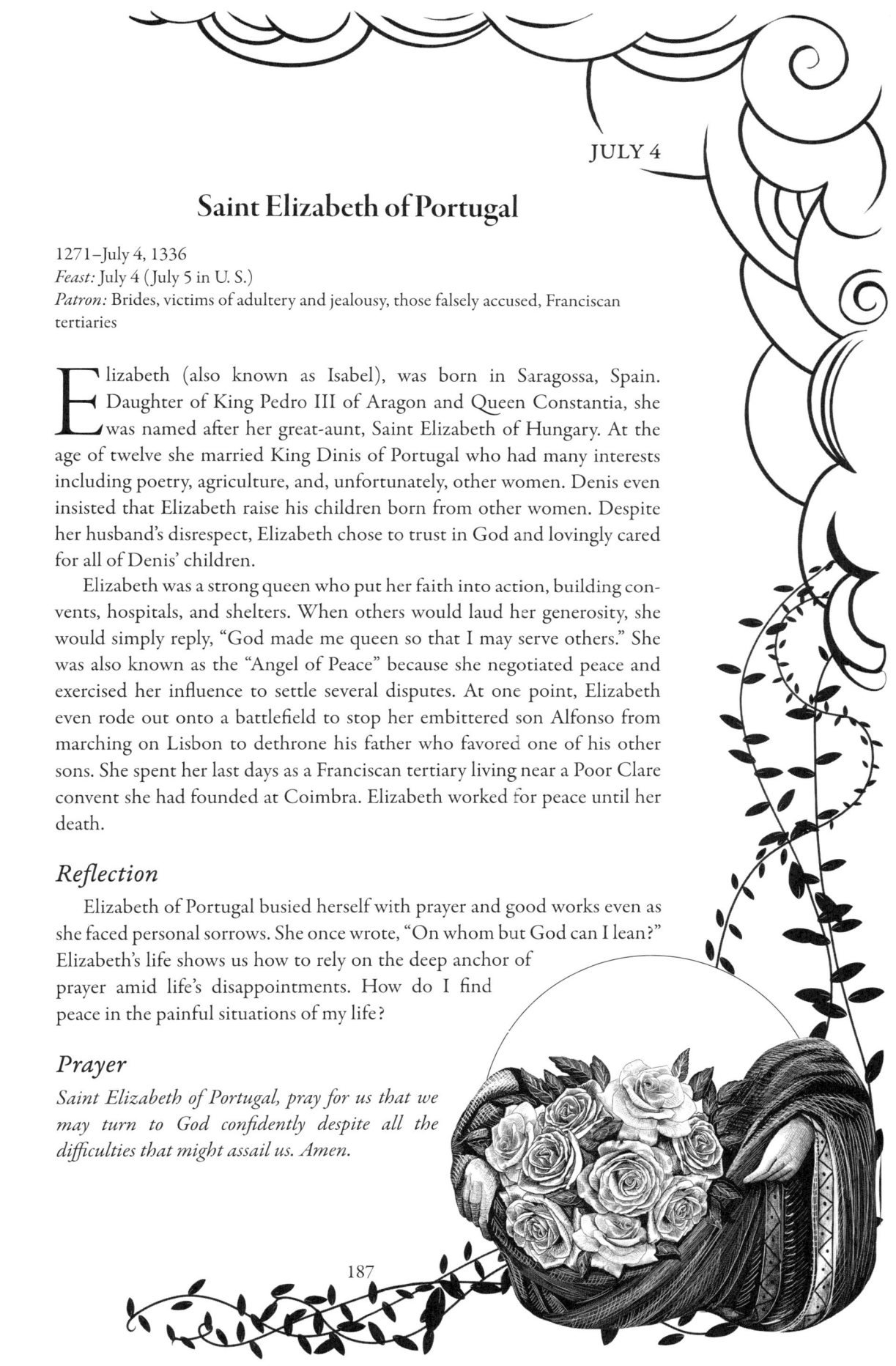

JULY 5

Saint Anthony Mary Zaccaria

1502–July 5, 1539
Feast: July 5
Patron: Physicians, the Barnabite Order

Born to a wealthy family in Cremona, Italy, Anthony became a doctor and worked with the poor. But he soon gave up medicine to become a priest. He saw the need for renewal in the Church and dedicated himself with great zeal to preaching the word. Anthony based his spirituality on Saint Paul's teachings. It was focused on Christ, especially the crucified Christ, along with a great devotion to the Holy Eucharist.

Anthony attracted followers and founded the Clerics Regular of Saint Paul, or Barnabites, a religious congregation of priests; the Angelic Sisters of Saint Paul, a congregation of women religious; and the Laity of Saint Paul for married couples. Anthony and his followers encouraged the practice of ringing church bells at 3:00 p.m. on Fridays to honor Jesus' passion. They also promoted the Forty Hours devotion for adoration of the Eucharist. Anthony's work to reform the Church provoked some opposition; twice he was put on trial for heresy but acquitted. Undaunted, Anthony continued preaching and working until he became seriously ill and died when he was only thirty-six. Almost three decades after his death, Anthony's body was found to be incorrupt.

Reflection

Saint Paul was a great inspiration for Anthony. Like him, Anthony could say, "I regard everything as loss because of the surpassing value of knowing Christ Jesus my Lord" (Phil 3:8). We too can find in Saint Paul a model for our life in Christ. The letters of Saint Paul make up a good part of the New Testament. What can I do to get to know him better?

Prayer

Saint Anthony Mary Zaccaria, pray for me that, like you, I may follow the example of Saint Paul and work to bring to others the knowledge of Jesus Christ. Amen.

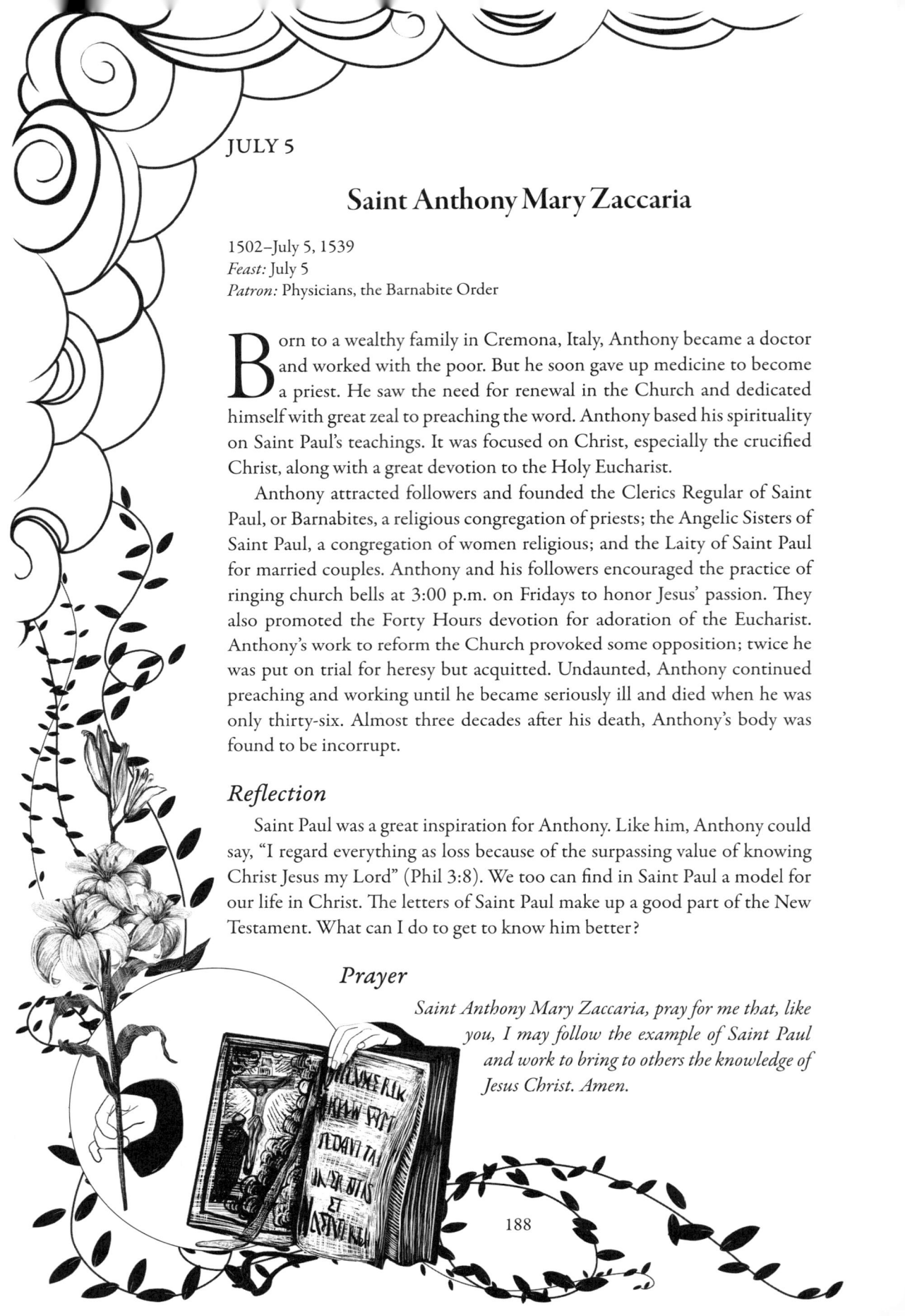

JULY 6

Saint Maria Goretti

October 16, 1890–July 6, 1902
Feast: July 6
Patron: Youth, victims of sexual assault

Maria was the third of seven children in a poor farming family in Italy. Her father, Luigi, died when she was only nine years old. She remained at home to manage the house and take care of her younger sister while her mother, Assunta, and older siblings worked. Maria's family shared their home with a widower, Giovanni Serenelli, and his teenage son, Alessandro. The two families helped one another, working together and sharing household expenses.

Over time, Alessandro became attracted to Maria and was aggressive in his advances, which Maria refused. One day when Alessandro was twenty, he cornered the eleven-year-old Maria while they were alone and attempted to rape her. Maria resisted and told him that he was committing a sin. In his anger, Alessandro stabbed her multiple times. Maria was hospitalized, but she died the next day. With her last words, Maria forgave Alessandro and expressed her desire that they see one another in heaven. Alessandro experienced a deep conversion in prison and lived a holy life from that day forward. He was present at Maria's canonization in 1950.

Reflection

Maria's desire for purity and aversion to sin are certainly virtues to imitate, but perhaps her greatest virtue was her capacity to forgive her murderer. Forgiveness is required of all Christians. However, forgiveness is not a feeling or a willingness to let someone hurt us again. Above all, it is an act of the will to desire the best for that person, as Maria did when she expressed her hope that Alessandro would go to heaven. Do I hope for the good of those who have hurt me?

Prayer

Saint Maria Goretti, pray that I may receive the grace I need to forgive those who have hurt me, and to receive forgiveness from those whom I may have hurt. Amen.

JULY 7

Blessed Peter To Rot

1912–July 1945
Feast: July 7
Patron: Married couples, catechists, Oceania

An ordinary family man, Peter To Rot was from an island village in what is now Papua New Guinea. Trained as a lay catechist, Peter took his responsibilities seriously and was known for being affable and compassionate. Peter's wife, Paula, was also a faithful Catholic and the couple prayed together regularly. A proud father, Peter would often take his two children with him as he attended to his duties as a catechist.

In 1942 during World War II, the Japanese military invaded and terrorized the island, imprisoning all the priests. Peter became the primary spiritual guide for his village—at first openly, and then secretly as Christian worship was forbidden. He visited the priests in prison and brought the Blessed Sacrament back to the village with him. When the village church was destroyed, Peter built a hidden one from tree branches.

When the military police instigated and encouraged polygamy, Peter openly took a stand against it. He was imprisoned and sentenced to two months. But Peter knew something else was planned for him. He told both his wife and his mother that the prison authorities informed him they were sending a doctor to see him soon though he was not sick. Another prisoner witnessed Peter's martyrdom by lethal injection. His wife was expecting their third child.

Reflection

The day Peter died, he asked his wife to bring him his crucifix. He could sense his future and told her that he was not afraid to die to protect the sanctity of marriage and family life. Marriage is often misunderstood and undervalued in today's world, but Peter saw clearly its importance. What support can I offer to couples I know who are struggling in their marriage?

Prayer

Blessed Peter To Rot, pray that all might recognize the sanctity and beauty of marriage, and for all married couples experiencing problems. Amen.

JULY 8

Saints Priscilla and Aquila

First Century
Feast: July 8
Patrons: Catholic marriage and family, lay evangelists

The married couple Priscilla and Aquila collaborated with Saint Paul, both in his manual labor of tentmaking, and in his work of evangelizing. From the Acts of the Apostles and Paul's letters, we know that Priscilla and Aquila met Paul in Corinth after they had left Rome. The three worked together making tents, which involved cutting and sewing goat-hair cloth or leather to make shelters and canopies. Tentmaking was practical employment for Paul and his friends as they could carry the necessary tools easily and purchase supplies when needed.

Priscilla (also called Prisca) and Aquila traveled with Paul to Ephesus. When Paul writes to the Corinthians from Ephesus, he mentions the couple and "the church in their house" (1 Cor 16:19). In this time before Christian churches were built, believers would meet in their houses for the celebration of the Eucharist. The couple ended up in Rome with Paul, and in his letter to the Romans from prison, Paul writes, "Greet Prisca and Aquila, who work with me in Christ Jesus, and who risked their necks for my life, to whom not only I give thanks, but also all the churches of the Gentiles" (Rom 16:3–4).

Reflection

Priscilla and Aquila are among the first married couples to work together for the Gospel. When they are mentioned in the New Testament, it is always together (mostly with Priscilla's name first, which was unusual in that Greco-Roman society). This couple's loving and respectful relationship helped them to effectively preach the Gospel. How can my relationships help me to tell others about Jesus?

Prayer

Saints Priscilla and Aquila, please intercede for all married couples. Pray that our society today will recover a full understanding and appreciation of the beauty of marriage. Amen.

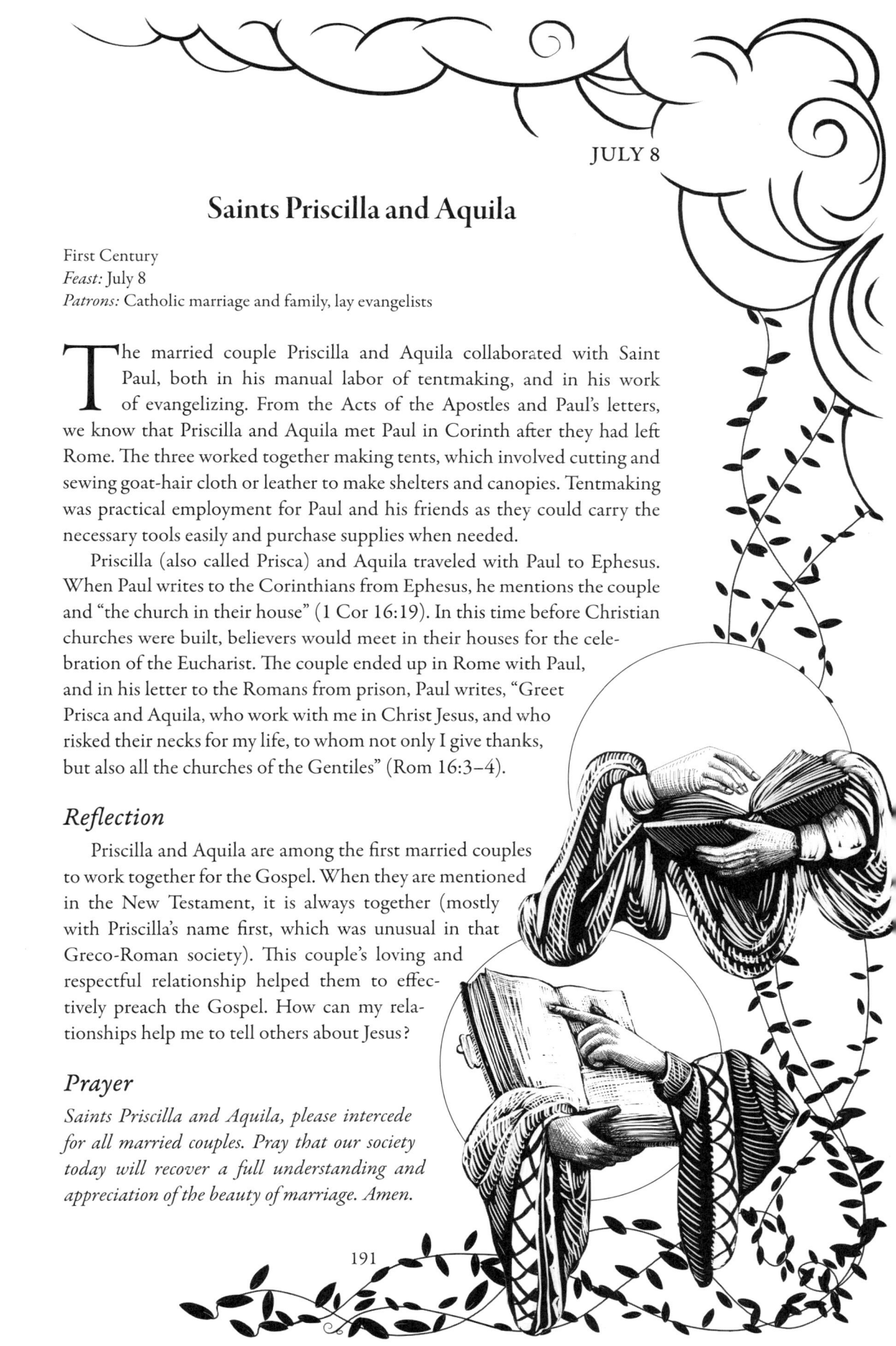

JULY 9

Saint Augustine Zhao Rong and Companions

c. 1746–1815
Feast: July 9
Patron: China

On October 1, 2000, Saint John Paul II canonized a group of 120 martyrs who died from 1648 to 1930. Eighty-seven were Chinese and thirty-three were missionaries. The group included priests, religious, and laity, even children. Augustine Zhao Rong was a Chinese soldier assigned to escort Bishop Gabriel Dufresse to his death. Profoundly moved by the bishop's heroism, Augustine converted to Christianity and was soon ordained a priest. He was tortured and killed that same year. Many of the martyrs honored on this day were killed at the turn of the twentieth century, during the Boxer rebellion. One of them was fourteen-year-old Anna Wang. Before she was beheaded, Anna declared, "The gate of heaven is open to all," and then she whispered, "Jesus, Jesus, Jesus."

Mark Ji Tianxiang, also honored in this group, was a doctor and an opium addict. He became addicted after using opium as a treatment for his own stomach ailment. At the time, addiction was not well understood, so his confessor forbade him to receive the Sacraments. Mark obeyed for thirty years but kept going to Mass and praying. When rounded up with his family by the Boxer rebels, Mark asked to be killed last, so that none of his family members would die alone.

Reflection

Martyrs are ordinary people of faith who show extraordinary courage in the face of death. The martyrs honored in this group included a French bishop, a Chinese soldier, a fourteen-year-old girl, and an opium addict who never overcame his addiction. These people had little in common except that, through God's grace, they all accepted death for the sake of the Gospel.

Prayer

Saints Augustine, Anna, Mark, and all those martyred in China, pray for us that we might allow the power of God's grace to transform our ordinary lives into powerful testimonies to the Gospel. Amen.

JULY 10

Blessed Pier Giorgio Frassati

April 6, 1901–July 4, 1925
Feast: July 4
Patron: Youth, students, mountaineers, Dominican tertiaries, World Youth Day

Pier Giorgio Frassati was the only son of a prominent Italian family. He easily could have led a life of indulgence, but instead chose to model his life on the Beatitudes. From a young age, Pier Giorgio was exuberant, and his enthusiastic love for God overflowed in a zest for life, jokes with friends, and acts of charity. He would lead mountain climbing trips in order to breathe in the beauty of God's creation. And he once presented a friend with a box of chocolates he had tied together so that when one was pulled out, all of the chocolates in the box came along with it.

The characteristic that most marked Pier Giorgio's life, however, was his love for the poor. As a child, he gave away his shoes to the needy, and as a young man, he joined the Saint Vincent de Paul Society. While pursuing an engineering degree, he frequently visited the slums of Turin. He said that just as Jesus visited him every day in the Eucharist, he wanted to return the favor by visiting Jesus in the poor. During one of his visits to the slums he contracted virulent polio that consumed his life within a few days. After his death, friends and family were surprised to discover the extent of Pier Giorgio's charitable activities. At the twenty-four-year-old's funeral, the streets were crowded with the people he had served.

Reflection

Like many young people, Pier Giorgio was idealistic and energetic. He used this energy to discover generous and ingenious ways to be of service. The power of the Gospel message and the attraction of Eucharistic adoration resonated deeply in his soul. His life is a compelling example for us of the joy of Christian discipleship.

Prayer

Blessed Pier Giorgio, pray for all young people. Show them how to live as true disciples of Christ in today's world. Amen.

JULY 11

Saint Benedict

c. 480–c. 543
Feast: July 11
Patron: Europe, monastic life, protection against poisoning

Benedict came from a wealthy, devout family—his sister, Scholastica, is also a saint. Benedict went to Rome for his studies. But dismayed by the lack of good morals, he left school and became a hermit for three years. He battled his weaknesses, renouncing sin and seeking to live wholly for Jesus Christ. Only then did he establish his first monastic community in Subiaco. Many young men were drawn to this way of life, and Benedict's order grew and flourished.

As Europe faced a great crisis after the fall of the Roman Empire, the monasteries Benedict established throughout Europe became centers not only of prayer and spiritual life but also of learning and culture. His monks preserved the great classic works of Greece and Rome. The Rule that Benedict wrote for his monks has guided monastic life ever since. With exceptional maturity, spiritual insight, and balance, Benedict crafted a way of life dedicated to love and service of God and neighbor. Benedict put God at the heart of everything and thus helped to build the foundation for the culture of faith that would later flourish in Europe.

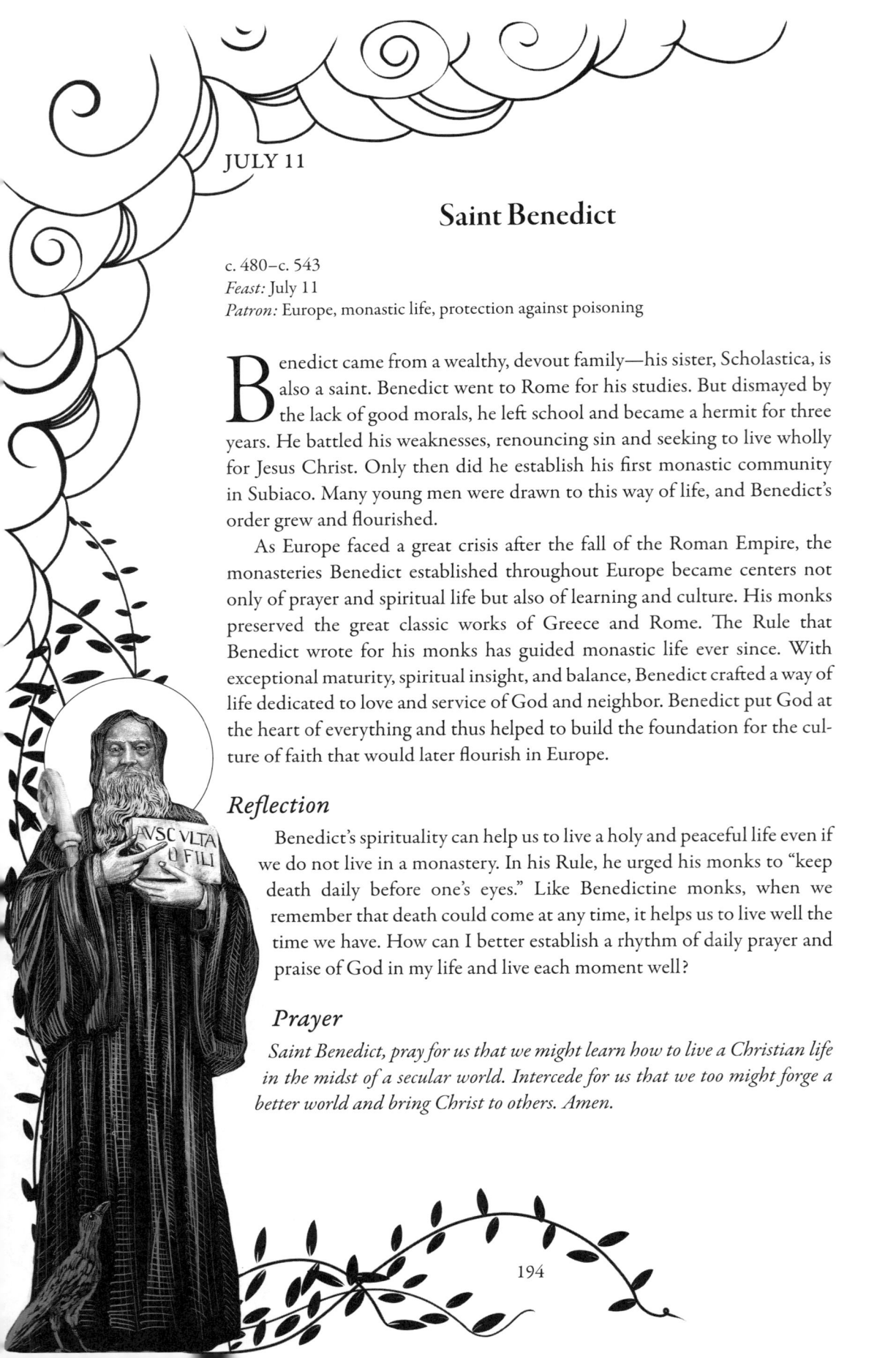

Reflection

Benedict's spirituality can help us to live a holy and peaceful life even if we do not live in a monastery. In his Rule, he urged his monks to "keep death daily before one's eyes." Like Benedictine monks, when we remember that death could come at any time, it helps us to live well the time we have. How can I better establish a rhythm of daily prayer and praise of God in my life and live each moment well?

Prayer

Saint Benedict, pray for us that we might learn how to live a Christian life in the midst of a secular world. Intercede for us that we too might forge a better world and bring Christ to others. Amen.

JULY 12

Saints Louis and Zélie Martin

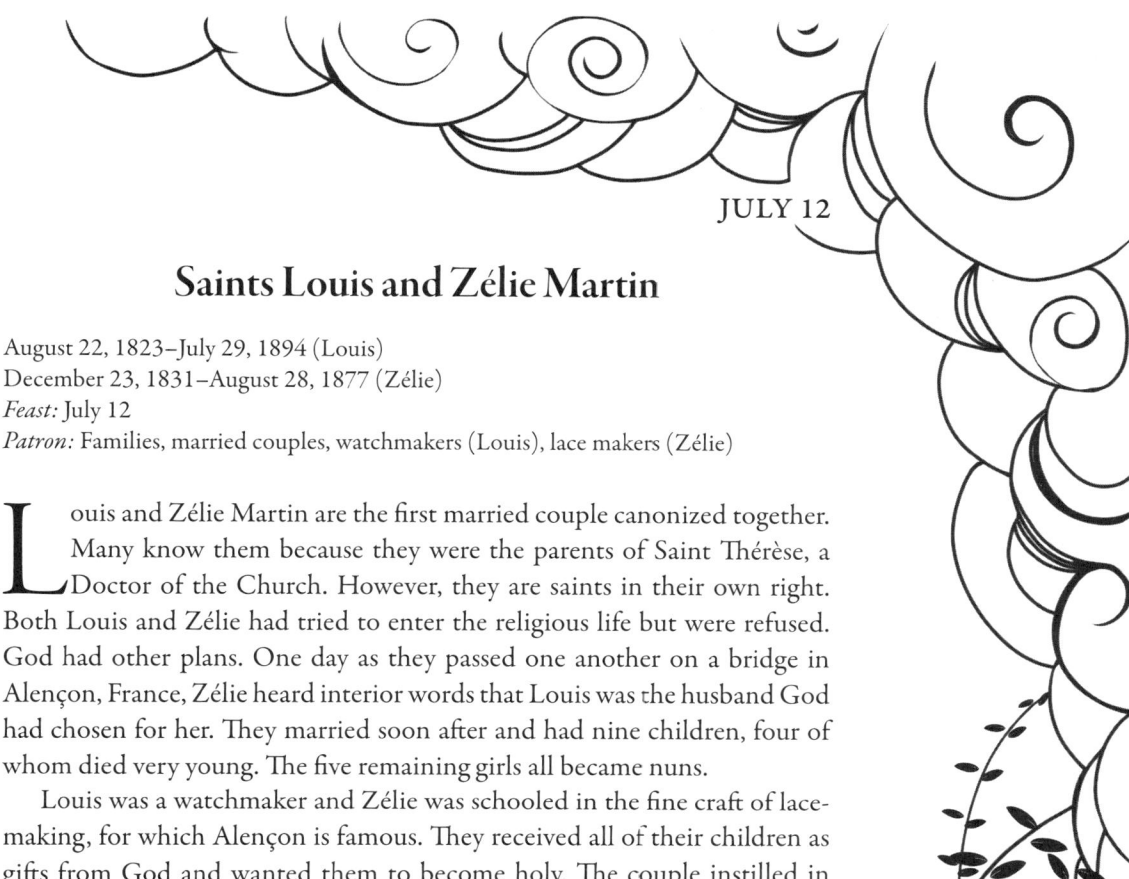

August 22, 1823–July 29, 1894 (Louis)
December 23, 1831–August 28, 1877 (Zélie)
Feast: July 12
Patron: Families, married couples, watchmakers (Louis), lace makers (Zélie)

Louis and Zélie Martin are the first married couple canonized together. Many know them because they were the parents of Saint Thérèse, a Doctor of the Church. However, they are saints in their own right. Both Louis and Zélie had tried to enter the religious life but were refused. God had other plans. One day as they passed one another on a bridge in Alençon, France, Zélie heard interior words that Louis was the husband God had chosen for her. They married soon after and had nine children, four of whom died very young. The five remaining girls all became nuns.

Louis was a watchmaker and Zélie was schooled in the fine craft of lace-making, for which Alençon is famous. They received all of their children as gifts from God and wanted them to become holy. The couple instilled in them a deep love for the Catholic faith, especially by their example of holiness. Their family was truly a domestic church in which faith, hope, and love reigned. Zélie was diagnosed with breast cancer when she was forty-two years old. After her death a few years later, Louis moved to Lisieux with the girls and raised them alone. He never remarried and, though it cost him greatly, he gave all his daughters permission to enter the convent.

Reflection

Louis and Zélie found holiness through the Sacrament of Matrimony. They dealt with the ordinary business of life involved in raising their children and providing for their material and spiritual needs. Most importantly, however, they prized the gift of faith and transmitted it to their children.

Prayer

Saints Louis and Zélie Martin, pray for families everywhere that they may be true havens of love and holiness. May all parents receive children from God with love and teach them the domestic virtues that can make family life a blessing for all. Amen.

JULY 13

Blessed Carlos Manuel Cecilio Rodríguez Santiago

November 22, 1918–July 13, 1963
Feast: July 13
Patron: Liturgical studies

Carlos is a man of distinctions: first Puerto Rican, first Caribbean-born, and first layperson in U.S. history to be beatified. He was born in Caguas, Puerto Rico, the second of five children of Manuel Rodríguez and Herminia Santiago. Born on the feast of Saint Cecilia, he was given the middle name "Cecilio." As a boy, Carlos rescued a younger cousin from a dog attack. The traumatic incident may have triggered his ulcerative colitis, from which he would suffer for the rest of his life.

Due to his illness, Carlos was unable to complete his studies. However, he continued to read avidly. His special love was for the liturgy and he dedicated time and resources to publishing the magazines *Liturgy* and *Christian Culture*. He also organized discussion groups around liturgy and culture. He celebrated when Pope Pius XII made important changes to the Easter Vigil in 1951, including moving it to the evening instead of the morning of Holy Saturday.

As his spiritual joy and fervor grew, however, Carlos' physical health continued to decline. During the year before his death, Carlos experienced a personal liturgy of the "dark night of the soul." Shortly before his death from cancer, the darkness dissipated and he expressed his hope in the resurrection by saying, "The thirteenth is a good day." No one knew what he meant until he died a few days later on July 13.

Reflection

Charlie, as he was affectionately called by his friends, loved the Mass and spent his energy working toward liturgical renewal. The Easter light remained alive in his heart until death, and not even the inner darkness of confusion could extinguish it. May God fan the Easter light in our souls and lead us to endless celebration in God's kingdom!

Prayer

Blessed Carlos Manuel Cecilio Rodríguez Santiago, ask the Lord of Light to fill us with the flame of love for worship, for community, and for communion with him. Amen.

JULY 14

Saint Camillus de Lellis

May 25, 1550–July 14, 1614
Feast: July 14 (July 18 in U. S.)
Patron: Sick, doctors, nurses, hospitals, health-care workers

Even as a boy Camillus had a rough character. His mother died when he was twelve, and a few years later he became a soldier, fighting alongside his father. The towering Camillus, who was six feet six inches, took to drinking and gambling excessively. Trying to seek healing for a leg wound that wouldn't mend, Camillus started working in a hospital in Rome. But he was let go on account of his bad temper and coarse ways.

While doing manual labor at a Capuchin monastery, a priest spoke to Camillus and something he said induced Camillus to turn his life around. Back at the San Giacomo Hospital in Rome, he began in earnest to care for the sick and was even named the hospital's director. Camillus also found a good spiritual director in Saint Philip Neri. Camillus was ordained a priest when he was thirty-four. He then began a congregation originally known as Fathers of a Good Death—now known as the Order of the Ministers of the Sick, or Camillians. Their work flourished and Camillus and his men nursed the victims of the plague with great dedication. Camillus used to encourage the men helping him by saying, "We want to assist the sick with the same love that a mother has for her only sick child."

Reflection

As a young man, Camillus certainly seemed like an unlikely candidate for sainthood. Yet the grace of God can do wonders with those who turn themselves over to God. What about me? What part of my life do I need to turn over to God?

Prayer

Saint Camillus de Lellis, pray for us that we may have the same compassion toward those we are called to serve. Amen.

JULY 15

Saint Bonaventure

c. 1221–July 15, 1274
Feast: July 15
Patron: Those with bowel disorders

One of the great lights of the Franciscan Order, Bonaventure is called the Seraphic Doctor because he wrote with such intense zeal and love for God. He was born Giovanni di Fidanza in Bagnoregio, Italy. While studying in Paris as a young man, he got to know the Franciscans and joined their order in 1243. With his keen intellectual gifts, he became a Master of Theology at the university of Paris. But due to the suspicions over their mendicant way of life (which blends contemplative and active life), both he and his classmate Thomas Aquinas had to wait until 1257 to be formally installed as masters.

But Bonaventure didn't stay there long. He was elected the Minister General of the Franciscans in that same year. He held that office for seventeen years. At that time the Franciscans had greatly expanded, having over thirty thousand friars. Controversy was also brewing with the Franciscan Spirituals. They were following a radical direction that would lead them away from Church teaching. Bonaventure carefully guided the friars to a correct understanding of Saint Francis and his vision for the Church. In 1273, Bonaventure was made a bishop and the cardinal of Albano. He was washing dishes when the papal legates came to bring him the red hat, so he asked them to hang it on a nearby bush. He died while attending the Second Council of Lyons.

Reflection

One of Bonaventure's greatest works is *The Journey of the Mind to God*. In it he writes that God's illumination of the human mind far outstrips mere human wisdom. Though Bonaventure was intelligent, he knew that prayer must be joined to study if we want to attain to God. Do I try to direct my study toward God?

Prayer

Saint Bonaventure, pray for us that, like you, our hearts may burn with an ardent love of God. Amen.

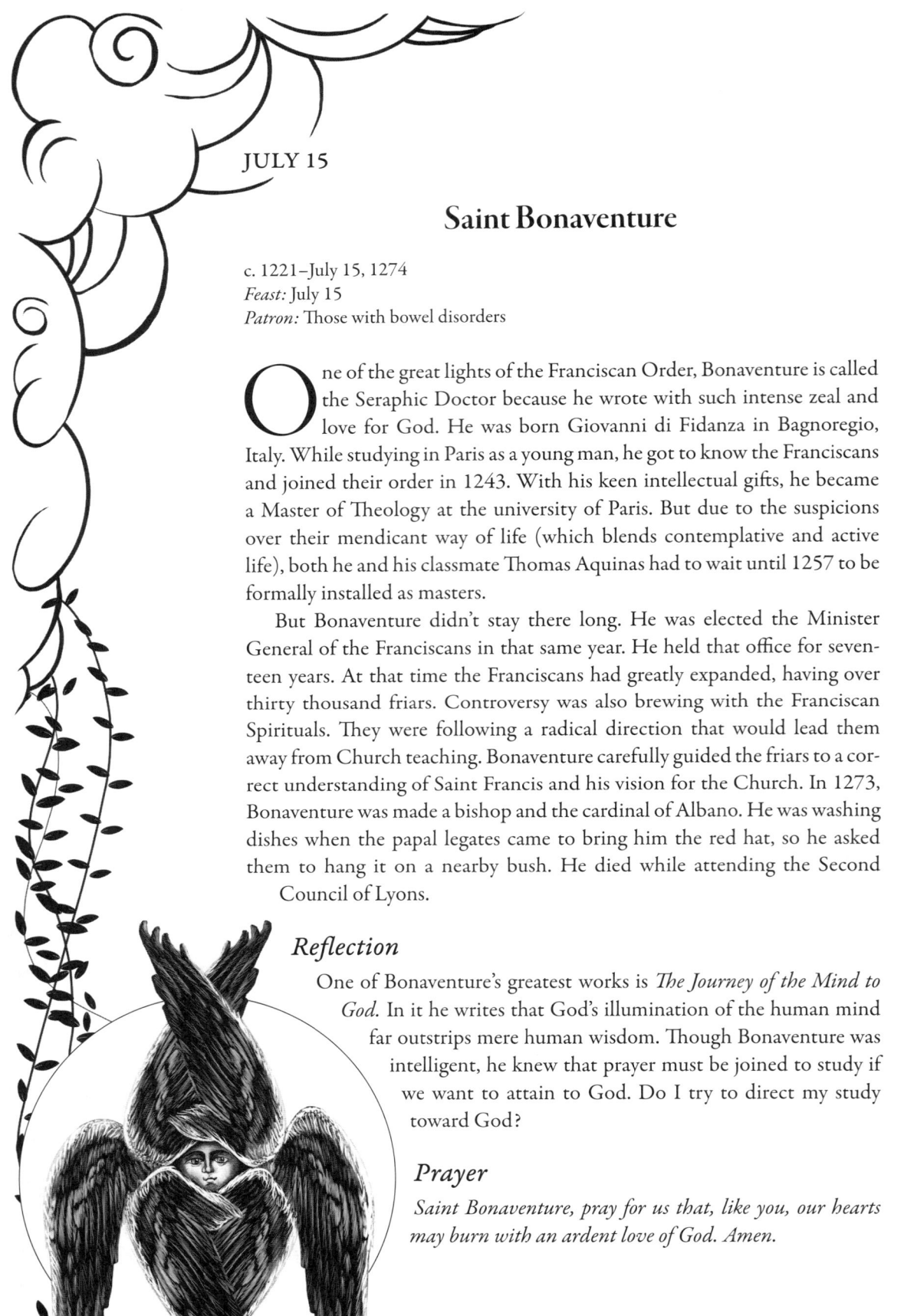

JULY 16

Saint Simon Stock

c. 1165–May 16, 1265
Feast: May 16
Patron: Bordeaux, those who wear the brown scapular, tanners

Simon was born in Kent, England, and was pious from a young age. It is said that he first became a hermit at the age of twelve and lived for many years in a tree stump, or "stock," from which his name derives. After twenty years, Simon felt called by God to join the Carmelites. As a Carmelite he traveled widely and established monasteries throughout Europe. In 1247, Simon was elected the superior general of the order. A competent leader, he did much to solidify its growth.

However, Simon also faced difficulties in adjusting the Carmelite life to changes in society. When the order faced any difficulty, Simon would kneel in prayer and ask the Blessed Mother to aid him. On July 16, 1251, Mary appeared to Simon and gave him the brown scapular as a sign of her protection of the Carmelite Order. After a long life, Simon died in Bordeaux, France.

Reflection

The brown scapular that Mary gave to Simon can help us reflect on the Biblical theme concerning garments of salvation. The Bible contains many references to garments, beginning in Genesis: "And the Lord God made garments of skins for the man and for his wife, and clothed them" (3:21). The need for clothing was an effect of their sin. God's tender action can be seen as symbolizing the garments of grace that he would bestow through Jesus Christ. In the same way, the brown scapular is a sign of the salvation that Jesus won for us.

Prayer

O Beautiful Flower of Carmel, most fruitful vine, splendor of heaven, holy and singular, who brought forth the Son of God, still ever remaining a pure virgin, assist us in our necessity. O Star of the Sea, help and protect us. Show us that you are our Mother.

— From a prayer attributed to Saint Simon Stock

JULY 17

Blessed Solanus Casey

November 25, 1870–July 31, 1957
Feast: July 30
Patron: Apparent failure and setbacks

Bernard Francis Casey was the sixth of sixteen children born to Irish immigrants in the state of Wisconsin. As a young man, he longed to be a priest, but struggled academically in the seminary. He was thus advised to look into religious orders and decided to become a Capuchin, receiving the name Francis Solanus. Barely passing his classes, he was finally ordained a "simplex" priest, which meant he could not preach or hear confessions. Still, he took great joy in celebrating the Holy Mass.

After his ordination, Father Solanus spent twenty years in Yonkers, New York, and New York City, doing simple jobs in various Capuchin monasteries. While he was serving as the doorkeeper, people noticed his gifts as a counselor and intercessor and began seeking his advice. As his popularity grew, he was transferred to Detroit, Michigan, where he continued to work as the porter. He spent long hours listening to everyone who came to the monastery door and became known for his wisdom, compassion, and humility. Those he prayed for often received miraculous cures, but he always emphasized that all miracles came from God. After his death at age eighty-six, Father Solanus' funeral was attended by thousands of the people he had helped during his life.

Reflection

Solanus Casey is not known for being academically gifted. But he is known for always having time for those who approached him. He made a difference just by listening with compassion and offering honest advice without passing judgment. How much do I value attentively listening to others? Do I view unexpected conversations as interruptions or blessings?

Prayer

Dear Lord, help us to communicate you in what we say and in the way we listen. May those who come to us find you. Amen.

JULY 18

Blessed Titus Brandsma

February 23, 1881–July 26, 1942
Feast: July 27
Patron: Journalists, Friesland

Anno Sjoerd Brandsma was born into a devout family in Friesland, Netherlands. He entered the Carmelites in 1898 and became a priest, taking the religious name "Titus," after his father. In 1923, he was appointed professor at the Catholic University of Nijmegen. He was popular there for his attention to and care for his students. With his great heart, Brandsma had a special sensitivity to the poor and was extremely generous.

When the Nazis occupied Holland in 1940, Titus was spiritual adviser to the Roman Catholic Association of Journalists. He fully backed the Dutch bishops' policy of refusing to publish Nazi propaganda in Catholic papers. On January 19, 1942, he was arrested and imprisoned for his leading role in this opposition, and then sent to the Dachau concentration camp on June 19. The guards regularly beat him and left him bleeding in the mud. Yet Brandsma prayed for his persecutors and tried to inspire and encourage fellow prisoners. His health broken, he had to go to the camp hospital where the Nazis used him for medical experiments, finally giving him a lethal injection on July 26, 1942.

Reflection

The concentration camp did not conquer Titus' spirit because he had a profound spiritual attitude. He knew that Jesus was always with him and that one can always pray. Titus would often say, "Prayer is life; not an oasis in the desert of life." And in a letter from prison, before being sent to Dachau, he wrote, "Our dear Lord is everywhere." Prayer enables us to live in the presence of God, who carries us through all the difficulties of life.

Prayer

Blessed Titus Brandsma, pray that our spirits may not be crushed under the burdens of life but that we might always trust in the Lord as you did. Amen.

JULY 19

Saint Macrina the Younger

c. 330–379
Feast: July 19
Patron: Penitents, nuns

Macrina came from a family of saints: her grandmother was Saint Macrina the Elder, her parents Saints Basil the Elder and Emmelia, and her brothers included Saints Peter of Sebaste, Gregory of Nyssa, and Basil the Great. Her brother Gregory wrote a life of Macrina, in which he says that while she was still in the womb, an angel appeared to her mother and gave the child the private name of Thecla, an early martyr associated with Saint Paul.

Macrina was known for her beauty. She was betrothed to marry at a young age, but the young man died suddenly. Macrina saw that as a sign from God that she was to lead a virginal life. She dedicated herself to helping her family in domestic work, to prayer, and the study of Scripture. After her father died, she and her mother led a monastic style of life on a family estate in the country. Gregory says that when her brother Basil returned from his studies with a conceited attitude, Macrina schooled him in humility.

Reflection

Macrina was noted for her ascetical practices and spirit of penance. Today we are less inclined to emphasize the need for penance. Yet it remains a requirement of the Gospel: "Unless you repent, you will all perish" (Lk 13:3). Its purpose is not to punish but to purify us. By denying ourselves small comforts, we can more easily say "no" to sin. Perhaps the best penances are to hold back a biting word, extend a helping hand, or to patiently listen when we'd rather speak.

Prayer

Saint Macrina, pray for us that we might better understand the true goal of our lives: to love God and our neighbor as we journey toward eternal life. Help us to value the things that really matter and to say no to everything else. Amen.

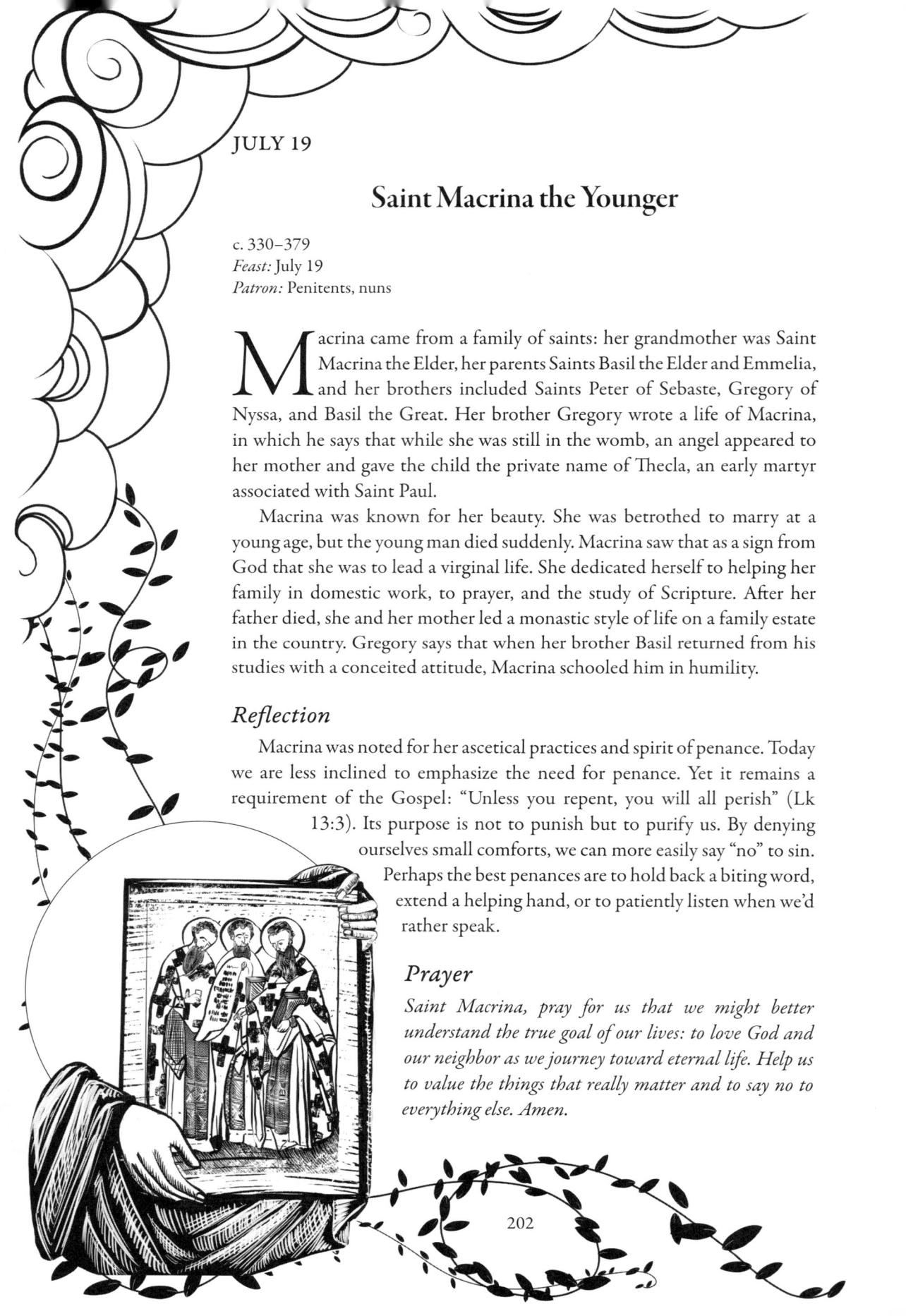

Saint Lawrence of Brindisi

July 22, 1559–July 22, 1619
Feast: July 21
Patron: Brindisi, preachers

Julius Caesar de Rossi was born in Brindisi, Italy, and lost his father at an early age. He entered the Capuchins when he was sixteen. Ordained in 1582, he had an extraordinary gift for languages and fluently spoke at least eight, including Latin, Hebrew, and Greek. That enabled him to study the Bible in its original languages, which proved an invaluable resource for preaching. Lawrence wrote extensively, including important treatises on the Blessed Virgin Mary as well as biblical writings. A cardinal once wrote that Lawrence knew Scripture so well that were it ever lost, he could rewrite the Bible from memory!

Lawrence was an important figure in the Catholic Counter-Reformation. He led the Capuchin Order and implemented reforms of the Council of Trent. His preaching was so riveting that he attracted great crowds. And when he went to Austria and Bohemia, he brought many Lutherans back to the Catholic faith by his preaching and zeal. He was also an excellent diplomat and helped forge greater unity among the countries of Europe. In 1959, in recognition of his many contributions, Saint John XXIII named him a Doctor of the Church, with the title "Apostolic Doctor."

Reflection

Lawrence responded to the needs of his time with apostolic methods that attracted people. He used his gifts to the maximum, especially his great learning and his fluency in languages. The Church today needs new evangelizers who can speak to people in a way they will understand. How can I be an authentic witness of my faith?

Prayer

Saint Lawrence of Brindisi, pray for us that we may study and deepen our knowledge of Sacred Scripture, in which you found the riches of God's word. Amen.

JULY 21

Saint Paul VI

September 26, 1897–August 6, 1978
Feast: May 29
Patron: Ecumenism

Giovanni Battista Montini was born in Brescia, northern Italy, to a well-to-do family. He was ordained a priest on May 29, 1920, the day on which his future feast day would be celebrated. In 1922, he began a long period of service in the Vatican Secretariat of State. During World War II, he was a key aide to Pope Pius XII and headed Vatican efforts to help refugees and others suffering from the war. He was appointed archbishop of Milan in 1954. There he sought to bring the Gospel to working people and to involve the Church in social action.

After Saint John XXIII died, Montini was elected pope on June 21, 1963 and took the name Paul VI. His major task was to complete the Second Vatican Council, and then to implement its teachings and decrees. Great turmoil shook the Church and the world in the post-conciliar years. Paul VI tried to bring about balance and peace but was often criticized. His most famous encyclical was the prophetic *Humanae Vitae*, in which he articulated Catholic teaching on sexual morality and contraception. The document was not well received in many quarters, and Paul VI suffered very much because of it. But, trusting God, he forged ahead with his papal mission until his death in 1978.

Reflection

As a young priest, Father Montini probably never dreamed that he would become pope during such a critical time in Church history. Yet through all the crises and trouble, he trusted that Jesus would guide the Church. If we ever find ourselves in turmoil, we too can trust that Jesus will guide us through the storm.

Prayer

Saint Paul VI, pray for the Church in our day, that it may continue to be a beacon of light and hope for all. Amen.

JULY 22

Saint Mary Magdalene

First Century
Feast: July 22
Patron: Converts, women, hair dressers, penitent sinners, people ridiculed for their piety, those troubled by sexual temptation, the contemplative life

Mary Magdalene was from the town of Magdala, on the shore of the Sea of Galilee. Tradition has identified Mary with several women in Scripture. According to one tradition, Mary Magdalene is Mary of Bethany, the sister of Lazarus and Martha. She is also identified with the penitent woman who washes and anoints Jesus' feet and dries them with her hair. Jesus cast seven demons out of Mary Magdalene, bringing her into his active public ministry (see Lk 8:2; Mk 16:9). Nothing in Scripture, however, suggests she was a prostitute as is often mistakenly thought.

When most of the disciples ran away in fear, Mary Magdalene stayed by the foot of the Cross with John and the Blessed Virgin Mary. In faith, she went to the tomb on Easter Sunday and found it empty (see Mk 16:1–7). As the first witness to the resurrection, God entrusted her with the task of announcing the news of the risen Lord to the rest of the disciples. According to tradition, Mary Magdalene was in the Upper Room at Pentecost and she traveled to Ephesus with Mary and John the Beloved, where she died and was buried. Another tradition holds that she died in France after spending many years there in prayer and solitude.

Reflection

Mary Magdalene plays an important role as the first witness to the Resurrection. For this reason, the Eastern Church calls her *isapostolos* (equivalent to an apostle), and the Western Church has traditionally called her *apostola apostolorum*, or "the Apostle to the Apostles." Each member of the Church has a different role, but we all share the important responsibility of spreading the Gospel. Am I open to how God is calling me to spread the Gospel?

Prayer

Saint Mary Magdalene, pray for me, that I may fulfill my call to witness joyfully to the signs of the love of God in my life. Amen.

JULY 23

Saint Bridget of Sweden

1303–July 23, 1373
Feast: July 23
Patron: Europe, Sweden, widows, scholars

As a wife, mother, and foundress, Saint Bridget lived a remarkable life. Born of a noble family in Finster, Sweden, she married at a young age and had eight children. She and her husband, Ulf, devoutly practiced their faith, worked to help the poor, and became Third Order Franciscans. In 1344, they made a long pilgrimage to the shrine of Saint James in Compostela, Spain. Shortly after, Ulf became sick and died.

Bridget remained four years in the Cistercian monastery where Ulf had died. There she had many mystical revelations, especially about the passion of Christ. She also felt called by God to begin the Order of the Most Holy Savior (later known as the Brigittines.) To obtain the pope's approval for this, she went on pilgrimage to Rome in 1349. The popes at that time, however, were living in Avignon. So, Bridget had to wait a long time and never returned to Sweden. In Italy she continued her good works, dedicating herself to helping the sick and those in need. She was canonized on October 7, 1391, by Boniface IX. In 1999, Saint John Paul II named her a co-patroness of Europe.

Reflection

Bridget was a strong woman of faith who knew how to direct people to God. She preached the Gospel by word and example within and outside of her own family. One of her daughters, Catherine, is also a canonized saint. Though Bridget lived in high society, she kept her focus on Jesus Christ. She is a model of how to bring the Gospel to every part of society. How can I be a witness to the Gospel for the people in my corner of the world?

Prayer

Saint Bridget of Sweden, intercede for us that the Gospel may penetrate our culture. May Christian families, including my own, follow your holy example. Amen.

JULY 24

Saint Charbel Makhlouf

1828–December 24, 1898
Feast: July 24
Patron: Lebanon

The youngest of five children, Youssef Makhlouf was born in a mountain village in northern Lebanon. His father died when Youssef was only three years old. After his father's death, his mother eventually remarried a man who became a Maronite priest. Youssef assisted at his stepfather's Masses in the Maronite Rite and the family was very devout, dedicated to prayer and fasting. Youssef spent a lot of time caring for the family's sheep and goats and would often retreat into a little grotto to pray. As Youssef grew older, his mother wanted him to marry. But Youssef knew he was called to the monastic life.

At the age of twenty-three, he left home without telling anyone and entered the monastery. He took the religious name Charbel, after an early Syrian martyr. After living in the monastery for sixteen years, Charbel received permission to move to a nearby hermitage. Charbel dedicated his life completely to prayer. Many people came to visit him, seeking his spiritual advice as well as healings. During Mass one day, Charbel fell ill. He died eight days later on Christmas Eve. Since his death, many miraculous healings have been attributed to his intercession.

Reflection

Charbel prayed with great devotion. His dedication to prayer inspired and strengthened the spiritual lives of the many people who knew him. His example shows us how our own daily fidelity to the Lord's call brings life not only for ourselves but also for those with whom we live and work. How can I be more faithful to daily prayer?

Prayer

Saint Charbel Makhlouf, your life of prayer helped you to remain close to Jesus. Help me to strengthen my prayer life so that I too may be generous in responding to the Lord's call in my daily life. Amen.

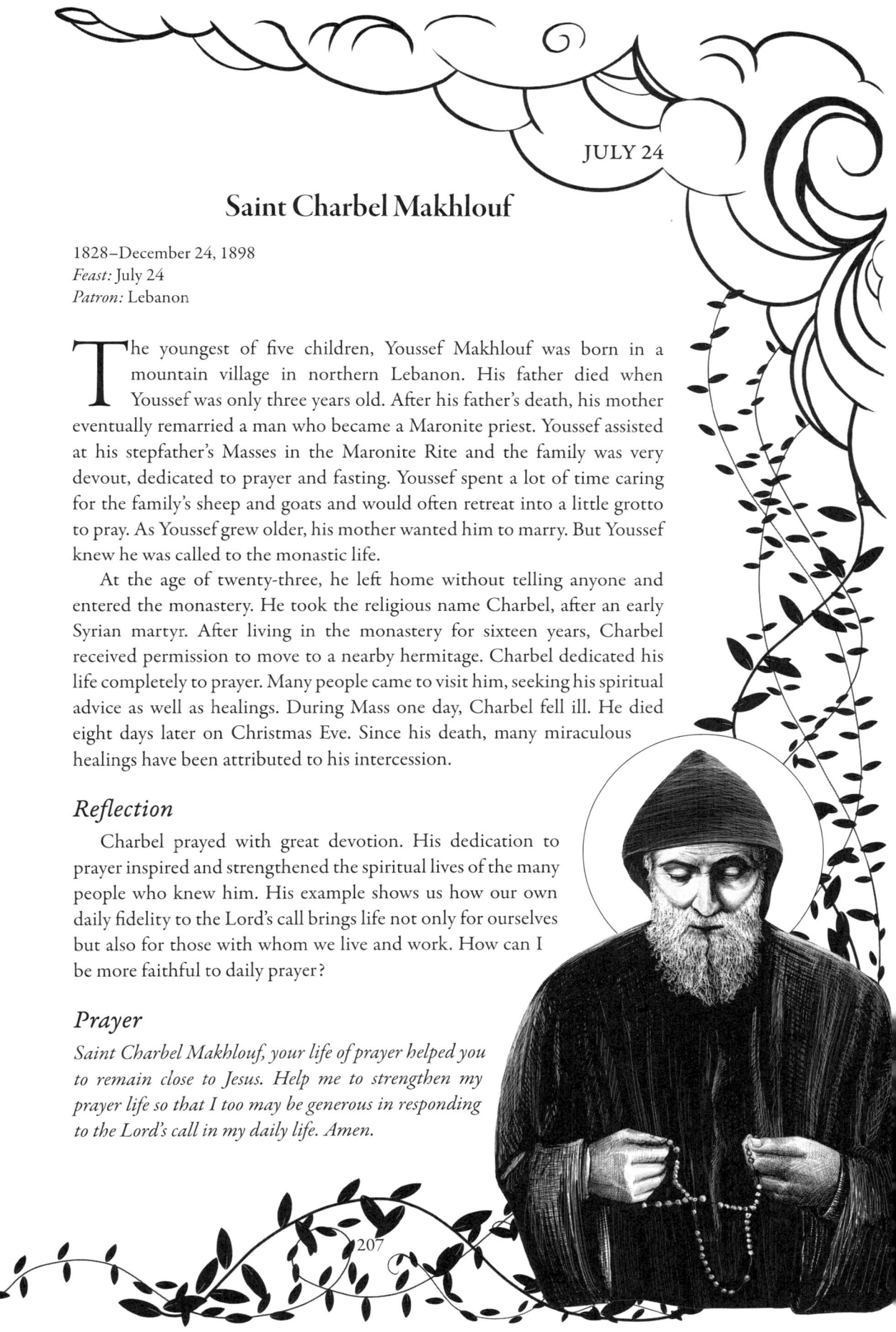

JULY 25

Saint James, the Apostle

First Century
Feast: July 25
Patron: Spain, Guatemala, pharmacists, pilgrims, against arthritis

James, the son of Zebedee and brother of John the Apostle, is known as "James the Greater," probably because he was older than the other James, who was the head of the Church in Jerusalem. Jesus called James and his brother John from their fishing boat to become "fishers of men" (see Mt 4:19). The brothers immediately left their nets and their father to follow Jesus—which they would do until the end of their lives. Along with Peter, John, and sometimes Andrew, James was given a prominent place among the apostles. He was present at the Transfiguration and for several miracles that seem to have been witnessed "by invitation only." He was also among the apostles whom Jesus asked to stay awake with him in the garden of Gethsemane (see Mt 26:36–46). After Pentecost, some traditions hold that he preached in Spain, but then returned to Judea where King Herod Agrippa ordered his beheading. James is traditionally honored as the first of the apostles to die for his faith. The famous shrine to him in Compostela, Spain, has drawn countless pilgrims who have walked the *camino de Santiago*.

Reflection

James was a close friend of Jesus, privileged to accompany him very closely during his public ministry. He witnessed the Lord's love and compassion for each person he encountered. Jesus continues to invite us to accompany him closely! He promised to be with us always and fulfills this promise in a special way in the Blessed Sacrament. How might Jesus be inviting me into a closer relationship to "keep watch" with him (see Mt 26:40)?

Prayer

Saint James the Apostle, pray that I may come to know Jesus more personally and hear and respond to his invitations so that I may grow closer to him. Amen.

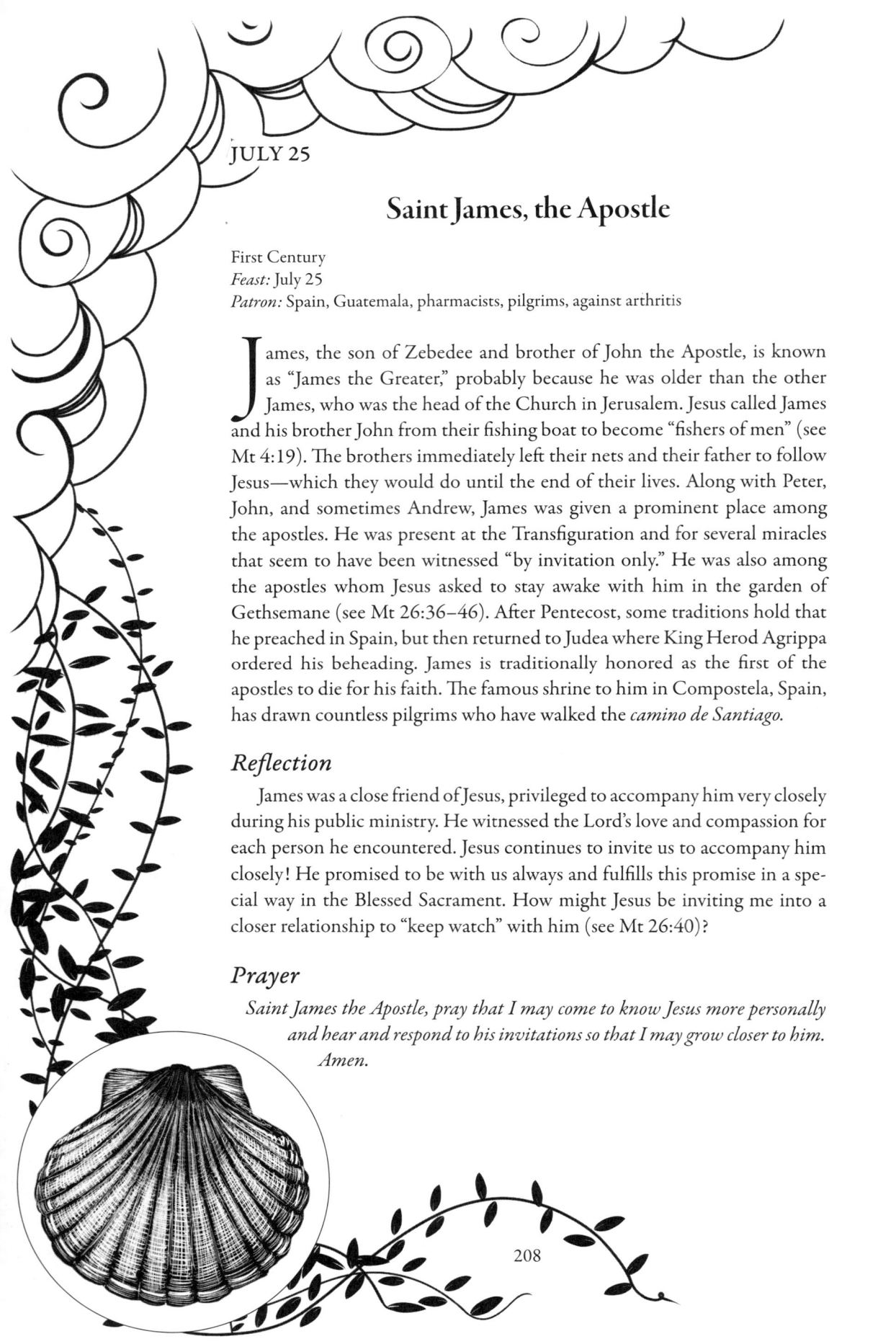

JULY 26

Saints Joachim and Anne

First Century
Feast: July 26
Patron: Grandparents
Joachim: Fathers, married couples, cabinetmakers, linen traders
Anne: Christian mothers, housewives, expectant mothers, childless couples, infertility

Joachim and Anne have been honored from the early centuries of the Church as the parents of Mary and the grandparents of Jesus. Devotion to Joachim and Anne spread first in the East and then in the West. A church dedicated to Saint Anne was built in Jerusalem in the twelfth century. What we know of Joachim and Anne comes from the Protoevangelium of James, an apocryphal work. Although these writings are not authoritative like the Bible, they do tell us what early Christians thought about Mary's parents.

According to tradition, Joachim and Anne suffered greatly because they were childless. Finally, in their old age, an angel of the Lord appeared to Anne and told her she would have a child. Overwhelmed, Anne praised God and promised to give the child back to God. As the angel had said, Mary was born and when she was three her parents presented her to the Temple. It is said that little Mary danced before the Lord's altar, and all of Israel loved her.

Reflection

Joachim and Anne can help us reflect on the beauty of marriage and the gift of children. Their inability to conceive gave them great pain because they viewed children as a precious gift of marriage. Family life today is under great stress. The example of these two saints inspires us to value our family relationships and to make our homes true domestic churches where everyone can learn to give and receive love.

Prayer

Saints Joachim and Anne, pray for us, especially for married couples and families. Pray that all families will follow your example of a life centered on love. You helped to prepare the way for Christ, the Lord. May our families be places where Jesus dwells among us. Amen.

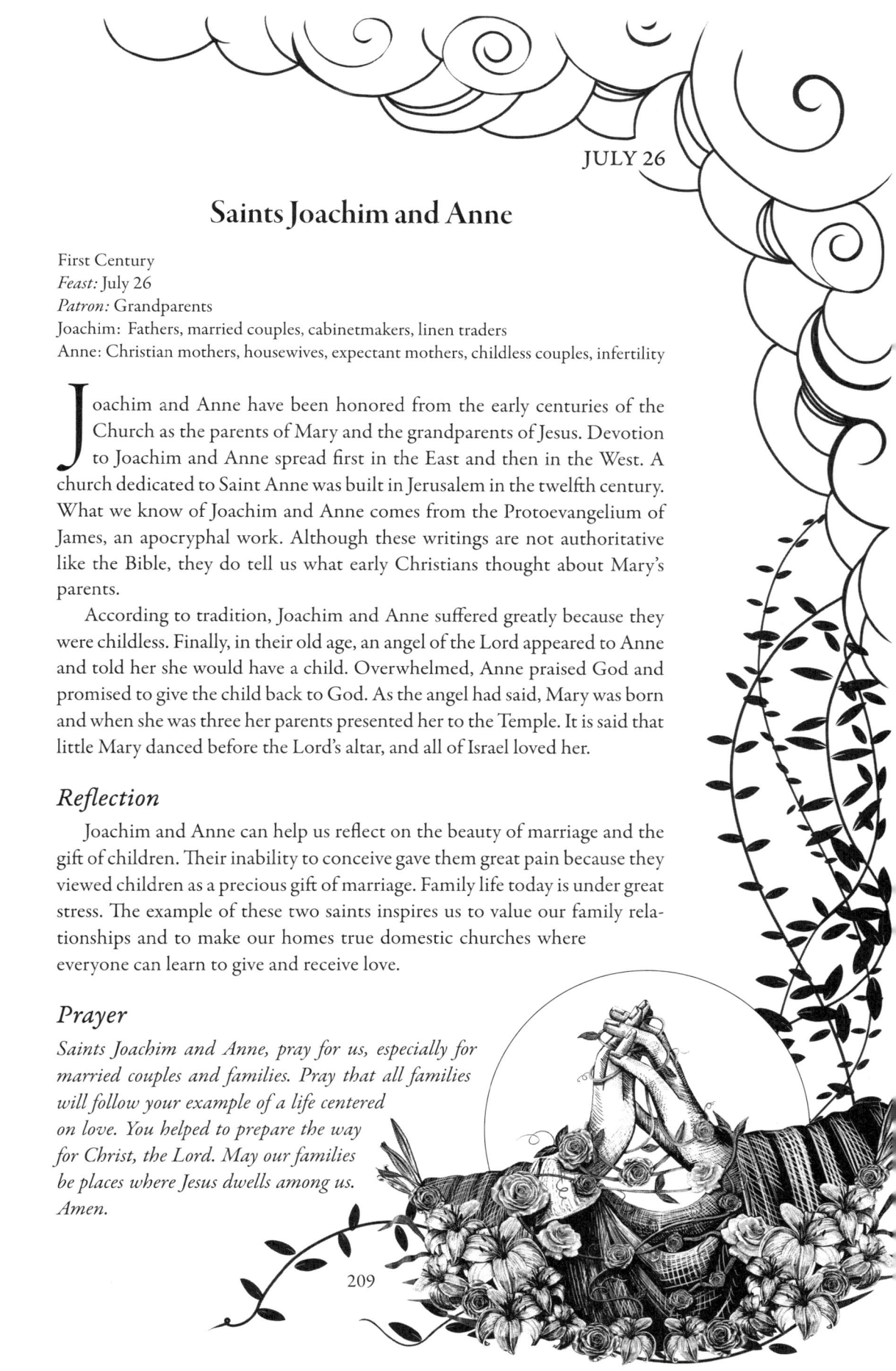

JULY 27

Saint Alphonsa of the Immaculate Conception

August 19, 1910–July 28, 1946
Feast: July 28
Patron: Against sickness, against the death of parents

Born in India, Alphonsa, known as Annakutty, was the last of five children. Her mother died three months after her birth and so her earliest years were lived with her grandmother. These were years of joy in which she drank in her grandmother's love for the faith and prayer. When she was ten years old, she went to live in the house of her aunt Anna Murickal, a severe and demanding woman who was determined to procure an advantageous marriage for the girl despite her desire to be a nun. Annakutty patiently and firmly resisted her aunt's attempts to marry her off.

In 1928, Annakutty entered the postulancy of the Congregation of the Franciscan Clarists, taking the name Alphonsa of the Immaculate Conception. Two years later, however, ill health knocked on the door of Alphonsa's life, never to leave. Before her perpetual profession, she was miraculously and instantaneously cured. Alphonsa made her profession in 1936 with great joy. Shortly thereafter, however, she again began to suffer painful illnesses. Nevertheless, she always tried to accept her sufferings with faith in the Lord's goodness. She wrote shortly before her death, "I feel that the Lord has destined me to be an oblation, a sacrifice of suffering."

Reflection

Sister Alphonsa of the Immaculate Conception was never far from illness, frustration, and sorrow, and yet her life was also a song of determination and self-gift. She knew her suffering was not worthless. She accepted it out of love for her Suffering Savior, knowing that because of him her suffering would lead to the resurrection. How can I more trustingly accept whatever sufferings I may experience in my life?

Prayer

Saint Alphonsa of the Immaculate Conception, help me to discover God's love for me even when I have difficulty dealing with the frustration and sorrow in my life. Amen.

JULY 28

Blessed Stanley Rother

March 27, 1935–July 28, 1981
Feast: July 28
Patron: Farmers, missionaries, missions, Oklahoma

Born on a farm in Okarche, Oklahoma, Stanley Francis Rother was the first native-born priest from the United States to be martyred and beatified. As a young man, he went to Assumption Seminary in San Antonio. But like Saint John Vianney, the Curé of Ars, Stanley also had difficulties academically and was sent home. With the support of his bishop, he tried again to become a priest at Mount Saint Mary's Seminary in Emmitsburg, Maryland. He succeeded and was ordained on May 25, 1963.

After serving in several parishes, Stanley volunteered to go to a diocesan mission in Santiago Atitlán, Guatemala. Despite his past difficulties learning Latin, he learned Spanish and Tz'utujil, the local Mayan language. His penchant for hard work coupled with his farming skills helped him to serve the people in many ways. Among other things he founded a co-op, a nutrition center, the first Catholic radio station in the area, and a clinic.

However, a civil war brought violence to the country, and Stanley's name appeared on a death list because of his work for his poor parishioners. He returned to Oklahoma, but soon he felt called to go back to the people he had served. He said, "The shepherd cannot run at the first sign of danger." Upon his return, three men broke into his rectory and shot him. Stanley is now entombed in Oklahoma City, but his heart is buried in Santiago Atitlán, where he selflessly served for so many years.

Reflection

Stanley Rother is a shining example of the virtue of courage. He was a good shepherd, just like Jesus, who said, "The good shepherd lays down his life for the sheep" (Jn 10:11). How can I show courage in the face of difficulties?

Prayer

Blessed Stanley Rother, your heart was formed after the heart of Jesus. Pray that I might also walk according to the ways of the Lord and seek justice for all. Amen.

JULY 29

Saint Martha

First Century
Feast: July 29
Patron: Cooks, dieticians, domestic servants, servants

Everything we know about Martha of Bethany is found in the Gospels of Luke and John. Jesus was a regular guest of Martha, her sister, Mary, and their brother, Lazarus.

On one of Jesus' visits Martha was busy with many domestic chores. She complained to Jesus that Mary was not helping her. Jesus responded, "Martha, Martha, you are worried and distracted by many things; there is need of only one thing. Mary has chosen the better part" (Lk 10:41–42). Martha must have taken to heart Jesus' words about the primacy of sitting still to listen to him, as evidenced in her growth in contemplative prayerfulness revealed in the face of her brother's death. Grieving, she still was able to profess her faith in Jesus, "Yes, Lord, I believe that you are the Messiah, the Son of God" (Jn 11:27). And Jesus raised Lazarus from the dead.

Reflection

Jesus' words to Martha were not in any way a condemnation of work or even of busyness. It was not about what she was doing but how Jesus wanted her to change. He said, "You are worried and distracted." We can hear in this an invitation: "Be calm. Have peace. Stay focused on me and on my presence here with you!" How can I be more aware of Jesus' presence with me, even in the midst of all my other responsibilities?

Prayer

Jesus, you counted Martha among your closest friends. Teach me to recognize your presence and friendship in my life, even—and especially—in moments of anxiety and busyness. Amen.

JULY 30

Saint Peter Chrysologus

c. 380–c. 450
Feast: July 30
Patron: Preachers

Peter was called Chrysologus ("golden word" in Greek) because of his eloquent preaching. A convert to the Catholic faith, he was ordained a deacon and later appointed as bishop of Ravenna, Italy. Peter was a bold and fervent pastoral leader. He cared for his flock in a way that nurtured their faith and weaned them away from the vestiges of paganism. He also cultivated relationships with notable people of his time, including the empress Gallia Placidia, other bishops, and Pope Saint Leo the Great.

Peter's preaching was short and well-focused. He said that people would benefit more from a short homily that makes a point well than from long-winded preaching. He often focused on the meaning of the Incarnation due to the errors that were circulating in his time, especially Arianism. As a concerned pastor, Peter wrote a letter to the priest Eutyches, who was erroneously teaching that Jesus had only one nature, the divine nature, and was not fully human. Peter urged him to follow the teaching authority of the pope.

Reflection

Peter was made a Doctor of the Church in 1729 and became known as the "Doctor of Homilies." Pope Francis has said that people often suffer from bad homilies: the clergy because they have to give them, and the congregation because they have to listen to them (see *Joy of the Gospel*, 135). How can I look beyond a homily that doesn't interest me and listen to God's voice within?

Prayer

Saint Peter Chrysologus, you often preached about the incarnate Word of God, Jesus Christ, hiding his divinity behind his human flesh. Pray for me now that my eyes may be opened to see Jesus hidden in each person I meet. Amen.

JULY 31

Saint Ignatius of Loyola

1491–July 31, 1556
Feast: July 31
Patron: The Society of Jesus, soldiers, educators, spiritual retreats, spiritual directors

Ignatius was born to a wealthy and noble family in Loyola, Spain. Seeking fame and glory, he became a knight and immersed himself in the indulgences of courtier life. But then he was gravely injured at the Battle of Pamplona. While convalescing, Ignatius reluctantly read the only books available, the life of Christ and the lives of saints. As he read them, he noticed that he experienced a happiness that was deeper and longer lasting than when he daydreamed about worldly pursuits. Ignatius realized true fulfillment is only found in God—so after his recovery, he left his former life and spent long hours in prayer.

Ignatius' classic work, *The Spiritual Exercises,* began to take shape based on his experiences of the spiritual life. After a trip to Jerusalem, Ignatius sought higher education and was ordained a priest. He started to attract followers, and, over time, these men banded together and were informally known as "the Company of Jesus." They dedicated themselves to preaching, teaching, hearing confessions, and caring for the outcasts of society. They soon became a formal religious order, the Society of Jesus, and Ignatius was chosen as their first superior. At the time of his death, the Jesuits had a thousand members and had already spread throughout much of the world.

Reflection

Ignatius' initial conversion was largely due to spiritual books. Reading about Christ and the saints inspired him to cultivate a deeper relationship with God. The media we consume has great power to influence us for good or for ill. How does media impact me? Am I a better person because of my media consumption?

Prayer

Lord, help me to use media in a way that will bring you glory and draw me closer to you. Amen.

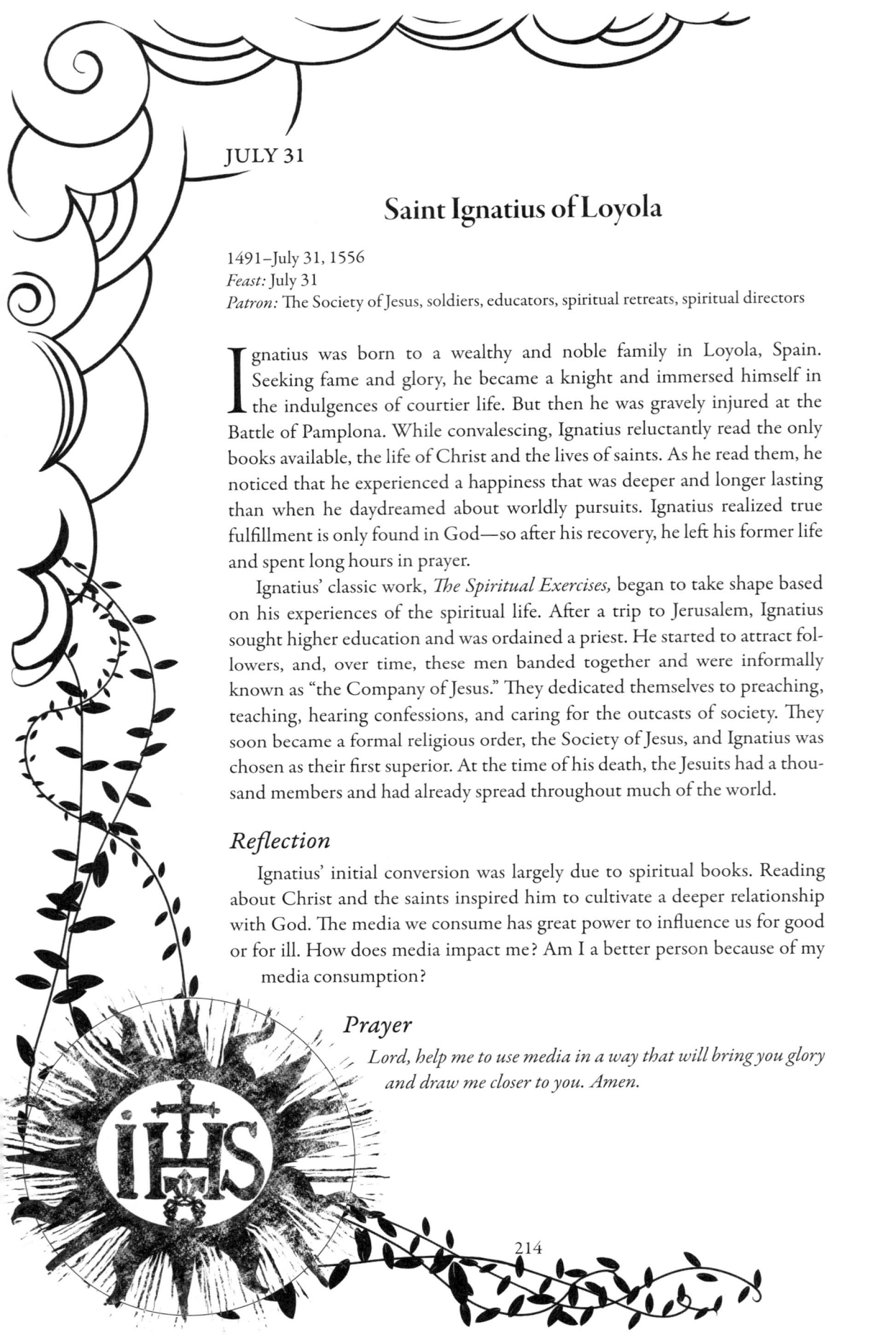

AUGUST 1

Saint Alphonsus Liguori

September 27, 1696–August 1, 1787
Feast: August 1
Patron: Moral theologians, confessors, and those suffering from arthritis

Alphonsus was born near Naples, Italy. His wealthy family provided him with the finest education, and by age sixteen, he had earned doctorates in both civil and canon law. Two years later, he joined the Confraternity of Our Lady of Mercy and cared for the sick at the hospital for "incurables." At the same time, he began to practice law. However, after several years, Alphonsus left the bar, disgusted by the unscrupulous machinations of the court system.

Alphonsus entered the seminary and was ordained in 1726. He soon became known for his sermons, which were eloquent and persuasive. His great compassion led him to evangelize everyone, especially the poor, with patience and love. Due to his untiring efforts, groups in which people would pray and reflect on the word of God began to arise throughout the city. In 1732, Alphonsus founded the Redemptorists, dedicated to evangelizing the materially and spiritually poor the world over. Despite resisting the office, Alphonsus was made a bishop when he was sixty-six years old. He wrote over one hundred books, including classics such as *The Practice of the Love of Jesus Christ* and *The Glories of Mary*. Known for his strong devotion to Mary, Alphonsus died at the age of ninety-one, just as the Church bells tolled the Angelus.

Reflection

Alphonsus used every means at his disposal to instruct and form the faithful in holiness. He aimed both to instruct them in the basic truths of faith and to live that same faith ardently with the help of the Eucharist and devotion to Mary. How do I allow Mary to help me to grow closer to Jesus?

Prayer

Saint Alphonsus Liguori, pray that I may strive to live the Gospel of Jesus Christ with the help of the Virgin Mary. Amen.

AUGUST 2

Saint Peter Julian Eymard

February 4, 1811–August 1, 1868
Feast: August 2
Patron: Those who promote devotion to the Holy Eucharist

Born in the small French town of La Mure d'Isere, Peter felt God's call from a young age. After some difficulties due to poor health, he was ordained as a diocesan priest. Peter always had a strong devotion to Mary, which led him to enter the Marists in 1839. He was also developing a strongly Eucharistic spirituality. On the feast of Corpus Christi in 1845, an intense spiritual experience gave him the idea to form a congregation of priests devoted to Jesus in the Eucharist.

As his love for the Eucharist grew, Peter discerned that God was calling him to leave the Marists and to establish the Congregation of the Blessed Sacrament. He did this in 1856. The beginnings were lived in great poverty. Peter evangelized people in the streets and prepared them for their first Communion. He involved lay people in this work. And in 1858, with Marguerite Guillot, he began the Congregation of the Servants of the Blessed Sacrament, a contemplative community for women. His writings that emphasize the Eucharist as a Sacrament of love are still popular today.

Reflection

Peter Julian Eymard's charism joined Marian devotion with a strong emphasis on the importance of Eucharistic prayer. The Eucharist is Jesus, the source of all grace. Peter's example can help us to reflect on our own love for and appreciation of the wonderful gift that Jesus has given us in the Eucharist. How can I make time in my week for prayer before the Blessed Sacrament?

Prayer

Saint Peter Julian Eymard, you were filled with such love for the real presence of Jesus in the Eucharist that you wanted to share him with everyone. Pray that we too may find in the Eucharist—the source of all grace and blessings—our strength and our peace. Amen.

AUGUST 3

Saint Peter Faber

April 13, 1506–August 1, 1546
Feast: August 2
Patron: Those who suffer depression

Born at Savoy in the French Alps, Peter was gifted with an astounding memory. As a young man, he went to Paris to study, where he roomed with Saints Francis Xavier and Ignatius of Loyola. Peter tutored Ignatius in philosophy and also told him about the self-doubt and mental torments he suffered. Ignatius guided him in dealing with those issues. Peter soon joined Ignatius and his companions as a founding member of the Society of Jesus.

Known for his gentle spirit and warmth, Peter was sent on many apostolic trips. By leading spiritual retreats in the style taught to him by Ignatius, Peter helped many people live their faith more fully. Peter continued to battle his own inclinations to depression and distress. In the last four years of his life, he kept a journal called the *Memoriale,* in which he recorded his dialogues with God and prayer experiences. In 1546, Pope Paul III asked him to attend the Council of Trent as a theologian; however, exhausted from his travels and work, the forty-year-old Peter died in the company of his good friend Ignatius before the council started.

Reflection

Peter Faber battled depression, mood swings, and self-doubt, just as many people do. In his spiritual journal Peter explained that he found that recalling God's presence with him helped him to know he was not alone in his suffering. In times of struggle we can recall that the Holy Spirit dwells in us by grace and will strengthen us in our needs.

Prayer

Saint Peter Faber, you knew firsthand how hard it is to deal with the depression and sadness that can drag us down. Pray for us that when we experience times of darkness, we may feel the light, warmth, and comfort of the Holy Spirit, who always guides us. Amen.

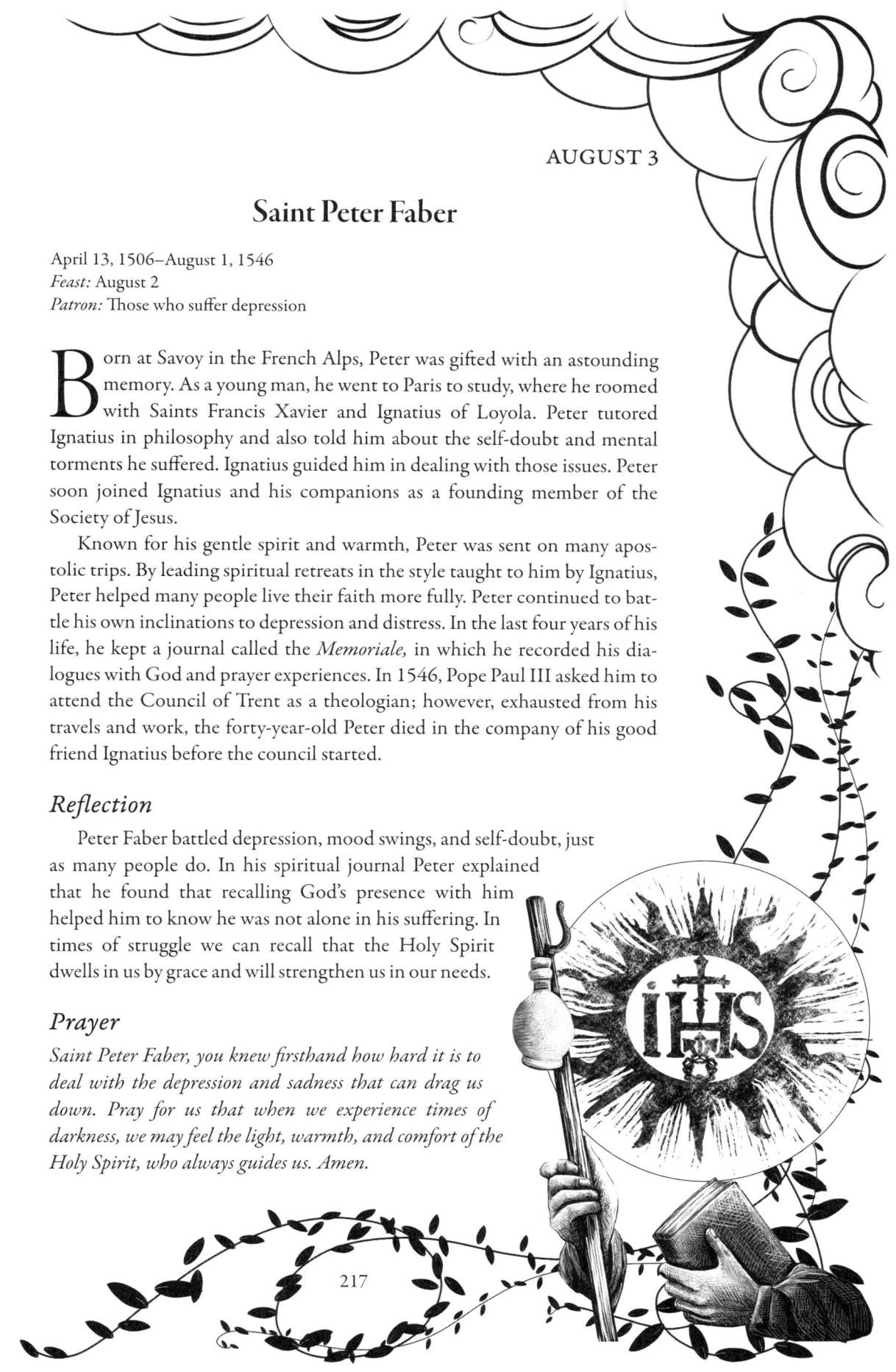

AUGUST 4

Saint John Vianney

May 8, 1786–August 4, 1859
Feast: August 4
Patron: Priests, especially parish priests

No one expected that John Vianney would go far in life. He wasn't a good student, partly because he entered the seminary with little preparation and partly because he had been raised for the practical life of a French farmer. However, John persevered even through the humiliation of being sent home in failure. His parish priest tutored him until he was ready for ordination.

John was then assigned to a tiny, faithless village named Ars, which was considered a "non-parish" by the clergy. The people of Ars either ignored or ridiculed their new priest. In response, John preached and prayed, performing endless acts of penance. He cajoled the people to revive their religious fervor. His heroic efforts were met with the constant harassment of the devil, even to the point of setting the rectory on fire. However, by 1855, some twenty thousand pilgrims came every year to confess to the humble Curé (pastor) of Ars. He spent sixteen hours every day hearing confessions. The grace of God worked so powerfully through the ministry of John Vianney that his gentle glance alone could bring the sinful to repentance.

Reflection

The Curé of Ars helps us to see the efficacy of prayer and penance. Often, we are tempted to categorize our failures or those of others as inevitable. We do not expect change. Having been a farmer, the Curé knew the possibility of growth, but he also knew that change required hard work: digging, plowing, planting, weeding, watering, even defending, until the harvest was ready. The grace of God brings about spiritual growth. Do I trust that God's grace is active in me?

Prayer

Saint John Vianney, pray for the Church today that priests may follow your example and that parishes may be alive in the grace of God. Amen.

AUGUST 5

Saint Mary MacKillop

January 15, 1842–August 8, 1909
Feast: August 8
Patron: Australia, abuse victims, the falsely accused

Mary Helen was the eldest child of Scottish parents who were immigrants to Australia. Due to the family's poverty, she began work at fourteen and later became a teacher and governess. In 1864, with the help of Father Julian Tenison Woods, Mary opened a boarding school for girls in Portland, Victoria. Two years later, they opened that country's first Catholic school in Penola, South Australia. Seeing the urgent need for Catholic education, in 1867 Mary founded the first native Australian religious order, the Sisters of Saint Joseph of the Sacred Heart, or the Josephites. She took vows as Sister Mary of the Cross, perhaps not suspecting how greatly the Cross would impact her life in the near future.

As happens so often to the saints, misunderstandings and jealousy led to opposition. Mother MacKillop was accused of disobedience and misappropriation of funds. This led first to her banishment from her order and finally, in 1871, to excommunication. With a broken heart but an unbroken spirit, Mother MacKillop remained peaceful and continued to spend herself serving others. Eventually, the excommunication was revoked and when the truth came out, she was reappointed to her congregation's leadership and promoted good works until her death.

Reflection

It is hard to imagine being maligned, as was Mary MacKillop, without seeking to turn the tables on the accusers. Yet Mary constantly exhorted her sisters to refrain from criticizing the bishop and the others involved. Because she greatly respected the opinions and viewpoints of others, Mary MacKillop is an attractive example for us when we feel tempted to be judgmental of others.

Prayer

Saint Mary MacKillop, you were a woman of many firsts in serving the people of Australia. May we, too, embrace everyone in charity. Amen.

AUGUST 6

Saint Sixtus II and Companions

Died August 6, 258
Feast: August 7
Patron: Persecuted Christians

Named in the Roman Canon of the Mass, Sixtus was pope for just one year. He was a peaceful pope who strove to maintain unity in the Church. Sixtus helped to heal a rift that had developed with the Church in Africa over the question of rebaptizing those who had lapsed from the faith. He determined that they could be reconciled without being rebaptized.

Before the beginning of Sixtus' pontificate, the emperor Valerian had begun to persecute the Church, and the violence gradually grew worse. First, he demanded that prominent Christians sacrifice to the Roman gods. Some capitulated to the emperor's demands, but many people, including most of the clergy, refused. Eventually, the Emperor issued a decree that all bishops, priests, and deacons should be put to death. Sixtus and the priests of Rome held secretive Masses in the catacombs to evade the emperor's soldiers. Several days later, however, some soldiers broke in as Sixtus was celebrating Mass. Sixtus and four of his deacons were beheaded. Three more deacons were killed within a few days, including Saint Lawrence. Sixtus was buried in the Catacombs of Saint Callistus.

Reflection

The early centuries of the Church were marked by fierce persecution by the Roman Empire. Though the persecution was not constant, it made life extremely perilous for Christians. However, Rome slowly collapsed and lost its political power, while Christianity perdured. Though it takes time, love and truth triumph over hate and falsehood. We can keep this in mind when we see our own culture slip further away from its Christian roots.

Prayer

Saint Sixtus, pray for us who live in a world that often opposes Jesus and the truth of the Gospel. Help us to be authentic witnesses to the faith, for which you willingly gave your life. Amen.

Saint Cajetan

AUGUST 7

1480–August 7, 1547
Feast: August 7
Patron: Unemployed

A man of great academic and political ability, Tommaso Gaetano received his degree in civil and canon law at age twenty-four. He served as a diplomat under Pope Julius II but resigned after the pope's death to study for the priesthood. Taking the name Cajetan, he was ordained in 1516, just one year before Martin Luther launched the Protestant Reformation. After his ordination, Cajetan founded, directed, and worked in hospitals in his hometown of Vicenza and in Verona and Venice.

Amidst the changing political and religious climate, Cajetan's priestly life began to take a new direction. Like Luther and his followers, Cajetan saw a great need for renewal in the Church, especially among clergy. Unlike them, Cajetan believed that renewal could take place from within the Church Jesus had founded. In 1524, with a few companions, he founded the Clerics Regular who later would be called the Theatines. They committed themselves to preaching, helping the sick, promoting the Sacraments, and renewing the life of the clergy. The order grew slowly, and Cajetan encountered much opposition. But his personal holiness and his commitment to clerical holiness was a light in a time of darkness and confusion.

Reflection

In a time of great turmoil in the Church, Cajetan dedicated himself to serving the people of God and renewing the priesthood. Our Church always needs people who put holiness first and provide a good example to others. When scandal causes people to lose trust in the Church, we can offer others the witness of a living relationship with God. This witness is more powerful than we could ever know.

Prayer

Saint Cajetan, pray for me so that I can be the yeast of God's love in the unleavened bread of my society and culture. Amen.

AUGUST 8

Saint Dominic

1170–August 6, 1221
Feast: August 8
Patron: Astronomers, preachers, the Dominican Order

Dominic de Guzmán was born in Spain in 1170, a time when feudal society was changing, cities were expanding, and major universities were being founded in Europe's urban centers. From childhood, Dominic felt drawn to the word of God. To read and pray with Scripture became his passion. He studied for the priesthood and was ordained around 1195. While traveling through southern France with his bishop, Diego d'Azevedo, Dominic saw Albigensians, who incorrectly maintained that all material creation was evil, and understood the need for sound preaching..

Gradually, Dominic conceived the idea of starting an order of poor mendicant friars who would study so as to more effectively preach the Gospel. He also gathered a group of women to establish the female branch of the order. He traveled widely and had many miracles attributed to him. He tried his best to stay out of the limelight but had little luck; people knew he was a saint. When Dominic was fifty-one, he fell seriously ill. On the Feast of the Transfiguration, as his brothers prayed, he stretched his arms upward and died.

Reflection

Dominic was quick to adopt new ways of pastoral care for the people of his time. Yet he was always grounded in the word of God. The Dominican motto *Veritas* (truth) aptly sums up Dominic's spirituality. We too live in an age of great change, which can sometimes uproot people from their faith. We can learn from Dominic's example of prayer and contemplation as we make our way through a chaotic world.

Prayer

Saint Dominic, pray that we may always have a deep love for truth, especially for the word of God. May we ground our lives on divine teaching so as to share with others the light of Jesus Christ. Amen.

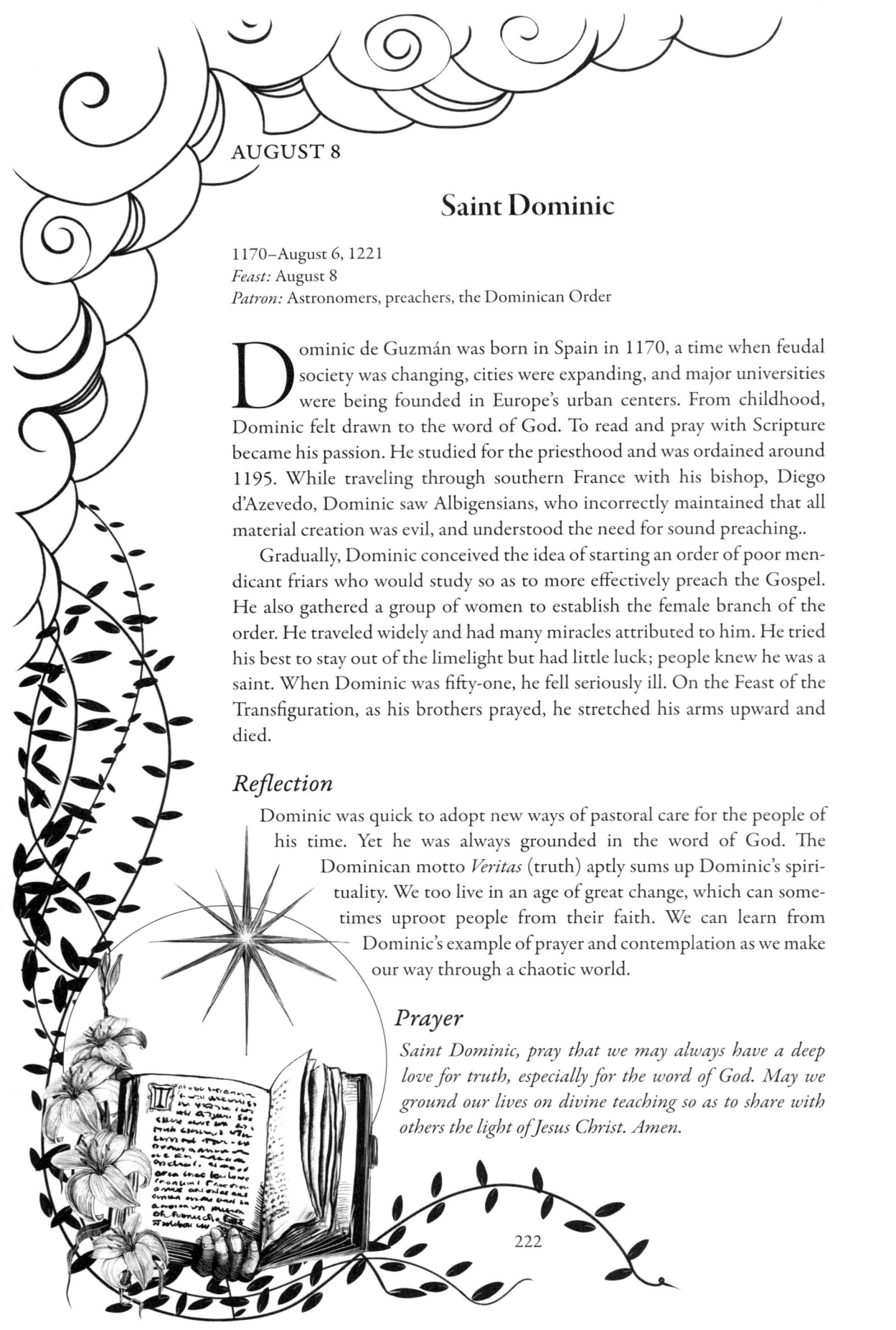

AUGUST 9

Saint Teresa Benedicta of the Cross

October 12, 1891–August 9, 1942
Feast: August 9
Patron: Jewish converts, philosophers, Europe

Edith Stein was born in Breslau, Prussia, on the Jewish Day of Atonement. An inquisitive child who always searched for what was true, Edith excelled in school. She eventually pursued a doctorate in philosophy, which was unusual for a woman at that time. In 1916, she became a research assistant to Edmund Husserl, the founder of phenomenology. Although a professed atheist since the age of fourteen, one day Edith powerfully encountered what she instinctively knew was true while reading Saint Teresa of Ávila's autobiography. This led her to the Catholic Church.

On January 1, 1922, Edith was baptized. She spent some years as a teacher and lecturer, but in 1933 she entered the Carmelite Monastery in Cologne, taking the name Teresa Benedicta of the Cross. To her surprise, her superiors asked her to continue writing. She finished her last book, *Science of the Cross*, in Echt, Netherlands, where she had fled with her sister Rosa. When the bishops of the Netherlands publicly condemned the persecution of Jews, the Gestapo retaliated by sending priests and religious of Jewish origin to the death camps. As Edith was led away, she said to her sister, "Come, we are going for our people."

Reflection

Edith Stein's doctoral dissertation, *On the Problem of Empathy*, was, in a sense, a summary of her life. It came naturally to her to enter into the experience of others. Her conversion and vocation as a Carmelite allowed Edith to experience an even deeper communion with others through the mystery of God's love. Edith's embrace of this divine love was demonstrated in her Christ-like willingness to die in solidarity with her people as a martyr in Auschwitz.

Prayer

Saint Teresa Benedicta of the Cross, inspire us with your same generous and sacrificial love of the Cross. Amen.

AUGUST 10

Saint Lawrence

Died c. 258
Feast: August 10
Patron: Deacons, fire, cooks, comedians, the poor

Lawrence was one of the most popular of the Roman martyrs. The great devotion to him indicates his martyrdom must have been extraordinarily heroic, even if some of the details include elements of legend. Lawrence was from Spain, and while studying at Saragoza he met a teacher who would later become Pope Sixtus II. They became good friends and later both went to Rome. There, Sixtus ordained Lawrence a deacon and put him in charge of all the deacons.

In this capacity, Lawrence showed an extraordinary care and love for the poor. In 258, when Emperor Valerian ordered the death of all Roman clergy, Sixtus and four deacons were executed on August 6. According to tradition, Lawrence wept when he saw Sixtus being led to martyrdom because he wanted to die with him. He cried out, "Father, where are you going without your son?" Sixtus replied, "I am not abandoning you, my son. You will face a more difficult trial." Soon after, the authorities demanded that Lawrence give them the Church's riches. Losing no time, Lawrence gathered Rome's poor and presented them to the emperor saying, "Here are the treasures of the Church." Enraged, the emperor had Lawrence burned to death on a gridiron.

Reflection

In a sermon on the martyrdom of Lawrence, Saint Augustine noted that the holy deacon ministered Christ's blood at the celebration of the Eucharist and willingly shed his own blood for the sake of Christ. When we participate at Mass, we can offer ourselves to Jesus and ask him to join our actions and sufferings to his for the salvation of the world.

Prayer

Saint Lawrence, pray for us that we might have the courage to put our faith into practice, especially through love of the poor and neglected. Amen.

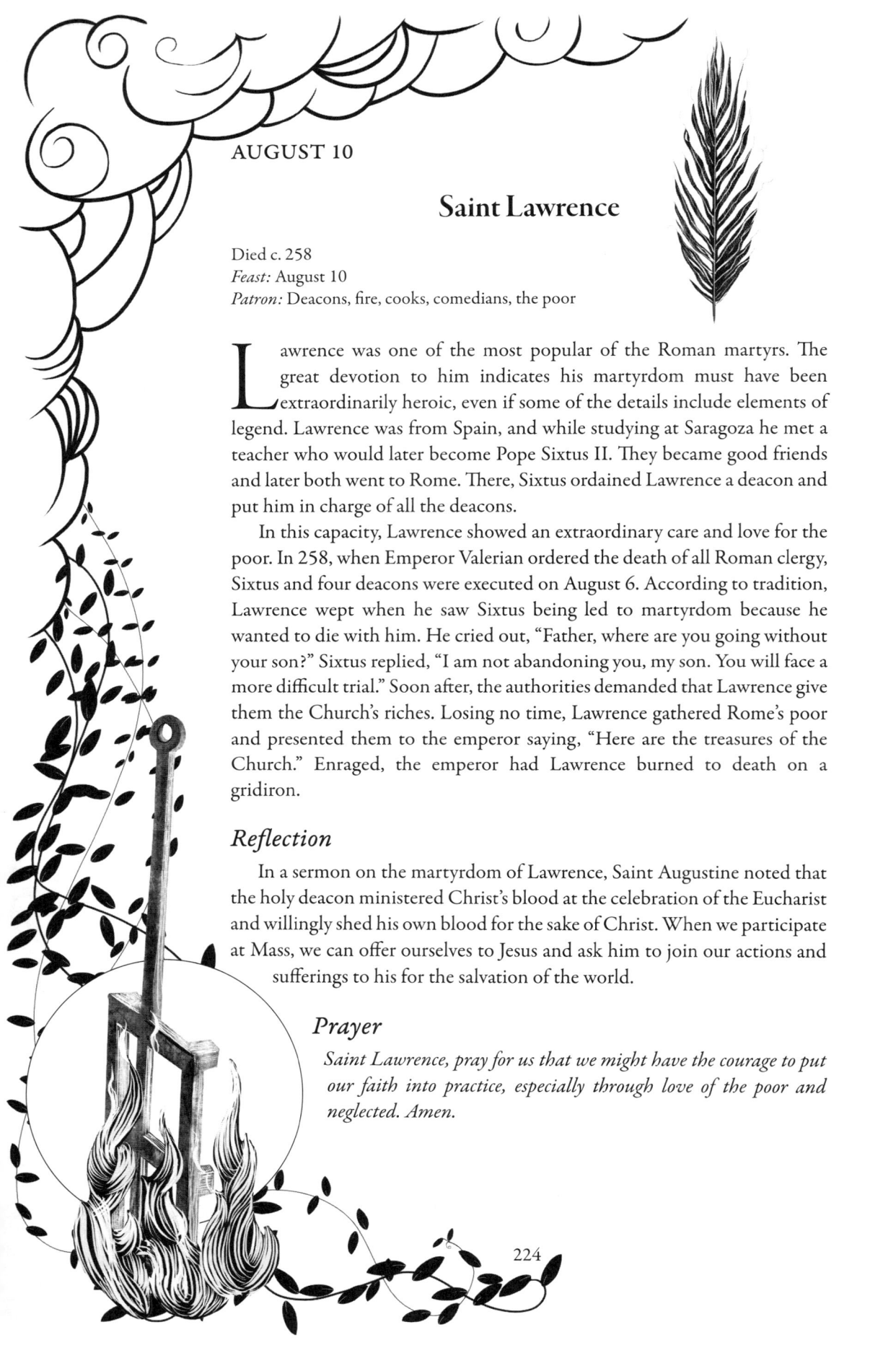

AUGUST 11

Saint Clare of Assisi

c. 1194–August 11, 1253
Feast: August 11
Patron: Television, the Poor Clares

On Palm Sunday night in the year 1212, a young woman ran away from home. Clare Offreduccio wanted to follow Jesus Christ by living a radically evangelical life. Her desire for this way of life was inflamed by the preaching of a charismatic young man of Assisi named Francis Bernardone. Over her family's objections, Clare left her life of comfort to join Saint Francis in his new movement. Clare trusted in God and pledged to follow Jesus Christ in a life of total poverty.

Soon, Clare's sister Catherine joined her, and little by little more women came. They established poor convents and slowly began to spread throughout Italy and beyond. Their new religious order came to be known as the Poor Clares. As Clare's reputation for holiness grew, people flocked to the convent with requests for prayer. Clare struggled when Church authorities resisted the idea of a group of nuns living in complete poverty without a source of income. But she always stood firm on this point, and after great opposition, official approval of her order's Rule arrived just as Clare neared death.

Reflection

In establishing the Poor Clares, Clare collaborated with Saint Francis in a spiritually fruitful way that shows her as a strong, wise woman. Her strength of character enabled her to withstand pressure from Church authorities who wanted her to follow a less austere way of life. The strength of Clare teaches us that the great works of God spring from the root of poverty and prayer.

Prayer

Saint Clare of Assisi, you followed Jesus Christ in complete poverty and love. Pray for us that we may not set our hearts on material possessions but on Jesus, and to use our goods in a way that will benefit others. Amen.

AUGUST 12

Saint Jane Frances de Chantal

January 23, 1572–December 13, 1641
Feast: August 12
Patron: Forgotten people, widows, parents separated from their children, forgiveness

A native of Dijon, France, Jane married the Baron Christophe de Chantal. Unfortunately, in less than a decade, her husband was accidentally shot while he was hunting. After his death, Jane was inconsolable, and for many years she struggled to forgive the man who had killed her husband. Her father-in-law demanded that the young widow move onto his estate with her four young children. She suffered greatly there due to a conniving servant who had power over the household. In the midst of her grief and humiliations, Jane prayed for a faith-filled guide to help her.

During Lent of 1604, Jane met the young bishop of Geneva, Saint Francis de Sales, in Dijon. Francis became her spiritual director and a close friendship developed. Soon the bishop revealed to Jane his intention to found a religious congregation of women devoted to works of charity among the sick. After arranging for the care of her children, Jane worked with Francis to begin the Order of the Visitation of Holy Mary, also known as the Visitation Order. Jane established many foundations, and admiring crowds often met her with applause. Jane's response: "These people do not know me; they are mistaken." Before her death she had founded more than eighty monasteries.

Reflection

The spiritual friendship between Jane and Francis bore great fruit for themselves and for others. Jane had the spiritual sensitivity to see where God was leading her through her wise spiritual director. To her, nothing mattered but that God's designs for her life be lovingly accepted. How is God intervening in my life—perhaps in unexpected ways—and pointing me to his love?

Prayer

Saint Jane Frances de Chantal, obtain for me from the Lord an open heart, ready to give him everything in all that he desires. Amen.

AUGUST 13

Saints Pontian and Hippolytus

Died 235
Feast: August 13
Patron: Prison guards, prison officers, prison workers

Honored together in death, these two saints clashed with each other during life. Pontian became pope in 230, during the difficult times of Roman persecution. He also faced internal problems in the Church. Hippolytus had set himself up as an antipope some years earlier and continued his dissent under Pontian. Hippolytus was a rigorist who thought the popes were being too lenient toward Christians who had denied Christ during the persecution but later wanted to return to the Church. Despite this, Hippolytus was an important theologian who wrote many works on Scripture, liturgy, and Church teaching.

The Christian persecution under the emperor Maximinus, however, saw no distinction between Pontian and Hippolytus. They both were banished to hard labor in the salt mines of Sardinia. Pontian resigned his office so that another pope could be elected. Hippolytus reconciled with him, and then ended his schism by sending word to his followers in Rome to return to Church unity under the new pope. They both died from their sufferings in the harsh condition of the mines. Their feast is on August 13 because on that day in 235, their bodies were interred in the catacombs in Rome.

Reflection

The schism of Hippolytus shows us that the Church has always had problems, even in the early days of persecution and martyrs. The human element always threatens to break Church unity. Yet the reconciliation of Hippolytus and Pontian shows that the power of grace is greater. However harsh the character of Hippolytus may have been, his love for Jesus Christ was greater and led him to freely give up his life. Sometimes it is more important to listen lovingly rather than to voice our opinions and be recognized as right.

Prayer

Saints Pontian and Hippolytus, pray for us that we may always work for the greater unity of the Church. Amen.

AUGUST 14

Saint Maximilian Kolbe

January 8, 1894–August 14, 1941
Feast: August 14
Patron: Drug addicts, families, imprisoned people, journalists, pro-life movement

As a boy, Raymond Kolbe had a remarkable vision. The Blessed Mother appeared to him holding two crowns: one white, representing a life of purity, and the other red, signifying martyrdom. She asked him to choose. He replied, "I choose both." The young Pole later became a Franciscan, taking the name "Maximilian Maria." While studying in Rome, he founded the Militia of the Immaculata, an evangelization movement that promoted sanctity and devotion to Mary. Maximilian published a popular magazine, religious literature, and even broadcast radio programs. His use of the new media to evangelize attracted many of his fellow friars and laypeople who helped him in his mission.

After the Nazis invaded Poland in 1939, Maximilian and his Franciscan brothers hid two thousand Jewish refugees and published anti-Nazi literature. Furious, the Nazis suppressed their congregation and sent Maximilian to Auschwitz. One fateful day, some prisoners escaped. The Nazi guards decided to execute ten prisoners to deter future escape attempts. One of the men selected cried out, "My wife, my children!" Maximilian volunteered to replace him. The group was left to starve, but Maximilian remained calm, leading them in prayer and song. Clinging to life two weeks later, Maximilian was killed with an injection of carbonic acid. Franciszek Gajowniczek, the man Maximilian replaced, attended his canonization in 1982 surrounded by his wife, children, and grandchildren.

Reflection

As a child, Maximilian learned his life would require extraordinary sacrifice. He prepared himself by living a series of selfless acts culminating in his acceptance of the "red crown" of martyrdom. How do I accept the small daily sacrifices that come my way?

Prayer

Saint Maximilian Kolbe, pray that I may remember to call upon Mary, our powerful intercessor, and ask her to pray for me. Amen.

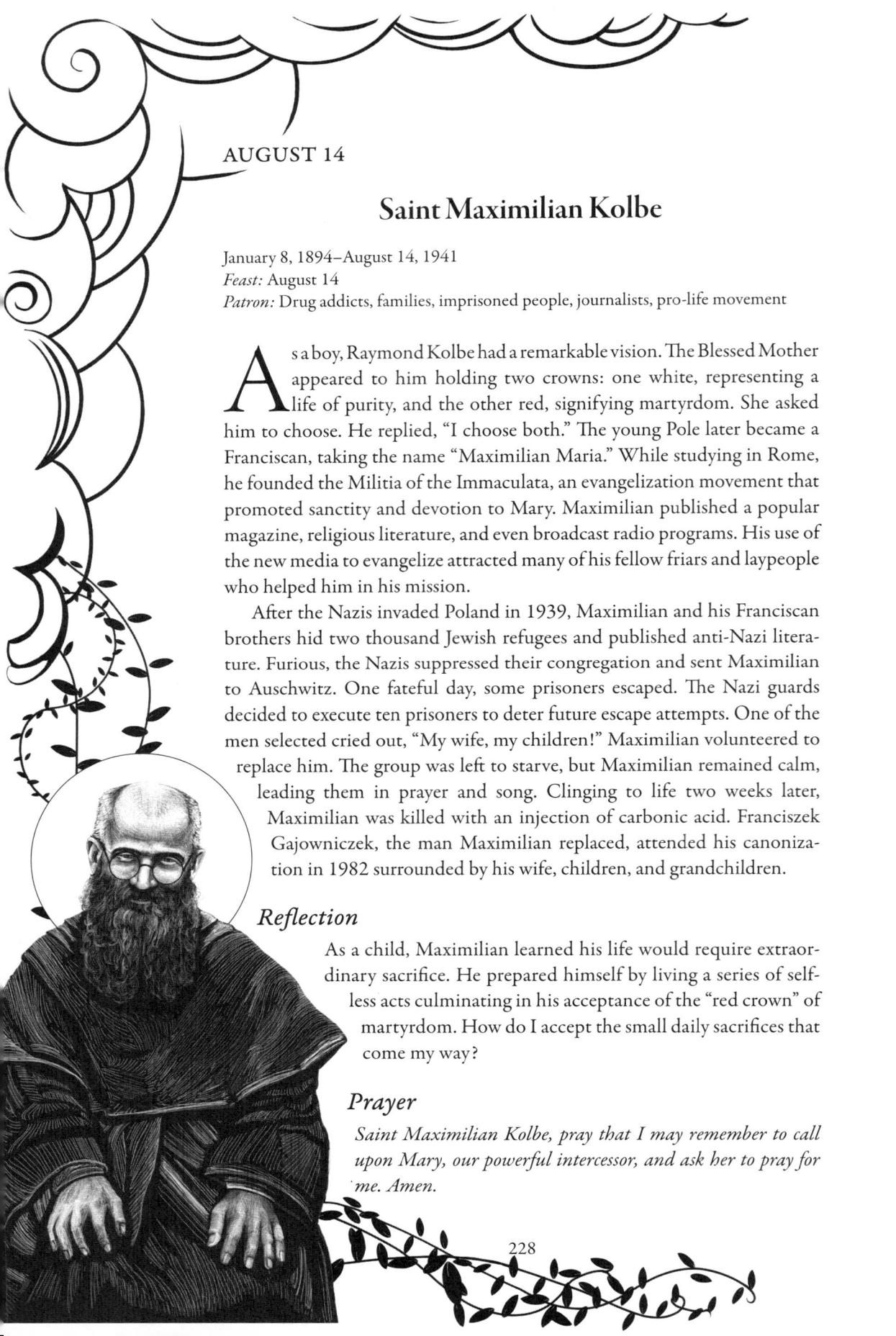

AUGUST 15

Our Lady of the Assumption

First Century
Feast: August 15
Patron: The dying

We honor Mary as the Mother of God because she is the mother of Our Lord Jesus Christ, who is both God and man. In the Old Testament, the Ark of the Covenant represented God's presence among his people. Mary is the new Ark of the Covenant, because she carried the Lord in her womb. The first reading on the Feast of the Assumption speaks of the woman "clothed with the sun" (see Rev 21:1). Mary is the "great sign" in the heavens, a sign of hope for the pilgrim people of God.

On Calvary, Mary stood by the Cross of Jesus and shared in his sufferings. God saw fit that Mary would share in Jesus' resurrection also, anticipating the resurrection of the body that will occur at the end of the world. As Mother of God, it was also fitting that Mary's body be preserved from decay. Therefore, at the end of her earthly life, God assumed her to heaven, body and soul. Mary's prophetic words in today's Gospel reflect the reality that we celebrate today: "From now on all generations will call me blessed; for the Mighty One has done great things for me" (Lk 1:48–49).

Reflection

As Christians, we need not fear death. Jesus has forged the way for us by his resurrection from the dead, leading us to eternal life. Our bodies too will rise again to happiness forever. When the sorrows of earthly life overwhelm us, it helps to remind ourselves that after a few short years, which pass quickly, we will enjoy the happiness of heaven forever.

Prayer

Our Lady of the Assumption, Mary our Mother, pray for us who are still on our pilgrimage through this earthly life. Remind us of our goal, that we are called to happiness in eternal life. Amen.

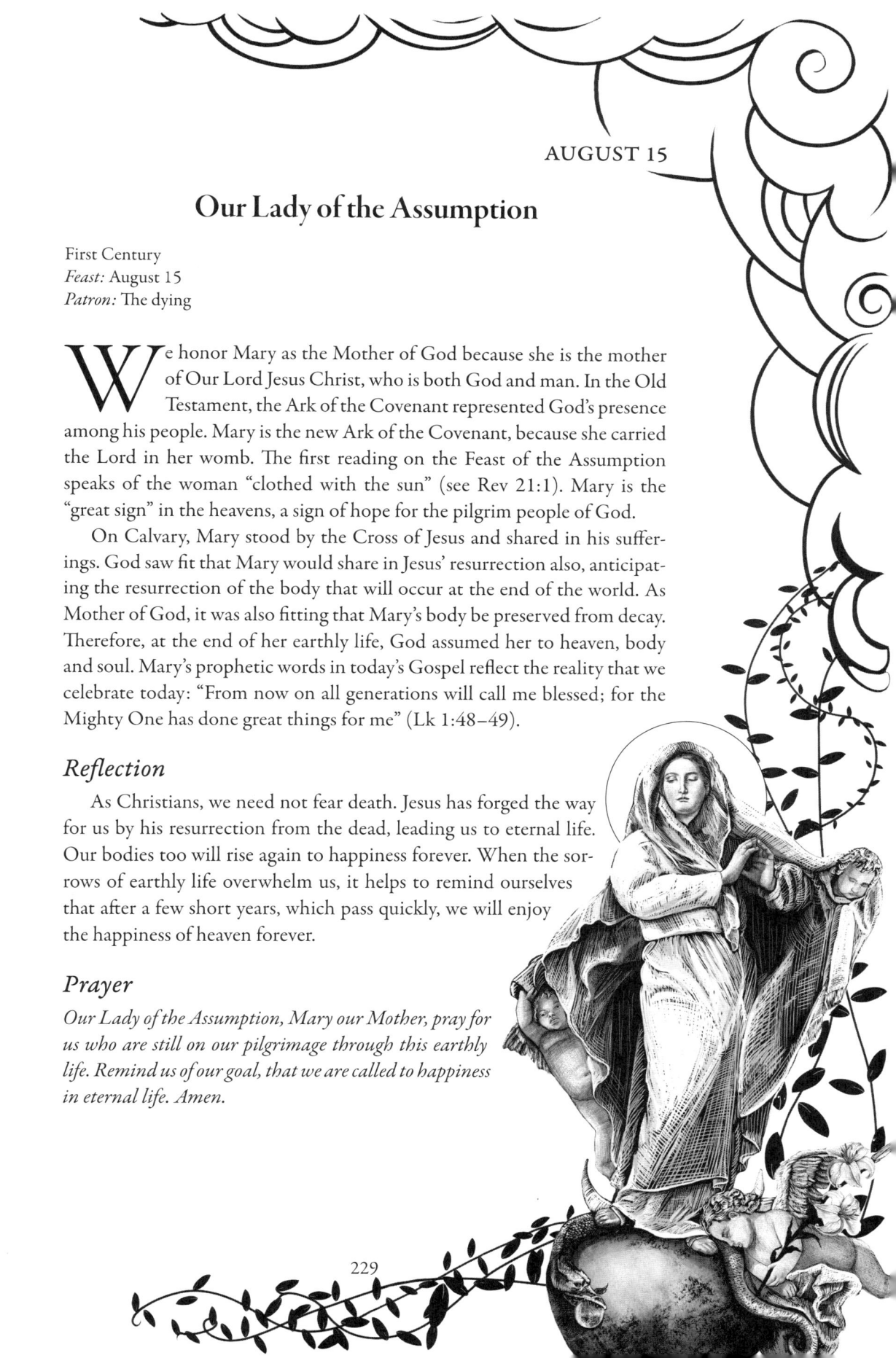

AUGUST 16

Saint Stephen of Hungary

c. 975–August 15, 1038
Feast: August 16
Patron: Hungary, bricklayers, stone masons

Born of the Magyars, Stephen was baptized with his father around 985 by Saint Adalbert of Prague. Paganism was still rampant in that difficult time. Stephen took his faith seriously and wanted to spread Christianity among his people. He succeeded his father as king in 997. It is said that on Christmas Day 1000, Stephen received a crown that he had requested from Pope Sylvester II and was made apostolic King of Hungary about a week later.

Stephen invited the Benedictines to evangelize in his country and established monasteries for them. He also established a system of tithes that supported the Church and the poor. Stephen's devotion to the faith was genuine and he sincerely wanted to help people become Christian. He brought up his son, Emeric, as a devout Catholic, but had the sorrow of seeing him die in a hunting accident. Stephen was canonized together with Emeric in 1083 by Pope Gregory VII.

Reflection

Stephen lived in a very different world than we do, and it might seem hard to relate to a saint who was a king in the early Middle Ages. Yet we can certainly admire and emulate his zeal to spread the Catholic faith, if not some of his methods. Evangelization takes different forms according to the needs of people and their culture. But it always starts from love for Jesus and a desire to make him known to others. In my daily life, what are some ways that I might invite others to learn more about Jesus?

Prayer

Saint Stephen, you always sought to rule with justice and zeal. Pray for us that in our day we might evangelize the modern world so as to make the Gospel known to the ends of the earth. Amen.

AUGUST 17

Saint Lydia

First Century
Feast: August 3
Patron: Dyers, hospitality, businesswomen

What we know about Lydia comes from the New Testament. In chapter 16 of the Acts of the Apostles, Paul and Luke begin their mission in the city of Philippi. Although located in Greece, Philippi was a Roman colony. Lydia seems to have been from the Greek-speaking merchant class of the city. The text says she was from Thyatira, which was a city in Asia Minor (what is now Turkey).

God was working in Lydia's life before she met Paul and Luke. She was not Jewish, but was already a "worshipper of God," that is, a non-Jewish person who believed in the God of the Jews. Luke describes how he and Paul met Lydia:

> On the sabbath day we went outside the gate by the river, where we supposed there was a place of prayer; and we sat down and spoke to the women who had gathered there. A certain woman named Lydia, a worshipper of God, was listening to us; she was from the city of Thyatira and a dealer in purple cloth. The Lord opened her heart to listen eagerly to what was said by Paul. When she and her household were baptized, she urged us, saying, "If you have judged me to be faithful to the Lord, come and stay at my home." And she prevailed upon us. (Acts 16:13–15)

Thus, Lydia became the first Christian convert in Philippi, and her home became a center of hospitality for other believers.

Reflection

Lydia was immediately open to Paul and Luke, a sign of her naturally hospitable nature as well as her generosity to the Christian community of Philippi. How welcoming am I upon meeting newcomers in my parish community?

Prayer

Saint Lydia, pray that I may follow your example of openness to each human being I meet. Amen.

AUGUST 18

Saint Alberto Hurtado

January 22, 1901–August 18, 1952
Feast: August 18
Patron: Chile, poor people, street children, social workers

Alberto Hurtado Cruchaga was born in Viña del Mar, Chile. When he was four years old, his father passed away, leaving his mother to care for two young sons. To pay off debts, his mother had to sell the family home. Due to his family's poverty, Alberto lived with various relatives and moved around often. This experience of homelessness in Alberto's youth would shape his future.

In 1923, Alberto entered the Jesuits. He studied a variety of subjects including philosophy, theology, and psychology in Argentina, Spain, and Belgium. He was ordained on August 24, 1933. A decade later, while he was giving a retreat, Alberto gave a rousing speech urging the attendees to consider the poor of Santiago, especially homeless children. This was the beginning of the charitable work for which Alberto became well known. First, he started *El Hogar de Cristo* or "Christ's House," which provided shelter and a familial atmosphere for the needy. Alberto went on to begin many more initiatives on behalf of the poor, who were so close to his heart. He died of pancreatic cancer and, despite the pain he suffered during his illness, he was often heard saying, "I am content, Lord."

Reflection

The evangelical commandment of loving God and loving one's neighbor was the rule by which Alberto lived. Many in our world still hunger for justice. God has given us particular gifts so that we may put them at the service of our most needful brothers and sisters. How do I feel God inviting me to do more for my brothers and sisters in need?

Prayer

O Lord, like Saint Alberto Hurtado, may I follow in your footsteps by serving those in need in my community, nation, and world. Amen.

AUGUST 19

Saint John Eudes

November 14, 1601–August 19, 1680
Feast: August 19
Patron: Retreatants, seminarians, victims of human trafficking

Born into a devout family in Normandy, John Eudes became a priest and entered the Oratorians, the order founded by Saint Philip Neri. For several years, John selflessly dedicated himself to helping people struck by the plague. Then, realizing that Catholics in rural France were drifting away from the faith, he began preaching missions. These intense times of faith formation lasted from six to eight weeks. John's preaching led to conversions and a great revival in the Church in France.

John deeply desired to provide the people he served with spiritual guidance and education. With these needs in mind, John founded the Congregation of Jesus and Mary to train priests and carry out parish missions. John also was moved by the plight of poor women who turned to prostitution out of desperation, so he founded a congregation of women religious under the patronage of Our Lady of Charity of the Refuge. Later, another group developed, the Good Shepherd Sisters, who had the mission of helping girls and troubled women. In all his work, John experienced great opposition, but he persevered and put the needs of the faithful before all else.

Reflection

John Eudes stressed how the Christian life must be lived in an intense union with Jesus. To this end, John developed devotion to the Sacred Heart of Jesus, as well as to the Heart of Mary. By preaching about the great love of Jesus for us, John was able to move people's hearts. His approach teaches us the importance of helping people connect with Jesus' great love for them. Am I in touch with God's great love for me?

Prayer

Saint John Eudes, please intercede for the great pastoral needs of our time. Help me to be a living witness of the burning love of the Sacred Heart of Jesus for all people. Amen.

AUGUST 20

Saint Bernard of Clairvaux

1090–August 20, 1153
Feast: August 20
Patron: Cistercians, Burgundy, beekeepers, candlemakers, climbers, Church reform

At times, an individual can dominate a century, influencing politics, intellectual thought, Church, and culture. Saint Bernard of Clairvaux was such a person. Born near Dijon, Burgundy, he was sent to study at Châtillon-sur-Seine. After his mother's death, Bernard felt prompted to enter religious life. Over thirty of his friends and family members decided to enter the monastery with him. Bernard thus presented himself with a crowd of other interested men to Saint Stephen Harding, the abbot of the struggling abbey of Cîteaux.

Three years later, Bernard was sent with twelve monks to found another abbey in a location he renamed "Clairvaux," or "valley of light." As the learned abbot's reputation for holiness grew, Bernard became involved in matters outside the monastery. A wise and skilled arbitrator, he was often called upon to settle disputes. Bernard's voice was deeply respected and so he wrote prolifically on many subjects, from the conduct of bishops to spiritual meditations on the Song of Songs. He was canonized twenty-one years after his death.

Reflection

Bernard of Clairvaux's writings reveal a profound mysticism. Contemplation poured forth from this great man's heart and became action for the sake of the world. In all his work both in his monastery and in the world, Bernard sought to be a communication of love. I may not be at the service of kings and popes, like Bernard, but others may request my time and attention. How do I respond?

Prayer

Saint Bernard of Clairvaux, pray that I may grow close to God's love and be generous in making a gift of myself to others. Amen.

AUGUST 21

Saint Pius X

June 2, 1835–August 21, 1914
Feast: August 21
Patron: First Communicants, immigrants

Though he rose to become a bishop, cardinal, and pope, Giuseppe Sarto always remained at heart a simple parish priest. Born into a poor family near Venice, he wrote in his last will and testament, "I was born poor, I lived poor, I die poor." As a priest, his extensive pastoral work made him aware of the acute need for religious instruction. After becoming pope in 1903, he still taught a weekly catechism class to children. He wrote what is now called the *Catechism of Saint Pius X* and worked to establish the Confraternity of Christian Doctrine in every parish.

Pius X's motto, "To restore all things in Christ," guided his entire papacy. He encouraged liturgical reforms, lowered the age for first Communion, and encouraged frequent Communion. Under his leadership, the *Code of Canon Law* was gathered in one volume. Pius also reacted strongly to the rise of modernism, which he saw as a synthesis of all heresies, and condemned its theological errors. Though he is sometimes remembered mainly for his strong anti-modernism, Pius' legacy includes his emphasis on pastoral work, concern for the poor, and clergy formation. He died on the eve of World War I and was the first pope to be canonized since the sixteenth century.

Reflection

Saint Pius X emphasized the Eucharist as the primary means to restore all things in Christ. As he liked to say, "Holy Communion is the shortest and safest way to heaven." Personal union with Jesus through the Eucharist can light a fire in our hearts, leading us to give of ourselves to others. How do I receive the inestimable gift of Jesus in the Eucharist?

Prayer

Saint Pius X, pray that the love of Christ in the Eucharist may always inflame my heart and spur me to share that love with others. Amen.

AUGUST 22

Blessed Victoria Rasoamanarivo

1848–August 21, 1894
Feast: August 21
Patron: Madagascar, lay ministers, victims of adultery

Born in Madagascar, Victoria came from a prominent family with connections to the monarchy. During her lifetime, depending on the king or queen, Catholic missionaries were either welcomed or expelled. When she was thirteen, she went to a new school run by Catholic sisters. Though she was raised in the traditional faith of her people, she was moved by the Gospel and soon decided to be baptized, taking the name Victoria. She was inclined toward religious life, but a marriage was arranged for her. Unfortunately, her husband was unfaithful and drank too much, but Victoria had the joy of seeing him repent and receive Baptism on his deathbed.

In 1883, another persecution of Catholics broke out and all the missionaries were expelled. The first Sunday after the missionaries left, soldiers tried to stop the faithful from entering the cathedral. Victoria bravely said to them, "If you must have blood, begin by shedding mine." She continued to use her status to protect believers during the few years during which there were no priests. She also spent a great deal of time helping the poor with her time and wealth. When missionaries returned, they found a flourishing Church, thanks in large part to Victoria's efforts. She died after a brief illness at the age of forty-six.

Reflection

Victoria worked to keep the Catholics of Madagascar united in times of great difficulty. She could have given up and practiced her faith privately, but she felt called to risk everything to help the larger Catholic community. Victoria had a deep sense of the Church and of her obligation not to abandon the Body of Christ. What gifts can I contribute to the Church?

Prayer

Blessed Victoria, pray that I may use all my gifts for the good of the Church. Amen.

AUGUST 23

Saint Rose of Lima

April 20, 1586–August 24, 1617
Feast: August 23 (August 30 in Peru)
Patron: Peru, indigenous peoples of the Americas, gardeners, florists

Born Isabel Flores de Oliva but called "Rose," this unique young woman was the first saint of the Americas to be canonized. Her life was quite unusual in that she practiced strict, even severe, penances from a young age. Though her family had marriage plans for Rose, she forcefully resisted. Finally, her parents relented and allowed her to live a contemplative life, as long as she remained in their home.

Rose took Saint Catherine of Siena as a model and became a Third Order Dominican. She built a little hut in the family garden and spent most of her time praying and fasting. To her family's bafflement, Rose spent only a few hours each night on a rough bed and denied herself any kind of comfort. However, Rose was not turned in on herself. She preferred to remain at home in part because as her reputation for sanctity grew, she received unwanted attention. But Rose nevertheless often tried to help the poor and needy, at times even bringing people to her hut to care for them herself. After Rose's death, many miracles occurred due to her intercession.

Reflection

Honoring the saints does not mean that we always must imitate all their penances and practices. As Saint Paul reminds us, the most important thing is love (see 1 Cor 13:1–13). Saint Thomas Aquinas said that virtue is essentially about doing what is good, not necessarily what is difficult. However, difficulty can sometimes call forth greater virtue from us as long as it is motivated by love. How does love motivate my spiritual practices?

Prayer

Saint Rose of Lima, pray for us that we may put holiness first in our lives, even when others do not understand. Amen.

AUGUST 24

Saint Bartholomew, the Apostle

First Century
Feast: August 24
Patron: Bookbinders, butchers, shoemakers, Armenia

Bartholomew, usually identified with Nathanael, was one of the twelve apostles. According to tradition, he preached in India and Armenia and was martyred by being skinned alive. When Philip told him about Jesus, Nathanael at first dismissed it, saying, "Can anything good come out of Nazareth?" But he went with Philip to see Jesus, who said to Nathanael, "Here is truly an Israelite in whom there is no deceit!" Nathanael replied, "Where did you get to know me?" And Jesus said, "I saw you under the fig tree before Philip called you." Nathanael then exclaimed, "Rabbi, you are the Son of God! You are the King of Israel!" (Jn 1:45–49).

What did Jesus mean by praising Nathanael as a true Israelite? Jacob, one of the great patriarchs, had been deceitful at first, but after struggling with God, his name was changed to Israel. The prophet Hosea spoke of Israel as being like a fig tree: "Like grapes in the wilderness, I found Israel. Like the first fruit on the fig tree" (9:10). Did Jesus have that text in mind? Perhaps under the fig tree Nathanael had been struggling with God in prayer and was changed, like Jacob, into a true Israelite. Thus, despite his initial skepticism about Jesus, Nathanael had a pure heart open to the truth.

Reflection

John's Gospel opens and closes with doubting apostles: Nathanael at the beginning and Thomas at the end. Despite their initial resistance, both apostles became great followers of Jesus. Their example can give us courage to keep on being disciples even when we feel inadequate.

Prayer

Saint Bartholomew, pray for us that, like you, we may have hearts that are true and good, free of any deceit, so that we may prove to be faithful disciples of Jesus despite any difficulties. Amen.

AUGUST 25

Saint Louis IX of France

April 25, 1214–August 25, 1270
Feast: August 25
Patron: Kings, soldiers, barbers, bridegrooms, parents of large families, prisoners

The only canonized king of France, Saint Louis IX was outstanding for his holiness and love for those in need. He was born into the House of Capet; his parents were Louis VIII and Blanche. His mother instilled in him a great love for God and devotion to the Catholic faith. Because Louis was only twelve when his father died, Blanche acted as a regent until her son was old enough to rule on his own. In 1234, he married Margaret of Provence. They had a loving marriage and raised eleven children.

Louis sought to base his rule on Christian principles. He helped the poor and established homes for the blind as well as several hospitals. Louis strove to act justly toward all and took seriously his duties in governing. He also built the lovely Sainte-Chapelle in Paris, a fine example of Gothic architecture. During his reign, the Sorbonne was established, which became an important theological college at the University of Paris. A man of his age, the king led two crusades, the sixth and seventh, that ultimately failed. He died of dysentery at Tunis in North Africa. Pope Boniface VIII canonized him in 1297.

Reflection

Louis lived his life focused on the needs of others. His example reminds us that we need to bring our faith into our daily lives as citizens. According to our means, we can help the poor, the suffering, and those who have no one to speak for them. Building a "civilization of love," as recent popes have termed it, calls us to bring Christian principles into every aspect of society.

Prayer

Saint Louis IX, pray for us that we may care for the poor and do all we are able for those in need. Amen.

AUGUST 26

Saint Genesius

Died fourth century
Feast: August 25
Patron: Actors, comedians, dancers, epilepsy

The life of this saint is mixed with legend. Genesius of Arles was a notary who declared he was a Christian after he had to record an edict that declared the persecution of Christians. He fled but was pursued by authorities and beheaded. Around the sixth century, Genesius' life story changed in the popular consciousness. At this time, he was reported to have been a stage actor, well known for his comedic acts.

According to the legend, Genesius was an actor in Rome. When an opportunity came to perform for Emperor Diocletian, he decided to appeal to Diocletian's hatred for Christians. The troupe of actors mimicked Genesius' reception of Baptism, intending to mock it. However, while play-acting the profession of faith, Genesius found himself answering the questions sincerely—he had a conversion in the middle of the performance! The other actors, not knowing Genesius' change of heart, led him before the emperor to make light of the way in which the Christian martyrs were treated at the time. To their surprise, Genesius berated Diocletian for his persecution of Christians and proclaimed his belief in the Gospel. A Christian for just a few hours, Genesius became a martyr for his newfound faith.

Reflection

Genesius' conversion story is a bit dramatic—in more ways than one. By God's grace, simply hearing and speaking aloud the truths of Christianity brought him to faith. How well do I know what the Church teaches? Does it excite me? Am I inspired to share it? Maybe today's story is an invitation for me to read (or re-read) a good book to refresh my understanding of what I professed in my own baptism.

Prayer

Jesus, you are the Truth. Help me to be growing always in my knowledge and love for you. Amen.

AUGUST 27

Saint Monica

c. 331–387
Feast: August 27
Patron: Wives, wives who suffer abuse, mothers, widows, alcoholics

Saint Monica is one of the first saints to grow up without being persecuted for her faith. Yet she suffered a spiritual martyrdom. Her parents gave her in marriage to a man who was not Christian and who had a terrible temper. Patiently, she sought to win over her husband to the faith with her virtues of forbearance, patience, and forgiveness. He finally became a Christian and a devoted husband. Monica had one happy year with him before he died.

Monica's son, Augustine, also gave her reason to worry. As a teenager, he had rejected his faith. Monica tried everything to help him—tears, cajoling, arguments, even briefly forbidding him to visit her. But she found that prayer was her most effective recourse. Strengthened by her faith, the courageous widow went after her wayward son when he traveled from Africa to Europe. Monica finally caught up with him in Milan, where she and Augustine found a spiritual guide in Saint Ambrose, bishop of Milan. After sharing the joy of Augustine's baptism and some intimate moments talking about faith and the joys of heaven, Monica fell ill and died. Her last request to Augustine was, "Remember me before God."

Reflection

Due in great part to Monica's prayers, Augustine became one of the greatest Fathers of the Church. Her loving determination gradually transformed her son's life. When we begin to lose hope for our loved ones who are away from the Church, we can look to Monica's life for inspiration. God listens to our prayers for our loved ones.

Prayer

Saint Monica, teach us to love with the heart of God. When we cannot directly help those we love, help us to persevere in trust and prayer. Amen.

AUGUST 28

Saint Augustine

November 13, 354–August 28, 430
Feast: August 28
Patron: Theologians, brewers, printers, sexual temptation

Augustine had a saintly mother, but that did not stop him from losing his faith. Falling in with intellectuals hostile to Christianity, he became a Manichean. He also fell in love with a woman and, without marrying her, had a son, Adeodatus. Resisting his mother's pleadings, Augustine searched for the truth. During the next fifteen years, his studies led him back toward Christianity. In addition to his mother's prayers, two turning points for Augustine were the preaching of Saint Ambrose, the bishop of Milan, and the prayerful reading of Scripture.

After his baptism, Augustine returned to his hometown of Hippo and began living a monastic life of prayer, chastity, and study with his friends. Augustine considered himself unworthy of ministry, but the bishop of Hippo insisted on ordaining him—first as a priest, and then as a bishop and his successor. Augustine became a tireless proclaimer of Christ and fearlessly addressed the errors of his day with a power and clarity that silenced his opponents. While he was bishop, he wrote the first spiritual autobiography, his *Confessions,* a moving, honest account of how God tirelessly sought him. After forty years, Augustine fell ill. He died while praying the psalms, in praise of God's tender mercy.

Reflection

Augustine is considered one of the greatest Western Fathers of the Church. He is called the "Doctor of Grace," because his writings emphasize our dependence on God's grace in our lives. Augustine was informed by reason, but his teachings also reflected his personal journey to Christ. How does my personal journey of faith influence how I understand and share the faith?

Prayer

Saint Augustine, God drew you to himself through truth, love, beauty, and goodness. Help me to discover God's grace in my life and to courageously respond to his invitations. Amen.

AUGUST 29

Saint John the Baptist

First Century
Feast: June 24 (Nativity) and August 29 (Beheading)
Patron: Builders, tailors, Baptism, conversion, people who suffer from seizures or spasms, many countries and cities including Jordan, Monaco, Puerto Rico, and Florence

John the Baptist's unusual life was intimately intertwined with Jesus' life and ministry. His birth was announced by the Angel Gabriel to John's father, Zechariah. Gabriel declared that Zechariah and his wife, Elizabeth, the cousin of Jesus' mother, Mary, would soon have a son despite their old age (see Lk 1:5–25). When John was born, Zechariah prophesied about his son: "And you, child, will be called the prophet of the Most High; for you will go before the Lord to prepare his ways" (Lk 1:76).

As an adult, John went to live in the desert, wearing clothing of camel's hair and eating locusts and wild honey (see Mt 3:1–4). He warned the people that the Messiah was coming. Crowds flocked to the desert to be baptized as a sign of their repentance. Though sinless, Jesus went to be baptized by John (see Mt 3:13–17). John was imprisoned after criticizing Herod Antipas for marrying Herodias, his half-brother's wife. Herodias hated John for speaking the truth and wanted him dead. Her opportunity came when Herod vowed to do anything for Herodias' daughter after she danced for him. At the behest of her mother, Herodias' daughter requested John's head on a platter. Thus, John was beheaded.

Reflection

John the Baptist's life ended tragically. Much like Jesus' death, it must have appeared to his disciples that evil had won. But John won the glorious crown of martyrdom. John had once said of Christ, "He must increase, but I must decrease" (Jn 3:30). How does my life point people to Jesus?

Prayer

Saint John the Baptist, please pray that my thoughts, words, and actions will point others directly to Jesus. Amen.

AUGUST 30

Saint Jeanne Jugan

October 25, 1792–August 29, 1879
Feast: August 30
Patron: The poor, the elderly, those who care for them

Born in Brittany, Jeanne grew up during the upheaval of the French Revolution. Her father, a fisherman, died at sea when she was three. Jeanne's mother, a fervent Catholic, taught her children to love God and put his will first. As Jeanne grew older, she told her mother that she did not want to marry saying, "God wants me for himself. He is keeping me for a work which is not yet founded." Jeanne quietly spent the next few decades working in nursing and domestic service, waiting for a sign of the Lord's plan.

When Jeanne was about forty-seven, her life's work finally became clear. She took in an elderly blind woman and then began to care for more destitute elderly people. This work led her to found a new religious congregation, the Little Sisters of the Poor. She took the name Sister Mary of the Cross. The order grew, but a priest whom the bishop put in charge forced Jeanne into obscurity until her death. Jeanne accepted her situation saying, "We are grafted into the Cross and we must carry it joyfully unto death." When she died, the younger sisters did not even know that she was the foundress.

Reflection

As foundress of the Little Sisters of the Poor, Jeanne Jugan could have demanded recognition. But with remarkable humility she accepted being put aside and only wanted to serve God in the poor. Her life exemplified Jesus' words, "the least among all of you is the greatest" (Lk 9:48). When I feel unrecognized, do I bring those feelings to Jesus, who always sees me?

Prayer

Jeanne Jugan, pray that I might not seek to be glorified of other people but only in the sight of God. Amen.

AUGUST 31

Saint Aidan of Lindisfarne

Died August 31, 651
Feast: August 31
Patron: Northumbria, firefighters, gentleness

Under the influence of Saint Aidan of Lindisfarne, much of northern England became Christian. As a young man, he lived as a monk at the island monastery of Iona, in present-day Scotland. Saint Oswald, king of Northumbria, then asked Aidan to bring Christianity to the peoples of Northumbria. The first bishop the king had sent was harsh with the people, and his methods met with little success. Seeing Aidan's gentle manner, the king believed the monk would have greater success.

Consecrated a bishop in 635, Aidan lived on Lindisfarne, a tidal island off the coast of England. He traveled on foot across Northumbria, establishing churches and preaching the Gospel to everyone he encountered. At first, he did not speak the native language, so the king accompanied him as an interpreter. Bishop Aidan was known for his gentleness and generosity to the poor. On one occasion, King Oswald had given him a fine horse for his travels. However, upon meeting a beggar in need, Aidan immediately gave away his horse. In his biography on this gentle bishop, who is honored for evangelizing much of England, Saint Bede wrote that Aidan was "inspired with a passionate love of virtue, but at the same time full of a surpassing mildness and gentleness."

Reflection

Aidan's predecessor claimed that the English were unwilling to receive the Gospel. However, Aidan realized that the problem was not the people but rather the methods being used. He changed tactics, living an ascetical life and attracting the people to God with his gentleness and holiness. When I fail, how quickly do I turn to God with trust in his mercy and love?

Prayer

Lord Jesus, when I encounter difficulties in life, help me to see the situation clearly and respond as you would. Amen.

SEPTEMBER 1

Blessed Francisco de Paula Victor

April 12, 1827–September 23, 1905
Feast: September 23
Patron: Those discriminated against because of their race or social status

Francisco was born in Brazil to a slave mother, Lourença Justiniana de Jesus, and an unknown father. Their slave owner, Marianna Santa Barbara Ferreira, had Francisco baptized and was his godmother. As a young man Francisco trained to be a tailor, but he always dreamed about becoming a priest. However, both his race and his status as a slave were legal impediments to the necessary schooling. But he never lost hope. When his godmother heard about Francisco's desire, she approached the local parish priest who then approached the bishop. Providentially, Bishop Antonio Viçoso was a committed abolitionist and he fought to have Francisco admitted to the seminary.

In the seminary, Francisco suffered severe discrimination due to his race. Little by little, however, his humility, determination, and love for God won him the respect of his teachers and fellow seminarians. He was ordained on June 14, 1851. In parish ministry, Francisco continued to suffer much of the same prejudice. Some of his parishioners even refused to receive Communion from him. But Francisco remained faithful to his vocation, loving Jesus above everything, and eventually he also won the love of his parishioners. When he died, the people of his territory were already calling him "the saint of the impossible." He was the first black male Brazilian to be beatified.

Reflection

Jesus said, "for God, all things are possible" (Mt 19:26). Along with the support of good people in his life, Francisco's faith, hope, and love were the instruments God used to move away the natural obstacles in his path. These virtues made him a great inspiration to everyone who knew him. What might God be asking me to entrust to him with a little more faith?

Prayer

Father, help me to face all life's obstacles with enduring hope and faith. Amen.

SEPTEMBER 2

Saint Solomon Le Clercq

November 14, 1745–September 2, 1792
Feast: September 2
Patron: Teachers

Nicolas Le Clercq entered the Brothers of the Christian Schools in Rouen, France, and took the name Solomon. Founded by Saint John Baptist de la Salle, the brothers were dedicated to teaching. Solomon threw himself wholeheartedly into this work. Besides teaching, he was put in charge of the formation of the novices and helped with other administrative tasks.

During the French Revolution, clergy and religious were ordered to sign "The Civil Constitution of the Clergy." Essentially, it gave the revolutionaries control over the Church. Along with many others, Solomon refused to sign it. The brothers soon lost their schools and their legal status, and Solomon was forced to live in hiding. On August 15, 1792, he was arrested and sent to a Carmelite convent that had been turned into a prison. On September 2, he and many others were killed. Solomon and 188 of his fellow martyrs were beatified in 1926. On October 16, 2016, Pope Francis canonized Brother Solomon.

Reflection

The Christian Brothers in France were dissolved by the revolutionary government, and its members were killed or had to flee. Yet it was soon re-established and recognized by the French government, and since then has spread throughout the world. As the ancient writer Tertullian said, "the blood of martyrs is the seed of Christians." The more that hostile forces try to stamp out Christ and his Church, the more it flourishes. If we have the freedom to practice our faith, we ought never to take it for granted.

Prayer

Saint Solomon Le Clercq, you dedicated your life to teaching others about Jesus and willingly gave your life for love of him. Pray for us in the trials we face each day, so that we may never lose heart but put our trust in Jesus. Amen.

SEPTEMBER 3

Saint Gregory the Great

c. 540–March 12, 604
Feast: September 3
Patron: Church musicians, singers, sacred music, teachers, victims of plague

Two circumstances marked the background of Gregory's life: his upper class, saintly Roman family, and the chaos of the fall and repeated sacking of Rome. As a young man, Gregory was a popular politician and became prefect of Rome at age thirty. When his father died, Gregory left politics, turned the family home into a monastery, and founded many other monasteries using the family fortune. He would later say that these short years spent as a simple monk were his happiest. But Gregory's talents did not remain unnoticed. Pope Pelagius II asked for his help, and Gregory reluctantly but obediently served as deacon of Rome and as papal delegate to Constantinople.

When Pope Pelagius died of the plague, Gregory was immediately selected as his successor. Gregory felt unworthy and deeply desired to return to monastic life. But at the people's and the emperor's behest, Gregory eventually gave in. As pope, he was a down-to-earth pastor who told stories in his homilies. He actively sought the spiritual and material welfare of the people. Despite his poor health, Gregory revitalized the Church's life in almost every area. Gregory died after almost fourteen years as pope, having already positively shaped the Church for the future.

Reflection

Gregory is one of the few popes given the title "the Great" because of his genius in leadership and immense accomplishments. Yet he always remained a humble monk at heart. He referred to himself in his role as pope as "servant of the servants of God." How willing am I to serve others without recognition?

Prayer

Saint Gregory the Great, pray that I might grow in your humble spirit of service. Amen.

SEPTEMBER 4

Blessed Dina Bélanger

April 30, 1897–September 4, 1929
Feast: September 4 (Canada)
Patron: Pianists, music students

Born in Quebec, Canada, Dina would later be known as the "Little Flower" of Canada because her life and spirituality were similar to that of Saint Thérèse. As a child, Dina showed remarkable skills as a pianist. Music became her special way of bringing glory to God. Dina's education and religious upbringing with the Sisters of Notre Dame intensified her love for prayer, natural goodness, and simplicity of life. Dina attended a conservatory in New York and became an accomplished concert pianist, but she always desired to give her life completely to God.

In 1921, Dina was received into the Congregation of Jesus and Mary in which she took the name Sister Marie Sainte-Cécile de Rome. She taught music for a time but contracted scarlet fever and then tuberculosis, which ultimately claimed her life at the age of twenty-four. Dina's short life would have been known only to her sisters, loved ones, and God, had her superiors not asked her to write an autobiography while she was ill. Published after her death, her *Autobiography* reveals a deep mystical interior life and a profound participation in the merciful love of Jesus and the life of the Trinity.

Reflection

Before Dina entered the convent, she heard Jesus say to her, "You will do good above all by your writing." She died without seeing the impact of her writing, trusting that Jesus would keep his word. The fruits of our relationship with God will only be fully known in heaven. Do I trust that my love for Christ bears fruit, even when I cannot see it?

Prayer

Blessed Dina Bélanger, help us to draw close to the merciful Heart of Jesus as you did. Amen.

SEPTEMBER 5

Saint Teresa of Calcutta

August 26, 1910–September 5, 1997
Feast: September 5
Patron: The poorest of the poor

God often calls simple, ordinary people to accomplish his great plans. Such a call transformed a young Albanian girl from Skopje named Agnes Gonxha Bojaxhiu into the beloved Mother Teresa of Calcutta. As a young woman, Agnes entered the Institute of the Blessed Virgin Mary, known as the Sisters of Loreto. She was missioned to India where she began teaching in Calcutta.

Then one day in 1946, Teresa was riding a train to Darjeeling and the Lord revealed a new plan for her. She was to establish a new religious order that would live and work among the poor in the streets of Calcutta. After obtaining permission to pursue her new mission, Teresa set out. She rented a little room and later obtained the use of a hostel where she brought the destitute and dying whom she rescued from the streets. Soon some former students joined her, and a new order was born: the Missionaries of Charity. Mother Teresa also founded communities of priests and brothers and gathered many cooperators and volunteers who also care for God's poor around the world.

Reflection

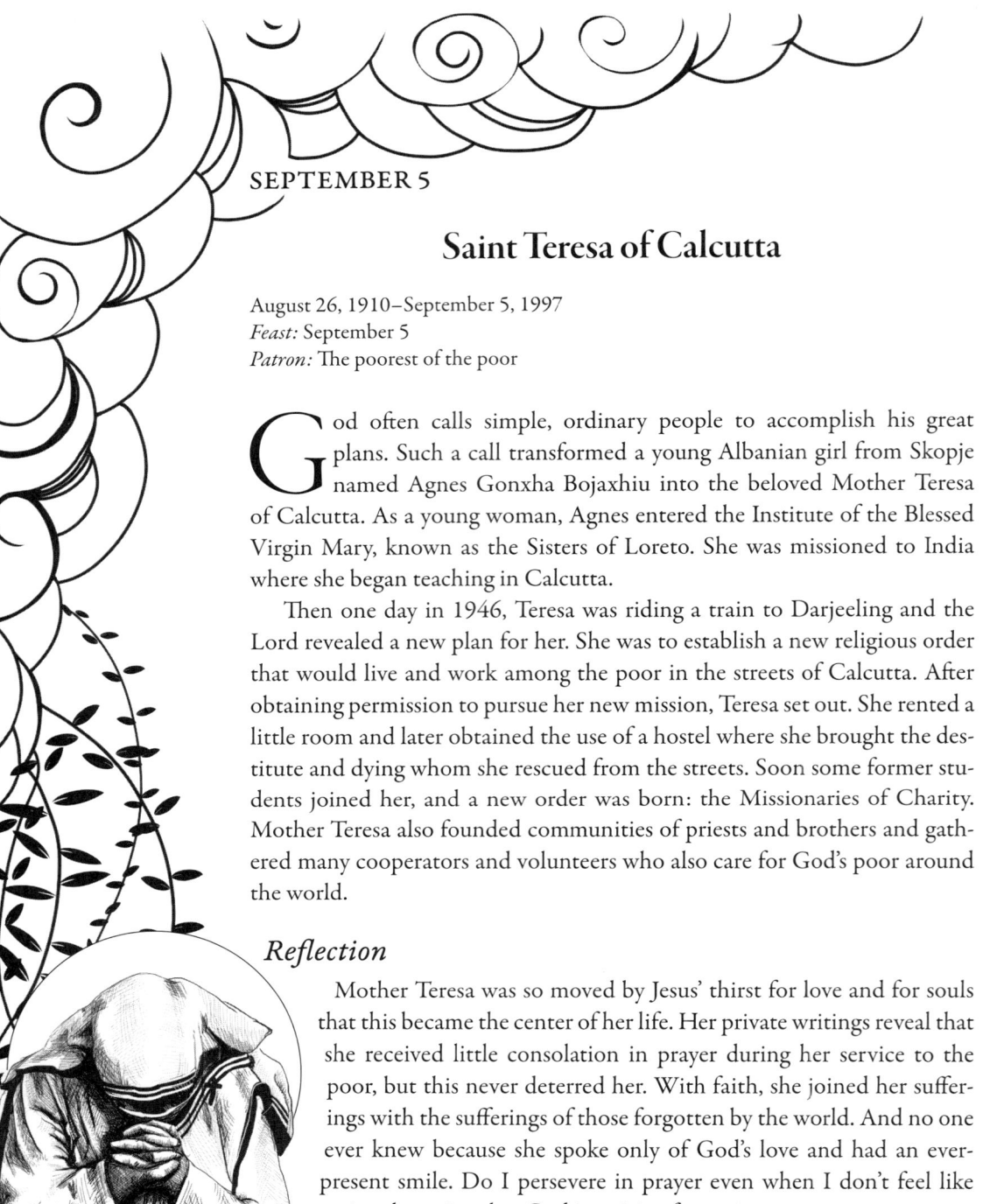

Mother Teresa was so moved by Jesus' thirst for love and for souls that this became the center of her life. Her private writings reveal that she received little consolation in prayer during her service to the poor, but this never deterred her. With faith, she joined her sufferings with the sufferings of those forgotten by the world. And no one ever knew because she spoke only of God's love and had an ever-present smile. Do I persevere in prayer even when I don't feel like praying, knowing that God is waiting for me?

Prayer

Saint Teresa of Calcutta, you have shown us how to love without counting the cost. Continue to inspire us to comfort the poor. Amen.

SEPTEMBER 6

Blessed Celine Chludzińska Borzęcka

October 29, 1833–October 26, 1913
Feast: October 26
Patron: Sisters of the Resurrection, widows, education

Celine Chludzińska Borzęcka was born in Antowil, Orsza, in what is now Belarus. One of three children, she grew up in a wealthy and devout Catholic family. From an early age, Celine felt a call to religious life. However, her parents counseled her to marry and so, at age twenty, she married Joseph Borzecki. Celine loved her husband deeply and they had four children, two of whom died in infancy.

After her husband's death in 1874, Celine and her two daughters traveled to Italy. In Rome they met the co-founder of the Resurrectionists, Father Peter Semenenko, who recognized in Celine a soul deeply in love with God. Eight years later, Celine and her youngest daughter, along with two other women, felt called to begin life in community under his spiritual guidance. When Father Peter died four years later, some questioned whether Celine and the sisters should join another community. However, Celine remained steadfast. With help from supporters, she opened a school for girls. A year later, in 1891, the Congregation of the Sisters of the Resurrection was officially founded. Mother Celine remained the superior general until she died. In the last days of her life, she would often say, "Be saints!"

Reflection

Celine sought God's will in her life from a young age and yet faced many difficulties: her parents insisted she marry when she felt called to religious life; her husband died; and when she again pursued religious life, she met more obstacles. Through each experience, Celine discovered how God remained faithful. Do I trust in God is faithful even when I feel as if everything is going wrong?

Prayer

Mother Celine Borzęcka, teach me how to trust God's ways even when they are mysterious and appear to contradict human understanding. Amen.

SEPTEMBER 7

Blessed Giuseppe Puglisi

September 15, 1937–September 15, 1993
Feast: October 21
Patron: Victims of organized crime, members of gangs and the mafia

Giuseppe Puglisi was born to a working-class family in Sicily. He was ordained a priest and later became a pastor in the same neighborhood of Palermo where he had grown up. The mafia was so ubiquitous that many people, including some Church leaders, tolerated it and considered it simply a part of the fabric of society. Father Giuseppe, however, considered it a scourge to be resisted. In his parish, he constantly encouraged the people not to be afraid nor to turn a blind eye to the crimes and violence.

Father Giuseppe forbade members of the mafia to have roles of honor in feast day processions, and he refused their donations. He worked especially with the youth—encouraging them not to drop out of school or to get involved in illegal activities. Unknown to others, Father Giuseppe received several death threats. However, he simply continued living his vocation and trying to bring peace to the people in his parish. On his fifty-sixth birthday, this brave priest was returning to his rectory when he was shot point blank by a mafia hit man.

Reflection

Father Giuseppe did not organize rallies or make public protests, but the mafia still considered him a serious threat. He simply did his job as a priest—living and preaching the Gospel. Several years after Father Giuseppe's death, the mafia member who confessed to killing him revealed the priest's last words were: "I've been expecting you." Even though Father Giuseppe knew his life could be in danger, he continued doing God's will. Do I follow God's will even when it might lead to undesired consequences?

Prayer

Blessed Giuseppe Puglisi, intercede for us to have the courage to do God's will. Please also intercede for those caught up in organized crime, that they will have the grace of repentance. Amen.

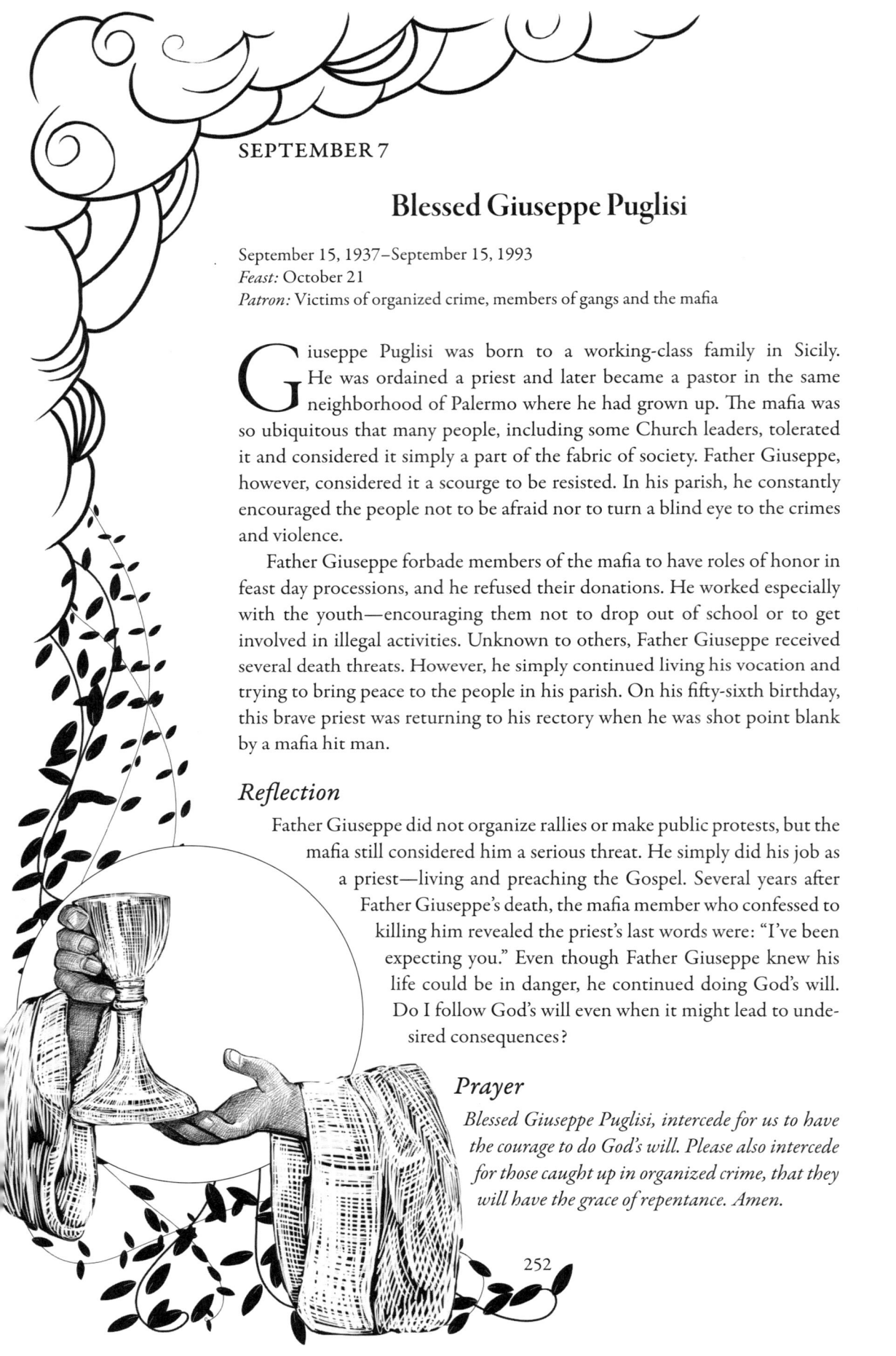

SEPTEMBER 8

Blessed Frédéric Ozanam

April 23, 1813–September 8, 1853
Feast: September 9
Patron: Saint Vincent de Paul Society, social workers

Born into a devout Catholic family, Frédéric struggled with doubts about the faith as a teenager. But a local priest, Father Noirot, helped him through this crisis. Frédéric went on to Paris to study law. There he defended the Catholic faith from critical professors, and he organized groups to discuss the faith. One day a student asked him what he was doing to live out his faith and not just talk about it. Frédéric took to heart the man's challenge and organized a group to visit and help poor families. His rallying call was, "Let us go to the poor!"

Frédéric's group slowly grew and became known as the Saint Vincent de Paul Society. Blessed Rosalie Rendu, a religious sister from the Daughters of Charity of Saint Vincent de Paul, guided Frédéric and his friends in their new work. In 1841, Frédéric married Amélie Soulacroix. Though he was a respected scholar, he continued to serve the poor and write on their behalf. His life's work was cut short when he died at the age of forty. By the time of his death, the small society he had founded to serve the poor had spread worldwide.

Reflection

Frédéric took to heart the words of Jesus, "Just as you did it to one of the least of these who are members of my family, you did it to me" (Mt 25:40). Frédéric's passion for social justice grew out of his great love for Jesus Christ and for each person, in whom he saw the face of Christ. Do I treat others as I would treat Jesus?

Prayer

Blessed Frédéric Ozanam, pray for us that we might always see the face of Christ in the poor and serve them as we would Christ. Amen.

SEPTEMBER 9

Saint Peter Claver

June 26, 1580–September 8, 1654
Feast: September 9
Patron: Colombia, victims of slavery, racial harmony

The son of a farming family, Peter was born and raised in Catalonia, Spain. After graduating from the university in Barcelona, he joined the Jesuits. He was still a student when his was assigned to Cartagena in what is now Colombia. Peter was ordained a priest there in 1616. He then assisted Father Alphonsus de Sandoval, a fellow Jesuit who ministered to Africans captured by slave traders. Together with interpreters, the priests would climb down ship holds to the men and women being treated as cargo, to bathe their wounds and speak to them words of comfort and faith.

In his forty years of ministry, Peter baptized an estimated three hundred thousand slaves. He also visited prisons, plantations, hospitals, and mines to follow up on the newly baptized. He avoided as much as possible the hospitality of slave owners and slept in the slave quarters. He continually took up collections of clothing, fruit, and other goods to distribute to his people. Since he only had a limited knowledge of the African languages, he devised a method of instruction using large drawings of the life of Christ. Even in his final years when incapacitated by illness, Peter Claver continued to receive visitors and offer his service as confessor.

Reflection

Peter Claver gave himself tirelessly to care for those in need. He even signed his profession document when he made his religious vows with the words, "Peter Claver, slave of the Africans." Even in our own day many people are victims of slavery, some actually held captive in forced labor, others enslaved by bad habits or addiction. Our world still needs self-forgetting and self-giving love. How am I called to show self-forgetting love to others?

Prayer

Saint Peter Claver, teach us to give expecting no return. May all our actions speak of Jesus. Amen.

SEPTEMBER 10

Saint Daniel Comboni

March 15, 1831–October 10, 1881
Feast: October 10
Patron: Africa, missionaries

Daniel Comboni was born in Limone sul Garda, Italy. At the age of twelve he was sent to Verona to study under Father Nicolas Mazza. He soon became avidly interested in the missions. By 1854, Daniel was ordained a priest and was missioned to Sudan. Great obstacles and ill health cut short his first missionary venture, and he returned to Verona. Though it seemed he had failed, Daniel knew that God had a plan for him, and he prayed for guidance.

In 1864, while before the tomb of Saint Peter in Rome, Daniel received an inspiration from God. He would submit his ideas for a missionary project for Africa to the Congregation for the Propagation of the Faith. His motto was: "Save Africa through Africa." In 1867 and 1872 respectively, he founded two missionary institutes of men and of women known as the Comboni Missionaries and the Comboni Missionary Sisters. In 1877, Daniel was consecrated bishop and named Vicar Apostolic of Central Africa. A few years later, he traveled to Africa for the eighth and last time to stand alongside his missionaries, many of whom were dying due to drought and famine. Fatigued and overcome with fever, Daniel died in Khartoum. His last words were, "I am dying, but my work will not die."

Reflection

Daniel's work in Africa often met with obstacles and disappointment instead of success, and he also experienced false accusations from supposed friends. Nevertheless, graced with the virtues of fortitude and patience, Daniel persevered, trusting in God's plan and love. How do I respond in the face of adversity?

Prayer

Saint Daniel Comboni, pray that I might press on in the face of failure, knowing that God is always with me. Amen.

SEPTEMBER 11

Blessed Sebastian Kimura

1565–September 10, 1622
Feast: September 10
Patron: Japan

Sebastian Kimura was one of the first Japanese natives to be ordained a priest. His grandfather was baptized by Saint Francis Xavier. From the time he was twelve years old, he worked closely with the Society of Jesus and formally entered the Jesuits at the age of nineteen. At the time, a seminary had not yet been established in Japan, so Sebastian completed his seminary studies in the Philippines. He was ordained in Nagasaki in September 1601.

During this time, a wave of persecution against Christians in Japan began and many foreign missionaries were forced to leave the country. His superiors urged Sebastian to flee, but he was captured before he could leave Nagasaki. Along with several others, Sebastian was slowly burned to death in 1622. He was the last of the group of martyrs to die. Alive for three excruciating hours, witnesses said that he finally knelt in the midst of the flames and died. Pope Pius IX beatified Sebastian and 204 companions in 1867.

Reflection

Sebastian's deeply rooted faith enabled him to courageously follow Christ in his vocation as a religious and a priest, even in the midst of persecutions and sufferings. All of us can recall with gratitude the people who have helped us to deepen our faith in Jesus. Their example reminds us that the Lord entrusts us anew each day with the marvelous gift of faith in Jesus in the Church. He calls us to share this gift with the people of our time.

Prayer

Blessed Sebastian Kimura, you dedicated yourself totally to following Christ. Help us by your prayers to follow Christ with this same faith and courage. Amen.

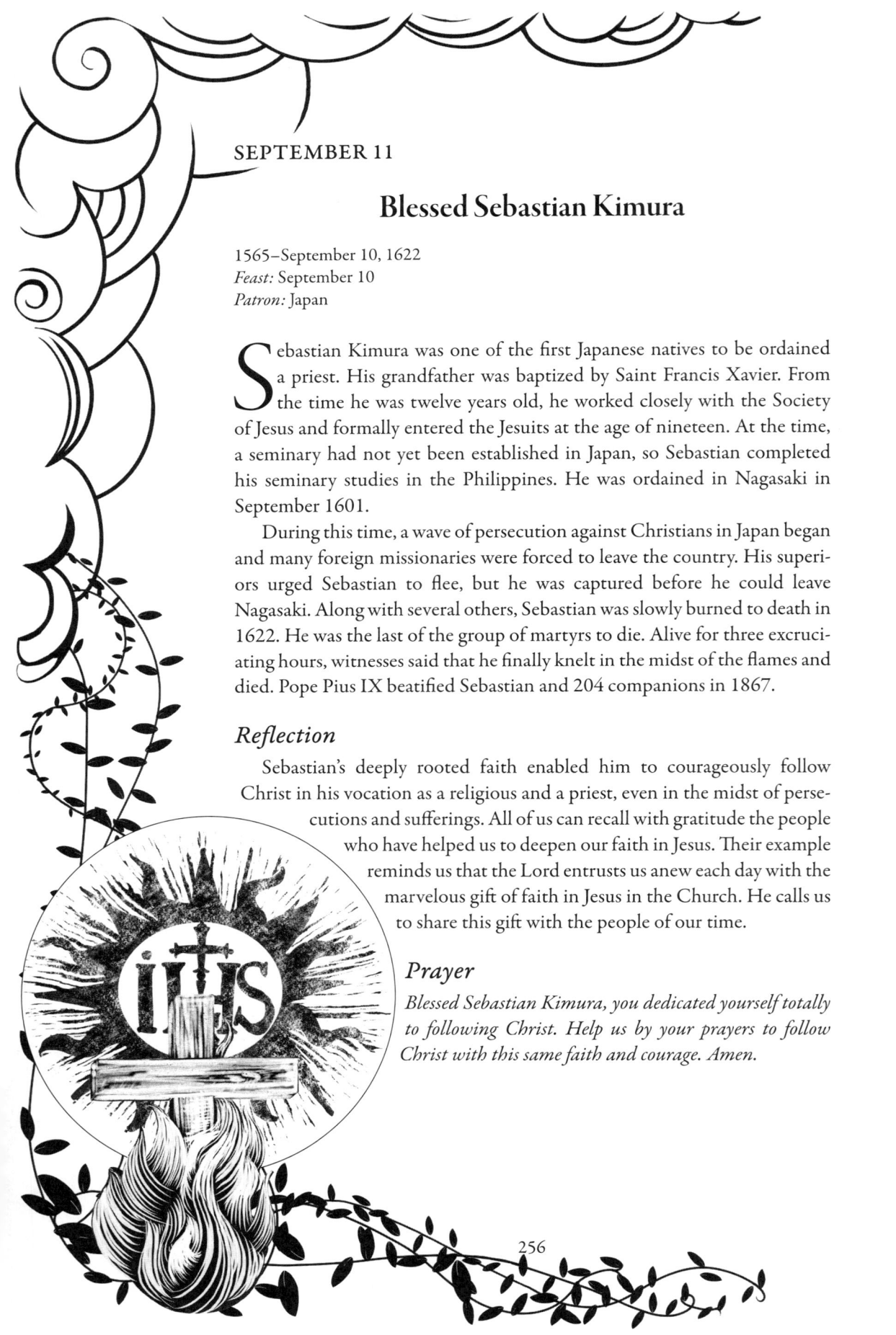

SEPTEMBER 12

Saint Hildegard of Bingen

1098–September 17, 1179
Feast: September 17
Patron: Ecology, musicians, writers, and herbalists

Though never formally educated, Hildegard was a woman of immense talent and religious insight. Before her death, among many other accomplishments, she would become the abbess of two monasteries, compose music, practice the art of herbal medicine, and offer biblical and theological commentary. As a child, Hildegard's family placed her with a family relative, Jutta, who lived as an anchoress. Jutta taught her to pray the psalms and to read and sing in Latin.

Hildegard also received visions and divine revelations from a young age. In fact, she was surprised when she discovered that most people did not have this experience! So, she kept her visions to herself. Later in life, when Hildegard finally confided to her confessor that she regularly received visions, he encouraged her to dictate them. These writings were eventually submitted to and approved by Pope Eugene III who convened a committee that included Saint Bernard of Clairvaux to examine the visions. Though Hildegard received no explicit training, she became a popular preacher—a shocking feat considering the times and the fact that she was a cloistered nun. On October 7, 2012, Pope Benedict XVI recognized Hildegard's wisdom and theological contributions by naming her a Doctor of the Church.

Reflection

Hildegard first considered her frequent communications with God to be normal occurrences—something to be expected. While her visions and union with God were in fact extraordinary, every Christian is invited to have a unique, intimate relationship with God. Do I experience the love of God in a personal way? How can this become a more ordinary part of my life?

Prayer

Lord Jesus, you desire union and friendship with me. Help me remember to invite you into my everyday activities and to trust in your constant presence. Amen.

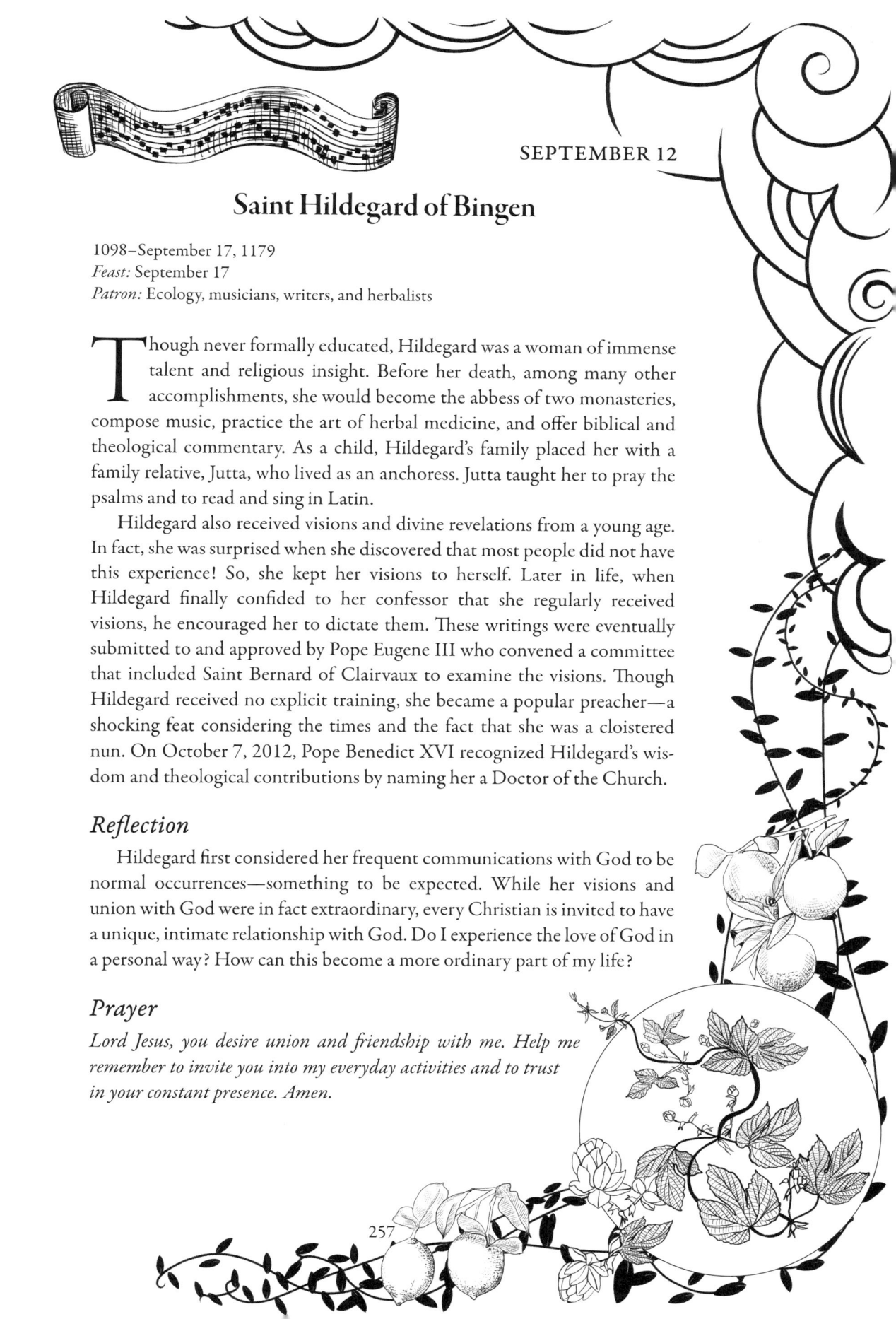

SEPTEMBER 13

Saint John Chrysostom

c. 349–September 14, 407
Feast: September 13
Patron: Education, epilepsy, lecturers, orators, preachers

John Chrysostom was born in Antioch, Turkey. His father died soon after his birth, but John's mother made sure he had the best schooling. Around 367, John met Saint Meletius and was impressed with the holy bishop's way of life. Soon, John decided to leave behind his secular studies and be baptized. John then devoted himself to manual labor, prayer, and studying Scripture. He even lived in the caves around Antioch for a time, but his extreme asceticism weakened his health, and he prudently decided to return to Antioch.

Around 381, Bishop Meletius ordained John a deacon, and five years later he was ordained a priest. His primary work was preaching, and he was extremely gifted in this. He came to be known as "Golden Mouth" ("Chrysostom" in Greek). In 398, John was consecrated archbishop of Constantinople. His fiery preaching and efforts to reform the imperial court, clergy, and the faithful were not always appreciated. Political intrigue led to attempts on his life and John's eventual permanent banishment. Despite efforts from two popes, John was never restored as bishop. He died while being marched farther to a place of extreme exile. His last words were, "Glory be to God for all things."

Reflection

John preached the Gospel both when it was popular and when it was not. Living our faith in today's world is not that different from centuries ago. Each day we must remain strong as our faith is put to the test. As Paul prayed for the Ephesians that they might "be strengthened in [their] inner being with power through his Spirit" (3:16), may we too, with God's help, give witness to what we believe.

Prayer

Saint John Chrysostom, pray that I may have the courage to live my life as a witness to the Gospel message. Amen.

SEPTEMBER 14

Saint Helena

c. 246–c. 329
Feast: August 18
Patron: Archeologists, converts, divorced people

Helena was said to be the humble daughter of an innkeeper. She also became the lawful wife of Constantius Chlorus, who became a general in the Roman army. Together they had a son, Constantine. However, when Constantius rose to power, he left Helena and remarried for political reasons. Abandoned, Helena focused her life on her son. When Constantine became emperor, he became fascinated with Christianity and ended the persecution against Christians. He also sent for his mother to join him in Rome.

Helena embraced Christianity enthusiastically and was baptized. As the beloved mother of the emperor, Helena generously and personally gave alms wherever she went. She also had some of the first churches in Rome built. Late in life, despite her age, Helena went on pilgrimage to the Holy Land—a long and difficult journey. According to tradition, Helena discovered Jesus' true Cross in Jerusalem. She determined it was the true Cross when a leper was healed after he touched it. Helena's great devotion also led her to restore several holy sites and build at least two churches, including the Church of the Nativity in Bethlehem. She died shortly after her pilgrimage.

Reflection

When Constantius left her, Helena could have allowed bitterness to poison her spirit. Instead, she shifted the focus of her life first to her son and later in life entirely to Christ. Her example can encourage us when we suffer betrayal. At such moments, we can find healing in Christ. How strongly do I believe Christ is with me in my difficulties?

Prayer

Saint Helena, help me to focus my gaze on Christ, discovering the power of his Cross in my daily life. Amen.

SEPTEMBER 15

Saint Catherine of Genoa

1447–September 15, 1510
Feast: September 15
Patron: Brides, widows, infertility, difficult marriages

Catherine is a remarkable saint whose life demonstrated a blend of deep prayer life with intense activity. Born into a wealthy Italian family, her marriage to Giuliano Adorno was arranged at the age of sixteen. Her husband was an unfaithful spendthrift who gambled away the family fortune. For ten years she suffered in her miserable marriage. Catherine sunk into depression and then turned to worldly pursuits for solace, but these left her even more unhappy.

In March 1473, Catherine decided to go to confession upon the advice of her sister. When she entered the confessional, suddenly an overpowering sense of her own sins overcame her, along with an intense, deeply-felt knowledge of God's incredible love. She couldn't finish confessing. After three days of weeping and soul-searching, she went back to confession. She gave herself totally to God, crying out, "Oh Love! No more sin!" Her profound interior life led her to the heights of mysticism. Meanwhile, her husband had a miraculous conversion, and they both lived in a small house near the Pammatone Hospital in Genoa. Together they spent the rest of their lives caring for the poor and the sick.

Reflection

Catherine's teachings on the spiritual life were collected by her followers and published after her death. She is best known for her teachings on purgatory, which she saw not as an exterior fire but an inner one. The soul's ardent love for God burns like a fire, until all the remnants of sin are removed. She reminds us, who live in an age that takes sin lightly, of the pressing need to repent of our sins and do penance for them.

Prayer

Saint Catherine of Genoa, pray that I may learn from your example to unite prayer with action. Amen.

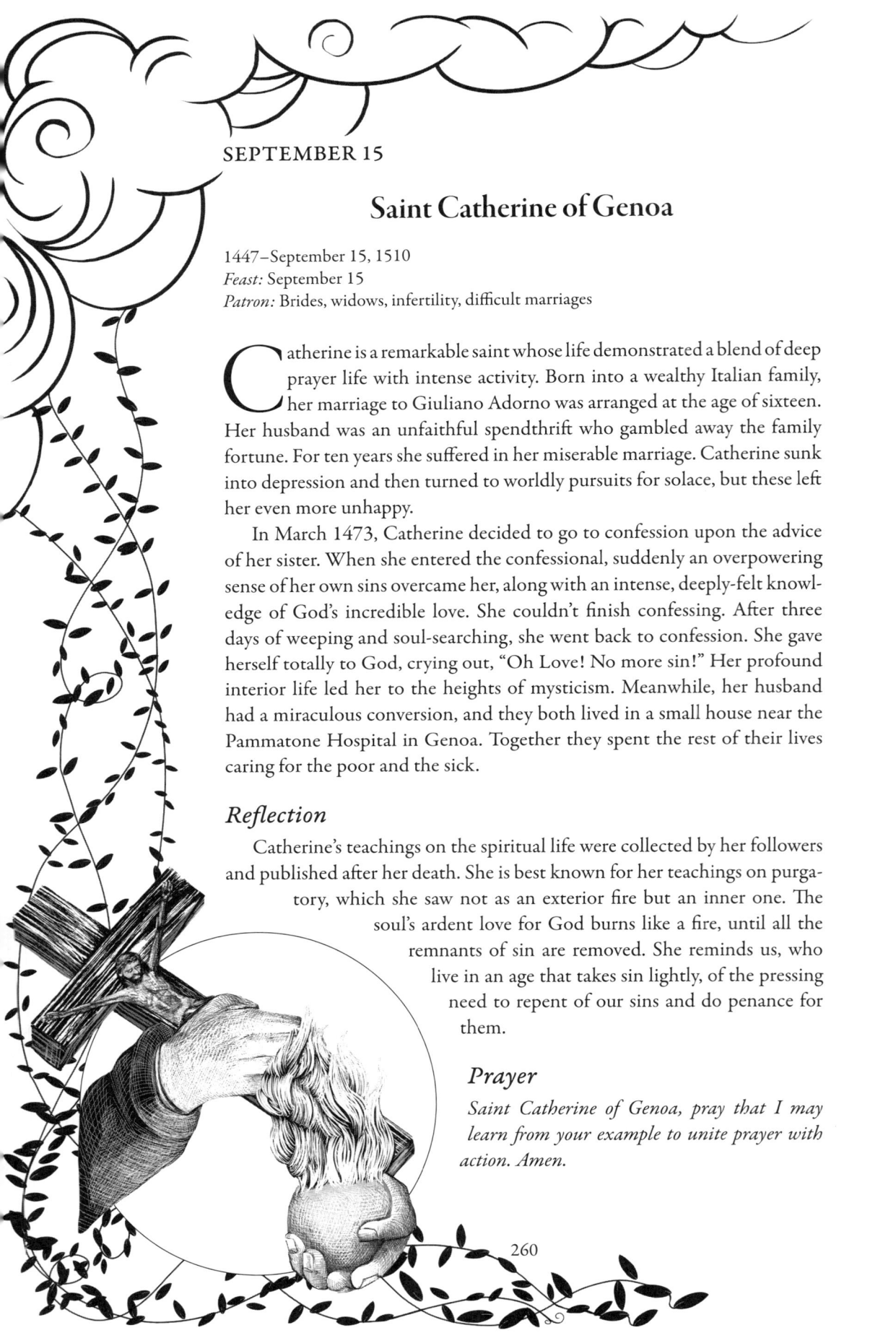

SEPTEMBER 16

Saint Cyprian

c. 210–September 14, 258
Feast: September 16
Patron: Church in North Africa

Cyprian was a well-to-do, middle-aged lawyer when he converted to Christianity in 246. About two years later, he was elected bishop of Carthage. In early 250, the emperor Decius began a persecution of the Church. Cyprian went into hiding so that he could continue to pastor the Church, but for this he was criticized. Many Christians renounced their faith in this persecution, and when it abated, Cyprian faced the problem of dealing with those who had lapsed. He strove to find a middle course between one group of priests who were too indulgent and another who refused absolution to those who had abandoned the faith. Cyprian suffered much opposition from both sides.

Soon after the persecution, a plague broke out in Carthage, and Cyprian took the lead in helping the sick, winning over some hearts. He wrote one of his many treatises, *On Mortality*, to comfort the faithful during this time. In 257, a new persecution broke out under the emperor Valerian. Cyprian was banished and later kept under house arrest at his own villa. He refused to flee or to be tried in another city. Before Cyprian was executed, the faithful spread cloths before him to catch the holy bishop's blood. He was the first bishop of Carthage to be martyred.

Reflection

Cyprian was known to be a serious but also a cheerful bishop. The Church has always faced problems and conflicts. But Cyprian's life shows us that, with God, it is possible to have peace in the midst of difficulty. What are some ways I have seen God's grace at work in his Church in the midst of sin??

Prayer

Saint Cyprian, pray for the Church in our day, that we may always live in closer unity with our fellow Christians and face problems with trust in God. Amen.

SEPTEMBER 17

Saint Robert Bellarmine

October 4, 1542–September 17, 1621
Feast: September 17
Patron: Catechists, catechumens

Because Robert was an excellent student, his father hoped that he would choose a career that could help their impoverished family become affluent. Instead, he became a Jesuit at the age of eighteen. Robert was ordained to the priesthood ten years later but had already developed quite a reputation as a preacher. He spent almost twenty years as a professor and spiritual director and, in the years following the Council of Trent, worked to help clarify theological questions arising from the Protestant Reformation.

Bellarmine was also a prolific writer. He wrote books explaining the role and rights of the pope, the Mystical Body of Christ, and many of the Church's traditions. He is said to have written the preface to the 1592 Vulgate Bible that was promulgated under Pope Clement VIII. His most popular writings, however, flowed from his experiences of the Ignatian spiritual exercises. In these writings, his intense love for Jesus and profound conviction of God's love are very evident. When he died, he was so admired for his sanctity that he was generally assumed to be numbered among the saints years before his canonization.

Reflection

In his public life and role as a cardinal, Robert Bellarmine always stressed that personal prayer and conversion had to precede any external actions. He was an extremely busy man who made invaluable contributions to the Church's understanding of her own teachings and responsibilities. However, none of that would have been possible without his faithfulness to prayer—after all, we can't give what we don't have. How can I dedicate a little more time to prayer today?

Prayer

Jesus, you are the Truth. Saint Robert Bellarmine found such joy and fulfillment in bringing others to know you. I too want to know you more. Amen.

SEPTEMBER 18

Saint Joseph of Cupertino

June 17, 1603–September 18, 1663
Feast: September 18
Patron: Astronauts, pilots, air travelers, students

Joseph was born in Cupertino in what is now modern-day Italy. Because of his father's debts, his mother had to give birth in a stable. Joseph was an awkward boy who was absent minded and clumsy. Joseph's pursuits often ended in failure. He tried to become a shoemaker, but it did not work out. He then tried to enter religious life with the Conventual Franciscans but was refused. The Capuchins accepted him in 1620 but sent him home after just eight months.

Finally, the Conventual Franciscans agreed to accept him as a tertiary and assigned him to the stables. In this humble place, so similar to where he was born, Joseph began to thrive. Finally, he was admitted to the novitiate and, to everyone's surprise—including his own—he managed to pass his examinations. Joseph was ordained a priest in 1628. Soon after, he began to experience levitations and increased ecstasies. Sometimes he even would levitate while he was celebrating Mass. Joseph's superiors eventually had to forbid him from offering Mass publicly because he was attracting throngs of people. To avoid the crowds, Joseph was shuttled to several remote monasteries in succession. When he arrived at the monastery in Osimo where he would soon die, he said, "This is my rest."

Reflection

Joseph was hardworking, prayerful, and full of joy in all circumstances. Despite the suffering that his special gifts caused, Joseph continued to serve God in humble faithfulness and trust. God often wants to show the power of his love through the simplest of people. How do I experience God's power and love in my life?

Prayer

Saint Joseph of Cupertino, help me not to despair in my failures but to rejoice and praise God for whatever good I am able to do. Amen.

SEPTEMBER 19

Blessed James Miller

September 21, 1944–February 13, 1982
Feast: February 13
Patron: Farmers, indigenous people, religious brothers, teachers

Raised on a farm in Wisconsin, James Miller thought of becoming a priest as a child. However, while attending a high school taught by the Christian Brothers, he felt called to become a religious brother instead. After his profession, James taught high school in Minnesota for five years. He was also the soccer coach and maintenance supervisor, earning him the nickname "Brother Fix-It." James was happy teaching, but he had a great desire to be a missionary and was pleased when his superiors sent him to Nicaragua.

Known as "Hermano Santiago," James taught, helped build schools, started a soccer team, and did maintenance work. In 1979, during the Sandinista revolution, James' superiors feared for his safety and asked him to return to the United States. Two years later, he was delighted to be sent to Guatemala. There he taught high school and helped train young indigenous students in job and leadership skills. Many of his students were the first in their families to have the opportunity to finish high school. However, the Christian Brothers' advocacy for the poor was not appreciated by the ruling powers. On February 13, 1982, while on a ladder making repairs to a wall, Hermano Santiago was shot by masked men and died instantly. His attackers were never identified.

Reflection

James Miller was an outgoing person who often smiled and showed interest in others. Hard working and humble, he never considered a job beneath him. Do I understand that all I do is important in God's eyes?

Prayer

Blessed James Miller, knowing the danger involved in your service to others, you went about your work trusting in God. Pray that I might not be deterred from what God asks of me. Amen.

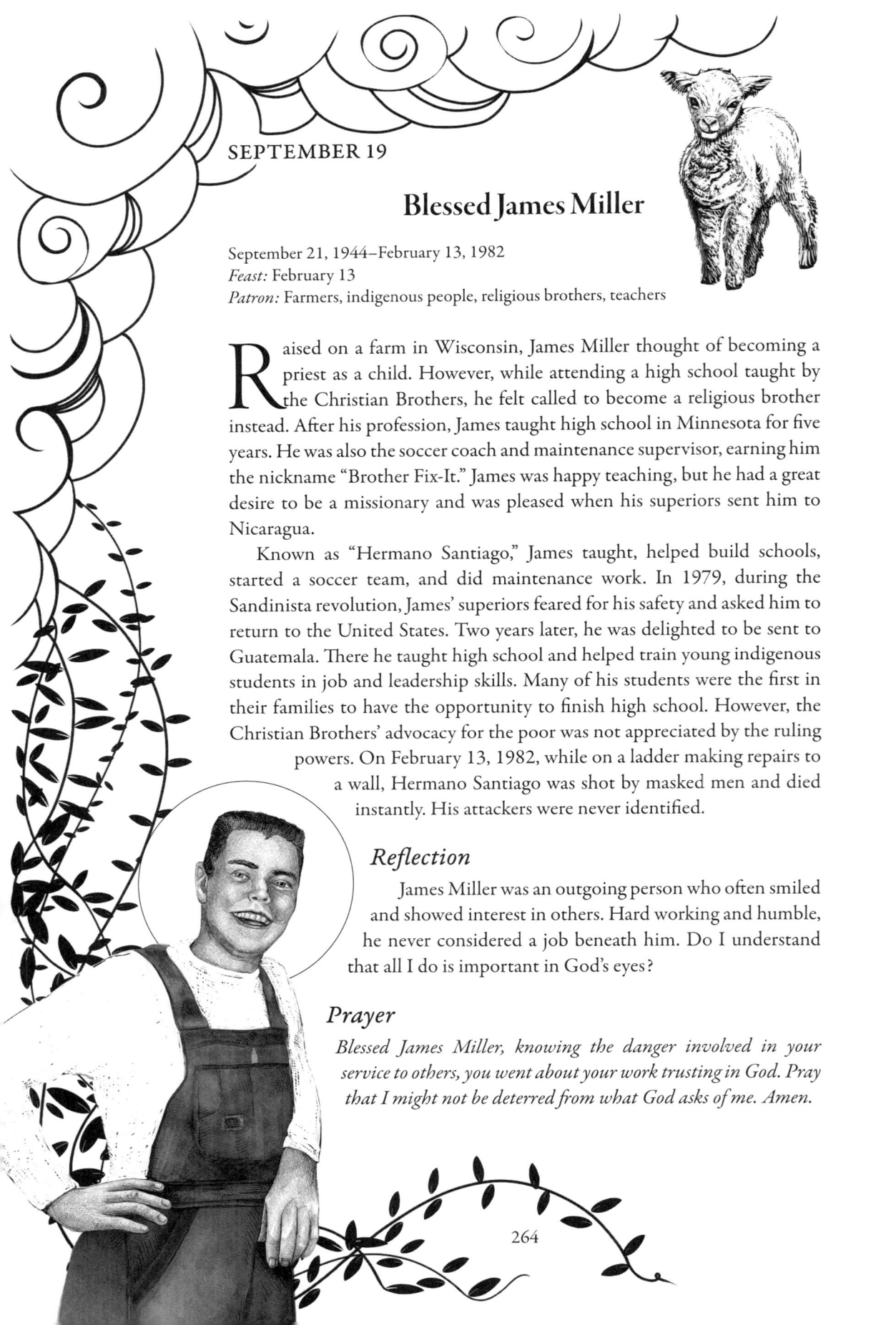

SEPTEMBER 20

Saint Andrew Kim Tae-gŏn, Paul Chŏng Ha-sang, and Companions

August 21, 1821–September 16, 1846 (Andrew Kim)
c. 1794–September 22, 1839 (Paul Chong)
1839–1867 (Companions)
Feast: September 20
Patron: Korea, farmers, indigenous people, religious brothers, teachers

The Catholic faith was brought to Korea not by missionaries but by books. In the late 1700s, a Korean man went to China and was baptized. He returned home with Catholic books, and other Koreans wanted to become Christian after reading them. The man baptized others, and, despite the lack of priests, the number of Christians grew. The first Western missionary priests arrived in 1836 to find a flourishing community. But before religious freedom became a reality in Korea, the Church endured a long persecution in which over ten thousand people were martyred.

Baptized at the age of fifteen, Andrew Kim traveled to Macau to study for the priesthood. He was ordained in 1845, the first Korean priest. A year later, he courageously gave his life for the faith after enduring horrible tortures. Paul Chŏng, born into a Catholic family, was a lay catechist whose father was also a martyr. When ordered to renounce his Catholic faith, Paul replied, "I have told you that I am a Christian and will be one until my death." The group of 103 martyrs to which Andrew and Paul belonged was canonized by Saint John Paul II on May 6, 1984 in Seoul.

Reflection

Despite intense persecution, the Church in Korea flourished. In this marvelous example of faith, Catholic books played a important role. People who had never heard about Jesus Christ read good books and were converted. With all the various digital media now available, we might ask ourselves how we too can witness to Christ by using those means.

Prayer

Saints Andrew Kim, Paul Chŏng, and all the Korean martyrs, pray for us that we might have the same kind of strong and living faith that inspired you to live and to die for Jesus Christ. Amen.

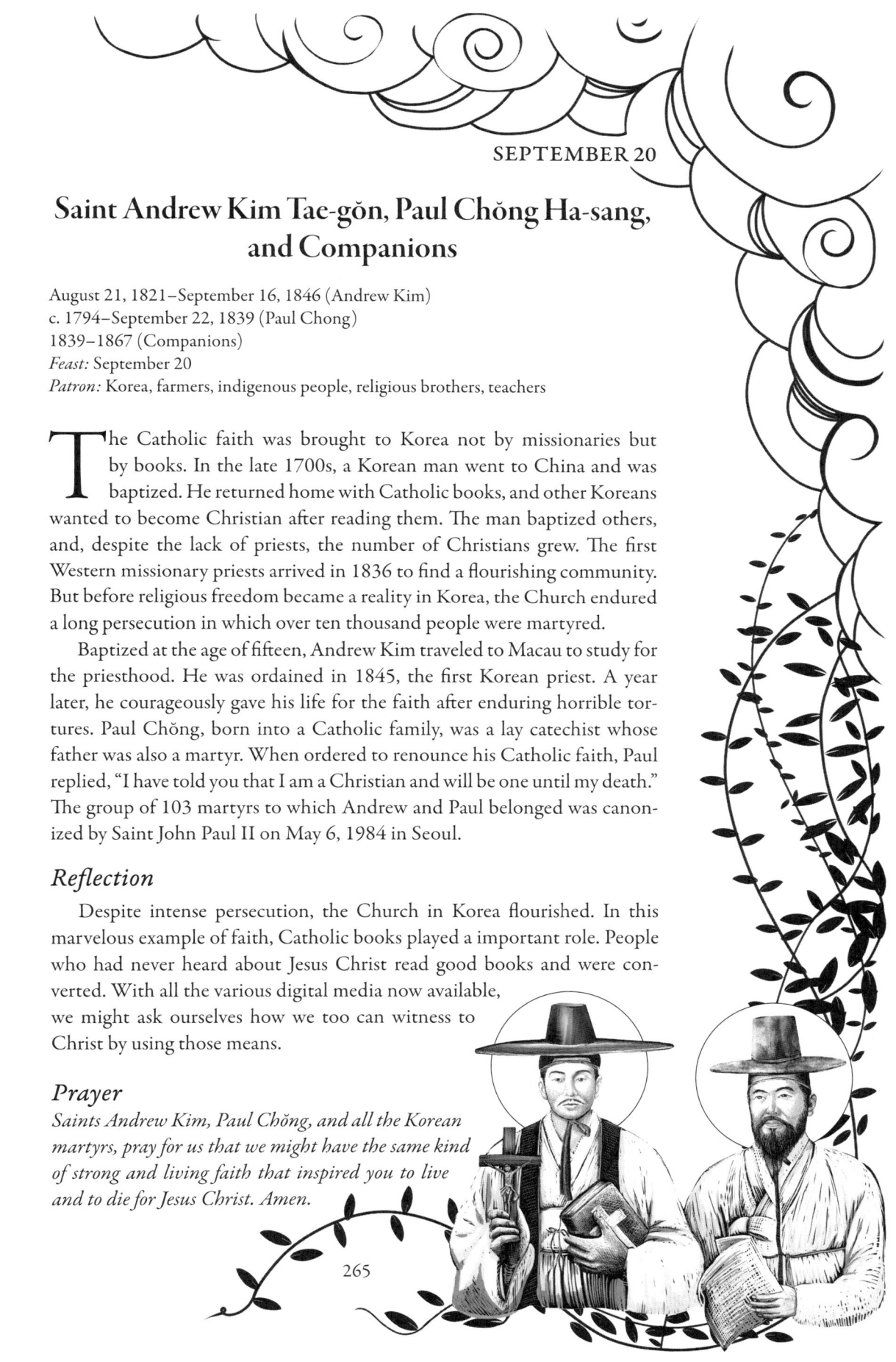

SEPTEMBER 21

Saint Matthew, the Apostle

First Century
Feast: September 21
Patron: Accountants, bankers, bookkeepers, stockbrokers, tax collectors

Also known as Levi, the son of Alphaeus, Matthew was a tax collector when he met Jesus (see Mk 2:13–14). Tax collectors were *persona non grata* in first-century Jewish circles. The villagers of Capernaum surely saw in Matthew a collaborator with the Roman occupying force, a man who made his living off of the hardship of others.

Jesus obviously saw more potential in Matthew. Jesus saw beyond appearances and knew that Matthew's heart was ready for a change. One day, as Jesus was walking along, he observed Matthew in his tax collector's booth and called him saying, "Follow me" (Mt 9:9). Matthew immediately got up and followed him, becoming one of the twelve apostles. He is commonly regarded as the author of the Gospel that carries his name. Ancient authors disagree as to where and how Matthew was martyred, but there is nearly unanimous agreement that he gave his life for the Gospel.

Reflection

Matthew's neighbors most likely had written him off as a lowlife profiteer. So, it's likely that Jesus' personal invitation caught both Matthew and those around him completely off guard. Nevertheless, Mathew chose to drop everything and follow this rabbi whom he must have been observing for a time from afar. We might write off friends and family who seem far from God, but their hearts can be changed by grace in an instant. How can I ready my heart to be changed by God at any moment?

Prayer

Saint Matthew, help me to treasure the gift of God's love and mercy above any earthly gain. Pray that I may believe in the power of God's grace to change hearts and reach out to friends and family who have fallen away from the faith. Amen.

SEPTEMBER 22

Saint Thecla

First Century
Feast: September 23
Patron: The dying

Thecla is traditionally honored as the first female martyr of the Church because she was sentenced to death for her faith, even though she was miraculously saved. Her legend is found in the ancient document, *The Acts of Paul and Thecla,* which dates from the mid to late second century. Thecla became immensely popular in the early Church.

As the story goes, she was born to noble parents at Iconium in Asia Minor. She heard Saint Paul preaching and resolved to consecrate her virginity to Jesus. That didn't go over well with her fiancé, nor her mother. They repudiated Thecla and had her condemned to death by burning. She was saved when a thunderstorm rolled in just in time to put out the flames. Thecla also survived two later attempts to put her to death, again by miraculous means. She then joined Paul's company of co-workers to spread the Gospel. Later she was said to have become a hermit and practiced great asceticism. Devotion to Thecla grew for many centuries and Saint Bede refers to her feast day on September 23 in his martyrology.

Reflection

Thecla's connection with the Apostle Paul is significant, as it puts her in the heart of the early Church's missionary efforts. Today, the Church is calling for a new evangelization, one that will not only reach those who have never heard the Gospel, but also those who have fallen away from the Church. Do I know someone who has left the Church? How can I witness to the beauty of the faith in an invitational way?

Prayer

Saint Thecla, just as you were drawn to the Good News by Saint Paul's preaching, pray that through the witness of our lives we may help others to find the light of Christ. Amen.

SEPTEMBER 23

Saint Pio of Pietrelcina

May 25, 1887–September 23, 1968
Feast: September 23
Patron: Civil defense volunteers, teens, relief of stress and depression

Francesco Forgione always wanted to be a priest, but his poor farming family couldn't send him to school. So, his father left Italy, seeking work in the United States to pay for his son's education. Francesco became a Capuchin and was ordained in 1910. Known as Padre Pio, he had poor health but many mystical gifts. He received the stigmata in 1918, which stirred controversy since some thought he was a fraud. His critics got the Vatican to forbid him from celebrating Mass publicly and from hearing confessions. Though Padre Pio suffered immensely from this, he accepted the Church's decision in humility. He would often say, "Pray, hope, and don't worry," and this summed up his simple yet profound stance in the face of constant criticism and rumors.

In the end, the truth won out, and Padre Pio was permitted to celebrate Mass and hear confessions. He spent countless hours listening to the confessions of the many people who flocked to him. He also felt called to help people in their bodily needs, so he raised funds to build a hospital, which opened in 1956. He died praying the Rosary, a favorite prayer he offered constantly. Saint John Paul II, who had once gone to him for confession, canonized Padre Pio in 2002.

Reflection

Padre Pio took sin seriously and always tried to bring his penitents to a deep sorrow. In our day the sacrament of Penance is rather neglected, but it is a great source of grace and spiritual renewal. How can I make this Sacrament a more regular part of my life?

Prayer

Saint Pio, pray for us that we might turn away from all sin and grow in love for God and our neighbor. Amen.

SEPTEMBER 24

Blessed Émilie Tavernier Gamelin

February 19, 1800–September 23, 1851
Feast: September 23 (September 24 in Canada)
Patron: Sisters of Providence, loss of children, devotion to Mary

Émilie Tavernier was born in Montreal, the youngest of fifteen children. Her mother died when she was four, and the young girl was placed in a boarding school operated by the Sisters of Notre-Dame. Her father also died during this time. At eighteen, Émilie left the sisters to help her widowed brother. He allowed her to keep a table set to feed the hungry people who knocked on their door. She called it "The Table of the King" after the example of her own mother.

At age twenty-three, Émilie married Jean-Baptise Gamelin, a prosperous farmer. Their nearly five-year marriage was marked by the death of all three of their children. At her husband's death, she sought consolation in meditating on Mary's sorrows at the foot of the Cross. In the meantime, she continued to reach out to the poor around her. She started a refuge for elderly, destitute women in 1830; cared for children orphaned by the 1832 cholera epidemic; and visited prisoners. In 1843, at the invitation of the bishop of Montreal, Émilie Tavernier-Gamelin founded the Sisters of Providence, then called Daughters of Charity, Servants of the Poor. Mother Gamelin lived only seven years after the foundation of the new religious community; she died in the cholera epidemic of 1851. Her dying words were a testimony of her entire life: "Humility, simplicity, charity."

Reflection

In human terms, life dealt Émilie an incredibly unfair set of circumstances. Death robbed her of both her parents early in life, and then of all of her children as well as her husband. However, rather than turn in on herself, Émilie looked to Mary for comfort and support. Her life shows us how deep sorrow can be transformed into profound simplicity and compassion for others.

Prayer

Blessed Émilie, I too want humility, simplicity, and charity to characterize my life. Help me to respond with generous love to those around me. Amen.

SEPTEMBER 25

Saint Lorenzo Ruiz

c. 1610–September 1637
Feast: September 28
Patron: The Philippines, Filipino and Chinese youth

The first Filipino to be canonized, Lorenzo Ruiz seems to have been quite ordinary by all accounts. He was born of a Chinese father and Filipino mother in Binondo, Manila. Raised Catholic and educated by the Dominicans, he served as an altar boy, became a clerk, married, and had three children. Then Lorenzo's life turned upside down when he was accused of murder by the Spanish authorities. He feared unjust execution, so he sought help from the Dominicans. Believing in his innocence, they arranged for Lorenzo's escape on a boat that was secretly leaving.

When they left Manila, Lorenzo discovered that the Dominicans were on a mission to Japan, where Christians were fiercely persecuted. Shortly after landing, they were captured by the Japanese government. Lorenzo and his companions were imprisoned under harsh conditions. Finally, they were brought to Nagasaki where their torture was so cruel that several of the missionaries wavered. Lorenzo feared he would apostatize, but his prayer gave him strength to endure both torture and death. When his judges gave him one last chance to renounce his faith, Lorenzo answered, "Never! If I had a thousand lives, I would offer them all to God!"

Reflection

Lorenzo Ruiz is not your typical martyr. He found himself in the wrong place at the wrong time. Nevertheless, when he could have denied his faith and save his life, he instead heroically affirmed his commitment to Christ at the cost of his life. What are the costs of faith that I experience in my life? How do I respond?

Prayer

Saint Lorenzo Ruiz, help us to discover God's faithful love for us in every circumstance of our lives, no matter how unexpected or difficult. Amen.

SEPTEMBER 26

Saints Cosmas and Damian

Died c. 287
Feast: September 26 (September 25 in Canada)
Patron: Pharmacists, doctors, surgeons, barbers

These two saints were brothers who worked as doctors in what is now Turkey. Refusing to take any money for their services, the people called them "the silverless ones." Prominent and highly sought out, they ministered to their patients and also evangelized them, making many converts. During the early stages of Diocletian's persecution, they were called before the prefect Lysias. The brothers were said to remain calm despite attempts to kill them by drowning, burning, and crucifixion. Finally, they were beheaded.

Many miracles occurred through Cosmas and Damian's intercession and their cult became very popular. They were honored both in the East and the West and many churches were built in their honor. Damian was immortalized in the Franciscan heritage when Saint Francis of Assisi rebuilt the chapel of San Damiano. Their names are included in the Roman Canon of the Mass. Their relics are believed to have been transported in the sixth century from Syria, the place of their execution, to the Church of Cosmas and Damian in Rome.

Reflection

Paintings of Cosmas and Damian often show them holding the tools of their trade as physicians of the body. Catholicism is about incarnational reality. With the Incarnation, God took a human nature, including a real body. Catholic theology recognizes how important the human body is in God's design. It is good; it is holy. That is also the basis for the Sacraments, which take simple things like bread, wine, oil, water, and make them bearers of divinity, the means by which Christ gives us grace.

Prayer

Saints Cosmas and Damian, pray for us that we may be faithful witnesses to the Catholic faith and that we may be free from bodily ailments. Amen.

SEPTEMBER 27

Saint Vincent de Paul

April 24, 1581–September 27, 1660
Feast: September 27
Patron: Works of charity, helping the poor and needy, hospital workers, prisoners

Born to a farming family in Gascony, France, Vincent was ordained a priest as a young man. But he was not a particularly fervent priest. In 1605, while on a trip by sea, he was captured and sold into slavery in North Africa. For the next two years he was sold to several masters, until he finally managed to escape. Returning to France around 1609, Vincent met Father Pierre de Bérulle, an important member of the French school of spirituality, who helped him deepen his spiritual life.

Soon Vincent was asked to be the chaplain for the wealthy Gondi family. While working with their servants and tenants, Vincent began to realize the pastoral needs of the poor. Vincent expanded his work and began to preach missions. He founded the Congregation of the Mission, now known as the Vincentians, for priests dedicated to this pastoral work. He also worked with Saint Louise de Marillac to begin the Daughters of Charity. After a life of hard work, Vincent peacefully passed away while sitting in his chair when he was eighty-five years old.

Reflection

Though Vincent did not always put God first, he was open to grace. Gradually, the Lord led him to seek holiness. Little by little, Vincent took steps to reform and instruct the clergy, to preach, and to help the poor. His work was so outstanding that many charitable works take him as their patron, such as the Saint Vincent de Paul Society. In what way has the Lord been leading me to grow in my own vocation and mission?

Prayer

Saint Vincent de Paul, pray for us that we might put our faith into action and change the world. Amen.

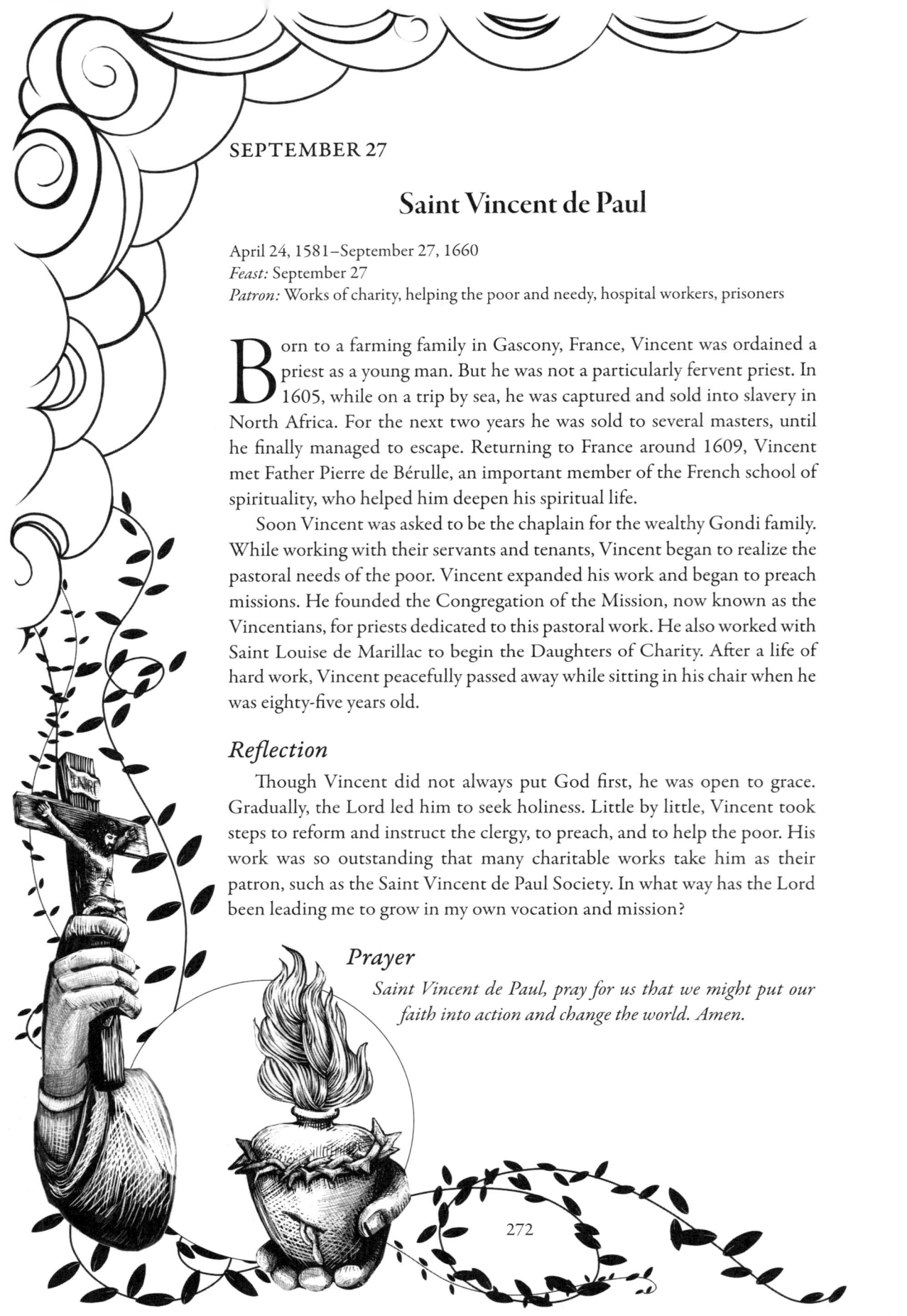

SEPTEMBER 28

Saint Wenceslaus

c. 907–c. 929
Feast: September 28
Patron: The Czech Republic

Wenceslaus was the eldest son of the Duke of Bohemia at a time when Christianity was new to the area and much of the country was still pagan. After his father's death, his mother, Drahomira, became regent and adopted anti-Christian policies. Wenceslaus was raised by his pious grandmother, Ludmilla, who opposed Drahomira's anti-Christian rule and was consequently murdered by pagan nobles. Because of her cruel and extravagant behavior, Drahomira was soon deposed and Wenceslaus assumed the throne when he was only fifteen or sixteen years old.

As a ruler, Wenceslaus had a reputation for helping the poor and supporting the Church, which greatly encouraged its growth in Bohemia. His foreign policy, however, was unpopular among some of his nobles, who banded together with Wenceslaus' malcontent brother, Boleslaus, to assassinate him. Boleslaus invited Wenceslaus to his home to celebrate a feast day and, along with a few supporters, attacked him on the way to church. With his dying breath, Wenceslaus asked God to forgive his brother. The people lamented their beloved king as a martyr and more readily converted to Christianity because of his example.

Reflection

Much of the opposition Wenceslaus faced came from his own family, particularly his mother and brother. And yet, he always treated them kindly and gave them the benefit of the doubt, seeing it as his duty as a Christian to love them and pray for their conversion. How do I deal with difficult family members? Do I pray for them daily and love them as they are?

Prayer

Dear Lord, help us to love our families in the moments when loving them isn't easy. May those moments be opportunities for all of us to grow in grace together. Amen.

SEPTEMBER 29

Saint Michael the Archangel

Feast: September 29
Patron: Battle, Germany, grocers, mariners, paratroopers, military, policemen, radiologists, sailors, seafarers, temptation

Michael, Gabriel, and Raphael are the only angels mentioned by name in Scripture. They have traditionally received the title of "saint" not because they are formally canonized but because they are in eternity with God. According to tradition, the angel Lucifer wanted Michael to join him in rebelling against God. Michael refused to rebel because turning against God would suggest that he knew better than God. Michael's name comes from his Hebrew response to Lucifer, "Who is like God?" Michael's name is both a question and a battle cry against evil.

Revelation describes another battle that will take place at the end of time when Michael will lead the armies of God against Satan (see Rev 12:7–12). Because of his role as general of the angelic armies in the fight against evil at the beginning and end of time, Michael is honored in Catholic tradition and liturgy as the protector of the Church. He has traditionally been called upon to intercede for and protect people who are in the grip of the devil. Michael also assists people in their struggle against evil in the hour of death. He is believed to have appeared in several locations around the world, and many shrines have been built in his honor.

Reflection

In the Book of Daniel, Michael is referred to as "the great prince" (12:1). Saint Leo XIII also promulgated a prayer to Michael that refers to him as the "prince of the heavenly hosts." Do I call upon the aid of this prince of the angels to protect me from evil?

Prayer

Saint Michael, defend me from the snares of the devil. Help me to worship and serve God at all times despite temptation, just as you did. Amen.

SEPTEMBER 30

Saint Jerome

c. 347–c. 420
Feast: September 30
Patron: Archaeologists, librarians, students, translators, Bible scholars

Jerome was born in Dalmatia and later went to Rome for studies. He converted to Christianity and was baptized by Pope Liberius. Attracted by the ascetical life, Jerome traveled widely and was ordained to the priesthood in Antioch. He studied for about two years under Saint Gregory Nazianzen in Constantinople. Back in Rome, Jerome became a secretary to Pope Damasus, who supported him although Jerome was an unpopular ascetic who stirred up opposition with his acerbic wit and criticisms of lax clergy. When the pope died, Jerome decided to travel to the Holy Land.

Eventually, Jerome took up residence in a cave in Bethlehem around 386. There he focused on writing and Scripture studies. An expert linguist, Jerome translated the Bible from the original Hebrew and Greek into Latin. Known as the Vulgate, this translation became standard in the Church for many centuries. Jerome also directed a group of women ascetics and helped those in need. But for the most part, this brilliant man lived out his last years in quiet solitude, meditating on and translating the word of God.

Reflection

Jerome liked to say, "Ignorance of Scripture is ignorance of Christ." He immersed himself in the Bible because it is the word of God. His example can help us to reflect on the importance that we give to the Scriptures. How well do I know the Bible? Do I read and meditate on it daily? In what ways can I grow in my appreciation for this gift of God so that it will guide my life?

Prayer

Saint Jerome, pray for us that we, like you, may take delight in studying the Scriptures. May God's word always be a lamp to our feet and light to our path (see Ps 119:105). Amen.

OCTOBER 1

Saint Thérèse of Lisieux

January 2, 1873–September 30, 1897
Feast: October 1
Patron: Missionaries, France, Russia, florists, gardeners, loss of parents, tuberculosis

Thérèse was born to Saints Louis and Zélie Martin. The youngest of five girls, her childhood was in many ways idyllic, but also touched by profound suffering. In 1877, when she was four, Thérèse's mother died. Greatly impacted, she became sensitive and overly attached to her older sister Pauline who then entered the Carmelite monastery. The bereft Thérèse fell seriously ill until, miraculously, she was healed after having a vision of the Blessed Virgin Mary. On Christmas Eve 1886, Thérèse experienced another miracle of a deep healing of her extreme sensitivity. Soon after, she felt drawn to religious life, but she was too young to enter.

Thérèse's desire to become a Carmelite was finally granted when she was fifteen years old. She professed her vows in 1890 and took the name Thérèse of the Infant Jesus and the Holy Face. Her time in Carmel was not always easy, but Thérèse showed quiet heroism in simple ways. In a time when much emphasis was put on individual effort in the spiritual life, Thérèse pioneered a spirituality of trust in God's mercy that she called "the little way." On Holy Thursday night, 1896, Thérèse felt a stream of blood rise to her lips. The stained handkerchief she examined the next morning confirmed her in joy: her Divine Spouse would be coming to take her to heaven soon. Thérèse died of tuberculosis the next year, after a time of deep spiritual darkness that she endured by relying on her trust in God.

Reflection

Thérèse was a little soul who trusted that God would bring her to great holiness. She likened her spiritual approach to an elevator that brings the weak straight to the top, while others climb the stairs. How often do I remember that doing little things with great love is pleasing to God?

Prayer

Saint Thérèse, help me to trust in God's great love for me. Amen.

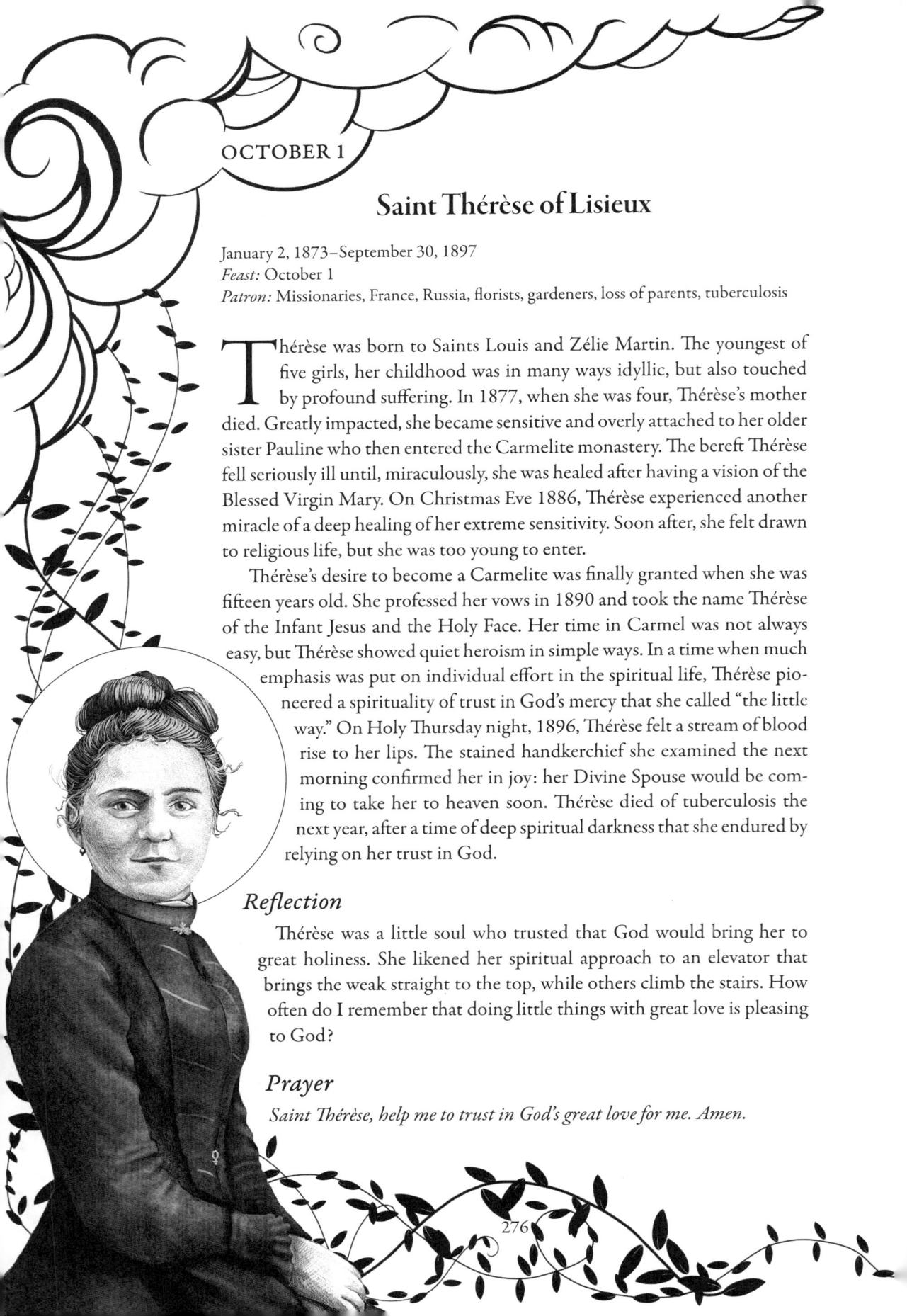

OCTOBER 2

Saint Raphael the Archangel

Feast: September 29
Patron: Pharmacists, eye diseases, safe journey, healing, finding one's future spouse

Angels are not—and never have been—human. They are a creation completely distinct from us; whereas we are both body and spirit, they are pure spirit. Angels live in God's presence and sing his praises unceasingly. And some angels, such as our own guardian angels and the archangels, are given special missions from God for our sake. In the delightful biblical Book of Tobit, the Archangel Raphael is sent by God to help a man named Tobit and his family.

Tobit is a good, faithful, and generous man who becomes blind. He sends his son, Tobias, on a journey to reclaim a loan. The Archangel Raphael then appears, disguised as a man, and offers to be Tobias' guide. On the way, they meet Sarah, a young woman whose seven husbands had been killed one after the other by a demon. With Raphael's help, the demon is expelled, and Tobias and Sarah get married. Returning home, Tobias cures his father's blindness with a remedy provided by Raphael, who reveals his true identity as "one of the seven angels who stand ready and enter before the glory of the Lord" (Tob 12:15). Raphael then encourages them to give thanks to God and ascends to heaven.

Reflection

The Archangel Raphael exercises many roles in the story of Tobit: guide through unknown lands, victor over evil, supporter of the beauty of marriage, and miraculous healer. But perhaps the most striking of Raphael's actions was his final reminder to Tobias and Sarah to express gratitude to God. Even in the midst of trial, do I praise God with thanksgiving?

Prayer

Saint Raphael, pray that I may follow God's will for my life in a spirit of deep gratitude. Amen.

OCTOBER 3

Saint Mother Théodore Guérin

October 2, 1798–May 14, 1856
Feast: October 3
Patron: Educators, pharmacists, writers, those away from the Church

Despite family tragedy, faith in divine providence marked Anne-Thérèse Guerin's entire life. Growing up, Anne-Thérèse grieved the death of her two brothers and then the murder of her father, a French naval officer, when she was fifteen. Anne-Thérèse took care of her grieving mother and sister for about ten years. She then entered the Sisters of Providence of Ruillé sur-Loir, France, taking the name Théodore.

Despite ill health, Mother Théodore was then asked to lead five other sisters on a new mission to the United States, to Indiana, to be exact. Imagine the sisters' surprise when they arrived only to find themselves in the middle of the woods! Overcoming many hardships, they managed to open a school in less than a year. Mother Théodore faced many challenges: great poverty, a harsh climate, her continuing poor health, and interference from Church authorities. A bishop even excommunicated Mother Théodore, who had always treated him with respect, but had also insisted that he not exercise undue control over her sisters. Thankfully, that bishop resigned, and the new bishop set things right. With trust in God's help, Mother Théodore successfully established the congregation, now known as the Sisters of Providence of Saint Mary-of-the-Woods.

Reflection

Mother Théodore would often say, "With Jesus, what have we to fear?" Though she had poor health, her indomitable spirit overcame every trial. She did not focus on the difficulties but on the source of her strength: Jesus Christ. How does Mother Théodore's example speak to me as I strive to grow in faith in Divine Providence?

Prayer

Mother Theodore, intercede for us in our difficulties. Ask the Lord that we might always trust in the tender and loving providence of God, who works through all things. Amen.

OCTOBER 4

Saint Francis of Assisi

c. 1182–October 3, 1226
Feast: October 4
Patron: Animals, merchants, ecology, Italy

A young, handsome nobleman from Assisi, Italy, Francis was frivolous, fun-loving, and generous. A glory-seeking knight, his life was interrupted when he was captured and imprisoned for over a year. This event pushed Francis to start searching for something more. Gradually, Francis recognized the emptiness of his carefree life and embraced Jesus' invitation to leave everything and follow him. But not everyone understood Francis' new way of life. Disowned by his father and ridiculed by the townspeople, Francis nevertheless rejoiced in his suffering because it united him with Christ.

The lighthearted cheerfulness of Francis' youth now blossomed into a deep, persistent joy that captivated others. Within ten years, Francis had over five thousand followers. Following Francis' example, his friars' preaching, spirit of poverty, and commitment to peace began to renew the Church. Toward the end of his life, Francis received the wounds of Christ on his hands, feet, and side. While in excruciating pain, he composed his famous hymn, "Canticle of Brother Sun." Francis' quiet joy, however, always remained. When a doctor told him that death was near, Francis exclaimed, "Welcome, Sister Death!" He died at age forty-four, lying on the floor of a hut near the little chapel called the Portiuncula, surrounded by his friars.

Reflection

Two of the most striking aspects of Francis' life were his joy in suffering and his immense sensitivity to all of God's creatures. His vision of the goodness and connectedness of all creation in Christ is a unique legacy that we can learn to apply to aspects of our own lives. How might I show more love and care for the gift of God's creation?

Prayer

Saint Francis of Assisi, help us to follow Christ more closely: in joy, in service, in peace with others, and in harmony with all creation. Amen.

OCTOBER 5

Blessed Francis Xavier Seelos

January 11, 1819–October 4, 1867
Feast: October 5
Patron: missionaries, preachers

Francis Xavier was one of twelve children born to a devout family in Bavaria. He wanted to become a priest and after reading about the need for German-speaking priests in the United States, he entered the Redemptorists in 1842. The following year he was sent to New York to finish his studies for the priesthood. After his ordination, his first assignment was in Pittsburgh, where he had the privilege of working with Saint John Neumann, another Redemptorist. Francis' time with Neumann formed him in many ways, especially in pastoral work and the spiritual life.

Though Francis was proposed as a candidate for bishop of Pittsburgh, he narrowly avoided the office—to his great relief. From 1863 to 1866, Francis then traveled and worked as an itinerant preacher in ten states in the east and Midwest. He was known for spending long hours in the confessional and always showing great concern for the poor. Because of his happy disposition and life of penance, he was called the "cheerful ascetic." Francis died in New Orleans after contracting yellow fever while caring for people during an epidemic.

Reflection

Francis was a renowned confessor who highlighted the sacrament of Penance in his ministry because he knew that it was a prime means to encourage people to holiness. When Saint John Paul II beatified Francis on April 9, 2000, he said that this humble priest invites us to grow in our union with Christ through the sacraments of Penance and the Eucharist. How can I take full advantage of these sacraments for my spiritual growth?

Prayer

Blessed Francis Xavier Seelos, pray for us that we might cheerfully dedicate ourselves to helping our neighbor in times of need and giving God first place in our life. Amen.

OCTOBER 6

Blessed Marie-Rose Durocher

October 6, 1811–October 6, 1849
Feast: October 6 (U. S. and Canada)
Patron: Congregation of the Holy Names of Jesus and Mary, poor children

Like many of us, Marie-Rose Durocher lived a life of constantly changing circumstances. Born Eulalie Durocher, the tenth of eleven children, she had a happy childhood on her family's farm in Quebec. She enjoyed school, horseback riding, and visiting Jesus in the Eucharist. She had dreams of becoming a religious sister, but poor health prevented her.

When she was eighteen, her mother died. Eulalie grieved for her mother. Not sure what to do next, she gratefully accepted her brother's invitation to come and live with him. He was the pastor of a nearby parish, and Eulalie became not only housekeeper and rectory manager, but also catechist and liturgy coordinator! Her attentiveness to people helped her excel during her twelve years of work in the parish

At the parish, she saw the great need for evangelization and catechesis. She agreed to join a religious community that Bishop Ignace Bourget was bringing to Canada from France. When the French community was unable to come, Bishop Bourget asked Eulalie to found a community. She resisted at first, aware of her poor health, her brother's need for her, and her own insufficiency. Eventually, however, she agreed and founded the Congregation of the Holy Names of Jesus and Mary. Under the guidance of Mother Marie-Rose, as she was now called, the fledging congregation provided education and catechesis for poor children. Mother Marie-Rose died only six years after the congregation's foundation.

Reflection

Mother Marie-Rose followed where God led her through the circumstances of her life. She allowed her time at her brother's parish to open her heart to the needs of God's people. May we, too, allow our experiences to open our hearts to God's call to us today.

Prayer

Blessed Marie-Rose, pray for me and for all the people I will encounter today—let our experiences bring us closer to God. Amen.

OCTOBER 7

Blessed Chiara Badano

October 29, 1971–October 7, 1990
Feast: October 29
Patron: Cancer patients, young people

Born in Savona, Italy, Chiara Badano's parents welcomed the gift of a child with immense gratitude after eleven years of prayer for one. While very young, Chiara developed a close relationship with Jesus and readily entrusted the needs of others to him in prayer. When she was nine, she attended an event put on by the Focolare Movement and later told a friend that she had "rediscovered the Gospel in a new light."

As a teenager, Chiara radiated beauty inside and out. She enjoyed sports and dancing with her friends, but also experienced normal teenage challenges including failures in school. Nevertheless, the Gospel was Chiara's daily nourishment, moving her to reach out to the lonely, sick, and elderly. When she was seventeen, Chiara was diagnosed with a rare form of bone cancer. She struggled with the diagnosis, but after she had surrendered her pain to the Lord, the cancer only strengthened her bond with Jesus. Everyone who met her during this time was touched by the light radiating from her presence. Knowing that heaven was coming quickly, Chiara joyfully prepared to meet Jesus face to face. Like a bride about to meet her spouse, she asked to be buried in a wedding dress.

Reflection

The founder of Focolare nicknamed Chiara "Luce" since she radiated Christ's presence. Chiara Luce's life became so illumined with the light of Christ because she united all her joys and sorrows, illnesses and sufferings to Jesus. Our lives are full of opportunities to draw near to the Lord and experience his love. How is God inviting me to be united to him today?

Prayer

Lord, help me to live every moment of my life with you so that our life together may give life to others. Amen.

OCTOBER 8

Blessed Giuseppe Toniolo

March 7, 1845–October 7, 1918
Feast: September 4
Patron: Teachers, economists, workers

Born in Treviso, Italy, Giuseppe Toniolo was inspired to study law and economics. He became a well-known and beloved lecturer at the university level. Giuseppe promoted a Christian vision of economics that kept the needs of the human person at the center. He advanced proposals for days of rest from work, limits on working hours, and protections for women and children in the workplace. When the now widespread organization known as Catholic Action was taking root in Italy, Giuseppe became involved. Soon his gifts led him to leadership positions and frequent interactions with the Holy See, including with Pope Leo XIII and Saint Pius X.

A convincing speaker and prolific writer, Giuseppe used his prominence to encourage Catholics to become more active in the nation's political life. He also urged Catholics to take up the emerging forms of media in order to communicate the truth. Giuseppe was also a devoted father. He and his wife, Maria, raised seven children. The word of God held a prominent place in their home. Throughout his life, Giuseppe maintained a strong devotion to Our Lady of the Rosary; he died on her feast day at the age of seventy-three.

Reflection

Giuseppe was a family man who excelled in his field and applied his expertise for the advancement of Christian ideals in the public sphere. He is a beautiful example of the fullness of the Christian life that the Church invites every person to live, regardless of his or her vocation. What is my area of expertise? How might the Lord be inviting me to share my gifts on behalf of the Gospel?

Prayer

Blessed Giuseppe Toniolo, pray for us and for our society, that we may always be attentive to the needs of others, serving the Lord in all circumstances. Amen.

OCTOBER 9

Saint John Leonardi

1541–October 9, 1609
Feast: October 9
Patron: Pharmacists

Born in Lucca, Italy, John Leonardi studied for ten years to become a pharmacist. Something else was tugging at his heart, however, and he left that profession to become a priest in 1572. John saw that Christ was the medicine, so to speak, that would heal the spiritual difficulties people faced in the tumultuous times after the Reformation. He believed that true renewal must be rooted in love for Christ and the Church.

According to John, reform in the Church must occur in all its members, from top to bottom. But he saw the importance of forming young people in particular. In 1574, John founded an order of priests to teach and work with youth, the Clerics Regular of the Mother of God. He went to Rome, where he became a friend of Saint Philip Neri who assisted him in his new work. Then in 1609, the former-pharmacist-turned-priest, who had brought spiritual health to so many, died after nursing those sick with the plague.

Reflection

Today, many people take up second careers, but that was unusual in John's day. He made a great act of faith by leaving his pharmacy to become a priest. But nothing we give to God is ever lost. John was able to use his training to enhance his priestly work, seeing it as God's medicine for the soul. How can I use everything I have learned for the glory of God?

Prayer

Saint John Leonardi, you spent your life preaching about Jesus Christ, the healer of our souls. Pray for us that despite whatever wounds we may bear, we too may be effective witnesses to the Gospel. Amen.

OCTOBER 10

Saint John Henry Newman

February 21, 1801–August 11, 1890
Feast: October 9
Patron: Converts, scholars, and students

One of the most brilliant minds in nineteenth-century England, John Henry Newman helped revive Roman Catholicism by his intellectual wrestling and humble submission to the truth. He was born into a middle-class family in London, received an excellent education at Oxford, and was ordained an Anglican clergyman in 1825. While carefully studying the Fathers of the Church, John unexpectedly found himself convinced that the Church of Rome and early Christianity were one and the same. With friends, he anonymously distributed tracts, hoping to convince others of this find.

In the ensuing controversy, John had to renounce his prestigious position as vicar at the Oxford University church, Saint Mary the Virgin. In 1845, he was quietly received into the Catholic Church and later went to Rome to study for the priesthood. While in Rome, he joined the Oratory of Saint Philip Neri and later established it in England. Even though all his energies were now spent among Catholics, some of them still misunderstood and distrusted him. As a result, he wrote the classic on conversion, *Apologia Pro Vita Sua*, in 1864. Because of his constant devotion and defense of the faith, Pope Leo XIII made him a cardinal.

Reflection

John's clear and compelling sermons, as well as his theological masterpieces, such as *An Essay in Aid of a Grammar of Assent*, prove him an intellectual giant. But even more than his intellectual prowess, he stood out for his humility in seeking the truth. His devotion and humility made him a model of Christian and priestly life. Do I humbly seek the truth?

Prayer

Saint John Henry Newman, inspire us to find the conviction to adhere to our faith when it is easy to believe and when it is not. Amen.

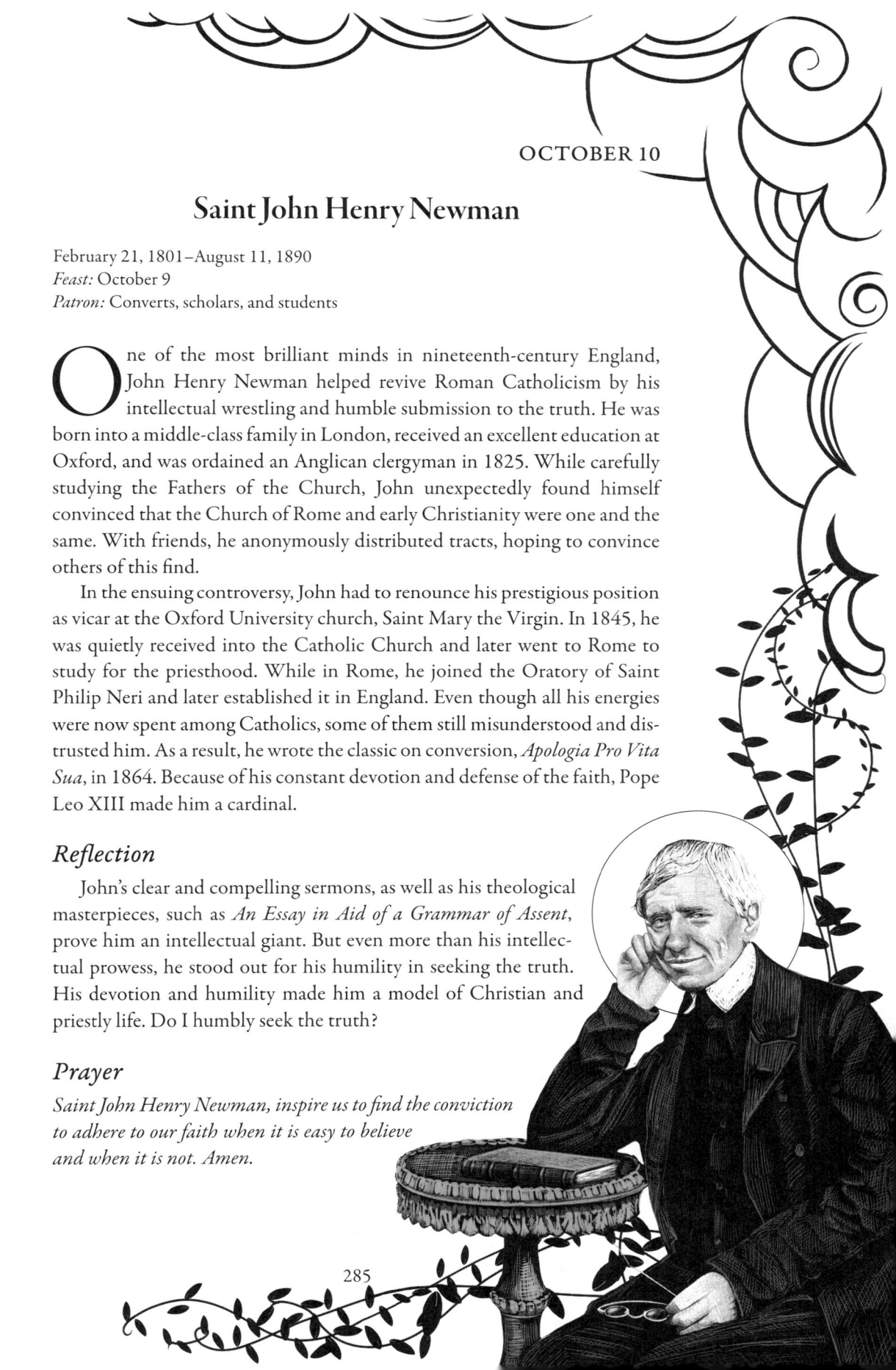

OCTOBER 11

Saint John XXIII

November 25, 1881–June 3, 1963
Feast: October 11
Patron: Christian unity

Known as "Good Pope John," Angelo Roncalli's simplicity of heart endeared him to the world. Born into a poor family of sharecroppers in northern Italy, Angelo was ordained a priest in 1904. He became a secretary to Bishop Radini Tedeschi of Bergamo, and taught Church history and patristics in the seminary. When Italy entered World War I in 1915, he was drafted into the Italian army and served until the war ended.

In 1921, Angelo was called to Rome to reorganize the Society for the Propagation of the Faith. His long career as a Vatican diplomat in Bulgaria, Turkey, and France began in 1925 when he became a bishop. In 1944, he became a nuncio to Paris and used his influence to support Jewish refugees. Angelo was elected pope in 1958, when he was seventy-seven years old. Despite his age, Pope John XXIII had immense energy. He soon shocked everyone by calling an ecumenical council, which ushered in major changes in the Church. This pope—who said that he had felt called by the Holy Spirit to convoke Vatican II—died one day after Pentecost, just months after the council began.

Reflection

Pope John XXIII always sought to discern God's will and follow it throughout his life, even taking the episcopal motto "obedience and peace." Obedience to his heavenly Father and the inspirations of the Holy Spirit helped Pope John XXIII to develop a Christ-like love for all the faithful. How do I seek to know and to do God's will in my life?

Prayer

Saint John XXIII, we ask your intercession for the universal Church, that it may respond to God's word with faith and love. Pray for us that we may "hold fast to what is good" (1 Thes 5:21). Amen.

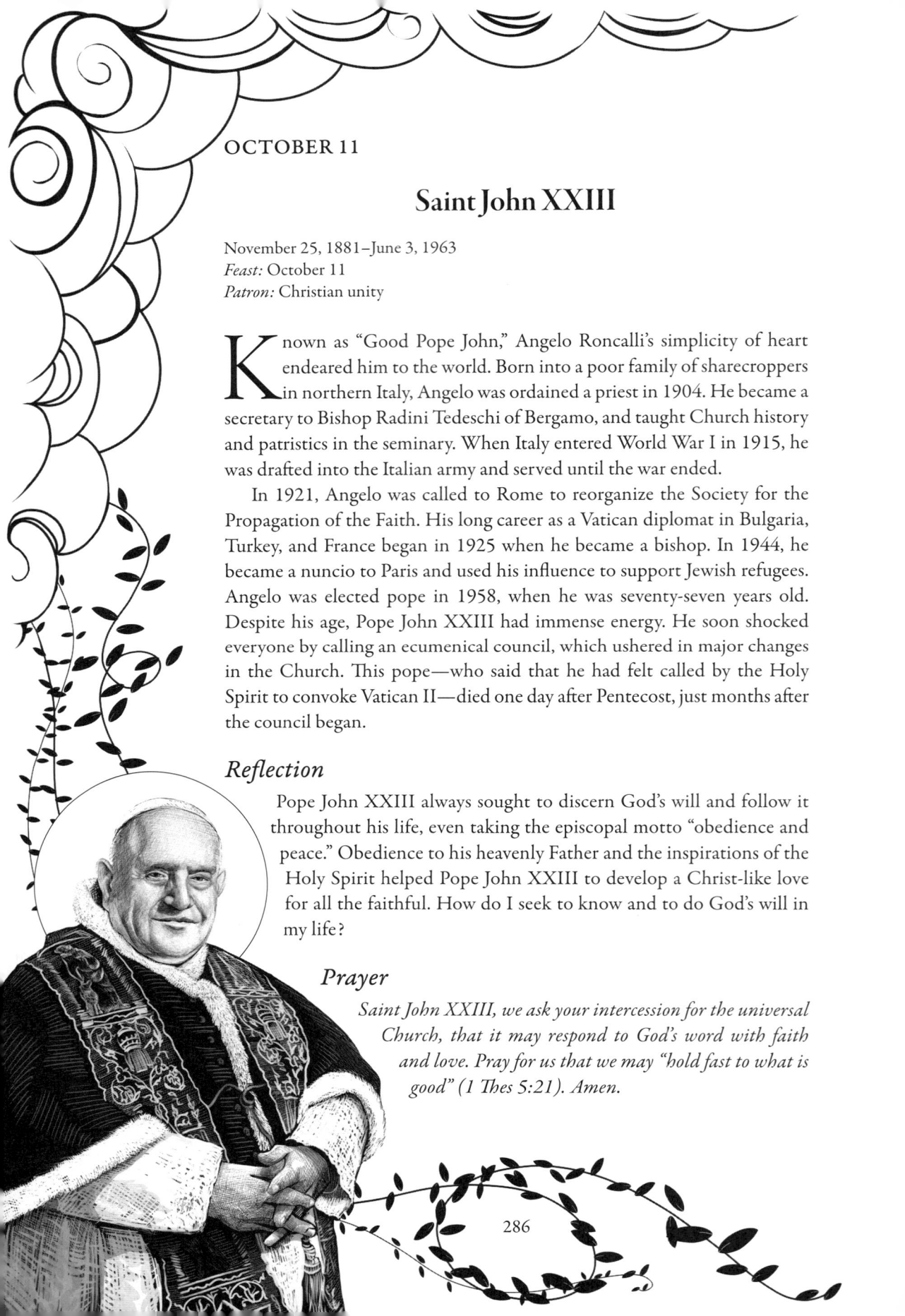

OCTOBER 12

Saint Gerard Majella

April 1726–October 16, 1755
Feast: October 16
Patron: Children, especially the unborn; expectant mothers; those trying to conceive; those falsely accused

Gerard was born in Muro, Italy, the youngest of five children. His father died when Gerard was twelve and he was sent to his uncle to learn how to be a tailor. Gerard was always devout, but ill health prevented him from entering the Capuchins. Finally, in 1749 he was permitted to enter the newly-founded Redemptorist Order. The unimpressed Redemptorist who sent Gerard to the rector wrote a note that said, "I send you a useless brother." Gerard instead would prove himself to be an invaluable brother who was extremely obedient and devoted to God.

Gerard once suffered the calumny of being falsely accused of fathering a woman's child, but he didn't defend himself. He accepted the penance imposed on him by Saint Alphonsus Liguori, the founder of the Redemptorists. Later, the woman who accused him admitted she had lied. Upon realizing how patiently Gerard had accepted the false accusation, Alphonsus exclaimed, "Brother Gerard is a saint!" Known for reading people's souls and other wonders, this humble brother died after predicting the day and hour of his death.

Reflection

Gerard is a very popular saint because he is the patron of expectant mothers and childbirths. He once gave his handkerchief to a girl and told her that she might need it someday. Some years later the woman was having a difficult time in childbirth, and it was feared the child would die. Remembering the handkerchief, she asked for it to be placed on her. Miraculously, she easily gave birth to a healthy child. How can I assist expecting mothers with prayer and material support, if possible?

Prayer

Saint Gerard Majella, pray that I may choose the road of humility and obedience to imitate Jesus better, as you did. Amen.

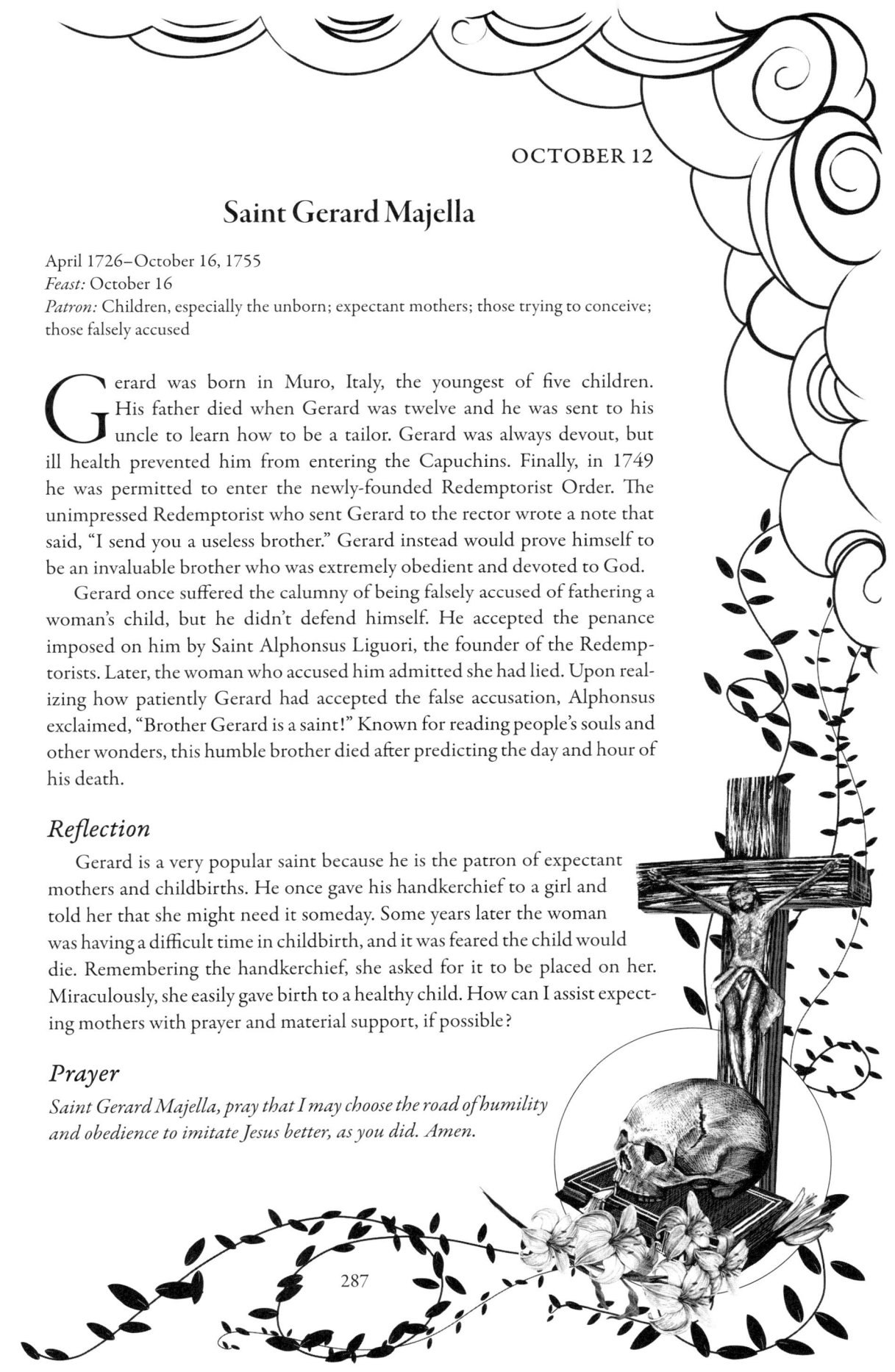

OCTOBER 13

Saint Hedwig of Silesia

1174–October 15, 1243
Feast: October 16
Patron: Poland, orphaned children

The daughter of a Bavarian count, Hedwig was married at the age of twelve to Henry, duke of Silesia (a region located mostly in modern-day Poland). The pious Hedwig soon enlisted her husband to help her build churches, convents, hospitals, and even a residence for lepers. Despite her privileged position, Hedwig knew pain and suffering: three of her seven children died at an early age. Hedwig did not retreat in her grief but went out of herself to help others. She prayed, fasted, and offered up penances. She also carried food to the sick and beggars, visited prisoners, and nursed lepers—unheard of activities for a woman of her status.

Eventually, both Henry and Hedwig felt called to make a vow of perpetual chastity. After Henry's death, Hedwig spent the final years of her life at the Cistercian convent that she and her husband had built in Trebnitz, which still stands in Poland. There she lived as a nun without ever taking the religious vows so that she could retain her wealth to spend on the poor. Hedwig died after a prolonged illness during which she had a consoling vision of the Blessed Mother who assuredly welcomed her into heaven.

Reflection

Thomas Merton once wrote that if the Cistercians had a third order, Hedwig would be their "most illustrious member." Her life shows us how much good one person with Jesus' priorities can do. Her example can help us find our own Gospel balance in an increasingly secular and consumerist society. By the wonderful providence of God, Karol Wojtyła, the first Polish pope, was elected on Saint Hedwig's feast day in 1978.

Prayer

Saint Hedwig of Silesia, please ask God to grant me unselfish love—for the Lord, for my family, and for those most in need. Amen.

OCTOBER 14

Saint Callistus I

Died 222
Feast: October 14
Patron: Cemetery workers

The life of Saint Callistus I—a man who went from slave to pope—has all the elements of a great adventure story. Callistus was likely a slave in a Roman imperial household. When he lost some money that was under his management, he had to flee. Eventually caught, he was imprisoned and released in order to reclaim the lost money. However, Callistus was promptly arrested again and sentenced to working in the mines after getting into a fight in a synagogue (presumably in an attempt to get someone to repay money owed). After his release, he was put in charge of the Roman Church's burial ground, known today as the Catacombs of Saint Callistus.

In an unlikely turn of events, at some point this former slave was ordained a deacon and eventually was made pope. A priest named Hippolytus was enraged when Callistus was elected pope because of Callistus' doctrinal positions. Callistus wanted to receive back into the Church those Christians who had repented of their serious sins. Because he thought that Callistus was too lenient, Hippolytus set himself up as an anti-pope. Thankfully, however, the more merciful way of Callistus prevailed. This unlikely slave-turned-pope was martyred, probably in a riot, and is today honored as a saint.

Reflection

The human element has always been present in the Church, even in the ancient Church of apostles and martyrs. Callistus I died before he could resolve his conflict with Hippolytus. Yet in the end, each of these adversaries gave their lives as martyrs. Though in conflict during their lives, both men are now honored as saints. This is something to keep in mind when we carry out our own debates over various aspects of Catholic life today.

Prayer

Saint Callistus I, pray for the Church, that we may always maintain unity in essentials, liberty in non-essentials, and charity in all. Amen.

OCTOBER 15

Saint Teresa of Ávila

March 28, 1515–October 4, 1582
Feast: October 15
Patron: Headache sufferers, writers, those in need of grace, religious, Spain

At seven years old, little Teresa from Ávila, Spain, greatly desired to become a martyr. She told her parents, "I want to see God." When she was about twelve, her mother died. Distraught, Teresa turned to the distractions of a worldly life. Her father enrolled her in a convent school until she could be married. But Teresa began to feel a call to religious life. Against her father's wishes, she joined the Carmelites at Incarnation Monastery, taking the name Teresa of Jesus.

Life at the monastery was relatively lax and, at times, Teresa neglected her prayer life. However, her spiritual life changed during Lent in 1554. At thirty-nine years of age, Teresa began to experience a deeper sense of God's presence within her, as well as visions and ecstasies. This divine influence convinced her to begin the great Carmelite reform. She founded monasteries where a simpler, more authentic Carmelite spirit was lived. Her reform was taken up by the men's monasteries through Saint John of the Cross. Teresa died as she traveled back from founding a monastery in Burgos. Her last words were, "O my Lord and my Spouse, the hour that I have longed for has come. It is time to meet one another."

Reflection

Amid all the practical details of reform, Teresa wrote several timeless guides for spiritual progress including *Way of Perfection* and *The Interior Castle*. This Doctor of the Church constantly advised her sisters to be authentic in prayer and contemplation. From her, we learn how to pray from within our own reality. God already knows us through and through, so pretense in prayer is useless.

Prayer

Saint Teresa of Ávila, pray that I may always be more open to God's presence in my life. Amen.

OCTOBER 16

Saint Margaret Mary Alacoque

July 22, 1647–October 17, 1690
Feast: October 16
Patron: Those suffering from polio, devotion to the Sacred Heart

Saint Margaret Mary Alacoque's life exemplifies Saint Paul's words: "I can do all things through him who strengthens me" (Phil 4:13). From childhood, she suffered many hardships. When she was eight years old her father died. Then she developed rheumatic fever and was unable to walk for four years. She also suffered greatly when relatives took over her father's property and treated her and her mother with cruelty. But through these sufferings she found strength in her faith.

Margaret Mary was finally cured of her paralysis when she prayed to the Blessed Virgin Mary and promised to enter religious life. It took her some time to follow through on her promise, but she finally decided to become a Visitation sister at the convent in Paray-le-Monial, France. Between 1673 and 1675, she received visions in which Jesus revealed his Heart to her. He also told Margaret Mary that he had chosen her to spread devotion to his Sacred Heart. She tried to share Jesus' message with others, but many of her sisters did not believe her. Fortunately, her spiritual director, Saint Claude de la Colombière, discerned that her visions were from God. With his help, devotion to the Sacred Heart began to spread and today is practiced by Catholics around the world.

Reflection

After Margaret Mary's death, it took the Church seventy-five years to officially recognize and approve devotion to the Sacred Heart. While alive, she experienced bitter opposition from those who did not believe that her visions were from God. Sometimes, except perhaps for a few friends and mentors, others may not understand how God is working in our lives. But God is always with us, even when we experience misunderstanding.

Prayer

Saint Margaret Mary Alacoque, help me to respond to Christ's love with courage and trust. Amen.

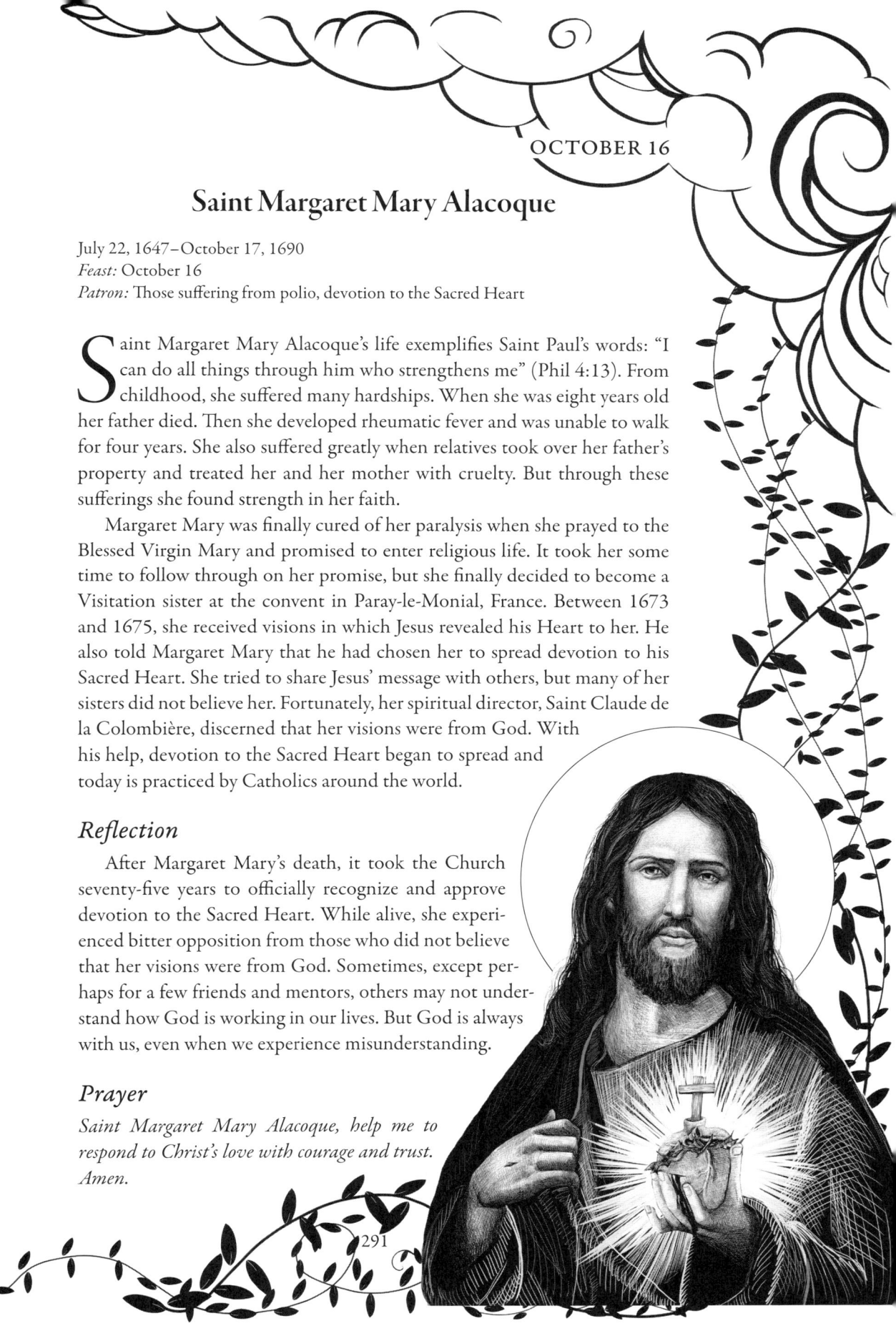

OCTOBER 17

Saint Ignatius of Antioch

Died c. 107
Feast: October 17
Patron: Church in eastern Mediterranean, sacred music, healing of throat diseases

An important witness to the faith of the early Church, Ignatius was a Syrian convert to Christianity. He became bishop of Antioch and is reported to have known the Apostle John. Little is known of Ignatius' life, except that when he was bishop, he was arrested for being a Christian and marched to Rome. On his way to martyrdom, Ignatius wrote seven letters. He addressed the letters to various churches, and they are now an invaluable source of information about Christian life at that time.

In his letter to the Roman Christians, Ignatius describes the rough treatment he endured on the long journey to Rome. He writes that his Roman soldier captors were like "ten leopards" who only grew fiercer when treated kindly. In a stirring way, he appealed to the Romans not to try to prevent his martyrdom: "Allow me to become food for the wild beasts, through whose instrumentality it will be granted me to attain to God. I am the wheat of God, and let me be ground by the teeth of the wild beasts, that I may be found the pure bread of Christ."

Reflection

The freshness and vigor of Ignatius' faith and ardent love for Jesus Christ shine through his writings. The faith of the early Christians, who did not shrink from martyrdom but desired to give their lives for the love of Christ, can inspire us in our day. We can still read the words of Saint Ignatius and let his burning faith enrich ours. The letters can easily be found online and do not take long to read.

Prayer

Saint Ignatius of Antioch, pray for us that we may see in the troubles of this life a pathway that leads to God. Amen.

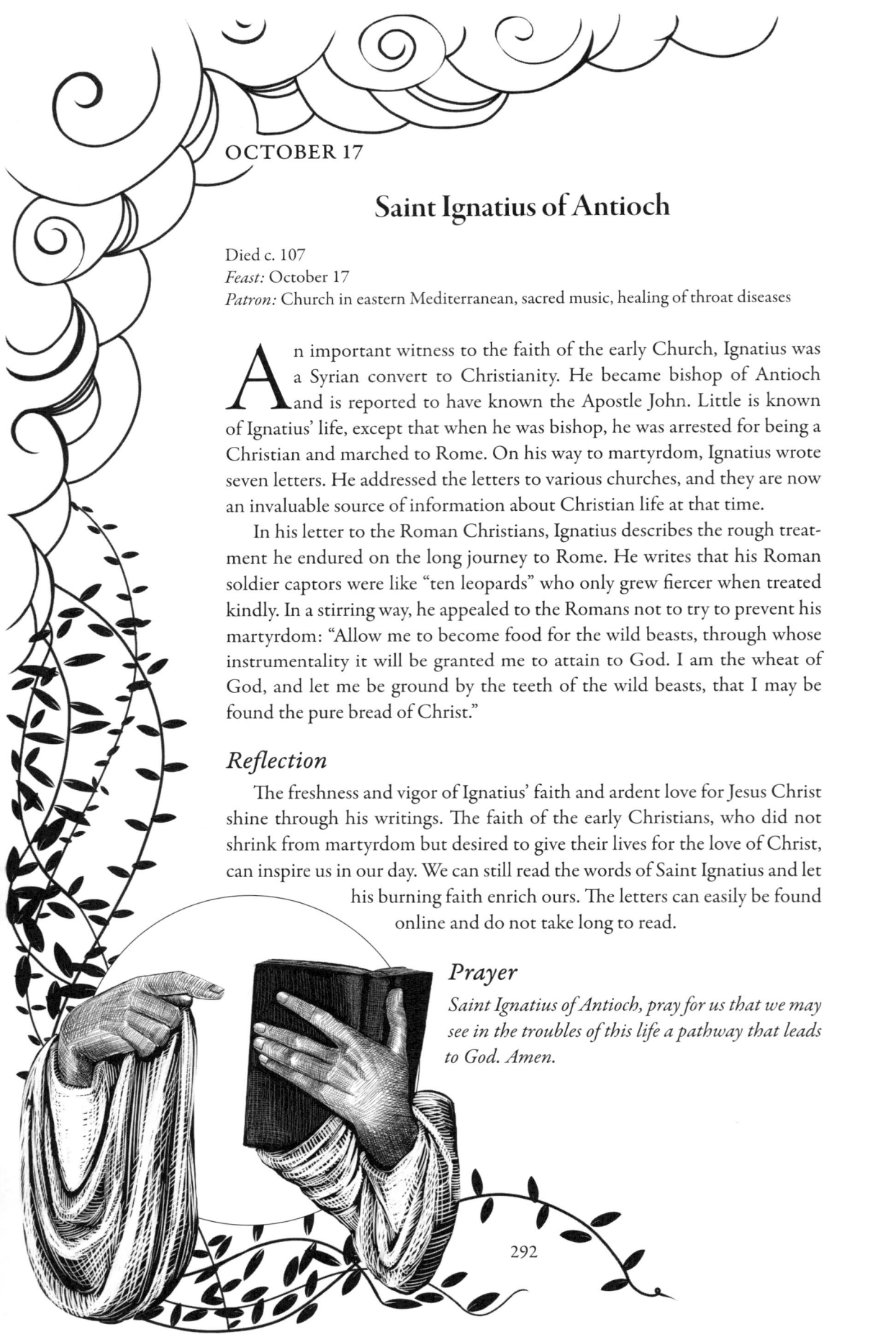

OCTOBER 18

Saint Luke, the Apostle

First Century
Feast: October 18
Patron: Physicians, surgeons, artists, bookbinders

Luke wrote a large part of the New Testament, including the third Gospel and the Acts of the Apostles. Scholars believe that Luke likely was not Jewish and was from Antioch. Paul refers to Luke as "the beloved physician" who was his traveling companion (Col 4:14). Luke indicates his presence on Paul's missionary journeys in Acts by switching to the use of "we" to describe their adventures. Luke points to his presence in this way on Paul's journey to Troas in Acts 16.

Some scholars believe Luke wrote his Gospel during Paul's imprisonment in Caesarea. The evangelist's symbol is the calf or ox, because these animals were offered in sacrifice in the Temple, and Luke's Gospel begins with the account of Zechariah, a Temple priest, the father of John the Baptist. Luke remained Paul's faithful companion through many dangerous journeys. While imprisoned in Rome before his martyrdom, Paul wrote, "Only Luke is with me" (2 Tim 4:11). Some traditions hold that Luke died a martyr. Others hold that he lived to old age in Greece.

Reflection

Legend has it that Luke was an artist and though this is not certain, he was definitely an artist with words. Luke was not simply a secretary or editor, recording events in the life of Jesus and the early Church—he was a true evangelist. He not only wrote the word of God but proclaimed it in word and deed. From Luke we can learn a profound love for the word of God, which inspires us to use all our talents in service of the Gospel.

Prayer

Saint Luke, help me to love the word of God, proclaim it, and live it in my life as you did. Help me find ways to reach the people of our times with the Gospel. Amen.

OCTOBER 19

Saints Jean de Brébeuf, Isaac Jogues, and Companions

March 25, 1593–March 16, 1649 (Jean de Brébeuf)
January 10, 1607–October 18, 1646 (Isaac Jogues)
Died 1642–1649 (Companions)
Feast: October 19 (United States), September 26 (Canada)
Patron: Missionaries, evangelizers, United States, Canada

This group of six Jesuit priests (Jean de Brébeuf, Isaac Jogues, Noel Chabanel, Anthony Daniel, Charles Garnier, Gabriel Lalemant) and two lay assistants (René Goupil and Jean de la Lande) were zealous missionary martyrs in Canada and upstate New York. The *Jesuit Relations* record in great detail their work and sufferings as they evangelized the native peoples.

Isaac Jogues was captured, tortured, and held as a prisoner in the Mohawk village of Ossernenon for over a year. He managed to escape and returned to France. But, in his zeal, he asked to return to the missions. Jean de Brébeuf was outstanding for his courage, missionary zeal, and efforts to understand the native peoples. He and Gabriel Lalemant were martyred together after suffering extreme torture. The martyrs' shrines at Midland, Ontario, and Auriesville, New York, recall the dedication and heroism of these brave men.

Reflection

One can only stand in awe of these holy martyrs' courage in the face of tremendous suffering. A moving area of the Auriesville shrine is the ravine where a grief-stricken Isaac Jogues, praying the psalms for the dead, sought in vain for the body of René Goupil. He had returned to bury his friend after the two men had been attacked as they walked back to the village. He relates, "Finally on the fourth trip I found René's head and some half-gnawed bones. These I buried. Reverently did I kiss them as the bones of a martyr of Jesus Christ...."

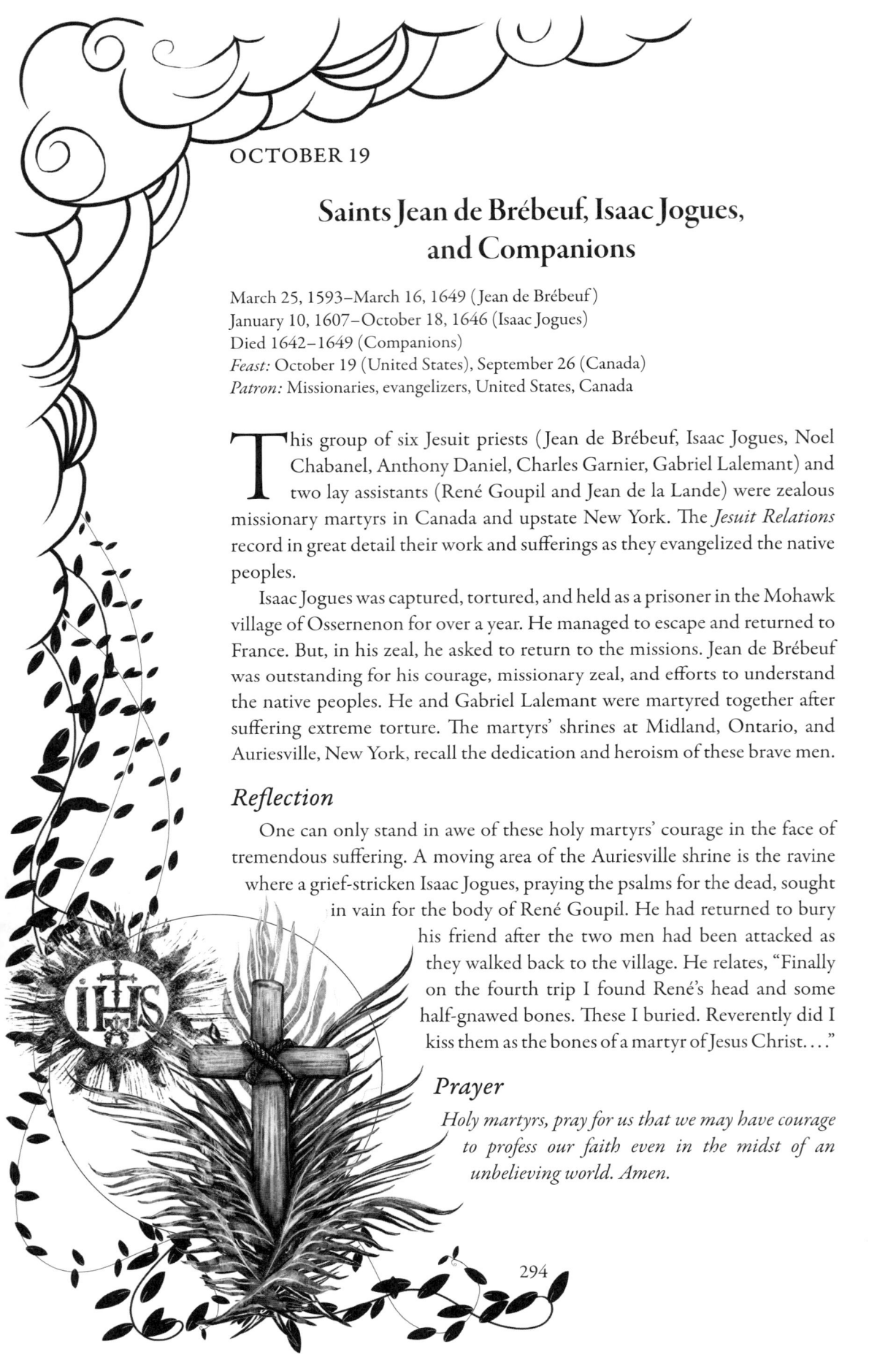

Prayer

Holy martyrs, pray for us that we may have courage to profess our faith even in the midst of an unbelieving world. Amen.

OCTOBER 20

Saint Paul of the Cross

January 3, 1694–October 18, 1775
Feast: October 20 (United States), October 19 (elsewhere)
Patron: The Passionist Congregations, preachers, devotion to the Passion of Christ

Paul was born Paolo Francesco Danei in Ovada, Italy, the second of sixteen children. As a young man, Paul became a soldier, but he soon realized that this was not his call. When he returned home, one of his uncles tried to arrange a marriage for him. He declined, knowing that God's will for him was not marriage. In the summer of 1720, Paul had a vision that gave him clarity. He saw himself dressed in a black garment with a white cross and heart. The Lord was asking Paul to begin a religious community committed to spreading devotion to the Passion of Jesus.

Paul climbed Mount Argentario with his brother John Baptist, and they lived in an abandoned hermitage. The two men prayed and came down the mountain on Sundays to preach. Soon they attracted many followers. In 1741, Pope Benedict XIV gave his approval to the Congregation of the Most Holy Cross and Passion of Our Lord Jesus Christ, often called the Passionists. Paul also founded an order of contemplative Passionist nuns with a similar spirituality. After living to see the fruits of a life of trust in God's will, Paul passed away in Rome.

Reflection

Paul patiently followed the path that God illuminated for him one step at a time. He once wrote, "If you correspond to the designs of God, he will make a saint of you. Be generous, and remember that we ought to walk in the footsteps of Jesus crucified. The servant of God who is not crucified with Jesus Christ, what is he?"

Prayer

Saint Paul of the Cross, pray that I may always persevere in listening to the voice of the Lord and find inspiration in his Passion as you did. Amen.

OCTOBER 21

Saint Laura Montoya

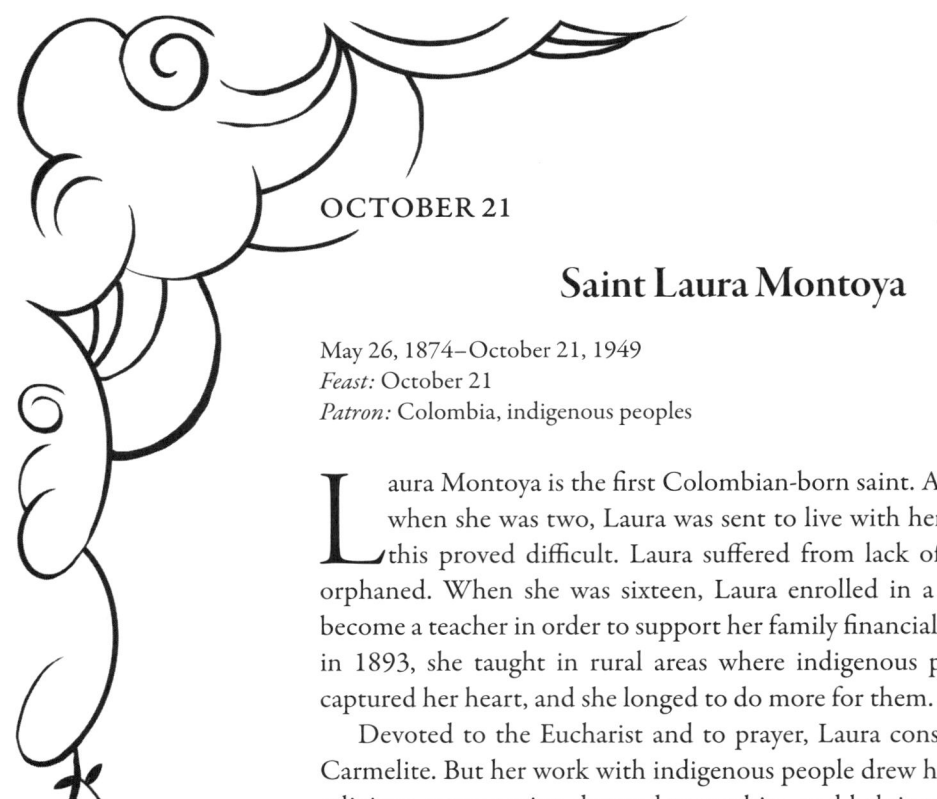

May 26, 1874–October 21, 1949
Feast: October 21
Patron: Colombia, indigenous peoples

Laura Montoya is the first Colombian-born saint. After her father died when she was two, Laura was sent to live with her grandmother, but this proved difficult. Laura suffered from lack of affection and felt orphaned. When she was sixteen, Laura enrolled in a school to train to become a teacher in order to support her family financially. After graduating in 1893, she taught in rural areas where indigenous peoples lived. They captured her heart, and she longed to do more for them.

Devoted to the Eucharist and to prayer, Laura considered becoming a Carmelite. But her work with indigenous people drew her instead to start a religious congregation devoted to teaching and helping them. In 1914, she founded the Congregation of the Missionary Sisters of Mary Immaculate and Saint Catherine of Siena. The bishop approved it but, sadly, Laura still faced opposition due to racism even within the Church. Laura pressed forward despite this, and slowly her congregation grew and flourished. Her last years were marked by a painful illness.

Reflection

Laura often said that she wanted to become an indigenous person and live among them in order "to win them all for Christ." In this she followed the spirit of Saint Paul, who wrote "I have become all things to all people, that I might by all means save some" (1 Cor 9:22). Whatever their race or ethnic origin, each person we meet is made in the image and likeness of God and called to holiness. What effort do I make to try to see Christ in everyone?

Prayer

Saint Laura Montoya, pray for us that our hearts, like yours, may be filled with the love of Christ. Help us to turn away from sin so that we may radiate Christ to all whom we meet. Amen.

OCTOBER 22

Saint John Paul II

May 18, 1920–April 2, 2005
Feast: October 22
Patron: Archdiocese of Kraków, World Youth Day, youth, families, new evangelization

The man many now call "Saint John Paul the Great" was baptized Karol Józef Wojtyła in Wadowice, Poland. Karol's entire immediate family had died by 1941. During World War II, he entered a clandestine seminary in German-occupied Kraków. A poet and playwright, Karol also acted in underground theater. After his ordination on November 1, 1946, he studied in Rome. Soon recognized for his intellectual and spiritual gifts, Karol was consecrated bishop and later archbishop of Kraków, and then was elevated to cardinal.

Following Pope John Paul I's unexpected death in 1978, the world was shocked when then-relatively-unknown Cardinal Wojtyła was chosen as the first non-Italian pope in 455 years. Taking the name John Paul II, this energetic, charismatic pope made numerous international trips. A noted moral theologian and philosopher, John Paul II issued several encyclicals, apostolic letters, and other writings. He is particularly known for his integrated vision of the human person, defense of marriage and family, and human rights. Millions attended his funeral, crying out: "Sainthood now!"

Reflection

Only six years into his pontificate, John Paul II wrote an apostolic letter entitled *Salvifici Doloris* (On the Christian Meaning of Human Suffering). He wrote that each person in his or her own suffering can "also become a sharer in the redemptive suffering of Christ." When diagnosed with Parkinson's disease years later, he would live out his earlier words in a way that he might never have imagined. In his final years, John Paul II bore witness to the value of all human life, even in the midst of suffering.

Prayer

Saint John Paul II, pray that I may remember that my value as a person flows from God's love for me, not from my worth in the eyes of the world. Amen.

OCTOBER 23

Saint John of Capistrano

1386–October 23, 1456
Feast: October 23
Patron: Chaplains, jurists, judges, military chaplains

John was born in Capistrano, Italy. His father died when he was young, so he was raised by his faith-filled mother. He then studied law in Perugia and was appointed governor in 1412. During this time, war broke out between Perugia and a prominent Italian family, the Malatesta. Sent to propose peace to the family, John was seized and imprisoned. While imprisoned, Saint Francis of Assisi appeared to John and invited him to enter the Franciscans.

After his release from prison, John entered the Franciscans in Perugia. He was ordained in 1425 and then began traveling on missions with Saint Bernardine of Siena. While Bernardine preached, John would hear confessions. Soon John was traveling and preaching all over Europe. John's abilities to move hearts as well as to cure the sick were renowned—entire towns were said to come out to meet him. A promoter of the Franciscan reform, John was appointed by Pope Martin V to resolve the conflict between the Franciscans and the "Fraticelli," a heretical branch of the order. John was so well respected that he was often sent on behalf of the pope to restore the faith and peace to regions in turmoil. After a life of tireless preaching, John died at the age of seventy.

Reflection

John spent his life in imitation of the poor, chaste, and obedient Christ. Traveling by foot from town to town was not an easy life. Nevertheless, John persisted and used his God-given talents to promote virtuous living, justice, and peace. How willing am I to follow Christ when the road is difficult?

Prayer

Saint John of Capistrano, your love for Christ overcame all obstacles. Help me to cherish God's call and to follow him wherever he might lead. Amen.

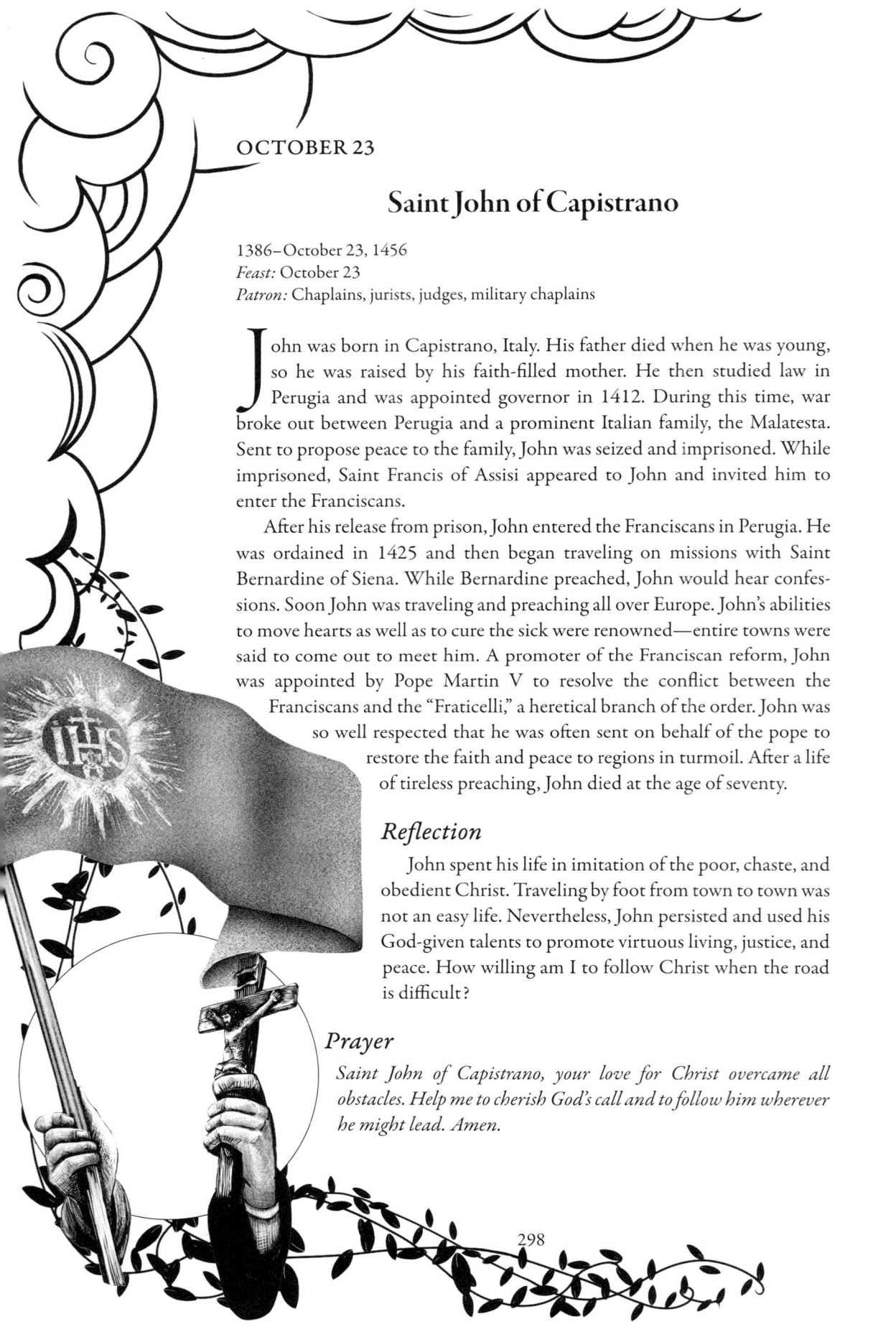

OCTOBER 24

Saint Anthony Mary Claret

December 23, 1807–October 24, 1870
Feast: October 24
Patron: Catholic press, textile merchants, weavers, savings (he taught the poor how to save money)

Anthony's life was an incredible journey marked by his great apostolic zeal and devotion to Mary. Born in the village of Sallent in northeast Spain, he worked as a weaver from the age of twelve. Anthony wanted to be a Jesuit, but ill health prevented him, so he was ordained a secular priest in 1835. He was sent to Catalonia and the Canary Islands as an apostolic missionary. He was such an eloquent preacher that great crowds came to hear him.

In 1849, Anthony founded a religious order of priests, the Missionary Sons of the Immaculate Heart of Mary, commonly known as the Claretians. Shortly after, he was sent to Cuba as the archbishop of Santiago. His immense pastoral activity focused on both the spiritual life and the social needs of the people. He pursued social justice, founded trade schools and credit unions, and helped families establish farms. This stirred up opposition and Anthony survived several assassination attempts. Despite all this, he pressed on. In 1857, he was called back to Spain to serve as the confessor for Queen Isabella II. He also attended the First Vatican Council. Just days after the council was adjourned, Anthony died in a Cistercian monastery in southern France.

Reflection

A great preacher, Anthony also understood the power of the press to preach the Gospel. He founded a Catholic publishing house in Spain and wrote over two hundred books and pamphlets. Today through social media, each of us can influence many others for good. When I go online, do I consider how I can be a positive influence for God's greater glory?

Prayer

Saint Anthony Mary Claret, pray for us that we may live in a way that will attract others to Jesus, the Light of the World. Amen.

OCTOBER 25

Blessed Mary Angela Truszkowska

May 16, 1825–October 10, 1899
Feast: October 10
Patron: Sisters of Saint Felix of Cantalice (Felicians), homeless, abandoned children

Sophia Truszkowska was born in Poland to devout parents who promoted virtue both in and outside of the home. At the age of sixteen, Sophia suffered from tuberculosis and was sent to Switzerland to recover. After she returned to her family in Warsaw, her father fell ill, and Sophia accompanied him to Germany for treatment. In the Cathedral of Cologne, she had an experience in prayer that gave her some vocational direction. She felt called to join the Saint Vincent de Paul Society in 1854.

Sophia soon decided to rent a flat and care for orphaned girls and elderly women in what the locals affectionately called "The Institute of Miss Truszkowska." Sophia's cousin Clothilde Ciechanowska joined her and they both eventually left their homes to live with the people they were serving. Soon the Congregation of the Sisters of Saint Felix of Cantalice, or Felicians, came into being. Sophia, now known as Mother Mary Angela, was superior general of the order for three terms. When she was only in her mid-forties, Mother Angela was forced to step down because of health issues. She spent the last thirty years of her life praying humbly in the background as the congregation she founded grew.

Reflection

Blessed Mary Angela Truszkowska discerned God's call in her life through her strong urge to serve the poor. As she followed her passion, she discovered her place in God's vineyard. Our passions and talents are great gifts from God that are not meant to be hidden but used to build the kingdom of God. What is my passion in life?

Prayer

God, help me discern how you are calling me to use my passions to glorify you and to make your love known in the world. Amen.

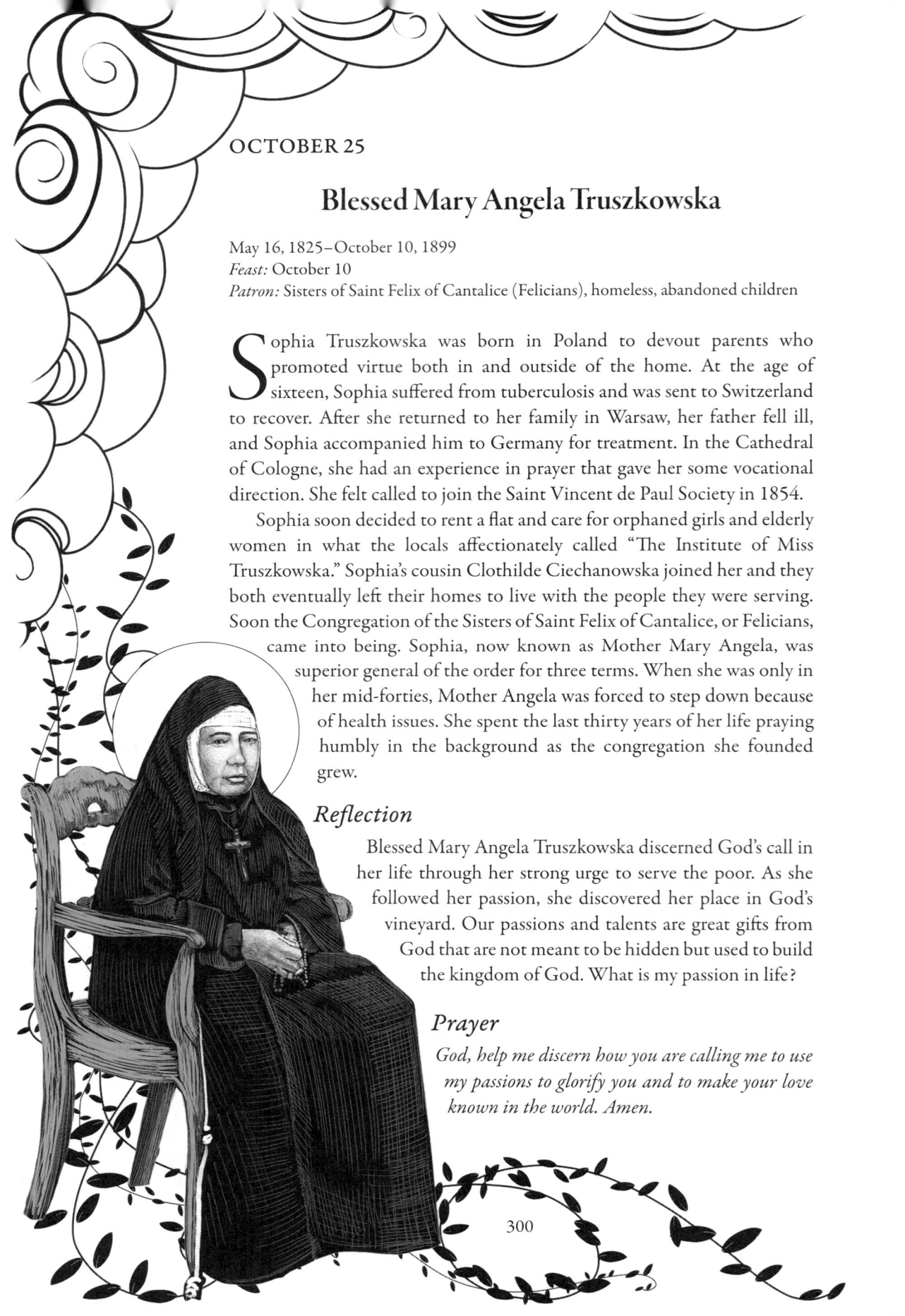

OCTOBER 26

Blessed Franz Jägerstätter

May 20, 1907–August 9, 1943
Feast: May 21
Patron: Conscientious objectors, family, youthful conversion

Born in Saint Radegund, Upper Austria, Franz was a wild youth who enjoyed riding his motorcycle more than going to church. He even fathered a child out of wedlock. But then he returned to practicing his Catholic faith, married, and settled down. He and his wife, Franziska, had three daughters and lived happily on the family farm. His life might have gone on to old age, but storm clouds were gathering.

In 1938, Hitler and his Nazis moved into Austria. Franz was the only person in his town to vote against the takeover. Franz reported for mandatory military training in 1940, but was released to attend to his farm. Later he was called and excused again. Becoming more alarmed at what the Nazis were doing, Franz decided that if called again, he would not serve. Franz knew what his refusal would mean for his family, but Franziska supported his decision to follow his conscience, despite her grief. When he was conscripted in early 1943, Franz offered to serve as a medic but refused to fight. For that he was imprisoned for several months and then beheaded.

Reflection

Franz received little support for his decision of conscience; even his pastor and bishop told him he should fight. At times we too have to stand up for our faith even if other people think we're crazy. Peer pressure can be very hard to resist. But the Holy Spirit will give us the grace and strength we need to stand fast. That is the fruit of the sacrament of Confirmation.

Prayer

Blessed Franz, you followed your conscience despite the great suffering you knew would come to you. Pray for us that in the daily trials of life, we will have the strength to be faithful witnesses to the Gospel. Amen.

OCTOBER 27

Saint Marie of the Incarnation

October 28, 1599–April 30, 1672
Feast: April 30 (Canada)
Patron: Canada, Quebec, educators, missionaries

From her humble beginnings in Tours, France, Marie Guyart became a wife, mother, and missionary nun. Though she wanted to enter the convent, her parents made her marry at age seventeen. But her husband, Claude Martin, died about two years later, leaving her with their six-month-old son. When her son, Claude, was twelve, Marie felt called to entrust him to the care of her sister and enter the Ursulines, taking the name Marie of the Incarnation. Claude was incredibly distressed at his mother's departure, but he would later grow to accept her decision.

Gradually, Marie discerned God's call to become a missionary to Canada. Landing in Quebec in 1639, she was indefatigable in her work. She organized the building of a monastery and school to teach both French and native girls. Incredibly, Marie learned the Montagnais, Algonquin, Huron, and Iroquois languages. She also wrote many letters to friends and relatives in France, including her son, who had become a Benedictine. Her letters were widely circulated in France because of the accounts they gave of life in Canada. Just before her death, Marie sent a message to her beloved son: "Tell him that I am carrying him with me in my heart."

Reflection

Marie once wrote, "God never led me by a spirit of fear, but by love and trust." She could have let herself be overwhelmed by fear, but she trusted in God, not in her own efforts. If we find life overwhelming at times, her example can help us to take one step at a time, as God gives us the light.

Prayer

Saint Marie of the Incarnation, pray that we may bring the light of faith even to those places where it seems to be fading. Amen.

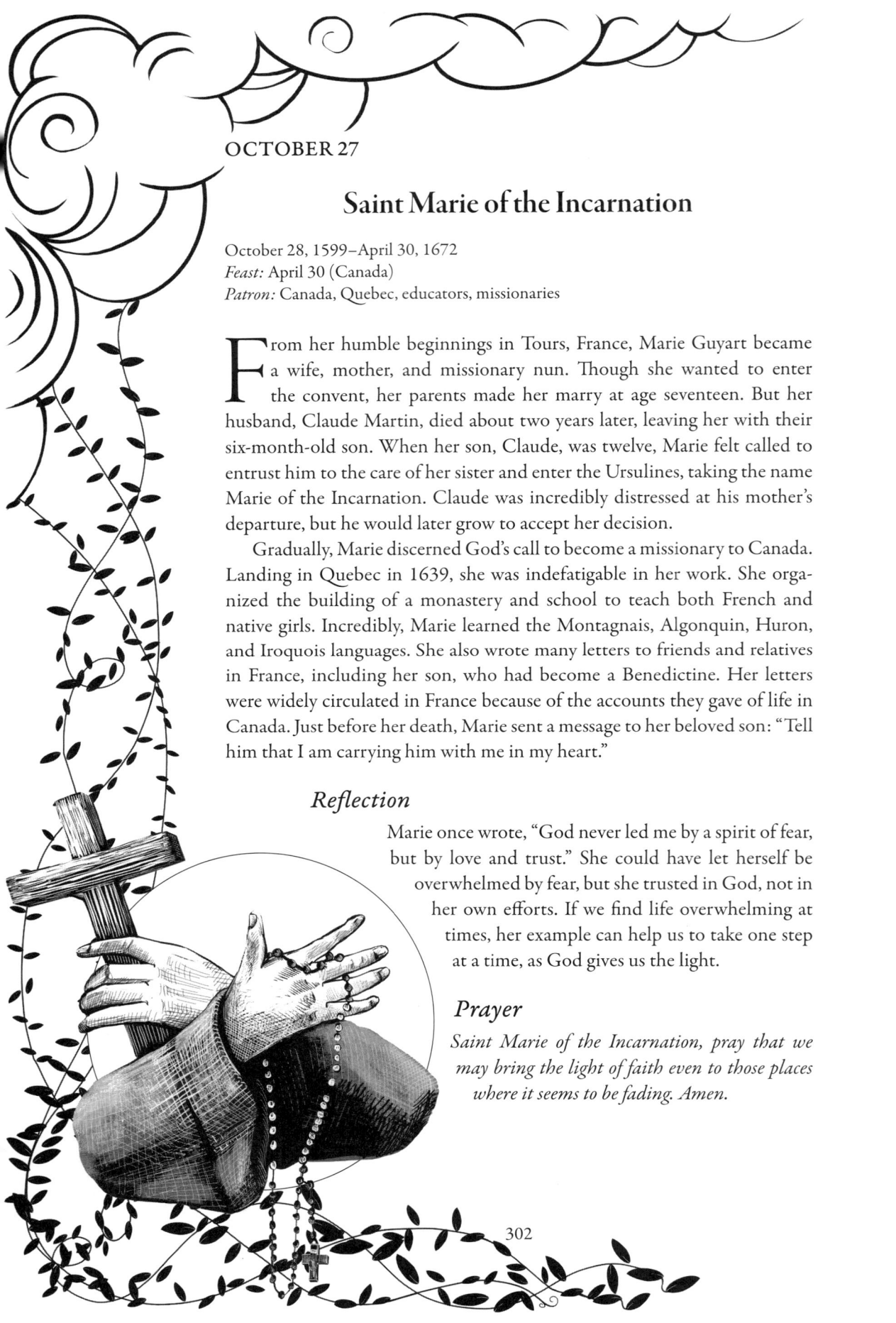

OCTOBER 28

Saints Simon and Jude, Apostles

First Century
Feast: October 28
Patron: Jude: Desperate situations, hopeless cases; Simon: tanners

The Gospels mention Simon and Jude together in the lists of the apostles. Jude, son of James, is also called Thaddeus. Simon is called the Zealot. Not much else is known about the lives of Simon and Jude. But we do know the most important event of their lives: Jesus called them to be his apostles. Somehow, Simon and Jude went to hear Jesus speak, met him, and their hearts began to burn with a fire.

At the Last Supper, Jude had asked Jesus, "Lord, how is it that you will reveal yourself to us, and not to the world?" (Jn 14:22). In going forth to preach, both Simon and Jude understood that the Lord was asking them to be his voice, so that he would be revealed not just to them but to the whole world. Tradition holds that they gave their lives in martyrdom, witnessing to Jesus even with their blood. Jude, known as the saint of the impossible, has become a favorite saint of many people today.

Reflection

The name "Thaddeus" can refer to a gentle, sweet character, while a zealot is someone who is zealously on fire for a cause. By celebrating the feast of Jude Thaddeus and Simon together, the Church shows us how to blend the best of both traits. Mercy without principle can degenerate into fear of standing up for the good. Zeal without love can degenerate into harshness. But zeal joined to mercy and love can lead people to God in a most effective way.

Prayer

Saints Simon and Jude, pray for us that we too may witness to Jesus in our lives. Show us how to share the truth of the Gospel with zeal, mercy, and love. Amen.

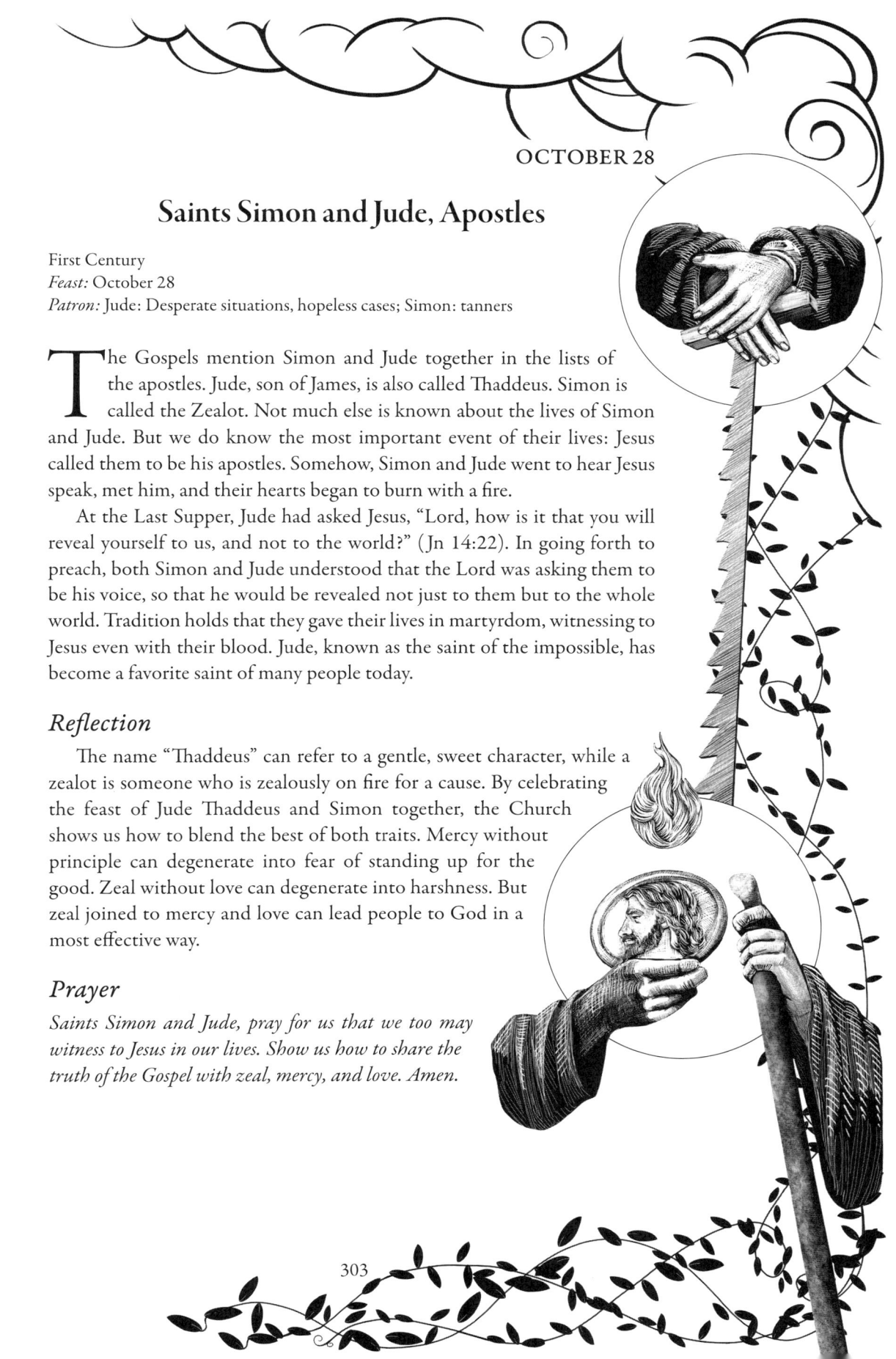

OCTOBER 29

Saint Narcisa de Jesús Martillo Morán

October 29, 1832–December 8, 1869
Feast: August 30
Patron: Ecuador

From Nobol, Ecuador, Narcisa was born to a farming family, the sixth of nine children. Both her parents were devout. Her mother died when Narcisa was six, and in this event Narcisa first met the suffering of the Cross. When she received the sacrament of Confirmation, she felt an interior grace calling her to live a life of union with the Cross. She responded to this call by increasing her prayer, penance, and efforts to practice virtue.

Narcisa sought spiritual direction and made private vows of virginity, poverty, and obedience, but she always felt called to remain a laywoman. When she was nineteen, her father died, and Narcisa moved to the city of Guayaquil and worked as a seamstress. There she also began to help the poor, the sick, and abandoned children. Meanwhile, no one knew that she also spent hours of her day in prayer and penance. Some years later, she moved to Peru and lived as a lay member in the Dominican convent of Patrocinio. On the Solemnity of the Immaculate Conception, light and a beautiful aroma streamed from Narcisa's bedroom. On entering the room the sisters discovered that this holy, simple woman had died.

Reflection

Although Narcisa engaged in severe penances that few are called to, we can still look to her as an example. Narcisa knew that our smallest sacrifices could draw down graces upon the world. Like her, we can share in Jesus' redemption of the world by doing penance and accepting life's little and big moments of suffering.

Prayer

Saint Narcisa de Jesús Martillo Morán, pray that when trials come, I may not be discouraged but hand everything over to Jesus with great trust. Amen.

OCTOBER 30

Saint Alphonsus Rodriguez

c. 1533–October 31, 1617
Feast: October 31
Patron: Majorca, receptionists, phone operators, greeters

Born in Segovia, Spain, Alphonsus was the son of a wool merchant. His father once gave hospitality to a visiting Jesuit—Saint Peter Faber—who helped Alphonsus prepare for his first Holy Communion. Alphonsus worked in the family business and married. But tragedy struck. His wife and two of his three children died by the time he was thirty-one. When his remaining son died a few years later, Alphonsus decided to enter religious life. After some setbacks, he succeeded in becoming a Jesuit brother.

Alphonsus spent more than forty-six years as the doorkeeper at the Jesuit college in Majorca. He became a saint in a humble, hidden way. When answering the door, Alphonsus would often say, "I'm coming, Lord!" to remind himself that Jesus was waiting for him in that person. Everyone who met him went away happier. Alphonsus often befriended the young Jesuits and encouraged them in their vocations. In fact, he told a future saint, Peter Claver, that he should ask to go to the missions in South America. After a life of humility and love, Alphonsus died at age eighty-four, and his last words were, "Jesus, Jesus, Jesus!"

Reflection

During his life, Alphonsus crossed paths with many holy people, including at least two who would become canonized saints. But no matter who he met, he always spread love and goodness to all. It is wonderful to reflect on how other people can help us on our journey to God. Who has helped me most in my own faith journey? Spend some time thanking God for that person.

Prayer

Saint Alphonsus Rodriguez, you lived the Jesuit motto to do everything for the greater glory of God. Pray for us that we may give glory to God in all we do. Amen.

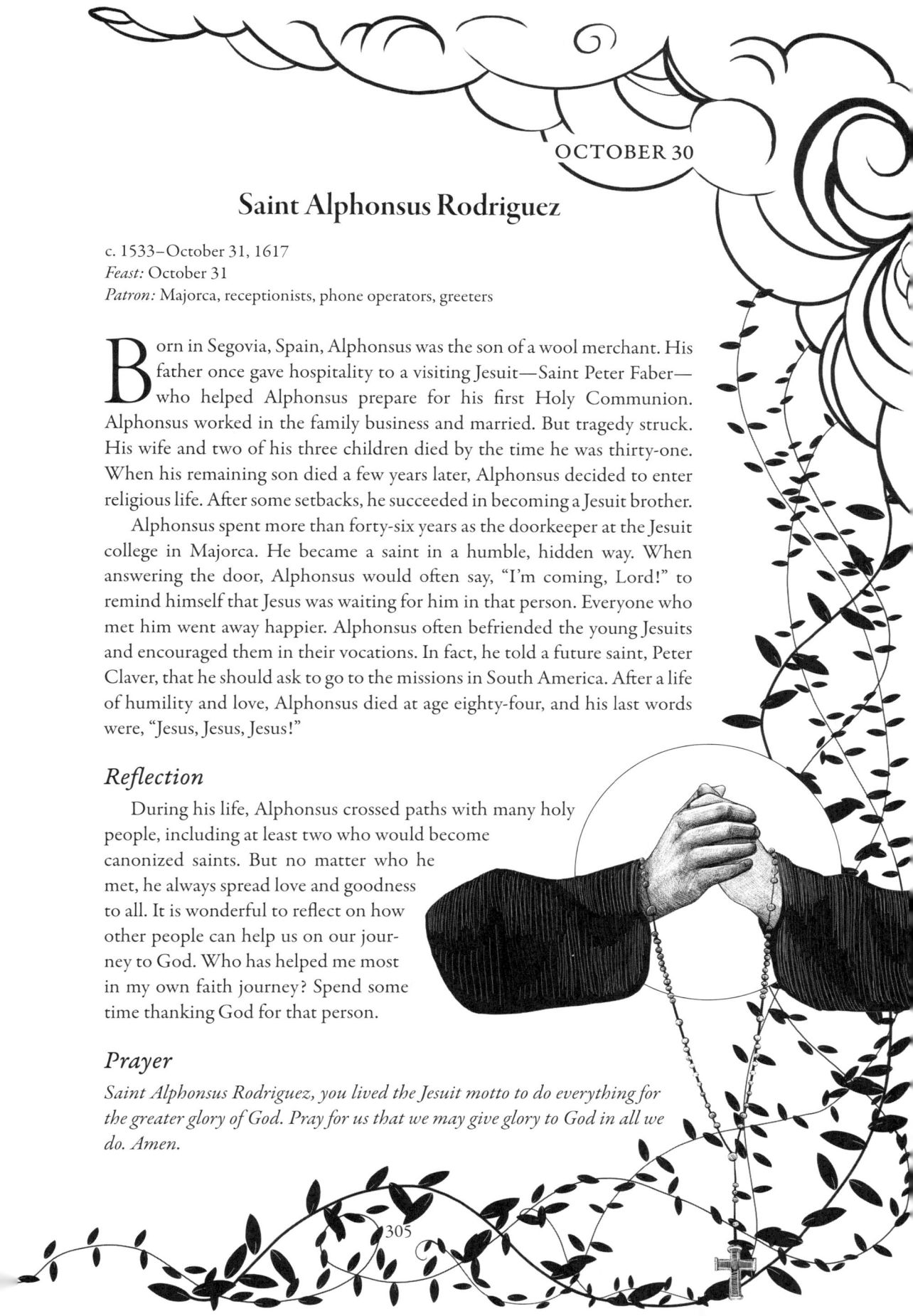

OCTOBER 31

Blessed Benedict Daswa

June 16, 1946–February 2, 1990
Feast: February 1
Patron: Against the occult, against witchcraft, persecuted Christians, teachers

Tshimangadzo Samuel Daswa belonged to the Lemba tribe in rural Limpopo, the northernmost province of South Africa. He grew up observing Jewish customs but converted to Catholicism when he was seventeen, taking the baptismal name Benedict. A respected member of the community, Benedict served on the village council and was the principal of the village school. He was very active in his Catholic community as well and was instrumental in building the parish church. A loving father, Benedict and his wife had eight children.

After his conversion, Benedict made no secret that he was against the traditional local belief in witchcraft. When unusually severe weather caused lightning damage to multiple homes, he made clear that he would not pay a *sangoma*, a diviner, to determine who was responsible. Benedict knew that when a "witch" was identified, the villagers would either drive off or kill the person. The people's anger then turned against Benedict. A week after his refusal, Benedict stopped the car he was driving because the road had been blocked by tree logs. When he got out of his car, a mob attacked and killed him. According to the diocesan investigation of his death, Benedict's last words were, "God, into your hands, receive my spirit."

Reflection

Benedict refused to go along with the prevailing mindset, even though he knew he would make enemies by his refusal. We can follow his example by recognizing when generally accepted beliefs are contrary to our faith. We can also ask God for the grace to courageously resist those beliefs, even when they are taken for granted by those around us.

Prayer

Saint Benedict Daswa, intercede for us that we may have the courage to stand against the attitudes or opinions of our contemporaries that contradict Christian faith. Amen.

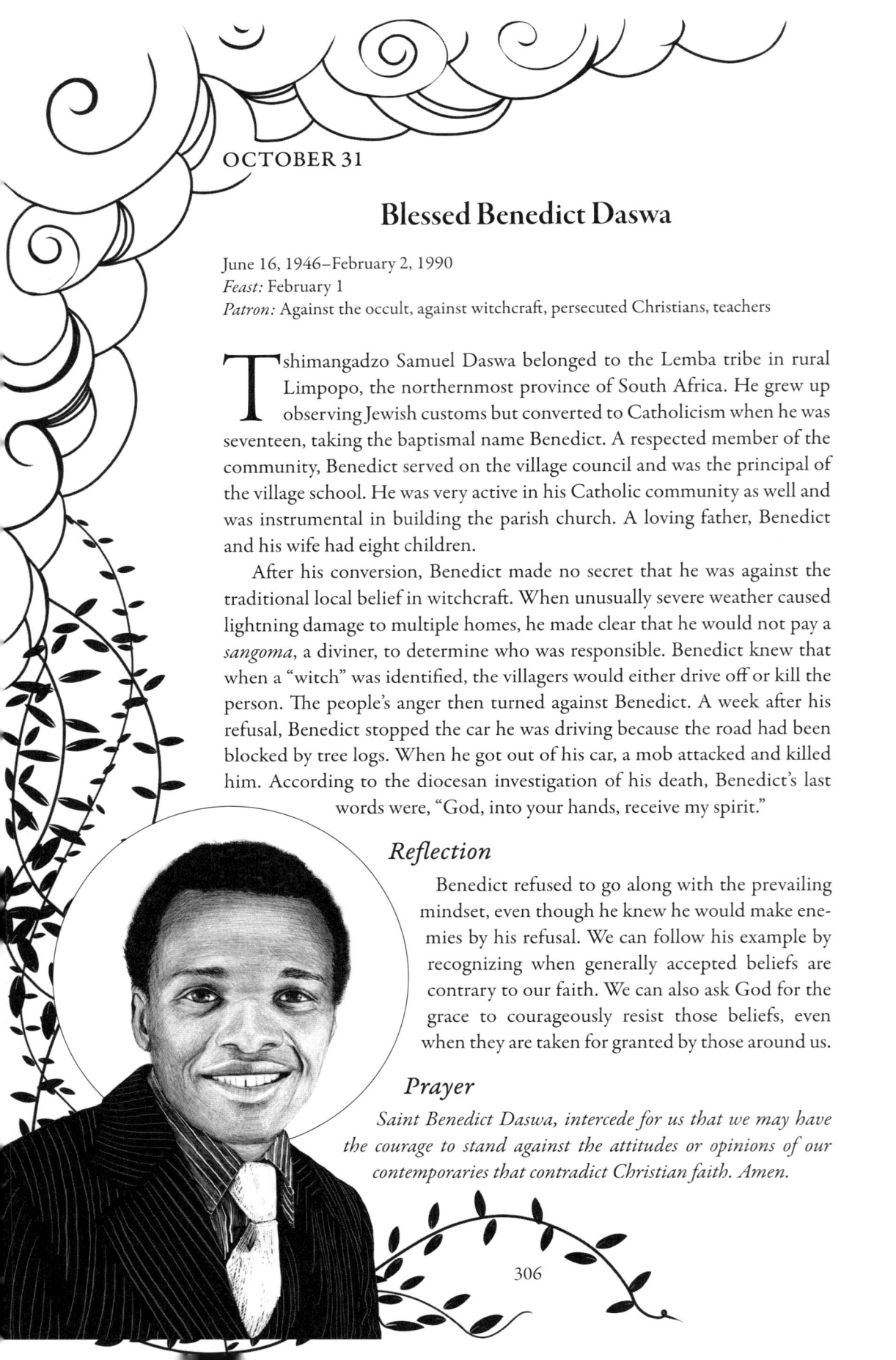

NOVEMBER 1

The Martyrs of Compiègne

Died July 17, 1794
Feast: July 17
Patron: Religious freedom

During the Reign of Terror in France, a group of sixteen Carmelites—eleven choir sisters, three lay sisters, and two externs—were brought to the guillotine in what is now the *Place de la Nation* in Paris. Dressed in their habits, they sang hymns as the cart carrying them to their deaths lurched through the streets. *Salve Regina. . . . Veni, Sancte Spiritus. . . .* Almost two years prior, the nuns had made an act of consecration to offer their lives to restore peace to France and to the Church.

That day, as the cart came to a stop, the raucous, bloodthirsty crowd fell strangely silent. The youngest, who had just made her first vows, Sister Constance, was the first to climb up to the guillotine. She intoned Psalm 117, "Praise the Lord, all you nations!" The nuns sang along as each one went willingly to her death until the prioress, Blessed Teresa of Saint Augustine, the last one, had fallen. No one in the crowd cheered as usual, or even said a word. Darkness had fallen over France. But eleven days after the sisters' sacrifice, the bloodshed stopped, and the Reign of Terror ended.

Reflection

The offering of the Carmelite Martyrs of Compiègne draws us into the mystery of atoning love. As Saint Paul wrote, "In my flesh I am completing what is lacking in Christ's afflictions for the sake of his body, that is, the church" (Col 1:24). The sisters understood that their baptism had made them members of Christ and that, through them, Jesus could act to bring life to the world. Do I believe in the power of my baptism?

Prayer

Jesus, accept the small offerings I can give you in my life and work each day. Unite them to your own offering through the Mass. Amen.

NOVEMBER 2

Saint Claudine Thévenet

March 30, 1774–February 3, 1837
Feast: February 3
Patron: Poor children, forgiveness

Claudine (nicknamed "Glady") was born in Lyon, France, and grew up in a family of silk merchants. The French Revolution began when she was fifteen and brought intense suffering. The city of Lyon rebelled against the government and endured a siege and much destruction. After the city fell, two of her brothers were among the many executed. Claudine witnessed their death by firing squad. Their last words made a lifelong impression on her: "Forgive, Glady, as we forgive."

Inspired by her brothers' last words, Claudine dedicated the rest of her life to helping those suffering from the effects of the French Revolution. She began her work by taking in two abandoned children, entrusted to her by her mentor, Father Coindre, who had found them shivering on the steps of a church. She and some companions started a group called the Association of the Sacred Heart, but this later became the Congregation of the Religious of Jesus and Mary. The sisters took in poor children and educated those of all classes. Mother Claudine encouraged her sisters, "Be mothers to these children."

Reflection

Despite her great desire to do good, things often went wrong for Mother Claudine. Father Coindre and some of the first sisters died soon after the congregation received approval. She also had to resist an attempt to have her congregation merged with another. At the time of her death, her congregation seemed to be declining. But soon after Mother Claudine's death, the sisters began missionary endeavors to other countries. How can adversity help me to grow in my trust that God is at work in everything?

Prayer

Saint Claudine Thévenet, help us to have the strength and conviction you had in following God's plan, despite setbacks and apparent lack of success. Amen.

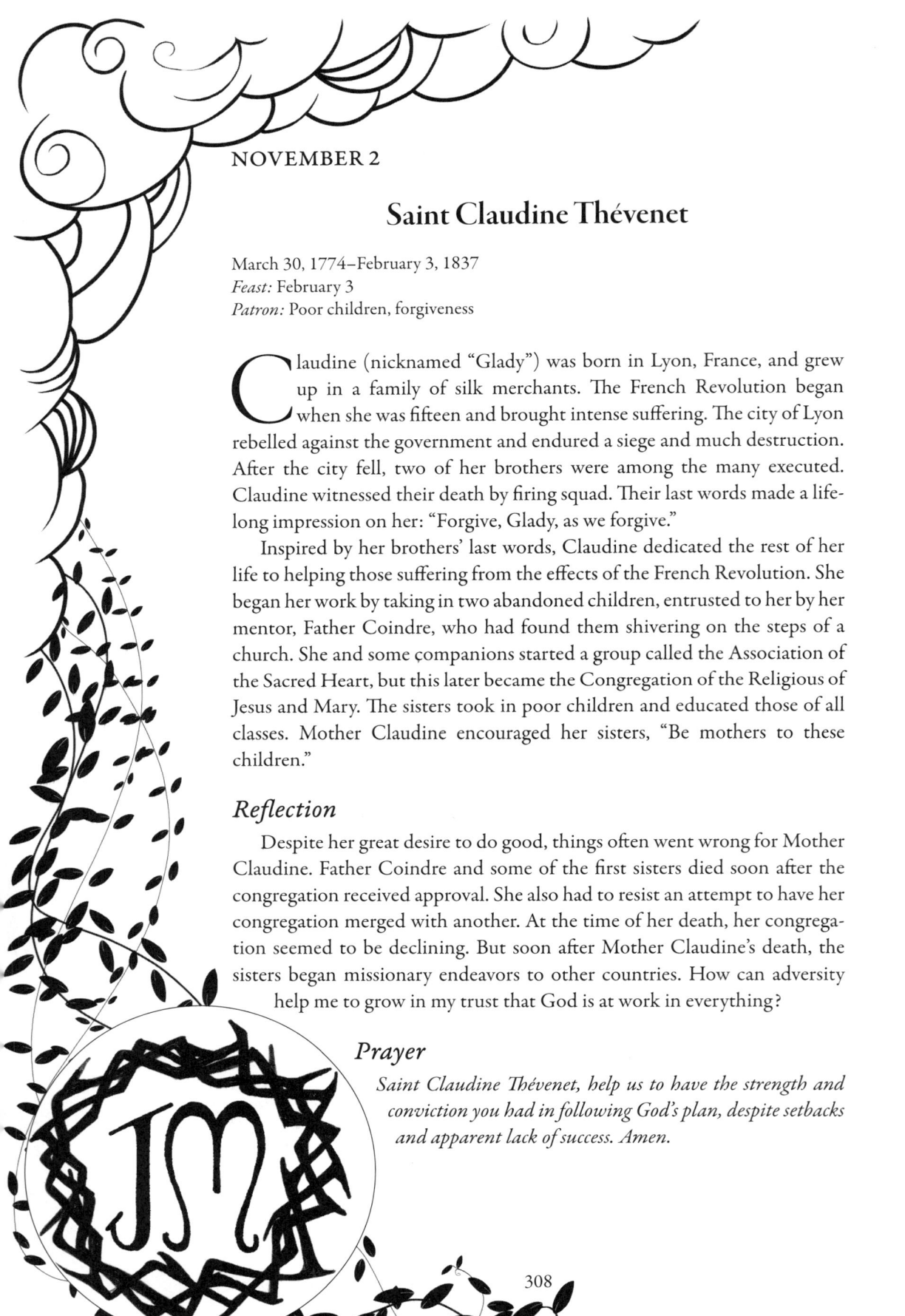

NOVEMBER 3

Saint Martin de Porres

December 9, 1579–November 3, 1639
Feast: November 3
Patron: Social justice, racial harmony, barbers, surgeons, animals, Peru

Martin grew up in Lima, Peru, with his mother and younger sister. His father, a Spanish nobleman, was not a constant presence. However, when Martin was eight, his father took him to Ecuador to study. Back in Peru four years later, Martin was apprenticed to a barber-surgeon and learned how to draw blood and care for wounds. His mother, Ana, also taught him herbal medicine. And so, Martin's expertise was soon sought after.

When he was around sixteen years old, Martin joined the Dominicans as a lay helper. Unfortunately, he was not allowed to take religious vows because he was of mixed racial heritage. Later, however, this rule was changed, and Martin was able to become a professed Dominican brother. As a young brother, people called him "Martin the Charitable" because of his gentle concern for everyone, including animals. His legacy of kindness included politely asking the monastery mice to relocate to the outer courtyard—which they did. He remained a humble man even though his life was filled with miraculous cures and unusual phenomena, such as passing through locked doors to visit the sick. When he was sixty years old, Martin came down with a fever and died as his fellow friars sang the *Salve Regina* around his bed.

Reflection

Martin was friends with two other saints, Rose of Lima and Juan Macías. One might wonder if holiness was contagious in the seventeenth century! Martin's life shows us the value of developing life-giving relationships of service and love with those around us.

Prayer

Saint Martin de Porres, you were a wise companion and a humble worker of wonders. May we also be open to God's grace and available to all. Amen.

NOVEMBER 4

Saint Charles Borromeo

Oct 2, 1538–Nov 3, 1584
Feast: November 4
Patron: Apple orchards, catechists, catechumens, clergy, colic, seminarians, spiritual directors, stomach trouble, ulcers

One of six children, Charles was born in a castle in northern Italy. His father was a count and his mother died when he was only nine years old. As a child, Charles developed a speech impediment, which caused people around him to assume he was unintelligent. However, Charles loved to study, and by the time he was twenty-one he had obtained a doctorate in civil and canon law. Despite pressure from his family to get married, Charles decided to become a priest. He was ordained when he was twenty-five years old and soon became bishop of Milan.

Charles was instrumental in helping his uncle, Pope Pius IV, to reconvene the Council of Trent, which led to important reforms in the Church. After the Council, Charles began working tirelessly to reform his own diocese of Milan. He also worked to ensure that the poor were well cared for and personally nursed victims when Milan was struck by the plague. When he was only forty-six years old, this zealous bishop fell ill and died. He was canonized only twenty-six years after his death by Pope Paul V.

Reflection

Charles Borromeo easily could have chosen to live a very comfortable life. He was intelligent, likeable, and born into a wealthy family. Instead, he chose a life of simplicity and humility, focusing above all on the material needs of others and their spiritual good. May his example of generosity inspire us to be generous in working for the good of others.

Prayer

Saint Charles Borromeo, pray that I may love the Church and all her members as you did. Amen.

NOVEMBER 5

Saint Longinus

First Century
Feast: October 16
Patron: The blind, people with poor eyesight, soldiers

Saint Longinus is not named in Scripture, but legend gives this name to the Roman centurion who was present at the crucifixion and death of Jesus. All four Gospels indicate that Roman soldiers were present at the foot of the Cross. In the Gospel of Mark, Jesus gave a loud cry before he died, and, "when the centurion, who stood facing him, saw that in this way he breathed his last, he said, 'Truly this man was God's son!'" (15:39). In the Gospel of Matthew, the centurion and the men with him utter these same words (27:54). In the Gospel of Luke, the centurion declares, "Certainly this man was innocent" (23:47).

Tradition also indicates that Longinus is the soldier in the Gospel of John who "pierced [Jesus'] side with a spear, and at once blood and water came out" (19:34). The Gospel writer does not record the soldier's reaction, but this is traditionally thought to be the moment of Longinus' conversion. According to legend, Longinus was going blind, but when he pierced Jesus' side, the blood that fell on his eyes healed him.

Reflection

Longinus was moved to belief at that moment when blood and water gushed forth from the Heart of Jesus. We too can be moved to convert our hearts each time we meet Jesus in the Eucharist. When we read the accounts of the passion of Jesus in the Gospels or pray the Stations of the Cross, we can imagine ourselves present in that scene.

Prayer

Saint Longinus, converted by the Sacred Heart of Jesus, pray that we may open our hearts to know and love Jesus Christ more completely each day. Amen.

NOVEMBER 6

Blessed Josefa Naval Girbés

December 11, 1820–February 24, 1893
Feast: February 24 (November 6—Discalced Carmelites)
Patron: Third Order Carmelites

Josefa Naval Girbés was born to a devout Catholic family in Valencia, Spain. People recognized her piety from a young age. She was allowed to receive her first Communion two years before the standard age because of her exceptional enthusiasm for the spiritual life. When she was thirteen, her mother passed away. After her death, Josefa heard in prayer that the Blessed Mother would always be with her, and she nourished a close relationship with Mary for her entire life.

After consulting with a spiritual director, Josefa made a vow of chastity when she was eighteen and eventually entered the Third Order Carmelites. She lived the life of a consecrated virgin in the world. Josefa took this secular calling seriously, using her domestic skills and religious formation to evangelize. As a skilled housekeeper, she opened her home as a place to teach girls needlework, prayer, virtue, and the faith. She also taught religious formation to young mothers, that they might effectively pass on the faith to their children. At the time of Josefa's death, she was well-known for her sanctity and her home had become a center of religious formation and prayer. She was buried in her Third Order Carmelite habit, as she had requested.

Reflection

The Christian life is not meant to be lived alone. Josefa lived as a single, secular, consecrated woman, but community was an important part of her life and mission. Genuine community is not built upon such things as gossip, mere circumstance, or even just shared interests. Real community and friendship are centered on Christ, who is love and mercy. Are my relationships centered on Christ?

Prayer

Lord, give me the courage to build genuine community with the people in my life, that we may witness to the unifying power of your love. Amen.

NOVEMBER 7

Blessed Luigi and Maria Beltrame Quattrocchi

January 12, 1880–November 9, 1951 (Luigi)
June 24, 1884–August 26, 1965 (Maria)
Feast: November 25
Patron: Married couples

Today we honor a relatively contemporary example of holiness lived in marriage. When this couple was beatified together in 2001, three of their four children were still alive and present at the beatification. Luigi was born into a large family, and a childless uncle asked Luigi's parents if he could raise one of their children, so Luigi grew up in his uncle's home. He was given ample educational opportunities and went on to study law. Maria was the intelligent daughter of an army officer. She studied culture, music, and languages, and she later became a professor and writer on the topic of education.

Luigi and Maria were married in 1905 and had four children. Their doctors told them they should end a particularly difficult pregnancy in abortion, but the couple refused and their daughter, Enrichetta, was born healthy. Luigi and Maria were extremely active members of their parish, participating in daily Mass, prayer services, and catechetical opportunities. But they also made plenty of time for vacations, sports, and entertaining friends. Of their four children, two became priests, and one became a Benedictine nun.

Reflection

Luigi and Maria provide a beautiful example of a simple, loving couple striving for holiness. They knew that it was important for a family to pray together and have fun together. Though their own family life was not without its own moments of pain and difficulty, they always lived in a spirit of joyful trust in God. How might the Lord be inviting me to a greater sense of joyful trust in my daily life?

Prayer

Heavenly Father, help me to live out holiness in my everyday life, both in times of joy and difficulty. Amen.

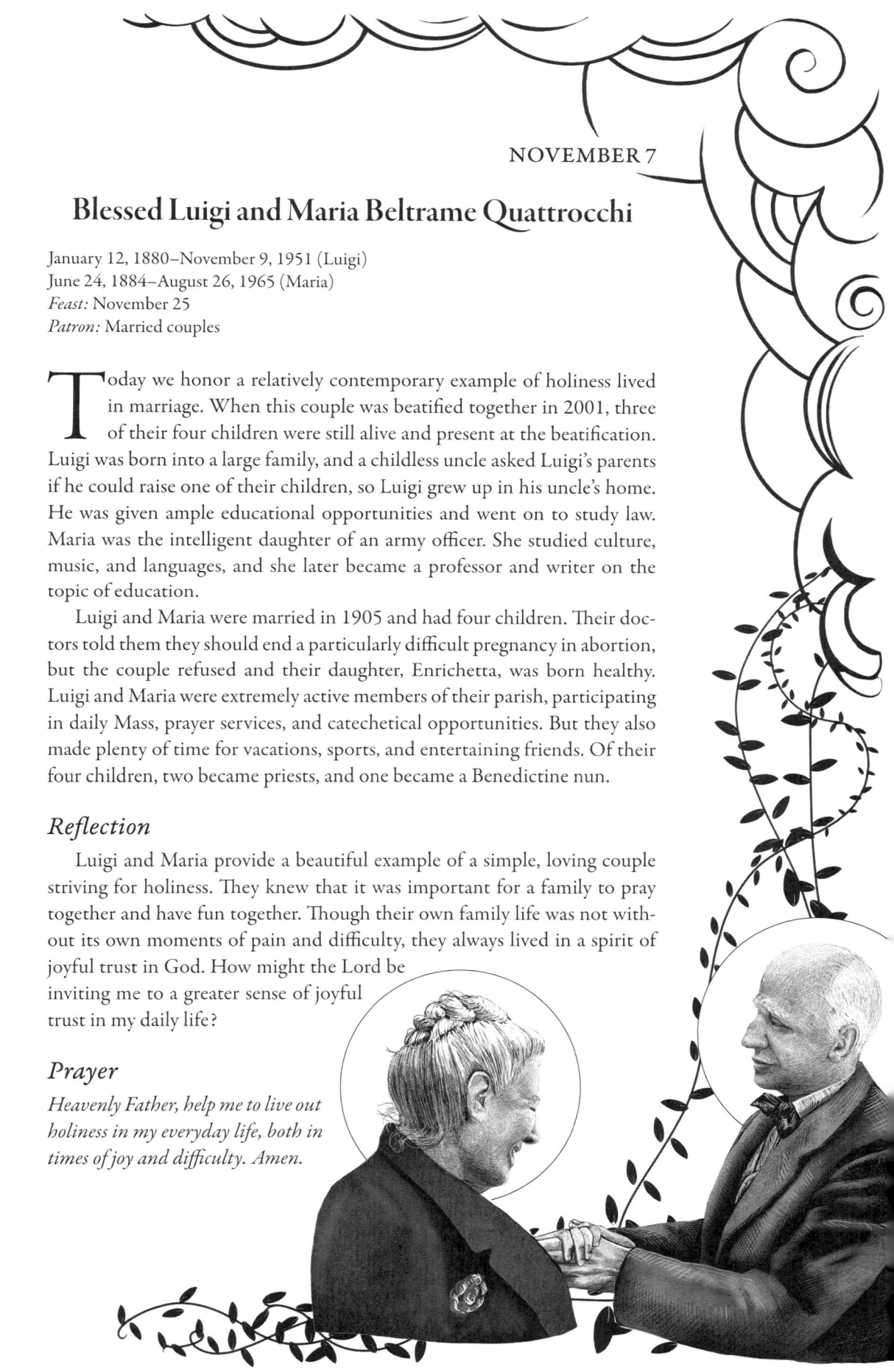

NOVEMBER 8

Saint Elizabeth of the Trinity

July 18, 1880–November 9, 1906
Feast: November 8
Patron: Sick persons, loss of parents, against illness

The daughter of Captain Joseph Catez and Marie Rolland, Elizabeth was born in a military camp in the Avor district of Farges-en-Septaine, France. Her father died when she was only seven and her mother moved the family to Dijon. Elizabeth was lively and quick-tempered as a little girl, but she gradually learned better self-control. On the occasion of her first Communion, Elizabeth met the prioress at the Carmel of Dijon, who told her that the name Elizabeth means "House of God." Elizabeth was deeply impressed by this meaning, and reflecting on it helped her grow spiritually.

Elizabeth became an accomplished pianist. A beautiful girl with a vivacious personality and attractive appearance, she had many suitors. Her mother urged her to consider marriage. However, Elizabeth felt an invitation from the Lord to join Carmel. In 1901, Elizabeth entered the Discalced Carmelite Monastery in Dijon. Her life in Carmel over the next five years fanned her contemplative thirst for God. She was gifted with a deep awareness and attentiveness to the indwelling of the Trinity in her soul through baptism. Elizabeth suffered from health problems for much of her time in Carmel, but she still radiated joy and peace. She died of Addison's disease at the age of twenty-six. Her last words were, "I am going to Light, to Love, to Life!"

Reflection

Elizabeth of the Trinity's spiritual writings beautifully describe her relationship with the Trinity. She experienced the Three Divine Persons as a community of love dwelling within her and she tried daily to focus all her energies on God's presence. Am I in touch with God's presence in my soul through baptism?

Prayer

Saint Elizabeth of the Trinity, pray that I may be attentive to the presence of God dwelling within me. Amen.

NOVEMBER 9

Blessed John Duns Scotus

c. 1266–November 8, 1308
Feast: November 8
Patron: Theology students

Born in Duns, Scotland, John entered the Franciscans and was ordained in 1291. As a philosopher and theologian, he spent his life teaching, mainly in Oxford and Paris. He is best known for his role in defending the doctrine of the Immaculate Conception of Mary—which teaches us that Mary was conceived without original sin and filled with grace. Some theologians—even the great Saint Thomas Aquinas—objected that this doctrine seemed to detract from the effectiveness of the redemption won for us by Christ. John Scotus came up with the solution: Mary was redeemed by Christ but ahead of time; she was preserved from sin in view of the merits of Christ.

Called the Subtle Doctor because of the fine quality of his thought, John was also known as a holy priest who lived well his Franciscan vocation. In the last year of his life his superiors suddenly asked him to leave Paris and go to Cologne to teach, and he quickly obeyed. John died at the age of forty-three and was buried in the Franciscan church in Cologne.

Reflection

Like Thomas Aquinas, Bonaventure, and other great theologian-saints, John sought to find God in theology. For John theology was not merely academic study but a path to holiness. We don't have to be theologians to profit from study of the faith. All of us are called to learn as much as we can about God, through both study and prayer, a journey that will last our whole life.

Prayer

Blessed John Duns Scotus, as a Franciscan friar you sought Jesus in a spirit of poverty and detachment, and you taught him to others. Pray for us that the light of faith may illuminate our minds and direct us on the path of true love of God. Amen.

NOVEMBER 10

Saint Leo the Great

c. 400–November 10, 461
Feast: November 10
Patron: Confessors, popes, moral theology, vocations

Not much is known of Leo's early years. It is believed he was born at the end of the fourth century in Rome to parents from Tuscany. He was ordained to the diaconate and advised popes Celestine and Sixtus III. He was quickly recognized for his energy and many talents, and in 440 he was elected bishop of Rome. As pope, Leo made many efforts to unify the Church. He defended the primacy of Peter and taught that the bishop of Rome's authority is universal.

When the Council of Chalcedon was convened in 451, Leo read a letter to those gathered. He affirmed the union of Jesus' two natures, human and divine, in his one divine Person, without confusion and without separation. The bishops responded to Leo's letter in unison: "Peter has spoken through the mouth of Leo." In 452, Leo was asked by the emperor to meet with Attila the Hun to convince him not to attack Rome. Leo, an experienced diplomat, met with Attila and persuaded him to withdraw from Italy and negotiate peace. When Leo died, he had served as pope for over two decades. He was buried in Saint Peter's Basilica in Rome.

Reflection

Inspired by the Holy Spirit, Leo embraced and promoted the bishop of Rome's authoritative role in the Church. His love for the Church's teachings also enabled him to instruct with clarity. He was particularly known for his clear and profound letters and homilies, many of which have been preserved and handed down through the centuries. How can I better understand the Church's authority in matters of faith and morals?

Prayer

Saint Leo the Great, help me to spread the Gospel and love the Church's teachings with the same fire of love you had in your heart. Amen.

NOVEMBER 11

Saint Martin of Tours

c. 316–November 8, 397
Feast: November 11
Patron: Soldiers, the poor, tailors, France

When Martin was still a catechumen and a Roman soldier in Gaul, he met a shivering beggar outside the city of Amiens. Moved with compassion, Martin cut his own warm military cloak in two and gave half to the beggar. That night, he had a dream in which he saw Jesus Christ appear wearing the half cloak, saying, "Here is Martin, the Roman soldier who is not baptized; he has clad me." Martin was soon baptized—he was only eighteen—and not long after, left the Roman military.

Seeking a life of holiness, Martin became a disciple of Saint Hilary of Poitiers. But when Hilary was exiled, Martin traveled to northern Italy and lived as a hermit. In 361, Hilary was able to return to Tours, so Martin also returned. Hilary gave him some land outside the city and there Martin established the first monastery in Gaul. He probably would have remained there for the rest of his life, but, by popular acclaim, he was made bishop of Tours in 371. Martin continued to promote the monastic life, establishing a famous monastery at Marmoutier. After his death, Martin was one of the first non-martyrs widely recognized for his holiness and venerated as a saint.

Reflection

The relic of Martin's cloak became one of the most prized possessions of the Frankish kings. The keeper of the cloak—the *cappellanus*—was a priest, called in French the *chapelain*. From this we get the English word "chaplain." To give spiritual counsel, comfort, and support is the role of a chaplain. Even if we are not chaplains, we can each give spiritual assistance to others in some small way.

Prayer

Saint Martin of Tours, intercede for us that the Christian faith may continue to spread throughout the world. Amen.

NOVEMBER 12

Saint Josaphat Kuncevyc

c. 1580–November 12, 1623
Feast: November 12
Patron: Christian unity

Josaphat was born John Kuncevyc in the Ukraine. Upon seeing the enmity that religious difference in his area caused, John had a great desire for unity in the Church from a very young age. When he was in his twenties, he joined the Monastery of the Holy Trinity and took the name Josaphat. After he was ordained, he was known for his preaching on unity with Rome. He became bishop of the Eparchy of Vitebsk in 1617 and also archbishop of Polotsk the next year. His diocese was divided between the Orthodox and those who were faithful to Rome, churches were in disrepair, and there was laxity among the clergy. But far from being intimidated, he immediately set to work.

Under Josaphat's leadership, synods were organized in the main cities, a catechism was issued to help the people learn their faith, and churches were rebuilt. He continued to work for harmony with the Orthodox. But in 1620, the Orthodox appointed a rival bishop in the same area and declared Josaphat an invalid bishop. Determined to bring unity to an tense situation, Josaphat traveled to the city of Vitebsk, one of the strongholds of anti-Rome sentiment. He tried to encourage peace among the people, but he was attacked by an angry crowd, struck in the head with a halberd, shot, and then thrown into the river. He was canonized in 1867 by Pope Pius IX.

Reflection

Josaphat's attempts to bring unity to the Church were opposed by many. But he so greatly desired that all people would come to Christ's Church that he was willing to give his life for this cause. What can I do to build up the Body of Christ?

Prayer

Saint Josaphat Kuncevyc, please pray for unity in the Church. Where there are divisions, let me be a force of charity and peace. Amen.

NOVEMBER 13

Saint Frances Xavier Cabrini

July 15, 1850–December 22, 1917
Feast: November 13
Patron: Immigrants

Mother Cabrini was a woman of great determination, profound holiness, superb business skill, and immense faith. Born in Lombardy, Italy, Maria Francesca received a strong faith from her parents and dreamed of becoming a missionary to China. But her poor health prevented her from entering religious life. In 1874, her bishop asked her to teach at a girls' orphanage in the city of Codogno in northern Italy. There, she and five other women began preparation for religious vows. They professed vows in 1877, and three years later, in collaboration with the local bishop, founded the Missionary Sisters of the Sacred Heart of Jesus.

Mother Cabrini's dream to serve in China found new direction in Pope Leo XIII's advice to her: "Not to the East, but to the West." She arrived in New York in 1889 and immediately began to work with the Italian immigrants. Over the next twenty-eight years, she opened sixty-seven institutions from New York to California, Chicago to Argentina. Her radical trust in God coupled with her business savvy worked miracles. She died in one of her congregation's hospitals in Chicago at age sixty-seven, as she was preparing Christmas candy for the local children. In 1946, she became the first United States citizen to be canonized.

Reflection

Mother Cabrini tried to be faithful and available to God in each moment of her life. Her trusting response to God's will led her to do both big and small things for the Lord. In what ways can I grow in trust as I respond to God's invitations in my life?

Prayer

Saint Frances Xavier Cabrini, you manifested remarkable faithfulness in each circumstance of your life. Help me to have a missionary heart in my daily life. Amen.

NOVEMBER 14

Saint Gertrude the Great

January 6, 1256–November 17, 1301/2
Feast: November 16
Patron: The West Indies, Devotion to the Sacred Heart

Born on the Feast of Epiphany and likely orphaned at a young age, Gertrude grew up in a Benedictine abbey in Germany. She was entrusted to the care of Saint Mechtilde, who was a mentor and like a mother to the gifted young girl. Soon Gertrude decided to join the convent as a nun. As a young woman, she had a particular love for studying. Occasionally, she even shortened her times of prayer in favor of time in the library.

When she was about twenty-five years old, Gertrude had her first of many visions of Jesus, who made it clear that she was allowing her study to come between them. She immediately began to focus on her prayer life and became especially focused on Jesus' Sacred Heart. Gertrude believed strongly that the messages she received from the Lord were not for her alone but for the good of others. So, she spent much of her time writing down her reflections and conversations with Jesus. She even considered writer's block a blessing, because she felt it was Jesus inviting her to spend more time with him in prayer!

Reflection

Gertrude was very aware of her own imperfections and weaknesses. However, she never lost her deep trust and incredible joy in Jesus' love and mercy toward her. When we are feeling weak or unworthy, Gertrude's example can help us to refocus on the love of Jesus, and perhaps motivate us to do something generous for someone else.

Prayer

Sacred Heart of Jesus, your love for us is so powerful, you poured yourself out completely so that we could live with you in eternity. Through the intercession of Saint Gertrude the Great, help me to love you more and more. Amen.

NOVEMBER 15

Saint Albert the Great

c. 1206–November 15, 1280
Feast: November 15
Patron: Students, teachers, philosophers, scientists

Saint Albert the Great was a person to whom people would go whenever a question came up. He knew almost everything there was to know in the medieval world. An outstanding philosopher and theologian, he also studied the natural sciences. He painstakingly observed and recorded facts about insects, birds, astronomy, and many other fields.

Born in Germany, Albert entered the then recently-founded Order of Dominicans. His talents made him an important asset, and he became a professor in Paris and Cologne. At that time the works of Aristotle were becoming better known in Europe, and Albert used the philosopher's thought to enhance understanding of Christian doctrine. In this, Albert influenced his student, Saint Thomas Aquinas. Albert became the provincial of the Dominicans and was appointed bishop of Regensburg in 1260. But being a bishop didn't suit him, and he resigned after two years. He returned to scholarly work and preaching, mainly in Germany. In 1931, Pope Pius XI canonized him and made him a Doctor of the Church.

Reflection

Throughout his life, Albert thirsted for knowledge of both human and divine things. He knew how to see the natural world in the light of God. Albert also knew himself. He realized that he was not well suited for the pastoral ministry of a bishop and resigned from that office. All the saints showed a passion for doing the will of God. But sometimes doing the will of God can mean turning down an offer rather than accepting it. How do we know the difference? Only by prayer and careful discernment.

Prayer

Saint Albert the Great, pray for us that we may grow in knowledge of God and of ourselves, so as to serve God in the best way we can. Amen.

NOVEMBER 16

Saint Margaret of Scotland

c. 1045–November 16, 1093
Feast: November 16
Patron: Those who suffer the death of a child, large families, learning, queens, Scotland, widows

Margaret was born in a time of political upheaval. Her father, Edward d'Outremer, heir to the English throne, was exiled to Hungary, where Margaret grew up. When she was twelve, her family was allowed to return to England, but then they were forced to flee again. Margaret's family was given refuge by King Malcolm III of Scotland. The king fell in love with the beautiful young Margaret, and the two were married at the royal castle in 1070.

By her good example and power of persuasion, Queen Margaret convinced the king that prayer and the spiritual life were important. Margaret also promoted a return to the practice of religion and education among her subjects. She also initiated synods of the bishops, which she participated in, to deal with abuses and scandals in the Church. Margaret was a devoted mother to her six sons and two daughters. She instructed them in the Catholic faith. Her son David went on to become king of Scotland and is also a canonized saint.

Reflection

Queen Margaret unselfishly used her privileged position for the good of her people. Her selfless care extended from her family circle, to the castle servants, and to the poor of her kingdom. Margaret and her husband regularly welcomed the poor into the castle, where they would wash their feet and then serve them. She personally nursed the sick and could not leave the castle without being surrounded by beggars, none of whom went away empty-handed. The source of Margaret's amazing charity was her deep prayer life. In what ways does my prayer life extend to Corporal and Spiritual Works of Mercy?

Prayer

Saint Margaret of Scotland, pray that my life may become Christ-like and truly make a difference for others. Amen.

NOVEMBER 17

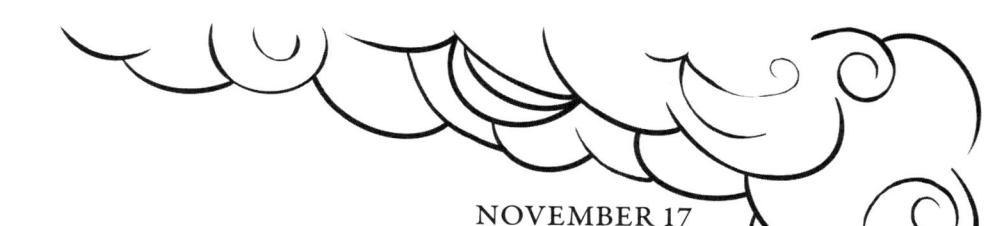

Saint Elizabeth of Hungary

1207–November 17, 1231
Feast: November 17
Patron: Brides, bakers, widows, Catholic Charities, Third Order Franciscans, Hungary

Princess Elizabeth's short life was not without suffering, yet it was remarkably full. At four years old, she was sent by her father to Thuringia in central Germany to be raised in the home of her betrothed. At fourteen, Elizabeth married Ludwig IV, whom she both loved and respected. Deeply in love, Ludwig admired Elizabeth's goodness and supported her works of mercy, even when they were costly or caused gossip. When Ludwig traveled without her, Elizabeth showed how much she missed him by wearing mourning clothes until he returned.

Yet Elizabeth never fully fit in at court. The self-absorbed nobles resented her Hungarian lineage, her simple lifestyle, and her generosity to those in need. When Elizabeth was expecting their third child, Ludwig was called to fight in a crusade. He died a few months later. Ludwig's brother Heinrich took power and banished Elizabeth in the middle of winter. The queen begged on the streets for food for her children. Some members of her husband's family mercifully began to provide for Elizabeth and her children. They urged her to remarry, but Elizabeth instead chose to renounce her title, become a Franciscan tertiary, and dedicate herself to works of mercy. She died at age twenty-three.

Reflection

The night Elizabeth was banished from the royal castle, she prayed in a Franciscan monastery and asked the friars to sing a hymn of thanksgiving to God for the trials she was experiencing. In every circumstance, this extraordinary woman kept her gaze focused on God. For what difficult circumstances of my life can I give thanks to God?

Prayer

Saint Elizabeth of Hungary, teach us not to be distracted by material things so that we can see the face of God in those around us. Amen.

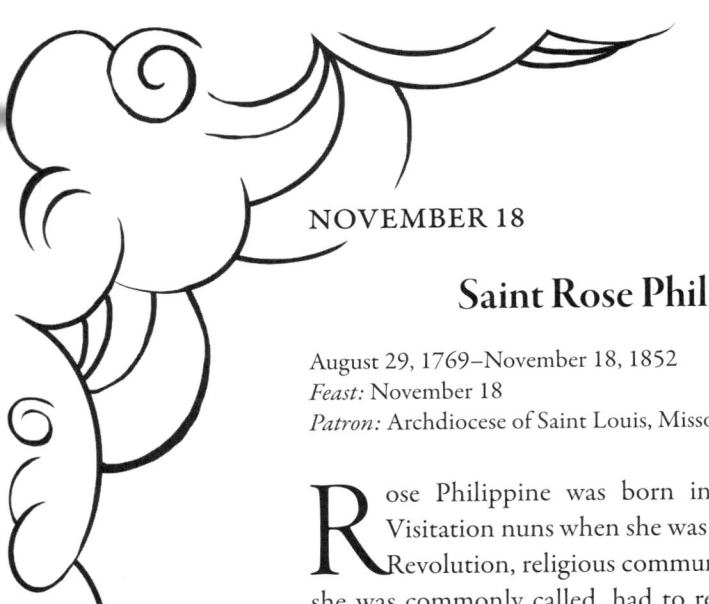

NOVEMBER 18

Saint Rose Philippine Duchesne

August 29, 1769–November 18, 1852
Feast: November 18
Patron: Archdiocese of Saint Louis, Missouri; missionaries, indigenous peoples

Rose Philippine was born in Grenoble, France, and entered the Visitation nuns when she was seventeen years old. During the French Revolution, religious communities were outlawed, and Philippine, as she was commonly called, had to return home. She continued to live her religious life, however, and proceeded to establish a school for poor children, nurse prisoners, and hide priests from revolutionaries. In 1801, Philippine and a group of sisters reclaimed their convent and unsuccessfully tried to reestablish their community.

In 1804, Philippine and some of the sisters decided to join the newly founded Society of the Sacred Heart. In 1818, she and four other sisters were sent as missionaries to the United States. The sisters suffered greatly from the extreme cold, grueling work, lack of funds, illness, and opposition. However, by 1828, Philippine had founded six convents with schools for young women in Missouri and Louisiana. When she was seventy-two, Philippine asked to go with four other sisters to open a school at the Jesuit mission for the Potawatomi people in Sugar Creek, Kansas. She prayed so much that the Potawatomi called her the "Woman-Who-Prays-Always." The following year, Philippine returned to Missouri, where she lived in humility and quiet prayer until her death.

Reflection

From surviving the French Revolution to becoming a missionary in a foreign land, Philippine learned to trust God in all the seemingly impossible challenges she encountered. Faithful to prayer, she knew that God was with her in every circumstance. How can I find peace in times of anxiety, trusting that God is always with me?

Prayer

Saint Rose Philippine Duchesne, help me to become aware that God is with me in my joys and sufferings and to believe that he will bring good out of every circumstance. Amen.

NOVEMBER 19

Blessed Frédéric Janssoone

November 19, 1838–August 4, 1916
Feast: August 4 (August 5 in Canada)
Patron: Preachers

Given his background, Blessed Frédéric Janssoone may someday be invoked as a patron saint for salespeople and fundraising professionals. Born to a wealthy Flemish family in Ghyvelde, France, Frédéric lost his father at a young age and became a traveling salesman to support his family. In this work he showed a genius for business that he would later use for the sake of the Gospel. After his mother's death, he entered the seminary and was ordained a Franciscan priest in 1870.

In 1876, Frédéric was sent to serve in the Holy Land and was elected its custodial vicar two years later. He had a church built in Bethlehem, reintroduced the practice of walking the Way of the Cross throughout Jerusalem's streets, and traveled the world to raise funds for the Holy Land. In 1888, Frédéric was sent to Canada and settled there for the rest of his life. There, he helped encourage Marian devotion by developing the shrine of Our Lady at Cap-de-la-Madeleine, Quebec. He was also noted for his missions, retreats, and preaching, and for his spiritual assistance to Third Order Franciscans. In 1902 he wrote, "I only desire one thing for which I have longed for forty years, to go and be with the Lord." Frédéric's desire was fulfilled when he was seventy-seven years old.

Reflection

Frédéric inspired support for sacred places like the Holy Land and Quebec's Marian shrine. His success certainly was due not only to his business acumen but also to his piety, devotion, and deep spiritual life. Frédéric aimed to save souls, not just buildings. How am I called to put my natural talents and skills at the service of the Gospel?

Prayer

Blessed Frédéric Janssoone, pray that I always direct my talents and skills toward furthering God's kingdom. Amen.

NOVEMBER 20

Saint Clement I

Died c. 97
Feast: November 23
Patron: Stonecutters, marble workers, mariners

Clement I has great importance as a saint of the early Church. He shepherded the early Christians during difficult times when they were suffering terrible persecution. Clement is acknowledged as an Apostolic Father, that is, one of the early Church writers thought to have had personal contact with the apostles. Tertullian believed that Clement was consecrated by Peter himself.

Clement wrote what is known as his *First Epistle to the Corinthians* around AD 96. The Church in Corinth, which had been founded by Saint Paul, was still troubled by divisions and conflicts. In his letter, Clement exhorted them to heal their divisions, and to recall their unity in Christ in order to give a more profound Christian witness to the world. At one point he writes, "Let us look steadfastly to the blood of Christ, and see how precious in the sight of God is his blood, which having been poured out for our salvation, brought the grace of repentance to the whole world." Clement suffered martyrdom during the persecution of Emperor Trajan. Because of the tradition that Clement was martyred by drowning, he is sometimes depicted with an anchor and is considered the patron of mariners.

Reflection

In his willingness to lay down his life for others, as Jesus the Good Shepherd did, Clement shows us the true meaning of leadership in the Church. In whatever ways we might exercise authority over others, we can follow Clement's example of faithful love and sacrifice. His call to the Corinthians to live in harmony and love needs to be heard today, especially where divisions and conflicts threaten to divide us.

Prayer

Saint Clement, may your example inspire us to be faithful and to witness to our faith despite difficulties. Amen.

NOVEMBER 21

Blessed Miguel Agustín Pro

January 13, 1891–November 23, 1927
Feast: November 23
Patron: Mexico, persecuted Christians

Miguel Agustín Pro was born to fervent Catholic parents in Guadalupe, Mexico. He was known for his cheerful, happy character, and he enjoyed games and practical jokes. When Miguel was twenty years old, he felt called to enter the Jesuits. The Mexican government, headed by Plutarco Calles, was fiercely anti-Catholic, so Miguel had to go abroad to finish his studies and was ordained in Belgium.

Returning to Mexico, Miguel secretly carried out his priestly ministry. It was like the Church of the catacombs. He met with small groups in secret locations to celebrate Mass and administer the other Sacraments. He used his nickname, "Cocol," when he wrote letters to avoid the notice of the secret police. In October 1926, he was arrested but not kept in custody for long. After his release, he was under constant surveillance. A year later he was arrested again under trumped-up charges. Without trial, he was sent to the firing squad. Facing the soldiers, Miguel held out a crucifix and rosary and said he forgave them. Then he raised his arms in the form of a cross and shouted, *"Viva Cristo Rey!"* ("Long live Christ the King!")

Reflection

Miguel risked his life and made the ultimate sacrifice in order to bring the Mass and the Sacraments to his flock. When we have regular access to the Sacraments, it can be easy to take them for granted. How can I better appreciate the blessing of the Mass? In what ways could I share about the Mass with others and perhaps invite them to attend with me?

Prayer

Blessed Miguel Agustín Pro, pray for us that we may always realize how important our faith is and never take it for granted. Amen.

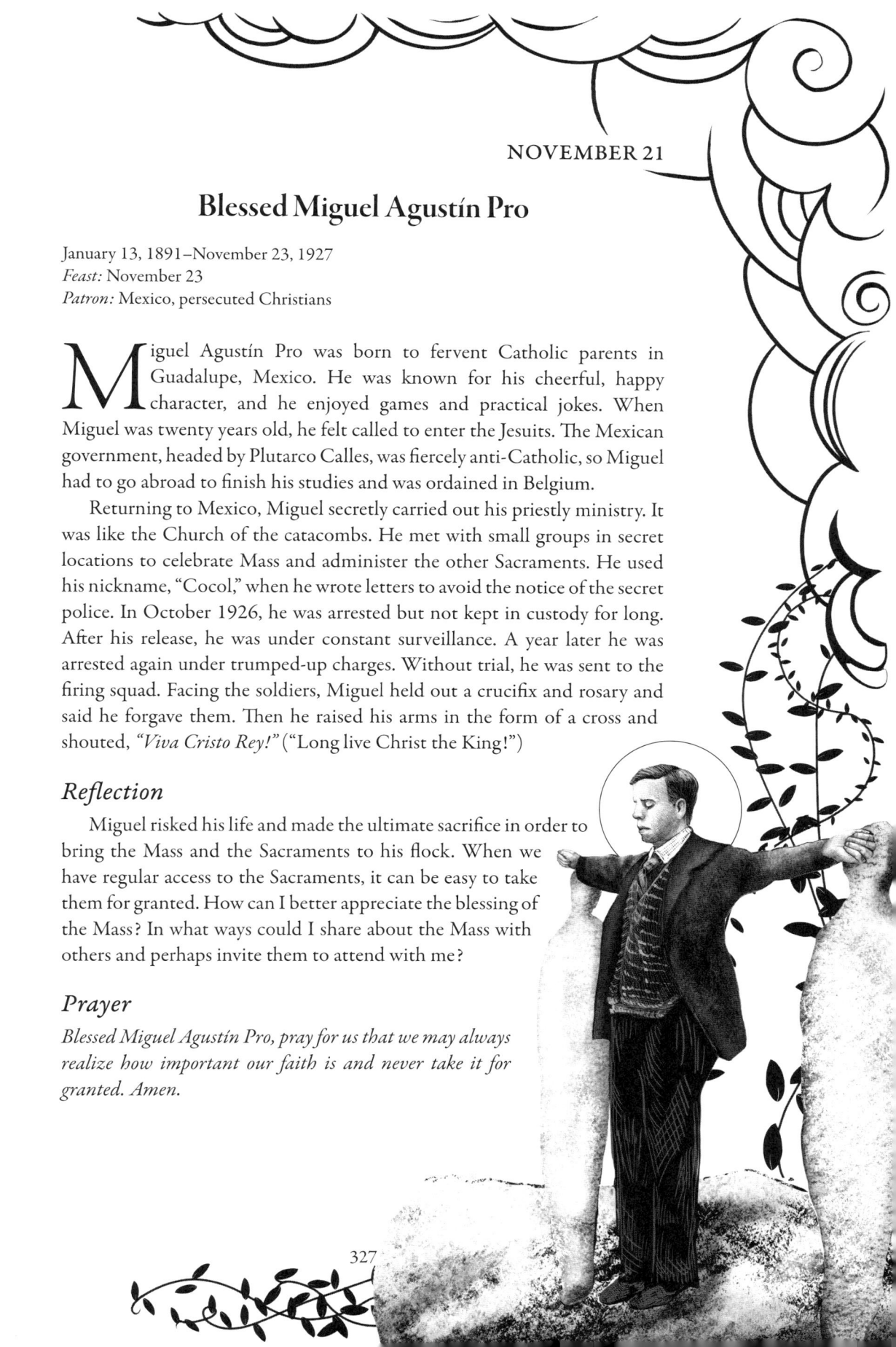

NOVEMBER 22

Saint Cecilia

Second Century
Feast: November 22
Patron: Composers, musicians, organ makers, poets, singers, vocalists

Although we know little about her life, Cecilia is a very popular saint because she is the patron of musicians. According to legend she became their patron because at her wedding she sang to the Lord in her heart. She was given in marriage as a young woman to a man named Valerian. But she had consecrated her virginity to Jesus Christ. On their wedding night, when she informed her husband of this, she said that she had an angel to guard her. Valerian asked to see the angel. Cecilia sent him to the Appian Way to meet Pope Urban, who lived among the poor.

Valerian was impressed by Pope Urban, converted, and was baptized. His brother Tiburtius also embraced the Christian faith. Before long, Valerian and his brother were captured and martyred for being Christians. Cecilia was then also condemned to death for believing in Jesus. Before her death, she arranged for her house to become a place of worship for Roman Christians. Cecilia was beheaded and heroically accepted her martyrdom after professing her faith. She was buried in the Catacombs of Saint Callistus, and her tomb remains a much-venerated place of pilgrimage.

Reflection

Few details are known about many of the early Roman martyrs, including Cecilia. Nevertheless, even saints known through legends can still speak to us today, sometimes in remarkable ways. Devotion to the saints does not depend on knowledge of exact historical details but on their presence interceding for us in heaven. Which saints do I feel a close connection to in my life? Which aspects of their lives inspire me?

Prayer

Saint Cecilia, you inspire us by the heroic example of your life. Pray for us that we may always have the courage to live our faith and the love to serve others in need. Amen.

NOVEMBER 23

Saint Columban

c. 530–November 23, 615
Feast: November 23
Patron: Motorcyclists, Missionary Society of Saint Columban (Columban Fathers)

This outwardly severe but warm-hearted monk has been called the greatest Irish missionary of his era. He was born in southeastern Ireland during a period of great thirst for holiness and learning. A handsome youth beset by temptations, he decided to become a monk. After studying under a holy teacher at Lough Erne, Columban entered the monastery at Bangor, on Ireland's northern coast. His later writings show that he became well-versed in Scripture and the Latin classics.

Columban asked to become a missionary. At first his abbot, Comgall, refused—probably viewing Columban as his successor. But later he relented and sent the monk off to the continent with several companions. The little band decided to go wherever the Lord would direct them. As a result, within the next two decades, three new monasteries began to flourish in the wilderness of Burgundy. They attracted penitent pilgrims as well as aspirants to their strict way of life. Eventually, Columban alienated the king, whom he wanted to convert from his immoral lifestyle. Banished with several of his companions, the aging monk founded yet another monastery at Lake Constance and finally settled south of the Alps at Bobbio, Italy. There he established his last monastic foundation and passed to his eternal reward.

Reflection

Before the coming of Patrick, Irish kings and chiefs had sought personal glory through warfare. In Columban's time, many Irish sought God's glory by battling their own passions. Columban exercised a rigorous self-mastery and asked the same of his monks. Our era is different, yet we, too, can seek God's glory by exercising self-discipline. The Lord is ready and eager to help us.

Prayer

Lord Jesus, I want to grow in self-discipline, but I know I'm weak. Help me day by day, I pray. Amen.

NOVEMBER 24

Saint Andrew Dũng-Lạc and Companions

c.1795–December 21, 1839 (Andrew Dũng-Lạc)
Died c. 1745–c. 1862 (Companions)
Feast: November 24
Patron: Vietnam

This group of 177 martyrs gave their lives for the faith during several persecutions in Vietnam. Ninety-six of them were native Vietnamese, and the others were European missionaries. Andrew Dũng-Lạc was baptized as a teenager. He studied for the priesthood and was ordained in 1823. With great zeal he fasted, preached, and brought many people into the Church. In 1832, Emperor Minh-Mang began to persecute Christians, demanding that they trample upon a crucifix to renounce their faith. Many resisted and were killed. Andrew was imprisoned but later released. In 1839, he was arrested again, together with another priest, Saint Peter Thi. They were tortured severely and beheaded.

Another martyr in this group was the priest Saint Paul Le Bao Tinh. While in prison, he wrote a beautiful letter in which he said, "Our master [Jesus Christ] bears the whole weight of the Cross, leaving me only the tiniest, last bit. . . . Behold, the pagans have trodden your Cross underfoot! Where is your glory? As I see all this, I would, in the ardent love I have for you, prefer to be torn limb from limb and to die as a witness to your love."

Reflection

An estimated 300,000 Christians were martyred in Vietnam in the eighteenth and nineteenth centuries. Their incredible courage and faith give abundant witness to the power of the Gospel to transform people's lives. Although the religious situation in Vietnam has improved, religion is still restricted. Do I support persecuted Christians with my prayers and offerings?

Prayer

Saint Andrew and companions, you courageously bore witness to Jesus Christ despite suffering and death. Pray that religious freedom might increase throughout the world, that the Gospel may be proclaimed to everyone. Amen.

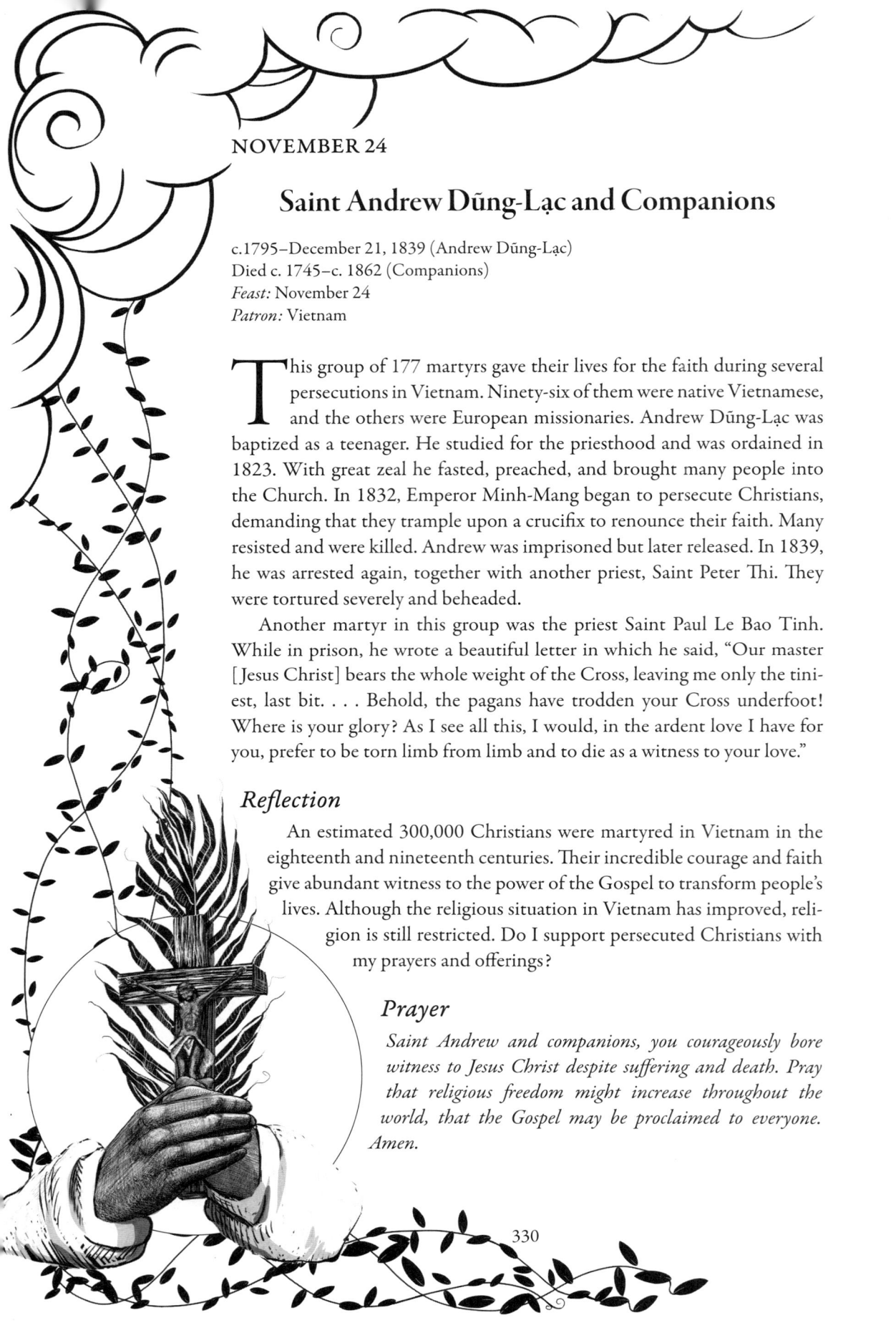

NOVEMBER 25

Saint Catherine of Alexandria

c. 287–c. 305
Feast: November 25
Patron: Young women, wheelwrights, lawyers, librarians, philosophers

Saint Catherine of Alexandria is honored as one of the Church's foremost virgin martyrs and counted among the Fourteen Holy Helpers, a group of saints often turned to for powerful intercessory help. During the Middle Ages, devotion to Catherine was immensely popular, and she was one of the saints who spoke to Saint Joan of Arc.

Despite her popularity, we know almost nothing about Catherine's life. According to legend, when she was about eighteen years old, she went to the Emperor Maximinus to upbraid him for persecuting Christians. The emperor brought in many pagan philosophers to debate with her, but Catherine outwitted them all. Enraged, the emperor had her scourged and imprisoned, but angels healed her wounds. Then he tried to kill her on a spiked wheel, but it broke when she touched it. Finally, she was beheaded. Angels brought her body to Mount Sinai, where a monastery was later built in her honor.

Reflection

Catherine's popularity can be said to be like something that goes "viral" on the internet. But we can see a deeper meaning in it. God raises up saints to give a specific witness of holiness to the whole Church. Catherine's vocation presents her as a model of feminine wisdom and scholarship at a time when many women received little education. She is an example of the "feminine genius" that Saint John Paul II spoke about so often. Ultimately modeled on Mary, the Mother of God, her life can show us all how to reach holiness by making a sincere gift of our lives to the Lord.

Prayer

Saint Catherine of Alexandria, pray for us that we may know how to use human wisdom in the service of God. Amen.

NOVEMBER 26

Blessed James Alberione

April 4, 1884–November 26, 1971
Feast: November 26
Patron: Evangelization with modern media, new evangelization

James Alberione grew up on a farm in northern Italy. When asked what he wanted to be when he was older, he told his first-grade teacher, "I want to be a priest!" As a young seminarian, James experienced a great grace during the night between the nineteenth and twentieth centuries. As he prayed before the Blessed Sacrament, he felt a deep personal call from God. He intensely felt Jesus' desire to draw everyone to himself. James was inspired to see that the Church would need apostles to proclaim the Gospel using all modern means of communication.

James was ordained a priest in 1907 and soon began teaching at the seminary. His bishop later asked him to manage the diocesan newspaper. Though many saw only the dangers of the media, Alberione believed that every new means of communication should be used by the Church for evangelization. For this reason, he began the Society of Saint Paul in 1914 and the Daughters of Saint Paul in 1915. He would go on to add an astounding eight more foundations to the Pauline Family. This prophetic apostle of the media died at the age of eighty-seven after receiving a blessing from Saint Paul VI.

Reflection

Alberione's experience before Jesus in the Blessed Sacrament as a young seminarian marked the rest of his life. His spirituality centered on the Eucharist and the word of God, with the Mass at the heart of each day. The religious communities he founded all have adoration as an essential aspect of their prayer. Is there a way I can integrate more Eucharistic prayer into my life?

Prayer

Blessed James Alberione, intercede that we may be holy apostles of the media. Pray that we may use every means available to share Jesus with others. Amen.

NOVEMBER 27

Blessed Marie-Clémentine Anuarite Nengapeta

November 29, 1939–December 1, 1964
Feast: December 1
Patron: Young people of Africa, vocations to religious life, victims of sexual assault

Anuarite Nengapeta was born in the Belgian Congo to a non-Christian family. She was baptized when she was four. Anuarite attended her village mission school, where she met the Holy Family Sisters. Feeling a call from God to become a religious, she entered their congregation, taking the name Marie-Clémentine. After her profession of vows, she worked as a teacher and also as a cook.

In 1964, a rebellion broke out in the Congo. One night, a group of rebel soldiers invaded the convent, herded the sisters into a truck, and drove them to another village. When they arrived, Colonel Ngalo demanded that Anuarite become his wife. She absolutely refused and he said, "Do you dare to refuse me?" Ngalo called another soldier, Colonel Olombe, who wanted Anuarite for himself. She continued to resist and Olombe beat her with a rifle and ordered some of the soldiers present to stab her with their bayonets. Olombe then shot her, and Anuarite died soon after, but not before she said, "I forgive you for you know not what you are doing."

Reflection

Anuarite was faithful to her vow of chastity because of her great love for Jesus. Her favorite expression, "Jesus alone," showed her great desire to love Jesus faithfully. Far from being a burden, consecrated chastity is a deep expression of love and a gift given to the Church as a sign of the world to come. Anuarite's witness is a beautiful testimony to the grace of the Holy Spirit, who never fails to raise up vocations to the religious life in the Church.

Prayer

Blessed Marie-Clémentine Anuarite Nengapeta, radiant martyr of purity, pray that the witness of consecrated chastity may flourish in the Church. Amen.

NOVEMBER 28

Saint Christopher

Died c. 251
Feast: July 25
Patron: Travelers, motorists, protection against storms and sudden death

Little is known of Christopher except that he was an early martyr who likely died in the third century under the persecution of Emperor Decius in Lycia. Churches were named for him within a century of his death, and devotion to the saint soon sprang up, along with numerous legends surrounding the details of his life. The most popular legend, written in the Middle Ages, relates how Christopher always sought to serve the strongest master he could find. After several wrong leads, he met a hermit who instructed him in the Christian faith. Christopher was baptized and determined to follow Christ.

Christopher wanted to live a holy life, so he decided to help those who were weaker than he was to cross a dangerous river. One day, he carried a small child across the river. The child was so heavy that Christopher could hardly lift him. Upon reaching the other side, the boy told Christopher that he had carried the weight of the world and the God who created it. The child whom Christopher had carried was Christ himself. Christopher then shared this encounter with everyone he met, and many hearts were converted.

Reflection

The name Christopher means "Christ bearer." The legend of Christopher interprets his name literally. But we are all called to bear Christ in our hearts and on our tongues, loving the Lord and speaking the Good News to others. Does what I say correspond to what is in my heart? When has there been a disconnect between what I say and what I feel in my heart?

Prayer

Lord, may our hearts and tongues be of one accord. Help us to carry you in all that we say and do. Amen.

NOVEMBER 29

Blessed Anne Catherine Emmerich

September 8, 1774–February 9, 1824
Feast: February 9
Patron: Organists, people who suffer from poor health

Born into a farming family in Westphalia, Germany, Anne Catherine wanted to enter the convent from a young age. After several orders refused her because of her poor health and lack of a dowry, the Augustinian nuns accepted her in 1802. She lived an exemplary life in the convent, but it closed in 1811, so she became a housekeeper for a priest. In 1813, she started to have signs of the stigmata. This caused controversy as doctors examined her to see if it was real. Apparently, it was, but it only lasted until 1818.

Anne had religious visions throughout her life, and the stigmata attracted people to her. A poet named Clemens Brentano visited her and he became involved in writing down her visions. These largely centered on the life of Christ, especially his passion, and the life of the Blessed Mother. However, scholars think that Brentano added many of his own thoughts to the manuscripts, so it's difficult to tell how much of what he wrote is authentic. The Vatican did not take account of these writings in her cause for beatification.

Reflection

While her mystical visions make her unusual, Anne was also very focused on serving others. She once said, "I have always considered service to my neighbor to be the greatest virtue." In his beatification homily, Saint John Paul II stressed that the central message of her life concerns the love of Christ, shown by his wounds for us: "He himself bore our sins in his body on the cross . . . by his wounds you have been healed" (1 Pet 2:24).

Prayer

Blessed Anne Catherine Emmerich, pray for us that we might be moved to repentance by meditating on the passion of Jesus Christ, and show to others his saving love. Amen.

NOVEMBER 30

Saint Andrew, the Apostle

First Century
Feast: November 30
Patron: Fishermen, fishmongers, rope-makers, Scotland, Russia, Greece, Barbados

One of the twelve apostles, Andrew was Simon Peter's brother. He was also a native of Bethsaida, a fisherman, and a disciple of John the Baptist. When John pointed out Jesus as the Lamb of God, Andrew followed him, and Jesus invited him to "Come and see" (Jn 1:39). Andrew then led his brother to Jesus. He went and "found his brother Simon and said to him, 'We have found the Messiah. . . .' He brought Simon to Jesus" (Jn 1:41–42).

After Pentecost, according to tradition, Andrew went east to spread the Gospel. He is said to have preached along the Black Sea and is honored as the founder of the see of Constantinople. He was martyred near Patras in Greece, on an X-shaped cross known as Saint Andrew's cross. An ancient document puts these words in Andrew's mouth as he approached his martyrdom: "Hail, O Cross, inaugurated by the Body of Christ and adorned with his limbs like precious pearls. Before the Lord was nailed to you, you inspired an earthly fear. Now, instead, endowed with heavenly love, you are accepted as a gift."

Reflection

Even among the apostles, Andrew is outstanding since he was the first to be called and he brought Peter to Jesus. Meeting Jesus changed Andrew, and from then on, he was set afire. He wanted to bring others to Jesus so they too could meet their Savior, the one who would set them free. How might I bring others to Jesus today?

Prayer

Saint Andrew the Apostle, you teach us that to know Jesus means to share him with others. Pray for us that with you, we too may have a holy fire to make known to others the difference that Jesus makes. Amen.

DECEMBER 1

Blessed Charles de Foucauld

September 15, 1858–December 1, 1916
Feast: December 1
Patron: Muslim-Christian dialogue, orphans, atheists

Charles de Foucauld was born into an aristocratic family in Strasbourg, France. He was orphaned when he was six. As a young man, Charles was self-centered and did not believe in God. When his grandfather enrolled him in military college, he had a difficult time taking it seriously. He was a playboy, drank heavily, and, to the great delight of his friends, threw many ostentatious parties. Charles was eventually discharged from the army for his bad behavior. Then he had a change of heart and reenlisted—this decision led him to greater maturity.

After a dangerous trip to Morocco, Charles returned to France and began to seriously search for God. One day he met a holy priest, Father Henri Huvelin, who told him to make a good confession and receive Holy Communion. Even though Charles did not believe, he obeyed, and this experience rekindled his faith. He became a Trappist, living first in France and then Syria. Then he felt called to live a solitary life in Nazareth and was ordained a priest in 1901. He spent the last years of his life in Algeria, where he lived alone with the Blessed Sacrament among the Tuareg people. Charles died when bandits raided his home and shot him.

Reflection

In many ways, Charles' life after his conversion could appear to some to be a failure. But he fulfilled his inner calling to be the presence of Christ to Christians, Jews, and Muslims in the solitude of the desert where Christ would not otherwise have been known. Do I look for how God is present to me even when he seems absent?

Prayer

Blessed Charles de Foucauld, pray for us that we may live in a way that attracts people to the Lord. Amen.

DECEMBER 2

Blessed Manuel Lozano Garrido

August 9, 1920–November 3, 1971
Feast: November 3
Patron: Journalists, spondylitis sufferers, Eucharistic devotees

Manuel, nicknamed Lolo, was one of eight children. As a teenager during the Spanish Civil War, he smuggled the Eucharist to prisoners. In 1937, he was caught and temporarily imprisoned, an event that foreshadowed his lifelong struggle with spondylitis. This spinal deformity caused Manuel to be discharged early from military service. Gradually, the disease confined him to a wheelchair. Manuel was able to continue his professional work as a journalist from his room. As his condition worsened and he lost the use of his hands, his sister Lucia became his assistant. She set a recording machine before him and later transcribed his words.

Manuel's nine books and numerous articles continue to inspire devotion today. He was a man in love with the Blessed Sacrament. Mass was celebrated in his room daily. He acknowledged the Eucharist as his total inspiration. In later years he formed a prayer group named *Sinai*, which brought the infirm together in groups of twelve, joined with a monastic community, to pray for a particular journalist or newspaper. Manuel's apostolate continued even after he suffered total blindness in 1962. After twenty-eight years in a wheelchair, he died quietly and peacefully.

Reflection

Manuel understood and related effectively with the world because of his connection to Jesus, the source of life in the Eucharist. He knew intimately the joys and sorrows, the triumphs and tragedies of life and how God's love transforms them. For this reason, the Church offers him as patron of journalists.

Prayer

Blessed Manuel Lozano Garrido, ask Jesus to help us to respond generously to his unwavering love for us. Amen.

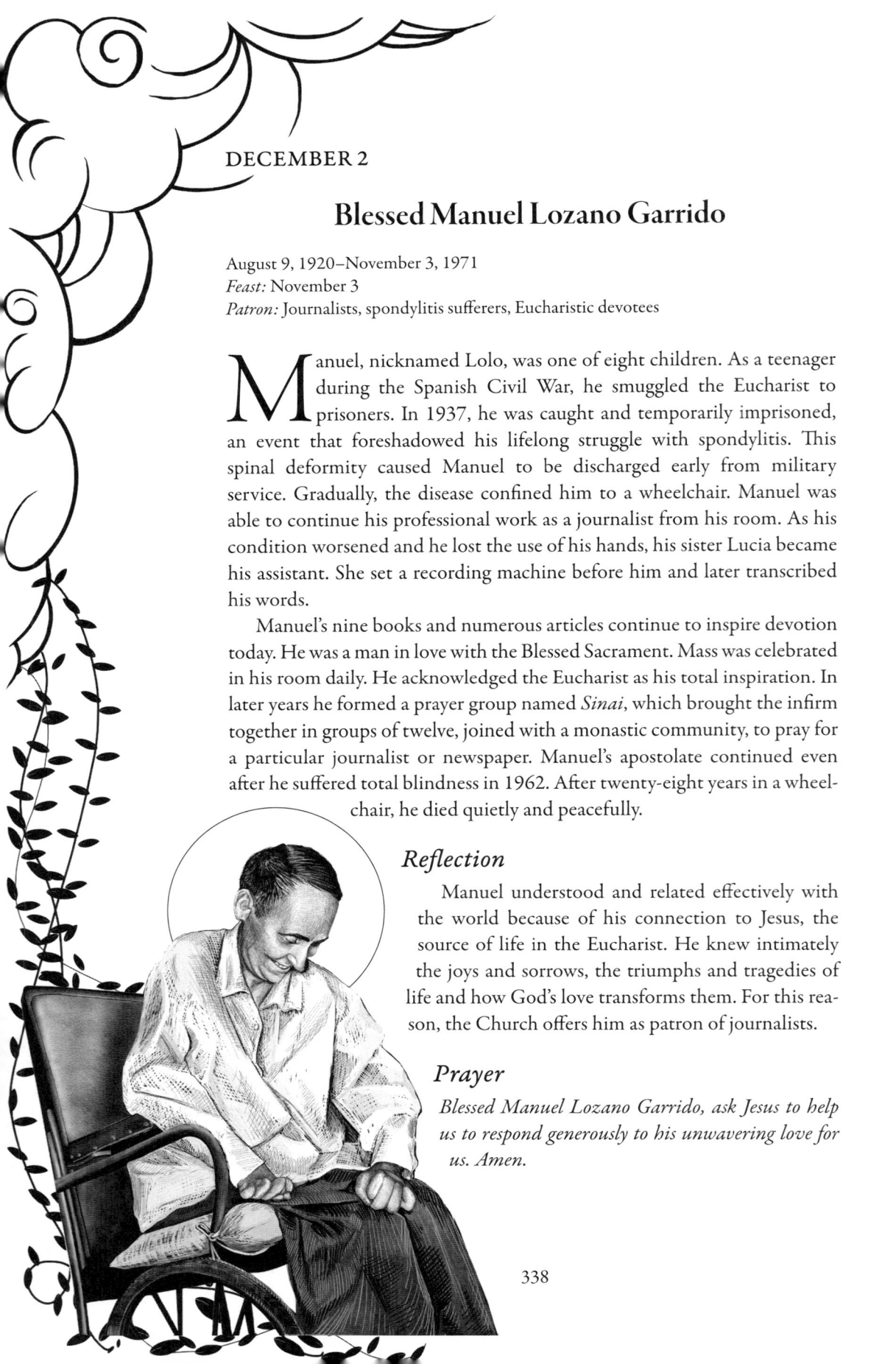

DECEMBER 3

Saint Francis Xavier

April 7, 1506–December 3, 1552
Feast: December 3
Patron: Asia, foreign missions, missionaries, and navigators

Born in northern Spain, Francis was the youngest son of a noble family. As the youngest, special attention was given to his education. He was sent to university to study theology. There he met Saint Ignatius of Loyola, and although Francis was skeptical of him at first, he eventually became one of Ignatius' closest friends and one of the first members of the Society of Jesus founded by Ignatius.

After his ordination, Francis was sent to the East Indies to teach, preach, baptize, and work among the poor. He traveled to India, the Malay Archipelago, the Spice Islands (present-day Indonesia), and Japan, living among the people and catechizing them. He served without regard to rank or class and was known for adapting his methods to suit the culture and character of the people he was evangelizing. Francis was always driven by the desire to teach more people about Christianity and God's love for them, and in his lifetime, he baptized approximately thirty thousand persons. After more than ten years as a missionary, he became ill and died at the age of forty-six, just as he was on the verge of entering the new missionary territory of China.

Reflection

Wherever Francis Xavier went, he would learn the language of the native people, believing it was the best way to connect with them. Unfortunately, he had no knack for languages and struggled a great deal with this! God does not always let us stay in our comfort zones, doing only what we are good at. Sometimes he asks us to serve him by stretching ourselves beyond our natural talents and abilities, trusting in him instead of ourselves.

Prayer

Dear Lord, teach me how to use both my talents and my limitations for your greater glory. Amen.

DECEMBER 4

Saint John of Damascus

c. 676–c. 749
Feast: December 4
Patron: Pharmacists, icon painters, theology students

John of Damascus was an outstanding theologian who wrote many important works. The breadth of his theological writing makes him an important bridge between East and West. Born in Damascus, Syria, to Christian parents, John received a good education, became a monk, and was ordained a priest. In the early eighth century, a major controversy broke out over the veneration of sacred images. The emperor, Leo III, was an iconoclast (those who opposed the veneration of icons). John vigorously defended the use of sacred images.

In other areas of theology, John carefully studied previous Church writers and gathered a treasury of their teachings. His masterful work *An Exact Exposition of the Orthodox Faith* became an important source for later writers. The great medieval theologians, including Thomas Aquinas, often relied on it to develop their own teachings. He is also an important writer in the field of Marian theology. His sermons on the Assumption of Mary testify to the development of this doctrine. After a very fruitful life of teaching and pastoral work, John died in his monastery, Mar Saba, near Jerusalem. In 1883, Pope Leo XIII declared him a Doctor of the Church.

Reflection

John was a great theologian and poet who wrote many beautiful hymns. Through his hymns and his eloquent defense of icons, John testified to the role of beauty in our faith and worship. Christian art and music not only enrich our understanding and practice of the faith, but they also enrich our culture. What are some ways I can incorporate the beauty of sacred art and music into my life?

Prayer

Saint John of Damascus, pray that we may always cherish the gift of faith. Help us to know how to express our faith in works of art and beauty. Amen.

DECEMBER 5

Blessed Niels Stensen

January 11, 1638–December 5, 1686
Feast: December 5
Patron: Scientists, doctors, geologists

If you've ever heard of Stensen's duct—which brings saliva from the parotid gland to the mouth—you might not know that it was discovered by Blessed Niels Stensen. His remarkable life testifies to the amazing variety of people whom the Church honors for their holiness. Born to a Lutheran family in Denmark, he spent most of his earlier years studying medicine and related subjects. He became a doctor and traveled widely in Europe, lecturing in various universities. Niels was an expert in anatomy, paleontology, and geology.

While living in Florence, Italy, he became interested in the Catholic Church. In 1666 he was in Livorno during a Eucharistic procession on Corpus Christi. He thought, "Either that host is just a piece of bread and these people are deluded, or it really is the Body of Christ—and I should worship it too!" That "either-or" dilemma haunted him, and he became a Catholic by the next year. He decided to study for the priesthood and was ordained in 1675. Two years later he was consecrated a bishop and was sent to Scandinavia and later Germany. Niels refused to live in luxury and gave away virtually everything he owned. He died in Germany after a painful illness.

Reflection

Niels' life reflected many beautiful facets of God's work. His scientific work joined with his role as a priest and bishop reminds us that, far from being opposed to science, the Catholic Church has a rich and fruitful scientific heritage. All truth comes from God, and no scientific truth detracts from the truth of faith.

Prayer

Blessed Niels Stensen, pray for us that we may use our knowledge of creation to deepen and sustain faith in the natural wonders that God has given us. Amen.

DECEMBER 6

Saint Nicholas

c. 270–c. 343
Feast: December 6
Patron: Children, sailors, fishermen, merchants, broadcasters, the falsely accused, repentant thieves, brewers, pharmacists, archers, pawnbrokers

Nicholas was born in what is now Turkey and became the bishop of Myra. Even if historical details are vague, popular stories about Nicholas reveal he was a devoted and well-loved pastor of his flock. He attended the Council of Nicea and upheld the orthodox faith about Christ against the errors of Arius. He was especially known for his care for the poor and needy. One legend is that Nicholas provided a dowry for three poor young girls by throwing three bags of gold coins into their house. This and similar stories gave rise to popular traditions of gift-giving on the feast of Saint Nicholas, which eventually evolved into the figure of Santa Claus.

Nicholas is also a popular saint in the East, and his cult spread in the West, especially after his relics were brought to Bari, Italy, in 1087. A forensic examination of those bones enabled researchers to reconstruct his features. It shows that his nose had been badly broken and didn't heal properly. Perhaps he was injured while he was imprisoned during the persecution of Diocletian.

Reflection

In a sermon on Saint Nicholas, Saint Thomas Aquinas says that he was an outstanding pastor for two reasons: his great piety and devotion, and his boundless generosity in doing good for others. Nicholas' love for God overflowed into good deeds for others. How do I allow the love I experience in my relationship with God to overflow into my daily life?

Prayer

Saint Nicholas, through your prayers, help us to grow in love of God and to spend ourselves for others just as you did. Amen.

DECEMBER 7

Saint Ambrose

c. 340–April 4, 397
Feast: December 7
Patron: Beekeepers, Milan

Born into a prominent Roman family, Ambrose studied law and became a governor in northern Italy. When the bishop of Milan died, Ambrose was elected by popular acclaim. He fled because he was still a catechumen and had not even been baptized yet! But then he accepted the position and was baptized and ordained a bishop. Despite his lack of theological education, he studied and became an outstanding theologian.

Ambrose was firm in opposing the Arian heresy. Showing great courage in upholding the truth of the faith, he did not fear to oppose even the Roman emperor Valentinian II. As a pastor, Ambrose also showed great compassion for the poor. He even melted down some of the Church's sacred vessels to ransom needy captives. He was well known for his eloquent preaching; it even impressed the young Saint Augustine of Hippo, who converted to the Catholic faith with the help of Ambrose. In his theology, Ambrose wrote extensively about the Blessed Virgin Mary. He emphasized her virginity and was also the first to speak of Mary as an image or symbol of the Church.

Reflection

The Arians denied the divinity of Jesus Christ. To counter this, Ambrose wrote about Mary and explained how she is truly the Mother of God. What the Church teaches about Mary aims at safeguarding what it teaches about Jesus. In other words, Mary leads us to Jesus. In my life as a disciple of Jesus, how have I allowed Mary to lead me closer to her Son?

Prayer

Saint Ambrose, you labored tirelessly in preaching the Gospel and helping the poor. Pray for us that we too may reach out to others with the Good News of Jesus Christ with courage and zeal. Amen.

DECEMBER 8

Saint Catherine Labouré

May 2, 1806–December 31, 1876
Feast: November 28
Patron: Miraculous medal, sick persons, the elderly

Shortly after her mother's death, nine-year-old Catherine clasped a statue of the Blessed Virgin and said, "You will be my Mother now!" The eighth of ten children, Catherine, nicknamed Zoé, worked on the Labouré family farm. Her special chore was caring for hundreds of doves! Catherine also frequently attended daily Mass, walking several miles each way. Overcoming great obstacles—including her father's opposition—she entered the Daughters of Charity in 1830.

On July 18 of that same year, the night before the feast of Saint Vincent de Paul, Catherine was awoken by a small child who summoned her to the convent chapel. There, the Blessed Mother appeared to her and they spoke for over two hours. Mary appeared to Catherine again on November 27. This time, she showed the young novice an image of a medal (now known as the Miraculous Medal) honoring her Immaculate Conception. Mary asked Catherine to have the medal made and distributed, promising many graces to those who wore it. Catherine told her confessor, Father Aladel, what Mary had asked. At first, he did not believe her, but after two years he went to the archbishop of Paris and they had 1,500 medals made. At the time of her death at seventy-one, Catherine rejoiced that millions of the medals had been distributed worldwide.

Reflection

For forty-six years, Catherine kept Mary's apparitions as her secret and told only her confessor. While the medal became hugely popular, Catherine humbly cared for the sick, answered the convent door, and did other menial labor. How can I imitate Catherine's profound devotion to the Blessed Mother and her deep humility?

Prayer

Saint Catherine Labouré, draw me closer to Mary, knowing that she will always lead me to Jesus. Amen.

DECEMBER 9

Saint Juan Diego

1474–May 30, 1548
Feast: December 9
Patron: Mexico, indigenous peoples, florists

Today's saint grew up in what is now Mexico City. He was known as Cuauhtlatoatzin, or "the talking eagle," for most of his life. When he was about fifty years old, he converted to Christianity and was baptized, taking the name Juan Diego. From that time on, he walked more than nine miles to attend Mass a few times each week. During one of these walks, the Mother of God appeared to him on a hill known as Tepeyac on December 9, 1531. She instructed him to tell the bishop to have a church built on that location. However, the bishop didn't believe his story.

On December 12, Mary appeared to Juan Diego again. This time, she showed him rose bushes flowering in the dead of winter. He collected the roses in his garment, known as a *tilma*, and took them to the bishop. When Juan Diego opened his *tilma*, the roses fell out and revealed the image of the Blessed Mother, now known as Our Lady of Guadalupe. Juan Diego lived as a hermit from then on, protecting the *tilma* and welcoming pilgrims who came to see the miraculous image. Less than seven years following Our Lady's appearances, some eight million Mexicans accepted the Christian faith.

Reflection

When Mary appeared to Juan Diego, she called out to him saying, "Juanito, Juan Dieguito!" This would be like calling a young child "sweet little Johnny." She also reassured him, "Am I not here who am your Mother?" Am I aware of how tenderly I am loved by Jesus and his Blessed Mother?

Prayer

Mary, you came to Juan Diego in the midst of his daily routine. May my daily routine always leave room for noticing your loving presence. Amen.

DECEMBER 10

Saint Barbara

Third Century
Feast: December 4
Patron: Field artillery crews, architects, mathematicians, miners

Although her biography is mostly legendary, Saint Barbara is still one of the most popular saints. She was born in what is now Turkey. Her father, Dioscorus, a pagan, shut her up in a tower in order to protect her from the outside world. He provided tutors for her education. Barbara was very intelligent and realized the pagan idols were nothing. She secretly became a Christian and was baptized one day when her father let her out of the tower. When Dioscorus found out, however, he was enraged and turned her over to the authorities to be put to death.

Despite horrible tortures, Barbara miraculously survived. Then her father himself beheaded her. He was immediately struck by a thunderbolt from heaven that killed him on the spot. Barbara's legend proved so popular that she was included among the Fourteen Holy Helpers, a group of saints invoked for their special powers of protection. The thunderbolt is the basis for her patronage of those who work with artillery and explosives.

Reflection

Barbara's liturgical feast was removed from the calendar after Vatican II, but her popularity lives on in unlikely circles, such as the U.S. Army Field Artillery, the Royal Regiment of Canadian Artillery, and similar groups in other countries. They celebrate Barbara's feast day in grand style, with honors, awards, and a great meal. This might seem a bit removed from the purpose of honoring saints, but it shows how faith can affect popular culture. As society becomes more secular, we can try to make faith relevant in ways that people will understand.

Prayer

Saint Barbara, you achieved divine glory by the holiness of your life. Pray for us that we may evangelize people today so that everyone might hear and accept what Jesus teaches us in the Gospel and through his Church. Amen.

DECEMBER 11

Saint Damasus I

c. 305–December 11, 384
Feast: December 11
Patron: Archeologists

Of Spanish descent, Damasus was born in Rome during the tumultuous fourth century. He was a child when Constantine issued the Edict of Milan, freeing Christians from persecution. Damasus became a priest and was elected pope in 366. He was very devoted to the cult of the martyrs, especially Saint Lawrence, and repaired the church dedicated to him.

From the beginning of his papacy Damasus faced great trials, for he was challenged by a rival anti-pope. Damasus did two things that had a long-lasting, major effect in the Church: he changed the language of the liturgy in the West from Greek to Latin, and he asked Saint Jerome to do a new translation of the Bible into Latin, the language of the people. The pope wanted them to better understand the liturgy and the word of God. Jerome's version of the Bible, known as the Vulgate, was the standard Catholic translation for centuries. Saint Jerome described Damasus as "an incomparable person, learned in the Scriptures, a virgin doctor of the virgin Church, who loved chastity and heard its praises with pleasure."

Reflection

Damasus reminds us of the importance of reading and praying with the Scriptures, and of centering our life on the Eucharist, which Vatican II described as the source and summit of Christian life. We find both in the Mass. How much importance do I give to Sunday Mass? In what ways can I make my participation in Mass more spiritually fruitful?

Prayer

Saint Damasus, pray for us that we may prayerfully read the word of God and allow the Holy Spirit to inspire us with a great love for the Lord. Help us also to grow in our understanding and love for the Mass. Amen.

DECEMBER 12

Saint Gianna Beretta Molla

October 4, 1922–April 28, 1962
Feast: April 28
Patron: Mothers, physicians, and unborn children

A devout Catholic, young Gianna desired marriage and children. She became a doctor first, specializing in pediatrics. She was also very involved with the evangelizing group Catholic Action and developed a deep spiritual life. Gianna prayed for a good husband, whom she found in Pietro Molla. They married on September 24, 1955, in her hometown of Magenta, Italy (near Milan). Three children soon followed. Gianna viewed practicing medicine as a mission and continued in her commitment to serving children, women, the elderly, and the poor. The Mollas regularly attended Mass and prayed together. Their recreation included skiing and mountain climbing.

During her final pregnancy in 1961, Gianna was diagnosed with a uterine tumor. She wanted to save the life of her child at all costs and chose to have only the tumor removed so that she could continue the pregnancy. She knew the risks involved in this decision, but she entrusted herself to divine Providence with much prayer. The pregnancy was difficult, but Gianna delivered a healthy girl, Gianna Emanuela, on Holy Saturday 1962. However, the mother developed complications from the Caesarean section. Gianna suffered for days in extreme pain. She would frequently whisper: "Jesus, I love you! Jesus, I love you!" She died at home a week after giving birth.

Reflection

Gianna and her husband, Pietro, worked to build a loving Christian marriage and family. A prayerful woman, she sought God's will in every aspect of her life. The decision she made to save her baby's life demonstrated her complete trust in God's providence. When I face especially difficult decisions, do I ask for God's guidance?

Prayer

Saint Gianna, you loved life and wanted to give life to others as a doctor, wife, and mother. Pray that my decisions may always be life-giving. Amen.

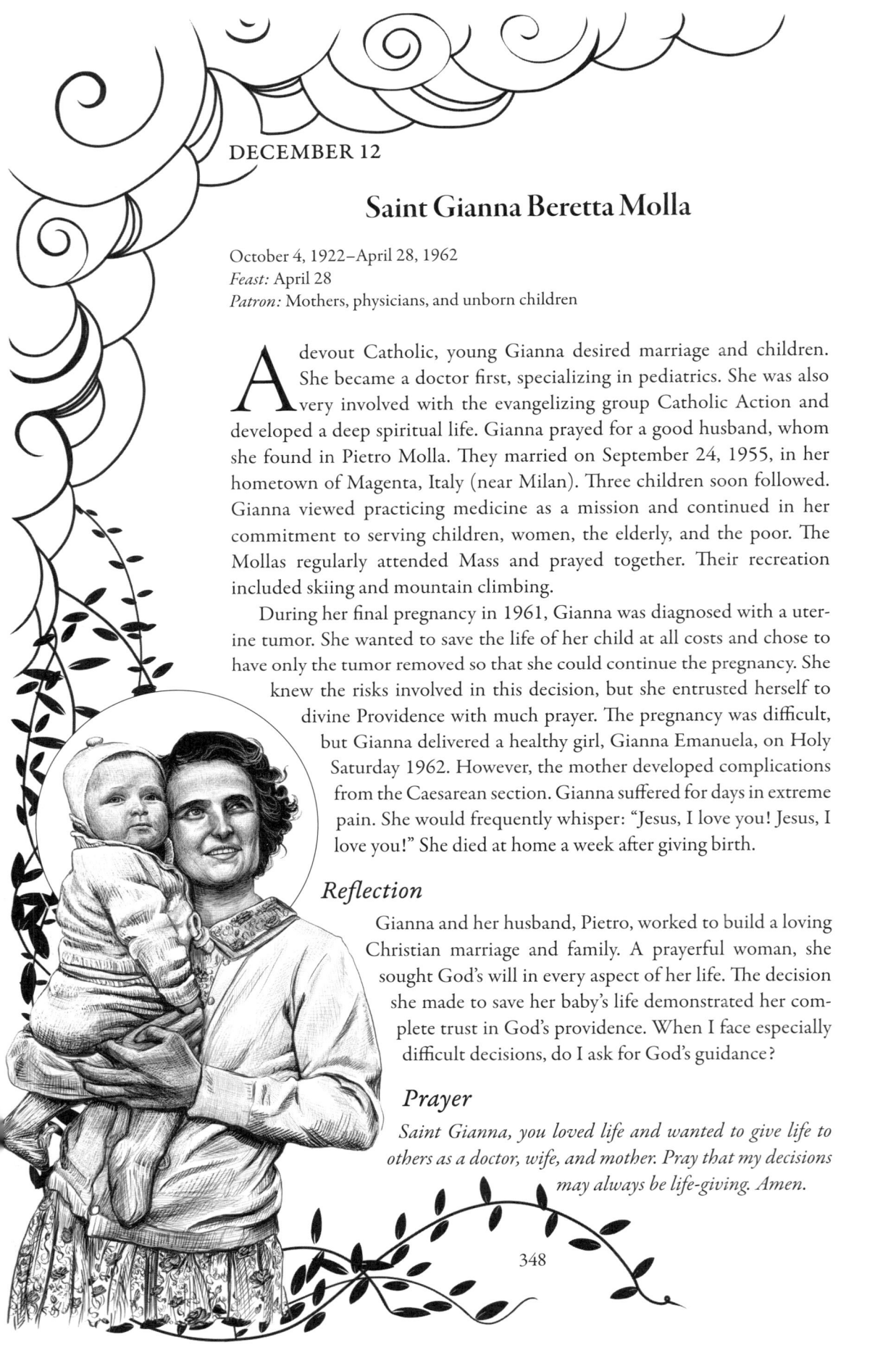

DECEMBER 13

Saint Lucy

c. 283–304
Feast: December 13
Patron: Those with eye trouble, writers, sales persons, Sicily

Lucy is one of the most popular saints from the early Church. Born in Sicily, in the Roman Empire, she gave her life for Christ during the persecution of Diocletian. That much is certain, but beyond that we know little. It is thought, however, that her father died when she was young. Her mother later arranged for Lucy to marry a young pagan man. But Lucy had already promised to live as a virgin for the love of Jesus.

Lucy's rejected suitor denounced her to the Roman authorities, who sentenced her to be forced into prostitution. According to legend, Lucy became immovable, and no effort was successful in moving her. She was martyred when her neck was pierced with a sword and she died. Devotion to Lucy spread widely, and her name was inserted into the Roman Canon of the Mass.

Reflection

The name Lucy comes from the Latin word for light (*lux*). Her feast appropriately occurs in Advent, near the winter solstice as the days grow shorter and darker. Lucy has thus become a symbol that points to Christ, the true light of the world. While she is widely invoked for help with physical eyesight, Lucy can also help us gain spiritual insight. Her life reminds us to keep our eyes on Jesus who told us, "I am the light of the world. Whoever follows me will never walk in darkness but will have the light of life" (Jn 8:12).

Prayer

Saint Lucy, your love led you to give your whole self to Jesus, and your courage enabled you to cling to that commitment despite persecution. Pray for us that we might have the same love and courage living our Christian faith as you did. Amen.

DECEMBER 14

Saint John of the Cross

June 24, 1542–December 14, 1591
Feast: December 14
Patron: Mystics, contemplative prayer, poets

John was born in 1542 in Spain and, at the age of twenty-one, he entered the Carmelite Order. In 1567, he was ordained and contemplated transferring from the Carmelites to enter the more austere Carthusians. He then met Saint Teresa of Ávila, who convinced him that the life John sought could be found within the Carmelite reform movement. She had already initiated this reform among the Carmelite nuns and wished to begin with the men. In 1568, the male Carmelite reform movement was initiated and John of the Cross was among the first members.

In 1577, some Carmelites who opposed the strict observance reform held John captive for nine months. During his imprisonment he began to write his famous poem, the *Spiritual Canticle*. After his escape, John continued to write and to serve in various offices in the reformed Carmelite Order. In particular, he was known for being a gifted confessor and spiritual director. This gentle man died in Ubeda, Spain, echoing Jesus' last words, "Into your hands O Lord, I commend my spirit."

Reflection

Of all the phrases that could be used to describe this saint, he probably would have chosen "Lover of the Beloved." From all his letters, poems, and commentaries, John of the Cross shows himself to be a person overwhelmingly in love with his beloved God. What is most inspiring about this Doctor of the Church is not so much the intellectual clarity of his written work but that his interior mystical experiences translated into radical exterior holiness. He models for us how to be transparent men and women of integrity.

Prayer

Saint John of the Cross, pray that I too may become an authentic witness to God's work in me. Amen.

DECEMBER 15

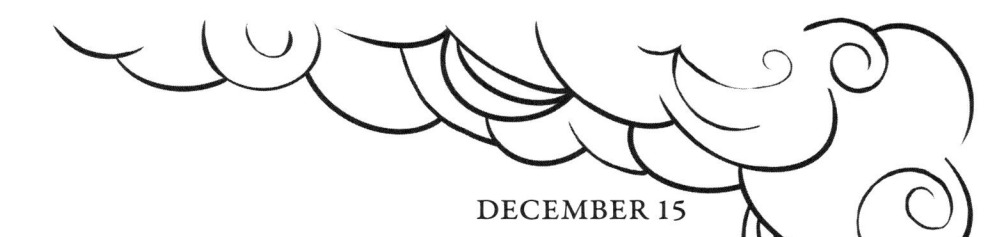

Blessed Anne-Marie Javouhey

November 10, 1779–July 15, 1851
Feast: July 15
Patron: Sisters of Saint Joseph of Cluny, social justice

Anne-Marie was born at a critical time in history, not long before the French Revolution brought turmoil to France and persecution to the Church. Shortly after her birth, her mother consecrated her to the Blessed Mother. That grace would bear great fruit. As a girl, Anne-Marie stood watch for priests who offered Mass secretly. She decided that she wanted to give her life to God, but most convents had been closed. Finally, she found one that accepted her, but she left it before her final vows because she realized that God was calling her to begin her own foundation. Gathering a group of young women, she began the Sisters of Saint Joseph of Cluny.

With her flair for leadership and organization, the congregation flourished and soon expanded to Africa and to French Guiana, South America. Anne-Marie had innovative ideas, such as bringing African men to France to prepare for ordination. In French Guiana she was entrusted with preparing a group of six hundred slaves for liberation and education. She handled this with great skill, but this provoked opposition from local farmers. The local bishop excommunicated her. Undaunted, she returned to France and guided her sisters as the congregation spread to five continents.

Reflection

Anne-Marie was remarkable in her ability to persevere in doing good despite tremendous obstacles. How did she succeed? She trusted God and divine providence and did not take opposition personally. She knew that she was doing God's will and that was all that mattered. How do I respond to opposition when I have prayerfully discerned God's will for me?

Prayer

Blessed Anne-Marie, pray for us that in our world today, more people will respond to the Lord's call to become workers in his vineyard. Amen.

DECEMBER 16

The Seven Thai Martyrs of Songkhon

† December 16 and 26, 1940
Feast: December 16
Patron: Thailand, catechists

The Seven Martyrs of Thailand were a group of Catholics who were martyred in the officially Buddhist nation during a time of intense political unrest. World War II was heating up, and there were strong anti-Western sentiments in the region. Christianity was seen as a foreign influence, so many Christians were coerced into renouncing the faith.

After their priests had been expelled, a group of the faithful in a small rice-farming village called Songkhon persevered in teaching the faith. Philip, a thirty-three-year-old married catechist with five children, led the efforts, joined by members of the Congregation of the Lovers of the Holy Cross: Sister Agnes Phila and Sister Lucia Khambang. In December of 1940, Philip was ordered to report to the local law enforcement. He knew it might be a trap but expressed his willingness to die for his faith. He was fatally shot. The two religious sisters boldly continued catechizing the children of the village despite threats. Shortly after, the two sisters, their housekeeper, and three young women were marched out to the village cemetery and shot. All seven were beatified together by Saint John Paul II in 1989.

Reflection

The Thai martyrs recognized the responsibility they had toward their community as the natural consequence of their baptism. Philip knew that the Church needed him. How aware am I of the responsibility that comes with my own baptism? Am I willing to witness to the love of Jesus, even when it's not popular? How do I view my own role within the Church, the Body of Christ?

Prayer

Father, in Baptism, you have made me your beloved child. Grant me the courage, faith, and love that I need to live according to that identity at every moment of my life. Amen.

DECEMBER 17

Blessed Karl Leisner

February 28, 1915–August 12, 1945
Feast: August 12
Patron: Priests and seminarians

Born in Germany during World War I, Karl Leisner died a martyr during World War II. While the Nazis were forcing children to join Hitler Youth, Karl led underground Catholic youth groups in discussions of the faith. As Hitler rose to power, Karl discerned a call to the priesthood. Soon after being ordained a deacon, Karl was diagnosed with tuberculosis. While recovering in a sanatorium, a patient reported Karl for making an anti-Hitler remark.

Karl was promptly arrested and eventually transferred to the Dachau concentration camp in 1941. Admired for his even temperament, he encouraged others in the camp. He even signed his letters to his parents with the phrase "ever joyful." Karl's fellow prisoner, a French bishop, secretly ordained him to the priesthood. Due to his debilitating illness, he celebrated his first and only Mass at Dachau on the Feast of Saint Stephen in 1944. Karl lived to see Dachau liberated by the Americans in April 1945. However, his health continued to deteriorate, and he died months later at age thirty. Saint John Paul II beatified him in 1996 during a Mass at Berlin's Olympic Stadium. Hitler had built the stadium as a showcase of the Nazi regime, but the stadium now showcased Blessed Karl Leisner's eternal triumph.

Reflection

From an early age, Karl recognized the anti-Christian nature of the Nazi regime. He helped young people learn and practice their faith even as the government prohibited such activities. Even in Dachau and gravely ill, Karl comforted others and joyfully lived his priestly vocation to the full. He inspires us to find joy in the Lord, even in the worst of circumstances.

Prayer

Blessed Karl Leisner, pray that I may live my faith as courageously as you did, and to do so with joy. Amen.

DECEMBER 18

Saint Angela of Foligno

1248–January 4, 1309
Feast: January 4 (January 7 in the U.S.)
Patron: Widows, those afflicted by sexual temptation

Until she was about thirty-seven years old, Angela's life was focused on enjoying pleasures and her social life. She married and had several children. But then events such as the violent earthquake of 1279 and ongoing wars in her area of Italy made her think more deeply about the purpose of life. She prayed to Saint Francis for guidance, and in 1285 he appeared to her in a vision and instructed her to make a general confession. Three years later her mother, husband, and children died within a few months of each other. This shock caused her great grief, but it also allowed her to completely change her life.

Angela became a Third Order Franciscan and dedicated herself to prayer, penance, and good works. She attracted followers and later began a community of women religious. Angela also quickly made progress in the spiritual life and became a great mystic. She described her mystical experiences to her confessor, who recorded them. These writings have a great place in the Church's legacy of spiritual wisdom. Her spiritual teachings were so respected in her time that she was known as "Teacher of Theologians."

Reflection

The steps of Angela's mystical journey show us the possible stages of the spiritual life. She began with a fear of hell, which made her turn away from her sinful life. But gradually she was drawn more into the love of Christ crucified. The spiritual life is a journey that continues our whole life. At whatever stage we are, we can always go forward, one step at a time, until we reach the goal of eternal life.

Prayer

Saint Angela of Foligno, pray for us that our hearts might be drawn away from earthly attractions and be more and more filled with love. Amen.

DECEMBER 19

Saint Giuseppe Maria Tomasi

September 12, 1649–January 1, 1713
Feast: January 3
Patron: Liturgical studies, language studies

Giuseppe Maria Tomasi was born in Sicily, Italy, to parents who were minor nobility. He was raised a devout Catholic, and as a child he loved the liturgy of the Church. He would even try to wear the liturgical color of the day! He learned many languages, particularly Spanish, because he was destined for the Spanish court. However, he felt the call to be a priest and entered the Theatine religious community after renouncing his considerable inheritance.

Giuseppe became a scholar of languages and the liturgy and published translations of ancient liturgical texts. He did not seek attention for his work and even published some of his books under a pseudonym to avoid acclaim. Nevertheless, universities around the world praised his books and influential people sought him out. In 1721, he was made a cardinal, much to his dismay. Despite the honor and attention, Giuseppe lived a modest, holy life, and people would flock to see the man they believed to be a living saint. When Giuseppe was alive, people who touched his clothes reported being cured.

Reflection

Giuseppe is considered a saint not only for his scholarly service to the Church but also for his holiness and piety, especially his humility and self-giving love. The holiness of Giuseppe's life impressed those around him and led others to Christ. At one point he studied with a rabbi to deepen his knowledge of Hebrew. The rabbi was so impressed with Giuseppe's holiness that he asked to be baptized. In what ways can my relationship with God lead others to Christ?

Prayer

Saint Giuseppe Tomasi, pray that we may see the beauty and value of the liturgy and celebrate it well. And pray that we may unite our natural gifts with a true spirit of humility. Amen.

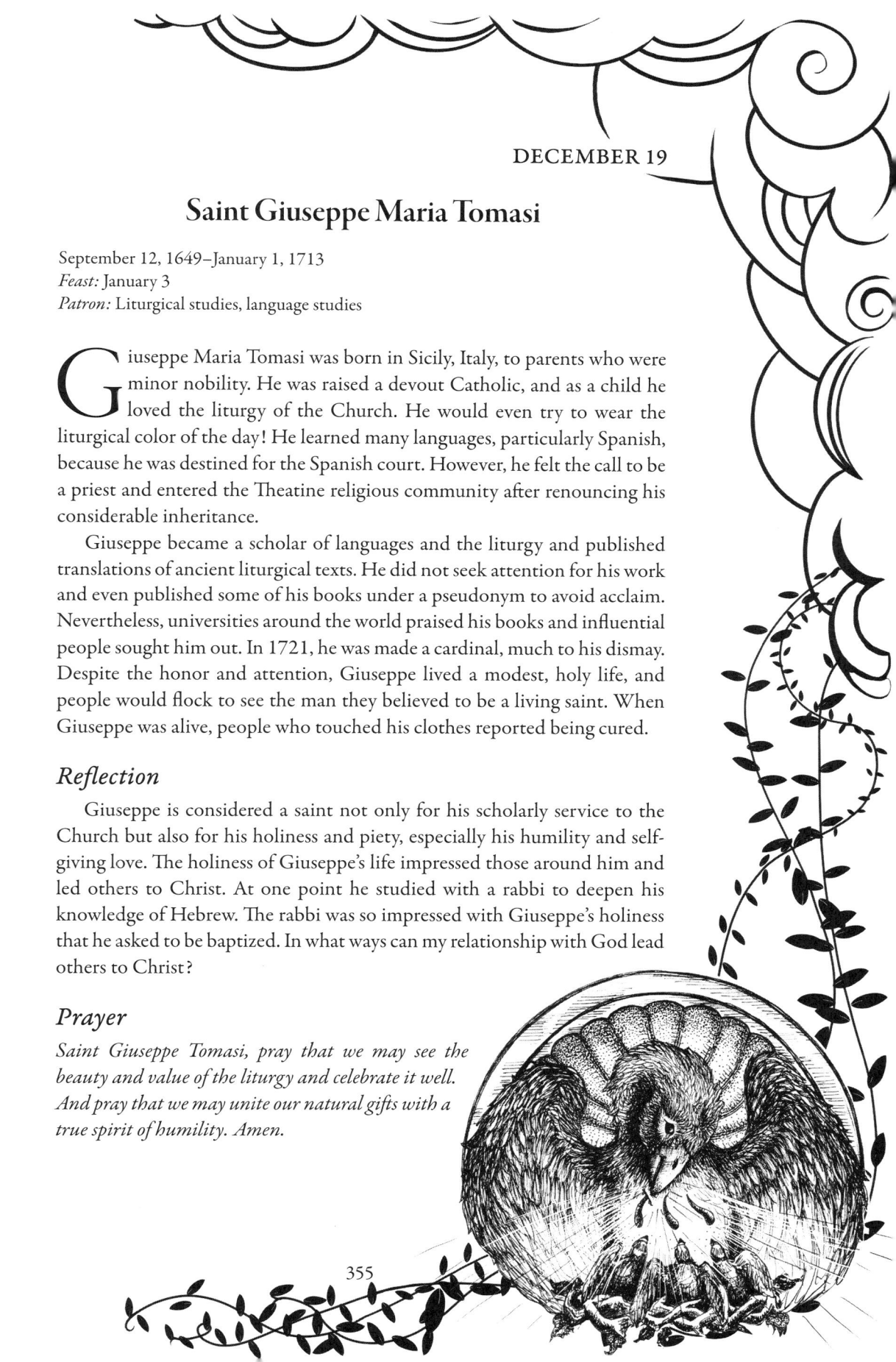

DECEMBER 20

Blessed Liduina Meneguzzi

September 12, 1901–December 2, 1941
Feast: December 2
Patron: The poor, sick, and suffering

Elisa Angela Meneguzzi was born near Padua, Italy. A devout girl, she fervently attended Mass and taught catechism to other children. At the age of fourteen she began to work as a domestic servant, but her dream was to serve God and give her life to him completely. In 1926, she entered the Sisters of Saint Francis de Sales, or Salesians, and was given the name Liduina. Her life seemed ordinary, just like that of the other sisters, but she nourished in her heart a profound love of God and neighbor.

Liduina always burned with an ardent zeal and desired to work in a mission land. In 1937, this dream came true when Liduina was sent to Dire Dawa, Ethiopia. She worked as a nurse in the hospital, helping the sick and talking to them about God. After World War II broke out, Liduina cared for many wounded soldiers, many of whom were Muslim. Through her holy example, many non-Christians were drawn to the Catholic faith. The people loved her so much that they called her "Sister *Gudda*," meaning "Great." She died of cancer at the age of forty.

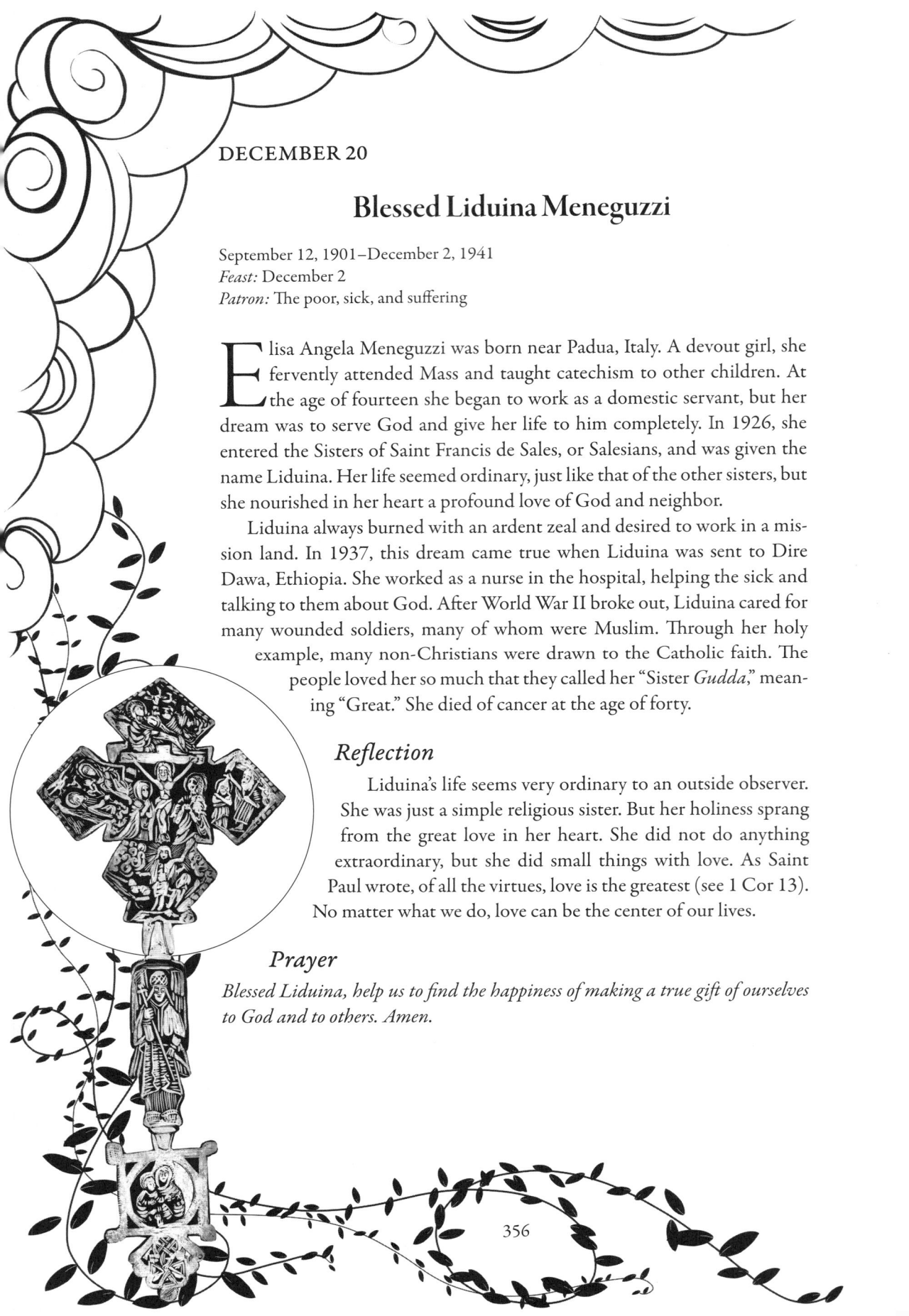

Reflection

Liduina's life seems very ordinary to an outside observer. She was just a simple religious sister. But her holiness sprang from the great love in her heart. She did not do anything extraordinary, but she did small things with love. As Saint Paul wrote, of all the virtues, love is the greatest (see 1 Cor 13). No matter what we do, love can be the center of our lives.

Prayer

Blessed Liduina, help us to find the happiness of making a true gift of ourselves to God and to others. Amen.

DECEMBER 21

Saint Peter Canisius

May 8, 1521–December 21, 1597
Feast: December 21
Patron: Catholic press, Germany

Peter Canisius was an outstanding pastor and evangelizer throughout the tumultuous sixteenth century. Born in the Netherlands, he became known as the "Second Apostle to Germany," after Saint Boniface. He studied law at the University of Cologne. Then in 1543, Peter made the spiritual exercises with Saint Peter Faber and decided to enter the Jesuits. As a Jesuit, Peter had a genius for combining academic work with a wonderful pastoral spirit. He founded the first German-speaking Jesuit college and published many academic works.

One of Peter's burning desires was to work for the renewal and spread of the Catholic Church in the wake of Protestantism. He tirelessly preached, taught, and wrote to help people understand the faith. The catechism that he wrote in Germany became hugely influential. Peter was a delegate to the Council of Trent and promoted its program of reform. He also spread devotion to the Blessed Virgin Mary and is credited with adding to the Hail Mary the words, "Holy Mary, Mother of God, pray for us sinners." Pope Pius XI canonized him in 1925 and declared him a Doctor of the Church.

Reflection

Peter lived in a time when many people were leaving the Church after the Protestant Reformation. Like Peter, we too live in an age where many Catholics are leaving the Church. This is often due to a lack of knowledge about the faith, which leaves people vulnerable to other voices. We can never stop growing in knowledge of the faith. How much time do I spend in serious study of the faith so as to grow in understanding?

Prayer

Saint Peter Canisius, inspire us with a love like yours for the truth and intercede for those who are seeking the light of Christ. Amen.

DECEMBER 22

Saint Marguerite d'Youville

October 15, 1701–December 23, 1771
Feast: October 16 (Canada)
Patron: Widows, difficult marriages, death of young children

Marguerite was born in Quebec, the eldest of six children. Seven years later her father died, leaving the family very poor. She married Francois d'Youville when she was twenty-one years old. Her mother-in-law made life miserable for Marguerite. Even worse, Francois was emotionally distant and was often away from home because he was involved in the illegal liquor trade. The couple had six children, four of whom died in infancy. When Marguerite was pregnant with their sixth child, she cared for her ill husband until his death in 1730, leaving her with a huge debt.

While she cared for her children, Marguerite also ran a shop to pay off her husband's debts. But she still found time to visit the poor in the hospital and to beg for money to bury hanged criminals. In 1737, three young women joined Marguerite in her work for the poor and thus began the Congregation of the Sisters of Charity of Montreal, or the "Grey Nuns." Marguerite was asked to take over Montreal's run-down Charon Brothers Hospital. She and the other sisters cared for everyone who needed help, including the poor, lepers, and orphans. The sisters' loving care for their patients set a high standard for hospital care in North America.

Reflection

When Saint John XXIII beatified Marguerite in 1959, he called her "Mother of Universal Charity." After enduring so much suffering in her own life, Marguerite was still able to receive and share God's love with others without counting the cost. Even in our suffering, God's grace can make it possible for us to reach out to others who are suffering.

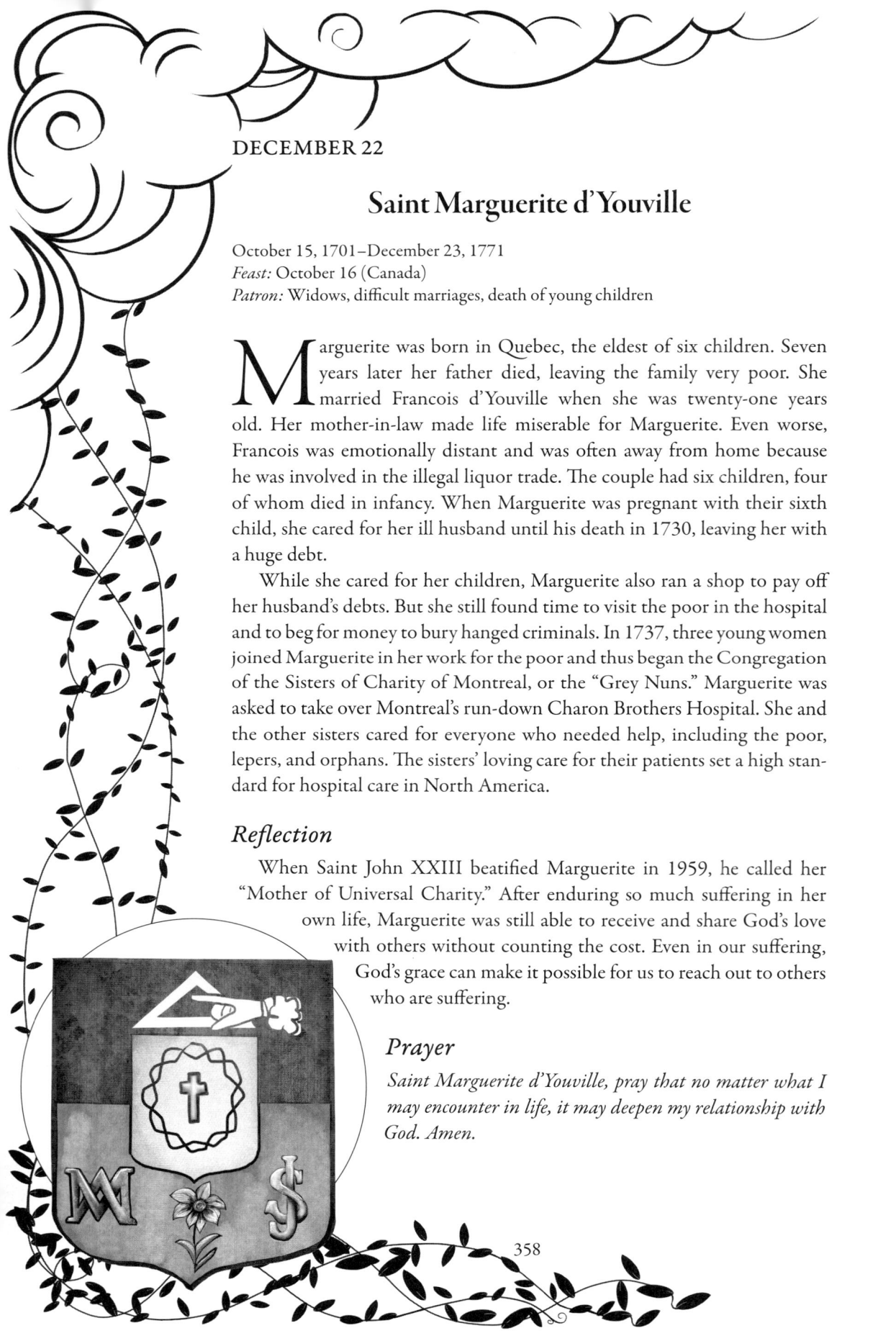

Prayer

Saint Marguerite d'Youville, pray that no matter what I may encounter in life, it may deepen my relationship with God. Amen.

DECEMBER 23

Saint John of Kanty

June 23, 1390–December 24, 1473
Feast: December 23
Patron: Poland and Lithuania, teachers, students, priests

John was a scholar-saint. He was born near Kanty in Poland and spent most of his life teaching in the University of Kraków. As a young man, he completed higher studies in philosophy and then studied for the priesthood. After ordination, John began teaching and was known for his profound understanding of Catholic doctrine. At one point, some rivals forced him out of his professorship, and he was assigned to a parish. He accepted this gracefully, and, although he was new to pastoral ministry, he gradually won the people's hearts with his goodness and kindness. After a few years he returned to teaching.

John's outstanding concern for the needy made him popular with the poor of Kraków, who always knew that his goods and money were at their disposal. By giving away most of what he owned and keeping only what he needed, John lived an austere and simple way of life. Once, he was even turned away from a restaurant because his cassock was so worn! When people worried that John's way of life would weaken his health, he always reminded them that the Desert Fathers lived long lives despite their penance and fasting. John indeed lived a long life, dying at the age of eighty-three on Christmas Eve.

Reflection

John's teaching often focused on Sacred Scripture. The word of God in the Bible nourishes our minds and hearts so that we may live as true Christians. How can I put aside some time every day to read and pray with Scripture?

Prayer

Saint John of Kanty, pray for us that we too may live a simple life, share our goods with others, and let God's word nourish us each day. Amen.

DECEMBER 24

Saint Antônio de Sant'Anna Galvão

1739–December 23, 1822
Feast: May 11
Patron: Vocational discernment, pregnant women

Antônio Galvão was born into a loving and devout Catholic family in São Paulo, Brazil. The fourth of ten children, he entered the Jesuit seminary when he was only thirteen years old. However, Anthony's plans were interrupted when the Jesuits had to return to Portugal. He decided to pursue religious life with the Franciscans instead and made his profession in 1761. He took the religious name Frei (or friar) Antônio de Sant'Anna out of respect for his family's great devotion to Saint Anne, the mother of Mary.

Frei Galvão, as he is known in Brazil, was ordained a priest in 1762 and was assigned to be the preacher, confessor, and porter of a convent. He went on to help found a new religious order for women, the congregation of Our Lady of the Conception of Divine Providence. He became so well-known in São Paulo that people would come to hear his preaching, to ask for his prayers, and even to receive physical healing. His tomb in São Paulo continues to be a destination for pilgrims to obtain graces through the intercession of this holy, simple friar.

Reflection

When Antônio first joined the Jesuits, he probably had no idea how many twists and turns his life would take. He would change religious orders, help found a religious congregation, be appointed novice master, and found a Franciscan convent, among other things! Amid all of these changes, Antônio trusted that holiness lies in being faithful to what the Lord asks. In what ways can I grow in my trust in God when my life takes a new turn?

Prayer

Saint Antônio de Sant'Anna Galvão, intercede for me, that I may trust in God in the ordinary moments of life. Amen.

DECEMBER 25

Saint Albert Chmielowski

August 20, 1845–December 25, 1916
Feast: June 17
Patron: Artists, the poor

In 1989, Saint John Paul II canonized Brother Albert Chmielowski, who had inspired his own vocation. Fellow Poles, both men had been immersed in the world of art and culture before answering God's call. Born near Kraków and named Adam, the future Brother Albert's parents died when he was young. At age eighteen, he lost a leg in the January Uprising against the rule of the Russian Empire. Adam then left Poland and became a painter. He returned to Kraków in 1874 and was one of Poland's most well-known artists. His most famous work is the *Ecce Homo*, depicting Christ wearing the crown of thorns.

A devout Catholic, Adam tried to join the Jesuits, but health problems forced him to leave, and he returned to painting. In 1887, Adam gave up his career as an artist to become "Brother Albert" as a Third Order Franciscan. He lived in Kraków's homeless shelter—and was soon running it. Within a year, he had founded the Servants of the Poor, a Franciscan Third Order congregation, now known as the Albertines. A few years later, he established the feminine branch with co-foundress Blessed Maria Jabłońska. The Albertine brothers and sisters devoted themselves to caring for the poor, sick, mentally ill, and elderly. Albert died in the Kraków homeless shelter on Christmas Day.

Reflection

As a young priest, Saint John Paul II wrote a play about Albert titled, "Our God's Brother." Truly this humble man was a brother of God. Not only was he attentive to the physical needs of the poor but, like Jesus, he also tended to their spiritual hunger. Am I attentive to the spiritual and material needs of others?

Prayer

Saint Albert Chmielowski, pray that I may have a heart open to helping others in any need. Amen.

DECEMBER 26

Saint Stephen

c. 34 AD
Feast: December 26
Patron: Deacons, horses, masons, protection against sudden death

As the first Christian martyr, Stephen holds a special place in early Christian history. His story is found in the Acts of the Apostles. He was probably a Hellenistic Jew, since his name is Greek (*"stephanos"* means "crown"), and he was one of those appointed as deacons to serve the Hellenist widows (see Acts 6:1–6). Full of zeal, Stephen publicly proclaimed Jesus and even disputed with people about the truth of the Gospel.

Angered at Stephen's boldness and effectiveness in preaching the Gospel, his opponents dragged him before the Sanhedrin. Stephen then gave a very long speech recounting the history of Israel and accused his fellow Jews of not keeping the Law when they failed to recognize Jesus as the Messiah. Enraged, his persecutors stoned him to death. As he died, he prayed, "Lord, do not hold this sin against them" (Acts 7:60). Saint Augustine recounts many miracles that occurred when Stephen's relics were brought to North Africa, including the conversion of an obstinate unbeliever (see *The City of God,* Book 22, chap. 8).

Reflection

When Stephen was being stoned, the witnesses "laid their coats at the feet of a young man named Saul. . . . And Saul approved of their killing him" (Acts 7:58, 8:1). Saul became Saint Paul. While we don't know the secrets of how God distributes graces, perhaps Paul was converted through Stephen's intercession. We belong to the Communion of Saints, that mysterious union of the Church on earth with the Church in heaven. When we offer our prayers and sacrifices to God, he can use them to bring graces to others.

Prayer

Saint Stephen, pray that we may be courageous witnesses of the Gospel in our day, so that many others will come to believe in Jesus. Amen.

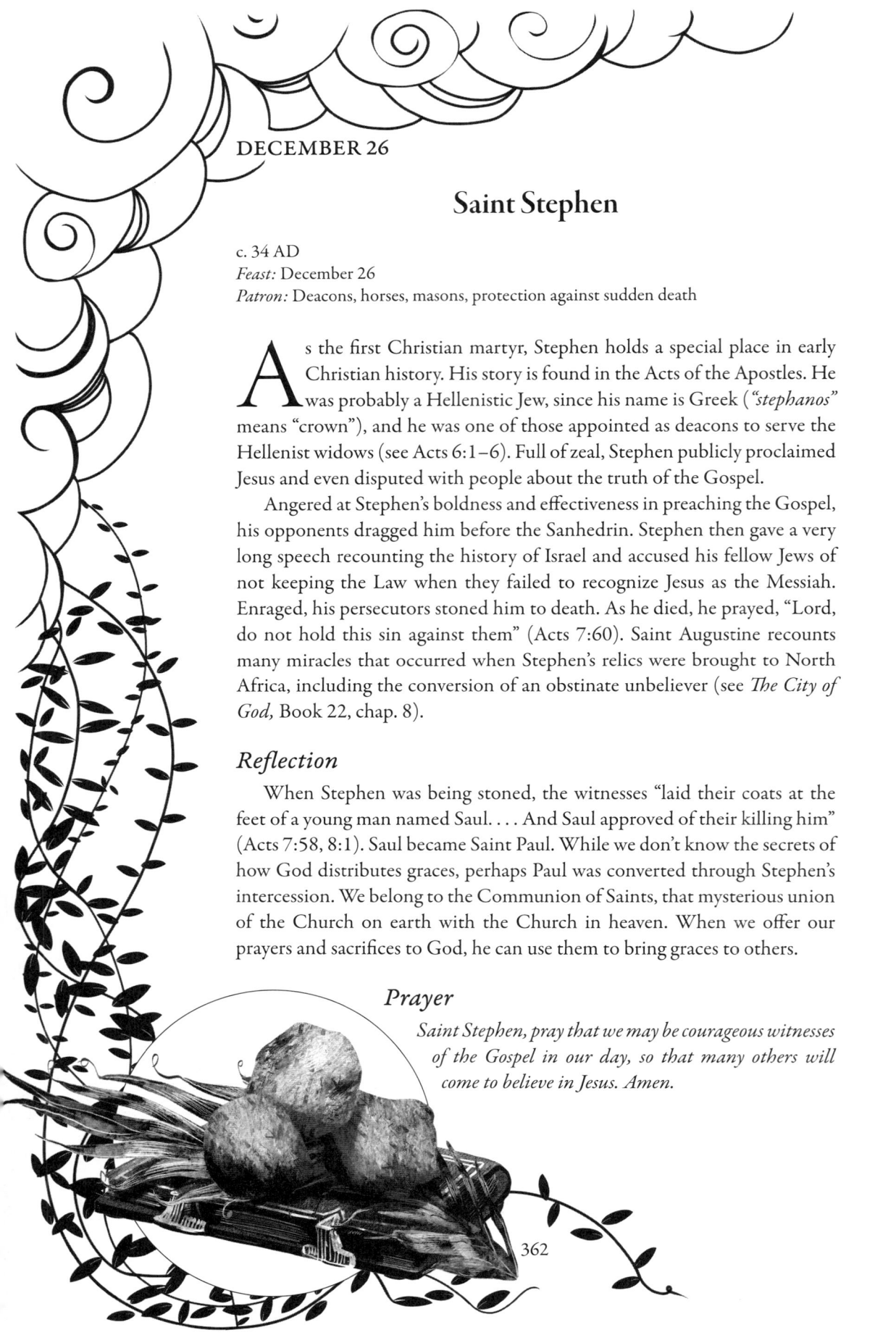

DECEMBER 27

Saint John, the Apostle

First Century
Feast: December 27
Patron: Art dealers, booksellers, engravers, paper makers, printers, publishers, writers

John the Apostle, traditionally held to be the author of the fourth Gospel, was probably the youngest of the twelve apostles. Explicitly named in the Gospels, his parents were Zebedee and Salome. Jesus called John and his older brother, James, to follow him after they witnessed a miraculous catch of fish (see Lk 5:1–11). Before following Jesus, John is believed to have been one of John the Baptist's disciples. As one of the apostles chosen by Jesus, John held a special place among the twelve. He was one of the few present at the Transfiguration (see Mt 17:1). John was also the only apostle to remain with Jesus at the Cross.

After Jesus' ascension, John worked with Peter and the other apostles to establish the Church in Jerusalem. According to second- and third-century testimony, John then went to Ephesus with Mary. Among his disciples was Saint Polycarp. In his old age, John was exiled to the island of Patmos, where it is believed he received the visions related in the Book of Revelation. According to Saint Jerome, in John's old age, his preaching consisted of a single message: "Little children, love one another."

Reflection

According to tradition, the "beloved disciple" named in the Gospel of John is believed to have been John himself. John knew he was loved by the Lord, and this became the foundation of his very identity. His familiarity with God's love for him made him an effective witness of the Gospel. Sometimes, it's easy to forget that I, too, am a beloved disciple of Jesus. How might the Lord be inviting me to a deeper faith in his love for me?

Prayer

Saint John the Apostle, pray that I may be ever convinced of God's love for me. Amen.

DECEMBER 28

Blessed Sára Salkaházi

May 11, 1899–December 27, 1944
Feast: May 11
Patron: Social workers, journalists

Strong-willed, chain-smoking Sára Salkaházi did not always want to be a nun. The talented daughter of hotel owners, Sára tried out many careers, including teacher, bookbinder, milliner, journalist, and activist. After ending a marriage engagement, Sára applied to enter the Sisters of Social Service and was admitted at age thirty. In her first years as a sister, she juggled an astounding number of roles, including teacher, editor of a Catholic women's journal, and manager of a bookstore and homeless shelter. Worn out, Sára was not permitted by her worried superiors to renew her vows. Discouraged, she nevertheless persevered until she was permitted to make vows again.

As the Nazi ideology gained steam in Hungary, Sára wrote against it. She and her sisters hid many Jewish refugees from persecution in their hostels. In 1943, recognizing the danger her community was in, Sára privately offered her life to Christ so that her sisters' lives might be spared. About a year later, Nazis invaded Hungary and soon raided one of the hostels she managed. Sára and her Jewish refugees were shot on the bank of the Danube and then thrown into the river. None of the other Sisters of Social Service were harmed. Sára is credited with saving one hundred Jews, and more than one thousand of her sisters.

Reflection

Despite personal setbacks and enormous challenges, Sára persevered in her vocation. She gave her life for others, first by sacrificing herself in small ways and ultimately by offering her very life. What daily challenges can I offer as small sacrifices to benefit others?

Prayer

Blessed Sára Salkaházi, may I seek and live out my personal vocation, as you did, and persevere in it despite my daily challenges. Amen.

DECEMBER 29

Saint Thomas Becket

December 21, 1118–December 29, 1170
Feast: December 29
Patron: Secular clergy

King Henry II of England relied greatly on his friend and chancellor, Thomas Becket. A minor cleric who had formerly served the archdeacon of Canterbury, Thomas showed himself wise and tireless in the service of his royal patron. But the proud and worldly Thomas was also a man of prayer. At the death of Theobald, archbishop of Canterbury, the king asked Thomas to take on the additional position. Thomas warned Henry that he could not serve Church and state with equal loyalties. However, at the urging of the papal legate, Thomas eventually gave in.

True to his word, Thomas soon abandoned his worldly lifestyle and, against Henry's wishes, resigned his chancellorship. A long period of struggle over the Church's rights followed. At one point, Thomas fled to France for seven years. When he returned to England, he continued upholding the Church's rights. King Henry raged, "Will no one rid me of this troublesome priest?" Taking this as a mandate, four knights traveled to Canterbury and slew Thomas in the cathedral. Thomas was soon canonized, and Canterbury became a destination for pilgrimages. Remorse and popular sentiment even pressured King Henry to do public penance at his former friend's tomb.

Reflection

Thomas could have enjoyed the pleasures and honors of friendship with King Henry II, but he preferred friendship with God. Sometimes we have to choose between what the Church teaches and what our culture encourages. Our choice may not involve a complete about-face such as Thomas experienced, but it still may be costly. At such moments, God's grace will be enough for us (see 2 Cor 12:9).

Prayer

Saint Thomas Becket, obtain for me the grace to always see clearly and do diligently what the Lord expects of me. Amen.

DECEMBER 30

Blessed Maria Gabriella Sagheddu

March 17, 1914–April 23, 1939
Feast: April 23
Patron: The sick and poor, death of parents, ecumenism

The daughter of a shepherd, Maria Sagheddu was born in Dorgali, Sardinia, in Italy. Strong-willed and stubborn as a child, Maria matured into a gentle and reserved young woman who devoted herself to prayer. She also joined the Catholic Action movement and committed herself to acts of charity. At twenty-one, Maria decided to enter a Trappist monastery. She had a spirit of simple humility and self-sacrifice, often saying to God, "Do what you want with me!"

One day the abbess, Mother Maria Pia Gullini, asked the community to pray and offer sacrifices on behalf of unity among Christians. Maria was moved by the request, and decided to offer her life for the cause of ecumenism. Soon after, Maria contracted tuberculosis. The once vibrant and healthy girl lived only fifteen more months. She spent her last months in prayer, offering up her suffering with the intention that all Christians might be united. In 1983 Saint John Paul II beatified Maria on the Feast of the Conversion of Saint Paul, which concludes the Week of Prayer for Christian Unity.

Reflection

Saint John Paul II hailed "Blessed Maria Gabriella of Unity" as a model for all Christians. In Maria's time, ecumenism was a novel concept in Italy, and Maria had never personally experienced the effects of disunity among Christians. Nevertheless, she understood the importance of Christian unity because she understood God's love and the Gospel message. Her selfless offering of her life was an act of love for her fellow Christians and for God. How can I help to promote Christian unity?

Prayer

Blessed Maria Gabriella Sagheddu, help me to be inspired to pray and offer sacrifices for unity among Christians. Amen.

DECEMBER 31

Saint Sylvester I

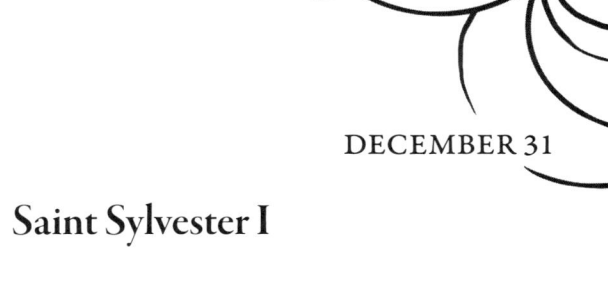

285–335
Feast: December 31
Patron: The Pontifical Equestrian Order of Saint Sylvester, new beginnings

Sylvester I was pope from 314 until his death at the end of 335. As a young man, he lived through Diocletian's terrible persecution of the Church. In 313, the Emperor Constantine issued the Edict of Milan, which ended the Roman persecutions against the Church. Sylvester became pope immediately after this monumental change and he wisely guided the Church through this crucial time of transition. Christians were now allowed to practice their faith freely, but the changes also precipitated the spread of heresies. In 325, the Council of Nicea was assembled and taught the orthodox faith against Arianism. Sylvester sent two papal legates who approved the Council's decrees.

Constantine took an active part in building some important churches in Rome, such as Saint Peter's and Saint John Lateran. Sylvester oversaw these projects; yet the danger of the emperor's meddling in Church affairs also started to emerge. As a holy pastor, Sylvester did his best to help the Church flourish in freedom and to inspire the faithful to greater fervor. One of the first non-martyr Christians to be canonized, the saintly pope was buried in the Catacombs of Saint Priscilla.

Reflection

With his feast on the last day of the calendar year, Sylvester can help us make the transition from year to year in a holy way. He reminds us of the value of time because our life on earth is fleeting. As we set goals and make resolutions for the coming year, we can ask him for the most important grace of all: eternal life with God.

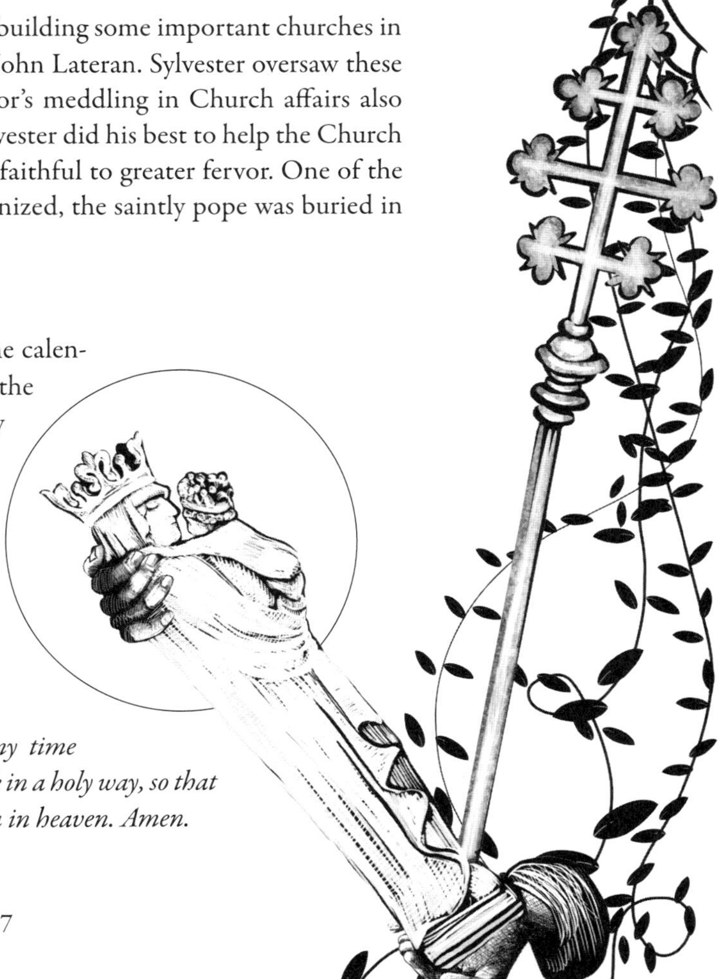

Prayer

Saint Sylvester, pray that I may use my time wisely. Help me to live this next year of life in a holy way, so that one day I may attain eternal life with you in heaven. Amen.

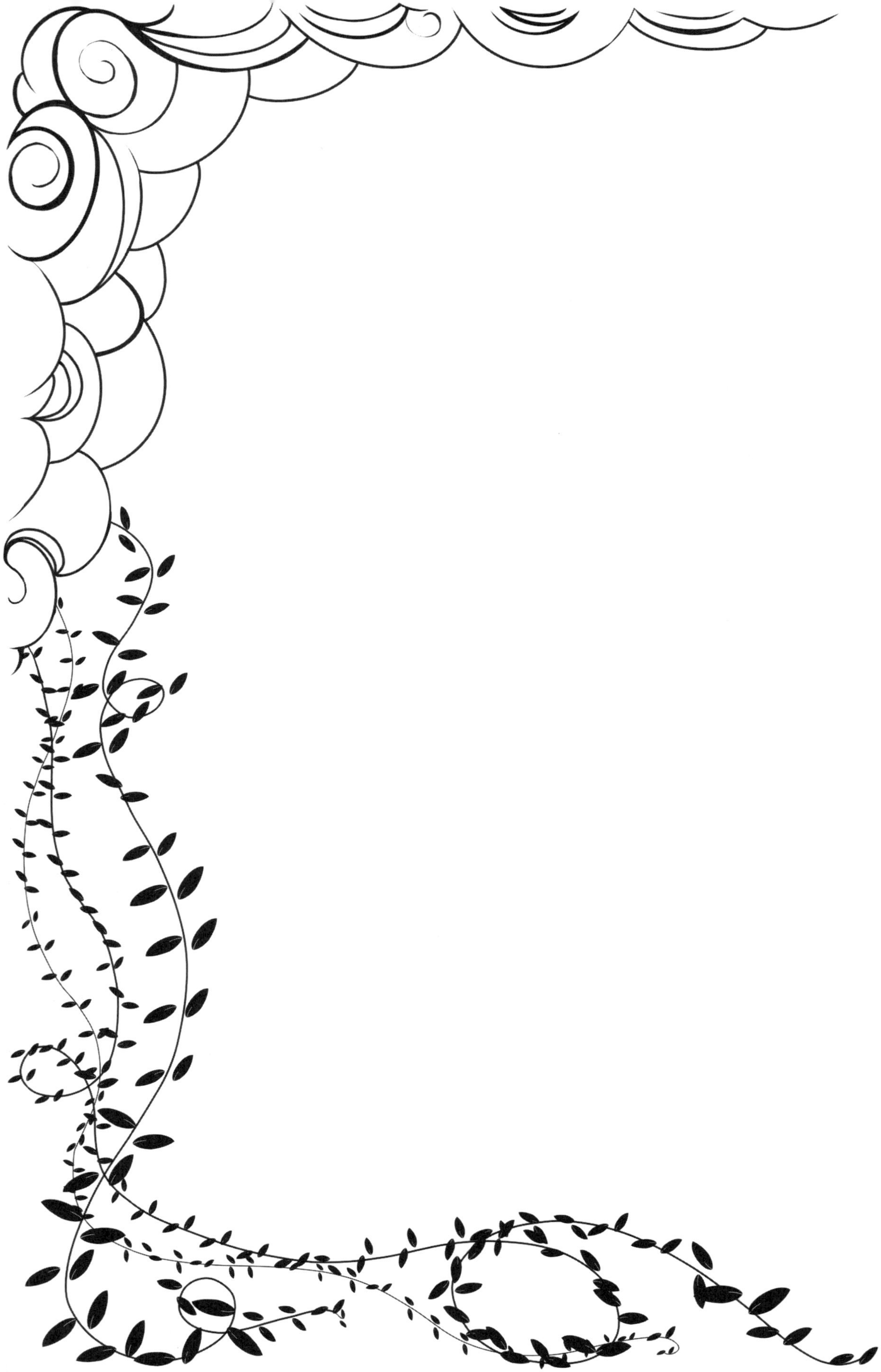

APPENDIX OF PRAYERS

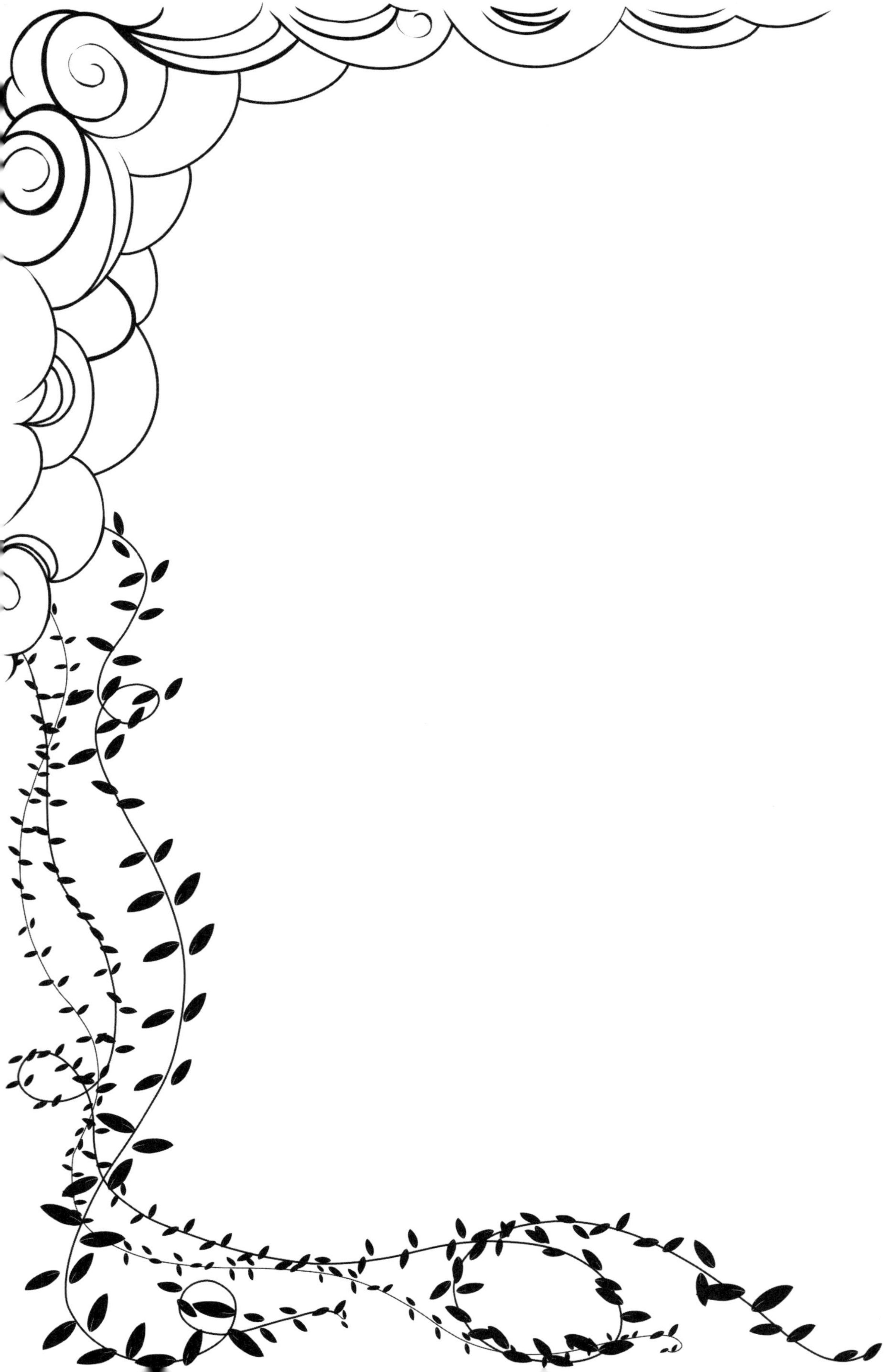

HOLINESS AS BEAUTY

There is unmistakable beauty at the very core of every human heart.

In our day-to-day lives we can feel pushed and pulled by the hundreds of things clamoring for our attention. Through all the noise, we easily miss the beauty that radiates from the center of our beings and tells the story that we are precious, unrepeatable children of Almighty God. We miss how our personal stories fit into the larger divine narrative of salvation history, and how our stories resemble the glorious paschal mystery: the life, death, and resurrection of Jesus Christ.

The saints in this book lived lives just like ours, but they lived in such a way that their interior beauty became more and more evident. They knew how it feels to hope, to be in distress, to worry, to pray and plead with God. They knew how hard it is to forgive, especially family. But they lived all of this in such a way that they allowed the beauty of God's grace to envelop and transform every aspect of their lives.

The bold, distinctive character of the art and relatable stories of this volume are meant to encourage and strengthen you in your inner self (see Eph 3:16). Each day includes a prayer to ask the saint's intercession, and this appendix provides prayers written *by* the saints so that you can learn from their way of praying.

May you become holy—boldly and uniquely who God created you to be in Christ. In this way, your unmistakable beauty will "shine like stars in the world, as you hold on to the word of life" (Phil 2:15).

Prayer to the Holy Trinity

O my God, Trinity whom I adore, help me to forget myself completely and to establish myself in you, as still and at peace as if my soul were already in eternity. Let nothing disturb my peace nor draw me away from you, O my unchangeable One, but let every minute carry me further into the depths of your mystery!

Give peace to my soul; make it your heaven, your beloved abode, and the place of your rest. Let me never leave you there alone; but keep me there totally present, completely vigilant in my faith, totally in adoration, and wholly surrendered to your creative action.

O my beloved Christ, crucified for love, I want to be the spouse of your heart. I long to cover you with glory, to love you . . . even unto death! But I feel my weakness. I ask you to clothe me with yourself, to identify my soul with all the movements of your soul, to submerge me, to fill me, to substitute yourself for me, so that my life may be only a radiance of your life. Enter me as Adorer, as Redeemer, and as Savior.

O Eternal Word, utterance of my God, I want to spend my life listening to you, I want to become totally teachable so that I might learn everything from you. Through all darkness, all emptiness, and all helplessness, I want to be centered on you always and remain in your great light; O my beloved Star, make me so captivated that I no longer move away from your radiance.

O consuming Fire, Spirit of love, let it be done that an incarnation of the Word may occur again in my soul. May I be for him another humanity in whom he may renew his whole mystery. And you, O Father, incline yourself toward your little creature, cover her in your shadow and see in her only the Beloved in whom you are well pleased.

O my "Three," my all, my beatitude, infinite Solitude, Immensity in which I lose myself, I surrender myself to you as your prey. Bury yourself in me so that I may bury myself in you, until I go to contemplate in your light the abyss of your grandeur.

Saint Elizabeth of the Trinity,
November 21, 1904

Invocations of Trust

O my God, my only hope, I have placed all my trust in you, and I know I shall not be disappointed (317).

I know the full power of your mercy, and I trust that you will give me everything your weak child needs (898).

O Jesus, concealed in the Blessed Sacrament of the Altar, my only love and mercy, I commend to you all the needs of my body and soul. You can help me, because you are mercy itself. In you lies all my hope (1751).

Saint Faustina

Prayer for Holiness of Life

Godhead! Godhead!
Eternal Godhead!
I proclaim and do not deny it:
you are a peaceful sea
in which the spirit feeds and is nourished
while resting in you.
Unite our will with your will
in love's affection and union
so that we will want for nothing
other than becoming holy.

Saint Catherine of Siena

God of All Glory

Great God of all glory and you, my Lord Jesus Christ, I beseech you to enlighten me and dispel the darkness of my spirit; to give me a pure faith, firm hope, and perfect charity. O my God, grant that I may come to know you better and do all things according to your light and in conformity to your most holy will. Amen.

Saint Francis of Assisi

My God, I Give You This Day

My God, I give you this day. I offer you, now, all the good that I do, and I promise to accept, for love of you, all the difficulties I may encounter. Help me to act this day in a manner pleasing to you. Amen.

Saint Francis de Sales

Lord, I Am Yours

Lord, I am yours, and I want to belong to no one but you.
My soul is yours, and I want to live only by you.
My will is yours, and I want to love only for you.

I want to love you as my first cause, since I am from you.
I want to love you as my final end and eternal rest, because I am for you.
I want to love you more than my own being, since my being subsists
    because of you.
I want to love you more than myself, because I am all yours
    and all in you. Amen.

Saint Francis de Sales

Enter My Life

Open, O doors and bolts of my heart, that Christ the King
    of Glory may enter!
Enter, O my Light, and enlighten my darkness;
Enter, O my Life, and resurrect my deadness;
Enter, O my Physician, and heal my wounds;
Enter, O Divine Fire, and burn up the thorns of my sins;
Ignite my inward parts and my heart with the flame of Thy love;
Enter, O my King, and destroy in me the kingdom of sin;
Sit on the throne of my heart and reign in me alone,
    O my King and Lord.

*Dimitri of Rostov (1651–1709),
canonized a saint in the Russian Orthodox Church*

A Morning Offering

O my God! I offer You all my actions this day for the intentions and for the glory of the Sacred Heart of Jesus. I desire to sanctify every beat of my heart, my every thought, my simplest works, by uniting them to his infinite merits; and I wish to make reparation for my sins by casting them into the furnace of his merciful love. O my God! I ask you for myself and for those whom I hold dear, the grace to fulfill perfectly your holy will, to accept for love of you the joys and sorrows of this passing life.

Saint Thérèse of Lisieux

You Are My Refuge

Hail, Sacred Heart of Jesus, living and strengthening source of eternal life, infinite treasury of the divinity, burning furnace of divine love! You are my refuge and my sanctuary. My loving Savior, consume my heart in that burning fire with which your own heart is inflamed. Pour into my soul those graces that flow from your love. Let my heart be so united with yours that our wills may be one, and my will in all things be conformed with yours. May your will be the guide and rule of my desires and of my actions. Amen.

Saint Gertrude the Great

Christ Has No Body But Yours

Christ has no body now on earth but yours,
no hands but yours, no feet but yours.
Yours are the eyes through which
Christ's compassion looks out on the world,
yours are the feet with which
he is to go about doing good,
and yours are the hands with which
he is to bless us now.
Christ has no body now on earth but yours.

Attributed to Saint Teresa of Ávila

In Thanksgiving

O Jesus, eternal God, thank you for your countless graces and blessings. Let every beat of my heart be a new hymn of thanksgiving to you, O God. Let every drop of my blood circulate for you, Lord. My soul is one hymn in adoration of your mercy. I love you, God, for yourself alone (1794).

Saint Faustina

Prayer of Trust

I fly to your mercy, compassionate God, who alone are good. Although my misery is great and my offenses are many, I trust in your mercy because you are the God of mercy; and, from time immemorial, it has never been heard of, nor do heaven or earth remember, that a soul trusting in your mercy has been disappointed.

O God of compassion, you alone can justify me, and you will never reject me when I, contrite, approach your merciful heart, where no one has ever been refused, even if he were the greatest sinner (1730).

Saint Faustina

Christ Be with Us

May the Strength of God direct us.
May the Power of God preserve us.
May the Wisdom of God instruct us.
May the Hand of God protect us.
May the Way of God lead us.
May the Shield of God defend us.
May the Host of God guard us
    against the snares of the evil ones,
    against temptations of the world.
May Christ be with us!
May Christ be before us!
May Christ be in us!
Christ be over all!
May your salvation, Lord,
always be ours,
this day, O Lord, and evermore.

Saint Patrick

Prayer of Saint John Paul II to Saint Pio

Saint Pio, teach us, we pray, humility of heart so that we may be counted among the little ones of the Gospel to whom the Father promised to reveal the mysteries of his kingdom.

Help us to pray without ceasing, certain that God knows what we need even before we ask him.

Obtain for us the eyes of faith that will help us recognize in the poor and suffering the very face of Jesus.

Sustain us in the hour of trouble and trial and, if we fall, let us experience the joy of the Sacrament of forgiveness.

Grant us your tender devotion to Mary, Mother of Jesus and our Mother.

Accompany us on our earthly pilgrimage toward the blessed homeland where we too hope to arrive to contemplate forever the glory of the Father, the Son, and the Holy Spirit. Amen.

On the occasion of Saint Pio's canonization

Help Me Spread Your Fragrance

Dear Jesus, help me to spread your fragrance everywhere I go. Flood my soul with your Spirit and Life. Penetrate and possess my whole being so completely that my life may only be a radiance of yours.

Shine through me, and be so in me that every person I meet may feel your presence in my soul. Let them see no longer me but only Jesus. Stay with me, and then I shall begin to shine as you shine, so to shine as to be a light to others. The light, Jesus, will be all from you; none of it will be mine. It will be you shining on others through me. Let me praise you in the way that you love best, by shining on those around me.

Let me preach you without preaching, not by my words but by my example; by the catching force, the sympathetic influence of what I do, the evident fullness of the love my heart bears for you. Amen.

Saint John Henry Newman

All Glory Be to God

O God, how immense is your richness, wisdom, and knowledge!
How unfathomable are your judgments, how inscrutable your ways!
For who can know your mind, O Lord?
Who could ever be your counselor?
Who could ever be the giver and you the One to repay the gift?
For all things are from you, through you, and in you.
To you, O God, be glory forever. Amen.

Based on Saint Paul's Letter to the Romans (11:33–36)

Grant Me Peace

Lord, grant me your peace, which is beyond all understanding
and which will keep my heart and mind in Christ Jesus.
Fill my heart and thoughts with all that is true,
honorable, just, pure, pleasing, gracious,
virtuous, and praiseworthy.
Grant me your peace, O Lord, and may it remain with me always.

Based on Saint Paul's Letter to the Philippians (4:7–9)

Make Us Worthy, Lord

Make us worthy, Lord,
to serve our fellow men
throughout the world,
who live and die in poverty and hunger.
Give them today, through our hands,
their daily bread,
and through our understanding love,
give peace and joy. Amen.

Attributed to Saint Paul VI

May I Be in You

May I see with your eyes.
May I speak with your tongue.
May I hear with your ears.
May I relish what you relish.
May my hands be yours.
May I pray with your words.
May I treat others as you do.
May I participate in the liturgy as you offered yourself: totally.
May I be in you and you in me, to the point that I disappear.
May you use my tongue to sing the praises of God through the ages.
May you use my heart to love him.
May you use me, in my weaknesses and limitations, to proclaim:
"I am the Good Shepherd; what I desire is mercy."

Blessed James Alberione

To Jesus, the Divine Healer

May you be blessed, Divine Master,
because you made yourself similar to us
in order to make us similar to God.
You repaired the ruin
caused by sin and disorder.
You showed us
that we can inherit divine happiness

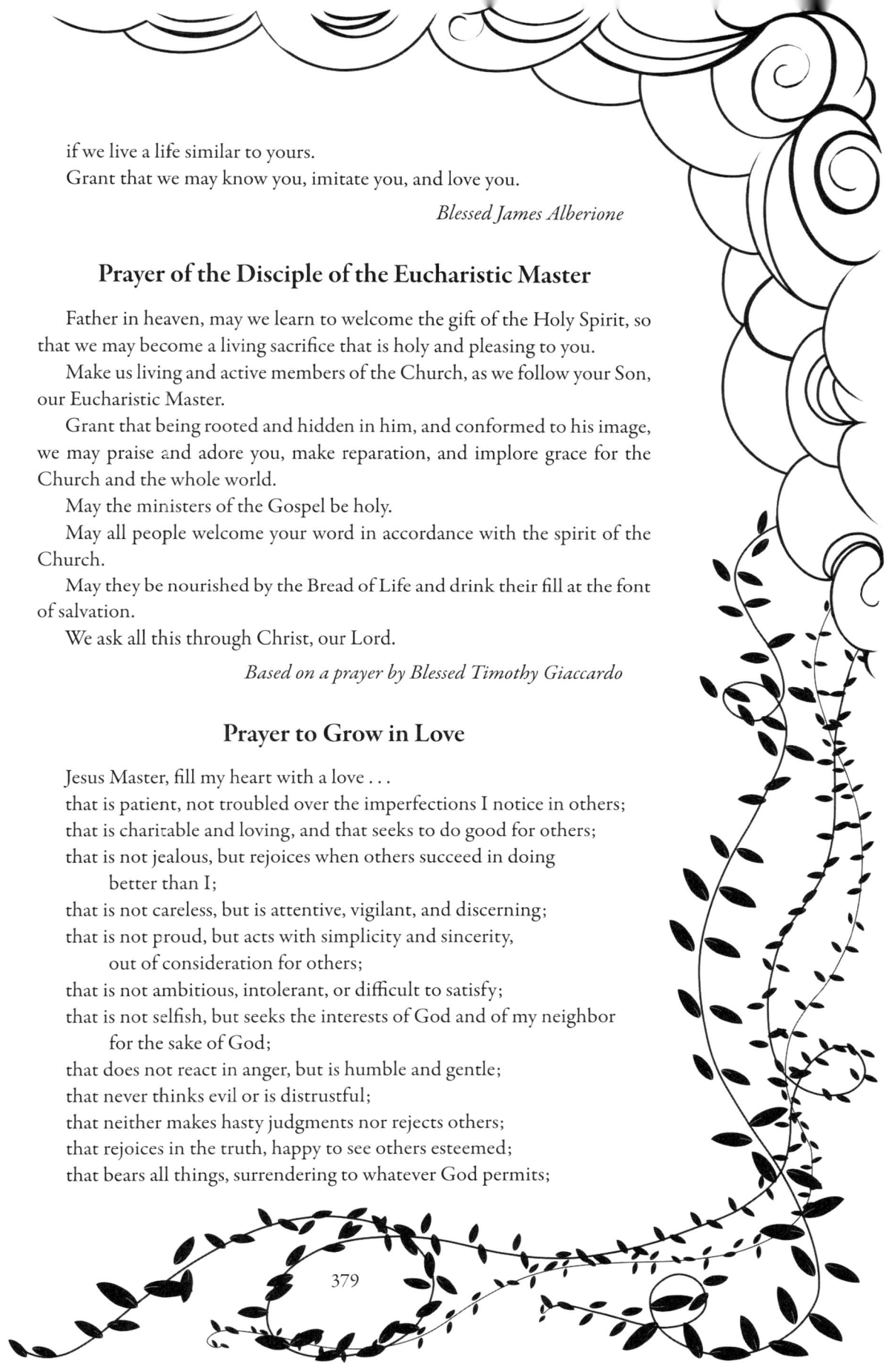

if we live a life similar to yours.
Grant that we may know you, imitate you, and love you.

Blessed James Alberione

Prayer of the Disciple of the Eucharistic Master

Father in heaven, may we learn to welcome the gift of the Holy Spirit, so that we may become a living sacrifice that is holy and pleasing to you.

Make us living and active members of the Church, as we follow your Son, our Eucharistic Master.

Grant that being rooted and hidden in him, and conformed to his image, we may praise and adore you, make reparation, and implore grace for the Church and the whole world.

May the ministers of the Gospel be holy.

May all people welcome your word in accordance with the spirit of the Church.

May they be nourished by the Bread of Life and drink their fill at the font of salvation.

We ask all this through Christ, our Lord.

Based on a prayer by Blessed Timothy Giaccardo

Prayer to Grow in Love

Jesus Master, fill my heart with a love . . .
that is patient, not troubled over the imperfections I notice in others;
that is charitable and loving, and that seeks to do good for others;
that is not jealous, but rejoices when others succeed in doing
    better than I;
that is not careless, but is attentive, vigilant, and discerning;
that is not proud, but acts with simplicity and sincerity,
    out of consideration for others;
that is not ambitious, intolerant, or difficult to satisfy;
that is not selfish, but seeks the interests of God and of my neighbor
    for the sake of God;
that does not react in anger, but is humble and gentle;
that never thinks evil or is distrustful;
that neither makes hasty judgments nor rejects others;
that rejoices in the truth, happy to see others esteemed;
that bears all things, surrendering to whatever God permits;

that believes and hopes in everything—especially in the good
    that exists within others.
Love never ends.

Venerable Mother Thecla Merlo (Based on 1 Corinthians 13)

God Alone Suffices

Let nothing disturb you.
Let nothing frighten you.
All things pass away:
God never changes.
Patience obtains all things.
One who has God lacks nothing.
God alone suffices.

Saint Teresa of Ávila

Mary, Our Guide to Heaven

Virgin full of grace, at Nazareth you lived a simple life, and did not desire anything more. You did not look for ecstasies, miracles, or anything out of the ordinary, O Queen of the elect.

The lowly, the many "little ones" on earth, turn their eyes to you with no fear.

You are the Mother beyond compare who walks by their side, to guide them along the path to heaven. Beloved Mother, in our sorrowful exile, I want to live with you day after day, following your example. I am drawn to contemplate you and to discover the depths of love in your heart. Under your motherly gaze, which teaches me to weep and to rejoice, all my fears vanish! Amen.

Saint Thérèse of Lisieux

To Mary, Mother of Mercy

Virgin full of goodness, Mother of mercy, I entrust to you my body and my soul, my thoughts and my actions, my life and my death.

O my Queen, come to my aid and deliver me from the snares of evil.

Obtain for me the grace to love my Lord Jesus Christ, your Son, with a true and perfect love, and after him, O Mary, to love you with all my heart and above all things. Amen.

Saint Thomas Aquinas

LIST OF CONTRIBUTORS

Mary Emmanuel Alves, FSP: *Jan* 14, *Aug* 1

Emi Magnificat Bratt, FSP: *Jan* 17, *Feb* 6, *Jul* 24, *Sept* 11

Cecilia Cicone: *Apr* 14; *Jun* 18; *Jul* 3, 22; *Aug* 29; *Oct* 25; *Nov* 6; *Dec* 24

Marie Paul Curley, FSP: *Jan* 25; *Apr* 17; *May* 22; *Jul* 7; *Aug* 27, 28; *Sept* 3, 14, 25; *Oct* 4; *Nov* 17

Maria Grace Dateno, FSP: *Feb* 29; *Mar* 27, 30; *Apr* 15, 16, 23; *May* 11; *Jun* 7; *Jul* 8; *Aug* 17, 22; *Sept* 7, 19; *Oct* 31; *Nov* 2, 5, 26; *Dec* 19

Barbara Gerace, FSP: *Sept* 13

Allison Gliot: *Feb* 13; *Mar* 23, 29; *Apr* 10, 27; *May* 1, 5, 10, 30; *Jun* 14; *Jul* 17, 31; *Aug* 31; *Sept* 28; *Nov* 28; *Dec* 3

Susan James Heady, FSP: *Sept* 4, 10

Anne Eileen Heffernan, FSP: *Jan* 5; *Feb* 1, 20; *Mar* 1, 3, 10; *Apr* 5, 19, 20; *May* 16, 19, 27; *Jun* 8; *Nov* 23; *Dec* 29

Kathryn James Hermes, FSP: *Jan* 13, 15; *Mar* 18; *Apr* 9; *Jul* 27; *Aug* 12, 20; *Sept* 6

Mary Lea Hill, FSP: *Apr* 25; *May* 26; *Jul* 10, 13; *Aug* 4, 5, 9; *Sept* 5, 9; *Oct* 10, 15; *Nov* 3; *Dec* 2

Patricia Edward Jablonski, FSP: *Jan* 6, *Feb* 22, *Mar* 4, *May* 13, *Jun* 30, *Oct* 13, *Nov* 16, *Dec* 8

Sandy Lucas: *Jan* 8; *Feb* 12, 24, 27; *Mar* 13; *Jun* 15, 17, 26; *Aug* 14; *Oct* 22; *Nov* 19; *Dec* 12, 17, 25, 28, 30

Emily Beata Marsh, FSP: *Jan* 11, 12, 21, 27, 31; *Feb* 4, 18; *Mar* 15; *Apr* 11, 12; *May* 25; *Aug* 7; *Oct* 6; *Nov* 13

Sean Marie David Mayer, FSP: *Sept* 21, 24

Marlyn Evangelina Monge, FSP: *Aug* 18, *Dec* 14

Mary Martha Moss, FSP: *May* 17, *Jul* 4, *Nov* 8

Theresa Aletheia Noble, FSP: *Jan* 2, 9, 10, 16, 18, 20, 22, 24, 30; *Feb* 2, 3, 7, 9, 10, 14, 15, 16, 19, 21, 26, 28; *Mar* 5, 7, 8, 14; *Jun* 29; *Sept* 18, 29; *Oct* 1, 20; *Nov* 10, 12

Carmen Christi Pompei, FSP: *Feb* 25, *Oct* 7

Susan Maria Sanchez, FSP: *Mar* 9; *Apr* 2; *May* 20; *Oct* 16, 23

Patricia Cora Shaules, FSP: *Jan* 4, *Mar* 17, *Jun* 21, *Nov* 18, *Dec* 22

Marianne Lorraine Trouve, FSP: *Jan* 1, 3, 7, 19, 23, 26, 28; *Feb* 11, 17, 23; *Mar* 2, 6, 11, 12, 16, 19, 21, 25, 26, 28; *Apr* 3, 4, 6, 7, 13, 18, 21, 22, 24, 26, 28, 30; *May* 2, 3, 4, 6, 7, 8, 9, 12, 14, 15, 18, 21, 23, 24, 28, 29, 31; *Jun* 1, 2, 3, 4, 5, 6, 9, 10, 12, 13, 16, 19, 20, 22, 23, 24, 25, 27, 28; *Jul* 2, 5, 9, 11, 12, 14, 15, 16, 18, 19, 20, 21, 23, 26, 28, 30; *Aug* 2, 3, 6, 8, 10, 11, 13, 15, 16, 19, 21, 23, 24, 25, 30; *Sept* 2, 8, 15, 16, 20, 22, 23, 26, 27, 30; *Oct* 3, 5, 9, 11, 12, 14, 17, 19, 21, 24, 26, 27, 28, 29, 30; *Nov* 1, 9, 11, 15, 20, 21, 22, 24, 25, 27, 29, 30; *Dec* 4, 5, 6, 7, 10, 11, 13, 15, 18, 20, 21, 23, 26, 31

Julie Benedicta Turner, FSP: *Jan* 29; *Feb* 5; *Mar* 20, 22, 24, 31; *Apr* 1, 8, 29; *Jun* 11; *Jul* 1, 6, 25, 29; *Aug* 26; *Sept* 1, 12, 17; *Oct* 2, 8; *Nov* 4, 7, 14; *Dec* 9, 16, 27

Christina Miriam Wedgendt, FSP: *Feb* 8

Susan Miriam Wolf, FSP: *Oct* 18, *Dec* 1

Editors: Sean Marie David Mayer, FSP; Maria Grace Dateno, FSP; and Theresa Aletheia Noble, FSP

Illustrator: Danielle Victoria Lussier, FSP

Design: Mary Joseph Peterson, FSP; Regina Frances Dick, FSP; and Linda Salvatore Boccia, FSP

INDICES

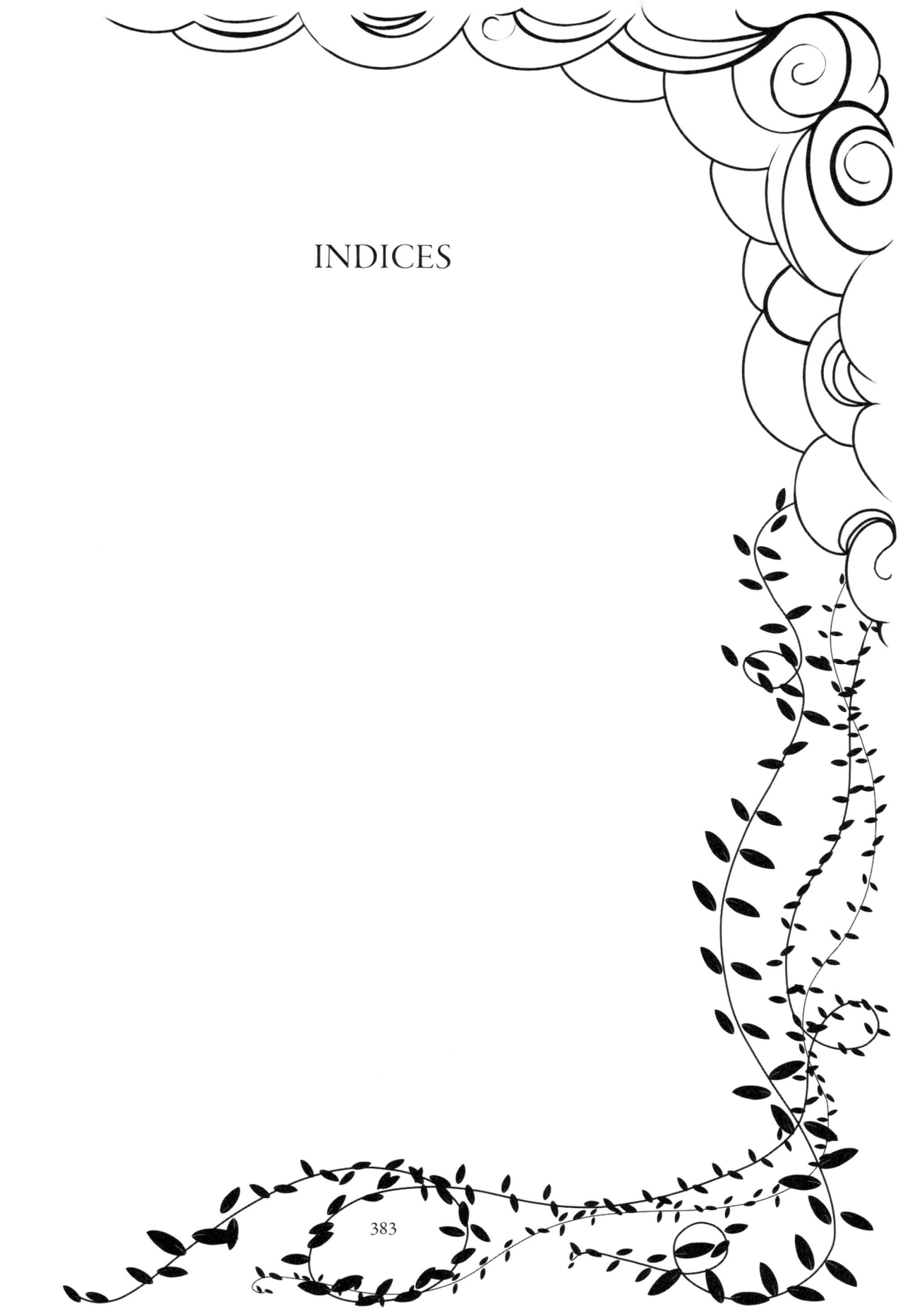

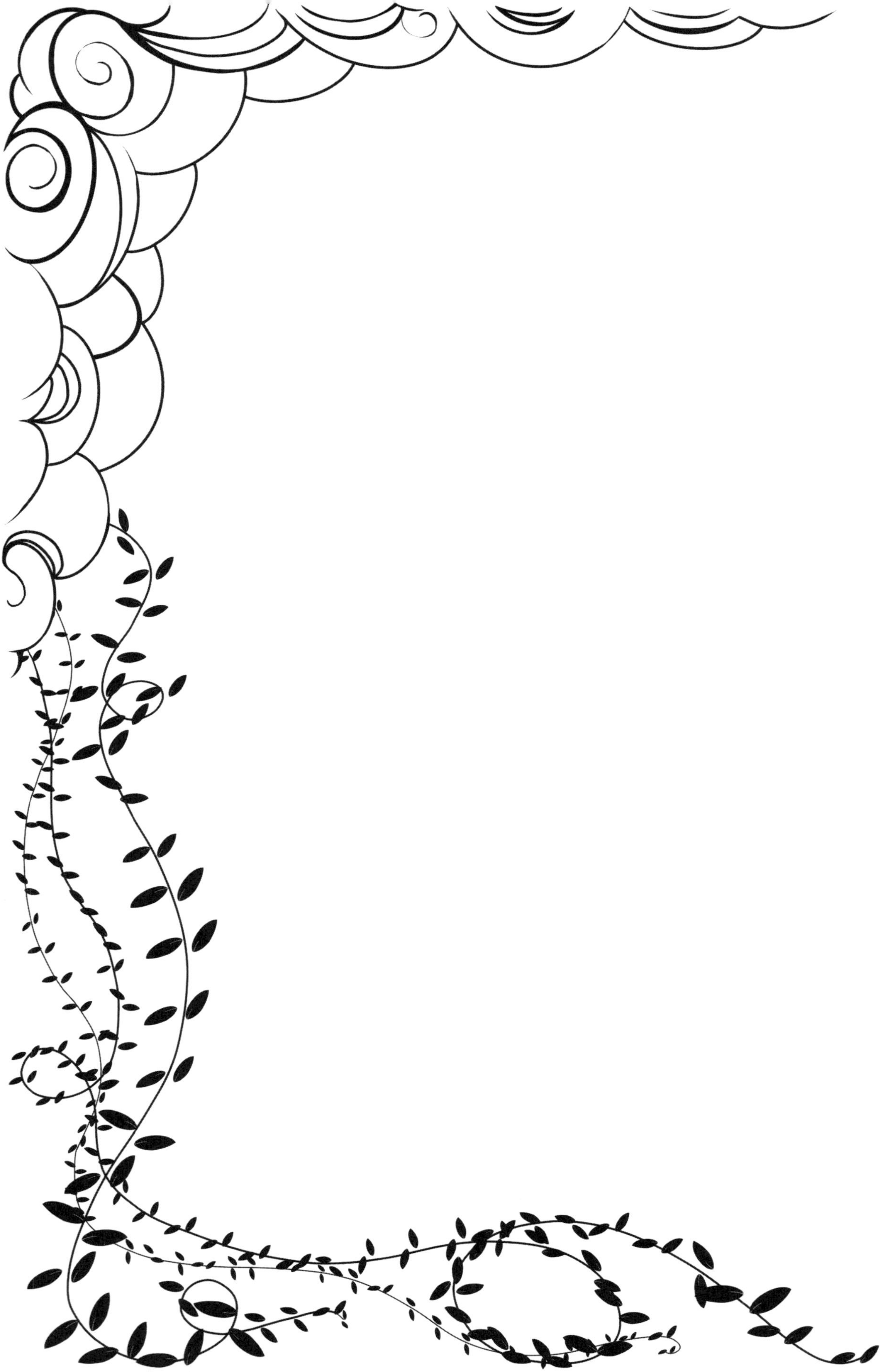

INDEX OF NAMES

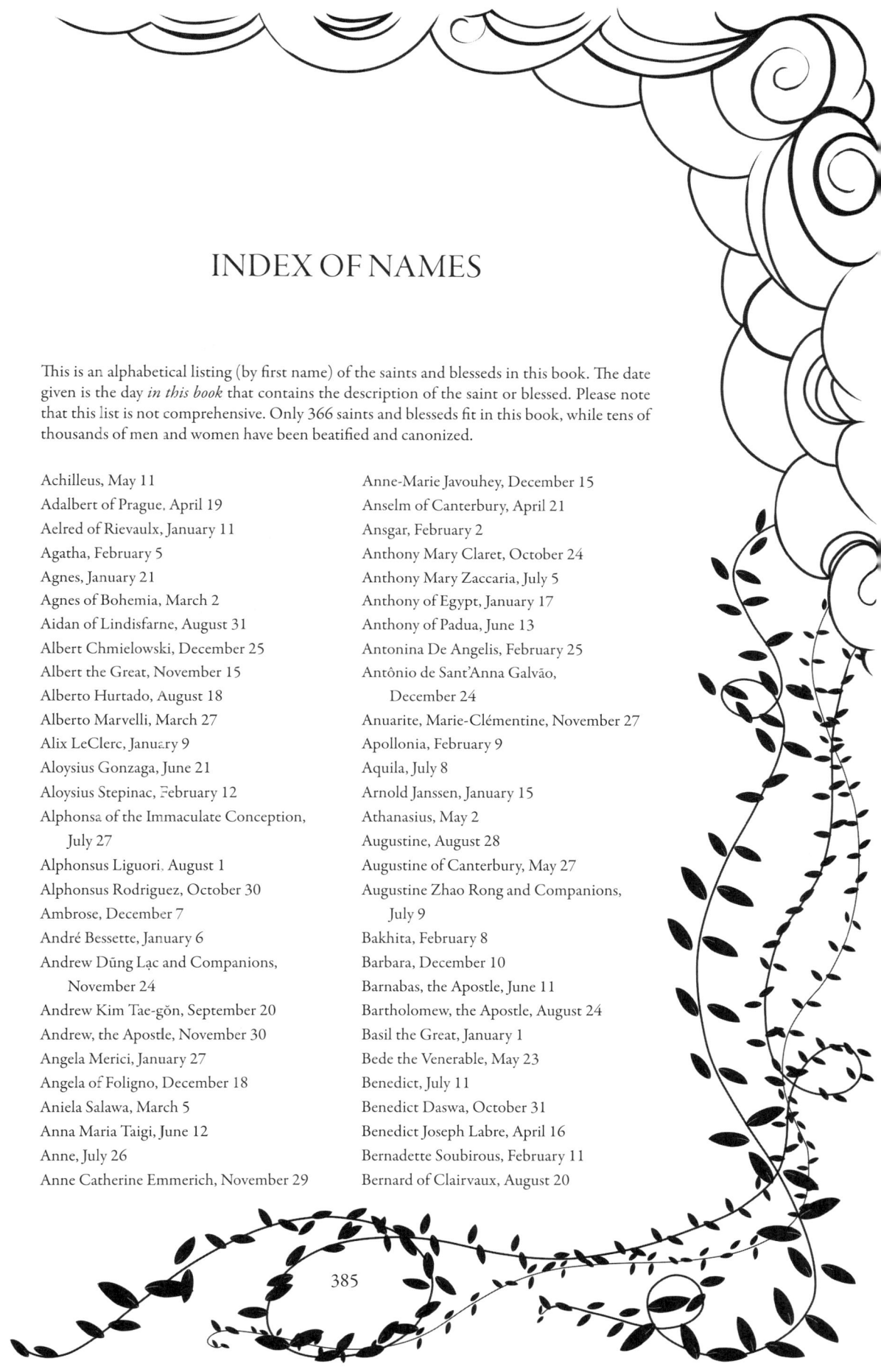

This is an alphabetical listing (by first name) of the saints and blesseds in this book. The date given is the day *in this book* that contains the description of the saint or blessed. Please note that this list is not comprehensive. Only 366 saints and blesseds fit in this book, while tens of thousands of men and women have been beatified and canonized.

Achilleus, May 11
Adalbert of Prague, April 19
Aelred of Rievaulx, January 11
Agatha, February 5
Agnes, January 21
Agnes of Bohemia, March 2
Aidan of Lindisfarne, August 31
Albert Chmielowski, December 25
Albert the Great, November 15
Alberto Hurtado, August 18
Alberto Marvelli, March 27
Alix LeClerc, January 9
Aloysius Gonzaga, June 21
Aloysius Stepinac, February 12
Alphonsa of the Immaculate Conception, July 27
Alphonsus Liguori, August 1
Alphonsus Rodriguez, October 30
Ambrose, December 7
André Bessette, January 6
Andrew Dũng Lạc and Companions, November 24
Andrew Kim Tae-gŏn, September 20
Andrew, the Apostle, November 30
Angela Merici, January 27
Angela of Foligno, December 18
Aniela Salawa, March 5
Anna Maria Taigi, June 12
Anne, July 26
Anne Catherine Emmerich, November 29

Anne-Marie Javouhey, December 15
Anselm of Canterbury, April 21
Ansgar, February 2
Anthony Mary Claret, October 24
Anthony Mary Zaccaria, July 5
Anthony of Egypt, January 17
Anthony of Padua, June 13
Antonina De Angelis, February 25
Antônio de Sant'Anna Galvão, December 24
Anuarite, Marie-Clémentine, November 27
Apollonia, February 9
Aquila, July 8
Arnold Janssen, January 15
Athanasius, May 2
Augustine, August 28
Augustine of Canterbury, May 27
Augustine Zhao Rong and Companions, July 9
Bakhita, February 8
Barbara, December 10
Barnabas, the Apostle, June 11
Bartholomew, the Apostle, August 24
Basil the Great, January 1
Bede the Venerable, May 23
Benedict, July 11
Benedict Daswa, October 31
Benedict Joseph Labre, April 16
Bernadette Soubirous, February 11
Bernard of Clairvaux, August 20

385

Bernardine of Siena, May 20
Beuno, April 20
Blaise, February 3
Bonaventure, July 15
Boniface, June 5
Brendan, May 16
Bridget of Sweden, July 23
Brigid of Ireland, February 1
Cajetan, August 7
Callistus, October 14
Camillus de Lellis, July 14
Canadian Martyrs, October 19
Caridad Brader, February 27
Carlo Gnocchi, February 28
Carlos Manuel Cecilio Rodríguez Santiago, July 13
Casimir, March 4
Catherine Labouré, December 8
Catherine of Alexandria, November 25
Catherine of Bologna, June 10
Catherine of Genoa, September 15
Catherine of Saint Augustine, May 8
Catherine of Siena, April 29
Catherine of Sweden, March 24
Cecilia, November 22
Celine Chludzińska Borzęcka, September 6
Charbel Makhlouf, July 24
Charles Borromeo, November 4
Charles de Foucauld, December 1
Charles Lwanga and Companions, June 3
Chiara Badano, October 7
Christopher, November 28
Clare of Assisi, August 11
Claude de la Colombière, February 15
Claudine Thévenet, November 2
Clement I, November 20
Clement Mary Hofbauer, March 15
Clemente Vismara, June 15
Clotilda, June 7
Colette, March 6
Columba, June 8
Columban, November 23
Compiègne, Martyrs of, November 1
Cosmas, September 26

Cristóbal Magallanes and Companions, May 21
Cyprian, September 16
Cyril, February 14
Cyril of Alexandria, June 27
Cyril of Jerusalem, March 18
Damasus I, December 11
Damian, September 26
Damien of Molokai, May 10
Daniel Comboni, September 10
David of Wales, March 1
Dina Bélanger, September 4
Dominic, August 8
Dominic Savio, May 6
Dulce Lopes Pontes, March 13
Dunstan, May 19
Dymphna, May 17
Edith Stein, August 9
Elizabeth, June 24
Elizabeth Ann Seton, January 4
Elizabeth Hesselblad, April 22
Elizabeth of Hungary, November 17
Elizabeth of Portugal, July 4
Elizabeth of the Trinity, November 8
Émilie Tavernier Gamelin, September 24
Ephrem the Syrian, June 9
Eurosia Fabris Barban, January 8
Fabian, January 19
Faustina Kowalska, February 22
Felicity, March 7
Fidelis of Sigmaringen, April 24
Filippo Smaldone, June 4
Florian, May 5
Fra Angelico, February 18
Frances of Rome, March 9
Frances Xavier Cabrini, November 13
Francis de Sales, January 24
Francis of Assisi, October 4
Francis of Paola, April 2
Francis Xavier, December 3
Francis Xavier Seelos, October 5
Francisca de Paula de Jesús, June 16
Francisco de Paula Victor, September 1
Francisco Marto, May 13

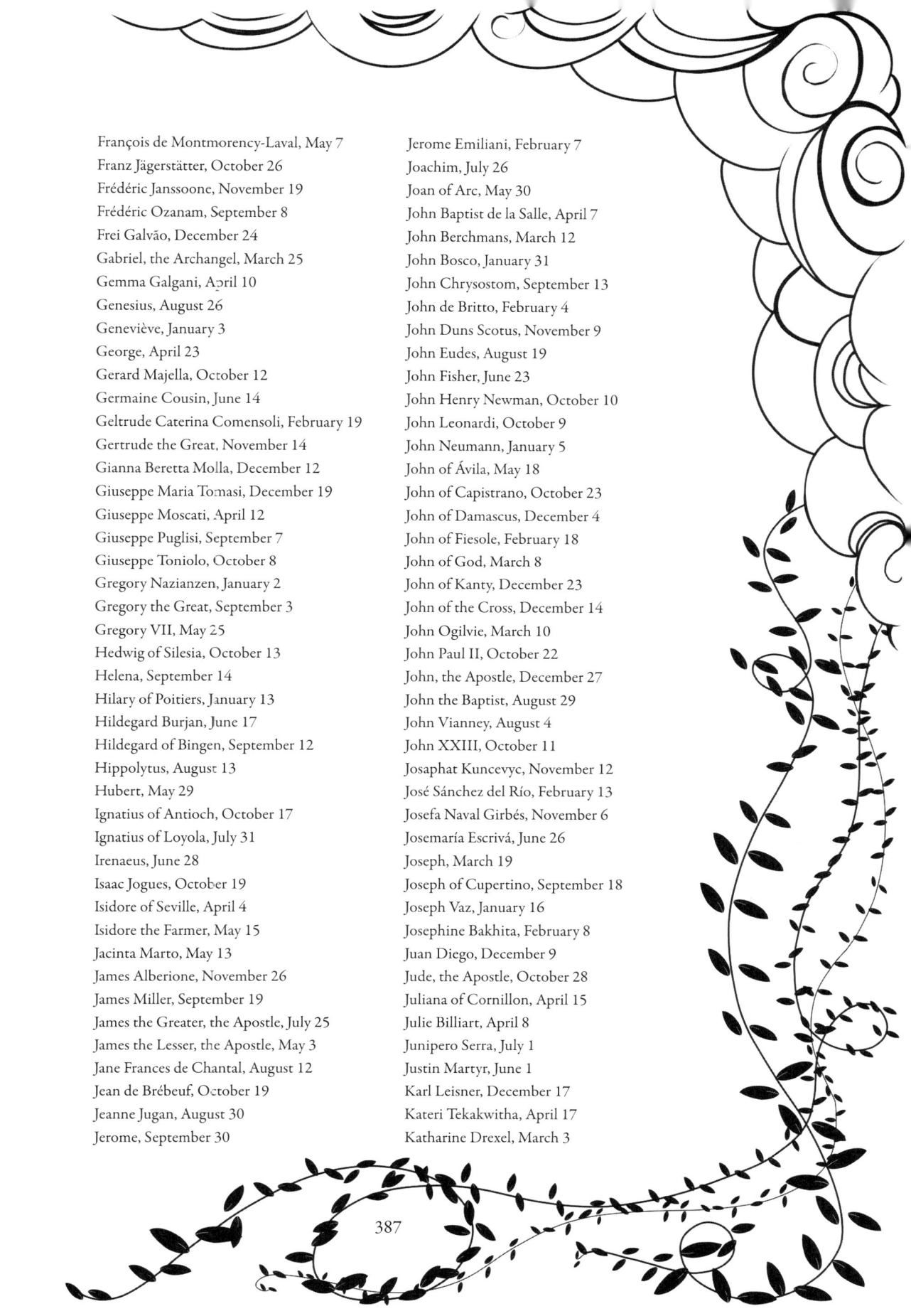

François de Montmorency-Laval, May 7
Franz Jägerstätter, October 26
Frédéric Janssoone, November 19
Frédéric Ozanam, September 8
Frei Galvão, December 24
Gabriel, the Archangel, March 25
Gemma Galgani, April 10
Genesius, August 26
Geneviève, January 3
George, April 23
Gerard Majella, October 12
Germaine Cousin, June 14
Geltrude Caterina Comensoli, February 19
Gertrude the Great, November 14
Gianna Beretta Molla, December 12
Giuseppe Maria Tomasi, December 19
Giuseppe Moscati, April 12
Giuseppe Puglisi, September 7
Giuseppe Toniolo, October 8
Gregory Nazianzen, January 2
Gregory the Great, September 3
Gregory VII, May 25
Hedwig of Silesia, October 13
Helena, September 14
Hilary of Poitiers, January 13
Hildegard Burjan, June 17
Hildegard of Bingen, September 12
Hippolytus, August 13
Hubert, May 29
Ignatius of Antioch, October 17
Ignatius of Loyola, July 31
Irenaeus, June 28
Isaac Jogues, October 19
Isidore of Seville, April 4
Isidore the Farmer, May 15
Jacinta Marto, May 13
James Alberione, November 26
James Miller, September 19
James the Greater, the Apostle, July 25
James the Lesser, the Apostle, May 3
Jane Frances de Chantal, August 12
Jean de Brébeuf, October 19
Jeanne Jugan, August 30
Jerome, September 30

Jerome Emiliani, February 7
Joachim, July 26
Joan of Arc, May 30
John Baptist de la Salle, April 7
John Berchmans, March 12
John Bosco, January 31
John Chrysostom, September 13
John de Britto, February 4
John Duns Scotus, November 9
John Eudes, August 19
John Fisher, June 23
John Henry Newman, October 10
John Leonardi, October 9
John Neumann, January 5
John of Ávila, May 18
John of Capistrano, October 23
John of Damascus, December 4
John of Fiesole, February 18
John of God, March 8
John of Kanty, December 23
John of the Cross, December 14
John Ogilvie, March 10
John Paul II, October 22
John, the Apostle, December 27
John the Baptist, August 29
John Vianney, August 4
John XXIII, October 11
Josaphat Kuncevyc, November 12
José Sánchez del Río, February 13
Josefa Naval Girbés, November 6
Josemaría Escrivá, June 26
Joseph, March 19
Joseph of Cupertino, September 18
Joseph Vaz, January 16
Josephine Bakhita, February 8
Juan Diego, December 9
Jude, the Apostle, October 28
Juliana of Cornillon, April 15
Julie Billiart, April 8
Junipero Serra, July 1
Justin Martyr, June 1
Karl Leisner, December 17
Kateri Tekakwitha, April 17
Katharine Drexel, March 3

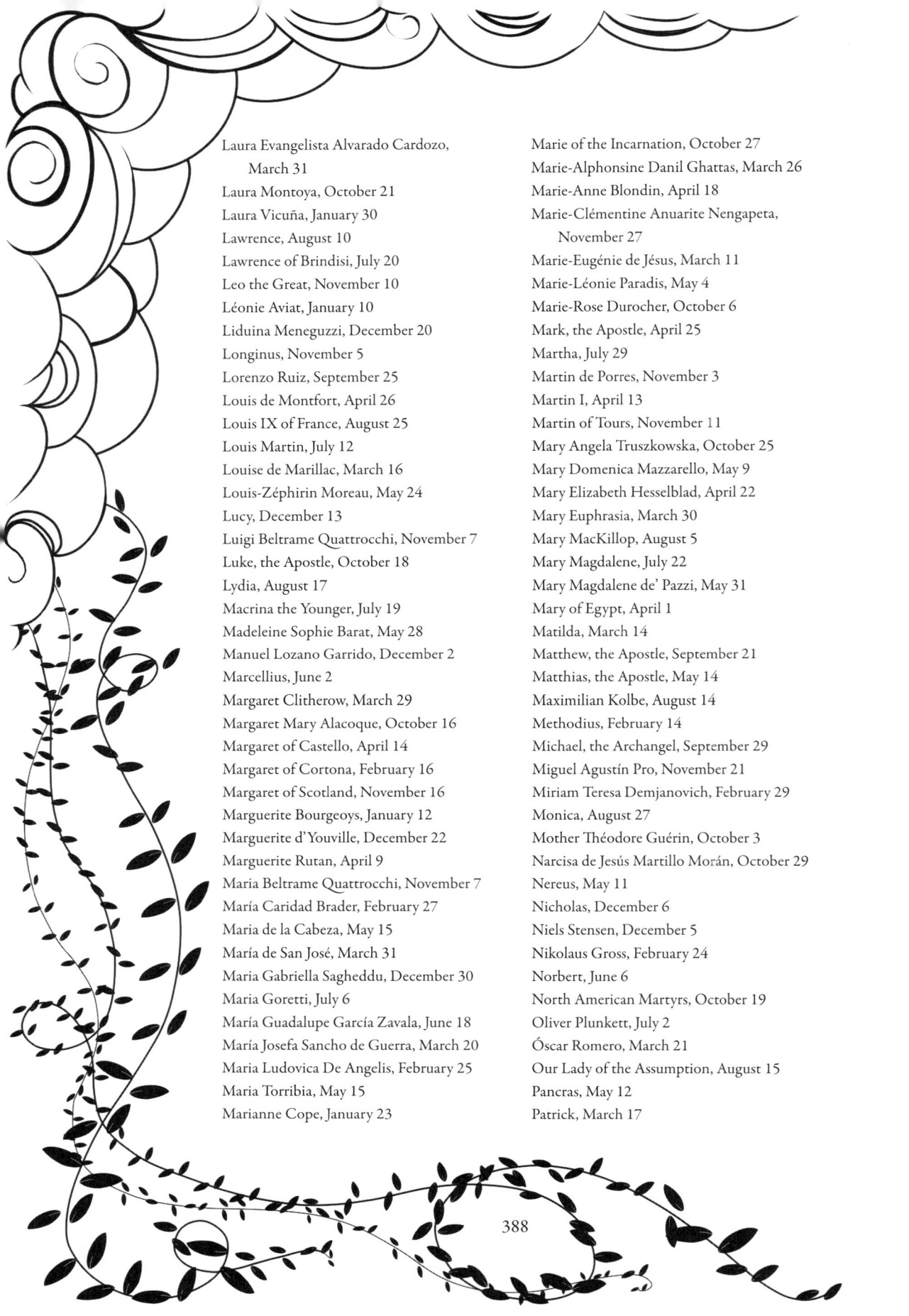

Laura Evangelista Alvarado Cardozo, March 31
Laura Montoya, October 21
Laura Vicuña, January 30
Lawrence, August 10
Lawrence of Brindisi, July 20
Leo the Great, November 10
Léonie Aviat, January 10
Liduina Meneguzzi, December 20
Longinus, November 5
Lorenzo Ruiz, September 25
Louis de Montfort, April 26
Louis IX of France, August 25
Louis Martin, July 12
Louise de Marillac, March 16
Louis-Zéphirin Moreau, May 24
Lucy, December 13
Luigi Beltrame Quattrocchi, November 7
Luke, the Apostle, October 18
Lydia, August 17
Macrina the Younger, July 19
Madeleine Sophie Barat, May 28
Manuel Lozano Garrido, December 2
Marcellius, June 2
Margaret Clitherow, March 29
Margaret Mary Alacoque, October 16
Margaret of Castello, April 14
Margaret of Cortona, February 16
Margaret of Scotland, November 16
Marguerite Bourgeoys, January 12
Marguerite d'Youville, December 22
Marguerite Rutan, April 9
Maria Beltrame Quattrocchi, November 7
María Caridad Brader, February 27
Maria de la Cabeza, May 15
María de San José, March 31
Maria Gabriella Sagheddu, December 30
Maria Goretti, July 6
María Guadalupe García Zavala, June 18
María Josefa Sancho de Guerra, March 20
Maria Ludovica De Angelis, February 25
Maria Torribia, May 15
Marianne Cope, January 23
Marie of the Incarnation, October 27
Marie-Alphonsine Danil Ghattas, March 26
Marie-Anne Blondin, April 18
Marie-Clémentine Anuarite Nengapeta, November 27
Marie-Eugénie de Jésus, March 11
Marie-Léonie Paradis, May 4
Marie-Rose Durocher, October 6
Mark, the Apostle, April 25
Martha, July 29
Martin de Porres, November 3
Martin I, April 13
Martin of Tours, November 11
Mary Angela Truszkowska, October 25
Mary Domenica Mazzarello, May 9
Mary Elizabeth Hesselblad, April 22
Mary Euphrasia, March 30
Mary MacKillop, August 5
Mary Magdalene, July 22
Mary Magdalene de' Pazzi, May 31
Mary of Egypt, April 1
Matilda, March 14
Matthew, the Apostle, September 21
Matthias, the Apostle, May 14
Maximilian Kolbe, August 14
Methodius, February 14
Michael, the Archangel, September 29
Miguel Agustín Pro, November 21
Miriam Teresa Demjanovich, February 29
Monica, August 27
Mother Théodore Guérin, October 3
Narcisa de Jesús Martillo Morán, October 29
Nereus, May 11
Nicholas, December 6
Niels Stensen, December 5
Nikolaus Gross, February 24
Norbert, June 6
North American Martyrs, October 19
Oliver Plunkett, July 2
Óscar Romero, March 21
Our Lady of the Assumption, August 15
Pancras, May 12
Patrick, March 17

Paul Chŏng Ha-sang, September 20
Paul Miki, February 6
Paul of the Cross, October 20
Paul, the Apostle, January 25
Paul VI, July 21
Paula Montal Fornés, February 26
Paulinus of Nola, June 20
Pedro Calungsod, April 3
Peregrine Laziosi, May 1
Perpetua, March 7
Peter, June 2
Peter Canisius, December 21
Peter Chanel, April 28
Peter Chrysologus, July 30
Peter Claver, September 9
Peter Damian, February 21
Peter Donders, January 14
Peter Faber, August 3
Peter Julian Eymard, August 2
Peter, the Apostle, June 29
Peter To Rot, July 7
Philip, the Apostle, May 3
Philip Neri, May 26
Pier Giorgio Frassati, July 10
Pio of Pietrelcina, September 23
Pius V, April 30
Pius X, August 21
Polycarp, February 23
Pontian, August 13
Priscilla, July 8
Rafqa Pietra Choboq Ar-Rayès, March 22
Raphael, the Archangel, October 2
Raymond of Peñafort, January 7
Regina Protmann, January 18
Rita of Cascia, May 22
Robert Bellarmine, September 17
Robert Southwell, February 20
Romuald, June 19
Rose of Lima, August 23
Rose Philippine Duchesne, November 18
Sára Salkaházi, December 28
Scholastica, February 10
Sebastian, January 20

Sebastian Kimura, September 11
Seven Holy Founders of the Servite Order, February 17
Seven Thai Martyrs of Songkhon, December 16
Simon Stock, July 16
Simon, the Apostle, October 28
Sixtus II and Companions, August 6
Solanus Casey, July 17
Solomon Le Clercq, September 2
Stanislaus of Szczepanów, April 11
Stanley Rother, July 28
Stephen, December 26
Stephen Harding, March 28
Stephen of Hungary, August 16
Sylvester I, December 31
Tarcisius, June 30
Teresa Benedicta of the Cross, August 9
Teresa of Ávila, October 15
Teresa of Calcutta, September 5
Teresa of the Andes, April 6
Thecla, September 22
Théodore Guérin, October 3
Thérèse of Lisieux, October 1
Thomas Aquinas, January 28
Thomas Becket, December 29
Thomas More, June 22
Thomas, the Apostle, July 3
Timothy, January 26
Timothy Giaccardo, January 29
Titus, January 26
Titus Brandsma, July 18
Turibius de Mogrovejo, March 23
Vasyl Velychkovsky, June 25
Victoria Rasoamanarivo, August 22
Vincent de Paul, September 27
Vincent Ferrer, April 5
Vincent of Saragossa, January 22
Wenceslaus, September 28
Zechariah, June 24
Zélie Martin, July 12
Zita, April 27

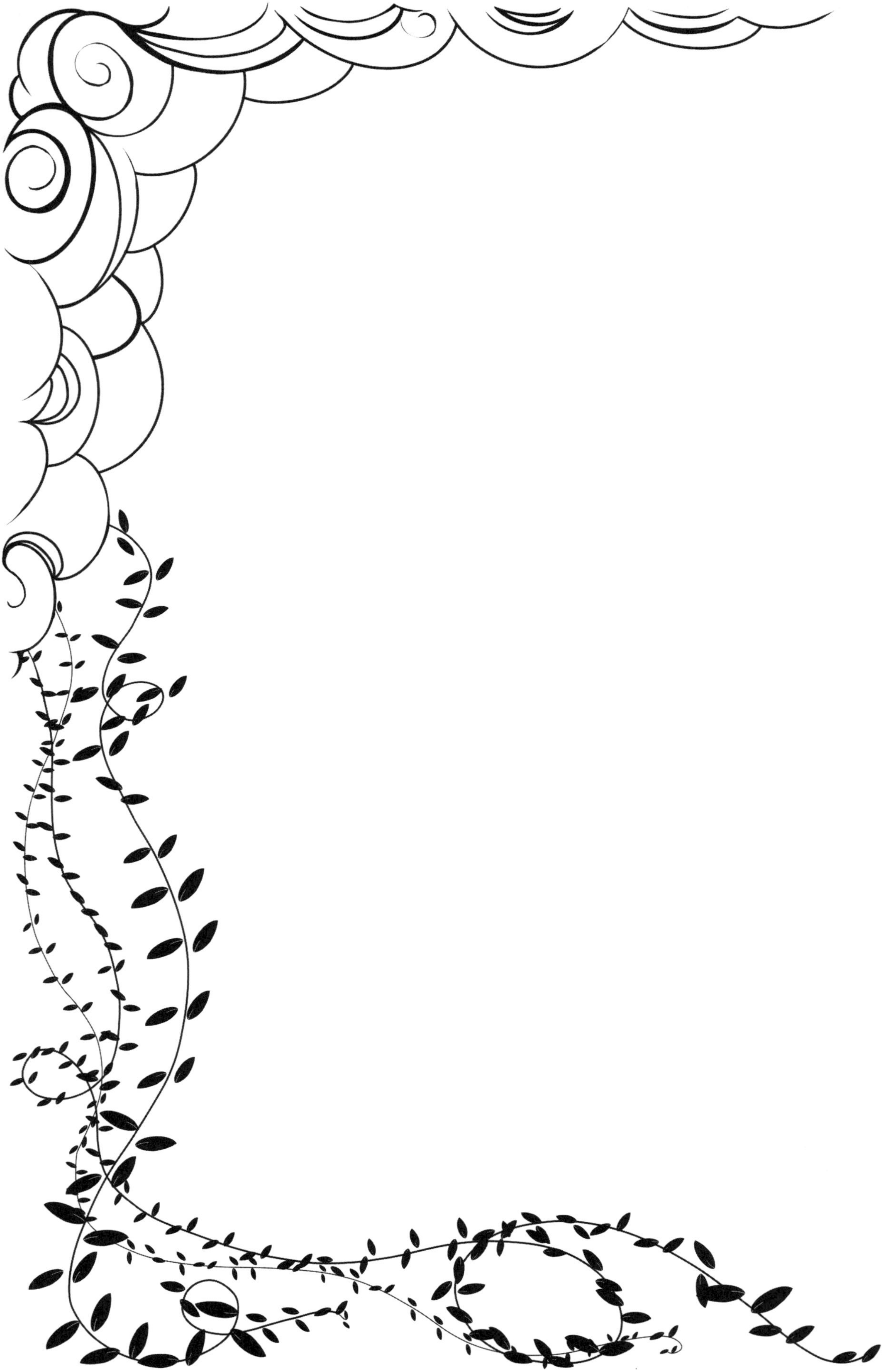

INDEX OF FEAST DAYS

This index notes the feast days of the saints and blesseds in this book. Because multiple saints have the same feast day, not all of them are on their own day. Therefore, the date in the first column is the feast day and the date in the third column is the date where you can find the saint or blessed's entry in this book.

- All caps: indicates major solemnities and feasts celebrated by the entire Church, (which are included in this list but are not necessarily described on the corresponding date in this book).
- Names in bold: indicate saints on the General Roman Calendar, which is for the whole Church. (No distinction is made between Memorials and Optional Memorials).
- Names in italics: indicate saints or blesseds celebrated by the Church in the United States or in Canada.
- Names in roman font: indicates saints or blesseds with a traditional feast day, but one not celebrated officially by the entire Church.
- *Not* indicated in this list are feasts and solemnities of the Church that do not fall on the same date each year, such as Epiphany, Easter, Pentecost, Holy Trinity, Corpus Christi, Christ the King, etc.

LITURGICAL FEAST DAY	SAINT NAME	DATE IN THIS BOOK
January 1	MARY, MOTHER OF GOD	
January 2	**Basil the Great**	January 1
January 2	**Gregory Nazianzen**	January 2
January 3	Geneviève	January 3
January 3	Giuseppe Maria Tomasi	December 19
January 4	*Elizabeth Ann Seton* (U.S.A.)	January 4
January 4	Angela of Foligno	December 18
January 5	*John Neumann* (U.S.A.)	January 5
January 6	*André Bessette* (U.S.A.) (January 7 in Canada)	January 6
January 7	**Raymond of Peñafort**	January 7
January 7	Angela of Foligno (U.S.A)	December 18
January 8	Eurosia Fabris Barban	January 8
January 8	*Raymond of Peñafort* (Canada)	January 7
January 10	Léonie Aviat	January 10
January 12	Aelred of Rievaulx	January 11

LITURGICAL FEAST DAY	SAINT NAME	DATE IN THIS BOOK
January 12	*Marguerite Bourgeoys* (Canada)	January 12
January 13	**Hilary of Poitiers**	January 13
January 14	Peter Donders	January 14
January 15	Arnold Janssen	January 15
January 15	Nikolaus Gross	February 24
January 16	Joseph Vaz	January 16
January 17	**Anthony of Egypt**	January 17
January 18	Regina Protmann	January 18
January 20	**Fabian**	January 19
January 20	**Sebastian**	January 20
January 21	**Agnes**	January 21
January 22	**Vincent of Saragossa**	January 22
January 22	Laura Vicuña	January 30
January 23	*Marianne Cope* (U.S.A.)	January 23
January 23	*Vincent of Saragossa* (U.S.A.)	January 22
January 24	**Francis de Sales**	January 24
January 25	CONVERSION OF ST. PAUL, THE APOSTLE	January 25
January 26	**Timothy and Titus**	January 26
January 27	**Angela Merici**	January 27
January 28	**Thomas Aquinas**	January 28
January 31	**John Bosco**	January 31
February 1	Brigid of Ireland	February 1
February 1	Benedict Daswa	October 31
February 2	PRESENTATION OF THE LORD	
February 3	**Ansgar**	February 2
February 3	**Blaise**	February 3
February 3	Claudine Thévenet	November 2
February 4	John de Britto	February 4
February 5	**Agatha**	February 5
February 6	**Paul Miki**	February 6
February 8	**Jerome Emiliani**	February 7
February 8	**Josephine Bakhita**	February 8
February 9	Apollonia	February 9
February 9	Anne Catherine Emmerich	November 29
February 10	**Scholastica**	February 10
February 10	Aloysius Stepinac	February 12
February 10	José Sánchez del Río	February 13
February 13	James Miller	September 19
February 14	**Cyril and Methodius**	February 14

LITURGICAL FEAST DAY	SAINT NAME	DATE IN THIS BOOK
February 15	Claude de la Colombière	February 15
February 17	**Seven Holy Founders of the Servite Order**	February 17
February 18	John of Fiesole (Fra Angelico)	February 18
February 18	Geltrude Caterina Comensoli	February 19
February 20	Francisco and Jacinta Marto	May 13
February 21	Robert Southwell	February 20
February 21	**Peter Damian**	February 21
February 22	CHAIR OF SAINT PETER	
February 22	Margaret of Cortona	February 16
February 23	**Polycarp**	February 23
February 24	Josefa Naval Girbés	November 6
February 25	Maria Ludovica De Angelis	February 25
February 26	Paula Montal Fornés	February 26
February 27	María Caridad Brader	February 27
March 1	David of Wales	March 1
March 2	Agnes of Bohemia	March 2
March 3	*Katharine Drexel* (U.S.A.)	March 3
March 4	**Casimir**	March 4
March 6	Colette	March 6
March 7	**Perpetua and Felicity**	March 7
March 8	**John of God**	March 8
March 9	**Frances of Rome**	March 9
March 9	Catherine of Bologna	June 10
March 10	John Ogilvie	March 10
March 10	Marie-Eugénie de Jésus	March 11
March 12	Aniela Salawa	March 5
March 14	Matilda	March 14
March 15	Clement Mary Hofbauer	March 15
March 17	**Patrick**	March 17
March 18	**Cyril of Jerusalem**	March 18
March 19	JOSEPH, SPOUSE OF THE BLESSED VIRGIN MARY	March 19
March 20	María Josefa Sancho de Guerra	March 20
March 23	Rafqa Pietra Choboq Ar-Rayès	March 22
March 23	**Turibius de Mogrovejo**	March 23
March 24	Óscar Romero	March 21
March 24	Catherine of Sweden	March 24
March 25	ANNUNCIATION OF THE LORD	
March 25	Marie-Alphonsine Danil Ghattas	March 26

LITURGICAL FEAST DAY	SAINT NAME	DATE IN THIS BOOK
March 26	Margaret Clitherow	March 29
April 1	Mary of Egypt	April 1
April 2	María de San José	March 31
April 2	**Francis of Paola**	April 2
April 2	Pedro Calungsod	April 3
April 4	**Isidore of Seville**	April 4
April 5	**Vincent Ferrer**	April 5
April 6	Juliana of Cornillon	April 15
April 7	**John Baptist de la Salle**	April 7
April 8	Julie Billiart	April 8
April 9	Marguerite Rutan	April 9
April 11	Gemma Galgani	April 10
April 11	**Stanislaus**	April 11
April 12	Teresa of the Andes	April 6
April 13	**Martin I**	April 13
April 13	Margaret of Castello	April 14
April 16	Bernadette Soubirous	February 11
April 16	Benedict Joseph Labre	April 16
April 17	*Kateri Tekakwitha* (Canada)	April 17
April 17	Stephen Harding	March 28
April 18	*Marie-Anne Blondin* (Canada)	April 18
April 21	Beuno	April 20
April 21	**Anselm of Canterbury**	April 21
April 23	**Adalbert of Prague**	April 19
April 23	**George**	April 23
April 23	Maria Gabriella Sagheddu	December 30
April 24	Mary Euphrasia	March 30
April 24	**Fidelis of Sigmaringen**	April 24
April 25	MARK, THE APOSTLE	April 25
April 27	Zita	April 27
April 28	**Louis de Montfort**	April 26
April 28	**Peter Chanel**	April 28
April 28	Gianna Beretta Molla	December 12
April 29	**Catherine of Siena**	April 29
April 30	**Pius V**	April 30
April 30	*Marie of the Incarnation* (Canada)	October 27
May 2	**Athanasius**	May 2
May 3	PHILIP AND JAMES, APOSTLES	May 3
May 4	Peregrine Laziosi	May 1

LITURGICAL FEAST DAY	SAINT NAME	DATE IN THIS BOOK
May 4	*Marie-Léonie Paradis* (Canada)	May 4
May 4	Florian	May 5
May 6	Dominic Savio	May 6
May 6	*François de Montmorency-Laval* (Canada)	May 7
May 8	Miriam Teresa Demjanovich	February 29
May 8	*Catherine of Saint Augustine* (Canada)	May 8
May 9	Louise de Marillac	March 16
May 10	*Damien of Molokai* (U.S.A.)	May 10
May 10	John of Ávila	May 18
May 11	Antônio de Sant'Anna Galvão	December 24
May 11	Sára Salkaházi	December 28
May 12	**Nereus and Achilleus**	May 11
May 12	**Pancras**	May 12
May 13	Mary Domenica Mazzarello	May 9
May 14	MATTHIAS, THE APOSTLE	May 14
May 15	*Isidore the Farmer* (U.S.A.)	May 15
May 15	Dymphna	May 17
May 16	Brendan	May 16
May 16	Simon Stock	July 16
May 19	Dunstan	May 19
May 20	**Bernardine of Siena**	May 20
May 21	**Cristóbal Magallanes and Companions**	May 21
May 21	Franz Jägerstätter	October 26
May 22	**Rita of Cascia**	May 22
May 24	*Louis-Zéphirin Moreau* (Canada)	May 24
May 25	**Bede the Venerable**	May 23
May 25	**Gregory VII**	May 25
May 25	Madeleine Sophie Barat	May 28
May 25	**Mary Magdalene de' Pazzi**	May 31
May 26	**Philip Neri**	May 26
May 27	**Augustine of Canterbury**	May 27
May 29	Paul VI	July 21
May 30	Joan of Arc	May 30
May 31	VISITATION OF THE BLESSED VIRGIN MARY	May 31
June 1	**Justin Martyr**	June 1
June 2	**Marcellinus and Peter**	June 2
June 3	**Charles Lwanga and Companions**	June 3
June 3	Clotilda	June 7

LITURGICAL FEAST DAY	SAINT NAME	DATE IN THIS BOOK
June 4	Mary Elizabeth Hesselblad	April 22
June 4	Filippo Smaldone	June 4
June 5	**Boniface**	June 5
June 6	**Norbert**	June 6
June 9	Columba	June 8
June 9	**Ephrem the Syrian**	June 9
June 9	Anna Maria Taigi	June 12
June 11	**Barnabas, the Apostle**	June 11
June 12	Hildegard Burjan	June 17
June 13	**Anthony of Padua**	June 13
June 14	Francisca de Paula de Jesús	June 16
June 15	Germaine Cousin	June 14
June 15	Clemente Vismara	June 15
June 17	Albert Chmielowski	December 25
June 19	**Romuald**	June 19
June 21	**Aloysius Gonzaga**	June 21
June 22	**Paulinus of Nola**	June 20
June 22	**Thomas More**	June 22
June 22	**John Fisher**	June 23
June 24	NATIVITY OF JOHN THE BAPTIST	
June 24	María Guadalupe García Zavala	June 18
June 26	Josemaría Escrivá	June 26
June 27	*Vasyl Velychkovsky* (Canada)	June 25
June 27	**Cyril of Alexandria**	June 27
June 28	**Irenaeus**	June 28
June 29	PETER AND PAUL, APOSTLES	June 29 and January 25
July 1	*Junipero Serra* (U.S.A.)	July 1
July 1	Oliver Plunkett	July 2
July 3	THOMAS, THE APOSTLE	July 3
July 4	Elizabeth of Portugal	July 4
July 4	Pier Giorgio Frassati	July 10
July 5	**Anthony Mary Zaccaria**	July 5
July 5	*Elizabeth of Portugal* (U.S.A.)	July 4
July 6	**Maria Goretti**	July 6
July 7	Peter To Rot	July 7
July 8	Priscilla and Aquila	July 8
July 9	**Augustine Zhao Rong and Companions**	July 9
July 11	**Benedict**	July 11

LITURGICAL FEAST DAY	SAINT NAME	DATE IN THIS BOOK
July 12	Louis and Zélie Martin	July 12
July 13	Carlos Manuel Cecilio Rodríguez Santiago	July 13
July 14	*Kateri Tekakwitha* (U.S.A.)	April 17
July 14	**Camillus de Lellis**	July 14
July 15	**Bonaventure**	July 15
July 15	Anne-Marie Javouhey	December 15
July 17	Martyrs of Compiègne	November 1
July 18	*Camillus de Lellis* (U.S.A.)	July 14
July 19	Macrina the Younger	July 19
July 21	**Lawrence of Brindisi**	July 20
July 22	MARY MAGDALENE	July 22
July 23	**Bridget of Sweden**	July 23
July 24	**Charbel Makhlouf**	July 24
July 25	JAMES, THE APOSTLE	July 25
July 25	Christopher	November 28
July 26	**Joachim and Anne**	July 26
July 27	Titus Brandsma	July 18
July 28	Alphonsa of the Immaculate Conception	July 27
July 28	Stanley Rother	July 28
July 29	**Martha**	July 29
July 30	Solanus Casey	July 17
July 30	**Peter Chrysologus**	July 30
July 31	**Ignatius of Loyola**	July 31
August 1	**Alphonsus Liguori**	August 1
August 2	**Peter Julian Eymard**	August 2
August 2	Peter Faber	August 3
August 3	Lydia	August 17
August 4	**John Vianney**	August 4
August 5	*Frédéric Janssoone* (Canada) (August 4 in the U.S.A.)	November 19
August 6	TRANSFIGURATION OF THE LORD	
August 7	**Sixtus II and Companions**	August 6
August 7	**Cajetan**	August 7
August 8	Mary MacKillop	August 5
August 8	**Dominic**	August 8
August 9	**Teresa Benedicta of the Cross**	August 9
August 10	LAWRENCE	August 10
August 11	**Clare of Assisi**	August 11
August 12	**Jane Frances de Chantal**	August 12

LITURGICAL FEAST DAY	SAINT NAME	DATE IN THIS BOOK
August 12	Blessed Karl Leisner	December 17
August 13	**Pontian and Hippolytus**	August 13
August 13	John Berchmans	March 12
August 13	Dulce Lopes Pontes	March 13
August 14	**Maximilian Kolbe**	August 14
August 15	ASSUMPTION OF THE BLESSED VIRGIN MARY	
August 15	Tarcisius	June 30
August 16	**Stephen of Hungary**	August 16
August 18	Alberto Hurtado	August 18
August 18	Helena	September 14
August 19	**John Eudes**	August 19
August 20	**Bernard of Clairvaux**	August 20
August 21	**Pius X**	August 21
August 21	Victoria Rasoamanarivo	August 22
August 23	**Rose of Lima**	August 23
August 24	BARTHOLOMEW, THE APOSTLE	August 24
August 25	**Louis IX of France**	August 25
August 25	Genesius	August 26
August 27	**Monica**	August 27
August 28	**Augustine**	August 28
August 29	**John the Baptist**	August 29
August 30	Jeanne Jugan	August 30
August 30	Narcisa de Jesús Martillo Morán	October 29
August 31	Aidan of Lindisfarne	August 31
September 2	Solomon Le Clercq	September 2
September 3	**Gregory the Great**	September 3
September 4	*Dina Bélanger (*Canada)	September 4
September 4	Giuseppe Toniolo	October 8
September 5	Teresa of Calcutta	September 5
September 8	NATIVITY OF THE BLESSED VIRGIN MARY	
September 9	*Peter Claver* (U.S.A.)	September 9
September 9	Frédéric Ozanam	September 8
September 9	Maria Torribia	May 15
September 10	Sebastian Kimura	September 11
September 13	**John Chrysostom**	September 13
September 14	EXALTATION OF THE CROSS	
September 15	Catherine of Genoa	September 15
September 16	**Cyprian**	September 16

LITURGICAL FEAST DAY	SAINT NAME	DATE IN THIS BOOK
September 17	**Robert Bellarmine**	September 17
September 17	Hildegard of Bingen	September 12
September 18	Joseph of Cupertino	September 18
September 20	**Andrew Kim Tae-gŏn, Paul Chŏng Ha-sang, and Companions**	September 20
September 21	MATTHEW, THE APOSTLE	September 21
September 23	**Pio of Pietrelcina**	September 23
September 23	Zechariah and Elizabeth	June 24
September 23	Francisco de Paula Victor	September 1
September 23	Thecla	September 22
September 24	**Émilie Tavernier Gamelin** (Canada) (September 23 in the U.S.A.)	September 24
September 26	**Cosmas and Damian** (September 25 in Canada)	September 26
September 26	*John de Brébeuf, Isaac Jogues, and Companions* (Canada)	October 19
September 27	**Vincent de Paul**	September 27
September 28	**Lorenzo Ruiz**	September 25
September 28	**Wenceslaus**	September 28
September 29	MICHAEL, GABRIEL, AND RAPHAEL, ARCHANGELS	
September 29	**Gabriel, the Archangel**	March 25
September 29	**Michael, the Archangel**	September 29
September 29	**Raphael, the Archangel**	October 2
September 30	**Jerome**	September 30
October 1	**Thérèse of Lisieux**	October 1
October 3	Mother Théodore Guérin	October 3
October 4	**Francis of Assisi**	October 4
October 5	Maria Faustina Kowalska	February 22
October 5	Alberto Marvelli	March 27
October 5	*Francis Xavier Seelos* (U.S.A.)	October 5
October 6	*Marie-Rose Durocher* (U.S.A. and Canada)	October 6
October 9	**John Leonardi**	October 9
October 9	John Henry Newman	October 10
October 10	Daniel Comboni	September 10
October 10	Mary Angela Truszkowska	October 25
October 11	John XXIII	October 11
October 14	**Callistus I**	October 14
October 15	**Teresa of Ávila**	October 15

LITURGICAL FEAST DAY	SAINT NAME	DATE IN THIS BOOK
October 16	Gerard Majella	October 12
October 16	**Hedwig of Silesia**	October 13
October 16	**Margaret Mary Alacoque**	October 16
October 16	*Marguerite d'Youville* (Canada)	December 22
October 16	Longinus	November 5
October 17	**Ignatius of Antioch**	October 17
October 18	LUKE, THE APOSTLE	October 18
October 19	*John de Brébeuf, Isaac Jogues, and Companions* (U.S.A.)	October 19
October 19	Timothy Giaccardo	January 29
October 20	*Paul of the Cross* (U.S.A.)	October 20
October 20	*Margaret Mary Alacoque* (Canada)	October 16
October 20	*Hedwig of Silesia* (Canada)	October 13
October 21	Giuseppe Puglisi	September 7
October 21	Laura Montoya	October 21
October 22	Alix LeClerc	January 9
October 22	John Paul II	October 22
October 23	**John of Capistrano**	October 23
October 24	**Anthony Mary Claret**	October 24
October 25	Carlo Gnocchi	February 28
October 26	Celine Chludzińska Borzęcka	September 6
October 28	SIMON AND JUDE, APOSTLES	October 28
October 29	Chiara Badano	October 7
October 31	Alphonsus Rodriguez	October 30
November 1	ALL SAINTS	
November 2	ALL SOULS	
November 3	**Martin de Porres**	November 3
November 3	Hubert	May 29
November 3	Manuel Lozano Garrido	December 2
November 4	**Charles Borromeo**	November 4
November 8	Elizabeth of the Trinity	November 8
November 8	John Duns Scotus	November 9
November 9	DEDICATION OF THE LATERAN BASILICA	
November 10	**Leo the Great**	November 10
November 11	**Martin of Tours**	November 11
November 12	**Josaphat Kuncevyc**	November 12
November 13	*Frances Xavier Cabrini* (U.S.A.)	November 13
November 15	**Albert the Great**	November 15
November 16	**Gertrude the Great**	November 14

LITURGICAL FEAST DAY	SAINT NAME	DATE IN THIS BOOK
November 16	**Margaret of Scotland**	November 16
November 16	Giuseppe Moscati	April 12
November 17	**Elizabeth of Hungary**	November 17
November 18	*Rose Philippine Duchesne* (U.S.A.)	November 18
November 22	**Cecilia**	November 22
November 23	**Clement I**	November 20
November 23	**Columban**	November 23
November 23	*Miguel Agustín Pro* (U.S.A.)	November 21
November 24	**Andrew Dũng Lạc and Companions**	November 24
November 25	Luigi and Maria Beltrame Quattrocchi	November 7
November 25	**Catherine of Alexandria**	November 25
November 26	James Alberione	November 26
November 28	Catherine Labouré	December 8
November 30	ANDREW, THE APOSTLE	November 30
December 1	Marie-Clémentine Anuarite Nengapeta	November 27
December 1	Charles de Foucauld	December 1
December 2	Liduina Meneguzzi	December 20
December 3	**Francis Xavier**	December 3
December 4	**John of Damascus**	December 4
December 4	Barbara	December 10
December 5	Niels Stensen	December 5
December 6	**Nicholas**	December 6
December 7	**Ambrose**	December 7
December 8	IMMACULATE CONCEPTION OF THE BLESSED VIRGIN MARY	
December 9	**Juan Diego**	December 9
December 11	**Damasus I**	December 11
December 12	*Our Lady of Guadalupe* (U.S.A. and Canada)	
December 13	**Lucy**	December 13
December 14	**John of the Cross**	December 14
December 16	The Seven Thai Martyrs of Songkhon	December 16
December 21	**Peter Canisius**	December 21
December 23	**John of Kanty**	December 23
December 25	CHRISTMAS	
December 26	STEPHEN	December 26
December 27	JOHN, THE APOSTLE	December 27
December 28	HOLY INNOCENTS, MARTYRS	
December 29	**Thomas Becket**	December 29
December 31	Sylvester I	December 31

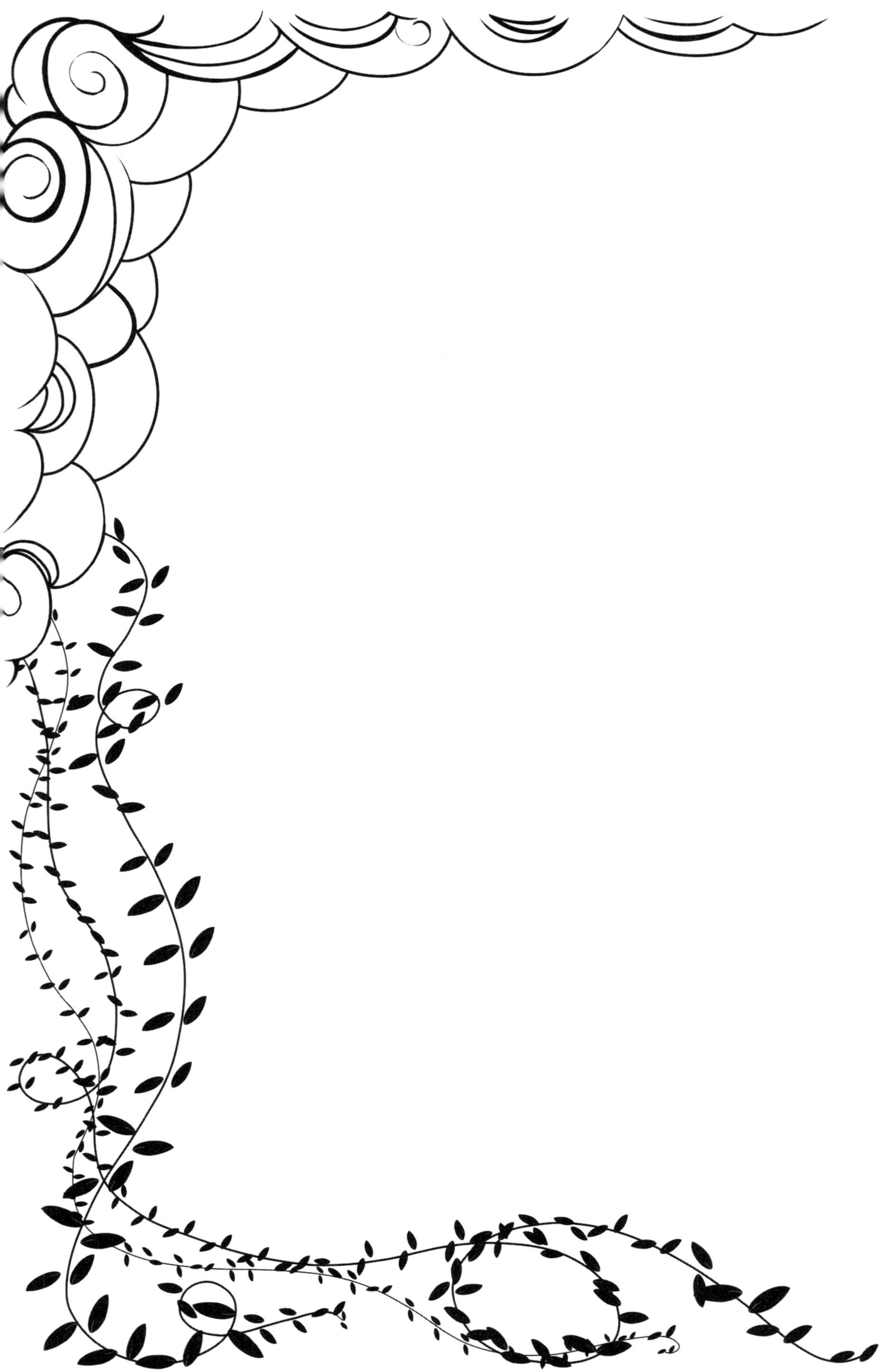

INDEX OF PATRON SAINTS

Just as we ask for prayers from family members or friends, so we ask the saints and blesseds in heaven to pray for us. Our Blessed Mother Mary's particularly powerful intercession is always available for everyone and in all circumstances. But we also can pray to any saint or blessed for assistance with any problem.

Often because of their life experiences, certain saints are considered "patron saints" for categories of people or certain problems. Catholics also often consider a saint their personal "patron saint" if he or she shares a name or birthday with them. This index lists various groups of people, problems, and virtues along with the saints and blesseds who can intercede for these needs in a special way.

abandoned and unwanted people   Margaret of Castello
abandoned children   Jerome Emiliani, Mary Angela Truszkowska
abuse victims   Germaine Cousin, Laura Vicuña, Mary MacKillop
accountants   Matthew the Apostle
actors   Genesius
addiction, overcoming   Mary of Egypt
adolescents   José Sánchez del Río, Maria Ludovica De Angelis, Pio of Pietrelcina
adopted children   Clotilda
adultery, victims of   Elizabeth of Portugal, Victoria Rasoamanarivo
advertising   Bernardine of Siena
Africa   Daniel Comboni
alcoholics   Monica, Matthias the Apostle
altar servers   John Berchmans, Pedro Calungsod, Tarcisius
amputees   Anthony of Padua
animals   Martin de Porres, Francis of Assisi
apologists   Justin Martyr, Irenaeus
apple orchards   Charles Borromeo
apprentices   John Bosco

archeologists   Damasus I, Helena, Jerome
archers   Sebastian, Nicholas
architects   Barbara, Thomas the Apostle
Armenia   Bartholomew the Apostle
art dealers   John the Apostle
arthritis   Alphonsus Liguori, James the Greater (the Apostle)
artists   Albert Chmielowski, Catherine of Bologna, John of Fiesole (Fra Angelico), Luke the Apostle
Asia   Francis Xavier
assault, sexual, victims of   Agnes, Maria Goretti, Zita
astronauts   Joseph of Cupertino
astronomers   Dominic
atheists   Charles de Foucauld
athletes   Sebastian
attorneys   *(see lawyers)*
Australia   Mary MacKillop
Austria   Joseph, Florian
authors   Paul the Apostle

bachelors   Giuseppe Moscati
back problems   Gemma Galgani

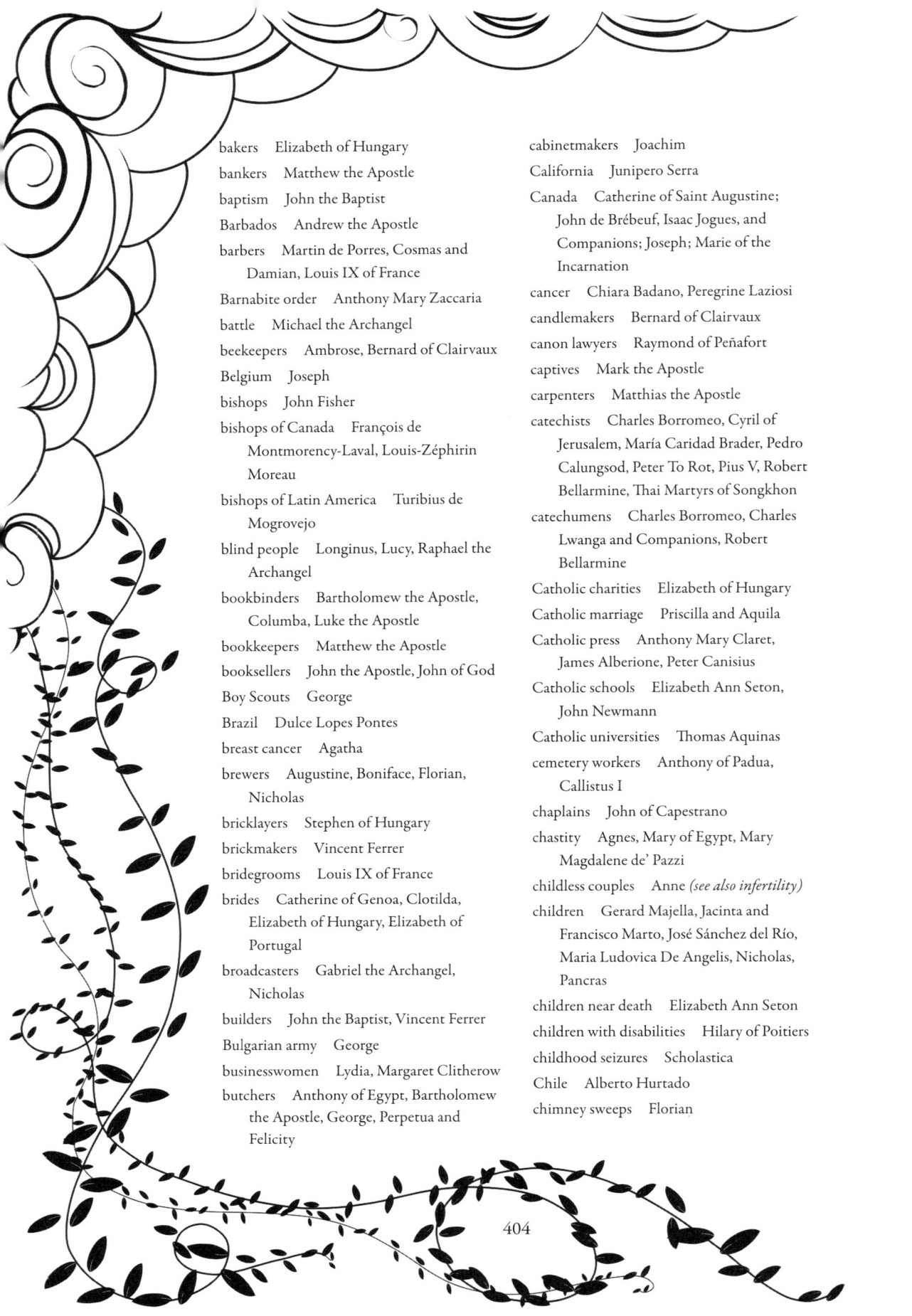

bakers   Elizabeth of Hungary
bankers   Matthew the Apostle
baptism   John the Baptist
Barbados   Andrew the Apostle
barbers   Martin de Porres, Cosmas and Damian, Louis IX of France
Barnabite order   Anthony Mary Zaccaria
battle   Michael the Archangel
beekeepers   Ambrose, Bernard of Clairvaux
Belgium   Joseph
bishops   John Fisher
bishops of Canada   François de Montmorency-Laval, Louis-Zéphirin Moreau
bishops of Latin America   Turibius de Mogrovejo
blind people   Longinus, Lucy, Raphael the Archangel
bookbinders   Bartholomew the Apostle, Columba, Luke the Apostle
bookkeepers   Matthew the Apostle
booksellers   John the Apostle, John of God
Boy Scouts   George
Brazil   Dulce Lopes Pontes
breast cancer   Agatha
brewers   Augustine, Boniface, Florian, Nicholas
bricklayers   Stephen of Hungary
brickmakers   Vincent Ferrer
bridegrooms   Louis IX of France
brides   Catherine of Genoa, Clotilda, Elizabeth of Hungary, Elizabeth of Portugal
broadcasters   Gabriel the Archangel, Nicholas
builders   John the Baptist, Vincent Ferrer
Bulgarian army   George
businesswomen   Lydia, Margaret Clitherow
butchers   Anthony of Egypt, Bartholomew the Apostle, George, Perpetua and Felicity

cabinetmakers   Joachim
California   Junipero Serra
Canada   Catherine of Saint Augustine; John de Brébeuf, Isaac Jogues, and Companions; Joseph; Marie of the Incarnation
cancer   Chiara Badano, Peregrine Laziosi
candlemakers   Bernard of Clairvaux
canon lawyers   Raymond of Peñafort
captives   Mark the Apostle
carpenters   Matthias the Apostle
catechists   Charles Borromeo, Cyril of Jerusalem, María Caridad Brader, Pedro Calungsod, Peter To Rot, Pius V, Robert Bellarmine, Thai Martyrs of Songkhon
catechumens   Charles Borromeo, Charles Lwanga and Companions, Robert Bellarmine
Catholic charities   Elizabeth of Hungary
Catholic marriage   Priscilla and Aquila
Catholic press   Anthony Mary Claret, James Alberione, Peter Canisius
Catholic schools   Elizabeth Ann Seton, John Newmann
Catholic universities   Thomas Aquinas
cemetery workers   Anthony of Padua, Callistus I
chaplains   John of Capestrano
chastity   Agnes, Mary of Egypt, Mary Magdalene de' Pazzi
childless couples   Anne *(see also infertility)*
children   Gerard Majella, Jacinta and Francisco Marto, José Sánchez del Río, Maria Ludovica De Angelis, Nicholas, Pancras
children near death   Elizabeth Ann Seton
children with disabilities   Hilary of Poitiers
childhood seizures   Scholastica
Chile   Alberto Hurtado
chimney sweeps   Florian

China   Augustine Zhao Rong and Companions
Chinese youth   Lorenzo Ruiz
Christian unity   John XXIII, Josaphat
Church in eastern Mediterranean   Ignatius of Antioch
Church in North Africa   Cyprian
church musicians   Gregory the Great
Church reform   Bernard of Clairvaux, Gregory VII, Pius V
Cistercians   Bernard of Clairvaux, Stephen Harding
civil defense volunteers   Pio of Pietrelcina
civil servants   Thomas More
clergy   *(see priests)*
climbers   Bernard of Clairvaux
colic   Charles Borromeo
Colombia   Laura Montoya, Peter Claver
comedians   Genesius, Lawrence, Philip Neri
communications media   Gabriel the Archangel, James Alberione
communicators   Bernardine of Siena, Óscar Romero
composers   Cecilia
compulsive gambling   Bernardine of Siena
confessors   Alphonsus Liguori, Francis de Sales, Leo the Great
conscientious objectors   Franz Jägerstätter
construction workers   Thomas the Apostle
contemplative life   Mary Magdalene, Romuald
contemplative prayer   John of the Cross
converts   Franz Jägerstätter, Helena, John Henry Newman, John the Baptist, Margaret Clitherow, Mary Magdalene
cooks   Lawrence, Martha
Coptic Church   Mark
court workers   Thomas More
Croatia   Aloysius Stepinac, Joseph

Cyprus   Barnabas the Apostle
Czech Republic   Adalbert of Prague, Agnes of Bohemia, Wenceslaus

dairy workers   Brigid of Ireland
dancers   Genesius
deacons   Lawrence, Stephen
deaf people   Filippo Smaldone, Francis de Sales
dentists   Apollonia
depression   Peter Faber, Pio of Pietrelcina
desperate situations   Jude the Apostle, Rita of Cascia
devotion to Mary   Bernadette Soubirous, Catherine Labouré (Miraculous Medal), Émilie Tavernier Gamelin (her sorrows), Louis de Montfort, Marie-Alphonsine Danil Ghattas (rosary), Seven Holy Founders of the Servite Order, Simon Stock (brown scapular)
devotion to Saint Joseph   André Bessette
devotion to the Divine Mercy   Maria Faustina Kowalska
devotion to the Eucharist   Anthony of Padua, Juliana of Cornillon, Manuel Lozano Garrido, Peter Julian Eymard
devotion to the Passion of Christ   Paul of the Cross
devotion to the Sacred Heart of Jesus   Claude de la Colombière, Gertrude the Great, Margaret Mary Alacoque
diabetics   Josemaría Escrivá
dieticians   Martha
difficult marriages   Catherine of Genoa, Marguerite d'Youville, Rita of Cascia
disabled, the   Angela Merici, Germaine Cousin
divorced, the   Helena
doctors   Anthony Mary Zaccaria, Camillus de Lellis, Cosmas and Damian, Gianna Beretta Molla, Giuseppe Moscati, Luke, Niels Stensen

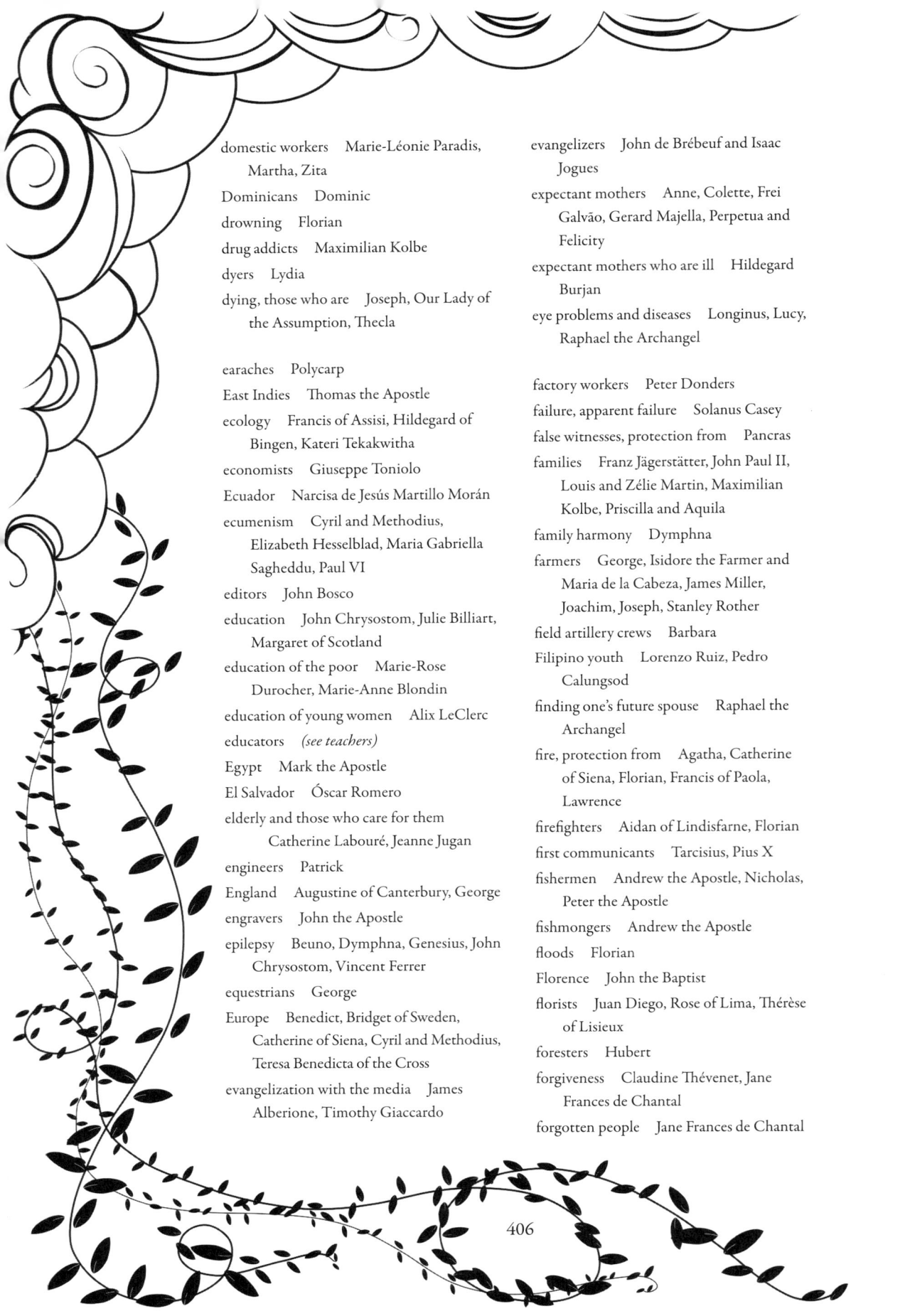

domestic workers   Marie-Léonie Paradis, Martha, Zita
Dominicans   Dominic
drowning   Florian
drug addicts   Maximilian Kolbe
dyers   Lydia
dying, those who are   Joseph, Our Lady of the Assumption, Thecla

earaches   Polycarp
East Indies   Thomas the Apostle
ecology   Francis of Assisi, Hildegard of Bingen, Kateri Tekakwitha
economists   Giuseppe Toniolo
Ecuador   Narcisa de Jesús Martillo Morán
ecumenism   Cyril and Methodius, Elizabeth Hesselblad, Maria Gabriella Sagheddu, Paul VI
editors   John Bosco
education   John Chrysostom, Julie Billiart, Margaret of Scotland
education of the poor   Marie-Rose Durocher, Marie-Anne Blondin
education of young women   Alix LeClerc
educators   *(see teachers)*
Egypt   Mark the Apostle
El Salvador   Óscar Romero
elderly and those who care for them   Catherine Labouré, Jeanne Jugan
engineers   Patrick
England   Augustine of Canterbury, George
engravers   John the Apostle
epilepsy   Beuno, Dymphna, Genesius, John Chrysostom, Vincent Ferrer
equestrians   George
Europe   Benedict, Bridget of Sweden, Catherine of Siena, Cyril and Methodius, Teresa Benedicta of the Cross
evangelization with the media   James Alberione, Timothy Giaccardo

evangelizers   John de Brébeuf and Isaac Jogues
expectant mothers   Anne, Colette, Frei Galvão, Gerard Majella, Perpetua and Felicity
expectant mothers who are ill   Hildegard Burjan
eye problems and diseases   Longinus, Lucy, Raphael the Archangel

factory workers   Peter Donders
failure, apparent failure   Solanus Casey
false witnesses, protection from   Pancras
families   Franz Jägerstätter, John Paul II, Louis and Zélie Martin, Maximilian Kolbe, Priscilla and Aquila
family harmony   Dymphna
farmers   George, Isidore the Farmer and Maria de la Cabeza, James Miller, Joachim, Joseph, Stanley Rother
field artillery crews   Barbara
Filipino youth   Lorenzo Ruiz, Pedro Calungsod
finding one's future spouse   Raphael the Archangel
fire, protection from   Agatha, Catherine of Siena, Florian, Francis of Paola, Lawrence
firefighters   Aidan of Lindisfarne, Florian
first communicants   Tarcisius, Pius X
fishermen   Andrew the Apostle, Nicholas, Peter the Apostle
fishmongers   Andrew the Apostle
floods   Florian
Florence   John the Baptist
florists   Juan Diego, Rose of Lima, Thérèse of Lisieux
foresters   Hubert
forgiveness   Claudine Thévenet, Jane Frances de Chantal
forgotten people   Jane Frances de Chantal

France   Joan of Arc, Martin of Tours, Thérèse of Lisieux
Franciscan tertiaries   Elizabeth of Portugal
Franciscans   Francis of Assisi
friendship   Aelred of Rievaulx

gang members, mafia members   Giuseppe Puglisi
gardeners   Agnes, Rose of Lima, Thérèse of Lisieux
gentleness   Aidan of Lindisfarne
geologists   Niels Stensen
Georgia (the country of)   George
Germany   Boniface, Michael the Archangel, Peter Canisius
glaziers   Mark the Apostle
goldsmiths   Dunstan
grandparents   Anne, Joachim
gravediggers   Anthony of Egypt
Greece   Andrew the Apostle, George
greeters   Alphonsus Rodriguez
grief   *(see loss, widows)*
grocers   Michael the Archangel
Guam   Pedro Calungsod
Guatemala   James the Greater
hailstorms   Barnabas the Apostle
hair dressers   Mary Magdalene
Hansen's disease   Damien of Molokai, Marianne Cope
Hawaii   Damien of Molokai, Marianne Cope
headaches   Pancras, Peter Damian, Teresa of Ávila, Vincent Ferrer
healing   Raphael the Archangel
healing of wounds   Rita of Cascia
healthcare workers   Aniela Salawa, Camillus de Lellis
heart ailments   John of God
herbalists   Hildegard of Bingen
historians   Bede the Venerable

HIV/AIDS patients and caregivers   Aloysius Gonzaga, Damien of Molokai, Marianne Cope, Peregrine Laziosi
home health care workers   Elizabeth Hesselblad
homebound   María Josefa Sancho de Guerra
homeless   Benedict Joseph Labre, Mary Angela Truszkowska
hope   Matthias the Apostle
hopeless cases   Jude the Apostle
horses   George, Stephen
hospital workers   Vincent de Paul
hospitality   Lydia
hospitals   Camillus de Lellis, John of God
housewives   Anne
human trafficking   John Eudes, Josephine Bakhita
humor   Philip Neri
Hungary   Adalbert of Prague, Elizabeth of Hungary, Stephen of Hungary
hunters   Hubert
hunting dogs   Hubert
hymn writers   Ephrem the Syrian

icon painters   John of Damascus
illness   *(see sick people, cancer, and other specific health problems)*
immigrants   Frances Xavier Cabrini, John Neumann, Joseph, Pius X
India   Thomas the Apostle
indigenous peoples, rights of   Turibius de Mogrovejo
indigenous peoples   James Miller, Juan Diego, Kateri Tekakwitha, Laura Montoya, Rose of Lima, Rose Philippine Duchesne
infants   Brigid of Ireland
infertility   Anne, Anthony of Padua, Catherine of Genoa, Colette, Francis of Paola, Gerard Majella, Zechariah and Elizabeth

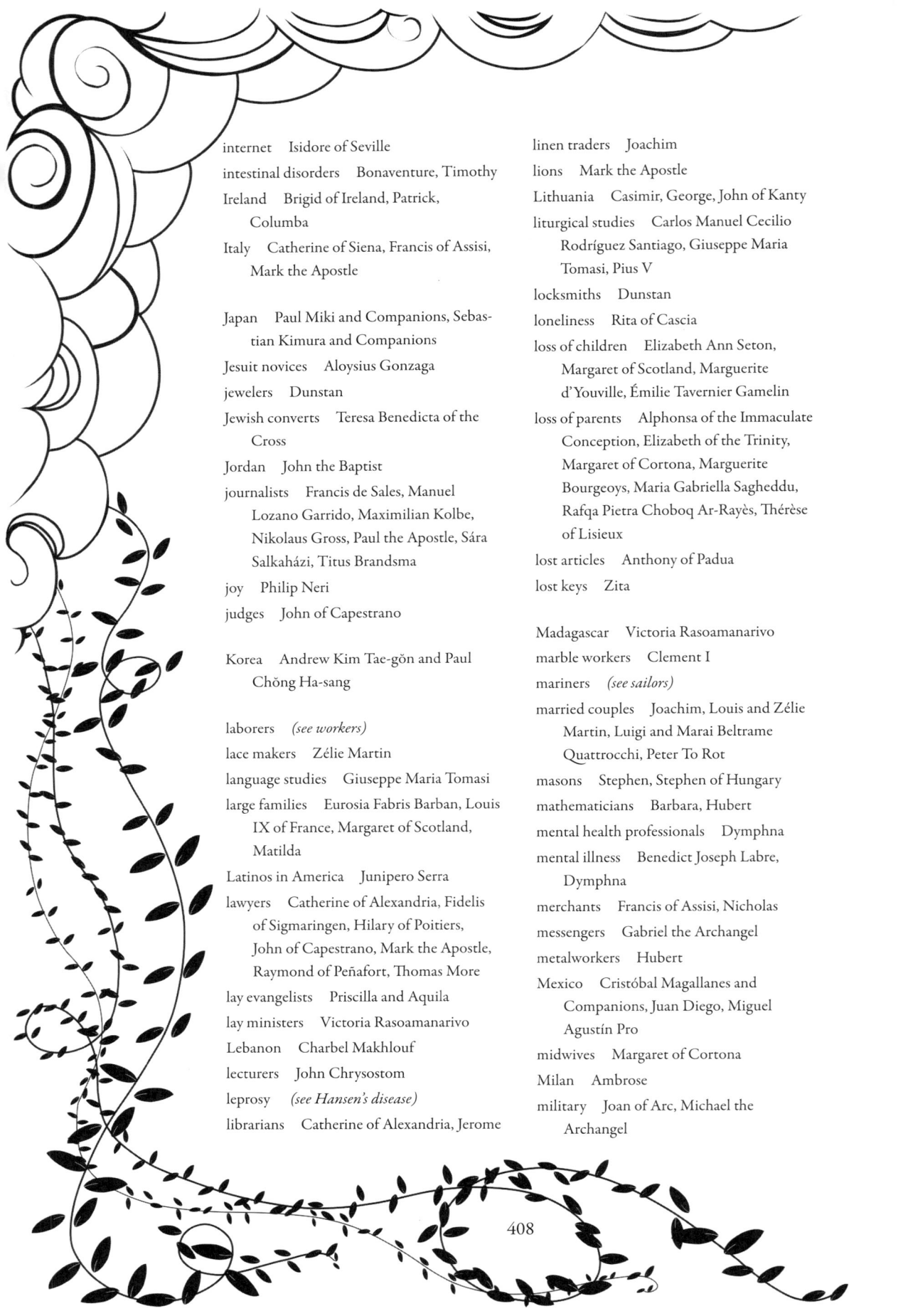

internet   Isidore of Seville
intestinal disorders   Bonaventure, Timothy
Ireland   Brigid of Ireland, Patrick, Columba
Italy   Catherine of Siena, Francis of Assisi, Mark the Apostle

Japan   Paul Miki and Companions, Sebastian Kimura and Companions
Jesuit novices   Aloysius Gonzaga
jewelers   Dunstan
Jewish converts   Teresa Benedicta of the Cross
Jordan   John the Baptist
journalists   Francis de Sales, Manuel Lozano Garrido, Maximilian Kolbe, Nikolaus Gross, Paul the Apostle, Sára Salkaházi, Titus Brandsma
joy   Philip Neri
judges   John of Capestrano

Korea   Andrew Kim Tae-gŏn and Paul Chŏng Ha-sang

laborers   (see workers)
lace makers   Zélie Martin
language studies   Giuseppe Maria Tomasi
large families   Eurosia Fabris Barban, Louis IX of France, Margaret of Scotland, Matilda
Latinos in America   Junipero Serra
lawyers   Catherine of Alexandria, Fidelis of Sigmaringen, Hilary of Poitiers, John of Capestrano, Mark the Apostle, Raymond of Peñafort, Thomas More
lay evangelists   Priscilla and Aquila
lay ministers   Victoria Rasoamanarivo
Lebanon   Charbel Makhlouf
lecturers   John Chrysostom
leprosy   (see Hansen's disease)
librarians   Catherine of Alexandria, Jerome

linen traders   Joachim
lions   Mark the Apostle
Lithuania   Casimir, George, John of Kanty
liturgical studies   Carlos Manuel Cecilio Rodríguez Santiago, Giuseppe Maria Tomasi, Pius V
locksmiths   Dunstan
loneliness   Rita of Cascia
loss of children   Elizabeth Ann Seton, Margaret of Scotland, Marguerite d'Youville, Émilie Tavernier Gamelin
loss of parents   Alphonsa of the Immaculate Conception, Elizabeth of the Trinity, Margaret of Cortona, Marguerite Bourgeoys, Maria Gabriella Sagheddu, Rafqa Pietra Choboq Ar-Rayès, Thérèse of Lisieux
lost articles   Anthony of Padua
lost keys   Zita

Madagascar   Victoria Rasoamanarivo
marble workers   Clement I
mariners   (see sailors)
married couples   Joachim, Louis and Zélie Martin, Luigi and Marai Beltrame Quattrocchi, Peter To Rot
masons   Stephen, Stephen of Hungary
mathematicians   Barbara, Hubert
mental health professionals   Dymphna
mental illness   Benedict Joseph Labre, Dymphna
merchants   Francis of Assisi, Nicholas
messengers   Gabriel the Archangel
metalworkers   Hubert
Mexico   Cristóbal Magallanes and Companions, Juan Diego, Miguel Agustín Pro
midwives   Margaret of Cortona
Milan   Ambrose
military   Joan of Arc, Michael the Archangel

military chaplains   John of Capestrano
miners   Barbara, Nikolaus Gross
misbehaving children   Matilda
miscarriage   Catherine of Siena, Catherine of Sweden
missionaries   Arnold Janssen, Clemente Vismara, Columba, Daniel Comboni, Francis Xavier, Francis Xavier Seelos, John de Brébeuf and Isaac Jogues, John de Britto, Junipero Serra, María Caridad Brader, Marie of the Incarnation, Rose Philippine Duchesne, Paul the Apostle, Stanley Rother, Thérèse of Lisieux
missions   Francis Xavier, Stanley Rother
Monaco   John the Baptist
monastic life   Benedict, Basil the Great
Montenegro   George
moral theologians   Alphonsus Liguori, Leo the Great
mothers   Anne, Anna Maria Taigi, Gianna Beretta Molla, Monica, Perpetua and Felicity
motorcyclists   Columban
motorists   Christopher
mountaineers   Pier Giorgio Frassati
music students   Dina Bélanger
musicians   Cecilia, Hildegard of Bingen
Muslim-Christian dialogue   Charles de Foucauld
mute people   Filippo Smaldone
Myanmar   Clemente Vismara
mystics   John of the Cross

National Catholic Rural Life Conference (U.S.A.)   Isidore the Farmer and Maria de la Cabeza
Naval officers   Francis of Paola
navigators   Francis Xavier
nervous breakdown   Dymphna
net makers   Peter the Apostle
new beginnings   Sylvester

new evangelization   Cyril and Methodius, John Paul II, James Alberione
Nigeria   Patrick
notaries   Mark the Apostle
nuns   Brigid of Ireland, Macrina the Younger, Scholastica
nurses   Catherine of Siena, Camillus de Lellis, John of God, Elizabeth Hesselblad, Liduina Meneguzzi, Marguerite Rutan, María de San José, María Guadalupe García Zavala

occult, against the   Benedict Daswa
Oceania   Peter Chanel, Peter To Rot
Oklahoma   Stanley Rother
opticians   Hubert
ordinary life   Josemaría Escrivá
organ makers   Cecilia
organists   Anne Catherine Emmerich
organized crime, victims of   Giuseppe Puglisi
orphans   Carlo Gnocchi, Charles de Foucauld, Gemma Galgani, Hedwig of Silesia, Jerome Emiliani
outcasts   Damien of Molokai, Marianne Cope

painters   Luke
Palestine   George
paper makers   John the Apostle
paralysis   Julie Billiart
paratroopers   Michael the Archangel
parents   Louis IX of France, Matilda, Rita of Cascia
parents separated from their children   Jane Frances de Chantal
Paris   Geneviève
Passionist Congregations   Paul of the Cross
pastors   Ephrem the Syrian
pastry chefs   Philip
pawnbrokers   Nicholas

peace   Norbert, Oliver Plunkett

peacemakers   Barnabas the Apostle

penitents   Macrina the Younger, Mary Magdalene, Mary of Egypt

ridiculed for their piety, those who are   Mary Magdalene, Zita

perjury, protection from   Pancras

persecuted Christians   Benedict Daswa, Martyrs of Compiègne, José Sánchez del Río, Marcellinus and Peter, Marguerite Rutan, Miguel Agustín Pro, Óscar Romero, Robert Southwell, Sixtus II and Companions

perseverance   Matthias the Apostle

Peru   Joseph, Martin de Porres, Rose of Lima, Turibius de Mogrovejo

pharmacists   Cosmas and Damian, Gemma Galgani, James the Greater, James the Lesser, John Leonardi, John of Damascus, Raphael the Archangel, Mother Théodore Guérin, Nicholas

philanthropists   Katharine Drexel

Philippines   Lorenzo Ruiz, Pedro Calungsod

philosophers   Albert the Great, Anselm of Canterbury, Catherine of Alexandria, Gregory Nazianzen, Justin Martyr, Teresa Benedicta of the Cross

phone operators   Alphonsus Rodriguez

physically unattractive people   Germaine Cousin

physicians   *(see doctors)*

pianists   Dina Bélanger

pilgrims   James the Greater

pilots   Joseph of Cupertino

plague   Francis of Paola, Geneviève, Gregory the Great

poets   Cecilia, John of the Cross

poisoning   Benedict

Poland   Adalbert of Prague, Casimir, Florian, Hedwig of Silesia, John of Kanty, Stanislaus

policemen   Michael the Archangel

polio   Margaret Mary Alacoque

politicians   Alberto Marvelli, Hildegard Burjan, Paulinus of Nola, Thomas More

Poor Clares   Clare of Assisi

poor people   Albert Chmielowski, Alberto Hurtado, Claudine Thévenet (particularly children), Dulce Lopes Pontes, Francisca de Paula de Jesús, Jeanne Jugan (particularly the elderly), Lawrence, Liduina Meneguzzi, Marguerite Bourgeoys, Maria Gabriella Sagheddu, Martin of Tours, Martin I, Teresa of Calcutta (particularly the poorest of the poor)

popes   Leo the Great, Peter the Apostle

Portugal   George

postal employees   Gabriel the Archangel

potters   Fabian

preachers   Anthony of Padua, Dominic, Francis Xavier Seelos, Frédéric Janssoone, John Chrysostom, Lawrence of Brindisi, Louis de Montfort, Peter Chrysologus

pregnancy   *(see expectant mothers)*

press, the   Francis de Sales, Paul the Apostle

priests   Charles Borromeo, John of Ávila, John of Kanty, Karl Leisner, Thomas Becket

priests, especially parish priests   John Vianney

printers   Augustine, John the Apostle

prison ministry   Vasyl Velychkovsky

prison workers   Pontian and Hippolytus

prisoners   Jacinta and Francisco Marto, Joan of Arc, Louis IX of France, Marguerite Rutan, Mark the Apostle, Maximilian Kolbe, Vincent de Paul

pro-life groups   Margaret of Castello, Maximilian Kolbe

public relations   Paul the Apostle

410

publishers   John the Apostle, Paul the Apostle
Puerto Rico   John the Baptist

Quebec   Marie of the Incarnation

racial harmony   Francisco de Paula Victor, Josephine Bakhita, Katharine Drexel, Martin de Porres, Peter Claver
radio workers   Gabriel the Archangel
radiologists   Michael the Archangel
ranchers   Perpetua and Felicity
receiving the last sacraments   Stanislaus
receptionists   Alphonsus Rodriguez
reconciliation   Oliver Plunkett, Vincent Ferrer
rejection and persecution for the Catholic faith   Athanasius, Elizabeth Ann Seton, Margaret Clitherow
rejection by religious orders   Peter Donders
relationships, especially sibling   Scholastica
religious brothers   James Miller
religious brothers and sisters   Teresa of Ávila
religious freedom   Compiègne, Martyrs of
repentant thieves   Nicholas
respiratory problems   Bernardine of Siena
retreatants   John Eudes
retreats, spiritual   Ignatius Loyola
rhetoricians   Gregory Nazianzen
Romani peoples of Europe   George
Romania   Andrew the Apostle
Rome   Philip Neri, Peter the Apostle
roofers   Vincent Ferrer
rope makers   Andrew the Apostle
rural communities   Isidore the Farmer and Maria de la Cabeza
Russia   Andrew the Apostle, Basil the Great, Thérèse of Lisieux

sacred music   Gregory the Great, Ignatius of Antioch
saddle makers   George
safe delivery of babies   Norbert, Gerard Majella
sailors   Brendan, Clement I, Francis of Paola, Michael the Archangel, Nicholas
Saint Vincent de Paul Society   Frédéric Ozanam
sales persons   Frédéric Janssoone, Lucy
savings   Anthony Mary Claret
Scandinavia   Ansgar
scholars   Bede the Venerable, Bridget of Sweden, John Henry Newman, Thomas Aquinas
scholars of the Bible   Jerome
schools   Thomas Aquinas
scientists   Albert the Great, Niels Stensen
Scotland   Andrew the Apostle, Columba, John Ogilvie, Margaret of Scotland
seekers of truth   Elizabeth Hesselblad, Thomas the Apostle
seizures or spasms   John the Baptist
seminarians   Charles Borromeo, John Eudes, Karl Leisner
Serbia   George
Serra Club   Junipero Serra
servants   Martha
service women   Joan of Arc
setbacks   Solanus Casey
sexual temptation   Angela of Foligno, Augustine, Catherine of Siena, Mary Magdalene, Thomas Aquinas
shepherds   Bernadette Soubirous, George
ship builders   Peter the Apostle
shoemakers   Bartholomew the Apostle
Sicily   Lucy
sick animals   Beuno
sick children   Carlo Gnocchi, Colette, John Neumann

sick, the   Alphonsa of the Immaculate Conception, André Bessette, Angela Merici, Anne Catherine Emmerich, Bernadette Soubirous, Camillus de Lellis, Catherine of Siena, Catherine Labouré, Elizabeth of the Trinity, Hilary of Poitiers, Jacinta and Francisco Marto, John of God, Liduina Meneguzzi, Maria Gabriella Sagheddu, Mary Domenica Mazzarello, Mary Magdalene de' Pazzi, Rafqa Pietra Choboq Ar-Rayès, Teresa of the Andes

singers   Cecilia, Gregory the Great

single laywomen   Margaret of Cortona, Zita

single mothers   Margaret of Cortona

skin diseases   Anthony of Egypt, Mary of Egypt

slavery, victims of   Francisca de Paula de Jesús, Peter Claver

Slavic peoples   Cyril and Methodius

Slovenia   Joseph

snakebite   Patrick

soap makers   Florian

social justice   Martin de Porres, Katharine Drexel, Turibius of Mogrovejo, Anne-Marie Javouhey

social workers   Alberto Hurtado, Frédéric Ozanam, Louise de Marillac, Sára Salkaházi

Society of Jesus   Ignatius of Loyola

soldiers   Achilleus and Nereus, George, Ignatius of Loyola, Longinus, Louis IX of France, Martin of Tours, Sebastian

South Sudan   Josephine Bakhita

Spain   James the Greater, Teresa of Ávila

speakers   John Chrysostom, Justin Martyr

spinal pain, injuries, and illnesses   Gemma Galgani

spiritual directors   Charles Borromeo, Ephrem the Syrian, Ignatius of Loyola

spondylitis   Manuel Lozano Garrido

Sri Lanka   Joseph Vaz

stained-glass workers   Mark the Apostle

stockbrokers   Matthew the Apostle

stomach problems   Charles Borromeo, Timothy

stonecutters   Clement I

storms   Christopher, Scholastica

street children   Alberto Hurtado

stress relief   Pio of Pietrelcina

students   Albert the Great, Aloysius Gonzaga, Jerome, John Bosco, John Berchmans, John Henry Newman, John of Kanty, Joseph of Cupertino, Madeleine Sophie Barat, Marie-Eugénie de Jésus, Pier Giorgio Frassati, Thomas Aquinas

Sudan   Josephine Bakhita

sudden death, protection from   Christopher, Stephen

surgeons   Cosmas and Damian, Luke the Apostle, Martin de Porres

Sweden   Bridget of Sweden

Syria   George

tailors   Basil the Great, John the Baptist, Martin of Tours, Matthias the Apostle

tanners   Simon the Apostle, Simon Stock

tax collectors   Matthew the Apostle

teachers   Anselm of Canterbury, Albert the Great, Benedict Daswa, Francis de Sales, Giuseppe Toniolo, Gregory the Great, Ignatius of Loyola, James Miller, John Baptist de la Salle, John of Ávila, John of Kanty, Léonie Aviat, Marie-Eugénie de Jésus, Madeleine Sophie Barat, María Caridad Brader, Marie of the Incarnation, Mary Domenica Mazzarello, Paula Montal Fornés, Solomon Le Clercq, Théodore Guérin

telephone workers   Gabriel the Archangel

television   Clare of Assisi

temptation   Michael the Archangel

textile merchants   Anthony Mary Claret

Thailand   Thai Martyrs of Songkhon

theologians   Anselm of Canterbury, Athanasius, Augustine, Irenaeus, Thomas Aquinas

theology students   John Duns Scotus, John of Damascus

Third Order Carmelites   Josefa Naval Girbés

Third Order Dominicans   Pier Giorgio Frassati

Third Order Franciscans   Elizabeth of Hungary

those away from the Church   Fidelis of Sigmaringen, Monica, Théodore Guérin

those falsely accused,   Elizabeth of Portugal, Gerard Majella, Mary MacKillop, Nicholas

throat   Blaise, Ignatius of Antioch

tilemakers   Vincent Ferrer

toothaches   Apollonia

translators   Jerome

travelers   Brendan, Christopher, Francis of Paola, Mary Euphrasia, Paul the Apostle, Raphael the Archangel

travelers, by plane   Joseph of Cupertino

troubled teens   Dominic Savio

trying to conceive   *(see infertility)*

tuberculosis   Thérèse of Lisieux

Uganda   Charles Lwanga and Companions

Ukraine   Andrew the Apostle

Ukrainian Catholic Church   Vasyl Velychkovsky

ulcers   Charles Borromeo

unborn children   Catherine of Sweden, Gerard Majella, Gianna Beretta Molla, Joseph

unemployed   Cajetan

United States   The Immaculate Conception, John de Brébeuf and Isaac Jogues

United States Army Chaplain Corps   Titus

unity   Cyril of Alexandria

universal call to holiness   Miriam Teresa Demjanovich

universal Church   Joseph

Uruguay   James the Lesser, Philip

U.S. Army Special Forces   Philip Neri

vegetarians   John de Britto

Venice   Mark the Apostle

Vienna   Clement Mary Hofbauer

Vietnam   Andrew Dũng Lạc and Companions

vinedressers   Vincent of Saragossa

vinegar makers   Vincent of Saragossa

virgins   Agnes, Joan of Arc, Joseph

vocalists   *(see singers)*

vocational discernment   Eurosia Fabris Barban, Frei Galvão

vocations   Leo the Great

waiters   Zita

Wales   David of Wales

watchmakers   Louis Martin

weavers   Anthony Mary Claret, Barnabas the Apostle

West Indies   Gertrude the Great

wheelwrights   Catherine of Alexandria

widows   Angela of Foligno, Bridget of Sweden, Catherine of Genoa, Celine Chludzińska Borzęcka, Elizabeth of Hungary, Frances of Rome, Jane Frances de Chantal, Louise de Marillac, Margaret of Scotland, Marguerite d'Youville, Monica

wild animals   Blaise

wine makers   Vincent of Saragossa

witchcraft, against   Benedict Daswa

wives   Anna Maria Taigi, Monica

wives who suffer abuse   Monica

women   Mary Magdalene

wool combers   Blaise

workers   Giuseppe Toniolo, John Bosco, Joseph

works of charity, service   Elizabeth of Hungary, Louis de Montfort, Regina Protmann, Vincent de Paul

World Youth Day   John Paul II, Pier Giorgio Frassati

writers   Francis de Sales, Hildegard of Bingen, John the Apostle, Lucy, Théodore Guérin, Teresa of Ávila

young people   Alberto Marvelli, Aloysius Gonzaga, Charles Lwanga and Companions, Chiara Badano, Dominic Savio, Geltrude Caterina Comensoli, John Paul II, Maria Goretti, Pier Giorgio Frassati, Teresa of the Andes

young people of Africa   Charles Lwanga and Companions, Marie-Clémentine Anuarite Nengapeta

Pauline
BOOKS & MEDIA

A mission of the Daughters of St. Paul

As apostles of Jesus Christ, evangelizing today's world:

We are CALLED to holiness
by God's living Word and Eucharist.

We COMMUNICATE the Gospel message
through our lives and through all
available forms of media.

We SERVE the Church
by responding to the hopes and needs
of all people with the Word of God,
in the spirit of St. Paul.

For more information visit us at
www.pauline.org.

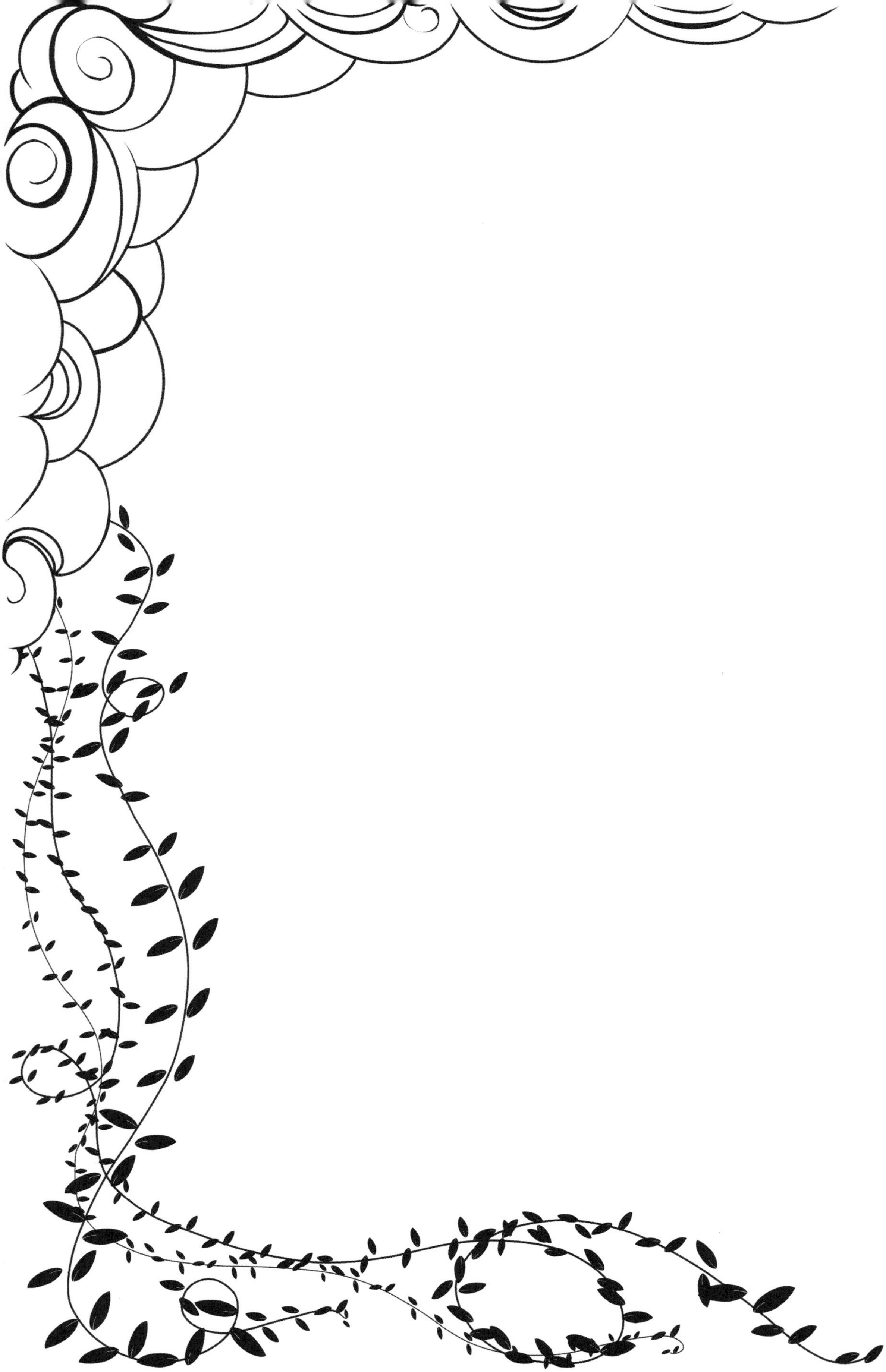

Pauline BOOKS & MEDIA

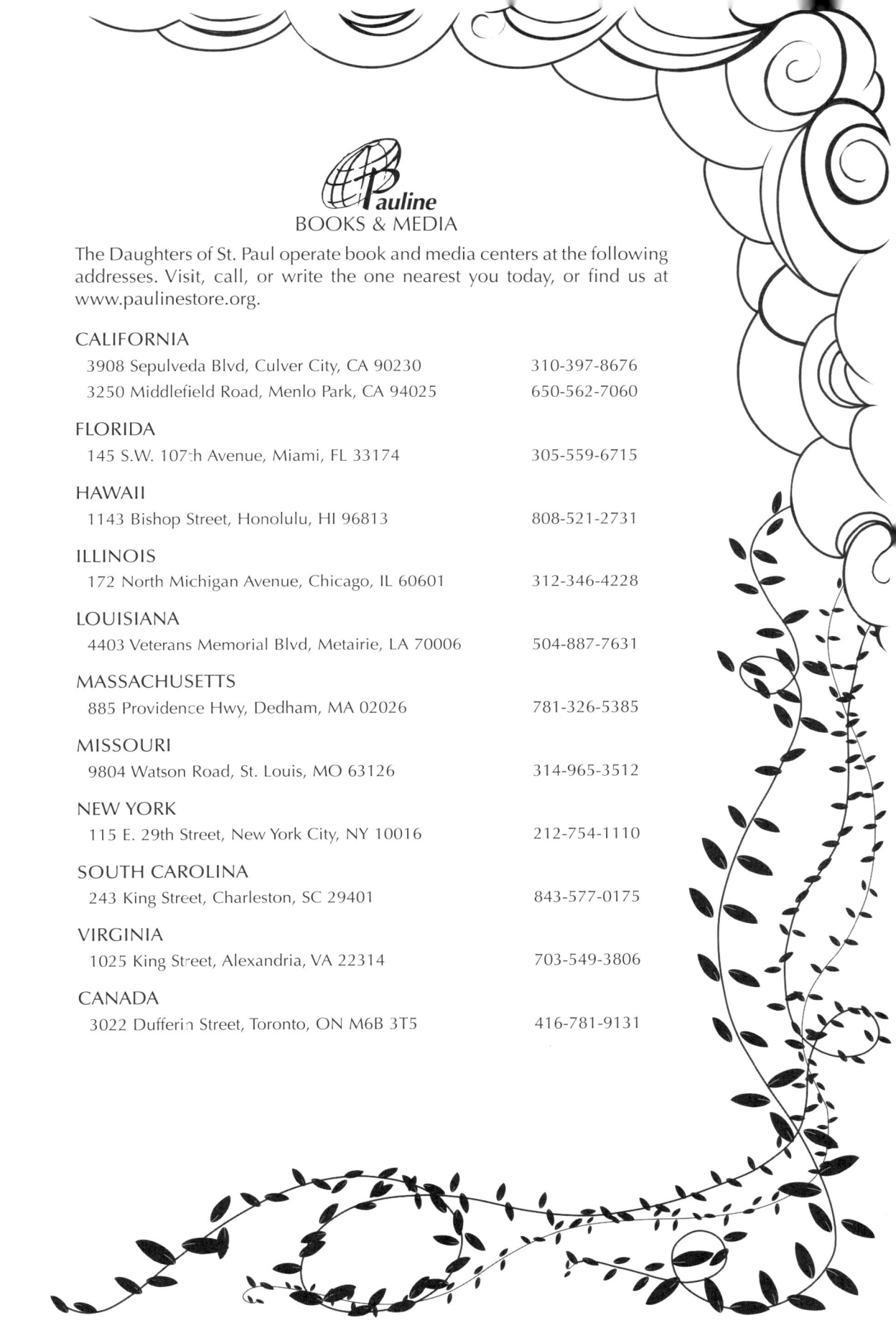

The Daughters of St. Paul operate book and media centers at the following addresses. Visit, call, or write the one nearest you today, or find us at www.paulinestore.org.

CALIFORNIA
3908 Sepulveda Blvd, Culver City, CA 90230 — 310-397-8676
3250 Middlefield Road, Menlo Park, CA 94025 — 650-562-7060

FLORIDA
145 S.W. 107th Avenue, Miami, FL 33174 — 305-559-6715

HAWAII
1143 Bishop Street, Honolulu, HI 96813 — 808-521-2731

ILLINOIS
172 North Michigan Avenue, Chicago, IL 60601 — 312-346-4228

LOUISIANA
4403 Veterans Memorial Blvd, Metairie, LA 70006 — 504-887-7631

MASSACHUSETTS
885 Providence Hwy, Dedham, MA 02026 — 781-326-5385

MISSOURI
9804 Watson Road, St. Louis, MO 63126 — 314-965-3512

NEW YORK
115 E. 29th Street, New York City, NY 10016 — 212-754-1110

SOUTH CAROLINA
243 King Street, Charleston, SC 29401 — 843-577-0175

VIRGINIA
1025 King Street, Alexandria, VA 22314 — 703-549-3806

CANADA
3022 Dufferin Street, Toronto, ON M6B 3T5 — 416-781-9131